www.mygrammarlab.com

Contents

		Introduction		vi
		Glossary		ix
UNIT				

1 — MUSEUMS AND GALLERIES

		Nouns and articles	DIAGNOSTIC TEST	1
	1	Nouns	tourist/tourists; some advice, a litre of petrol	2
	2	Articles *a/an*, *the*, no article	a café/an hour; I've got the photos.	6
	3	Special uses of *a/an* and *the*	She's a student at art school. The rich/poor/French	8
	4	Article or no article?	in the 1950s, on the left/right, at three o'clock, by train	10
	5	Demonstratives *this*, *that*, *these*, *those*	Is this seat free? I remember that day.	12
		Review		14
		Test		16

2 — FOOD AND DRINK

		Possessives, pronouns and quantifiers	DIAGNOSTIC TEST	17
	6	Possessive forms of nouns	Matt and Jane's new house, a map of the city	18
	7	Possessive adjectives and pronouns	your/yours, our/ours	20
	8	Pronouns *one/ones*; *another/the other (one)*	Which ones would you like?	22
	9	Reflexive and other pronouns	yourself, ourselves; each other; you/one/they	24
	10	*some, any, all, most, no, none of*	None of the bread is fresh.	26
	11	Indefinite pronouns	someone/anyone/no one/everyone	28
	12	*much, many, a lot of, (a) little, (a) few*	too many people, not enough food	30
	13	*both, either, neither; each, every*	Both dishes are tasty and neither is expensive.	32
		Review		34
		Test		38

3 — TRAVEL

		Prepositions	DIAGNOSTIC TEST	39
	14	General form and use; prepositions of place	at, in, above, beside, between	40
	15	Prepositions of movement	into, onto, off, along, across	44
	16	Prepositions of time	at, on, until, for, during	46
	17	Prepositions with other meanings	I'm working as a tour guide.	48
	18	Common prepositional phrases	by chance, on time, out of date	50
		Review		52
		Test		54

4 — ANIMALS

		Adjectives and adverbs	DIAGNOSTIC TEST	55
	19	Adjectives with nouns and verbs; *-ed* and *-ing* forms	He seems interested/interesting.	56
	20	Order of adjectives; stronger and weaker meanings	a comfortable old chair; really beautiful, rather cold	58
	21	Comparison of adjectives	large, larger, (the) largest	60
	22	Comparative structures	the same as/different from; a lot bigger than	62
	23	Types of adverb	slowly, usually, last week, upstairs, straight on	64
	24	Adverbs and word order	They usually work here. He's often late.	66
	25	Comparison of adverbs	more/less often; Who's been there the most?	68
		Review		70
		Test		74

5 — JOBS

		Present tenses	DIAGNOSTIC TEST	75
	26	*be*, *have* and *have got*	I'm married and I've got/I have two children.	76
	27	Present simple	My sister lives in Oxford. I don't live there.	78
	28	Present continuous	Are you watching TV?	80
	29	Present simple or continuous?	Sue works in a factory. She isn't working today.	82
		Review		86
		Test		88

CONTENTS

Past tenses — DIAGNOSTIC TEST — 89 — Unit 6 EXPLORERS

Unit	Topic	Example	Page
30	Past simple	I saw that film. Which film did you see?	90
31	Past continuous	We were living in Paris then.	92
32	Past simple or continuous?	He saw an accident while he was driving to work.	94
33	*used to* and *would*	I used to work on a farm and I would get up at 4 a.m.	96
34	Past perfect simple	She had been there before.	98
35	Past perfect continuous	They hadn't been working hard.	100
	Review		102
	Test		104

Present perfect — DIAGNOSTIC TEST — 105 — Unit 7 CARS

Unit	Topic	Example	Page
36	Present perfect for past experiences and present results	Have you driven an automatic car before? I haven't found that book yet.	106
37	Present perfect for situations up to the present	He's worked here for two years.	110
38	Present perfect or past simple?	He's bought a new car. He bought it yesterday.	112
39	Present perfect continuous	I've been waiting for hours.	114
40	Present perfect simple or continuous?	We've played six games. We've been playing for three hours.	116
	Review		118
	Test		120

Future forms — DIAGNOSTIC TEST — 121 — Unit 8 HOLIDAYS

Unit	Topic	Example	Page
41	*going to*, present continuous and *will*	We're going to buy a tent. We're camping this summer. Will you come with us?	122
42	Future continuous	I'll be sailing all day tomorrow.	126
43	Future perfect: simple and continuous	They will have finished by tomorrow. When I get home, I'll have been travelling for 35 hours.	128
44	Present simple with future meaning	Our flight arrives at 9.45.	130
45	Other ways to talk about the future	They were going to … (but) … It's likely to/due to/about to leave.	132
	Review		134
	Test		136

Modal verbs — DIAGNOSTIC TEST — 137 — Unit 9 TECHNOLOGY

Unit	Topic	Example	Page
46	Ability and possibility	can, could, be able to	138
47	Making a guess (1)	may, might, could, must, can't, should	142
48	Making a guess (2)	must, might, could, should + have	144
49	Rules	must, mustn't, have (got) to	146
50	Necessary and unnecessary actions	need, needn't, don't have to/need to Everything's fine – you needn't have worried.	148
51	Advice and criticism	should, ought to, must, had better	150
52	Permission	can, may, might, could, be allowed to	152
53	Requests and suggestions; offers, promises and warnings	can, could, would, will, shall	154
	Review		156
	Test		160

Conditionals — DIAGNOSTIC TEST — 161 — Unit 10 CRIME

Unit	Topic	Example	Page
54	Present and future conditions	If we talk to the baby, she smiles. If it rains tomorrow, we won't go.	162
55	Unlikely/unreal conditions	If we moved out of the city, we'd be safer.	164
56	Past conditions	If we'd arrived on time, we wouldn't have missed the flight.	166
57	Mixed conditionals	If you hadn't woken me, I might still be in bed.	168
58	*I wish, if only, it's time …*	I wish we were still on holiday. It's time you did this yourself.	170
	Review		172
	Test		174

iii

CONTENTS

UNIT

11 BUILDINGS — Word order and sentence patterns — DIAGNOSTIC TEST — 175

Unit	Topic	Example	Page
59	Word order in statements	The museum has made people interested in Bilbao.	176
60	*there* and *it*	There's a new cinema in town. It's got six screens.	180
61	*Yes/No* questions	Is the water from a bottle? Yes, it is.	182
62	*Wh-* questions	When was the Taj Mahal built?	184
63	*how*, *which/what*, *who* and *whose*	How did they build it? What was it like?	186
	Review		188
	Test		190

12 HOBBIES AND ACTIVITIES — Verbs with *-ing* forms and infinitives — DIAGNOSTIC TEST — 191

Unit	Topic	Example	Page
64	Verb + *-ing* form	Has he given up smoking?	192
65	Verb + infinitive	We decided to leave. We'd rather go by plane.	194
66	Verb (+ object) + infinitive; *make* and *let*	We asked them to leave. She makes him practise every day.	196
67	Verb + infinitive or *-ing* form	I remember learning to swim. Remember to lock the door.	198
	Review		200
	Test		202

13 THE MEDIA — Reported speech — DIAGNOSTIC TEST — 203

Unit	Topic	Example	Page
68	Reported statements	They said they worked for the town council.	204
69	Reported questions	He asked if I was going to buy the book.	208
70	Reported orders, requests and advice	The lifeguard warned us not to swim there.	210
71	Reporting verb patterns	He reminded me to book the hotel. She apologised for losing my umbrella.	212
	Review		214
	Test		216

14 BOOKS AND LITERATURE — Relative, participle and other clauses — DIAGNOSTIC TEST — 217

Unit	Topic	Example	Page
72	Relative clauses (1)	This is the book that he wrote.	218
73	Relative clauses (2)	The play, which he wrote in 1922, is still famous today.	222
74	Clauses after the noun	It's a novel based on a true story.	224
75	Participle clauses	They escaped, leaving everything behind.	226
76	Infinitive clauses	It was the first book to sell a million copies.	228
77	Other noun structures	It describes what life was like then.	230
	Review		232
	Test		236

15 THE WEATHER — Linking words — DIAGNOSTIC TEST — 237

Unit	Topic	Example	Page
78	Reason and purpose	*because*, *since*, *in order to*, *so that*, etc.	238
79	Causes and results	*therefore*, *so*; There's not enough rain to grow crops.	240
80	Adding information and giving alternatives	*not only … but also*; *either … or*	242
81	Showing differences	*while*, *whereas*, *even though*, *however*	244
82	Ordering events	*before*, *as soon as*, *when*, *while*	246
	Review		248
	Test		250

16 CLOTHES AND FASHION — Passive forms — DIAGNOSTIC TEST — 251

Unit	Topic	Example	Page
83	The passive	This dress was designed by Armani.	252
84	Passives with modal and other verbs	This shirt must be washed by hand.	256
85	*have something done*	We had our house painted last year. We got them to paint the walls.	258
86	Passive reporting verbs	He's thought to be very rich. They are expected to win.	260
	Review		262
	Test		264

CONTENTS

UNIT	Word combinations		DIAGNOSTIC TEST	265
87	Common collocations	run a business, make friends with, a little light rain		266
88	Adjective or noun + preposition	surprised by, keen on; What's the matter with …?		268
89	Verb + preposition (1)	He congratulated her on her success.		270
90	Verb + preposition (2)	We ran into some friends at the shops.		272
91	Phrasal verbs	work out, take off, look forward to, put up with		274
92	Confusing verbs (1)	make/do, have/take, get		278
93	Confusing verbs (2)	come/go, bring/take, live/stay, keep, leave		280
94	Confusing adjectives	injured/hurt, amusing/enjoyable		282
	Review			284
	Test			288

17 SPORTS

	Word formation		DIAGNOSTIC TEST	289
95	Forming nouns	visit/visitor, Poland/Polish, decide/decision		290
96	Forming adjectives	music/musical, comfort/comfortable; honest/dishonest		292
97	Forming verbs	modern/modernise, short/shorten; pay/repay		294
98	Compound nouns and adjectives	dishwasher, shopping centre; self-employed		296
	Review			298
	Test			300

18 EDUCATION AND TRAINING

	Formal and written English		DIAGNOSTIC TEST	301
99	Punctuation	Louise bought a CD; Andy, who hates music, didn't buy anything.		302
100	Ways to avoid repeating words	I play the violin, but my brother doesn't.		304
101	Using linking words in writing	after that, finally, in the end; furthermore		306
102	Using word order for emphasis	In fact it was Pink Floyd who recorded that album.		308
103	Organising information in writing	The song was written in 1988. It was recorded by more than fifty artists over the next twenty years.		310
104	Using nouns instead of verbs	They decided to split up → Their decision to split up …		312
105	Formal language	Your application will be assessed by the manager.		314
	Review			316
	Test			320

19 MUSIC

	Spoken English		DIAGNOSTIC TEST	321
106	Spoken question forms	The doctor didn't say much, did he?		322
107	Agreeing and disagreeing	So/Neither do I. No it isn't.		326
108	Expressing our feelings and ideas	That's awful/wonderful! To be honest …		328
109	Emphasis	You **do** say some silly things! That was **such** a good holiday.		330
110	Other spoken features	Don't know. Really? He's kind of shy.		332
	Review			334
	Test			336

20 HEALTH

	Grammar check			337
APPENDIX 1	QUICK CHECK 1	Pronouns		338
	QUICK CHECK 2	Prepositions		338
	QUICK CHECK 3	Verb tenses		340
	QUICK CHECK 4	Modal verbs		342
	QUICK CHECK 5	Conditionals		344
	QUICK CHECK 6	Verbs + -ing form and infinitive		345
	QUICK CHECK 7	Linking words		346
	QUICK CHECK 8	Verbs + prepositions		347
	QUICK CHECK 9	Phrasal verbs		347
APPENDIX 2	Irregular verbs			348
APPENDIX 3	Spelling rules			350
APPENDIX 4	British and American English			352
	Index			354
	Pronunciation table			inside back cover

Introduction to MyGrammarLab

Welcome to **MyGrammarLab** – a three-level grammar series that teaches and practises grammar through a unique blend of book, online and mobile resources. We recommend that you read this introduction along with the guide on the inside front cover to find out how to get the most out of your course.

What level is MyGrammarLab?

The **MyGrammarLab** series takes learners from elementary to advanced grammar, each level benchmarked against the Common European Framework and providing grammar practice for Cambridge ESOL exams:

	Level description	CEFR level	Grammar practice for exams
Elementary	elementary to pre-intermediate	A1/A2	KET
Intermediate	pre-intermediate to upper intermediate	B1/B2	PET FCE
Advanced	upper intermediate to advanced	C1/C2	CAE IELTS

What is unique about MyGrammarLab?

MyGrammarLab offers every learner of English the opportunity to study grammar in the way that best suits their needs – and provides as much practice as necessary to ensure that each grammar point is learnt and can be used in the context of real communication.

At each level, learners have access to a variety of materials:

book

- **clear and simple explanations** based on the Longman Dictionaries Defining Vocabulary of just 2000 words to ensure full understanding of the grammar
- **natural examples** to illustrate the grammar points, based on the Longman Corpus Network
- a topic-based approach that presents **grammar in context**
- a **variety of exercise types** – from drills to contextualised and personalised practice
- a **review section** at the end of each module to revise the key grammar points
- an **exit test** at the end of each module to check that the grammar has been fully understood
- information on the **pronunciation** of grammar items
- information on **common errors** and how to avoid making them
- a **grammar check section** for quickly checking specific grammar points
- a **glossary** of grammar terms used in the explanations

online

- a **grammar teacher** who explains key grammar points through short video presentations
- a full **diagnostic test** to identify the grammar points that need to be learnt
- **more practice** for every unit of the book
- regular **progress tests** to check that the grammar has been understood
- **catch-up exercises** for learners who fail the progress tests – to ensure that every learner has the opportunity to master the grammar
- a full **exit test** at the end of each module
- automatic marking and feedback
- **pronunciation practice** of grammar items
- the option to **listen and check** the answers for practice exercises from the book
- additional **grammar practice for exams**

mobile

- downloadable exercises for **practice anywhere, any time**
- the ability to **create exercises** from a bank of practice questions
- automatic marking and **feedback** for wrong answers

INTRODUCTION

What is a MyLab?
A MyLab is a Learning Management System – an online platform that enables learners and teachers to manage the learning process via a number of online tools such as automatic marking, the recording of grades in a gradebook and the ability to customise a course.

How can I get the most out of MyGrammarLab?

To the Student:
If you are using MyGrammarLab in class, your teacher will tell you which units to study and which exercises to do.

If you are using MyGrammarLab for self study, you can work through the book from Module 1 to Module 20. Or you can choose a grammar point that you want to study and go to a specific unit. Here is a good way to study a complete module:

📖	The modules in the book start with a text such as an advert, an email or a magazine article. The text introduces the grammar for the module. The grammar is highlighted in the text, and then there is a short exercise. The exercise shows you the units you need to study in order to learn more about the main grammar points.
⏻	**Go online for a full diagnostic test** Look for this instruction at the bottom of the first page of each module. Take the diagnostic test then click on the feedback button to see which unit to go to for more information and practice.
📖	The grammar information in the book is usually on the left, with the practice exercises on the right. It is therefore easy to check and read the grammar while you are doing the exercises. In a few units, there are two pages of grammar information followed by two of practice exercises.
⏻	For more information about the grammar, go online to watch the grammar videos in each unit and listen to your grammar teacher.
⏻	If you would like more grammar and listening practice, you can listen to the correct answers for some of the practice exercises in the book. Look for this symbol: 🔊 2.10 **Listen and check.** If you have the book with answer key, you can check all the answers at the back of the book.
⏻	**Go online for more practice** Look for this instruction at the end of the practice exercises in the book. All the online exercises are different to the exercises in the book. They are marked automatically. Your grades are recorded in your own gradebook.
📖 ⏻	Look for this symbol on the grammar information pages in the book: 🔊 1.10 . This means that there is some information on a pronunciation point. Go online to hear the information and practise the pronunciation.
📖 ⏻	**Go online for a progress test** Look for this instruction at the end of the practice exercises in the book. The online progress tests show you if you have understood the grammar points in the units that you have studied. If your grade is low, do the catch-up exercises online. If your grade is good, you probably don't need to do these.
📱	For practice away from your computer, download the catch-up exercises questions to your mobile phone. You can create your own practice tests. Go to www.mygrammarlab.com to download.
📖	At the end of each module there is a two-page review section. The review exercises bring together all the grammar points in the module.
📖	At the end of each module, there is also a test. The test shows you how much you know and if you need more practice.
⏻	**Go online for a full exit test** Look for this instruction at the end of the exit test in the book.

INTRODUCTION

To the Teacher:

If you are using MyGrammarLab with a class of students, you can either work through the book from the first to the last module, or you can select the areas that you would like your students to focus on.

You can work through a module as outlined on the previous page – but as a teacher, you are able to assign tests and view all the scores from your class in one gradebook. This will enable you to see at a glance which areas are difficult for your students – and will let you know which of your students are falling behind.

For pronunciation practice in class, audio CDs are available. The disk and track number for each explanation are given in the book. Look for this symbol: ◀) 1.10.

All tests (diagnostic, progress and exit) are hidden from students. Assign these when you want your class to take the test. Marking is automatic – as is the reporting of grades into the class gradebook.

Some practice exercises – such as written tasks - require teacher marking. These are hidden from your students so you should only assign these if you want them to submit their answers to you for marking. The grades are reported automatically into the gradebook.

Key to symbols

⚠	This highlights a grammar point that learners find particularly difficult and often gives common errors that students make.
NATURAL ENGLISH	Sometimes a sentence may be grammatically correct, but it does not sound natural. These notes will help you to produce natural English.
FORMALITY CHECK	This introduces information about the formality or informality of a particular grammar point or item of vocabulary.
GRAMMAR IN USE	This indicates an exercise which practises grammar in a typical context, often a longer passage or dialogue.
◀) Pronunciation ▶ 1.10	This indicates where you will find pronunciation practice on the audio CDs and in the MyLab.
◀) 2.10 Listen and check.	This indicates that there is a recorded answer online. You can check your answer by listening to the recording, or, if you are using the edition with answer key, by looking in the key at the back of the book.
short form	Some words in the explanations are shown in blue. This indicates that they are included in the glossary on p. ix. Look in the glossary to find out what these words mean.

Glossary

action verb a verb that describes an action rather than a state, e.g. *walk, drive, cook*. We can usually use action verbs in both simple and continuous forms.
→ state verb

active a verb or sentence is active if the person or thing doing the action is the subject of the verb. In the sentence *The player dropped the ball*, the verb *drop* is active. → passive

adjective a word that describes a noun, e.g. *friendly, valuable, interested, tropical*

adverb a word that describes or adds to the meaning of a verb, an adjective, another adverb, or a sentence. There are different types of adverbs: **manner**: *quickly, kindly, beautifully*; **degree**: *completely, definitely*; **frequency**: *always, often, never*; **place**: *here, there*; **time**: *now, then*; **sentence adverb**: *apparently, fortunately*

adverbial a word or phrase that is used as an adverb and answers questions, such as *How? When?* and *Where?* e.g. *by train, yesterday, in the south of France*

article the word *the* (definite article), or the words *a* or *an* (indefinite article)

auxiliary verb a verb that we use with another verb to form questions, negative sentences, tenses and the passive. Common auxiliary verbs are *be, do* and *have*.
→ main verb, modal verb

capital letter the large form of a letter of the alphabet, that we use at the beginning of a name or sentence, e.g. *B* not *b*

clause a group of words that contains a verb and usually a subject. A clause may be a sentence or part of a sentence. → main clause, relative clause, subordinate clause, infinitive clause, participle clause

collocation a combination of words that are often used together, e.g. *make the bed* (verb + noun), *heavy traffic* (adjective + noun)

comparative adjective *nicer, hotter, better, more comfortable*, etc. We use comparative adjectives for comparing two people or things.
→ superlative adjective

complement a word or phrase that follows a particular type of verb, e.g. *be, become, look, seem, appear, remain* and *describe*. In the sentence *That cake looks delicious*, the adjective *delicious* is a complement.

compound adjective an adjective that is made from two or more words, e.g. *well-known* (well + known), *user-friendly* (user + friendly)

compound noun a noun that is made from two or more words, e.g. *whiteboard* (white + board), *dining room* (dining + room), *office manager* (office + manager)

consonant any of the sounds and letters of the English alphabet, except *a, e, i, o, u* → vowel

continuous the form of a verb in tenses we make with *be* and the *-ing* form. We use the continuous, for example, for things we are doing now or at a particular time, or for a temporary period of time. **present continuous**: *I'm using my computer at the moment*; **past continuous**: *They were living in Japan at the time*; **present perfect continuous**: *I've been waiting here for an hour*; **past perfect continuous** *We'd been climbing for eight hours when we reached the top*; **future continuous** *The band will be practising all day tomorrow*; **future perfect continuous** *By the end of this week, I'll have been working here for three months.* → simple

contraction a short form of a word or words. *Haven't* is a contraction of *have not*. → short form

countable a countable noun has a singular and a plural form: *table/tables, man/men*. → uncountable

defining (relative) clause → relative clause

demonstrative adjective/pronoun *this, that, these, those*: **adjective**: *Please take these flowers – they're for you.* **pronoun**: *That's my brother in the photo.*

direct object a noun or pronoun that usually comes after the verb and shows who or what is affected by the action. In the sentence *She gave the book to me*, the direct object is *the book*. → indirect object

direct speech the exact words a person says, in quotation marks, e.g. *Mark said, 'I can't come to your party.'* → reported speech

first conditional a sentence with *if* that describes a future situation. We can use the first conditional with other words, too, e.g. *unless, as long as, when*: *If it's sunny tomorrow, we'll go to the beach.*

future continuous → continuous

future perfect continuous → continuous

future perfect (simple) the tense of a verb that we form with *will + have + past participle*. We use the future perfect for an action that will be complete by a time in the future: *I'll have finished my essay by this evening.*

imperative the form of a verb that we use to tell someone to do something or to stop doing something. *Give me that book! | Don't sit there!*

indefinite pronoun *someone, anyone, everywhere, nothing*, etc: *I've looked everywhere for my key.*

indirect object a noun or pronoun that comes after the verb, or after a preposition and shows who or what something is given to, said to, made for, etc. In the sentence *She gave the book to me/She gave me the book*, the indirect object is *me*. → direct object

indirect question a question that begins with *Could you tell me, Do you know*, etc.

infinitive the base form of a verb, e.g. *be, read, talk, write*. The infinitive with *to* is *to* + the base form: *to be, to read, to talk, to write*.

infinitive clause a (subordinate) clause which begins with an infinitive. In the sentence *It's a good idea to discuss your problems*, the infinitive clause is *to discuss you problems*.

-ing form the form of a verb that ends in *–ing*. We use the *-ing* form in continuous tenses, but we can also use it as the subject or object of a clause: *He's reading. | Reading is relaxing. | I like reading.*

intonation the way that our voice level changes to add meaning to what we say. For example, the voice often goes up at the end of a question.

intransitive verb a verb that has a subject but no object, e.g. *come, go, happen* → transitive verb

ix

GLOSSARY

irregular an irregular verb does not have a past tense and past participle that end in *-ed*, e.g. *go/went/gone*; an irregular noun does not have a plural that ends in *-s*, e.g. *man/men*; an irregular adverb does not end in *-ly*, e.g. *fast/fast* → regular

linking word a word such as *and*, *but* or *because* that we use to connect one part of a sentence with another, or to show how one sentence is related to another: *We paid the bill and went home.* | *I like summer because the weather's warm.*

main clause a clause that we can use alone or connect to another clause. In the sentence *It was raining so I went to the gym*, the main clause is *it was raining*.
→ clause, subordinate clause

main verb a verb that we can use with or without an auxiliary verb, e.g. *cost* in *How much does it cost? It costs $20.* → auxiliary verb, modal verb

modal verb a verb such as *can*, *should* or *might* that we use with another verb to show ideas such as ability (*can*), advice (*should*) or possibility (*might*): *I can swim.* | *We should leave now.* | *You might be right.*

negative a negative sentence contains a word such as *not* or *never*, e.g. *Shakespeare wasn't French.* | *I've never liked coffee.* → positive

non-defining (relative) clause → relative clause

noun a word for a person, animal, thing, place or idea, e.g. *tourist*, *horse*, *pen*, *China*, *happiness*

noun phrase a phrase which has a noun as its most important word. In the noun phrase *the tall man with a beard*, the other words all describe the man, so the word *man* is the most important. A noun phrase can act as subject, object or complement in a sentence. It can also follow a preposition.

object a noun or pronoun that usually follows a verb. In the sentence *The player dropped the ball*, the noun *ball* is the object. → subject

object pronoun *me*, *you*, *him*, *her*, *it*, *us*, *them*. We use object pronouns after the verb. → subject pronoun

participle clause a (subordinate) clause which begins with a present or past participle, e.g. *They left in the night, **taking all their luggage*** (present participle clause). | ***Built in 1720*** (past participle clause), *the house is now a hotel.*

passive if a verb or sentence is passive, the subject of the verb is affected by the action of the verb. In the sentence *The house was built ten years ago*, the verb *was built* is passive. → active

past continuous → continuous

past participle a form of a verb that we use to make past tenses and passives. Regular verbs have past participles that end in *-ed*, e.g. *arrived*, *called*. Irregular verbs have different forms, e.g. *gone*, *spoken*, *sold*.

past perfect continuous → continuous

past perfect (simple) the tense of a verb that we form with *had* and the past participle. We use the past perfect in reported statements or to show the order of events in the past: *He said he'd already seen that film.*

past simple the tense of a verb that we form by adding *-ed* to regular verbs. Irregular verbs have different forms, e.g. *go/went*. We use the past simple for single or repeated actions in the past: *I called you yesterday.* | *I called you twice yesterday.*

phrasal verb a verb + preposition/adverb combination. A phrasal verb has a different meaning from the verb alone: *I'm going to give up eating chocolate.* (*give up* = stop). With phrasal verbs, we can separate the verb + preposition/adverb: *I'm going to give it up.*
→ prepositional verb

plural the form of a word that we use for more than one person or thing. *Students* is the plural of *student*. *They* is a plural pronoun. → singular

positive a positive sentence describes what something/someone is or does. It does not contain a word such as *not* or *never*. *Shakespeare was English.* | *I've always liked coffee.* → negative

possessive adjective *my*, *your*, *his*, *her*, *its*, *our*, *their*. Possessive adjectives show who something belongs to, or who someone is related to: *my house*, *her brother*.

possessive pronoun *mine*, *yours*, *his*, *hers*, *ours*, *theirs*. A possessive pronoun replaces a possessive adjective + noun: *It's hers.* (her car) | *That's mine.* (my mobile)

prefix a group of letters that is added to the beginning of a word to change its meaning and make a new word, e.g. *happy/unhappy*, *like/dislike*. → suffix

preposition a word such as *on*, *at* or *into* that we use before a noun to show the position of something or someone, or its relationship with the noun, for time or purpose: *Put it on the table.* | *He disappeared into the shop.* | *Meet me at six o'clock.* | *This key is for the front door.*

prepositional verb a verb + preposition combination. A prepositional verb can have a different meaning from the verb alone: *They soon arrived at a decision.* With prepositional verbs, we cannot separate the verb + preposition. → phrasal verb

present continuous → continuous

present perfect continuous → continuous

present perfect (simple) the tense of a verb that we form with *have* and the past participle, e.g. *has gone*. The present perfect has many uses, for example for a situation that started in the past and continues now: *I've been at university for two years now.*

present simple the tense of a verb that uses the base form, or the base form + *s* for *he*, *she* and *it*: *I live*, *he lives*. We use the present simple, for example, for regular activities and facts. *I go to work by bus.* | *The Earth goes round the Sun.*

pronoun a word that replaces a noun, e.g. *I*, *she*, *they*, *me*, *her*, *them*, *it*. → object pronoun, subject pronoun, demonstrative pronoun, relative pronoun

punctuation the marks used to divide a piece of writing into sentences, clauses, etc. Capital letters and commas are examples of punctuation. (For a list of common punctuation symbols and their names ➤ page 302)

question tag *isn't it? doesn't she? have you?* etc. We add question tags to the end of a statement to make it a question, or to check that someone agrees. *You're from Poland, aren't you?*

reflexive pronoun *myself, yourself, himself,* etc. We use reflexive pronouns when the subject and object of the verb are the same: *She calls herself Tina.*

regular a regular verb has a past tense and past participle that ends in *-ed: finish/finished;* a regular noun has a plural that ends in *-s: book/books;* a regular adverb ends in *-ly: quick/quickly.* → irregular

relative clause a part of a sentence that gives information about someone or something in the main clause. A **defining relative clause** tells us exactly which person or thing we are talking about: *He's the man **who lives in the top flat**.* A **non-defining relative clause** gives us extra information about the subject or object of the main clause: *The book, **which was written in five weeks**, was a huge success.*

relative pronoun a pronoun that connects a relative clause to the main clause in a sentence, e.g. *who, which, that.*

reported speech the words someone says to report what another person has said: *Mark said that **he couldn't come to my party**.* → direct speech

reporting verb a verb used to report what another person says, e.g *say, ask, tell, advise, admit, order*

second conditional a sentence with *if, unless,* etc. that describes a situation we are imagining in the present or an unlikely situation in the future. We use the past tense after *if* in the second conditional: *If I was rich, I'd buy a Ferrari.*

short answer an answer to a *Yes/No* question that does not repeat the main verb: *Are you waiting for the bus? Yes, I am.* | *Did you buy it? No, I didn't.*

short form the form of verbs we usually use when we are speaking, e.g. *I've* (not *I have*), *weren't* (not *were not*). → contraction

simple simple tenses are not formed with *be* and the *-ing* form. → continuous

singular the form of a word that we use for only one person or thing. *Student* is a singular noun. *Am* and *is* are singular forms of the verb *be.* → plural

state verb a verb that describes a state rather than an action. e.g. *believe, love, belong, seem, hear.* We do not usually use state verbs in continuous forms.
→ action verb

statement a sentence that is not a question or an imperative: *I'm British.* | *It's three o'clock.* | *The play hasn't started.*

stress the force that we use to say a part of a word. In the word *coffee,* the stress is on the first syllable. If we stress a word or part of a word, we say it with more force.

subject a noun or pronoun that usually comes before the main verb in the sentence. The subject shows who is doing the action. In the sentence *The player dropped the ball,* the noun *player* is the subject.
→ object

subject pronoun *I, you, he, she, it, we, they.* We usually use subject pronouns before the verb.
→ object pronoun

subordinate clause a clause that is introduced by a linking word, e.g. *because, although, so that,* and that gives us more information about the main clause: ***Although the weather wasn't very good***, *we enjoyed our holiday.* → main clause, relative clause

suffix a letter or group of letters that is added to the end of a word to form a new word, e.g. *write/writer, move/movement, use/useless.* → prefix

superlative adjective *nicest, hottest, best, most comfortable,* etc. We use superlative adjectives when we compare one person or thing with several others.
→ comparative adjective

syllable a part of a word that contains a single vowel sound. *Dad* has one syllable and *butter* has two syllables.

third conditional a sentence we use with *if* to imagine a situation in the past that we know is not true. *If you hadn't left the gate open, the dog wouldn't have got out.*

time expression a word or phrase such as *today, every day, on Mondays, once a week.* Time expressions describe when or how often we do regular activities.

transitive verb a verb that must have an object, e.g. the verb *break* in the sentence *She broke the glass.*
→ intransitive verb

uncountable an uncountable noun does not have a plural form, e.g. *water, advice, music.* → countable

verb a word which describes an action or a state, e.g. *go, eat* or *understand.*

vowel one of the sounds that are shown by the letters *a, e, i, o, u* → consonant

Wh- clause a clause that begins with *who, what, where, when, why, how, whose* or *which.* In the sentence *I don't agree with what they decided,* the *wh-* clause is *what they decided.*

Wh- question a question that begins with a *wh-* word: *What's your name?*

Wh- word *who, what, where, when, why, how, whose, which*

Yes/No question a question which only needs the answer *yes* or *no,* e.g. *Are you a student?* | *Do you like pasta?*

zero conditional a sentence with *if* or *when* that shows that one action always follows another: *If you press this button, the light comes on.*

Nouns and articles

MODULE 1

Before you start

1 Read the guidebook page. Look at the <mark>highlighted</mark> grammar examples.

> **PLACES TO VISIT**
>
> This is <mark>the Hermitage Museum</mark> in St Petersburg. It has one of <mark>Europe's</mark> greatest art collections. The Hermitage was built in <mark>the eighteenth century</mark>; but in <mark>those</mark> days it wasn't an art gallery, it was a royal palace. <mark>The</mark> palace was used by the Tsars until the revolution of 1917. The building is now <mark>an enormous museum</mark> which contains <mark>art</mark> from many different <mark>countries</mark>, but mainly from Italy and France.
>
> Lots of <mark>information is</mark> available from the website: www.hermitagemuseum.org
>
> For phone numbers and opening times turn to <mark>page 106</mark>.

2 Now read the sentences and choose the correct words in *italics*. The <mark>highlighted</mark> grammar examples will help you.

1 Most museums encourage *familys / families* to visit them. ▶ Unit 1
2 Did you visit any interesting museums in *asia / Asia*? ▶ Unit 1
3 'The tourist office gave me lots of advice.' 'Really? *Was it / Were they* useful?' ▶ Unit 1
4 Which kind of *art / the art* do you prefer – paintings or sculpture? ▶ Unit 2
5 We bought a sculpture and a painting from that gallery. *A / The* painting is in our living room. ▶ Unit 2
6 It's *a beautiful / beautiful* picture. ▶ Unit 3
7 There's a new exhibition at *National Gallery / the National Gallery*. ▶ Unit 4
8 The picture was painted in *sixteenth / the sixteenth* century. ▶ Unit 4
9 The best paintings are in *room / the room* 18. ▶ Unit 4
10 In *those / these* days the royal family lived in the palace. ▶ Unit 5

3 Check your answers below. Then go to the unit for more information and practice.

1 families 2 Asia 3 Was it 4 art 5 The 6 a beautiful 7 the National Gallery 8 the sixteenth 9 room 10 those

⏻ Go online for a full diagnostic test

1 Nouns

Tourists enjoy shopping at the British Museum. There are lots of postcards and books for sale.

1 Types of noun

Nouns are the words we use for
- people, things and places: *a tourist, a postcard, a museum*
- activities, ideas and feelings: *shopping, information, love*

When nouns are names of people, places, dates, events, languages, religions and books, plays or films, they begin with a capital letter: *Professor Grey, the British Museum, Glasgow, Africa, Monday, April, May Day, Russian, Spanish, Islam, 'The Lord of the Rings', 'War and Peace', 'Avatar'*

Compound nouns, e.g. *bookshop, washing machine* ➤ Unit 98.1

2 Singular and plural nouns

Most nouns have a singular and plural form. To make plural forms
- add *-s* to most nouns: *books, postcards, days, houses*
- add *-es* to nouns ending in *-s, -ss, -sh, -ch, -o, -x* and *-z*: *buses, dishes, watches, potatoes, boxes* (BUT *videos, pianos*)
- for nouns ending in consonant + *-y*: *country → countries*
- for most nouns ending in *-f* or *-fe*: *life → lives   thief → thieves*

Spelling rules ➤ page 350

A few plural forms are irregular, and some nouns do not change:

SINGULAR	man	woman	child	person	foot	tooth
PLURAL	men	women	children	people	feet	teeth
SINGULAR AND PLURAL	aircraft	series	fish	sheep		

🔊 Pronunciation ➤ 1.02

3 Noun + verb

Some nouns end in *-s* but are singular, so we use a singular verb:

athletics   economics   gymnastics   politics   maths   physics   news

Athletics is an Olympic sport.   Today's **news isn't** very exciting.

Some nouns describe things with two parts, so they are plural:

jeans   pants   pyjamas   shorts   tights   trousers   glasses   scissors

These **jeans are** too tight.   My **glasses are** broken.

To talk about one or more of these things we can use *pair(s) of*:
I need **a pair of trousers** and **three pairs of** shorts.

2

Some nouns (e.g. *company, family, government, team*) describe groups of people.
We use a singular OR plural verb when we are talking about the people in the group:
*The Spanish team **is/are** playing brilliantly.* (all the Spanish players)
But we only use the singular verb when we are talking about the group as one thing:
✗ *A football team have eleven players.* ✓ *A football team **has** eleven players.*

British and American English ➤ page 352

⚠ The group noun *police* is ALWAYS plural:
✗ *The police has arrested the thieves.* ✓ *The police **have** arrested the thieves.*

4 Countable and uncountable nouns

Countable nouns are things we can count:
***How many museums** are there in Paris?* *There are **10,000 paintings** in the Louvre.*
Uncountable nouns are things we can't count.
- food and drink: *bread, butter, meat, tea, coffee, milk, oil, pasta, salt, rice*
- materials: *water, oil, air, oxygen, metal, cotton, wood, plastic, paper*
- school subjects and languages: *geography, art, music, English, Spanish*
- ideas and feelings: *education, work, advice, beauty, love, knowledge, fun*
- activities: *shopping, cycling, swimming*
- groups of similar things: *furniture, luggage, money*

COUNTABLE NOUNS	UNCOUNTABLE NOUNS
have a singular and a plural form: one **shop** → two **shops**	don't normally have a plural form: petrol → ✗ two petrols ✓ some petrol
We use a singular or plural verb: That **painting is** beautiful. Those **paintings were** expensive.	We only use a singular verb: Swimming **is** a popular sport. That **petrol was** expensive.
We use *a/an*, *the* or *this/that* before a singular noun: Is there **a museum** here? Where's **the museum**? **This museum** is enormous!	We don't use *a/an* before an uncountable noun. We can use *some* or *this/that*: ✗ This table is made of a plastic. ✓ This table is made of **plastic**. ✗ Can you give me an advice? ✓ Can you give me **some advice**? **This rice** isn't cooked!
We use words like *some*, *the*, *these/those* before a plural noun: I'd like **some apples**, please. **Those books** look interesting.	

5 Nouns that can be countable or uncountable

COUNTABLE MEANING	UNCOUNTABLE MEANING
We keep **six chickens** in our garden. (animals)	Do you like **chicken** and rice? (food)
A coffee and **two teas**, please. (cups of tea)	Sam prefers lemon **tea**. (drink)
Did you get **a paper** today? (a newspaper)	I need some writing **paper**. (material)
Those were easy **exercises**. (tasks)	Do you do much **exercise**? (physical activity)
I had some interesting **experiences** on holiday. (things that happened to me)	**Experience** is more important than qualifications. (learning by doing something)
The gallery has two **works** by Goya. (paintings)	My **work** is really interesting. (job)

6 Ways of counting uncountable nouns

We use different expressions to 'count' some uncountable nouns.
- units: *a **bar of** soap, a **bit of** information/fun, an **item of** news, a **loaf of** bread, a **piece of** furniture/luggage/paper, a **sheet of** paper, a **slice of** bread/cake/meat*
- containers: *a **bottle of** water, a **can/tin of** soup, a **carton of** milk, a **cup of** coffee, a **glass of** orange juice, a **jar of** jam, a **packet of** sugar, a **tub of** butter/margarine, a **tube of** toothpaste*
- measurements: **half a kilo of** meat, **a litre of** petrol, **two metres of** silk

1 NOUNS

Practice

1 **GRAMMAR IN USE** Find twelve more capital letters missing from the invitation.

> You are invited to a reception at the British museum at 7.30 p.m. on friday, 20th april.
> There will be a talk by professor ernest brand, author of 'tribal Art', to introduce our new exhibition of art from new guinea.
> Drinks will be served.
>
> Please reply to Ms helena summers on 02243 77689 before 28th march.

2 Write the plural form of the nouns.

car child ~~country~~ family house life loaf person potato series sheep watch

+ -s	+ -es	+ -ies	+ -ves	no change	irregular
		countries			

3 Choose the correct words in *italics*.  Listen and check.

0 I can't read his writing. I think I need new *glass* / (*glasses*).
1 How often do you brush your *tooth / teeth*?
2 I think physics *is / are* the most difficult subject at college.
3 How many *aircrafts / aircraft* does British Airways own?
4 *Was / Were* the news interesting yesterday?
5 The police *is / are* trying to find the missing girl.
6 There are three *women / womans* and two men in the new medical team.
7 I like your new jeans. *Was it / Were they* expensive?
8 Do you have *a pair of / a* scissors in your kitchen?
9 Some farms in New Zealand have a million *sheep / sheeps*.
10 Our neighbours have six *childs / children*.

4 Match sentences 1 and 2 with A and B in each pair.

0 1 I'd like some tea. ⟶ A And could I have two coffees, please?
   2 I'd like a tea. ⟶ B Could I have two packets of sugar, too?
1 1 Can you get me some paper?   A I want to write a letter.
   2 Can you get me a paper?   B I want something to read.
2 1 Do you have any chicken?   A There isn't any on the menu.
   2 Do you have any chickens?   B Or do you have only cows on your farm?
3 1 You should try a skiing holiday. A It will give you lots of experience.
   2 You should take that job.   B You will have a great experience.
4 1 I need to do some exercise.   A I want to improve my grammar.
   2 I need to do some exercises.   B I want to get fit.
5 1 I don't have a lot of work today. A I'm not busy.
   2 I don't have many of his works.   B I'm not very keen on his books.

5 **GRAMMAR IN USE** Choose the correct answer, A, B or C below. 🔊 2.03 Listen and check.

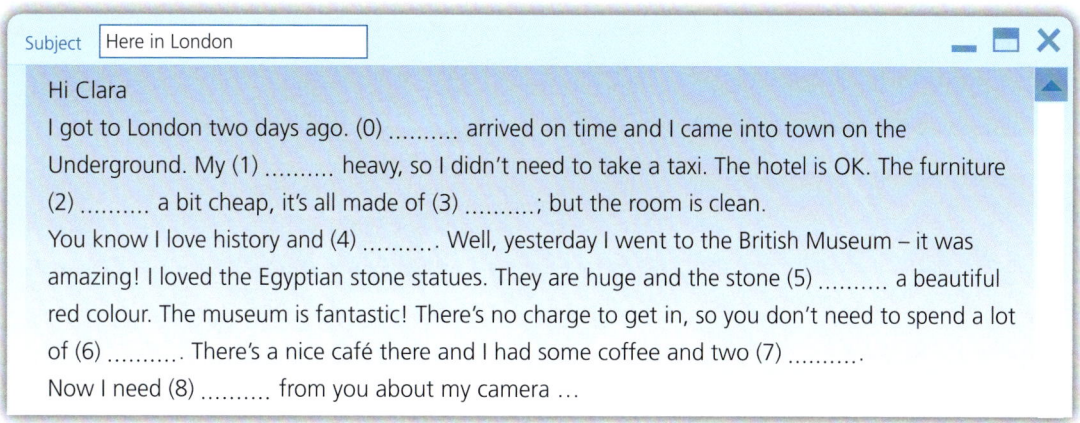

Subject: Here in London

Hi Clara
I got to London two days ago. (0) .... arrived on time and I came into town on the Underground. My (1) .... heavy, so I didn't need to take a taxi. The hotel is OK. The furniture (2) .... a bit cheap, it's all made of (3) ....; but the room is clean.
You know I love history and (4) .... Well, yesterday I went to the British Museum – it was amazing! I loved the Egyptian stone statues. They are huge and the stone (5) .... a beautiful red colour. The museum is fantastic! There's no charge to get in, so you don't need to spend a lot of (6) .... There's a nice café there and I had some coffee and two (7) ....
Now I need (8) .... from you about my camera …

0 A Flight   B Some flight   **C The flight**
1 A luggages weren't   B luggage wasn't   C luggage weren't
2 A is   B are   C were
3 A plastic   B a plastic   C the plastic
4 A an archaeology   B archaeology   C the archaeology
5 A are   B were   C is
6 A money   B moneys   C the money
7 A sandwichs   B sandwichies   C sandwiches
8 A an advice   B some advice   C advices

6 Complete the descriptions with the words from the box.

a bar   a bottle   a can   ~~a carton~~   a jar   a packet   a piece   a slice   a tub

0 *a carton* of milk

1 .... of soup

2 .... of water

3 .... of soap

4 .... of jam

5 .... of furniture

6 .... of meat

7 .... of butter

8 .... of rice

Go online for more practice

2 Articles a/an, the, no article

1 a or an? the /ə/ or the /iː/?

A, *an* and *the* are **articles**. We use *a* before consonant sounds (*b, d, k, t, s,* etc.):
a café, **a t**ourist, **a m**useum
- AND before *u* or *eu* when they sound like /j/ (as in *you*): **a u**niform, **a Eu**ropean city

We use *an* before **vowel** sounds (*a, e, i, o, u*): **an i**nteresting book, **an u**nusual job
- AND before words that begin with a silent *h*: **an h**our /ən aʊə/

We pronounce *the* with /ə/ before consonant sounds: the book, the tourist
Before vowel sounds we pronounce *the* with /iː/: the art gallery, the English teacher

🔊 **Pronunciation ➤ 1.03**

2 General or particular meaning?

We use *a/an* or no article when we are talking about things in general:

a/an + SINGULAR NOUN	no article + PLURAL NOUN	no article + UNCOUNTABLE NOUN
Is there **a café** here? (any kind of café)	**Sandwiches** aren't expensive. (sandwiches in general, all sandwiches)	I don't like **music**. (music in general, all music)

We use *the* to talk about something particular:

the + SINGULAR NOUN	the + PLURAL NOUN	the + UNCOUNTABLE NOUN
Yes, **the café**'s on the ground floor. (there is only one café here)	Did you get **the sandwiches**? (we know which sandwiches)	I don't like **the music** on that CD. (only the music on the CD, not music in general)

⚠️ We don't use *the* when we are talking about things in general:
✗ ~~Is there the cash machine near here?~~ ✓ Is there a cash machine near here?
✗ ~~I prefer the films to the books.~~ ✓ I prefer films to books.

3 New information or known information?

We use *a/an* or no article when we mention something for the first time.
We use *the* when we mention it again:
I've just bought **a new suit**. It's **the grey suit** we saw in the shop window last week.
'Carla asked her teacher for **advice**.' 'Really? Was **the advice** useful?'
'Have they filled in **entry forms**?' 'Yes, I've got **the forms** here.'

We use *the* when the listener knows which particular person or thing the speaker is talking about:
It was a great holiday. Have you seen **the photos** yet? (the photos of the holiday)

Practice

1 Complete the sentences with *a* or *an*. 🔊 2.04 Listen and check.

0 My teacher went to *an* American university. It's quite *a* famous one, I think.
1 Excuse me, Dr Taylor. There's .... urgent message for you. It's from .... patient.
2 There's .... bus stop on the corner. But you'll have to wait .... hour for the next bus.
3 She's got .... young son. He has .... unusual name.
4 My parents have .... elderly friend who owns .... small cottage by the sea.
5 Detectives don't wear .... uniform. But they always carry .... badge.
6 We can find you .... European holiday at .... excellent price.

2 Complete the notices with *a*, *an*, *the* or – (no article).

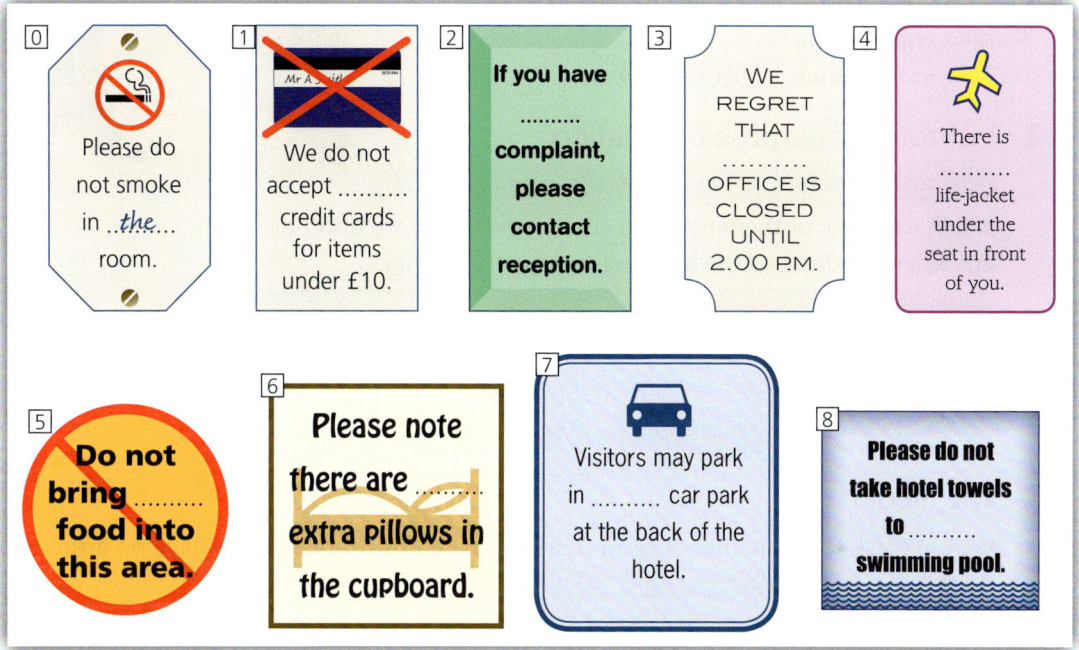

3 GRAMMAR IN USE Find nine more mistakes in the conversation and correct them.
🔊 2.05 Listen and check.

JENNY Hello, Karl. How are ~~the~~ things? Have you found *a* job yet?
KARL Hi, Jenny. Yes, I have.
JENNY Great! Is a job near here?
KARL Yes. It's at a hotel in a city centre.
JENNY That's very convenient. Which hotel is it?
KARL It's hotel opposite bus station: The Regent.
JENNY Oh, yes. I know it. By the way, how is Maria?
KARL She's OK now, but she's been quite sick. She had operation last month.
JENNY Oh dear. Was an operation serious?
KARL No, don't worry – nothing serious. She's better now.
JENNY I'm glad to hear it – the health is so important, isn't it?
KARL Yes. It was shock when she became ill.
JENNY I can imagine. Has she got the good doctor?
KARL Yes. The doctor's very helpful.

Go online for more practice

3 Special uses of *a/an* and *the*

> Michelle's **a student** at **art school**. She's in the museum copying **a beautiful painting**.

1 Jobs and descriptions

We use *a/an* with the names of jobs:
Michelle's **a student**.
I want to be **an engineer**.

We also use *a/an* to describe a person or thing, usually with an adjective:
She's copying **a beautiful painting**.
He's **a nice person**.
That was **an interesting exhibition**.

2 Institutions: purpose or building?

| institution | school college university prison hospital |

When we think of the purpose of these institutions we don't use *the*.
But when we think of the building, we use *the* or *a/an*.

PURPOSE	BUILDING
Michelle is a student at **art school**.	**The art school** is in North Street.
My brother's sick in **hospital**.	Excuse me, where's **the hospital**?
The murderer was sent to **prison**.	**The prison** has stone walls.

3 The media

We use *the* with the names of most newspapers, but most magazines have no article:

| newspapers | the Daily News the Sun the New York Times |
| most magazines | Vogue Newsweek Time Hello |

'Did you see her photo in **Vogue**?' 'No, it was in **the Sun**.'

We say *the cinema*, *the theatre* and *the radio*. We don't normally use *the* with *television* or *TV* when we are talking about the programmes:
In the mornings I like listening to **the radio** but in the evenings I prefer watching **TV**.

But we use *a* or *the* if we are talking about the machine:
There's something wrong with **the television** in my bedroom.

4 *the* + adjective for groups and nationalities

| the young the old the elderly the rich the poor the sick the homeless
the disabled the unemployed the blind the deaf the injured the dead |

Some adjectives can be used as nouns if they describe a particular group, e.g. all the people who are rich = *the rich*. We use a plural verb:
The rich are getting richer and **the poor** are getting poorer.

We can use nationality adjectives that end in *-ch/-sh/-ese* in the same way, e.g. French, Spanish, Dutch, Japanese (▶ Unit 95.2):
The French have elected a new president. (all the French people)
The Irish are voting on the new European Union tomorrow. (all the Irish people)

⚠ We can't use other nationality words in this way:
✗ ~~The Brazilian are used to hot weather.~~   ✓ **Brazilians** are used to hot weather.

Practice

1 GRAMMAR IN USE There are ten more places in the letter where *a* or *an* is missing. Write *a* or *an* in the correct places. 🔊 2.06 Listen and check.

I come from /ᵃ close family. I've got two sisters and a brother. Emily's the eldest sister. She's dentist and she's lovely person. Caroline is student. She's studying French at university. She isn't good student; she prefers to spend her time enjoying herself! My brother has got interesting job, he's architect. He designed beautiful new house for my uncle. I live with my parents in old house in small village. It's quiet place so I'm glad I've got lots of friends on the Internet!

2 Match the sentences 1–7 with the questions A–H.

0 Derek's at university. ⟶ B Is he studying to be a doctor?
1 Mr Rogers is going to the school.   A Is he on holiday?
2 My brother is in hospital.   C Is he the famous murderer?
3 Ali visited the university.   D Did he see the new physics building?
4 James isn't at school today.   E Is he going to see the school play?
5 He's working at the hospital.   F Is he visiting a prisoner?
6 Derek Sutcliffe is in prison.   G Is he a doctor?
7 Karl's going to the prison today.   H Is he having an operation?

3 GRAMMAR IN USE Complete the information with *the* or – (no article). 🔊 2.07 Listen and check.

PRINT MEDIA FACTSHEET

- The most widely read English language newspaper in the world is *USA Today*. The most popular magazine is (0) ...–... *AARP Magazine*. It is an American magazine for (1) .... elderly.

- (2) .... Japanese are the world's most enthusiastic newspaper readers. *Yomiuri Shimbun* sells more than 14 million copies every day.

- The most popular daily newspaper in Britain is (3) .... *Sun*, which sells over 3 million copies.

- One of the most unusual magazines is *The Big Issue*, which is sold by (4) .... homeless on the streets of London and other towns in the UK.

- (5) .... *Variety* is an international magazine that specialises in news about (6) .... cinema.

- In many countries magazines that give information about (7) .... television are very popular. Americans buy several million copies of (8) .... *TV Guide* each week.

Go online for more practice

4 Article or no article?

1 No article

We don't usually use *a/an* or *the* with:

people's names and titles	David Mr Brown Professor Smith Uncle John
named shops and companies	Harrods Tesco Microsoft United Airlines
cities, towns, states and regions	London Sydney Madrid Florida Tuscany
most countries and continents	Russia Japan Turkey Australia Asia Europe Africa
mountains, hills and lakes	Mount Vesuvius Box Hill Lake Placid
most roads, streets, squares and parks	Park Lane Oxford Street Trafalgar Square Times Square Central Park (BUT *the* M25 *the* high street)
named airports and stations	Miami Airport Birmingham Bus Station Victoria Station
schools, universities, etc.	Bradford Grammar School Yale University
times, days and months	at three o'clock at midday on Monday in December
languages, school subjects and sports	English Polish history basketball tennis football
means of transport and communication	by train by bus by email by phone (BUT *on foot* and *in person*)
meals	What time is dinner? Let's meet after lunch. (BUT *a snack*)
nouns + numbers	Go to check-in 3A. I'm in Room 334. Look at page 98.

We don't use an article for: *at home, at work, in bed, at school*

2 *the*

We usually use *the* with:

names of oceans, seas, rivers, mountain ranges	the Atlantic Ocean the Black Sea the Seine the Nile the Himalayas the Alps
countries with plural names, *Republic*, *Kingdom*, etc.	the United States the Netherlands the Republic of Ireland the United Kingdom
organisations	The International Monetary Fund the World Bank
names of museums, cinemas, theatres, hotels	the Getty Museum the Odeon Cinema the National Theatre the Ritz Hotel
places in a town, types of shops	the bank the hospital the post office the station the supermarket the chemist's
locations	on the left/right in the middle on the coast/border in the east/north/south/west
parts of a building	the ground floor the fifth floor the exit the entrance
times of the day	in the morning in the afternoon in the evening (BUT *at night*)
historical periods	the nineteenth century the 1950s the Middle Ages
musical instruments (British English)	Does she play the guitar? Can you play the violin?
noun + *of*	the House of Commons the University of London The Isle of Man

3 *a/an*

We use *a/an* to mean
- *one* with fractions and large numbers: *half a kilometre, one and a half, a thousand*
- *each* for frequency (how often) and measurements: *once a day, twice a month* (BUT *every hour*), *six euros a kilo, 100 kilometres an hour*

Practice

1 Match the two parts of the sentences.

0 I won't be able to see you in — A a year.
1 It can be quite cold here at   B the left.
2 The heart of a healthy adult beats 70 times → C the afternoon.
3 We go on holiday three times   D a minute.
4 The speed of light is 300 million metres   E night.
5 Our house is the one on   F a second.

2 **GRAMMAR IN USE** Read the conversation and choose the correct words in *italics*. 🔊 2.08 Listen and check.

MANAGER   What's my diary like for next week?
ASSISTANT Pretty busy. You're travelling to (0) *the Manchester /(Manchester)* on (1) *the Monday / Monday*.
MANAGER   From (2) *the Euston / Euston* Station?
ASSISTANT Yes. The train leaves at 8.15 in (3) *the morning / morning*. You have an appointment with (4) *the Mr / Mr* Grey at 11.30. He's our manager for (5) *the United / United* Kingdom.
MANAGER   Where am I meeting him?
ASSISTANT At (6) *the Carlton / Carlton* Hotel, in (7) *the centre / centre* of Manchester. It's in (8) *the St Peter's / St Peter's* Square. He said he would wait for you near (9) *the entrance / entrance* of the hotel. He wants to talk to you about the contract.
MANAGER   The one that begins in (10) *the December / December*?
ASSISTANT Yes, and I've made an appointment for you in (11) *the afternoon / afternoon* at (12) *the bank / bank*.

3 **GRAMMAR IN USE** Complete the information with *a*, *an*, *the* or – (no article). 🔊 2.09 Listen and check.

Newman's Tours

Lisbon Highlights Day 1

- When you get to (0) ..–.. Stansted Airport check in at (1) .... 8.45 a.m. and go to (2) .... Gate 56 for (3) .... flight EZ1221. Our tour guide, Katrina, will be there to greet you.

- Arrive at our hotel – all our rooms are on (4) .... third floor with great views of (5) .... River Tagus.

- In (6) .... afternoon we will visit (7) .... Gulbenkian Museum. The museum has an amazing collection of art from all periods, especially (8) .... eighteenth century.

  We will take you back to your hotel at 6.00 p.m. and you will have (9) .... hour and (10) .... half to relax before (11) .... dinner.

- Later in (12) .... evening you will be free to explore (13) .... centre of (14) .... Lisbon on (15) .... foot.

Go online for more practice

5 Demonstratives *this, that, these, those*

1 Demonstrative adjectives and pronouns

	ADJECTIVE (+ noun)	PRONOUN (without a noun)
singular	*This museum is interesting.* *That sculpture is beautiful.*	*This is interesting.* *That is beautiful.*
plural	*These tickets are expensive.* *Those sculptures are very old.*	*These are expensive.* *Those are very old.*

We often use *this/that one* or *those/these ones*:
Which shirt do you prefer? **This one** or **that one**? (= This shirt or that shirt?)

2 Near or far?

We use *this* and *these* to describe things that are near us:
Excuse me. Is **this** *seat free?* (the seat near me)
***These** are the tickets.* (the tickets I am holding)

We use *that* and *those* for things that are further away:
***That**'s an African elephant.* (the one I am pointing at in the distance)
Look at **those** *mountains, they're huge.* (the ones in the distance)

3 Now or then?

We also use *this/these* to describe a time that is now or in the near future:
I'm doing a lot of exercise **these** *days.* (around now)
What are you doing **this** *weekend?* (the weekend that is coming/has just started)

We use *that/those* for a time in the past:
There were no mobile phones in **those** *days.*
Do you remember **that** *weekend at the seaside?* (a weekend in the past)

4 Describing a person, thing or idea

We use *this/that/these/those* to describe a person, thing or idea:
***This** lesson is interesting.* (the lesson we are in now)
I hate **these** *dark nights.* (the winter nights we are having now)
I didn't know **that**! ***That**'s amazing!* (the information you've just given me)
***Those** people we met on holiday were really nice.* (people we met in the past)

We use *this is/these are* to introduce people:
Mum, **these are** *my friends from college.* **This is** *Jan and* **this is** *her sister, Frieda.*

On the phone we usually use *it's* to identify ourselves:
'Hi! **It's** *me/***It's** *Sarah here.'*

We use *this is* when we don't know the person we are speaking to:
'Hello. **This is** *Sarah Smith. May I speak to the manager?'*

Practice

1 Choose the best answer, A or B.

0 Do you like that dress?
  (A) The dress in the shop window.   B The dress I am wearing.
1 I don't like this very much.
  A The food I am eating.   B The food you are eating.
2 Are these your children?
  A The children in the photograph I'm looking at.   B The children playing in the garden.
3 That's very interesting.
  A The book I'm reading.   B The information you've just given me.
4 Are those the correct answers?
  A The answers in my book.   B The answers in your book.
5 I've already seen that one.
  A The DVD I'm holding.   B The DVD you're holding.
6 Can I have two of these, please?
  A The pens on the counter here.   B The pens on the top shelf.

2 Choose the correct words in *italics*. 🔊 2.10 Listen and check.

0 These *is /(are)* very comfortable seats.
1 *This / These* class is for advanced students.
2 Have you got any other colours? I don't like those *one / ones*.
3 I'm feeling nervous. *This / That* is my first day here.
4 Can you see *these / those* beautiful birds on top of the roof?
5 Did you enjoy *this / that* Indian meal we had last week?
6 *These / Those* shoes are very tight. Do you mind if I take them off?
7 'Hello, is that Stephen?' 'Yes, *this is / it's* me. How are you?'
8 Let me introduce my boss. Alex, *this / it* is Hilary.

3 **GRAMMAR IN USE** Complete the conversation with *this*, *that*, *these* or *those* and a suitable form of the verbs in brackets, if necessary. 🔊 2.11 Listen and check.

JAN Wow! We're here at last. So, (0) _this is_ (be) the famous Grand Canyon!
ANA It's amazing, isn't it? And (1) .... (be) a fantastic place to see it from.
JAN Can you see (2) .... river down at the bottom?
ANA Yes, I can.
JAN (3) .... (be) the Colorado River. It's wider than the River Thames.
ANA But (4) .... (be) impossible. It looks tiny!
JAN (5) .... (be) because it's so far away from us.
ANA Look at (6) .... rocks on the other side of the valley. Is (7) .... a cave over there?
JAN Yes, I think so. I read in the guidebook that the people here lived in caves before the Europeans arrived. In (8) .... days lots of people lived in this area.
ANA (9) .... (be) really interesting. Can we visit the caves?
JAN I don't think it's allowed (10) .... days.

Review MODULE 1

1 UNITS 1 AND 2 Match sentences 1 and 2 with A and B in each pair.

```
0  1  Did you do much exercise?         A  Did you finish your homework?
   2  Did you do all the exercises?     B  You went to the gym, didn't you?
1  1  I don't like children.            A  I mean all children.
   2  I don't like the children.        B  I mean my neighbour's children.
2  1  Did you get a book?               A  I asked you to find it for me.
   2  Did you get the book?             B  You'll need something to read on the train.
3  1  We had turkey.                    A  It lived in our garden when I was a child.
   2  We had a turkey.                  B  It was delicious.
4  1  Do you sell papers?               A  I want to look at the advertisements.
   2  Do you sell paper?                B  I want to write a letter.
5  1  Did you listen to the music?      A  Did you take your iPod with you?
   2  Did you listen to music on the train?  B  It was on that CD I gave you last week.
6  1  Will you apply for a job?         A  You know, the one you saw in the paper.
   2  Will you apply for the job?       B  Or don't you want to start work yet?
```

2 UNITS 2, 3 AND 4 Read the TV programme information and choose the correct words in *italics*.

Today's best programmes

Subtitled programmes are available on (0) *channel* / *the channel* 29.
Programmes include hand signing for (1) *deaf* / *the deaf*.

18.00 Channel 16	**TV International**
	A weekly look at (2) *television* / *the television* around (3) *a* / *the* world.
19.15 BBC 4	**The Bridge on (4) *River* / *the River* Kwai**
	Award-winning war film. (5) *A* / *The* list of actors includes Alec Guinness and William Holden.
21.30 Channel 5	**Job Watch**
	What is the government doing to help (6) *unemployed* / *the unemployed*? This programme examines (7) *a* / *the* latest job creation policies and a new plan to help students at (8) *university* / *the university* find jobs.
22.00 CNN	**The Energy Crisis**
	(9) *Chinese* / *The Chinese* are investing in coal-powered electricity. Is this the best way to protect (10) *an* / *the* environment? This documentary examines the facts.

3 UNITS 2, 3 AND 5 Complete the three conversations with *a*, *an*, *the*, – (no article), *this*, *that*, *these* or *those*. In five places, more than one answer is possible.

1 JOHN   This place is amazing. Look, (0) *that* 's the Mona Lisa over there, on the other side of the room.
  ALICE   (1) .... painting behind the thick glass?
  JOHN   Yes, (2) ....'s it. Let's get a bit nearer.
  ALICE   I still can't really see it. All (3) .... tourists are standing in the way. Why don't we get a coffee and come back later?
  JOHN   OK. Is there (4) .... café in (5) .... museum?
  ALICE   I'm sure there is. Let's ask (6) .... security guard over there.

14

2 TOURIST   Excuse me. I'm looking for (7) .... Tate Gallery.
  DAN   Which one? There are two.
  TOURIST   Er, (8) .... one with all the modern art.
  DAN   I think you mean the Tate Modern.
  TOURIST   Yes, (9) ....'s the one I want.
  DAN   Well, it's on the other side of (10) .... river. You have to cross over (11) .... Millennium Bridge.
  TOURIST   Where's (12) ....?
  DAN   It's not far. Just turn left at (13) .... corner of (14) .... street.

3 SILVIA   Hello, Cambridge Tourist Office? Right, I'm coming to (15) .... Cambridge next week and I'm looking for (16) .... information.
  GUIDE   Sure. What would you like to know?
  SILVIA   Well, I quite like (17) .... history and (18) .... architecture. Are any of (19) .... university buildings open to the public?
  GUIDE   Yes, and some of (20) .... colleges are very old.

4 ALL UNITS Read the text and choose the correct answer, A, B or C below.

BOSTON. Museums and Galleries

(0) ..... Stewart Gardner Museum is one of the most unusual museums in (1) ..... .

It was built by the millionairess Isabella Stewart Gardner at the end of (2) ..... century. In (3) ..... days wealthy Americans often travelled to Europe and bought fine paintings and sculptures. Isabella went to Europe many times and bought a lot of (4) ..... . She visited Venice in 1884 and fell in love with (5) ..... Barbaro. She decided that one day she would build (6) ..... in her home town, Boston, which would be (7) ..... of a Venetian palace. As she collected more and more art she decided her new home should also become (8) ..... .

In 1898 Isabella's husband, John Gardner, died and she began building her new home/museum. It opened to the public in 1903. Isabella kept (9) ..... floor of the museum as a private home for herself and she lived there until she died in 1924. (10) ..... days the museum contains more than 2,500 works of art and is open to the public from Tuesday to Sunday, from 11 a.m. to 5 p.m.

 0 A Isabella   (B) The Isabella   C An Isabella
 1 A North America   B the North America   C a North America
 2 A nineteenth   B the nineteenth   C a nineteenth
 3 A that   B these   C those
 4 A art   B some art   C the art
 5 A a Palazzo   B the Palazzo   C this Palazzo
 6 A house   B the house   C a house
 7 A copy   B the copy   C a copy
 8 A museum   B a museum   C the museum
 9 A the top   B that top   C a top
10 A The   B These   C Those

15

Test MODULE 1

Nouns and articles

Choose the correct answer, A, B or C.

1. She has two young .... so she's always tired!
   A babys   B babyes   C babies ▶ Unit 1

2. The police .... questions about the bank robbery.
   A are asking   B is asking   C asks ▶ Unit 1

3. Do you have suitable .... for this job?
   A experiences   B piece of experience   C experience ▶ Unit 1

4. Excuse me. Is there .... near here?
   A some art gallery   B an art gallery   C art gallery ▶ Unit 1

5. There was an interesting .... on the radio this morning.
   A news   B item of news   C one news ▶ Unit 1

6. The artist has .... name.
   A unusual   B a unusual   C an unusual ▶ Unit 2

7. Living in .... city can be expensive.
   A an European   B a European   C European ▶ Unit 2

8. My parents don't like travelling on ....
   A trains   B train   C the trains ▶ Unit 2

9. .... between Lisbon and Madrid is very slow.
   A Train   B A train   C The train ▶ Unit 2

10. Please call me back. .... is 090744454.
    A The number   B A number   C Number ▶ Unit 2

11. Isn't your cousin .... ?
    A the musician   B a musician   C musician ▶ Unit 3

12. The judge sent the murderer to .... for thirty years.
    A prison   B a prison   C the prison ▶ Unit 3

13. The Paralympics are special Olympic games for ....
    A some disabled   B the disabled   C disabled ▶ Unit 3

14. .... usually take their holidays in August.
    A French   B A French   C The French ▶ Unit 3

15. I go to the dentist ....
    A twice a year   B twice the year   C twice in year ▶ Unit 4

16. They have a lovely house near Malaga. It's just on ....
    A the coast   B coast   C a coast ▶ Unit 4

17. Caroline's studying law at .... University.
    A the Harvard   B a Harvard   C Harvard ▶ Unit 4

18. I'm going to take a photo of .... mountains over there.
    A this   B these   C those ▶ Unit 5

19. What was the name of .... hotel we stayed at last year?
    A that   B this   C a ▶ Unit 5

20. 'Hello. Can I speak to Mrs Gupta?'
    '.......... Mrs Gupta. How can I help you?'
    A It is   B This is   C That is ▶ Unit 5

Go online for a full exit test

Possessives, pronouns and quantifiers

MODULE 2

Before you start

1 Read the review of a restaurant. Look at the highlighted grammar examples.

The Sultan's Palace
★★★★

This Turkish restaurant is in a small side road at the end of the high street, so it's easy to miss it. I went there on Friday evening with a friend of mine. Expecting little choice, we went in for a quick meal and we were pleasantly surprised. We helped ourselves to several cold starters from the self-service display, and we ordered a couple of hot ones from the menu. Most of them were vegetarian and they were all excellent. We felt quite full so we asked the waiter to recommend something small for our main course. Well, I had a small lamb kebab, and my friend had a small chicken kebab – and both of them were really quite large! The meat tasted very good, and the rice and salad with it was just right. We looked at the desserts on the menu – and wanted to try every one of them – but we simply couldn't eat any more! And all this, with Turkish coffee at the end, was less than £25.00. I'd really recommend the Sultan's Palace – it's friendly and inexpensive, and I'm certain that anything on the menu will be just perfect!

2 Now read the sentences and choose the correct words in *italics*. The highlighted grammar examples will help you.

1 There's an excellent French restaurant at *the top of the road / the road's top*. ▶ Unit 6
2 Keith is going on holiday in the summer with a cousin of *him / his*. ▶ Unit 7
3 I love most cakes but I really don't like cream *one / ones*. ▶ Unit 8
4 The boys fell over while they were playing football and hurt *them / themselves*. ▶ Unit 9
5 The desserts were very expensive but all *them / of them* looked really good. ▶ Unit 10
6 *Anyone / Anything* can use the tennis courts here – you don't have to join the club. ▶ Unit 11
7 I always like *something sweet / sweet something* at the end of a meal. ▶ Unit 11
8 Her letter wasn't long because she had *little / a little* time to write it. ▶ Unit 12
9 Gerri's got two brothers and both *of them / them* are very good-looking. ▶ Unit 13
10 We went to every *of / one of* the physics lectures, but we still don't understand! ▶ Unit 13

3 Check your answers below. Then go to the unit for more information and practice.

1 the top of the road 2 his 3 ones 4 themselves 5 of them 6 Anyone 7 something sweet 8 little 9 of them 10 one of

⏻ Go online for a full diagnostic test

17

6 Possessive forms of nouns

I'd better go now. I've got to finish making the **children's** dinner.

1 Possessive forms

singular noun	+ 's	Jane**'s** apartment my uncle**'s** job the bus**'s** front lights
names that end in -s	' or 's	James**'** school OR James**'s** school
plural nouns that end in -s	'	boys**'** team workers**'** union
plural noun (irregular)	+ 's	children**'s** dinner people**'s** rights

2 Noun +'s or '

We usually use noun + 's (or ' only) for people and animals: *It's the **children's** dinner. Where are the **cats'** bowls? **John's wife's** dress is lovely.*

If there are two people, we usually only add 's to the second person:
*What do you think of **Matt and Jane's** new house?*

We can use noun + 's without another noun
- when the meaning is clear: *'Can I borrow your pen?' 'It's **Steve's**. Ask him.'*
- for people's homes: *There's a party after the exam at **Abbi's**.*
- for some businesses and services: *Lester is at the **dentist's**. Can you buy me some chocolate at the **newsagent's**?*

We can add 's / ' to a period of time:
*a **week's** holiday* (= a holiday of a week) *six **months'** travelling* *yesterday's news*

3 of + noun

We usually use *of* + noun for things and places:
*Would you like a map **of the city**? I don't know the time **of the next train**.*

With cities, countries and organisations, we can use 's or *of*:
London's parks *are very pleasant. / The **parks of London** are very pleasant.*
China's economy *is growing fast. / The **economy of China** is growing fast.*
*That needs the **World Bank's** approval. / That **needs the approval of the World Bank**.*

We can use *of* + noun and noun + 's together:
*It's the Lord Mayor **of London's** residence.   She's the Head **of Marketing's** wife.*

⚠️ We don't usually use *of* + noun for people:
✗ He's the uncle of Joan.   ✓ *He's **Joan's** uncle.*
We don't usually use noun + 's for things:
✗ I've broken my shoe's heel.   ✓ *I've broken the heel **of my shoe**.*
We often leave out *the* in *time of (the) day/night/year*, especially in spoken English:
*I'm usually working at this **time of day**.*

4 Compound nouns

Some **compound nouns** describe one person or thing that belongs to another:
table leg (= the leg of the table), *bedroom ceiling* (= the ceiling of the bedroom)
book cover (= the cover of the book), *college principal* (= the principal of the college)
✗ The bedroom's ceiling needs painting.   ✓ *The bedroom ceiling needs painting.*

More on compound nouns ➤ Unit 98.1

2

Practice

1 Write an apostrophe (') in the correct places in each sentence.

0 Is Marian's niece a teacher at the boys' school or the girls' school?
1 Tess's husband works at Microsoft's head office in California.
2 Mark and Sarah's children are staying at their grandparents'.
3 In the UK, you can usually buy women's perfumes at a chemist's.
4 What's the Prime Minister's wife's name? I've forgotten.
5 The country's economic situation may lead to a reduction in people's salaries.

2 Match the nouns in Box A and Box B to make compound nouns. Then write the words under the pictures.

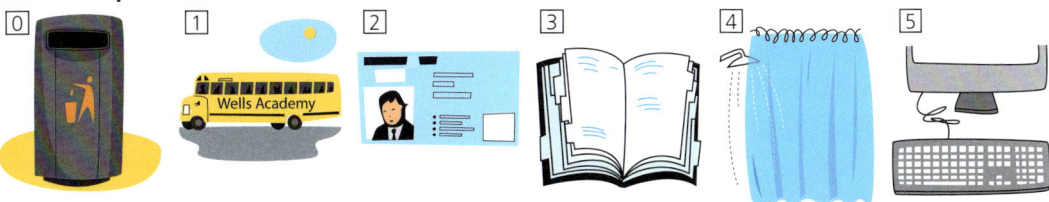

rubbish bin

A address computer identity
   rubbish school shower

B bin book bus card
   curtain keyboard

3 **GRAMMAR IN USE** Choose the correct words in *italics*. In one place, both answers are possible. 🔊 2.12 Listen and check.

Review: **Garlic and Shots Restaurant**

It was (0) *the end of a working week* / *a working week's end* and several of us decided we wanted a good night out. So, John, Lou, Charles, (1) *Charles'* / *Charles's* cousin and I got into (2) *the car of Lou* / *Lou's car* and went to (3) *London Soho district* / *London's Soho district* looking for an unusual restaurant. We found one. Garlic and Shots is a really interesting place to eat. Clearly, (4) *the idea of the restaurant* / *the restaurant's idea* is that all of the food contains garlic, and I mean <u>all</u> of the food! You can get garlic bread, garlic pasta, garlic drinks and even garlic ice cream! The (5) *food's variety* / *variety of the food* is amazing, but of course you have to be a (6) *garlic lover* / *garlic's lover*. We all had two courses, drinks and coffee (garlic coffee of course) and the (7) *bill's size* / *size of the bill* wasn't bad for central London.

4 Use the nouns in brackets to complete each sentence with **'s, '** or **of** + noun. In one sentence, two answers are possible. 🔊 2.13 Listen and check.

0 We can have the barbecue in *Anne's garden* – it's the biggest. (Anne + garden)
1 I can probably do work experience in .... after university. (Nick + father + business)
2 We have to provide .... every year by law. (four weeks + holiday)
3 I read an interesting magazine in the .... (doctor + waiting room)
4 We're collecting money so that the .... can stay open. (children + hospital)
5 It's the .... to provide homes for the homeless. (government + job)
6 Who's that at the door at this ....? (time + night)

7 Possessive adjectives and pronouns

1 Possessive adjectives and pronouns

Possessive adjectives and possessive pronouns tell us who things belong to.
*Are these **your** coffees?*
*Yes, thanks, they're **ours**.*

	SINGULAR					PLURAL		
subject pronouns	I	you	he	she	it	we	you	they
possessive adjectives	my	your	his	her	its	our	your	their
possessive pronouns	mine	yours	his	hers	– *	ours	yours	theirs

* There is no possessive pronoun form of *it*: *The green bowl is* (✗ *its*) *the cat's.* (= It belongs to the cat.)

2 Possessive adjectives

We use possessive adjectives to replace a noun + *'s* (➤ Unit 6.2):
*Lewis is **Yolanda's** son.* → *Lewis is **her** son.*
*That's **my grandparents'** house.* → *That's **their** house.*

The possessive adjective depends on the noun it replaces:
***Brad's** son = **his** son   **Brad's** daughter = **his** daughter* (✗ *her daughter*)
***Anna's** son = **her** son* (✗ *his son*) ***Anna's** daughter = **her** daughter*

We usually use possessive adjectives with parts of the body:
*Please raise **your** hand if you need more paper. **My** back is really painful today.*

 Remember that *its* is different from *it's* (= it is):
*The cat hasn't eaten **its** food. I think **it's** ill.* (= it is ill)

3 Possessive pronouns

If it's clear who/what we are talking about, we can use possessive pronouns. They replace a possessive adjective and noun:
*The cappuccino is **mine**.* (my cappuccino)
*I didn't have a seat so Brad offered me **his**.* (his seat)

 We don't use *a, an, the* or *'s* with possessive adjectives and pronouns:
✗ *That's my passport and this is the your's.*   ✓ *That's my passport and this is **yours**.*

4 a friend of John's, mine, hers, etc.

When someone has more than one of something, we can use *a/an* + noun +
- *of* + noun + *'s*: *'That's a good idea.' 'Actually, it was **an idea of John's**.'* (one of John's ideas)
- *of* + possessive pronoun: *Gerald is **a cousin of mine** from Devon.* (one of my cousins)
   ✗ *a cousin of me / a cousin of my*   ✓ *a cousin **of mine***

To emphasise that something belongs to someone, we use *a/an* + noun + *my/your/our*, etc. *own*:
*I don't like sharing – I've always wanted **a flat of my own**.* (my flat, for me only)
*Fran and Chris have got **a small business of their own**.* (not owned by anyone else)

Practice

1 **GRAMMAR IN USE** Read the information below. Then complete the conversation with the words from the box. 🔊 2.14 Listen and check.

Three friends are in a café. Amy orders a large cappuccino and a tuna sandwich. Olivia orders a cup of tea, a pasta salad and a piece of carrot cake. Maria orders a cola, a cheese omelette and a piece of carrot cake.

| hers hers ~~mine~~ mine is my Olivia's ours that yours yours |

WAITER	Here, we are. One large cappuccino.
AMY	That's (0) *mine*, thanks.
WAITER	And a cup of tea.
AMY	Maria, isn't that (1) ....?
MARIA	No, (2) .... the cola.
WAITER	Whose is the tea, then?
AMY	I think it's (3) ....
OLIVIA	Yes, that's right, it's mine.
WAITER	What about this pasta salad?
AMY	Oh, that's (4) ...., too. Olivia, take your salad.
WAITER	OK, two carrot cakes. Who are they for?
OLIVIA & MARIA	Oh, they're (5) .... Mmm, they look good.
WAITER	And, finally, a tuna sandwich. Is (6) ...., madam?
MARIA	No, I think it's (7) .... Amy?
AMY	Oh, yes. Thanks.
MARIA	Where's (8) .... cheese omelette?

2 Find and correct the mistake in each sentence.

0 We're going on holiday with some friends of ~~our~~ *ours*.
1 My daughter argues all the time with his new boss.
2 Clark couldn't come on the walk because he'd broken the ankle.
3 'Whose car is parked in the drive?' 'It's the mine. I'll move it.'
4 'Does this book belong to Maggie?' 'Yes, it's her.'
5 Sue and Jim suggested this restaurant. It was a good idea of them.
6 'Does this basket belong to your cat?' 'Yes, it's its.'

3 Complete the second sentence so it means the same as the first. Use two to five words in your answer. 🔊 2.15 Listen and check.

0 I don't have a calculator. Can I borrow yours?
Can I borrow your calculator? I don't have one *of my own*.
1 One of my uncles has given me tickets to the music festival next weekend.
An .... has given me tickets to the music festival next weekend.
2 My grandparents had a villa in Spain and they used to spend every summer in it.
My grandparents used to spend every summer in .... in Spain.
3 I bought two yoghurts. I've eaten mine and yours is in the fridge.
.... is in the fridge. I've eaten mine.
4 'Do you need a towel?' 'No, I've brought one of mine, thanks.'
'Do you need a towel?' 'No, I've brought a towel ...., thanks.'
5 Have you met Louise? She's one of Laura's friends.
Have you met Louise? She's a ....

⏻ Go online for more practice

21

8 Pronouns *one/ones*; *another/the other (one)*

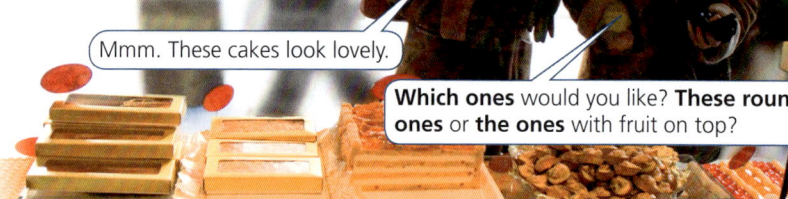

Mmm. These cakes look lovely.

Which ones would you like? **These round ones** or **the ones** with fruit on top?

1 one/ones

We can use *one/ones* to replace a noun:
SINGULAR   *I'd like a colour printer but I can't afford **one**.* (a colour printer)
PLURAL   *We've got lots of red apples on the tree but I prefer green **ones**.* (apples)

⚠ We use *one*, not *it* to mean 'one of many':
I need a stamp for this letter. ✗ *Have you got it?*   ✓ *Have you got **one**?*
We don't use *one* or *ones* to replace an uncountable noun:
✗ *I prefer brown rice to white one.*   ✓ *I prefer brown rice to **white** (rice).*

🔊 **Pronunciation** ➤ 1.04

2 this one, the + adjective + one(s)

We use *this/that/these/those* + *one(s)* to talk about particular things, and *which one(s)* to ask about them:
'**Which ones** would you like? **These ones** with fruit on top?'

We can use *a/an/the/some* + adjective + *one(s)*:
*The train was full so we decided to catch **a later one**.*
*The best computer games are **the most powerful ones**.*
*Dark trousers make me look thinner so I'd better get **some black ones**.*

⚠ If we add a phrase after *one* to describe it, we don't use *a/an* before it:
I'm looking for a new TV. ✗ *I'd like a one with a built-in DVD.*
✓ *I'd like **one** with a built-in DVD.*
But if we use an adjective before *one*, then we do use *a/an*:
✓ *I'd like **a big one** with a built-in DVD.*

3 another (one), the other one(s)

We use *another (one)* to talk about one more thing of the same type:
*That game was really good fun. Let's play **another (one)**.*
*I've appeared on one chat show and I'll never do **another (one)**!*

We can also use *another (one)* for a different thing of the same type:
'*I don't like this blue jumper.*' '*Well, exchange it for **another one**. There were lots of different colours in that shop.*'

⚠ We don't use *another one* with a noun:
✗ *I'd like another one coffee.*

We use *the other(s)/the other one(s)* for the second of two that are the same:
*I'll take this box. Can you take **the other one**?* (= the second of two boxes)
*Some of the students are in the gym and **the others/the other ones** are waiting in the hall.*

⚠ ✗ *We can put the others ones in the car.*   ✓ *We can put **the other ones** in the car.*

FORMALITY CHECK *Another one/the other one(s)* is less formal than *the others*:
*I think I prefer this payment plan to **the other ones** he showed me.* (informal)
*I assure you that this payment plan is better than **the others** on offer.* (formal)

Practice

1 Choose the correct words in *italics*. In three places, both answers are possible.

0   The local aerobics class is full so I'll have to find (*another*) / (*another one*).
1   'Would you like a cup of tea?' 'No, thanks. I've just had *one / ones*.'
2   'How did you do in the exam?' 'Which *one / ones*? I took six exams.'
3   If you miss the morning ferry, you can travel on *a later / a later one*.
4   These grapes are really sweet. Do you want to try *one / it*?
5   These paintings are for exhibition only, but all the *others / other ones* are for sale.
6   Would you prefer black pepper or *white / white one* on your meal?
7   I've packed two bags. Can you take *this / this one* and I'll take *the other / the other one*?
8   If you organise the team games at the children's party, I'll do all *the others / the others ones*.

2 **GRAMMAR IN USE** Find six more places where you can use *one* or *ones* instead of a noun. Write the correct word. 🔊 **2.16** Listen and check.

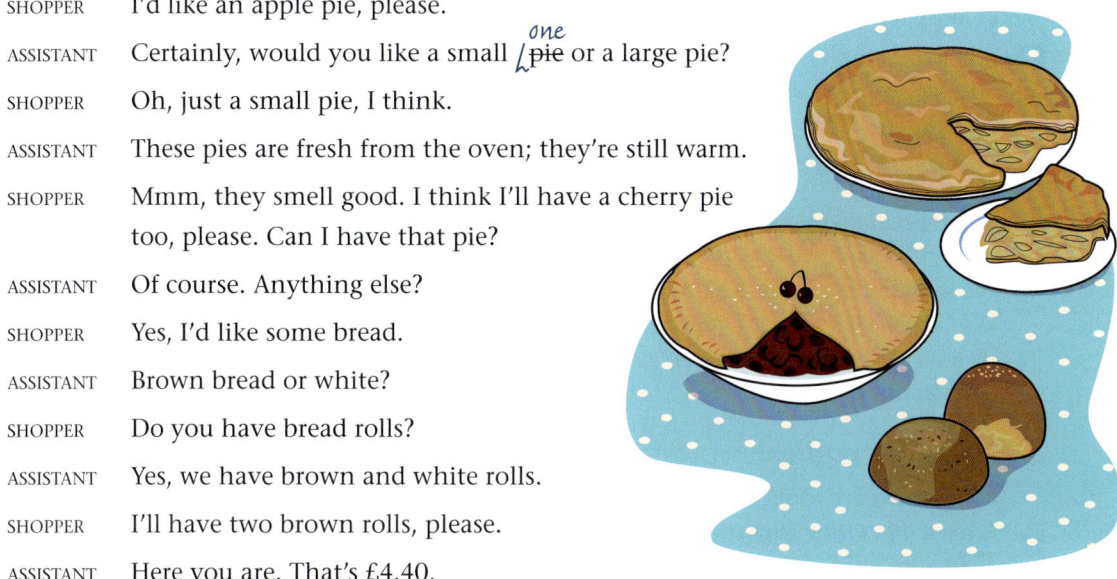

SHOPPER   I'd like an apple pie, please.
ASSISTANT   Certainly, would you like a small ~~pie~~ *one* or a large pie?
SHOPPER   Oh, just a small pie, I think.
ASSISTANT   These pies are fresh from the oven; they're still warm.
SHOPPER   Mmm, they smell good. I think I'll have a cherry pie too, please. Can I have that pie?
ASSISTANT   Of course. Anything else?
SHOPPER   Yes, I'd like some bread.
ASSISTANT   Brown bread or white?
SHOPPER   Do you have bread rolls?
ASSISTANT   Yes, we have brown and white rolls.
SHOPPER   I'll have two brown rolls, please.
ASSISTANT   Here you are. That's £4.40.

3 Complete a sentence for each situation.

0   You're planning a holiday with friends. They ask you whether you prefer quiet or lively holidays.
    You say: I prefer *quiet ones*.
1   You're trying on a jumper. It's too big. You call the assistant and say: Can I try ....?
2   A friend offers you a choice of egg sandwiches or cheese sandwiches. You say:
    I'll have ....
3   You have looked at two hotels on a website. Your friend prefers the first hotel but you don't. You say: I prefer ....
4   The hotel receptionist asks if you'd like a room with a bath or with a shower. You say:
    I'd like ....
5   There are two films on at your local cinema. One of them is very violent and you don't want to watch it. You say to your friend: Let's watch ....
6   You're looking at mobile phones. The shop assistant asks whether you want a phone with Internet access or not. You say: I'd like ....

⏻ Go online for more practice

9 Reflexive and other pronouns

1 Alice and Imogen are looking at **each other**.

2 Alice and Imogen are looking at **themselves**.

1 Reflexive pronouns

Compare the form and use of object pronouns and reflexive pronouns:

OBJECT/REFLEXIVE   *me/myself   you/yourself   him/himself   her/herself   it/itself*
us/ourselves   you/yourselves   them/themselves

*Her name is Christine but **her friends** call **her** Tina.* (*her* = object pronoun)

*Her name is Christine but **she** calls **herself** Tina.* (*herself* = reflexive pronoun)

We use reflexive pronouns (*myself, yourself*, etc.) when the subject and object of a sentence are the same person or thing: *Have **you** hurt **yourself**?*

We can also use reflexive pronouns to emphasise the subject of the sentence:
*Why do I have to do everything **myself**? Dentists use this toothpaste **themselves**.*

By myself/himself, etc. means 'alone/on your own' or 'without help':
*'Do you live **by yourself**?' 'No, I share a flat.' The children did the drawing **by themselves**.*

2 Verbs with reflexive pronouns

Some verbs are often used with reflexive pronouns, for example:
*They didn't **enjoy themselves** on the activity holiday – it was hard work!*
***Help yourself** to some food – there's plenty of it!*
*Did the children **behave themselves** at the zoo?*
*I **blame myself** for the mistakes in the report – I didn't check it carefully.*

⚠️ *Complain, feel, remember, rest, relax, get up* and *stand up* do not have a reflexive pronoun:
✗ ~~Do you remember yourself the hotel?~~ ✓ *Do you **remember** the hotel?*
But we can use a reflexive with *wash, shave* and *dress* if the situation is unusual:
✓ *After my operation I couldn't **dress myself** for three weeks.*

3 each other, one another

We use *each other* and *one another* when the subject and object are different:
*Alice and Imogen are looking at **each other/one another**.*
(= Alice is looking at Imogen and Imogen is looking at Alice.)
Compare: *Alice and Imogen are looking at **themselves**.*
(= Alice is looking at Alice and Imogen is looking at Imogen.)

4 you, one and they

We often use *you* for people in general: ***You** can't park here after 8.30 in the morning.*
We can also use *one* but it is very formal: ***One** needs to be careful when travelling alone.*

We often use *they* for the people in government or in charge of organisations:
***They're** putting taxes up again. **They** closed the factory in 2008.*

We also use *they* to talk about someone when we don't know who he or she is.
*Someone left this note for you, but **they** didn't leave **their** name.*

2

Practice

1 Complete the second sentence so it means the same as the first. Use reflexive pronouns and any other words that are necessary. 🔊 2.17 Listen and check.

0   We hope that all our guests have a good time.
    We hope that all our guests enjoy *themselves*.
1   Children under twelve must be with an adult.
    Children under twelve can't see the film ....
2   Danger! Hard hats must be worn to prevent injury.
    If you don't wear a hard hat, you may ....
3   This is a self-service restaurant.
    In this restaurant, we have to get the food ....
4   Any of the team's supporters found causing problems will be removed.
    All the supporters must behave ....

2 Match the sentences 1–5 with the pictures A–F.

0   Ryan brought his brother home and made him a cup of coffee.   .D......
1   Ryan got home late and made himself a cup of coffee.   ....
2   Jane went out with her daughter and bought her an ice cream.   ....
3   Jane went out this afternoon and bought herself an ice cream.   ....
4   The elephants frequently wash themselves.   ....
5   The elephants enjoy washing one another.   ....

3 **GRAMMAR IN USE** Read the conversation and choose the correct words in *italics*.
🔊 2.18 Listen and check.

TONI   Hi, Jan. Did you have a good holiday?
JAN   Oh yes, thanks. We really enjoyed (0) *us /(ourselves)*! We were in one of those really big holiday clubs, you know, where (1) *you / they* pay before you go. There were a lot of activities, so the twins could look after (2) *them / themselves* and we didn't have to worry about (3) *them / themselves*.
TONI   They're old enough to play with (4) *them / each other* now, anyway, aren't they?
JAN   Oh, of course, we can leave them (5) *by / on* themselves now for short periods and not worry. Oh, how's your roof, by the way? Did you get it fixed?
TONI   Well, the builder started, but he fell off a ladder and hurt (6) *hisself / himself*. He wasn't badly hurt but he couldn't finish the roof.
JAN   It's true what (7) *one / they* say – if you want a job done well, do it (8) *yourself / your own*!

10 some, any, all, most, no, none of

That's **all** the shopping – we've got **some** fruit and **some** vegetables ...

But we haven't got **any** bread. I'll go and get **some**.

1 some and any

We use *some* and *any* + noun when we don't know the exact number/amount, or it is not important:
*We've got **some** vegetables. Have we got **any** milk?*

We usually use *some* in positive sentences and *any* in questions and negative sentences.
- We can use *some* in questions if they are requests, offers or suggestions:
  *Can I have **some** information? Would you like **some** brochures? Shall we do **some** work now?*
- We can use *some* and *any* without a noun, when it is clear what we are talking about:
  *We haven't got any bread. I'll go and get **some**.*
  *'We need some coins for the ticket machine.' 'Oh dear, I haven't got **any**.'*
- We can use *any* to mean 'it doesn't matter which':
  *'Which flavour ice cream do you want?' 'Oh, get me **any** flavour – I don't mind which.'*

🔊 Pronunciation ➤ 1.05

2 all, most, some and no/none

We can use *all*, *most*, *some* and *no* before the subject or object in a sentence:
***All** the tickets cost £30.00. I've got **all** the tickets.*

They can go before plural or uncountable nouns:
***All fruit** contains sugar. **Most vegetables** contain a lot of vitamins.*
***Some fish** is expensive. **No sugary food** is good for you.*

We use *all (of)*, *most of*, *some of* and *none of* for particular people or things:
***All (of)** the vegetables in this soup are fresh.*
***Most of** our customers like the vegetarian dishes.*
*Do you want **some of** this white chocolate?*
***None of** our jam contains extra sugar.*

NATURAL ENGLISH We don't usually say *all people* or *no people*. We say *everyone/everybody* and *no one/nobody*: *Is **everyone** ready? **Nobody** called for you today.*

3 no, none of

No and *none of* mean 'not any'. We use them in negative statements, with a positive verb:
✗ *None of the advice he gave wasn't useful.*   ✓ ***None of** the advice he gave **was** useful.*

	SINGULAR COUNTABLE NOUN	PLURAL NOUN	UNCOUNTABLE NOUN
none of	—	**None of** the machines *is/are* working.*	**None of** the bread *was* fresh.
no	**No** reason *was* given.	**No** reasons *were* given.	**No** information *was* given.

* A singular verb after *none of* + plural noun is more formal.

Practice

1 **GRAMMAR IN USE** Read the conversation about a TV programme and choose the correct words in *italics*. 🔊 2.19 Listen and check.

LIZ   What's *The Restaurant*? Have you seen it?

LINDA Yes, it's a TV show for people who want to open a restaurant with Raymond Blanc. Nine teams start, but (0) *all / most* of them have to leave during the series as only one team can win.

LIZ   What do they have to do?

LINDA Well, each week (1) *all / any* of the teams do a task in their restaurant, but only (2) *none / some* of them can succeed.

LIZ   What do you mean? Do (3) *any / none* of them have to leave the show?

LINDA No, (4) *most / none* of them have to leave at this point, but (5) *some / most* of the teams – the worst two or three – do another task, and then the worst team has to leave.

LIZ   Do the teams come from different restaurants or are they amateur cooks?

LINDA I don't think (6) *some / any* of them are complete amateurs – they all have some professional experience.

Raymond Blanc shares his love of good food in *The Restaurant* tonight on BBC2.

2 Find and correct the mistake in each sentence. 🔊 2.20 Listen and check.

0 ~~There's any~~ milk left in the fridge. We need to buy some.
   There isn't any / There's no

1 'How many of these books should we bring?' 'All them, please.'

2 Can I have any mineral water with my meal, please?

3 There weren't no phone calls for you today.

4 'Where are the drinks?' 'We didn't buy none.'

5 Can I borrow a pen, please? Some colour will be fine.

6 'How many songs have you got on your iPod?' 'I've got any. I've just bought it.'

7 None of the visitors didn't enjoy the exhibition. They all hated it.

8 Most information the guide gave us was very useful.

3 Write sentences with the words below. Change the verbs as necessary.

0 Cathy / have / any / close friends / her class   *Cathy hasn't got any close friends in her class.*
1 Arnaud / like / most / music   ....
2 Fran / have / some / designer clothes   ....
3 John / read / all / Shakespeare's plays   ....
4 Ellen / visit / any / foreign countries   ....

4 Now make the sentences in Exercise 3 true for you.

0 I *'ve got some close friends in my class* .
1 I ....
2 I ....
3 I ....
4 I ....

11 Indefinite pronouns

1 Indefinite pronouns

We use indefinite pronouns to talk about a person, thing or place, when we don't know who or what they are, or it is not important.

PEOPLE	THINGS	PLACES
someone/somebody	something	somewhere
anyone/anybody	anything	anywhere
everyone/everybody	everything	everywhere
no one/nobody	nothing	nowhere

2 Use of indefinite pronouns

We use indefinite pronouns with *some* in positive sentences:
Someone will help you. (It doesn't matter who.)
My wallet is **somewhere** in this room. (I don't know where exactly.)
We can use them in requests, offers or suggestions (➤ Unit 10.1):
Shall we order **something** to drink?

We usually use indefinite pronouns with *any* in questions and negative sentences:
It's very dark – can you see **anything**? There isn't **anyone** at home.

We use indefinite pronouns with *every* to mean 'all people/things/places':
I've met **everyone** in the company now. **Everything** is ready.
Have you looked **everywhere** for your glasses?

We use indefinite pronouns with *no* with positive verbs, but the meaning is negative:
There was **no one** in the hotel who could help me.

⚠ We don't use two negatives: ✗ *No one wasn't there.* ✓ **No one was** there.

3 Indefinite pronouns + verb

Indefinite pronouns take a singular verb when they are the subject of a sentence:
Someone's waiting outside. **Something smells** good! What are you cooking?
Has anyone got a menu? 'What would you like to drink?' '**Anything is** fine. I'm really thirsty.'
Nobody was at home. **No one expects** you to be perfect.
Everything here **is** expensive. **Is everyone** here?

4 Other uses

We often use adjectives after indefinite pronouns: I'd like **something cool**, with ice.
Is there **anywhere quiet** round here? We need **someone reliable** for this job.

We also use *to* + verb after indefinite pronouns: Shall we order **something to drink**?
There's **nowhere to sit** inside the restaurant – it's full. I haven't got **anything to wear**.

We often use *else* after indefinite pronouns. It means 'another person/thing/place' or 'a different person/thing/place':
This club is boring. Let's go **somewhere else**. (to another club)
Don't you have **anything else** on the menu? (something different)

Practice

1 GRAMMAR IN USE Complete the review with the words from the box.
🔊 **2.21** Listen and check.

> anything everyone ~~everything~~ everything everywhere
> nothing nowhere somebody something

Review of the week – *Harrods Food Hall*

(0) *Everything* I had heard about this place was good. So on the last day of our trip to London, my wife and I visited this famous store. Well, we couldn't believe it! We've been (1) .... in the world, but (2) .... was as good as this! My wife wanted to buy (3) .... special for some friends, and there was so much to choose from. Harrods sells (4) .... – from seafood to chocolates. Of course, the only problem is that (5) .... is cheap. Still, we wanted to eat at Harrods – (6) ...., it didn't matter what – so we had an ice cream, and it was fantastic! The staff are so good, too; we asked (7) .... in uniform for some information and she was very helpful. My only real criticism was that it was very crowded – it seemed that (8) .... in London was in Harrods that day!

2 Choose the correct indefinite pronouns in the lines from songs.
0 *Nothing /(Everything)* I do, I do it for you.
1 *Anything / Something* you can do, I can do better.
2 *Somewhere / Anywhere* over the rainbow, skies are blue.
3 I can't run from myself; there's *anywhere / nowhere* to hide.
4 *Anything / Nothing* means more than the truth.

3 Rewrite sentences 1–4. Use an indefinite pronoun to replace the underlined words. Then rewrite sentences 5–8. Use an indefinite pronoun + adjective/*else* or *to* + verb.
🔊 **2.22** Listen and check.

0 I know I left my keys <u>in a place</u> in this room.
I know I left my keys somewhere in this room.

1 <u>Not one person</u> came to the school open day.
....

2 Jelena had <u>no belongings at all</u> when she came to this country.
....

3 I'd like a volunteer from the audience – <u>any person</u> will be OK.
....

4 The police searched <u>all the rooms</u> in the building but didn't find the murderer.
....

00 I'm bored with toast. I want <u>a different breakfast</u> this morning.
I want something else this morning.

5 I don't feel like a hot drink. Have you got <u>a cold drink</u>?
....

6 All these cameras are too expensive. Don't you have <u>a cheaper one</u>?
....

7 I'd rather not see Mr Knightley. Can I see <u>a different person</u>?
....

8 Can I have <u>a book or magazine that I can read</u>?
....

12 much, many, a lot of, (a) little, (a) few

1 much, many, a lot of (lots of)

We use *much*, *many* and *a lot of* to talk about a large amount; we don't know the exact amount.
- We usually use *much* and *many* in negative sentences and questions:
  + UNCOUNTABLE NOUN We haven't got **much water**.
  + COUNTABLE NOUN   There aren't **many cans** of cola.
- We use *a lot of* or *lots of* in positive and negative sentences and questions:
  We've got **a lot of** orange juice.
  Hurry up! We haven't got **a lot of** time.
  Were there **lots of** people at the swimming pool?

We can use these words without a noun, when it is clear what we are talking about:
*I've got some money with me but not **much**. I've got **a lot** to do today.* (✗ *a lot of to do*)

FORMALITY CHECK *Much* and *many* in positive sentences are formal. We prefer *a lot of* or *lots of* for informal use:
Many of the experiments produced useful results. (formal)
Come on. We've got **a lot of** work to do. (informal)

2 too much, too many, not enough

Too much and *too many* have a negative meaning. They mean 'more than we want':
We've got **too many** pizzas for only three people. We can't walk here – there's **too much** snow.
Not enough is the opposite of *too much/many*. It means 'less/fewer than we want':
We have**n't** got **enough** cola for the children. We did**n't** have **enough** people to play football.

3 (a) little, (a) few

We use *a little* instead of *some* to talk about a small amount; we use *a few* instead of *some* to talk about a small number; we don't know the exact amount or number:
+ UNCOUNTABLE NOUN Add **a little** butter to the potatoes.
+ COUNTABLE NOUN   There are **a few** good restaurants near here.

When we use *little* (without *a*), it means 'not much/not enough': *You will have **little** difficulty in finding my house. There's **little** hope of finishing this today.*

When we use *few* (without *a*), it means 'not many/not enough': ***Few** tourists come to the island. There are **few** good hotels near here.*

FORMALITY CHECK *Little* and *few* can sound quite formal on their own. In everyday English, we prefer to use *very little/very few* or *not much/not many*:
There are **very few** good restaurants near here. There are**n't many** good restaurants near here.

Practice

1 Match the beginning of each sentence with the correct ending, A or B.

0 There was a little rice left, so …
   A we couldn't have any with our curry.   (B) we had a spoonful each with our curry.
1 There was a lot of rice left, so …
   A we made a really big salad with it.   B we had to have potatoes with our curry.
2 There was very little rice left, so …
   A we all had a lot with our curry.   B we had to have potatoes instead.
3 There were a few potatoes left, so …
   A we had one each with our meal.   B we had to have rice with our meal.
4 There were very few potatoes left, so …
   A we had to have rice with our meal.   B we had two or three each with our meal.

2 **GRAMMAR IN USE** Read the article and choose the correct words in *italics*.
🔊 **2.23** Listen and check.

Crisis in science education

Companies are complaining there aren't (0) (*enough*) / *much* students taking science subjects now, especially physics. The problem, it seems, is that (1) *few / many* students see science subjects as too difficult, when there are (2) *a lot / a lot of* easier options, such as media studies. Professor Jennifer Cousins of Exmouth University comments: "This is becoming a serious problem. (3) *Very few / A few* students are choosing to study science subjects these days, which means that there (4) *are enough / aren't enough* graduates applying for jobs in the industrial sector. The way I see it, there are (5) *too many / too much* new courses at university level, and there's so (6) *much / many* competition between graduates that most students 'play safe' and take courses they feel more confident in. At present they have (7) *a little / little* incentive to choose scientific subjects because science is seen as both difficult and boring. We must introduce (8) *a little / a few* more excitement into science in schools."

3 **GRAMMAR IN USE** Complete the conversation with the words and phrases from the box.
🔊 **2.24** Listen and check.

a little   a lot   not much   ~~many~~   much   many   not many

JEZ Let's get something to eat. Are there (0) ..*many*...... restaurants here?

ALI Yes, there are quite (1) ...., but there's (2) .... variety. What kinds of food do you like?

JEZ Well, I eat too (3) .... junk food so I'd prefer something different. Are there any British restaurants here?

ALI Yes, but (4) .... There are only two, I think, and they're expensive. Do you eat much Indian food?

JEZ Well, I have tried (5) .... Indian food before, but I'm not very keen on it – sorry, Ali. I know you love it. What about Chinese?

ALI Oh, there are so (6) .... Chinese restaurants here that everyone gets bored with Chinese food! I know – we both like Italian. Let's go to Giovanni's.

⏻ Go online for more practice   31

13 *both, either, neither; each, every*

Both these dishes are very different from British food, partly because **neither** contains meat or potatoes.

1 Form

	+ NOUN	+ *of* + *the/those/my*, etc. + NOUN	+ (NOUN) + VERB (as a subject)
both	both dishes[1]	both the dishes/both of the dishes	both (dishes) **are** tasty
either	either dish	either of the dishes	either (dish) **is** tasty
neither	neither dish	neither of the dishes	neither (dish) **is** tasty
each	each dish	each (one) of the dishes	each (dish) **is** tasty
every	every dish[2]	every one of the dishes	every dish **is** tasty

[1] *Both* is followed by a plural noun and a plural verb. The others are usually singular.
[2] We do not use *every* as a pronoun: ✗ *Every is tasty.* ✓ *Every dish / Every one is tasty.*

2 *both, either, neither*

Both, *either* and *neither* can be objects (*I like **both** dishes*) or subjects (***Both** dishes are tasty*).
- *both* means 'one and the other': ***Both** these dishes are different from British food.*
- *either* (often + *or*) means 'one or the other': *I'm happy with **either** Chinese or Indian food. My husband's mad about both football and cricket, but I don't enjoy **either of them**.*
- *neither* (often + *nor*) means 'not one or the other':
  ***Neither** Indian nor Chinese food is expensive.*

With *either* and *neither* we sometimes use a plural verb, especially after *of the* + plural noun:
***Neither of the children are** learning French this year.*

3 *each, every*

We use *each* and *every* to talk about ALL the people or things in a group:
*You can find **every** type of food in London. I've tried **each** dish on the menu.*

If there are only two people or things in the group we use *each*, not *every*:
*The bride had several bracelets on **each** wrist and rings on **every** finger.*

When we use *each*, we think of each member of the group separately:
***Every** student in the room stood up when the new Principal came in.* (as a group)
*He then went round the room and spoke to **each** student individually.* (one by one)

⚠ We do not use *each* or *every* + *not* in negative sentences; we use *neither (of)* or *none of*:
✗ *Every/Each player didn't try hard.*
✓ ***Neither** player tried hard / **None of the** players tried hard.*
But we can use *not every*: ***Not every** player tried hard.* (= Most tried hard, but not all.)

4 *all* or *a/the whole*

We use *all the* before plural or uncountable nouns for something 'complete':
*He's eaten **all the** bread. Have you finished **all the** olives?*
We also use *all* after pronouns: *They **all** arrived at the same time. He's eaten it **all**.*
We use *a whole/the whole* before singular nouns:
*I've used **a whole** tank of petrol going to the hospital this week.*
*Have you eaten **the whole** cake?*

Practice

1 Use the pictures to correct the sentences. Use a word from the table on the opposite page and make any other changes if necessary.

Only $4.99

for main course + dessert!

Meal deal 1: beef steak, French fries, green beans + ice cream

Meal deal 2: lamb burger, French fries, salad + apple pie

0 One of the meals includes a dessert.   *Both of the meals include a dessert.*
1 Both of the meals are vegetarian.   ....
2 Neither meal contains vegetables.   ....
3 Both pictures show the whole meal.   ....
4 One of the meals includes French fries.   ....

2 **GRAMMAR IN USE** Complete the conversation with the words from the box.
🔊 **2.25** Listen and check.

all ~~both~~ both either either every neither neither whole

ANN   There are two good holidays on this website, and they're (0) *both* on popular
       islands, Tenerife and Corfu. I haven't been to (1) .... of them.
KELLY Really? I've been to (2) .... Are the flight times good or are they night flights?
ANN   No, (3) .... of them involves a night flight.
KELLY Oh, that's good. How much are they?
ANN   Well, (4) .... is very expensive. The Tenerife one is all-inclusive, and it's £499.
KELLY So it's £499 for the (5) .... holiday, including all meals and drinks?
ANN   Yes, that's right.
KELLY That's good. How much is the other one?
ANN   It's cheaper; it's £389, but that only includes breakfast, so we'd have to buy
       (6) .... other meal.
KELLY Yes, but (7) .... the restaurants in Greece that I've ever been to are fairly
       cheap. I'm happy to go on (8) .... of the holidays.

3 Complete the second sentence so it means the same as the first. Use one to three words.
🔊 **2.26** Listen and check.

0 I've seen all the Coen brothers' films.   I've seen *every* Coen brothers' film.
1 She's got burns on each hand.   She's burnt .... her hands.
2 Did he eat all the chocolate?   Did he eat .... bar of chocolate?
3 Both of the restaurants are expensive.   .... is cheap.
4 Every student passed the exam.   .... students passed the exam.
5 She saw neither of the candidates.   She .... either of the candidates.

⏻ Go online for more practice and a progress test

33

Review MODULE 2

1 UNITS 6 AND 7 Read Anya's email and choose the correct words in *italics*. In three places, both answers are possible.

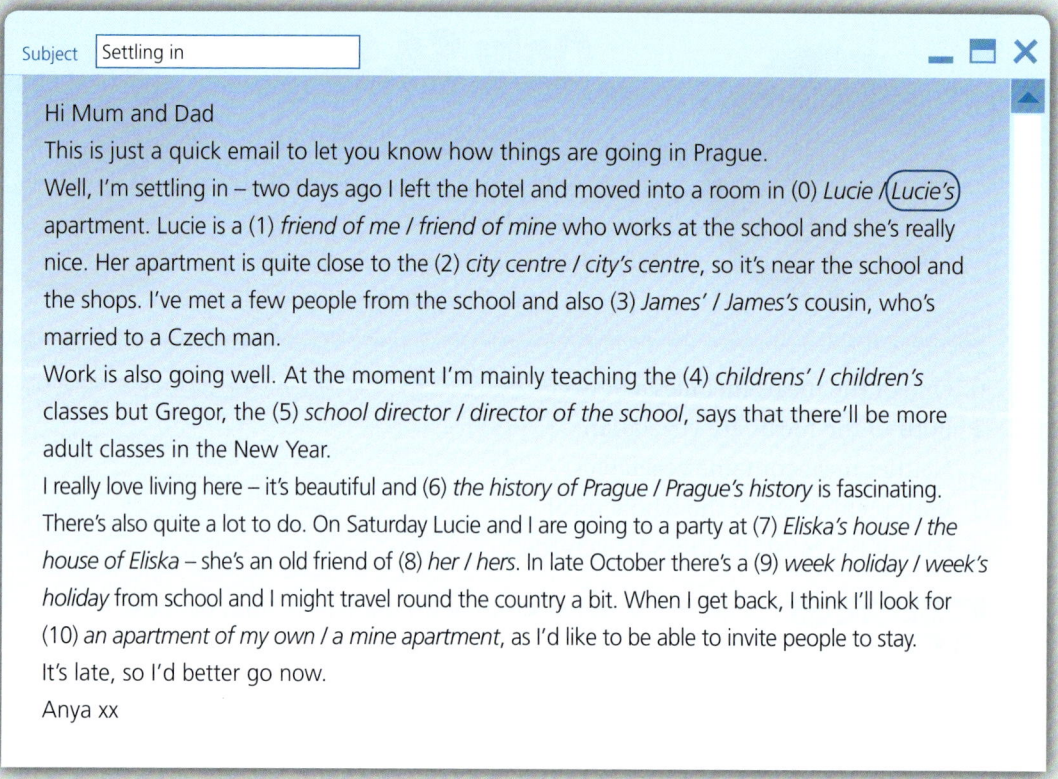

Subject: Settling in

Hi Mum and Dad

This is just a quick email to let you know how things are going in Prague.

Well, I'm settling in – two days ago I left the hotel and moved into a room in (0) *Lucie / (Lucie's)* apartment. Lucie is a (1) *friend of me / friend of mine* who works at the school and she's really nice. Her apartment is quite close to the (2) *city centre / city's centre*, so it's near the school and the shops. I've met a few people from the school and also (3) *James' / James's* cousin, who's married to a Czech man.

Work is also going well. At the moment I'm mainly teaching the (4) *childrens' / children's* classes but Gregor, the (5) *school director / director of the school*, says that there'll be more adult classes in the New Year.

I really love living here – it's beautiful and (6) *the history of Prague / Prague's history* is fascinating. There's also quite a lot to do. On Saturday Lucie and I are going to a party at (7) *Eliska's house / the house of Eliska* – she's an old friend of (8) *her / hers*. In late October there's a (9) *week holiday / week's holiday* from school and I might travel round the country a bit. When I get back, I think I'll look for (10) *an apartment of my own / a mine apartment*, as I'd like to be able to invite people to stay.

It's late, so I'd better go now.

Anya xx

2 UNITS 8, 9 AND 11 Rewrite the sentences, using the words in brackets.

0 That cake was delicious. I'd really like a second cake. (another / one)
  That cake was delicious. I'd really like another one.

1 Jimmy likes Ben and Ben likes Jimmy. (each)
  ....

2 There are no seats left in the hall. (nowhere / sit)
  ....

3 Some of the students are staying with us and the remaining students are in the hostel. (others)
  ....

4 Alexei was badly injured when he fell down the stairs. (himself)
  ....

5 The council is always digging the road up! (they)
  ....

6 Did you go to the cinema without any other people? (by)
  ....

7 I'd like a banana but I don't want that green banana. (one)
  ....

8 The letter was sent to all the people in this district. (everyone)
  ....

3 UNITS 10, 12 AND 13 Complete the answers to the questions. Use a word or phrase from Box A and a word or phrase from Box B.

A   a few   all the   any   both   every   much   ~~no~~   too much   very few

B   day   his numbers   homework   petrol   ~~reason~~   seats   station   students   travel documents

0 Why are you angry?
   Because there was really *no reason* for you to be late!
1 Do you want Mr Gould's home or work phone details?
   Can you give me ....?
2 Why can't I watch *My Name is Earl* tonight, Dad?
   Because you've got .... to do!
3 How often do you have to practise the guitar?
   Oh, ... Otherwise your fingers get stiff.
4 Samia can't find her train ticket. Where is it?
   It's OK. The teacher's got ....
5 Did many people come to your presentation?
   Well, ... came, but no lecturers.
6 You're driving slowly. Is there a problem?
   Yes, we haven't got .... left.
7 Where can I buy a travelcard?
   You can get one at .... or newsagent's.
8 Should I book that trip today?
   Yes, there are .... left on the coach.

4 UNITS 12 AND 13 Read the text and choose the correct answer, A, B or C below.

We're very lucky where we live because we've got (0) .... different shops nearby that sell interesting food. There are two butchers and they (1) .... sell very good meat, but unfortunately (2) .... of them sells fish. We can buy fish from a fresh fish van, but that doesn't come (3) .... day. There are two delicatessens: (4) .... sells different things, and (5) .... sell every kind of cheese you can think of! We've got three very good greengrocers and there are two supermarkets nearby, but we don't go to (6) .... because we prefer the smaller shops. There's also a market (7) .... weekend. Apart from the food shops, there are very (8) .... other shops, though – hardly any, in fact. There (9) .... clothes shops – only a shoe shop and a small boutique. However, there are (10) .... Indian restaurants! We've got three of them in the high street!

0   A much   B both   (C) a lot of
1   A both   B every   C all
2   A both   B neither   C every
3   A every   B either   C both
4   A each of   B each of them   C neither of them
5   A both them   B each them   C both of them
6   A neither   B either   C every
7   A every   B either   C neither
8   A many   B little   C few
9   A are many   B aren't enough   C are enough
10 A too many   B too much   C too few

35

5 ALL UNITS Match the sentences 1–6 with those in A–G that have the same meaning.

0 There wasn't anyone around.
1 It was my cousins' car.
2 We did that all by ourselves.
3 Our time off work is only a month.
4 There isn't enough for us all to have some.
5 We'd like something a little different.
6 We missed both of them.

A We get only four weeks' holiday.
B We didn't get to see either of them.
C It belonged to relatives of mine.
D Can you get us a different one, please?
E That was done entirely on our own.
F There was no one there.
G There's only a little left.

6 ALL UNITS Correct the sentences so that they describe the picture accurately.

0 Alicia has a lot of cola left.   *Alicia has a little cola left.*
1 Neither child has dark hair.
2 Carol has a bag of crisps.
3 The adults are talking to themselves.
4 Dennis is Paula's daughter.
5 One child isn't behaving himself.
6 They've eaten most of the cake.
7 They've eaten all the sandwiches.
8 One of the children is wearing a red T-shirt.

7 ALL UNITS Complete the conversation with words and phrases from A–L below. There are three extra phrases.

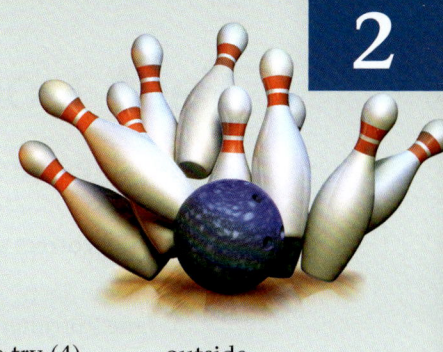

ALAN   Shall we go bowling this evening?
DAVE   I've never been bowling. Have (0) .F..... been before?
ALAN   We've been (1) .... times, yes.
ROB   OK. Which bowling alley shall we go to?
ALAN   How about Rowan's, near the (2) ....? It's quite good.
DICK   Oh, but (3) .... there. It's always crowded. Why don't we try (4) .... outside town for a change?
ALAN   That's a good idea. (5) .... friend works there so we might get a discount.
ROB   I doubt it! We don't get on very well!
DAVE   Will I be OK in these shoes?
DICK   Yes. You have to wear (6) .... they give you at the bowling alley, anyway.
ALAN   (7) .... a membership card for that bowling alley?
ROB   You don't have to be a member to play; it just costs (8) .... to get in if you're a member.
ALAN   OK. Let's go then.

A Has anyone got	E few	I a few
B everyone goes	F all of you	J the one
C centre shopping	G Rob brother	K shopping centre
D a little less	H the special ones	L Rob's brother's

8 ALL UNITS Read the article and think of the best word for each gap. Write one word only.

Celebrity chefs

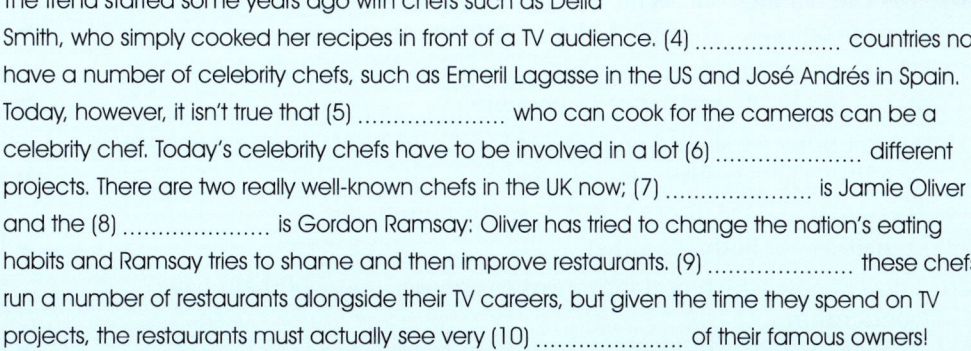

We have always had chefs, and we have celebrities, too. But now we have both in the rise (0) ....of...... the TV celebrity chef. These are chefs who usually run (1) .... own restaurants and may have written (2) .... few cookery books, but who also often turn up on the TV, appearing in cookery 'magazine' shows or presenting (3) .... of their own. The trend started some years ago with chefs such as Delia Smith, who simply cooked her recipes in front of a TV audience. (4) .... countries now have a number of celebrity chefs, such as Emeril Lagasse in the US and José Andrés in Spain. Today, however, it isn't true that (5) .... who can cook for the cameras can be a celebrity chef. Today's celebrity chefs have to be involved in a lot (6) .... different projects. There are two really well-known chefs in the UK now; (7) .... is Jamie Oliver and the (8) .... is Gordon Ramsay: Oliver has tried to change the nation's eating habits and Ramsay tries to shame and then improve restaurants. (9) .... these chefs run a number of restaurants alongside their TV careers, but given the time they spend on TV projects, the restaurants must actually see very (10) .... of their famous owners!

Test MODULE 2

Possessives, pronouns and quantifiers

Choose the correct answer, A, B or C.

1 Have you seen .... motorbike? It's really powerful.
   A Jane's brother   B Jane brother's   C Jane's brother's   ▶ Unit 6

2 We're going to stay with .... when we're in Madrid.
   A Kevin's cousin   B the cousin of Kevin   C Kevin cousin   ▶ Unit 6

3 Jules has painted the .... a dreadful shade of pink.
   A bedroom's walls   B bedroom walls   C wall bedrooms   ▶ Unit 6

4 I fell when I was running for the bus and twisted .... ankle really badly.
   A mine   B my   C the   ▶ Unit 7

5 I didn't know that Katherine was a colleague of ....!
   A you   B your   C yours   ▶ Unit 7

6 'Green or black olives?' 'Oh, black. I really don't like the ....'
   A green ones   B green one   C greens   ▶ Unit 8

7 That was a really good game. Do you want to play ....?
   A one other   B the other   C another one   ▶ Unit 8

8 'Did you get decorators to paint your lounge?' 'No, we did it ....'
   A ourselves   B by our own   C ourself   ▶ Unit 9

9 Sally had been working very hard and she decided to give .... a break.
   A her   B Sally   C herself   ▶ Unit 9

10 Our two children walk to school together, so they can look after ....
   A themselves   B one another   C another one   ▶ Unit 9

11 Have you heard that .... are going to close the hospital?
   A one   B we   C they   ▶ Unit 9

12 'Which type of envelope do you want?'
   '.......... envelope is fine; it's only to post a bill.'
   A Some   B No type   C Any   ▶ Unit 10

13 I can't believe it – the supermarket had .... fish again today!
   A any   B none   C no   ▶ Unit 10

14 Jez's party was boring. I didn't meet .... I knew there.
   A anyone   B no one   C someone   ▶ Unit 11

15 You missed .... really interesting on the news earlier today.
   A anything   B anybody   C something   ▶ Unit 11

16 You can tell me your secret. I promise I won't tell ....
   A someone else   B anyone else   C no one else   ▶ Unit 11

17 The problem with kids today is that they have .... free time.
   A too much   B too many   C enough   ▶ Unit 12

18 I don't think we should employ Mr Frank – he's got .... experience.
   A a little   B very little   C very few   ▶ Unit 12

19 'Do you prefer Picasso or Dali?' 'Frankly, I don't like .... of them!'
   A neither   B both   C either   ▶ Unit 13

20 I don't know which of the two cars to choose; .... of them have good features.
   A each   B both   C every   ▶ Unit 13

Go online for a full exit test

Prepositions

MODULE 3

Before you start

1 Read the email. Look at the <mark>highlighted</mark> grammar examples.

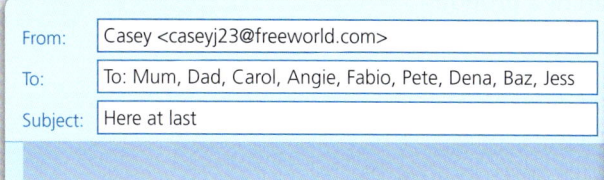

From: Casey <caseyj23@freeworld.com>
To: Mum, Dad, Carol, Angie, Fabio, Pete, Dena, Baz, Jess
Subject: Here at last

Hi guys
Well, my gap year has started! We landed <mark>in</mark> Nepal a few days ago after a long journey. I couldn't sleep at all <mark>during</mark> the flight because I was so excited! We flew <mark>over</mark> the Himalayas – that was just so beautiful. When we arrived, we went <mark>by</mark> bus to Chautara and we had to do the last part of the journey to this village on horses, would you believe? It's miles from anywhere. And it's freezing at night – the days are pleasant but I can only keep warm at night <mark>by wrapping</mark> up in clothes and getting <mark>under</mark> about fifteen blankets!
As you know, we're here to build a school for the community. All of our group are involved in the building work <mark>except</mark> me and Fran – we're lucky; we're working <mark>as</mark> the group cooks, so the others have to do the hard work! We're going to be here <mark>until</mark> about mid-November – the building will take <mark>at least</mark> two months – then we're moving south to India, before it gets too cold …

2 Now read the sentences and choose the correct words in *italics*. The <mark>highlighted</mark> grammar examples will help you.

1 You can register for the expedition by *complete / completing* a form online. ▶ Unit 14
2 We arrived *in / at* Crete in the middle of the night. ▶ Unit 14
3 The cat's *below / under* the blanket – he always hides there! ▶ Unit 14
4 We have to fly *through / over* the Andes when we come back. ▶ Unit 15
5 I was reading *during / for* the journey so I didn't see much of the scenery. ▶ Unit 16
6 I'd like to stay in this job *by / until* the end of the year. ▶ Unit 16
7 We prefer to travel *by / with* train – it's more comfortable than flying. ▶ Unit 17
8 Sophie worked *like / as* a French teacher when she came to London. ▶ Unit 17
9 I enjoy all Coldplay's music *besides / except* their first CD. ▶ Unit 17
10 Mum's going to pay me *at least / at last* £50.00 if I paint my room! ▶ Unit 18

3 Check your answers below. Then go to the unit for more information and practice.

1 completing 2 in 3 under 4 over 5 during
6 until 7 by 8 as 9 except 10 at least

⏻ Go online for a full diagnostic test

14 General form and use; prepositions of place

1 Form

Prepositions are usually one word, but some have two or more words:

one word	at	for	by	with	against	towards
two words	apart from	because of	due to	out of	away from	next to
three words	on top of	in front of	by means of	in spite of		

They are usually followed by a noun or a **pronoun**:
*Wait for me **at the bus stop**. I've had a terrible day. Let me tell you **about it**.*

If we use a verb after a preposition, we use the *-ing* form:
*You can lose weight **by eating** less and **doing** more exercise.*
*Marilyn got the job **in spite of being** late for the interview.*

We can use some prepositions on their own, as **adverbs**:
*Jason hasn't finished his work. He seems to be falling **behind**.*
*Have you been here **before**?*

We can put prepositions at the end of questions and **relative clauses**:
*Who are you looking **at**? This is Becky – she's the girl I used to share a flat **with**.*

Wh- questions + prepositions ▶ Unit 62.3 Prepositions in relative clauses ▶ Unit 72.4
For a full list of common prepositions ▶ page 338–9

2 Use

Prepositions show relationships (of place, time, etc.) between the parts of a sentence:

place	That's my bike – the one **against** the wall.
movement	Go **across** the bridge and **into** the station.
time	My grandfather was in hospital **during** the last days of the war.
means	You can contact us **by** phone or email.
instrument	Please complete the form **with** a black pen.
purpose	These little hooks are used **for** hanging pictures on the wall.

3 Prepositions of place: *in, on, at*

Prepositions of place describe where one person or thing is in relation to another:

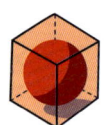
Your watch is **in** the drawer. The keys are **in** the car.
(+ town/country) **in** Warsaw/Poland; Paul's **in** Japan on business.
in prison/hospital; **in** the newspaper/a book

Your watch is **on** the table. My office is **on** the third floor.
London is **on** the River Thames.
on the floor/wall/ceiling; **on** the left/right;
on page 20; **on** a train/bus/plane (but **in** a car)

We use *at* to describe the exact or approximate position of something:
*It's **at** the end of the car park. The train stops **at** Preston. Can we sit **at** a window table?*
at the top/bottom/end of ...; at a wedding/concert/meeting; at the office/station/airport

We can use *at* or *in* with buildings, but the meaning is different. Compare:
*I can't talk. I'm **at** the cinema.* (I'm watching / going to watch a film.)
*I'm waiting for Karen **in** the cinema.* (I'm inside the building.)

40

4 under, below, over, above, on top of

		MEANING	EXAMPLES
under		in a lower position (close or touching)	The documents are **under** that file on the desk. Put the rubbish in the bin **under** the sink.
below		in a lower position	Arianne lives in the apartment **below** me. We have a big cupboard **below** the stairs.
over		in a higher position (close or touching)	The sign **over** the door said 'entrance'. Put covers **over** the furniture before you paint the room.
above		in a higher position	There's a helicopter flying round **above** the school. The dentist's is **above** the bank.
on top of		in a higher position, touching	Can you get my bag, please? It's **on top of** the wardrobe.

5 next to, by, beside, near

We use *next to, by* and *beside* to say that something is close:
The keys are **next to/by/beside** my bag, in the living room.
I'd love to live **by/beside/next to** the sea.

Near means 'not very far away'. Compare:
It's useful to live **near** an airport but I don't want to live **next to** one as the noise would be awful.

⚠ We usually use *near* with towns or cities, not *next to, by* or *beside*:
✗ Emin lives next to/by/beside Istanbul.   ✓ Emin lives **near** Istanbul.

6 in front of, opposite

Joanne always sits **in front of** Simone in class, and she always sits **opposite** her at lunch.

7 *between* and *among*

The prepositions *between* and *among* have different meanings.
- *Between* means 'with one or more people/objects on either side'.
- *Among* means 'surrounded by more than two people or objects'.

14 PREPOSITIONS OF PLACE

Practice

1 <u>Underline</u> the preposition in each sentence, then choose the correct word in *italics* to show the type of preposition.

0	Can you meet me <u>in front of</u> the snack bar later?	*place* / time
1	Can you meet me at half-past eight?	place / time
2	Can you get the spoons out of the drawer, please?	place / movement
3	They've been making cars for more than seventy years.	purpose / time
4	Joanna is moving away from home next year.	means / movement
5	You can contact us by email or text message.	means / purpose
6	Use a sharper knife for cutting meat.	time / purpose
7	The door can only be opened with a special key.	purpose / instrument
8	The refugees escaped by using false passports.	means / movement

2 Write a sentence about each picture, using the words and phrases below and a preposition from the box. Use the past simple tense. 2.27 Listen and check.

0  1  2

3  4  5

6  7  8

above   among   at   between   in   in front of   ~~on~~   opposite   under

0	Dana and Leona / meet / a plane	*Dana and Leona met on a plane.*
1	Derek / wait / the bus stop / for hours	
2	I / leave / my coat / the car / last night	
3	the cat / often sleep / the duvet	
4	they / live / the greengrocer's	
5	Lori / live / the greengrocer's	
6	we / park / the car / the cinema	
7	the girls / have / a picnic / pine trees	
8	Jacob / always / sit / the two girls	

3 Nine friends are taking a flight together to Stockholm. Read the sentences and write the names of the people by the correct seat numbers.

1a .... 1b .... 1c ....

2a .... 2b _Len_............ 2c ....

3a .... 3b .... 3c ....

- Jack and his wife, Jane, are sitting in the front row. Jane hates flying and never sits by the window. She's sitting between her sister, Ella, who loves looking out of the window, and her husband.
- Marga is sitting in row 3, between two other members of the group.
- Len is sitting in the centre seat of the second row – he's flying home to Sweden to celebrate his birthday, with his wife, Anna, who is sitting next to him.
- Steph is sitting in front of her husband, Vince, who always wants an aisle seat because of his long legs.
- Nils is also from Sweden. He's Len's brother-in-law. Nils' sister is sitting in front of him.

4 **GRAMMAR IN USE** Read the text and choose the correct answer, A, B or C below.
2.28 Listen and check.

The Amanjena Hotel is one of the finest luxury hotels (0) .... Morocco. Situated in beautiful grounds (1) .... the fascinating town of Marrakech, it is easy to get to. The standard rooms are all individual buildings and are all situated (2) .... palm trees and mature olive trees.
(3) .... each comfortable room there is a king-sized bed as well as a mini-bar, CD player, TV and DVD. There is also a small private garden with a fountain (4) .... each room, where guests can relax. Breakfast is served each morning (5) .... the swimming pool, and guests can have dinner (6) .... one of the hotel's two restaurants – serving Moroccan and international food. For those who want to shop, art, jewellery and handmade gifts are available (7) .... the three shops within the hotel complex, and there is a wide variety of shops (8) .... nearby Marrakech.

0 A at   B by   **C in**
1 A near   B at   C next to
2 A among   B in   C between
3 A At   B In   C On
4 A in front of B in   C at
5 A in   B over   C by
6 A at   B opposite   C between
7 A next to   B in front of C at
8 A in   B near   C on top of

5 Write about your bedroom, using the phrases in brackets to help you.

0 (next to my bed)   _There's a little table and a lamp next to my bed._
1 (next to my bed)   ....
2 (under the bed)   ....
3 (on the walls)   ....
4 (on top of the wardrobe)   ....
5 (opposite the bedroom window) ....

Go online for more practice

15 Prepositions of movement

We can **come off** the motorway here and drive **along** this road **into** the town centre.

1 into, out of, onto, off

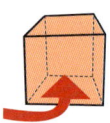
Into describes movement to the inside of something:
*It's raining. Let's go **into** the house now.*
*We can drive **into** the town centre this way.*

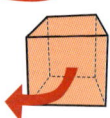
Out of is the opposite of *into*:
*Can you get my shoes **out of** the wardrobe?*
*Open the door and let me **out of** this room immediately!*

Onto expresses movement to a surface or 'line':
*The cat jumped **onto** the wall.*
*I think we should get **onto** the motorway here.*

Off is the opposite of *onto*:
*The cat jumped **off** the wall.*
*Let's get **off** the motorway and get something to eat.*

⚠ You may hear English speakers using *off of* rather than *off*, but many people think this is incorrect: [✗ *Please get off of the grass.*] ✓ *Please get **off** the grass.*

We get *into/out of* a car or taxi, but *on(to)/off* a bus, plane, train, ship, bike:
*Come on – jump **into the car**. We're late. I got **off the train** at the last stop.*

2 along, past, through

We use *along* when we follow the length of something (e.g. a path, a river, a road):
*We can drive **along** the Rhine to the south of Germany.*
*Walk **along** the path by the river – it's very pretty.*

We use *past* when we go up to something and then we pass it. We often use this with shops and buildings: *Go **past** the post office and the bookshop is on your left.*

We use *through* when we go from one side of something to the other side. We often use this with countries, open space, enclosed tunnels, etc. *We'll drive **through** Switzerland.*
*Go **through** the main entrance. I like to walk **through** the park on my way to work.*

3 across, over

Across and *over* both mean 'from one side to the other':
*Walk **across/over** the first bridge. We'll drive **across/over** the Alps.*
But we use *over* when we are not directly touching the surface we are crossing:
✗ ~~The horse jumped across the fence.~~ ✓ *The horse jumped **over** the fence.*

4 at, to

We usually use *to* to show direction: *Go **to** the bank and turn right. Give the book **to** Jamie.*
With some verbs (e.g. *throw, shout, point*), we can use *to* and *at*, but there is a difference in meaning:
*Throw those keys **to** me, will you? I need to lock the door.* (I want the keys.)
*She was so angry, she threw the keys **at** me.* (to try and hit me)

Practice

1 **GRAMMAR IN USE** Read the letter and choose the correct underlined words.
🔊 2.29 Listen and check.

> Our cycling holiday in the Lake District was great, thanks. We had one really lovely day when we cycled (0) into / (across) the Hardknott Pass (1) to / at the little village of Boot, then we went (2) along / past the River Esk for a while, going (3) across / into some lovely little bridges. We went (4) at / past the pretty village of Eskdale Green and cycled all the way to Ravenglass, on the coast. It's a long way, so we went (5) onto / into a really nice hotel for afternoon tea, and then put the bikes (6) onto / into the little train that goes back up to Boot.

2 Find five more mistakes with prepositions and correct them. Tick (✓) the correct sentences.
🔊 2.30 Listen and check.

0 I'll turn the TV on. Can you get the DVD ~~out~~ *out of* the case?
1 We flew across the Andes when we went from Argentina to Chile.
2 We're late! Hurry up and get onto the taxi.
3 Mike always runs along the canal path for half an hour every morning.
4 The bridge that goes through the railway line is in danger of collapsing.
5 Don't throw stones to the cat – you'll hurt her.
6 To get to the station from here, go along the school and turn left.

3 **GRAMMAR IN USE** Look at the map of London Zoo and complete the directions with one word in each gap. You are at the Snowdon Aviary.

Excuse me, how do I get to …

0 *the Oasis Café?* Go *along* the canal, *past* the owls and lovebirds, turn right, go *through* the tunnel. The Oasis Café is on the right.
1 *the woodland walk?* Turn right and go .... the bridge, then turn left and walk .... the canal.
2 *the gift shop?* Go straight on .... the owls and the lovebirds, turn right and go .... the canal, then go .... the tunnel under the road. It's on the left.
3 *the entrance?* Turn right and go .... the canal, go .... the Africa section and go .... the tunnel .... the information kiosk. Then turn left.
4 *the nearest toilets?* Go .... the canal and go right .... the bridge. Go .... the library, ... the tunnel and then go .... the café. The toilets are inside the café on the left.

16 Prepositions of time

What time's your connection?

It's at six, and I get to Australia in the morning on Thursday. I'll try to sleep during the flight.

1 at, in, on

We use
- *at* to introduce a time:
  The flight's at six o'clock.
- *in* for a point within a longer period of time:
  I get to Australia in the morning.
- *on* to introduce dates and days:
  We arrive on Thursday. The course ends on 11 July.

	COMMON USES	EXAMPLES
at	special occasions mealtimes + night/the weekend	We usually have fireworks **at** New Year. The managers have business meetings **at** breakfast. It's quiet here **at** night. We always sleep late **at** the weekend.
in	parts of the day months and seasons years and centuries	I never work well **in** the afternoon. Is your birthday **in** October? We don't go away **in** the summer. I was born **in** 1984. The world changed **in** the last century.
on	special days parts of days of the week	Do you have a birthday cake **on** your birthday? I last saw him **on** Thursday afternoon.

⚠️ With some *time expressions* (e.g. *this/last/next/every morning, week, year,* etc.) we don't use a preposition:
✗ *The French market comes in every March.*   ✓ *The French market comes every March.*
What time did you have breakfast this morning?   The new gym opened last month.

2 in, within, by, (from) ... until

We use
- *in* to talk about a completed period of time:
  They finished painting the hall in only two days.
- *within* to mean 'before a period of time has passed':
  You should have the results within 24 hours.
- *by* to mean 'not later than': *I need your essays by Friday.* (on or before Friday)
- *(from) ... until/to* for a period of time ending at a certain point:
  The play didn't finish until midnight.   Tickets are available to the end of the month.
  The holiday season runs from July until October.

NATURAL ENGLISH We often use *till* instead of *until* in everyday English:
We stayed in the club from about 9.00 till closing time.

American English *on the weekend, Friday through Sunday* ➤ page 352

3 for, during, last (for)

We use
- *for* with a period of time; it means 'the whole time': *We waited for the bus for an hour.*
- *during* to mean 'at one point in a period of time': *My bike was stolen during the night.*

We also use *during* when we mean 'for a while' or 'all through a period of time': *I'll try to sleep during the flight.*
Notice the difference between *during* and *for*: *We went away for two weeks during July. Jason was in hospital for several months during his childhood.*
With the verb *last for*, it is possible to leave out the preposition: *The course lasts (for) ten weeks.*

for and *since* with present perfect ➤ Unit 37.3

3

Practice

1 GRAMMAR IN USE Read the message and choose the correct words (or –) in *italics*.

> Mr Lewis – here are your flight details for later this week:
> You depart from Heathrow (0) *at* / *on* 8.30 (1) *–* / *in* the morning (2) *on* / *in* 23 April (Thursday). You arrive in Dubai (3) *to* / *at* 5.20 (4) *in* / *at* the evening. Unfortunately, you can't leave the airport (5) *during* / *for* this stopover. You then leave Dubai (6) *–* / *at* 8.45 and you arrive in Bangkok (7) *at* / *on* 6.30 (8) *in* / *–* the next morning. You're then going to fly to Hong Kong (9) *–* / *on* next Friday, and return to the UK (10) *in* / *during* ten days, but we haven't finalised those last two flights yet.

2 Replace the underlined words with a suitable preposition (if necessary) and a phrase from the box. 🔊 **2.31** Listen and check.

> four days   ~~the weekend~~   the summer   fifteen minutes   11 p.m. to 6 a.m.
> the afternoon   two hours   this evening   four o'clock

0 Will the gardens be open <u>on Saturday and Sunday</u>?   *at the weekend*
1 I find it really difficult to work <u>after lunch</u>.   ....
2 It's Monday now. We'll be in touch with your results <u>by Friday</u>.   ....
3 I'm working in Paris <u>from June until September</u>.   ....
4 Planes aren't allowed to take off or land <u>at night</u> at this airport.   ....
5 The oral exam was really short. It started at 9.00 and lasted <u>till 9.15</u>.   ....
6 It's 3.30 now. I'll wait <u>for another thirty minutes</u>, then I have to go.   ....
7 Don't worry, it's only 10.30 – we'll be finished <u>by lunchtime</u>.   ....
8 I met Luke this afternoon; he said he'd come round <u>in a few hours</u>.   ....

3 GRAMMAR IN USE Complete the text with prepositions from this unit. Write – if no preposition is necessary. 🔊 **2.32** Listen and check.

The Samaria Gorge Experience
Thank you for booking this trip with Andreas Travel. Please read these notes about your trip.

Your bus will meet you at your hotel at the time on your ticket. Please be at the meeting point (0) *by* this time, or you may have to take a taxi to the start of the walk. We will arrive at the top of the gorge (1) .... 7.00 a.m. We will stop here (2) .... about 30 minutes so that you can have breakfast and buy some snacks and some water. Please note that you will need to drink at least a litre of water (3) .... the day. The path through the gorge is easy to follow. We will meet you again at the bottom in Agia Roumeli, where you are welcome to join us at Stavros Restaurant (4) .... 3.00 p.m. for a drink and a snack. You are then free (5) .... 5.00 p.m., when the boat leaves for Paleochora. Please be at the harbour (6) .... 4.50 p.m. The boat trip lasts (7) .... about 40 minutes, and your bus will meet you for the journey back to your hotel.
Have a fantastic day!
PS We run tours (8) .... every day, including Sundays, so why not book another trip with us?

⏻ Go online for more practice   47

17 Prepositions with other meanings

This summer, Mark and Leo are travelling to Spain **with** some friends from university. They are all going on to Morocco **by** boat, **apart from** Mark who is staying in Spain to improve his Spanish.

1 by, with, for

We use *by*
- to talk about how we do something:
  *She makes extra money **by cleaning** houses. We pay for everything **by credit card**.*
  (BUT *We pay for everything **in/by cash**.*)
- to show how we communicate or travel: *Hardly anyone communicates **by letter** these days. I get the sports results **by text message**. They're going to Morocco **by boat**.*

⚠️ We say *by car, by plane, by bus*, etc. but we say *on foot* (= walking):
*We can get to the town centre either **by bus** or **on foot**.*

We use *with*
- to mean 'in the company of': *Are you going **with your friends** from university?*
- to show the instrument we use to do something: *Fill in the form **with a black pen**. We held the door open **with a book**.*

⚠️ We don't use *by* to say what instrument we use to do something:
✗ *I washed the car by an old T-shirt.*   ✓ *I washed the car **with an old T-shirt**.*

We use *for* to indicate the purpose of something: *We use this cloth **for cleaning** the tables.*

See also infinitive of purpose ➤ Unit 76.3

2 as or like?

We use *as*
- for a person's job or role: *I'm working **as a tour guide** this summer.*
- to describe what something can be used for: *Here – use this cushion **as a pillow**.*

We use *like* when we mean 'similar to' – it makes a comparison:
*Matt looks **like a film star**.* (He isn't a film star.)
*Your perfume smells **like roses**.* (It isn't roses.)

⚠️ We don't use *like* when we talk about someone's job. We use *as*:
✗ *Tony works like a taxi driver.*   ✓ *Tony works **as a taxi driver**.* (= He is a taxi driver.)

3 besides, except (for), apart from

Besides means 'in addition to': *I want to learn other languages **besides** my own.*

⚠️ Do not confuse *besides* and *beside* (preposition of place) (➤ Unit 14.5).

Except (for) means 'but not': *The shop is open every day **except (for)** Sunday.*
*We've invited everyone **except (for)** Nikki – so don't tell her about it!*

Apart from can mean
- 'besides': *I want to learn other languages **apart from** my own.*
- 'except': *All my friends are going **apart from** Mark.* (Mark isn't going.)

4 from, of

We use both *from* and *of* to show the material used in a product:
*My coat is made **of leather**. Our orange juice is made **from special Brazilian oranges**.*

There is very little difference, although we often use *from* when the material has been changed in some way: *Believe it or not, those shoes are made **from old car tyres**.*

Practice

1 **GRAMMAR IN USE** Read the conversation and choose the correct words in *italics*.
🔊 2.33 Listen and check.

RYAN   I've decided to go to Bangladesh for a few months before university.
TOM   Wow! What are you going to do there?
RYAN   I'm going to do voluntary work (0) *(as)/ like* a builder. You know, I want to do something (1) *apart / besides* travel – something to help people. But I'm going to travel, too. I'm going there (2) *on / by* plane, then after I finish the work, I'm going trekking in the Himalayas –
TOM   Horse-riding?
RYAN   No, trekking (3) *on / by* foot, then I'm going to travel back (4) *in / by* train.
TOM   It sounds amazing. How are you going to pay for it?
RYAN   Mainly (5) *for / by* doing lots of extra hours in the shop at weekends! I'm working every weekend before I go (6) *except / apart* from the weekend of Natalie's wedding.
TOM   Won't it be cold in the Himalayas?
RYAN   Yes, I think so. But I've got a really warm, light coat made (7) *of / with* wool.
TOM   Are you going (8) *from / with* anyone?
RYAN   No, on my own.

2 Write the words in the correct order to make sentences. Add a suitable preposition.

0 most older people read only glasses can   *Most older people can only read with glasses.*
1 people plane travelling hate a lot of   ....
2 worked for twenty years my a teacher uncle   ....
3 mobile phone an iPod looks my   ....
4 this computer you a DVD player use can   ....
5 every day is the centre New Year's Day open   ....

3 Find and correct the mistake in each sentence. 🔊 2.34 Listen and check.

0 'Are these shoes leather?' 'I'm not sure. They feel ~~as~~ *like* leather.'
1 In those days, there were few planes, and most people travelled on ship.
2 Don't clean the screen by detergent – you need a special fluid.
3 Everyone has completed the questionnaire apart for the head teacher.
4 Have you seen this handbag? It's made with crocodile skin!
5 It's getting very difficult to pay with cheque in shops and restaurants.
6 'What's this?' 'It's a garlic press. It's used to crushing garlic.'

4 Complete the sentences below with a preposition. Then change them to make them true for you. (Or write *So do I*.)

0 I always write my homework *with* a black pen.
   I always write my homework with a blue pen.
1 I prefer to keep in touch with my friends .... email.
   ....
2 I usually go on holiday .... my husband.
   ....
3 I don't often pay for things .... credit card.
   ....

Go online for more practice

18 Common prepositional phrases

PHRASE	MEANING	EXAMPLE
by chance by mistake	not planned do something wrong, but not on purpose	Julie and I met in the shopping centre **by chance**. This letter is for you – sorry, I opened it **by mistake**.
at last at least at the end (of)/beginning (of) at the latest at work (home, school)	after a long time not less than the last thing/the first thing no later than (place)	Dave is here **at last** – late as usual! It will take you **at least** an hour to get here. I always check homework **at the beginning** of the lesson. / The team collected the cup **at the end of** the match. We have to pay this bill by 1 June **at the latest**. Justin's **at work** now – why don't you call him there?
for ever (positive) for good (negative) for sale	always, starting from now you can buy it	This place is beautiful. I want to stay here **for ever**. I'm leaving this job **for good**. I hate it! Is all this furniture **for sale**?
in advance in charge (of) in love (with) in public/private in the end in time	before responsible for have romantic feelings for so everyone can see/so people can't see finally (after time and effort) early enough for an event	We don't need to pay for the hotel **in advance**. Terry is **in charge of** ten people in his new job. Erica fell **in love with** Stefan and they got married. I was very nervous the first time I spoke **in public**. I practised my speech for hours **in private**. It took a long time, but the technician found the fault **in the end**. Please arrive at the studio **in time** for the rehearsal.
on business on fire on holiday on purpose on time	for work burning away (for pleasure) intentionally at the correct time	Do you often travel **on business**? Help! The chip pan's **on fire**! Adrian's **on holiday** this week so he's not in the office. I didn't break the glass **on purpose**. It was an accident. The last bus always leaves (right) **on time**.
out of date out of order out of the question	old-fashioned not working not possible	Those flared trousers look really **out of date**! The coffee machine is **out of order** again. No, you can't go on holiday on your own. It's **out of the question**.

- We do not use *to* with *home*, *here* or *there*:
  ✗ <s>Come to here at six o'clock</s>.   ✓ Come **here** at six o'clock.
- *At last* and *at least* are different: *at last* means 'finally'; *at least* means 'not less than':
  'Sorry I'm so late. My train was cancelled.' 'Never mind. You're here **at last**.'
  I'll need **at least** three days to finish this project.
- *At the end* means 'the last thing'. *In the end* means 'finally' (after some time/effort):
  There's a really frightening scene **at the end** of that film – don't watch it before going to bed!
  My boss agreed to increase my salary **in the end**, but I had to ask him several times.
- *In time* means 'early enough for something'. *On time* means 'at the correct time':
  We were at the port **in time** for the first boat.
  The boat didn't leave **on time** because of engine trouble.

Practice

1 **GRAMMAR IN USE** Complete the email with prepositions. There is one more place where no preposition is needed. 🔊 2.35 Listen and check.

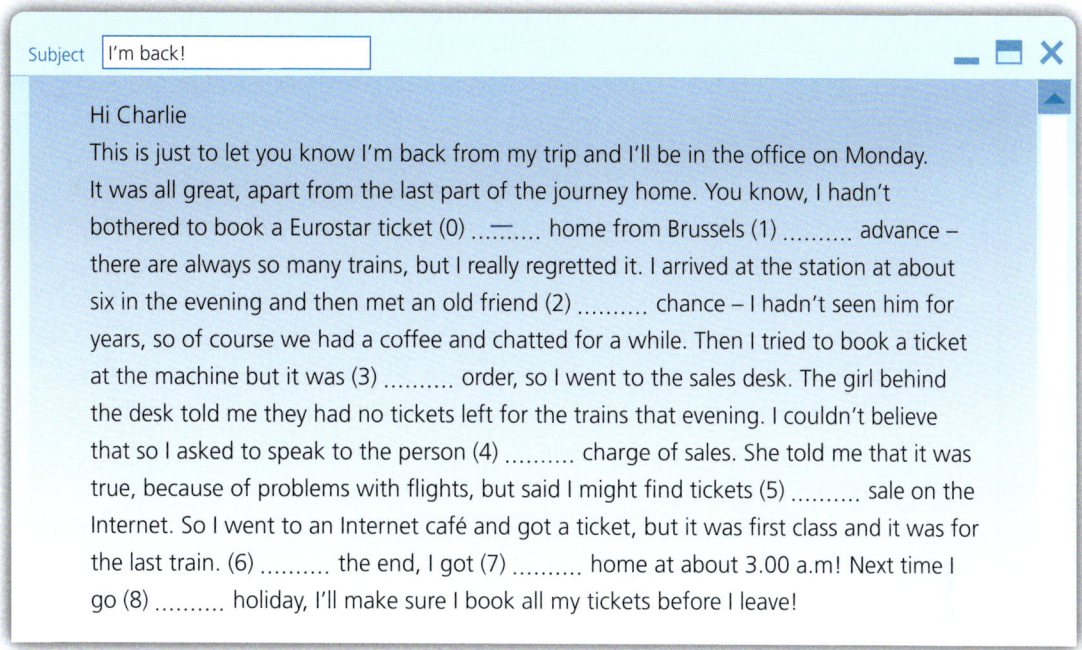

Subject: I'm back!

Hi Charlie

This is just to let you know I'm back from my trip and I'll be in the office on Monday. It was all great, apart from the last part of the journey home. You know, I hadn't bothered to book a Eurostar ticket (0) —— home from Brussels (1) .... advance – there are always so many trains, but I really regretted it. I arrived at the station at about six in the evening and then met an old friend (2) .... chance – I hadn't seen him for years, so of course we had a coffee and chatted for a while. Then I tried to book a ticket at the machine but it was (3) .... order, so I went to the sales desk. The girl behind the desk told me they had no tickets left for the trains that evening. I couldn't believe that so I asked to speak to the person (4) .... charge of sales. She told me that it was true, because of problems with flights, but said I might find tickets (5) .... sale on the Internet. So I went to an Internet café and got a ticket, but it was first class and it was for the last train. (6) .... the end, I got (7) .... home at about 3.00 a.m! Next time I go (8) .... holiday, I'll make sure I book all my tickets before I leave!

2 Match the underlined phrases with their meanings A–I.

0 Alice's new hairstyle looks really <u>old-fashioned</u>.
1 Sonia made a good impression <u>at first</u>.
2 Julie didn't do it <u>deliberately</u>.
3 Teresa dismissed her PA <u>in front of everyone</u>.
4 Gina finished the job <u>with days to spare</u>.
5 Maggie <u>finally</u> threw out the old sofa.
6 Fiona broke her leg when she was travelling <u>for work</u>.
7 Bryony is <u>responsible for</u> about twenty people.
8 Jodie reached the coach <u>at exactly the right time</u>.

A in charge of
B out of date
C in the beginning
D in public
E in the end
F in time
G on business
H on purpose
I on time

3 **GRAMMAR IN USE** Find six more mistakes with prepositional phrases and correct them. 🔊 2.36 Listen and check.

TANYA Hi, Cal. How are things?
CAL Fine, though I seem to spend about eighty hours a week ~~work~~ *at work* these days!
TANYA Poor you!
CAL Have you and Ines finished that project you were working on?
TANYA Yes, we finished it at the end. It took such a long time. We had to finish it by last Friday in the latest, and we sent it on Wednesday. Talking of Ines, have you heard the news?
CAL No, what news?
TANYA She's going back to the Spanish office. She says she's leaving London to good.
CAL No! I know she came here in business at the beginning of her stay, but I thought she loved London. How long has she been here?
TANYA At last three years – maybe longer.
CAL So why's she going back?
TANYA Well, she thinks it's too expensive here, and she misses her family. But it isn't off the question that she might come back for short visits.

Review MODULE 3

1 UNITS 14 AND 15 Read the email and follow the route on the map. (Not all the places are marked on the map.) Choose the correct prepositions.

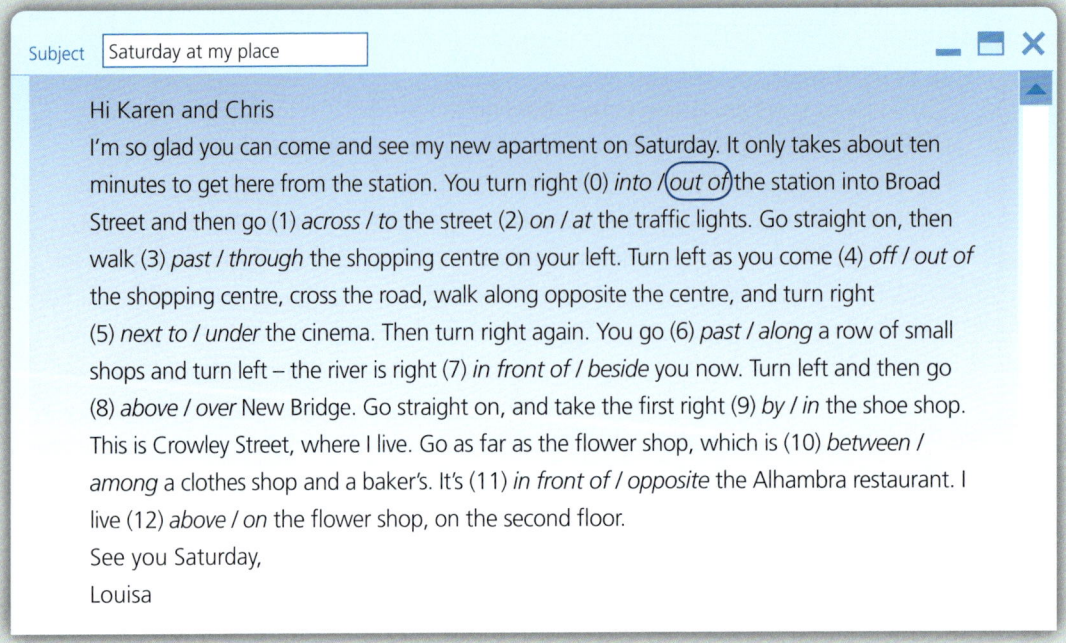

Subject: Saturday at my place

Hi Karen and Chris
I'm so glad you can come and see my new apartment on Saturday. It only takes about ten minutes to get here from the station. You turn right (0) *into / out of* the station into Broad Street and then go (1) *across / to* the street (2) *on / at* the traffic lights. Go straight on, then walk (3) *past / through* the shopping centre on your left. Turn left as you come (4) *off / out of* the shopping centre, cross the road, walk along opposite the centre, and turn right (5) *next to / under* the cinema. Then turn right again. You go (6) *past / along* a row of small shops and turn left – the river is right (7) *in front of / beside* you now. Turn left and then go (8) *above / over* New Bridge. Go straight on, and take the first right (9) *by / in* the shoe shop. This is Crowley Street, where I live. Go as far as the flower shop, which is (10) *between / among* a clothes shop and a baker's. It's (11) *in front of / opposite* the Alhambra restaurant. I live (12) *above / on* the flower shop, on the second floor.
See you Saturday,
Louisa

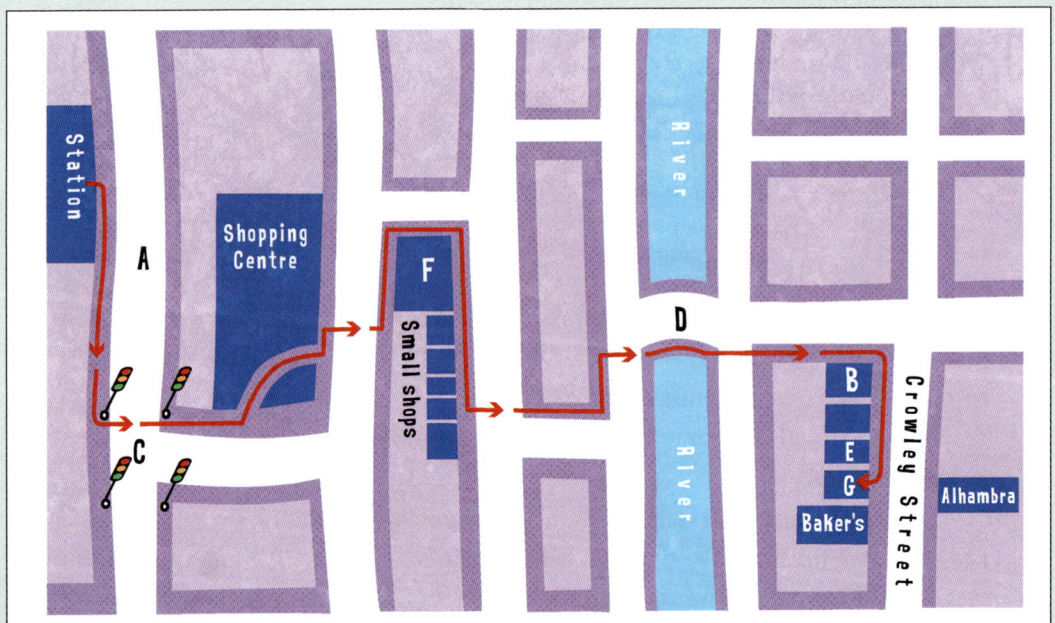

2 UNITS 14 AND 15 Now match A–G on the map with the places in the email.

0 Broad Street ....A....
1 the cinema ....
2 the flower shop ....
3 New Bridge ....
4 the traffic lights ....
5 the clothes shop ....
6 the shoe shop ....

52

3 **UNITS 15 AND 16** Complete the information with the words from the box.

along   by   during   ~~every~~   into   on   out of   through   until

Manningham Quiz Club Treasure Hunt
Join our quiz-based treasure hunts for some Sunday fun!
Follow the directions, and work out the clues to find out where the treasure is! Every correctly completed form wins a prize! Treasure hunts are held (0) ..*every*......... second Sunday (1) .... June, July and August.
Treasure hunt No. 4 will take place (2) .... Sunday 22 July, at 2.00 p.m.

Treasure hunt No. 4 – directions to clue 1
Start at the Manningham Woods car park. When you get (3) .... your car, turn left and go (4) .... the woods. Go (5) .... the woods for 400 metres to the stream. Walk (6) .... the stream for another 200 metres. The first clue is attached to the footbridge. You have (7) .... 5.00 p.m. to finish the treasure hunt. Completed forms must be handed to the organisers (8) .... 5.15 at the latest. Good luck!

4 **UNITS 16, 17 AND 18** Put a line through the incorrect word in each group.

0 We went by … car / ~~foot~~ / train.
1 It should last for … ever / hours / least.
2 That machine is out of … date / order / time.
3 He contacted me by … pen / email / text message.
4 They were on … business / time / work.
5 They arrived at … here / last / work.
6 We talked to each other in … plane / private / the end.
7 He completed the task with … a blue pen / email / some friends.

5 **ALL UNITS** Complete the second sentence so it means the same as the first, using the words in brackets. Use two to five words in your answer.

0 Maria told those lies intentionally, didn't she? (on)
   Maria told those lies ..*on purpose*.............., didn't she?
1 We were delayed on the motorway because a car was burning. (on)
   We were delayed on the motorway because there was a car ....
2 The performance starts at eight and finishes at ten in the evening. (from)
   The performance lasts .... in the evening.
3 I'd like to speak to the person responsible for sales. (in)
   I'd like to speak to the person .... sales.
4 Apart from Jonathan, the whole team played well. (for)
   The whole team played well .... Jonathan.
5 Jim always sits behind Alan in the class. (of)
   Alan always sits .... in the class.
6 Sandra always wears incredibly old-fashioned clothes. (out)
   Sandra's clothes are always incredibly ....
7 Meet us back at the car no later than six o'clock. (at)
   Meet us back at the car by six o'clock ....
8 You get a lot more exercise if you walk to work. (on)
   You get a lot more exercise if you go to work ....

Test MODULE 3

Prepositions

Choose the correct answer, A, B or C.

1. You can apply for a loan by .... the number below or in person at one of our branches.
   A call B called C calling ▶ Unit 14

2. It was pouring with rain outside so I had to wait for Joe .... the theatre.
   A at B in C on ▶ Unit 14

3. Don't put things .... the microwave when it's on as it gets very hot.
   A above B on top of C over ▶ Unit 14

4. It's impossible to find anything .... all these books and papers!
   A among B between C opposite ▶ Unit 14

5. Come down .... that wall immediately! It's too high to play on.
   A out of B off C off of ▶ Unit 15

6. There are lots of really lovely walks .... the River Thames.
   A past B through C along ▶ Unit 15

7. We flew .... the Rhine on the way to Berlin – it was really beautiful.
   A across B over C through ▶ Unit 15

8. Don't shout .... me! I hate it when you lose your temper.
   A to B on C at ▶ Unit 15

9. I prefer not to go to meetings .... Friday afternoons.
   A in B at C on ▶ Unit 16

10. I still haven't heard anything from the interview I had .... Monday.
    A at last B on last C last ▶ Unit 16

11. The hotel is closed for repairs .... the end of February.
    A until B within C by ▶ Unit 16

12. I sometimes fall asleep .... his lectures – they're so boring!
    A during B for C within ▶ Unit 16

13. Please don't cut your potatoes .... a knife – it's considered rude here.
    A for B by C with ▶ Unit 17

14. I love your perfume – it really smells .... roses.
    A like B as C from ▶ Unit 17

15. 'Have you got enough cash?' 'No, I'll pay .... credit card.'
    A with B in C by ▶ Unit 17

16. I like all flavours of ice cream .... for strawberry.
    A apart B besides C except ▶ Unit 17

17. Stay where you are. I'll come .... and pick you up immediately.
    A there B to there C at there ▶ Unit 18

18. It will take about three hours to do this work, at ....
    A last B least C the latest ▶ Unit 18

19. The film is good but there's a lot of violence .... the end.
    A in B on C at ▶ Unit 18

20. The plane was due to arrive at 5.15 and it landed right .... time.
    A on B in C at ▶ Unit 18

⏻ Go online for a full exit test

Adjectives and adverbs

MODULE 4

Before you start

1 Read the article. Look at the highlighted grammar examples.

Panda cubs arrive in Beijing Zoo

Following the recent earthquake, Chinese wildlife experts have moved eight giant panda bear cubs from the Wolong Nature Reserve in Sichuan province to Beijing Zoo. These attractive black and white animals are all less than two years old. The public rarely sees so many cute young panda bears in the same place, so there has been a lot of interest from the international media.

It seems that everyone thinks panda bears are fascinating. Perhaps it is because there are so few of them. But in fact pandas aren't as rare as they used to be. Their numbers have grown fairly fast since the Chinese opened the first nature reserves in 1958. New research methods mean it is less difficult to find the bears, and we can track the number of animals much more accurately than we could before. Although they are still few in number, their chances for the future are better than they have been for many years.

2 Now read the sentences and choose the correct words in *italics*. The highlighted grammar examples will help you.

1. What happened to your *blue and yellow / blue yellow* scarf? ▶ Unit 19
2. Do you think nature films on TV are *interested / interesting*? ▶ Unit 19
3. Lizzie has a *lovely old / old lovely* photograph of her grandparents. ▶ Unit 20
4. My exam results were *better / more good* than my sister's. ▶ Unit 21
5. They say the driving test is less *easier / easy* than it used to be. ▶ Unit 21
6. Tea isn't *expensive / as expensive* as coffee. ▶ Unit 22
7. I learnt to swim *fairly quickly / quickly fairly* because I was so young. ▶ Unit 23
8. We *visit often / often visit* our friends in Edinburgh. ▶ Unit 24
9. They *in the past treated animals badly / treated animals badly in the past*. ▶ Unit 24
10. Our cousins go there *much / many* more often than we do. ▶ Unit 25

3 Check your answers below. Then go to the unit for more information and practice.

1 blue and yellow   2 interesting   3 lovely old   4 better   5 easy   6 as expensive   7 fairly quickly   8 often visit   9 treated animals badly in the past   10 much

⏻ Go online for a full diagnostic test

19 Adjectives with nouns and verbs; -ed and -ing forms

Those **little white** lambs look **cute**.

Yes, they're **lovely**.

1 Adjectives with nouns

Adjectives give more information about nouns. Their form does not change for singular and plural nouns or for male and female:
*A **young** girl and two **young** boys came to the party.*

Adjectives usually come before a noun: ✓ *a white lamb* ✗ *a lamb white*

- We can put two or more adjectives before a noun. We don't usually use *and*:
  ✗ *a little and white lamb* ✓ *a little white lamb*
- But if both adjectives describe colours or two similar qualities, we put *and* between them:
  *a **black and white** horse* *a **long and boring** film*

2 Adjectives with verbs

We can use adjectives after the verbs *be, appear, become, get, feel, look, seem* and *taste*:
*The lambs **are lovely**.* (= They are lovely lambs.) *That lamb **looks cute**.*
*Our new teacher **seems nice**. Can we go home now? I'm **getting tired**.*

- We use *and* between two adjectives after a verb: *That flight was **long and tiring**.*
- The adjectives *alive, afraid, alone, asleep* and *awake* are always used after a verb.

⚠ We cannot use them in front of a noun:
✗ *They are asleep children.* ✓ *Be quiet. The children **are asleep**.*

Adjectives formed from nouns and verbs ➤ Unit 96.1

3 -ed and -ing forms

We sometimes use verbs ending in *-ed* and *-ing* as adjectives:
*I like **painted** furniture. Do you like **smoked** meat? The police are looking for a **missing** person. Some people say Leonardo da Vinci invented the first **flying** machine.*

Participle clauses ➤ Unit 75

Many *-ed* and *-ing* adjectives describe feelings, but we use them in different ways. We use
- *-ed* adjectives to describe how we feel: *I'm **confused**. The students are **interested**.*
- *-ing* adjectives to describe the thing that causes our feelings:
  *The rules are **confusing**. It's an **interesting** lesson.*

We often use *-ing* adjectives to ask about or give an opinion about something:
*Do you think horror films are **frightening**?* (= Do they frighten you?)
*My cousin is really **boring**.* (= He makes me feel bored.)

⚠ We don't use *-ing* adjectives to talk about how we feel:
Tell me more about the course. ✗ *I'm very interesting.* ✓ *I'm very **interested**.*

4

Practice

1 Write the words and phrases in the correct order. 2.37 Listen and check.

0 feels sweater soft this — *This sweater feels soft.*
1 bird is that alive ?
2 friendly new neighbours seem our
3 awake your guests are ?
4 weather and was hot the sunny
5 you car a getting are new ?
6 was it a long difficult and test
7 yellow we've orange got wallpaper and
8 in big lives old my aunt house a

2 Complete each sentence with a suitable *-ed* or *-ing* form of the verbs in brackets.

0 After a long day at work Jake always feels *tired*. (tire)
1 Jackie heard some .... news from her friend. (shock)
2 Dale and Fred think their new computer is really .... (excite)
3 There was a .... phone in the call box so Harry couldn't use it. (break)
4 Can you help me? I find these ticket machines very ....! (confuse)
5 Egyptian tombs usually have .... walls and ceilings. (paint)
6 Have you found the .... keys yet? (miss)

3 GRAMMAR IN USE Find eight more mistakes in the advertisement and correct them. 2.38 Listen and check.

JARROLD'S NATURE PARK

Do you think zoos are ~~bored~~ *boring* and unnatural?

Do you prefer to see beautiful and wild animals in their natural environment?

Jarrold's Nature Park is an excited new way of seeing animals. We know our animals are sensitive lived creatures so we keep them in enclosures that are large, open. There are no ugly cages or high fences.

We have animals beautiful from all parts of the world. Your children will love the amazed tropical forest with its birds and monkeys.

From enormous terrified spiders to cute panda bears. Jarrold's has them all.

Jarrold's Nature Park. It's much more than a zoo ordinary!

⏻ Go online for more practice

20 Order of adjectives; stronger and weaker meanings

Look at these **amazing multi-coloured tropical** fish. They're **really beautiful**.

1 Order of adjectives

We sometimes put more than one adjective in front of a noun. We put 'opinion' adjectives (what we think, not facts), e.g. *amazing, boring, comfortable*, before others:
Look at these **amazing** multi-coloured tropical **fish**.
I love my **comfortable** old leather **armchair**.

We put adjectives describing type or purpose (what something is for) next to the noun. These adjectives are often part of the noun (▶ Unit 98.1):
Amazing multi-coloured **tropical fish**. (= type of fish)
A long steel **hunting knife**. (= knife used for hunting)

When we use other adjectives we usually put them in this order:

opinion	size	shape	age	colour	origin	material	type/purpose	NOUN
(a) valuable	large	round			Italian		bedroom	mirror
			(an) old	red		silk	wedding	dress

We don't usually use more than three or four adjectives in front of a noun. If we want to give more information we use another clause or sentence:
✗ *My uncle has a really valuable large old black Italian sports car.*
✓ My uncle has a large black Italian sports car, which is old and really valuable.

2 Making adjectives stronger or weaker

We can use adverbs of degree, e.g. *really*, to make most adjectives stronger or weaker:
'I think they're **beautiful**.' 'Yes, I think they're **really beautiful**.' (stronger meaning).
'That film was **boring**.' 'Well, it was **slightly boring**, but some parts were OK.' (weaker meaning)

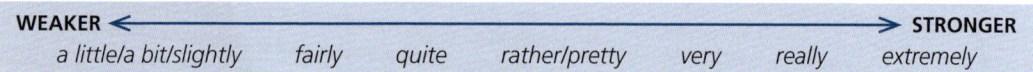

WEAKER ←   a little/a bit/slightly   fairly   quite   rather/pretty   very   really   extremely   → STRONGER

- We don't use *a little* and *a bit* with adjectives which come before a noun:
  ✗ *I bought a bit expensive watch.*   ✓ The watch I bought **was a bit expensive**.
- We often use *rather* with negative adjectives: It's **rather cold** today. She's **rather bossy**.
- When we use *quite* or *rather* with positive adjectives it often means something is surprising: That lesson was **rather interesting**. (more interesting than I expected)
- When a noun follows *quite/rather* + adjective we add *a/an*:
  He was quite nice. → He was **quite a nice** person.
  That's rather expensive. → That's **rather an expensive** hotel.

FORMALITY CHECK We don't usually use *a bit* or *pretty* in formal English:
✗ *The flight to Malaga will be a bit late due to bad weather.*
✓ The flight to Malaga will be **slightly late** due to bad weather.

Practice

1 Put the words in brackets in the correct order and complete the sentences.
🔊 2.39 Listen and check.

0 Samira owns a _lovely old French_ armchair. (French, lovely, old)
1 Tom lives in a .... cottage by the sea. (stone, little, pleasant)
2 We bought a .... chest of drawers for the bedroom. (wooden, big, new)
3 Did Melinda wear her .... dress to the party? (pretty, silk, blue)
4 Their new house has a .... room. (living, big, nice)
5 David gave her a .... picture frame. (round, silver, small)
6 Rembrandt was a .... artist. (seventeenth-century, Dutch, famous)
7 It's one of those .... machines. (German, washing, expensive)
8 Where's that .... T-shirt you used to wear? (cotton, red, horrible)

2 Read the sentences and choose the best words in *italics* for each meaning.

0 That meal was really expensive!   less / (more) expensive than I expected
1 I need something a little larger.   much / slightly larger
2 The weather's pretty hot here.   very / not very hot
3 I was shocked by that film – it was rather violent.   more violent than / not as violent as I like
4 I'm sorry I'm a bit late.   a few minutes / several hours late
5 She's quite a good artist, despite her lack of training.   better than / not as good as I expected
6 This train is extremely fast.   very / not very fast

3 GRAMMAR IN USE Complete the email with the words and phrases in the box. Be careful, only one of the phrases in each pair is correct. 🔊 2.40 Listen and check.

red big / big red   quite old / a quite old   old wooden / wooden old
(really good) / good really   rather expensive / a quite expensive   very / a bit
tourist nice / nice tourist   pretty late / late pretty   lovely large / large lovely

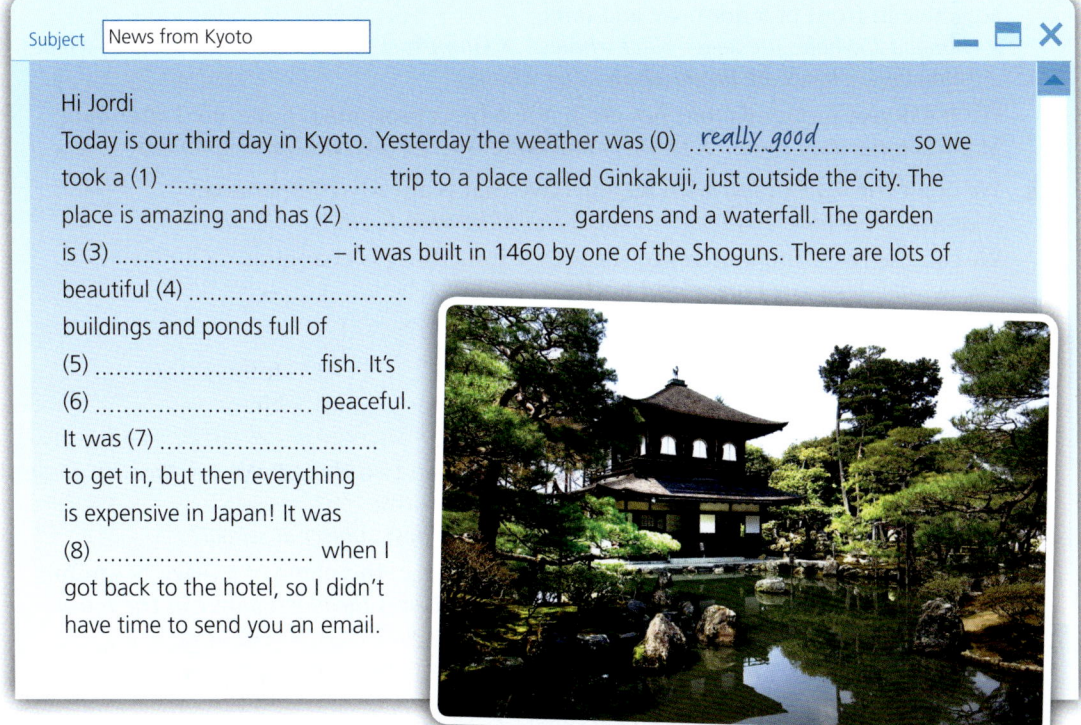

Subject: News from Kyoto

Hi Jordi
Today is our third day in Kyoto. Yesterday the weather was (0) _really good_ so we took a (1) .... trip to a place called Ginkakuji, just outside the city. The place is amazing and has (2) .... gardens and a waterfall. The garden is (3) .... – it was built in 1460 by one of the Shoguns. There are lots of beautiful (4) .... buildings and ponds full of (5) .... fish. It's (6) .... peaceful. It was (7) .... to get in, but then everything is expensive in Japan! It was (8) .... when I got back to the hotel, so I didn't have time to send you an email.

Go online for more practice

21 Comparison of adjectives

Humpback whales are **larger than** killer whales, but the blue whale is **the largest** of the whales.

1 Comparative and superlative forms

	COMPARATIVE (two things)	SUPERLATIVE (more than two things)
adjectives with one syllable[1]	add -(e)r : large → larg**er** small → small**er** young → young**er** fast → fast**er**	add -(e)st: large → **the** larg**est** small → **the** small**est** young → **the** young**est** fast → **the** fast**est**
adjectives with two or more syllables[2]	use *more/less* + adjective: useful → **more/less** useful expensive → **more/less** expensive interesting → **more/less** interesting	use *the most/the least* + adjective: useful → **the most/least** useful expensive → **the most/least** expensive interesting → **the most/least** interesting
irregular adjectives	bad → worse good → better far → farther/further well (= healthy) → better	bad → the worst good → the best far → the farthest/furthest

[1] Sometimes the spelling changes: *dry* → *drier/the driest*, *big* → *bigger/the biggest* (see page 351)
[2] Adjectives with two syllables where the second syllable is unstressed (often ending in *-y, -ly, -ow,* or *-l*) can sometimes form the comparative and superlative in the same way as one-syllable adjectives: *friendly* → *friendlier/the friendliest, gentle* → *gentler/the gentlest, funny* → *funnier/the funniest*

2 Comparative adjectives

We use comparative adjectives to compare two things. When we use a comparative adjective in front of a noun we add *than*:
✗ ~~Humpback whales are larger killer whales.~~   ✗ ~~Humpback whales are larger of killer whales.~~
✓ Humpback whales are **larger than** killer whales.

We use object pronouns (*me, her,* etc.), not subject pronouns (*I, she,* etc.) after *than*:
Maria is taller than Anna.   ✗ ~~Maria is taller than she.~~   ✓ Maria is taller than **her**.

 We don't use *more* or *less* with an adjective that is already comparative:
✗ ~~Kevin is more taller than Sue.~~   ✗ ~~Sue is less taller than Kevin.~~

We can use two comparatives to show that something is changing.
*The weather is getting **hotter and hotter**.*
*Food is becoming **more and more expensive** these days.*

 Pronunciation ➤ 1.06

3 Superlative adjectives

We use superlative adjectives to compare more than two things. We use *the* or a possessive adjective (*my/your/his,* etc.) before the superlative form:
*Blue whales are **the largest** whales.   What was **your best** subject at school?*

After superlatives we use *in* before singular nouns (i.e. the name of a place or group):
*The blue whale is the largest creature **in the world**.   Ben is the oldest player **in the team**.*

But we use *of* before plural nouns:
*The blue whale is the largest **of the whales**.   Ben is the oldest **of the players**.*

Making comparisons stronger and weaker   ➤ Unit 22.3

Practice

1 Use the words below to write comparative sentences.

0 Canada / big / Britain. *Canada is bigger than Britain.*
1 This towel / dry / that one
2 Magazines / interesting / newspapers
3 My spelling / bad / Lucy's
4 The airport / far / the railway station
5 Paris / beautiful / Berlin
6 Steak / good / lamb

2 Use the words below to write superlative sentences. 🔊 **2.41** Listen and check.

0 France / large country / the European Union *France is the largest country in the European Union.*
1 Mario / old student / my class
2 Selima / tallest / the athletes
3 New York / big city / North America
4 That / beautiful tree / the garden
5 Harry / experienced / the workers
6 Mine / nice / the rooms

3 **GRAMMAR IN USE** Find six more mistakes in the tour guide's statement and correct them. 🔊 **2.42** Listen and check.

> 'We only have four working elephants here at Songklan so it is ~~more small~~ *smaller* than the other elephant farms in the area. The largest elephant farm of this part of Thailand has 30 elephants! The four elephants here have different backgrounds and personalities. Mao-Mao travelled the most far; he came from Chaing Rai in the north of the country. Changra is the goodest worker, he loves lifting wood. But he's very greedy. He eats a lot more than the others! Selma is the most bad worker, she's very lazy. She's only eighteen years old but each year she gets lazier and more lazier! Tanan is friendlyer than the other elephants; she really loves people.'

elephant	age	weight
Changra	22 years old	4500 kg
Selma	18 years old	1750 kg
Mao-Mao	24 years old	5000 kg
Tanan	17 years old	1500 kg

4 Write sentences about the elephants. Use information from Exercise 3 and the words in brackets.

0 (the lightest) *Tanan is the lightest of the elephants.*
1 (the heaviest)
2 (Changra / younger)
3 (Selma / older)
4 (the youngest)
5 (greedier / the others)
6 (the friendliest)

Go online for more practice

22 Comparative structures

Pets for sale — Kittens €30 | Guinea pigs €20 | Rabbits €20 | Tortoise €100

The rabbits **aren't as expensive as** the kittens. The tortoise is **much more expensive than** the other animals.

1 *as* + adjective + *as*

To say that two things have the same quality we use *as* + adjective + *as*:

| The guinea pigs are €20. | = The guinea pigs are **as expensive as** the rabbits. |
| The rabbits are €20. | = The rabbits are **as expensive as** the guinea pigs. |

To describe a difference in quality we can use *not as* + adjective + *as*:

| The guinea pigs are €20. | = The guinea pigs **aren't as expensive as** the kittens. |
| The kittens are €30. | = The kittens **aren't as cheap as** the guinea pigs. |

If there is a big difference, we can use *not nearly as* + adjective + *as*:
I'm **not nearly as clever as** my brother. (= He's much cleverer than me.)

If there is a small difference, we can use *almost as/not quite as* + adjective + *as*:
My house is **almost as big as** yours. = My house isn't **quite as big as** yours. (slightly smaller)

🔊 **Pronunciation ➤ 1.07**

2 *the same (as)* and *different from*

We use *the same (as)* when two things are equal:
The price of the rabbits and the guinea pigs is **the same**. They both cost €20.
Mikal's motorbike is **the same as** mine. We both have Honda 250s.

We use *similar (to)* when something is nearly the same:
Indian elephants are **similar to** African elephants, but they're a bit smaller.

The opposite of *the same as* is *different from*. We can also use *different to*, but it is less common: Tigers are **different from** leopards. Tigers are much bigger.

American English *different than* ➤ page 352

⚠ We use nouns and pronouns after *the same (as)*, *similar (to)* and *different (from)*, not adjectives:
✗ They are the same expensive.   ✓ They are **the same price**.
✗ My brother and I are different tall.   ✓ My brother and I are **different heights**.

3 Making comparisons stronger or weaker

We can make comparisons stronger with *much*, *a lot* and *far*:
The tortoise is **much more expensive than** the other animals.
New York is **a lot bigger than** Paris.

We can make comparisons weaker with *a bit*, *slightly* or *a little*:
The rabbits are **slightly cheaper than** the kittens. My sister is **a bit younger than** me.

We can make superlatives stronger with *by far*. It means there is a big difference:
Fredrik is **by far the tallest** student in our class. (= He's much taller than all the others.)

We can make superlatives weaker with *one of* or *among*:
This is **one of the best** hospitals in the country. (Only a few hospitals may be better.)
Julie is **among the cleverest** of our students.

too, *enough* and *so/such* with adjectives ➤ Unit 79.2/3

4

Practice

1 Choose the best answer, A or B.

0 Your sunglasses are similar to mine.
   A They are exactly the same. (B) They are almost the same.
1 Jackie isn't as friendly as Lucy.
   A Lucy is friendlier than Jackie. B Jackie is friendlier than Lucy.
2 This bed is as comfortable as my old one.
   A My old bed was more comfortable. B The beds are both comfortable.
3 Ana isn't nearly as rich as Susie.
   A Susie is much richer than Ana. B Susie is a little richer than Ana.
4 Our TV is almost as big as Michael's.
   A Michael's TV is a little bigger than ours. B Michael's TV is much bigger than ours.
5 I had one of the best exam results in the school.
   A Nobody had a better result. B One or two people had a better result.

2 GRAMMAR IN USE The words in the box are missing from the text. Put them in the correct positions. (They are in the same order as in the text.) 2.43 Listen and check.

~~lot~~ of far to from not more

> Television viewers are sometimes surprised to learn that natural history programmes are often a *lot* more popular than soap operas or films. One the most famous presenters is David Attenborough. He has been making programmes about nature since the 1960s.
> In those days Jacques Cousteau was by the most famous TV presenter of nature programmes. Although Cousteau only made programmes about life in the sea, his style of presenting was similar Attenborough's – they both seem like friendly uncles who really love nature.
> Of course, today's programmes are different those of fifty years ago. In those days cameras were nearly as small and light as they are now. Today the technology is much advanced and there are digital special effects which can help us understand the complexity of the natural world.

3 Complete the second sentence so it means the same as the first, using the words in brackets. Use two to five words in your answer. 2.44 Listen and check.

0 Lions are stronger than tigers. (aren't)
   Tigers *aren't as strong as* lions.
1 I'm not as old as my sister. (than)
   My sister ....
2 Our cat is slightly smaller than Daniel's. (quite)
   Our cat isn't .... Daniel's.
3 Look, Melanie's dress is really similar to your mother's. (same)
   Look, Melanie's dress .... your mother's.
4 Nokia phones are not the same as Motorola ones. (from)
   Nokia phones .... Motorola ones.
5 The Metropole is much more expensive than any other hotel in our town. (far)
   The Metropole is .... hotel in our town.
6 Prices aren't quite as low as they used to be. (bit)
   Prices are .... they used to be.

Go online for more practice and a progress test   63

23 Types of adverb

When they are hunting, lions **usually** move **very slowly** and **silently through the grass**.

1 Types of adverb

Adverbs describe how, how often, when or where an action happens. They have many forms and they sometimes have more than one word.

TYPE OF ADVERB	EXAMPLES	
manner (how)	slowly quickly carefully well	Lions move **slowly** and **silently**.
frequency (how often)	often sometimes never usually	Lions **usually** move very slowly.
degree (how much)	very really a lot a little	Lions move **very** slowly.
time (when)	today soon last week at the weekends	We don't work **at the weekends**.
place (where)	here upstairs in an office	I work **in an office**.
direction (which way)	left right straight on across (the road) through (the grass)	Lions move **through the grass**.

already, yet ▶ Unit 36.5/6   *probably* ▶ Unit 41.5   *after that* ▶ Unit 82.2

Adverbs of manner have a regular form (except *well*); we add *-ly* to the adjective:
slow ➔ **slowly**, *silent* ➔ **silently**, *perfect* ➔ **perfectly**
Sometimes the spelling changes, e.g. *happy* ➔ *happ**ily***.

2 Irregular adverbs

The adverbs *fast, hard, high, long, low, near, late* and *early* have the same form as adjectives. Compare: *We got the **early** train.* (*early* = adjective)   *They arrived **early**.* (*early* = adverb)

The adverb for *good* is *well*:
*Sophia is a **good** writer.*   ✗ *Sophia writes good.*   ✓ *Sophia writes **well**.*

The words *friendly, lovely, silly* and *lonely* end in *-ly* but they are adjectives, not adverbs. We can't make them into adverbs so we say 'in a ..... way':
✗ *She talked to me friendlily.*   ✗ *She talked to me friendly.*
✓ *She talked to me **in a friendly way**.*

3 Adverbs of degree

We use *(very) much* and *a lot* to make verbs stronger. We use *a little* and *a bit* (spoken English) to make verbs weaker. We put these adverbs AFTER the verb and object:
*Steve **loves** his family **very much**.   Our customers **complain** about the service **a lot**.
He can **play** the guitar **a little**.   Her behaviour **annoys** me **a bit**.*

We can also use *really* to make verbs stronger. We put it BEFORE the verb and AFTER the subject: *I **really** hate him!   We **really** don't understand what you're saying.*

We use *really, very* and *extremely* to make adjectives, adverbs of manner and *often* stronger. We can use *fairly, rather* or *quite* to make them weaker:
*I can understand you if you speak **very slowly**.   My new car goes **really fast**.
We go to the cinema **quite often**.   I speak Arabic **fairly well**.*

4

Practice

1 Write the missing adverbs.

adjective	slow	happy	usual	early	fast	hard	good
adverb	slowly						

2 Complete the sentences, using the adverbs from Exercise 1.

0 Lift the weights *slowly* or you'll hurt yourself.
1 We found a good seat because we arrived ....
2 Jake's a fantastic artist. He can paint really ....
3 My parents have been .... married for more than thirty years.
4 If you want to pass the exam you need to work ....
5 I .... have a hot drink before I go to bed.
6 You shouldn't drive so .... – it's dangerous!

3 GRAMMAR IN USE Choose the correct words in *italics*. 2.45 Listen and check.

KEITH I thought you might be able to give me some advice on university courses. It's (0) (*really difficult*) / *difficult really* to choose one.
MIKE Which school subjects do you prefer?
KEITH Well, I'm (1) *a lot / very* good at science and I think biology is (2) *interesting quite / quite interesting*.
MIKE And what do you do in your free time?
KEITH I play (3) *computer games a lot / a lot computer games*. And I'm (4) *much / extremely* fond of animals. My parents own a farm and we've got two horses and a couple of cats. I can (5) *happy / happily* spend most of my free time with them!
MIKE So you like animals? Do you find it easy to control them?
KEITH Oh yes, it's (6) *easy fairly / fairly easy* for me. I know they sometimes behave badly or (7) *in a silly way / silly* but I seem to have a good relationship with them.
MIKE Do you have any special skills?
KEITH Yes, I play the piano (8) *rather / a little* well; and my mother's German so I can speak German (9) *perfectly / perfect*.
MIKE Have you thought about studying to become a vet?
KEITH No, but that's a (10) *really / lot* good suggestion. Do you think I'd get a place?

4 Complete the sentences with the phrases from the box. 2.46 Listen and check.

> very much   really slowly   ~~rather surprisingly~~   a little   quite often
> very carefully   extremely fast   rather hard   quite well

0 She behaved *rather surprisingly*; nobody expected her to do that.
1 I can sing ...., but my sister is better than me.
2 John was stopped by the police because he was driving ....
3 Palm trees grow ....; only one or two centimetres a year.
4 This is a dangerous machine. So make sure you read the instructions ....
5 We come here .... – about four or five times a year.
6 Clarissa loves her pet cat ....
7 Zack hit his head .... and got a really bad headache.
8 I hate going to the gym but I try to exercise .... every day to keep fit.

24 Adverbs and word order

Foxes **rarely** appear **in the daytime**.
They **usually** look for food **at night**.

1 Adverbs before the verb

We use adverbs of frequency to say how often we do something:

100% ←————————— HOW OFTEN —————————→ 0%
always   normally   usually   frequently   often   sometimes   occasionally   rarely   seldom   hardly ever   never

We usually put these adverbs BEFORE the main verb:
*Foxes **rarely appear** in the daytime.   They **usually look** for food at night.
Do you **always get up** late on Sundays?*

But we put them AFTER *be*, auxiliary verbs and modal verbs:
*My boss **is never** late for work.   We **are hardly ever** in this part of town.
I **have never** watched a rugby match.   You **should always** be polite to strangers.*

We can also put the adverbs *usually, normally, often, frequently, sometimes* and *occasionally* at the beginning or end of the sentence:
*I admit we go to fast food places **sometimes**.   **Occasionally** I like to eat really spicy food.*

⚠ We don't put *always, never, hardly ever, rarely* and *seldom* immediately before the subject at the beginning of a sentence (➤ Unit 102.2):
✗ *Always we go to the beach in August.*   ✓ *We **always go** to the beach in August.*

2 Adverbs after the verb

We usually put adverbs of manner (e.g. *well, badly, slowly, fast, easily, happily, carefully, fluently, perfectly*) after the main verb:
*Lions **move slowly** and silently.   Foxes **run fast**.   Did the interview **go well**?*

⚠ When there is an object after the verb, we usually put the adverb after the object:
✗ *She speaks fluently Russian.*   ✓ *She speaks **Russian fluently**.*
✗ *Did she drive fast the car?*   ✓ *Did she drive **the car fast**?*

When there is an object, adverbs of manner ending in *-ly* can sometimes go between an auxiliary or modal verb and a main verb:
*They **have badly damaged** your car.   You **can easily finish** that project in a day.*

3 Adverbs at the beginning or end of the sentence

We usually put adverbs and adverbials of place and time (e.g. *here, there, in London, yesterday, on Saturday, immediately, every day, at night*) at the end of the sentence:
*Foxes usually hunt **at night**.   Did you go to university **here**?   I didn't have lunch **yesterday**.*
If we want to give the adverb special emphasis, we can put it at the beginning:
*It's quite a large house. **Upstairs** there are three bedrooms.*
*'Do you drive to work on your own every day?' 'No. **On Mondays** a friend comes with me.'*

⚠ We don't put adverbs of place and time in front of the main verb:
✗ *I don't here live.*   ✗ *Foxes at night look for food.*   ✗ *We to Greece went for our holiday.*

Word order when there is more than one adverb   ➤ Unit 59.6

4

Practice

1 Write the words and phrases in the correct order.

0 always a shower do you in the morning have ?
Do you always have a shower in the morning?

1 dolphin I've seen never a
2 go to rarely the theatre we
3 go to work Christine this week didn't
4 speak I'd like to fluently French
5 live when there did you ?
6 late is the bus frequently
7 in London always bad the traffic is
8 the questions carefully answer

2 **GRAMMAR IN USE** Complete the text with words and phrases from A–L below. There are three extra words or phrases. ◆) 2.47 Listen and check.

Urban foxes

(0) ..H..... foxes were just a problem for farmers. They would attack chickens and sheep (1) .... They (2) .... into towns. But now they have become a serious problem for the residents of Britain's cities. (3) .... a lot of people live in houses with gardens. And many British cities have large parks. These are perfect places for foxes to live in. The foxes (4) .... serious diseases; and these can be passed on to cats and other pets. (5) .... raid rubbish bins. They can (6) .... plastic bags and their strong teeth and claws can (7) .... cut holes in fences. They leave food and rubbish all over the street and this encourages rats. (8) .... foxes can be aggressive towards people and children, especially if a mother is protecting her cubs.

A at night
B quickly
C open easily
D In Britain
E the foxes after dark
F often carry
G easily open
H ~~In the old days~~
I rarely came
J Occasionally
K came rarely
L After dark the foxes

3 In each sentence one adverb is in the wrong position. Circle the word and mark the correct position. If there is more than one possible position, show them all. ◆) 2.48 Listen and check.

0 In the wild foxes (rarely) are ↓ aggressive to people.
1 She occasionally is on the same train as me.
2 I don't like in the evenings eating a heavy meal.
3 Always we buy organic food.
4 I this morning received an interesting email.
5 Danny has often fruit for breakfast.
6 My sister and I during the daytime watch TV.
7 It's snowing so everyone is slowly driving.
8 You should wash your hands always before a meal.
9 We here hardly ever have lunch.
10 Samantha well sang at the concert on Friday.

⏻ Go online for more practice

25 Comparison of adverbs

The Arctic Tern can't fly **as fast as** some other birds, but it flies **the furthest**. Each spring it travels more than 20,000 kilometres.

1 Regular comparative and superlative forms

We use *more* + adverb (+ *than*) to make comparative forms of adverbs of manner and of the adverbs *often*, *rarely* and *frequently*:
*I eat **more slowly than** other people.*
*Can you speak **more quietly**? I'm trying to rest.*
*You see foxes in towns **more frequently** these days.*

We make superlative forms of adverbs with *(the) most* + adverb:
*Daniel has the highest phone bill because he uses his phone **(the) most often**.*

The opposite of *more/the most* + adverb is *less/the least* + adverb:
*I go to the dentist **less regularly than** I used to.*
*Of all the heaters in the test, the MaxHeat worked **the least efficiently**.*

2 Other comparative and superlative forms

Some adverbs have the same comparative and superlative forms as adjectives:

early → earlier/(the) earliest   high → higher/(the) highest   low → lower/(the) lowest
fast → faster/(the) fastest   late → later/(the) latest   near → nearer/(the) nearest
hard → harder/(the) hardest   long → longer/(the) longest   soon → sooner/(the) soonest

⚠ We don't use *more/the most* with these adverbs:
✗ ~~Cats can climb more high than dogs.~~   ✓ *Cats can climb **higher** than dogs.*
✗ ~~Borzov ran the most fast in the race.~~   ✓ *Borzov ran **the fastest** in the race.*

There are some irregular comparative and superlative adverbs:
well → better/(the) best   badly → worse/(the) worst   far → farther/further/(the) farthest/furthest

*Do you live **further** from college than me?   I played **worse** than usual yesterday.*
*The Arctic Tern flies **the furthest**.   Karl played **best** in last Saturday's match.*

NATURAL ENGLISH We often leave out *the* in superlative adverbs, especially irregular ones:
*Karl played **best** in last Saturday's match.*
We don't use superlative adverbs very often; we prefer to use a superlative adjective:
*Karl **played best** in last Saturday's match.* → *Karl was **the best player**.*

3 *as* + adverb + *as*

We use *(not) as* + adverb + *as* to compare two actions:
*I speak Polish **as fluently as** Tomas.   The Arctic Tern can't fly **as fast as** some other birds.*

4 Making comparisons stronger or weaker

We can make the meaning of comparative adverbs stronger with *much*, *a lot* and *far*:
*My grandmother has been walking **much more slowly** since her accident.*
*I exercise **far less often** than my brothers.   Athletes have to train **a lot harder** these days.*

We can make comparisons weaker with *a bit*, *slightly* or *a little*:
*Computers work **a little faster** if you add memory to them.   Can you come **a bit sooner**?*
*On Sundays trains run **slightly less frequently** than during the week.*

Practice

1 Complete the sentences with a comparative (C) or superlative (S) form of the adverb in brackets.

0. I'm putting on weight – I should go to the gym _more often_ (C often)
00. Which website sells airline tickets _the most cheaply_ ? (S cheap)
1. Which bird flies ....? (S high)
2. Children need to visit a dentist .... than adults do. (C frequent)
3. Who sang .... on the show yesterday? (S good)
4. Of all the cars in the test, the Mazda went .... (S fast)
5. Please speak .... – I can't understand you. (C slow)
6. Which type of battery lasts ....? (S long)
7. You've made lots of mistakes. Please work .... next time. (C careful)
8. Don't get the ten o'clock train. It arrives .... than the others. (C late)

2 Complete the second sentence so it means the same as the first, using the word in brackets. Use two to five words in your answer. 🔊 2.49 Listen and check.

0. I don't use the Internet as often as my colleagues. (less)
   I use the Internet _less often than_ my colleagues.
1. Computers work much faster than they used to. (as)
   Computers didn't use to .... they do now.
2. I think Carreras sang better than the others. (best)
   I think Carreras ....
3. Sue doesn't speak Spanish as fluently as I do. (more)
   I speak Spanish .... Sue.
4. Ali played the worst in the golf tournament. (player)
   Ali .... in the golf tournament.
5. People wear formal clothes less frequently these days. (as)
   People don't wear formal clothes .... they used to.

3 **GRAMMAR IN USE** Complete the text with suitable forms of the words in brackets. Add any other words that are necessary, e.g. *more, less, as, than*. 🔊 2.50 Listen and check.

Caring for elderly pets

As pets get older their needs change. You should be aware of these changes and treat older pets (0) _much more carefully than_ (much / careful) younger ones.

- Elderly cats and dogs don't see or hear (1) .... (good) young ones. As a result, they sometimes fall over or bang into things. Because of the dangers of traffic, don't allow them to travel (2) .... (far) a short distance outside your home.
- Older animals often have problems such as arthritis, so they can't move (3) .... (easy) they used to. Even if they are healthy, they can't walk or run (4) .... (quick) young animals. They exercise (5) .... (far / frequent) and get tired (6) .... (much / quick).
- Older pets eat smaller amounts but they need to eat (7) .... (often) young ones – as much as three times a day. You will notice that they eat (8) .... (slow) they did when they were young, but this is usually nothing to worry about.

⏻ Go online for more practice and a progress test

Review MODULE 4

1 UNITS 19 AND 20 Write the words and phrases in the correct order.

0 red a Melanie dress owns wonderful and evening gold
   Melanie owns a wonderful red and gold evening dress.

1 bath I at the market towel blue bought a beautiful
   ....

2 boring we in weren't Cathy's interested story
   ....

3 is new uncomfortable their sofa rather Italian
   ....

4 watches depressing often and on TV black films Alastair white
   ....

5 your grandmother still 1960s does that washing machine use enormous ?
   ....

6 quite was shocking behaviour Fred's
   ....

2 UNITS 19 AND 20 Read the letter and choose the correct underlined words.

Dear Mum,

The first day of the safari was really (0) excited / (exciting) and we set up camp in a (1) quiet place / place quiet by the river. This morning, as soon as (2) everyone was awake / was awake everyone we climbed up to the special viewing platform so we could see the animals drinking. Don't worry. The platform is (3) quite high / quite a high so it wasn't dangerous!

We have a group of (4) nice young / young nice guides who know all about the local animals. They know exactly where to find them at certain times of day. In the afternoon we were taken out in an (5) old uncomfortable / uncomfortable old jeep. But we saw beautiful (6) black white / black and white zebras and some lions, so I didn't mind about the rough ride. The lions were (7) a lot / rather frightening but I wasn't scared. It was a really (8) interesting / interested experience. I can't wait to show you my photos!

70

3 UNITS 21 AND 22 Complete the sentences, using comparative or superlative forms of the adjectives in the box.

> dangerous good greedy large lazy light long ~~poisonous~~ powerful short wide

Strange Animal Facts

- (0) *The most poisonous* animal is the poison dart frog. One frog has enough poison to kill 1,500 people. They are much (1) .... than most snakes and spiders. Try not to step on one!
- (2) .... bird in the world is the humming bird. It only weighs one gram.
- (3) .... animal is the sloth. It spends 80 percent of its life asleep!
- Falcons have (4) .... eyesight of any animal, even better than eagles. They can see small animals from more than a kilometre in the air. Their eyesight is seven times (5) .... than a human being's.
- The giant squid has enormous eyes – by far (6) .... eyes of any animal. They can be 39 cm wide – that's sixteen times (7) .... than a human eye.
- Tortoises have (8) .... life of any animal. They can live for up to 150 years. Flies, on the other hand, only live for 24 hours. That's 50,000 times (9) .... than the life of a tortoise.
- Vultures are one of (10) .... animals in the natural world. Sometimes they eat so much that they become too heavy to fly!

4 UNITS 21 AND 22 Rewrite the sentences so that they are true. Start with the words given.

0 Gold is slightly less valuable than steel.
   Gold *is much more valuable than steel.*

1 The mobile phone is a newer invention than the iPod.
   The mobile phone ....

2 A jet plane isn't as fast as a car.
   A jet plane ....

3 Five-star hotels are a little cheaper than four-star hotels.
   Five-star hotels ....

4 The Pacific Ocean is smaller than the Atlantic Ocean.
   The Pacific Ocean ....

5 Football is slightly more popular than cricket.
   Football ....

6 A tennis ball is similar in size to a rugby ball.
   A tennis ball ....

7 Salaries are much lower than they used to be.
   Salaries ....

8 A car isn't nearly as expensive as a motorbike.
   A car ....

5 UNITS 22, 23, 24 AND 25   Complete the survey questions with words or phrases from the box. There are four extra words or phrases.

> frequent   frequently   got better   got well   least   less   more
> much more   not very   ~~often~~   slightly worse   very bad   very well

Angel TV Market Research

○ Compared to last year, do you watch TV
a more (0) *often* ....? ☐   b (1) .... often? ☐   c about the same amount? ☐

○ In the last five years, do you think TV programmes have become
a (2) .... violent? ☐   b a little (3) .... violent? ☐   c less violent? ☐

○ Compared with five years ago, do you think the quality of TV programmes has
a got much worse? ☐   b got (4) ....? ☐
c (5) ....? ☐   d not changed? ☐

○ When you are watching TV, do you change channels
a very (6) ....? ☐   b (7) .... frequently? ☐   c never? ☐

○ How well do today's programmes match your viewing preferences?
a (8) .... ☐   b quite well ☐   c not very well ☐

Thank you for taking part in our survey.

6 UNITS 23, 24 AND 25   Find ten more mistakes in the conversation and correct them.

NURSE How are you ~~this morning feeling~~? *feeling this morning*

SUSIE Not fantastic. You know I feel hardly ever great at this time of day.

NURSE How about a cup of tea? Always that makes you feel more good.

SUSIE OK. That would be nice.

NURSE The doctor says that if you go slowly fairly, you today can have a walk around the gardens.

SUSIE I'm not sure. My leg still a lot hurts. Actually, I think it feels more bad than it did yesterday. Which doctor is coming today?

NURSE Well, it usually is Dr Marshall on Wednesdays.

SUSIE I don't like her. She a bit annoys me.

NURSE Why's that?

SUSIE She speaks so quickly. I don't understand really what she says at all.

7 ALL UNITS   Use the words in brackets to help you complete the sentences. Make changes and add words if necessary.

0 Computers are *not nearly as huge as they used to be.* (not nearly / huge / used to be)
1 The polar ice cap is melting .... (fast / ever before)
2 If you exercise .... (regular / you lose weight)
3 Sometimes politics can be .... (quite / bore)
4 In autumn .... (trees / become / red / gold)
5 In the 1960s people cut their hair .... (less / often / nowadays)

8 ALL UNITS Complete the second sentence so it means the same as the first. Use two or three words in your answer.

0 Horses don't live as long as elephants.
Elephants *live longer than* horses.

1 We weren't frightened by that film.
We didn't think that film ……………………… .

2 Is the Silver Line bus service a lot more frequent than the others?
Does the Silver Line bus service run ……………………… than the others?

3 Flights are a lot less expensive on the Internet.
Flights ……………………… nearly as expensive on the Internet.

4 The flight was boring and exhausting.
At the end of the flight we felt ……………………… .

5 We used to own an old French mirror which was beautiful.
We used to own a ……………………… mirror.

6 The Station Hotel is less expensive than the Holiday Inn.
The Station Hotel isn't ……………………… as the Holiday Inn.

7 I don't see my grandparents as often as I used to.
I see my grandparents ……………………… these days.

8 We had a long relaxing holiday.
Our holiday was ……………………… .

9 ALL UNITS Read the text and choose the correct answer, A, B or C below.

Running on ice

All over the world there are animals that (0) ……… for people. From dogs that control sheep in Scotland to elephants that carry wood and fuel in the jungles of Asia, animals are (1) ……… of human activity in the countryside. Perhaps (2) ……… of all these animals are the husky dogs that (3) ……… . For hundreds of years these creatures have been helping to move the native people around the snow and ice of Lapland. Despite the sub-zero temperatures they can (4) ……… sleds for distances of up to 130 kilometres a day. And they can move (5) ……… – in normal conditions the dogs run at speeds of about 30 kilometres per hour.

To keep warm, huskies have (6) ……… fur and they have feet which are (7) ……… than those of other dogs, making it easy to grip the slippery snow and ice. They live for 10 to 15 years and can survive in conditions of minus 60°C. Huskies love running and get very (8) ……… when they are attached to the sled for a journey.

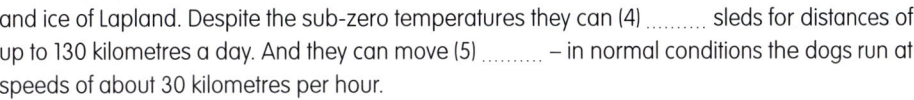

0 A hard work   (B) work hard   C work hardly
1 A a part important   B part importantly   C an important part
2 A more unusual   B the most unusual   C the unusualest
3 A in Finland pull sleds B pull in Finland sleds C pull sleds in Finland
4 A easily pull   B pull easy   C pull easily
5 A fastly   B fast quite   C quite fast
6 A a lot thick   B very thick   C very much thick
7 A far wider   B extremely wider   C more wide
8 A excitement   B exciting   C excited

Test MODULE 4

Adjectives and adverbs

Choose the correct answer, A, B or C.

1. Do you think this is ....?
   A an exercise difficult   B a difficult exercise   C difficult an exercise
   ➤ Unit 19

2. Dave's wearing a .... striped shirt today.
   A blue and white   B blue, white   C blue white
   ➤ Unit 19

3. I can't wait for my next holiday. I'm really .... about it!
   A exciting   B excite   C excited
   ➤ Unit 19

4. Elizabeth has a .... daughter.
   A young beautiful   B beautiful young   C young beautifully
   ➤ Unit 20

5. I love detective novels. I think they are .... interesting.
   A a bit   B slightly   C really
   ➤ Unit 20

6. It was .... experience.
   A quite a frightening   B quite frightening   C a frightening quite
   ➤ Unit 20

7. My exam results were .... I expected.
   A good as   B more good than   C better than
   ➤ Unit 21

8. We can run faster than ....
   A them   B they   C their
   ➤ Unit 21

9. Which is the most comfortable .... the seats?
   A of   B than   C in
   ➤ Unit 21

10. Motorbikes aren't as .... cars.
    A more expensive as   B expensive as   C expensive than
    ➤ Unit 22

11. Tania's mobile phone is .... mine.
    A the same as   B the same like   C the same with
    ➤ Unit 22

12. My sister is .... tallest students in her year.
    A as one of the   B the one of   C one of the
    ➤ Unit 22

13. My grandfather walks .... because he's quite old.
    A slow   B by slowest   C slowly
    ➤ Unit 23

14. I don't like the sea because I can't swim ....
    A good   B well   C better
    ➤ Unit 23

15. I don't like fish but I like ....!
    A steak a lot   B a lot steak   C a steak lot
    ➤ Unit 23

16. I .... football matches on TV.
    A watch hardly ever   B hardly watch ever   C hardly ever watch
    ➤ Unit 24

17. Elena gave a wonderful performance of the concerto; she ....
    A played it perfectly   B played perfectly it   C perfectly played it
    ➤ Unit 24

18. Do you know why the repair man ....?
    A yesterday didn't come   B didn't yesterday come   C didn't come yesterday
    ➤ Unit 24

19. Dexter jumped .... in the long jump competition.
    A most far   B most further   C the furthest
    ➤ Unit 25

20. People travel .... than they used to.
    A far more often   B far often   C more far often
    ➤ Unit 25

Go online for a full exit test

Present tenses

MODULE 5

Before you start

1 Read about Anouska, a TV extra. Look at the highlighted grammar examples.

I'm Anouska David – you don't know me, but you often see me on your TV! That's me on the left, in the picture. **I've got** a really interesting job as a TV extra. Yes, I **work in** TV! But **I'm not** a famous actor. You see, lots of TV productions need people for crowd scenes – and of course **they don't want** to pay famous actors, so they use ordinary people, like me. The only problem is the waiting – like now, **I'm sitting here** and I'm just waiting for someone to call me. **That happens all the time!** Still, I'm not complaining as **I usually have a really good time** at work. The other thing is that **I'm getting more and more jobs** at the moment, because there are so many TV companies these days.

2 Now read the sentences and choose the correct words in *italics*. The highlighted grammar examples will help you.

1 Alistair *isn't / not be* a famous actor. ➤ Unit 26
2 I *got / have got* an incredibly boring job. ➤ Unit 26
3 We always *have / have got* fun at your parties! ➤ Unit 26
4 Samantha and Frank both *live / living* near the office. ➤ Unit 27
5 'The bus is late.' 'I know. *It's coming / It comes* late every day. ➤ Unit 27
6 I can't go out yet. *I wait / I'm waiting* for the post. ➤ Unit 28
7 Food prices *climb / are climbing* higher and higher at the moment. ➤ Unit 28
8 *I don't want / I'm not wanting* to get up yet – I'm still tired. ➤ Unit 29

3 Check your answers below. Then go to the unit for more information and practice.

1 isn't 2 have got 3 have 4 live 5 It comes 6 I'm waiting 7 are climbing 8 I don't want

⏻ Go online for a full diagnostic test

26 be, have and have got

1 be

POSITIVE	I **am** (**'m**) English. You **are** (**'re**) early. She **is** (**'s**) a teacher. They **are** (**'re**) ill.
NEGATIVE	I **am** (**'m**) **not** French. He **is not** (**isn't**) a tennis player. We **are not** (**aren't**) from here.
QUESTIONS	**Are** you English? (No, I'm not.) **Are** they interesting? (Yes, they are.) Why **is** it a good job?

This **is** Karren Brady. She**'s** married and she **has** two children. She**'s** also a top business person and a director of West Ham Football Club.

NATURAL ENGLISH   In speech and informal writing, we usually use **short forms** e.g. *I'm, she's, he isn't, we aren't*. For negative questions with *I am*, we use *aren't I*: *Why* **aren't I** *on the list?*

We use the verb *be* to talk about
- people and things: *This* **is** *Karren Brady.   Ginny* **is** *very attractive.*
- current states: *It's really hot at the moment.   She's married.   I'm homesick.*
- qualities (adjectives): *My car* **is** *Japanese.   My children* **aren't** *rude!   I'm 1.75 metres tall.*
- opinions: *This book* **is** *boring.   Musicals* **are** *very popular.*
- position/location and time: *My flat's close to the city centre.   It's two o'clock.*
- someone's job/position: *Karren Brady* **is** *a business person.   We're students.*

 Pronunciation ➤ 1.08

2 have and have got

POSITIVE	I **have** two brothers. She **has** a sports car. They **have** a huge house.	I **have** (**'ve**) **got** two brothers. She **has** (**'s**) **got** a sports car. They **have** (**'ve**) **got** a huge house.
NEGATIVE	I **do not** (**don't**) **have** a sister. He **does not** (**doesn't**) **have** a motorbike. We **do not** (**don't**) **have** an apartment.	I **have not** (**haven't**) **got** a sister. He **has not** (**hasn't**) **got** a motorbike. We **have not** (**haven't**) **got** an apartment.
QUESTIONS	**Do** you **have** a niece? (Yes, I do.) **Does** she **have** a cat? (No, she **doesn't**.) Why **do** they **have** two cars?	**Have** you **got** a niece? (Yes, I have.) **Has** she **got** a cat? (No, she **hasn't**.) Why **have** they **got** two cars?

Pronunciation ➤ 1.09

⚠ We use forms of *have*, not *have got*, with past and future tenses:
✗ *When I was a child I had got a pet cat*.   ✓ *When I was a child I* **had** *a pet cat*.
✗ *One day we will have got our own house*.   ✓ *One day we* **will have** *our own house*.

We use both *have* and *have got* to talk about
- relationships: *I've got two brothers.   She* **has** *two children.*
- possessions: *I've got a good camera.* **Do** *they* **have** *a lot of money?*
- features: *Everyone in my family* **has got** *dark hair.   The apartment* **doesn't have** *a garden.*
- illness: *Sandra's got a cold.* **Does** *the baby* **have** *a temperature?*
- appointments: *I* **have** *an exam tomorrow.* **Has** *Fiona* **got** *an interview at Oxford?*

We can also use *have* + noun (but not *have got*) to talk about some things we do.
- hygiene and appearance: *have a haircut/a shower/a bath/a wash/a shave*
- food and drink: *have lunch/an evening meal/a snack/a drink/a meal out*
- experiences: *have fun/a good time/a bad time*
- special events: *have a party/a celebration/a holiday/a trip*
- activity (or lack of): *have a walk/a run/a swim/a sleep/a rest/a break*
- communication: *have a talk/a conversation/an argument/a word (with)*

Jack can't come to the phone; he's **having a shower**.   *I always* **have a good time** *at parties.*
Listen to that noise! The neighbours **are having a party**!   *I'm tired – let's* **have a break**.

American English *have/have got*   ➤ page 352

Practice

1 Complete the sentences with a form of *be*, *have* or *have got*. Put two answers if both *have* and *have got* are possible. 2.51 Listen and check.

0 Karren Brady 's a director of a football club.
00 She *doesn't have* / *hasn't got* (not) an easy job.
1 Simon and Jo often .... violent arguments!
2 I .... / .... an awful cold at the moment.
3 Peter .... (not) breakfast most mornings.
4 It .... really cold outside today.
5 .... you .... / .... you .... a sister?
6 They .... a New Year's party every year.
7 Fiona .... a shower before breakfast every morning.
8 The boss wants to .... a word with you.
9 .... that book interesting?
10 .... Sanjeev .... / .... Sanjeev .... dark hair?

2 GRAMMAR IN USE Read the email and choose the correct words in *italics*. In five places, both answers are possible. 2.52 Listen and check.

Subject: Missing you!

Hi guys

Well, here I (0) (am) / *are* at art college now, and I'm missing you all! You know, (1) *I'm* / *I've got* quite homesick – I didn't expect that at all.
(2) *I've got* / *I have* a room in an apartment with five other students. The apartment is quite big and it (3) *is* / *has* very nice. It's got a big kitchen, but it (4) *doesn't have* / *hasn't got* a dishwasher or washing machine!
Two of the rooms (5) *have got* / *are* still empty – I expect those people will come at the weekend. Two of the other girls here (6) *aren't* / *don't have* very friendly; they just stay in their rooms. But the other girl – Chris – is lovely. (7) *She's got* / *She has* long dark hair and looks a bit like Angelina Jolie. On Saturday we're going to (8) *have got* / *have* a dinner party – we're each going to find three more people to invite!
My timetable isn't too full – (9) *I've got* / *I have* about five lectures each week and eight classes.
Enough about me! How are you all? (10) *Have you got* / *Do you have* any news for me?
Love, Lucy

3 GRAMMAR IN USE Look at the notes about Martin O'Donnell and complete the sentences.

His name *is Martin O'Donnell.* He ....
He .... He .... and he's
got .... He .... tall and
he ....
He ....

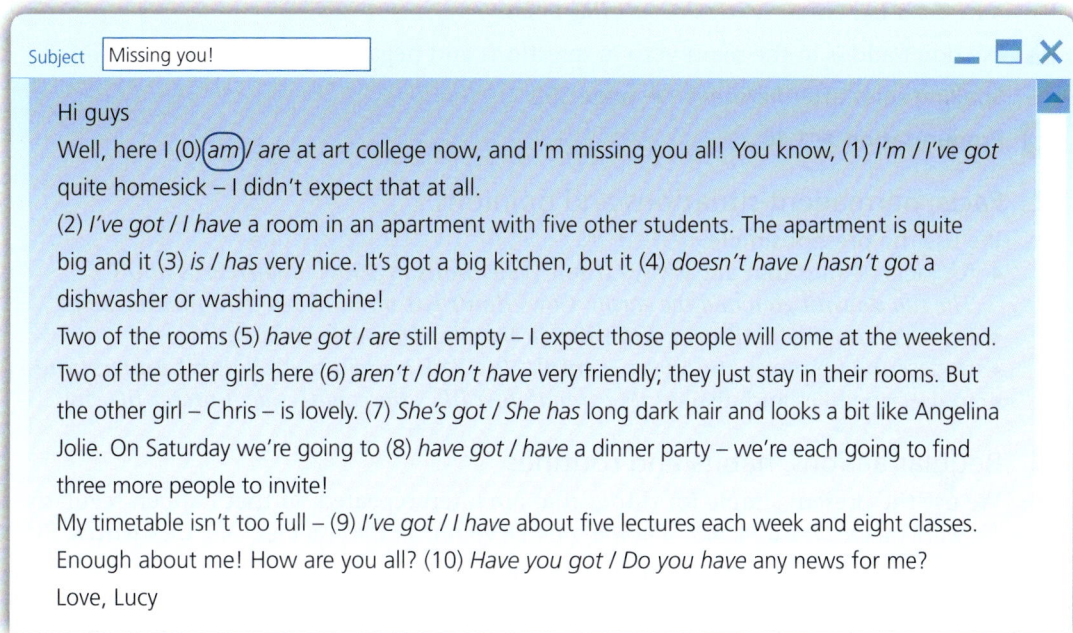

Martin O'Donnell, 29, Irish, married with two children.
1.82m, blond hair & beard.
Accountant in small finance company

Go online for more practice

27 Present simple

1 Form

POSITIVE	I **live** in London. My sister **lives** in Madrid. My parents **live** in Glasgow.
NEGATIVE	I **do not (don't) live** in an apartment. He **does not (doesn't) live** in a house. We **do not (don't) live** in a block of flats.
QUESTIONS	**Do** you **work** in an office? (No, I **don't**.) **Does** she **work** from home? (Yes, she **does**.) Where **do** they **work**?

Andrew Johnson **works** on a North Sea oil rig. He **works** there for two weeks every month. He regularly **climbs** to the top and **checks** that everything is safe.

⚠ Remember that the verb is different after *he*, *she* and *it*:
She **lives** near here. It **eats** a lot of meat.
✗ ~~Where do he work?~~ ✓ Where **does** he **work**?
✗ ~~He don't like cities.~~ ✓ He **doesn't like** cities.

⚠ We don't add *-s* to the main verb in questions and negatives: ✗ ~~Where does he works?~~

Spelling rules after *he/she/it* ➤ page 350

 Pronunciation ➤ 1.10

2 Facts, permanent situations and opinions

We use the present simple
- for facts (things that are always true): Water **boils** at 100°C and **freezes** at 0°C.
  The sun **doesn't go** round the earth. Cows **don't eat** meat. A red light **means** 'Stop'.
- for permanent situations: I **don't live** in the city. He **works** on an oil rig.
- to describe opinions and ideas: I **think** New York is exciting. You **don't understand**.
- to describe likes and dislikes: My grandfather **likes** the countryside. I **prefer** the city.

3 Regular actions, habits and routines

We use the present simple for things that are often repeated, or that happen regularly:
He **works** there once a month. **Do** the children **go out** in the evenings? No, they **watch** TV.

To say how often the action happens, we use
- adverbs of frequency (e.g. *always*, *often*) after *be* or before a main verb:
  Angelo is **often** late for work. He **always** climbs to the top.
  'Do you drive to work?' 'Not really, we **usually** use public transport. We **rarely** drive.'
- other time expressions. They usually go at the end of the sentence:
  Do you come to the studio **every day**? I go on holiday **once a year**.
  We go to our grandparents' for lunch **on Sundays**.
  These can also go at the beginning, for more emphasis:
  Every morning, I start work at 8.30.

More on adverbs and word order ➤ Unit 24

4 Describing films, plays and books

We usually use the present simple when we describe what happens in a film, play or book:
The story **takes** place in the United States. The main character **works** on a farm ...

When a sports game is described live on TV, the present simple is often used for quick actions:
Giggs **passes** to Rooney. Rooney **shoots** – he **scores**!

Practice

1 **GRAMMAR IN USE** Complete the book review with the present simple of the verbs in brackets. 🔊 2.53 Now listen and check.

Sepulchre is Kate Mosse's follow-up novel to her bestseller *Labyrinth*. It (0) ….*takes*…. (take) the same idea of two stories from different times which (1) ………….. (connect) with each other. The first story takes place in the late nineteenth century. Léonie Vernier (2) ………….. (live) in Paris with her mother and older brother, Anatole. Then an aunt in the south-west of the country invites Léonie to stay with her. Léonie (3) ………….. (not know) her aunt but she (4) ………….. (agree) to go, with her brother. When they (5) ………….. (arrive), things (6) ………….. (not be) as they seem …

In the second story, Meredith Martin is a young American university professor. Her research takes her to Paris, where she (7) ………….. (uncover) the sad story of Léonie and Anatole. (8) ………….. the novel ………….. (bring) nineteenth-century France to life? Yes, I think it (9) ………….. (do). (10) ………….. it ………….. (provide) a good successor to *Labyrinth*? No, I (11) ………….. (not think) so. The two stories (12) ………….. (not link) as well as the stories in *Labyrinth*; the second one didn't add anything, really.

2 Make questions from the words below. Then write true short answers. 🔊 2.54 Now listen and check.

0 horses / eat / meat? *Do horses eat meat? No, they don't.*
1 water / boil / 100°C?
2 the sun / always / rise / the west?
3 Switzerland / have / a coastline?
4 shops near you / usually / open / Sundays?

3 Read the information on the website. Then write about Derrick Coyle.

Unusual jobs: Ravenmaster, Tower of London

(0) Name: Derrick Coyle
(1) Age: 61
(2) Job: Ravenmaster at the Tower of London
(3) Lives: in an apartment at the Tower of London
(4) Hours: dawn to dusk (summer 05.30–21.30)
(5) Duties: look after ravens / prepare their food / give them water / lock them up at night

▶ Derrick Coyle, with one of his ravens

0 This *is Derrick Coyle.*
1 He …………………… years old.
2 He is the …………………………………….
3 ……………………………………………………
4 ……………………………………………………
5 ……………………………………………………

⏻ Go online for more practice

28 Present continuous

Trudi's a student. She**'s studying** animal behaviour. More people **are taking** their pets to the vet with behaviour problems these days, so Trudi should find a job when she graduates.

1 Form

POSITIVE	I**'m having** lunch. He**'s watching** TV. They**'re running** away.
NEGATIVE	I**'m not watching** TV. She **isn't having** lunch. We **aren't staying** there.
QUESTIONS	**Are** you **watching** TV? (No, I'm not.) **Is** she **running** away? (Yes, she **is**.) What **are** they **having** for lunch?

Some verbs change their spelling in the *-ing* form, e.g. *run* → *running*.

Spelling rules for *-ing* forms ➤ page 350

2 Actions happening now or around now

We use the present continuous for
- actions happening while we are speaking: *Hurry up. The taxi**'s waiting**.*
  *'Are you **watching** TV?' 'No. I**'m doing** my homework.'*
- actions happening around the time of speaking: *Trudi**'s studying** animal behaviour.*
- temporary situations:
  *We**'re staying** at my mother's while the builders **are repairing** the roof of our house.*

With these uses of the present continuous, we often use time expressions like *now, at the moment, today, this week*, etc: *I can't talk for long because I'm cooking **at the moment**.*
*Joe isn't working at home **this week** – he's at a conference in Germany.*

We sometimes use the present continuous with *always* to criticise another person's actions. In speech we stress *always* strongly in this type of sentence:
*Yolanda**'s always calling** me late at night. I'm getting really fed up with it.*
*'I've lost my keys. Can you come home and let me in?' 'You**'re always losing** your keys!'*

3 Changes and trends

We use the present continuous to talk about things that are changing as we speak:
*Harry's been really ill but he**'s getting better** now.   Prices **are going up** again.*
*More people **are taking** their pets to the vet with behaviour problems these days.*

4 Describing pictures

We use the present continuous to describe what is happening in pictures and photos:
*In the photo on page 81, the scientists **are tasting** food. The woman in the middle **is holding** a cup…*

Present continuous to talk about the future ➤ Unit 41.2

Practice

1 **GRAMMAR IN USE** Complete the phone conversation with present continuous forms of the verbs in brackets. 🔊 2.55 **Listen and check.**

WILL Hi, Amy. It's Will. Are you busy?
AMY   Will, hi. No, (0) *I'm watching* (I / watch) TV – nothing important. It's good to hear from you. What (1) .... (you / do) these days?
WILL That's why (2) .... (I / phone). I've just changed my job – I'm now a 'recipe tester'.
AMY   What fun! (3) .... (you / cook) all the time?
WILL No, I've only just started, so (4) .... (I / work) with another tester. (5) .... (I / not / cook) the food yet!
AMY   It'll be really interesting, though. (6) .... (I / find) work really boring now.
WILL Amy, (7) .... (you / always / complain) about your job, but it's really great!
AMY   Oh, yeah, standing in the street in the cold and wet, trying to persuade people to talk to me. Actually, (8) .... (I / not / spend) much time outside at the moment as (9) .... (I / plan) a new project. But I really want to get into acting.
WILL Yes, (10) .... (you / always / say) that, but you never do anything about it ...

2 Look at the table of changes in household spending in the UK. Use the words below + *because* to write sentences. 🔊 2.56 **Listen and check.**

CHANGES IN HOUSEHOLD SPENDING	% CHANGE
Food and drink	+ 9.2 ↑
Clothes	– 6.6 ↓
Domestic fuel (electricity, gas, etc.)	+ 65.0 ↑
Transport	+ 9.4 ↑
Communication (equipment, phones, etc.)	– 28.5 ↓
Eating out	+ 13.5 ↑

0 domestic fuel / increase / most / oil prices / go up
   Domestic fuel is increasing the most because oil prices are going up.
1 communication / decrease / most / equipment / get cheaper
   ....
2 the cost of clothes / decrease / the UK / buy / clothes from China
   ....
3 transport costs / go up / fuel prices / get higher
   ....
4 food and drink / go up / cost of transporting them / increase
   ....

3 Look at the photo on page 80 and describe what is happening.
In the photo, the vet is holding a kitten. He's ...

⏻ Go online for more practice

29 Present simple or continuous?

1 Basic differences in use

PRESENT SIMPLE	PRESENT CONTINUOUS
Permanent situations; things we do not expect to change: Janice **lives** in London with her husband and children.	Temporary situations, for a limited period of time: But Janice **is staying** in a hotel this weekend. Time expressions: *today, this week, at the moment*
Regular actions, habits and routines: Janice is a pilot. She **flies** all over the world. Time expressions: *usually, often, every day, once a month, at the weekend, most days*	Actions that are happening at/around the time we are speaking: Janice **is flying** to Sydney today. Time expressions: *(right) now, at the moment, today*
Permanent situations; things we do not expect to change: Pilots usually **train** for about two years to get their flying licence.	Something that is changing: More and more women **are training** to become pilots these days.
To describe events in a book, play or film: The story **starts** in Madrid. The main character **lives** there. One day, he **goes** out and …	To describe what is happening in a photo or picture: That's my niece in the photo. She**'s riding** her brother's bike.

2 Action verbs

Action verbs describe an action and can usually be used in both **simple** and **continuous** forms:
Janice **flies** around the world. She**'s flying** to Sydney today.
We usually **drive** to work, but at the moment we **aren't driving** because the car has broken down.

3 State verbs

State verbs describe states rather than actions, e.g. ways of thinking or feeling. These verbs are not usually used in the continuous form:
✓ I **prefer** *classical music to popular music.*
✗ *I'm preferring classical music to popular music.*
✓ Do you **understand** *the maths homework now?*
✗ *Are you understanding the maths homework now?*

	STATE VERBS	EXAMPLES
verbs of feeling/ wanting	like love dislike hate prefer need want wish (BUT we often use *enjoy* in the continuous)	**Does** she **like** her present? I **need** a little more time. (**Are** you **enjoying** that book?)
verbs of thinking/ believing	believe doubt forget know mean realise recognise remember think understand	I **don't believe** in luck. **Do** you **know** the answer? We **think** she's really nice.
verbs of being/ appearing	appear be seem	This door **appears** to be locked. Maria **seems** very helpful.
verbs of possessing/ relating	belong contain have (got) own possess	These drinks **contain** Vitamin C. Duncan **has** two Ferraris.
sense verbs	hear see smell taste	Listen! **Do** you **hear** music? This coffee **tastes** really good.

The verbs *agree, cost, promise* and *thank* are also rarely used in the continuous tense:
I **agree** *with you.*   *The hotel* **costs** *€100 a night.*
We **promise** *not to be late.*   *He always* **thanks** *us with a card or flowers.*

4 State verbs and the continuous form

We can use some state verbs in the continuous form, with a different and more active meaning:

	STATE (PRESENT SIMPLE)	ACTION (PRESENT CONTINUOUS)
have	I **have** two sisters. (= possess)	I'm **having** breakfast right now. (= eating)
think	What **do** you **think** of it? (= What's your opinion?)	What **are** you **thinking** about? (= considering at the moment)
appear	It **appears** that they're going to close the theatre. (= seems that/looks like)	The Gypsy Kings **are appearing** at the local theatre next week. (= performing)
taste	Your soup **tastes** wonderful! (= a quality of the soup)	I'm **tasting** the soup to check if it needs any more salt. (= I'm checking/testing it.)
see	Do you **see** the difference between the two pictures? (= can you notice it?)	**Are** you **seeing** your friends a lot at the moment? (= meeting regularly)

- We can also sometimes use state verbs in the continuous when we want to emphasise that the state is unusual or unexpected, and probably temporary:
  My new car uses a lot of petrol so it's **costing** *me a fortune.*
  (I don't usually spend this much on petrol.)
  I'm **finding** *it difficult to organise my time at the moment.*
  (This is unusual for me; I usually organise my time well.)
- Some verbs which express physical states (*feel, hurt, ache*) can be used in the simple or continuous forms with no (or very little) difference in meaning:
  'How **do** *you* **feel**/**are** *you* **feeling** *today?' 'I* **feel**/*I'm* **feeling** *a lot better, thanks.'*
  My back **aches**/**is aching** *this morning.*

FORMALITY CHECK It is becoming more common to use *like, love* and *hate* in the continuous form in informal English: *'How's the course going?' 'It's great! I'm really* **loving** *it!'* Some people consider this to be incorrect.

29 PRESENT SIMPLE OR CONTINUOUS?

Practice

1 Match the sentences 1–5 with the correct meaning, A or B.

0 Craig works in an architect's office.
 A This is a temporary position.
 B This is his permanent job.

1 Rhona is staying with her aunt this weekend.
 A She usually lives somewhere else.
 B This is her permanent home.

2 Max sings with a band on Friday evenings.
 A This is a changing situation.
 B This is something he does regularly.

3 Steve can't talk now. He's interviewing someone.
 A This is an action in progress.
 B This is something he does regularly.

4 More men are looking after their children these days.
 A This is a permanent situation.
 B This is a changing situation.

5 Berlin is one of Germany's sixteen states.
 A This is a fact – something permanent.
 B This is a changing situation.

2 **GRAMMAR IN USE** Read the information about HousesittersPro. Then complete John and Angela's statement with the verbs from the box.

> are enjoying are living are looking after are spending
> don't leave get go ~~live~~ spend visits work

HousesittersPro – the holiday solution
Going on holiday? Then you need HousesittersPro.

Our employees come and live in your home while you're away. They look after your property, including your garden and your pets, so that your home is safe. They are mostly retired people, and we have checked their background.

Meet John and Angela, two of our typical housesitters:

"We have both retired from responsible jobs. We (0) *live* in a small cottage in the country and we (1) .... our retirement. We (2) .... time in the garden most days and we often (3) .... to the cinema and theatre with our friends. Our daughter (4) .... us with our grandchildren now and again. But we sometimes (5) .... bored, so for three months every year we (6) .... for HousesittersPro. Then our life is very different. At the moment, we're in the home of a young couple who are travelling for three weeks. We (7) .... in their apartment in the city, and we (8) .... their pets. We (9) .... a lot of time in front of the TV, because as HousesittersPro employees, we (10) .... the house for more than a couple of hours at a time. You know that your house is safe when you have HousesittersPro in it!"

5

3 Choose the correct words in *italics*. In one sentence, both answers are possible. 🔊 2.57 Listen and check.

0 Fatima's a really good friend. She never *forgets / is forgetting* my birthday.
1 Selina *doesn't work / isn't working* in her office at the moment because the builders are there.
2 Mmm. Those roses *smell / are smelling* lovely. Are they from your garden?
3 I can't believe how difficult my new course is. *I find / I'm finding* it really hard to keep up with all the reading at the moment.
4 These are difficult times because food and fuel prices *go up / are going up* quickly.
5 *Do you believe / Are you believing* anything that child says?
6 Harry isn't at work because *he feels / he's feeling* unwell.
7 In the film 'Australia' two young people *meet / are meeting* and become friends during World War II.
8 Some of the students *don't understand / aren't understanding* basic mathematical ideas.

4 **GRAMMAR IN USE** Check the verbs in the list; write A for action, S for state or A/S for action/state. Then complete the conversation with the verbs in the present simple or present continuous. Use each verb once only. 🔊 2.58 Listen and check.

appear	A/S	be		enjoy		~~feel~~	
go		go well		have		know	
like		see		visit			

JULIET   I (0) *feel* exhausted after all that shopping!

KAREN   So do I. I usually (1) .... a coffee after shopping. This café looks nice.

JULIET   Mmm. I (2) (not often) .... shopping, but I really (3) .... it when I do!

KAREN   Let's sit here. Show me your new dress again. That's really nice. (4) .... it for a special occasion?

JULIET   No, I just need to cheer myself up!

KAREN   Oh, why? Everything (5) .... with your job, isn't it?

JULIET   Well, not really.

KAREN   Why's that? You usually (6) .... to be so happy in your work.

JULIET   Well, I was at first but as you know, I (7) .... my family in Scotland whenever I can, and these days, now that Dad's quite ill, I (8) .... them every weekend, so I'm leaving work early every Friday to get to Scotland. My boss (9) (not) .... that, although I work longer on other days, so we're always arguing at the moment.

KAREN   That's a shame. What are you going to do?

JULIET   Honestly, Karen, I (10) (not) .... I really like the job, but I need to be with my family at the moment, too.

5 Use the verbs in brackets to write about yourself. Choose the present simple or continuous.

0 (live) *I live with my parents but I'm planning to move into a flat with friends soon.*
1 (live) ....
2 (work/study) ....
3 (enjoy) ....
4 (believe) ....

⏻ Go online for more practice and a progress test

Review MODULE 5

1 UNITS 26 AND 27   Find six more mistakes and correct them. Tick (✓) the correct sentences.

  0 Does Melanie ~~has~~ *have* a lot of friends in her new school?
00 Lukasz always brings me a present when he comes back to London. ✓
  1 Sarah needs help with her homework. She don't understand the maths.
  2 Don't go in there! That sign means 'danger'!
  3 Yves is very good-looking. He got blue eyes and black hair.
  4 Do you have got any tickets left for tomorrow evening?
  5 I feel terrible; I think I'm having a cold.
  6 Children have often difficulty in sharing their toys.
  7 This laptop has a number of interesting features.
  8 Sorry, but we don't any lamb steaks today.

2 UNITS 27, 28 AND 29   Jeanette usually teaches English in London in the summer. This year she is giving English lessons to two children in Greece. Complete each sentence with a suitable form of the verbs in brackets.

0 Jeanette usually *works* .... all day in the summer but today *she's stopping* .... at 12.30. (work, stop)
1 She usually .... with friends, but now .... a house just for herself.   (live, have)
2 She usually .... trousers to work, but today .... a summer dress. (wear, wear)
3 She usually .... TV at the weekend, but this summer .... the sights in Athens.   (watch, visit)
4 Most summers she .... very much, but this summer .... more money.   (not earn, get)
5 Most summers she .... tired and overworked, but this summer .... really happy.   (feel, feel)

3 ALL UNITS   Match sentences 1 and 2 with their meanings, A or B, in each pair.

0 1 Nick's having a shower. ⟶ A There's a shower, not a bath, in his flat.
     2 Neil has a shower. ⟶ B He's wet.
1 1 Sally works from home.   A Her office is in her home.
     2 Samantha is working from home. B She is at home today to wait for a builder.
2 1 David's cold.   A He feels ill.
     2 Derek has a cold.   B The heating is turned off.
3 1 Steve always plays his guitar in the evening. A His guitar playing really annoys me.
     2 Simon is always playing his guitar in   B I don't mind his guitar playing.
         the evening.
4 1 Marianne's living in Edinburgh.   A She usually lives in London.
     2 Marie lives in Edinburgh.   B She doesn't live in London.
5 1 Teresa loses weight every year.   A She's on a good diet.
     2 Thea is losing weight.   B She always eats less in the summer.
6 1 Heidi is a good doctor.   A She visits her when she feels ill.
     2 Helen's got a good doctor.   B She has lots of experience.
7 1 Paul travels a lot on business.   A He's on a plane.
     2 Patrick is travelling on business. B He's an international salesman.

4 ALL UNITS Read the article and choose the correct answer, A, B or C below.

Diego Zeman – the human cannonball

It's a cold Saturday afternoon and I'm at Cottle and Austin's Circus to meet Diego Zeman, their human cannonball. When I (0) .... inside the Big Top, I (1) .... Diego immediately. His act is about to start and he (2) .... on top of the cannon. He then (3) .... inside it, and suddenly he shoots out, flies through the air and lands safely in the net. The whole act only (4) .... a couple of minutes, but I'm sure that Diego (5) .... nerves of steel – it's frightening stuff!

When we talk later on, Diego tells me that he (6) .... nervous at first, but then he feels free for the moments he (7) .... through the air – the whole two seconds! Diego (8) .... from a circus family, so he grew up amongst performers. His job may be glamorous, but it's hard work and Diego (9) .... a lot of money. He (10) .... with the circus and travels with them, and he (11) .... a couple of hours in the gym every day to control his weight and strengthen his legs and back. But he does it because he (12) .... the work.

0	A goes	B am going	C go
1	A see	B sees	C am seeing
2	A is standing	B has standing	C stands
3	A climbs	B climb	C is climbing
4	A is last	B is lasting	C lasts
5	A got	B has got	C is got
6	A feels always	B is feeling always	C always feels
7	A is fly	B is flying	C is flies
8	A comes	B is coming	C is come
9	A isn't earning	B don't earn	C doesn't earn
10	A is living	B lives	C live
11	A spends	B is spending	C does spend
12	A is loving	B is love	C loves

5 ALL UNITS Complete Neil and Jack's conversation about their flatmate, using the words in brackets. Decide whether to use the present simple or present continuous.

JACK You know, Laurence has been in the flat for three months now. What (0) *do you think* .... (you / think) of him?

NEIL Well, actually, (1) .... (I / get) really fed up with him. I mean, (2) .... (he / always / take) my food from the fridge.

JACK And mine. And (3) .... (he / never / do) the washing-up! It's not fair. Perhaps we should ask him to leave.

NEIL Well, I'm not sure that he wants to stay. (4) .... (he / not / seem) very happy here.

JACK Mmm. (5) .... (he / have) any friends? He doesn't go out much.

NEIL Mmm … you know that (6) .... (he / have) about three showers a day.

JACK That's because (7) .... (he / work) on a building site at the moment.

NEIL True, but the gas and water prices (8) .... (go up) all the time. We can't afford his three showers a day.

JACK I know, but (9) .... (he / have) some good points, too. He's quiet and (10) .... (he / usually / pay) the rent on time. Look, I'll have a word with him about the showers and so on, and we'll see how it goes.

Test MODULE 5

Present tenses

Choose the correct answer, A, B or C.

1. The meals here .... very expensive.
   A isn't   B aren't   C not are
   ▶ Unit 26

2. .... I invited to Jim's party?
   A Amn't   B Don't   C Aren't
   ▶ Unit 26

3. The shoe shop .... the shoes I saw last week.
   A doesn't have got   B hasn't got   C doesn't got
   ▶ Unit 26

4. I'm exhausted. I'm going to .... a sleep for half an hour.
   A have   B be   C have got
   ▶ Unit 26

5. Don't bother to invite Gerry – he .... musicals!
   A doesn't like   B doesn't likes   C isn't like
   ▶ Unit 27

6. I really like Leona Lewis – she .... so well.
   A sing   B is sing   C sings
   ▶ Unit 27

7. Most children .... enough green vegetables.
   A eatn't   B don't eat   C not eat
   ▶ Unit 27

8. We don't need to rush – this bus .... late!
   A is always   B always is   C always
   ▶ Unit 27

9. I .... on a colour printer, but mine is broken at the moment.
   A am usually print   B print usually   C usually print
   ▶ Unit 27

10. .... on the report for Grant Brothers at the moment?
    A Are you work   B You work   C Are you working
    ▶ Unit 28

11. 'Is Alana coming this evening?' 'No, she .... at home with the kids.'
    A staying   B stays   C is staying
    ▶ Unit 28

12. Let's put the heating on. The nights .... colder now.
    A are getting   B get   C is getting
    ▶ Unit 28

13. Can you tell the children to be quiet? They ....!
    A argue always   B are always arguing   C always argue
    ▶ Unit 28

14. In this picture, the woman .... a car that's broken down.
    A is repairing   B is repair   C repairs
    ▶ Unit 28

15. A student teacher .... our class while Ms Bennett has her baby.
    A takes   B does take   C is taking
    ▶ Unit 29

16. What .... when you're in bed at night?
    A you usually read   B do you usually read   C are you usually reading
    ▶ Unit 29

17. The film .... with a car crash, and then ...
    A is open   B opens   C is opening
    ▶ Unit 29

18. Older people .... more help from the government this year.
    A get   B are get   C are getting
    ▶ Unit 29

19. 'Is this the soup for the dinner party tonight? Mmm, it .... delicious!'
    A tastes   B is tasting   C is tasty
    ▶ Unit 29

20. .... the date of Dan's wedding anniversary? I've forgotten it.
    A Do you remember   B Are you remembering   C You remember
    ▶ Unit 29

Go online for a full exit test

Past tenses

MODULE 6

Before you start

1 Read the article about Marco Polo. Look at the highlighted grammar examples.

MARCO POLO

Marco Polo **lived** from 1254 to 1324. His father was a trader and often **travelled** to distant countries. In 1271 Marco left Venice with his father to go on a long voyage to the East. Clearly, journeys **used to take** much longer then than they do now, and it was only after they **had been travelling** for three years that they arrived in China, at the palace of the great Kublai Khan. The Emperor remembered Marco's father from when he **had visited** before and he welcomed the travellers. While he **was living** in China, Marco learned the language, and **would often travel** on business for the Emperor. After several years Marco and his father decided to leave China, and they **were discussing** their wishes with the Emperor **when** a message arrived from the King of Persia, who wanted to marry Kublai Khan's daughter. Marco and his father decided to accompany the wedding group, so, after twenty-four years away, Marco Polo arrived back in Venice in 1295.

2 Now read the sentences and choose the correct words in *italics*. The highlighted grammar examples will help you.

1 I *travelled / did travel* a lot when I was younger. ➤ Unit 30
2 We *have worked / worked* in Venice from 2006 to 2008. ➤ Unit 30
3 We visited a lot of museums while we *stayed / were staying* in Beijing. ➤ Unit 31
4 They *were having / had* dinner when the police knocked on the door. ➤ Unit 31
5 Fiona was working at Harrods *when / while* she met her husband. ➤ Unit 32
6 People *used to travel / used to travelling* by ship a lot in those days. ➤ Unit 33
7 When Simon was at college, he *had / would* sleep late every day. ➤ Unit 33
8 I didn't want to join you because I *saw / had seen* the film before. ➤ Unit 34
9 We had *been using / been used* the machine for days without any problems. ➤ Unit 35

3 Check your answers below. Then go to the unit for more information and practice.

1 travelled 2 worked 3 were staying 4 were having 5 when 6 used to travel 7 would 8 had seen 9 been using

Go online for a full diagnostic test

30 Past simple

Estevanico **was** the first black explorer to reach North America. He **lived** in the sixteenth century. He **travelled** to America with some Spanish explorers, as a slave. **When** they arrived, they **explored** Texas and New Mexico and he **learned** several native American languages. He **became** a free man in 1536 and **died** in 1539.

1 Regular and irregular verbs

Most verbs add -ed to the infinitive to form the past simple: stay → stay**ed**, learn → learn**ed**

POSITIVE	I **stayed** with my friend last night. He **learned** native American languages. They **failed** the exam.
NEGATIVE	I **did not (didn't) stay** with her last night. She **did not (didn't) learn** any languages. We **did not (didn't) fail** the exam.
QUESTIONS	**Did** you **stay** with her? (Yes, I **did**.) **Did** she **learn** any languages? (No, she **didn't**.) Which exam **did** they **fail**?

Many common verbs are irregular, e.g. be → **was/were**, do → **did**, go → **went**, have → **had**, make → **made**, put → **put**, say → **said**, see → **saw**, take → **took**, tell → **told**

Spelling rules for regular verbs ➤ page 350   Irregular verbs ➤ page 348

⚠ The pronunciation of the -ed ending depends on the sound that comes before it, for example
- /ɪd/ after /t/ and /d/: started, waited, added, ended
- /t/ after the sounds /p/, /f/, /k/, /s/, /ʃ/, /tʃ/: worked, stopped, passed, finished
- /d/ after all the other sounds: tried, planned, lived, listened

 Pronunciation ➤ 1.11

2 Past simple for past actions and situations

We use the past simple for
- a single completed action in the past: He **died** in 1539. **Did** you **see** the film last night?
- repeated actions in the past: He **learned** several native American languages. Caroline **phoned** her family every day when she was on holiday.
- a series of actions (when one thing happens after another) in the past: We **arrived** in Rome at eleven o'clock and **took** a taxi to Franco's apartment. Then we **went** to the square and **looked** round the shops, but we **didn't buy** anything.
- situations that finished in the past: He **lived** from 1500 to 1539. Children **didn't have** so many electronic toys when I **was** young.

3 Past simple + adverbs of time; *when, after*

We often use adverbs of time to say when a past action happened, for example
- *ago*: We **arrived** at the airport **ten minutes ago**. (ten minutes before now)
- *for* (with periods of time): The economic crisis **lasted for two years**.
- *last week/month/year*: Mariela **started** college **last month**. We **had** a general election **last year**.

We can also use *when/after* + past simple:
When they **arrived**, they **explored** Texas and New Mexico ...
After Rory **left** home that morning, he went to work as usual ...

6

Practice Use the list on page 348 to help you complete these exercises.

1 Write the past forms of these irregular verbs.

0 be   was/were
1 become ....
2 give ....
3 go ....
4 hear ....
5 meet ....
6 sell ....
7 take ....
8 travel ....

2 GRAMMAR IN USE Read more about Estevanico and put the verbs in brackets into the past simple. 🔊 2.59 Listen and check.

> Estevanico (0) _was_ (be) born in North Africa over 500 years ago, in 1490. He first (1) .... (become) a slave at the age of twenty-three after being captured by some Portuguese explorers, who later (2) .... (sell) him to Andres Dorantes de Carranza, a captain in the Spanish army.
> Dorantes (3) .... (hear) stories about the New World and in 1527, he and Estevanico (4) .... (join) an expedition to cross the Atlantic. Things (5) .... (not go) quite as planned and they (6) .... (go) first to Hispaniola, then Cuba, then Trinidad, and finally to what is now Florida and into Texas. For eight years Dorantes and Estevanico (7) .... (explore) the new land and (8) .... (trade) with the native Americans, then they (9) .... (travel) to New Spain (Mexico), where Dorantes finally (10) .... (give) Estevanico his freedom in 1536. Sadly, he (11) .... (not enjoy) it for long as he (12) .... (die) in 1539.

3 Write sentences in the past simple, using the words below. 🔊 2.60 Listen and check.

0   when / be / last major festival / your country?
    When was the last major festival in your country?

00 when / Kate / finish / race / feel / exhausted
    When Kate finished the race, she felt exhausted.

1   slave trade / stop / over 200 years ago
    ....

2   who / you / like most / your last school?
    ....

3   we / not understand / lecture / last week
    ....

4   when / you / take / your last exam?
    ....

5   when / Jack / arrive / tell / us the news
    ....

6   why / you / start / learning English?
    ....

4 Now answer questions 0, 2, 4 and 6 from Exercise 3 about yourself.

0 (0) _The last major festival in my country was New Year's Eve._
1 (0) ....
2 (2) ....
3 (4) ....
4 (6) ....

⏻ Go online for more practice

91

31 Past continuous

1 Form

POSITIVE	I **was waiting** for you. She **was travelling** in the Middle East. They **were living** at home.
NEGATIVE	I **was not (wasn't) waiting** long. He **was not (wasn't) travelling** then. We **were not (weren't) living** there.
QUESTIONS	**Were** you **waiting** long? (No, I wasn't.) **Were** they **living** at home? (Yes, they were.) Where **was** she **travelling**?

Spelling rules for *-ing* forms ➤ page 350

 Pronunciation ➤ 1.12

Freya Stark was a travel writer who spent much of her life travelling in the Middle East. While she **was travelling**, she **was** constantly **taking** notes and **photographing** places and people, so her travel books are very personal.

2 Past actions and situations

We use the past continuous
- to describe an action or situation happening at or around a time in the past:
  I **wasn't feeling** well that day, so I didn't go out with the others.
- for temporary past situations:
  We **were living** in Beijing at the time of the 2008 Olympics. (We don't live there now.)
- for two actions/situations happening at the same time:
  While Rob **was playing** his match, I **was waiting** in the car outside.

As with the present continuous (➤ Unit 28.2), we can use the past continuous to criticise another person's actions, often with *always*:
Karla **was always complaining** about something or other.

3 Interrupted actions

We use the past continuous and the past simple together to show that one action (past simple) interrupts another action (past continuous):

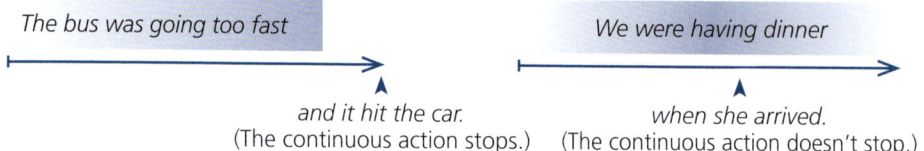

and it hit the car.
(The continuous action stops.)

when she arrived.
(The continuous action doesn't stop.)

4 Plans that did not happen

The past continuous of verbs like *plan, hope, intend* shows that the action did not happen:
We **were planning** to come to your party, but Mike was ill so we couldn't make it.
I **was hoping** to study medicine, but my grades weren't high enough so I couldn't.

was going to ➤ Unit 45.1

5 Background situations

We often use the past continuous to describe a 'background' situation in the past:
When we arrived at the beach, **the sun wasn't shining**.

We also use the past continuous to 'set the scene' for a story or account of something that happened; the actions that follow are in the past simple: Dana **was living** in Istanbul that summer. Isik **was working** at the same school as her. As soon as they **met**, they immediately **got on** with each other ...

⚠ We don't usually use continuous forms of state verbs (e.g. *like, see, hear, think, agree*). (➤ Unit 29.3)

Practice

1 Write the words in the correct order to make sentences. Put the verbs in the past continuous.

0 at that man you why stare ?   *Why were you staring at that man?*
1 not work during the strike there they ....
2 where you at the start of the year live ? ....
3 not feel yesterday evening I very well ....
4 heavily it rain and the rivers rise ....
5 she talk always while I watch TV ....

2 **GRAMMAR IN USE** Read the article and choose the correct words in *italics*. 2.61 Listen and check.

Meteorite crashes in Texas

At 3.30 p.m. yesterday a large meteorite (0) *crashed* / *was crashing* to Earth near the small town of Karlsville, Texas. Many local people (1) *was* / *were* doing things outside and (2) *were seeing* / *saw* it happen. Here are a couple of their reports:
"I (3) *washed* / *was washing* my car when I (4) *noticed* / *was noticing* a bright light in the sky. I (5) *didn't know* / *wasn't knowing* what it was."
"We (6) *were* / *did* driving home from the shopping mall when we (7) *heard* / *were hearing* a loud bang. When we looked up we could see smoke coming from the middle of a nearby field."
It seems that whatever people (8) *did* / *were doing*, they (9) *stopped* / *were stopping* and (10) *rushed* / *were rushing* to the site of the crash. Local police said that this was foolish but that nobody was hurt.

3 **GRAMMAR IN USE** Complete the conversation with words and phrases from the box. There are four extra words or phrases. 2.62 Listen and check.

> always asked   became   didn't know   fell   played   was always asking   was becoming
> was hoping   ~~was intending~~   was planning   was playing   wasn't knowing
> weren't planning

ALLA When's your trip to Namibia? Isn't it soon?
SUE Well, I (0) *was intending* to go in April, but everything's changed. You see, I
 (1) .... to go with Jana, from work, but she broke her wrist a while ago.
ALLA I (2) .... that.
SUE Yes, she (3) .... netball with some people from work in November when
 she (4) .... over. She landed on her wrist, and it was quite a bad break.
ALLA Mmm, but surely she's had enough time to recover?
SUE Yes, well, that wasn't the only problem. She was really starting to get on my nerves.
ALLA Oh, why?
SUE She (5) .... stupid questions, things like: 'Should I take my hairdryer?'
 We (6) .... to go to Ibiza, after all!
ALLA Oh dear ...
SUE So ... the broken wrist (7) .... a good excuse! Are you going away this year?
ALLA Oh, well, I (8) .... to visit my friend in Crete for a couple of weeks,
 but we hadn't discussed it and she's just told me that she's coming back soon ...

32 Past simple or continuous?

Dr Livingstone was a Scottish explorer, famous for his work in Africa. **While he was searching** for the source of the River Nile, he **disappeared**. He had been quite ill, so people were worried about him, but he was found by Henry Stanley. He **was still trying** to find the source of the Nile **when he died** in 1873.

1 Completed or unfinished actions?

PAST SIMPLE	PAST CONTINUOUS
We use the past simple for single or repeated **completed** actions in the past: We **arrived** at the hotel at three o'clock. He **went** on many expeditions to Africa.	We use the past continuous to describe an **unfinished** action at or around a time in the past: When we arrived at the hotel, the maid **was cleaning** our room. He **was searching** for the source of the Nile.

2 Interrupted past or series of past actions?

We use the past continuous for an action in progress when something else happened:
*While he **was searching** for the source of the River Nile, he **disappeared**.*
*'**Were** you **playing** football when you **sprained** your ankle?' 'No, I **wasn't doing** anything like that. I **was running** downstairs and I **tripped** over my trousers!'*

⚠ We use *when* + past simple, followed by past simple, when one action happened AFTER another one. Compare:
*When Isabel **joined** us, we **watched** a DVD.* (= Isabel came and then we watched a DVD.)
*When Isabel **joined** us, we **were watching** a DVD.* (= We were already watching a DVD at the time Isabel came.)

3 *when* and *while*

We can use either *when* or *while* before an unfinished action or the interrupted past. It means 'during the time':
*The post came **when** I **was having** my breakfast.*
*While he **was searching** for the source of the River Nile, he disappeared.*

We can use *when* before the unfinished (continuous) or the completed (simple) action:
*He was trying to find the source of the Nile **when** he **died** in 1873.*
*He died in 1873 **when** he **was trying** to find the source of the Nile.*

⚠ We don't use *while* before a completed action:
✗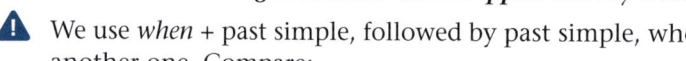
✓ **When the post came**, I was having my breakfast.
✓ *The post came **while/when** I **was having** my breakfast.*

We can use *as* instead of *while*:
As/While I was driving to work this morning, I saw a deer by the side of the road.

Practice

1 Look at the pictures and complete the sentences, using the verbs in brackets. Use the past simple or past continuous. 🔊 2.63 Listen and check.

0 When we *arrived* at the resort, *it was raining*. (arrive, fall)
1 We .... when the storm .... (run, start)
2 We .... for shelter when the storm .... (run, start)
3 I .... the bank when the robber .... (leave, arrive)
4 I .... the bank when the robber .... (leave, arrive)

2 `GRAMMAR IN USE` Read the article and choose the correct words in *italics*. 🔊 2.64 Listen and check.

Steve Fossett

MODERN ADVENTURER

Steve Fossett was always looking for adventure, even as a boy in the 1950s. After some years in business, he (0) (*began*) / *was beginning* his well-known adventures, from swimming the English Channel to sailing round the world. But Fossett is best-known for his adventures in the air – in hot-air balloons, gliders and light aircraft.
In 2005 he (1) *broke / was breaking* the record for non-stop flying when he flew round the world in 67 hours without stopping for fuel. A year later, as he (2) *attempted / was attempting* to break the record for the longest flight, he had to stop because part of his engine had failed – but he broke the record, anyway.
Fossett's adventures often put him in danger – in 1998, while he (3) *travelled / was travelling* around the world in a balloon, he almost died (4) *while / when* the balloon fell from the sky. In the end, it was a routine flight that (5) *took / was taking* his life – he was flying a small plane across the Nevada Desert in September 2007 when he (6) *disappeared / was disappearing*. No one could find him, then, some months later, a hiker (7) *walked / was walking* through the mountains in southern California when he (8) *noticed / was noticing* some personal items which (9) *belonged / were belonging* to the adventurer, and soon afterwards a search party (10) *found / was finding* the wreckage of the plane. Some time later, Fossett's body was found – his adventures were over.

3 Write true answers to the questions.
What were you doing, or what was happening when …
0 you received your last text message? *I was watching TV.*
1 you received your last text message? ....
2 you lost something important? ....
3 you saw something unusual? ....
4 you heard some shocking news? ....
5 you lost your temper? ....

⏻ Go online for more practice and a progress test

33 *used to* and *would*

Sir Ranulph Fiennes is an explorer. He **used to be** a soldier but started exploring in the 1960s. When he was younger, he **used to go** on very difficult expeditions and he **would take** risks that many other explorers wouldn't. In 2000, for example, he attempted to walk to the North Pole, alone and unsupported.

1 Form of *used to*

POSITIVE	I **used to** work there. He **used to** be a soldier. We **used to** have a cat.
NEGATIVE	I **did not (didn't) use to** work.* He **did not (didn't) use to** be an explorer. They **did not (didn't) use to** have a cat.
QUESTIONS	**Did** you **use to** work? (Yes, I did.) **Did** they **use to** have a cat? (No, they didn't.) Where **did** he **use to** work?

* It is also possible to form the negative and question with *used to*: **didn't used** to / **did** you **used to**?

 There is no present form of *used to*: ✗ *I use to go to work by bus.*   ✓ *I go to work by bus.*

 Do not confuse *used to do* with *be/get used to doing*:
I'**m used to spending** time on my own. (= I'm often alone; it isn't unusual for me.)
I **used to spend** time on my own. (= I spent time on my own in the past; I don't any more.)

2 *used to*

We use *used to* + infinitive to talk about regular past actions that do not happen now:
I **used to take** the bus to work every day. (But now I take the train.)
People **used to write** a lot of letters. (But now they send emails.)

We often use adverbs of frequency (e.g. *always, once a week, every year*) with *used to*:
I **always used to swim** before breakfast.   We **often used to hold** parties for our friends.
We **never used to stay up** late when we were young! (= We didn't use to stay up late.)

We also use *used to* + infinitive when we talk about past situations that are no longer true:
He **used to be** a soldier. (But now he's an explorer.) France **used to have** a king.

 Pronunciation ➤ 1.13

3 *would*

We can also use *would* + infinitive to talk about regular past actions that do not happen now: *When we first moved here, people* **would stop** *and talk in the street. They don't now.*
When we start descriptions of past actions with *used to*, we usually continue with *would*:
When he was younger, he **used to go** *on very difficult expeditions and he* **would take** *risks ...*

 Would is used for past actions, not situations:
✗ *France would have a king.*   ✓ *France* **used to have** *a king.*

 Pronunciation ➤ 1.14

4 *used to* or past simple?

We often use *used to*, not the past simple, when we want to emphasise a difference between the past and the present: *My sister works in an office now* **but she used to work** *on a farm.*
We use the past simple for
- single actions in the past: ✗ *I used to have an exam last week.*   ✓ *I* **had** *an exam last week.*
- periods of time: ✗ *He used to be in Greece for two years.*   ✓ *He* **was** *in Greece for two years.*
- a number of times: ✗ *We used to swim in the pool twice when we stayed there.*
  ✓ *We* **swam** *in the pool twice when we stayed there.*

6

Practice

1 Choose the correct words in *italics*. In two sentences, both answers are possible.
0   When we lived in the country, people in shops *would / used to be* much friendlier.
1   When I was a child we *didn't use / weren't used* to fly – we couldn't afford it.
2   *Do / Did* you use to wear a uniform at your last school?
3   When Matt was in his twenties, he *used to / would* play rugby every Sunday.
4   Last week we *interviewed / used to interview* over twenty candidates.
5   *Did you use to / Would you* have dark hair when you were a girl?
6   In the nineteenth century people *worked / used to work* longer hours than they do now.

2 **GRAMMAR IN USE** Complete the text with the verbs in brackets. Use the past simple, *used to* or *would*. (Remember not to repeat *used to* too much.) 🔊 **3.01** Listen and check.

The greatest mountain climber of all time?

Reinhold Messner is often called 'the greatest mountain climber of all time'; he was the first person to climb all fourteen peaks of over 8,000 metres.
Messner was born near Bolzano, Italy, in 1944. This area (0) ...*used to belong*... (belong) to the Austrian Empire, and is still German-speaking. When Reinhold was a child, he (1) .... (go) climbing in the Dolomite Mountains with his father and brothers. He (2) .... (become) a very good climber at a young age. He first (3) .... (climb) the Himalayas in 1970, though this expedition was a tragedy because his brother (4) .... (die) on the way down.
Messner was well-known for his attitude to the mountains: he (5) .... (climb) with only light equipment, he (6) .... (not request) any outside support and he (7) .... (not take) any extra oxygen – at a time when it was thought impossible to climb the highest peaks without oxygen. Apart from mountaineering, Messner (8) .... (make) a number of Arctic and Antarctic crossings.

3 Find six more mistakes and correct them. Tick (✓) the correct sentences. 🔊 **3.02** Listen and check.
0   Messner didn't use to ~~taking~~ *take* extra oxygen when he climbed.
1   When we went to Nepal, I used to climb to Everest Base Camp once.
2   When we were children, we'd often visit our grandparents at the weekends.
3   People today use to spend a lot of time on their computers.
4   Did they use to have electric lighting in the 1800s?
5   Centuries ago people would be a lot shorter than today.
6   We never use to stay at school for lunch in those days.
7   Before the 1960s men wouldn't have long hair.
8   Were you used to learn French when you were at school?

4 Use the words in brackets to write about things that have changed in your life.
0   (holidays)   *When I was young we would go to the mountains on holiday, but now I go abroad.*
1   (holidays)   ....
2   (music)   ....
3   (friends)   ....

⏻ Go online for more practice

34 Past perfect simple

In 1999, Eileen Collins became the first woman commander of a US space flight, but four years earlier, she **had** also **become** the first female American pilot in space.

1 Form

We form the past perfect with *had* + past participle. The regular past participle ends in *-ed* (e.g. *finished*).

POSITIVE	I **had** already **seen** the film. She **had met** him before. We **had finished** early.
NEGATIVE	I had not (**hadn't**) **seen** it before. He had not (**hadn't**) **met** her before. They had not (**hadn't**) **finished** the job.
QUESTIONS	**Had** you **seen** the film? (Yes, I **had**.) **Had** they **finished** the job? (No, they **hadn't**.) Where **had** he **met** her before?

Irregular past participles, e.g. *seen, met*, ➤ page 348

 Pronunciation ➤ 1.15

2 The order of past actions

We can use the past perfect to show which action happened first:
(2) *Before I finally found a job,* (1) *I* **had been** *to about thirty interviews.*

⚠ If one action happens immediately after the other, we use the past simple for both:
✗ *When Colin* **had arrived** *at the door, Sheila* **opened** *it straight away.*
✓ *When Colin* **arrived** *at the door, Sheila* **opened** *it straight away.*

We often use adverbs of time and linking words with the past perfect:
Four years **earlier**, *she* **had become** *the first American female pilot in space.* (adverb)
I'd never **liked** *Japanese food* **before** *but the meal Yuki cooked was lovely.* (adverb)
By the time *Grace decided to apply for the job, the position* **had been filled**. (linking phrase)

We often use the past perfect in stories to show a series of events in the past:
There was no answer from the house. No face at the window. Time **had stopped** *here ... Where was she? Where* **had** *she* **gone**? *The grass* **had grown** *thick ...* (from *Ghostwalk*, by Rebecca Stott)

3 Past perfect or past simple?

We usually use the past simple, not the past perfect
- if the order of actions is clear: *I* **got** *my first job after I* **left** *university.*
- if the order of actions is the same as the order of the verbs in the sentence. Compare:
  When I **got to** *the café, everyone* **ordered** *their drinks.*
  (= First, I got to the café, then everyone ordered their drinks.)
  When I **got to** *the café, everyone* **had ordered** *their drinks.*
  (= First, everyone ordered their drinks, then I got to the café.)

4 Giving reasons

We can use the past perfect to give a reason for an action or situation, often with *because*:
Eileen Collins became the commander **because** *she* **had already flown** *as a space pilot.*
Emily was unhappy – her husband **hadn't bought** *her a birthday present.*

5 Superlatives

We often use the past perfect (and *ever*) with superlative adjectives:
It was the **worst** *meal I* **had ever eaten**! *I never went there again.*

We also use the past perfect after *it was the first, second*, etc:
We went to Egypt in 1996. It was **the first time** *we'd travelled outside Europe.*

Present perfect + superlatives ➤ Unit 37.4

Practice

1 Which action comes first in each sentence? Write 1 or 2 after the verbs.

0 Russell realised [2] his mistake only hours after he had sent [1] the money.
1 When Kris arrived [ ] at the station, the group had already left [ ].
2 When Kris arrived [ ] at the station, the group left [ ].
3 Mandy had asked [ ] her father to lend her the car before, but this time he agreed [ ].
4 Sam had been [ ] in the room for some time before he realised [ ] it was the wrong class.
5 By the time the builders completed [ ] the work, we had already moved in [ ].
6 When the builders had completed [ ] the work, we moved in [ ].
7 Jelena started [ ] the course because she hadn't found [ ] a job.
8 Kevin got [ ] the job because he had been [ ] the best interviewee.

2 Read these sentences from novels and choose the correct words in *italics*.
🔊 **3.03** Listen and check.

0 Her mother *had* / (*had had*) a beautiful voice, both when she (*sang*) / *had sung* and when she (*talked*) / *had talked*.
1 The girls were still there, standing where he *saw* / *had seen* them earlier.
2 Liesel's treat was a ride in a car. She *was never* / *had never been* in one before.
3 The man was very pleasant, reminding him that they *met* / *had met* at Adam's wedding.
4 As Joe walked away, he *felt* / *had felt* that he *said* / *had said* goodbye to the last phase of his youth.
5 She stepped out of the bath, *reached* / *had reached* for the towel the maid *left* / *had left* for her and *wrapped* / *had wrapped* it around her.

3 **GRAMMAR IN USE** Complete the text with the verbs in brackets. Use the past simple or past perfect. 🔊 **3.04** Listen and check.

Leyton stared at the expanse of the Atlantic Ocean in front of him. He (0) *had finally come* (finally / come) to the end of his journey. Several months ago he (1) .... (not / know) whether the journey would really be possible. After all, he (2) .... (recover) from his illness only weeks before he (3) .... (make) the decision – well, it was because of the illness that he (4) .... (decide) to do this, to prove it was possible. Then, after a few weeks of planning and worrying, he (5) .... (set out), starting from the northernmost point of the country and walking, on his own, to the southernmost point. And here he was, at the end of his journey – he (6) .... (achieve) his aim. And he (7) .... (realise) now that it was the most exciting thing he (8) .... (ever / do) – and probably ever would do – in his life.

Go online for more practice

35 Past perfect continuous

> Francisco Pizarro **had been exploring** Central and South America for twenty years when he led the famous expedition to Peru which destroyed the Inca Empire.

1 Form

POSITIVE	I **had been watching** them. She **had been learning** the language. We **had been working** hard.
NEGATIVE	I **had not** (**hadn't**) **been watching** them. He **had not** (**hadn't**) **been learning** the language. They **had not** (**hadn't**) **been working** hard.
QUESTIONS	**Had** you **been watching** them? (Yes, I **had**.) **Had** they **been working** hard? (No, they **hadn't**.) Which language **had** she **been learning**?

2 Use

We use the past perfect continuous to talk about an action or situation that was happening in the past before another action or time:
*I **had been learning** French for five years when I went to live in Paris.*
*'How long **had you been living** in the house when you sold it?' 'Oh, about a year.'*

We usually introduce the second action with *when*:
*He'd been taking driving lessons for years **when** he finally passed the test.*

The first action can stop when the second action happens, or it can continue:

We'd been waiting for forty minutes → when the bus finally arrived. (The continuous action stops.)

Julia had been working there for two years → when Phil became the new sales manager. (The continuous action doesn't stop.)

 Pronunciation ➤ 1.16

3 Emphasising time and giving reasons

The past perfect continuous often emphasises a period of time:
*Pizarro **had been exploring for twenty years** when he went to Peru.*

We can use the past perfect continuous to give a reason for an action or feeling in the past:
*Derek was very tired when he arrived – he'**d been driving** in heavy traffic all afternoon.*

4 Comparison with other forms

Notice the difference between the past continuous and the past perfect continuous:
*When I arrived home, Brad **was washing** the car.* (He was still washing it.)
*When I arrived home, Brad **had been washing** the car and he was wet.* (He was no longer washing the car.)

The differences between the past perfect simple and continuous are similar to the differences between the present perfect simple and continuous (➤ Unit 40.1).
*I called Jane after I'**d written** my essay.* (The essay was finished.)
*I called Jane after I'**d been writing** my essay for two hours.* (The essay wasn't finished.)

- We use the past perfect simple with a number or amount:
  *I called Jane after I'**d read half the reports**.*
  *I gave up after I'**d phoned six times** without getting through.*
- We do not usually use the past perfect continuous with state verbs. (➤ Unit 29.3)

6

Practice

1 Write sentences in the past perfect continuous and the past simple using the words below. 3.05 Listen and check.

0 The explorers / sail / for days / when they / finally see / land
   The explorers had been sailing for days when they finally saw land.

1 How long / you / work there / when you / become / a director ?
   ....

2 I / not sleep / well / for weeks / when I / have / the accident at work
   ....

3 Paul / work / really long hours / for six months / when he / become ill
   ....

4 How long / Sarah / take / the medicine / before she / get better ?
   ....

5 We / not save / hard enough / so we / not can / go on holiday with the others
   ....

2 Complete the sentences with the past perfect continuous of the verbs from the box.

| not listen   not wear   play   rain   ~~run~~   work |

0 Jack was feeling exhausted because he *had been running* for three hours.
1 Barry and Gill were soaked when they arrived because it .... heavily.
2 Emma found the essay difficult because she .... in the lecture.
3 Yolanda fell asleep at her desk because she .... too hard.
4 The children were dirty because they .... in the garden.
5 Will had got really sunburnt because he .... any sunscreen.

3 **GRAMMAR IN USE** Complete the email with phrases from A–H below. 3.06 Listen and check.

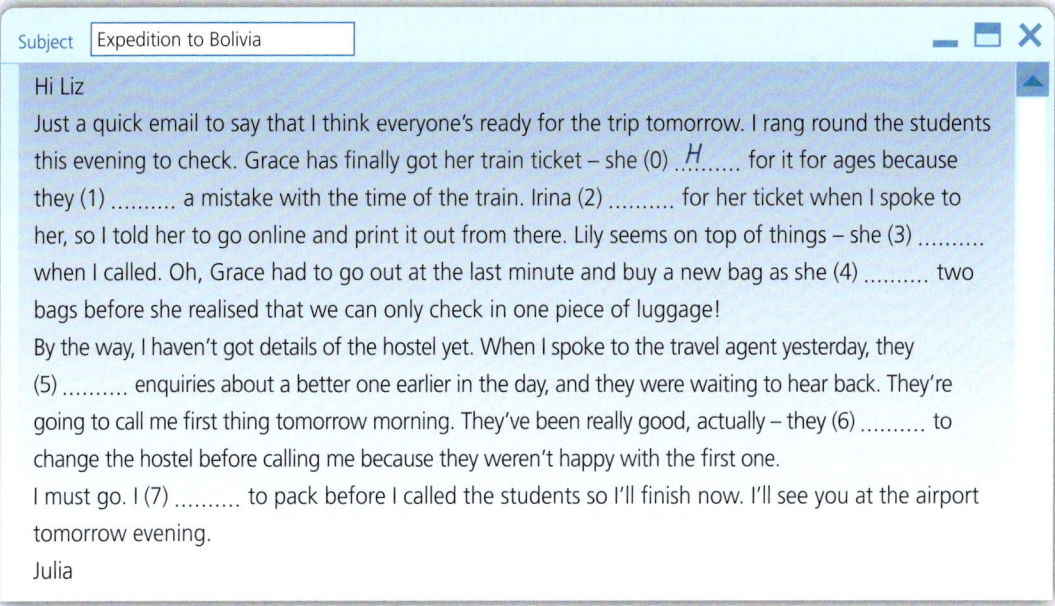

A was starting
B had made
C had been making
D was packing
E had packed
F was still waiting
G had decided
H ~~had been waiting~~

Go online for more practice and a progress test

Review MODULE 6

1 UNITS 30, 31 AND 32 Complete the two conversations. Use the correct form of the verbs in brackets – past simple or past continuous.

CLERK Castle Bank. How can I help you?
CALLER Hello. I'm afraid I've lost my debit card.
CLERK OK. What (0) *were you doing* (you / do) when you last (1) .... (have) it?
CALLER I (2) .... (get) cash out of a machine It wasn't stolen, though.
CLERK Right. When (3) .... (this / happen)?
CALLER Two days ago, I think.
CLERK OK. We'll check your account and get a new card to you within five days.
CALLER But I (4) .... (hope) to go away tomorrow. Can't you send it now?

ELLA How was your day at the beach?
BEN Well, when we (5) .... (arrive), the sun (6) .... (shine) brightly and it was really warm.
ELLA Great!
BEN But then it (7) .... (start) to rain and it (8) .... (not / stop) raining all day!

2 UNITS 30 AND 33 Find seven more mistakes in the story and correct them.

'I don't know what's happened to my best friend, Sarah. I'm quite worried about her. She ~~would~~ *used to* be a really fun-loving person but she's changed. It all started when she would go to Africa after college and worked in a village, helping poor children. She used to be there for two years. She obviously loved it there, but she's become really serious. She never use to be like that. When we were at college together, we would go out in the evenings – to the cinema, to cafés and so on, we weren't use to worry about anything. We would often go away at the weekend with a group of friends and Sarah used be ready to try anything – horse-riding, sailing, surfing – all that. But now she prefers to stay at home because she thinks we shouldn't spend money on these things. She is never used to criticise me so much – now she says that I need to take life more seriously. She used to tell me the other day that I was wasting my life! I know that she's learnt a lot from her work in Africa and that she's right in some ways, but you still need to have some fun, don't you?'

3 UNITS 30, 31, 34 AND 35 Match the sentences 1–5 with the correct meaning, A or B.

0 The plane had landed when we heard the noise.
  A We heard it before the plane landed. Ⓑ We heard it after the plane landed.
1 The children were preparing breakfast when I woke up.
  A Breakfast was ready. B Breakfast wasn't ready.
2 When Jeanette opened the door, I saw that she had been crying.
  A Her eyes were red. B There were tears running down her face.
3 When Boris and Angela arrived, we'd already eaten dinner.
  A Dinner was still in progress. B Dinner was over.

4 I'd already decided to leave the area when the new neighbours moved in.
   A I decided to leave before they came.   B I decided to leave after they came.
5 I decided to leave the area when the new neighbours moved in.
   A I decided to leave before they came.   B I decided to leave because of the neighbours.

4 ALL UNITS Read the article and choose the correct words in *italics*.

There haven't been many female explorers and adventurers but one of the best-known (0) *was* / *had been* Mary Kingsley. Born in London in 1862, Kingsley (1) *travelled / had travelled* to parts of Africa where few western women (2) *were ever travelling / had ever travelled* before.
Mary's father was a doctor who (3) *enjoyed / was enjoying* travelling, studying the different customs of people around the world. Her mother was an invalid, and much of Mary's early life (4) *was / had* spent nursing her, until she died in 1892, only a few weeks after Mary's father (5) *used to pass away / had passed away*.
As men in those days (6) *would / used to* be responsible for the women in their family, Mary stayed with her younger brother until he decided to travel to China in 1893. Now free, Mary travelled to West Africa with the intention of completing the book her father (7) *wrote / had been writing* at the time of his death.
From then to 1895, Mary travelled down the coast of West Africa. While she (8) *was travelling / used to travel*, she (9) *had collected / collected* specimens of tropical fish for the British Museum, as well as meeting the people and gathering material for her book. When she returned to England in 1895, she (10) *wrote / had been writing* her book 'Travels in West Africa', which immediately became a bestseller.
Mary (11) *had returned / returned* to Africa in 1899, this time to South Africa, where the Boer War (12) *had just broken out / just broke out*. She volunteered as a nurse, but after only a few months caring for Boer prisoners of war, she became ill herself, and died in 1900, at the age of only thirty-seven.

5 ALL UNITS Complete the second sentence so it means the same as the first, using the word in brackets. Use two to five words in your answer.

0 The car broke down when we were in the middle of our drive to Manchester.   (as)
   The car broke down *as we were driving* to Manchester.
1 It's Friday and I heard from Julian on Tuesday about the job application.   (ago)
   I heard from Julian .... about the job application.
2 Before we were aware of global warming, we drove bigger cars.   (drive)
   Before we were aware of global warming, we .... bigger cars.
3 They enquired at five hotels before they found one with a vacancy.   (had)
   After they .... at five hotels, they found one with a vacancy.
4 The play was cancelled when the group was in the middle of rehearsals.   (rehearsing)
   The group .... the play was cancelled.
5 Fuad finally mastered English after two years in New York.   (living)
   Fuad .... in New York for two years before he finally mastered English.
6 We spent the summers at the seaside when we were little, but we wouldn't swim in the sea very often.   (use)
   We spent the summers at the seaside when we were little, but we .... in the sea very often.

Test MODULE 6

Past tenses

Choose the correct answer, A, B or C.

1. After years as a classroom assistant, Alicia finally .... a teacher.
   A become B became C did became   ▶ Unit 30

2. 'I know about the timetable changes.' 'Oh, when .... you?'
   A they told B did they told C did they tell   ▶ Unit 30

3. Our friends were .... in France at the time of the floods.
   A living B live C liveing   ▶ Unit 31

4. Pablo and Pilar .... at the same hotel as us.
   A wasn't staying B not staying C weren't staying   ▶ Unit 31

5. Lucy called us with the news when we .... dinner.
   A prepared B were preparing C prepare   ▶ Unit 31

6. Although Sam spent four years studying maths, he .... it very well.
   A wasn't understanding B didn't understood C didn't understand   ▶ Unit 31

7. My boss .... to shout while we were discussing the sales figures.
   A was starting B was started C started   ▶ Unit 32

8. We were at the academy together – Harry .... to play the piano while I was learning to sing.
   A learns B was learnt C was learning   ▶ Unit 32

9. Jeff was working for a medical company .... he finished his PhD.
   A when B while C as   ▶ Unit 32

10. Meredith .... fluent Russian but she doesn't any more.
    A used to speak B used to speaking C use to speak   ▶ Unit 33

11. I recognise you – .... to go to Kingston Girls' School?
    A use you B didn't you use C don't you used   ▶ Unit 33

12. My mother's hair is grey now but she .... have beautiful red hair.
    A used to B would C had   ▶ Unit 33

13. When I lived in Bilbao, I .... the Guggenheim Museum several times.
    A would visit B visited C used to visit   ▶ Unit 33

14. Hilary .... as a doctor in Bangladesh for eighteen months.
    A used to work B would work C worked   ▶ Unit 33

15. Sony offered Neela a job before she .... her degree.
    A finish B had finished C was finishing   ▶ Unit 34

16. I had breakfast quite early, then I .... to the bus stop and caught the bus.
    A had gone B had went C went   ▶ Unit 34

17. We missed part of the concert because it .... when we got to the hall.
    A started B had started C hadn't started   ▶ Unit 34

18. Tony .... in China for long before the earthquake happened.
    A hadn't been working B hadn't working C hadn't been worked   ▶ Unit 35

19. We .... all the museums in the town by the end of the tour.
    A visited B had visited C had been visiting   ▶ Unit 35

20. Sorry I shouted at you. I was annoyed because I .... problems with the computer all morning.
    A had been having B was having C had   ▶ Unit 35

Go online for a full exit test

Present perfect

MODULE 7

Before you start

1 Read the extracts from a newspaper article and a letter. Look at the highlighted grammar examples.

NEW CAR SUPERMARKET IN DINGLEY

Lester's Car Supermarket has just opened a new supermarket at Dingley Corner. Lester's has been selling cars in Longton since 1998, but with sales of over fifty cars per week the company urgently needed a new and larger showroom.

Lester's car supermarket

Dear Customer,

Three years ago you bought a car from us. Have you thought about replacing it yet? Have you been looking for a car supplier that offers a huge range and incredible value? Well, look no further. We've been searching the country for the best buys and we already have over 500 used cars – all at amazing prices! We've reduced the prices on more than fifty different models this month – these really are the lowest prices we've ever offered.

And to celebrate the opening of our new car supermarket we are offering a 10% discount to all our customers.

2 Now read the sentences and choose the correct words in *italics*. The highlighted grammar examples will help you.

1. Has he *buying / bought* a car from a supermarket before? ▶ Unit 36
2. Have you looked *yet on the Internet / on the Internet yet*? ▶ Unit 36
3. Yes, we've *yet / just* looked at their website. ▶ Unit 36
4. This is the best car *I owned / I've ever owned*. ▶ Unit 37
5. My parents have had the same car since *2003 / eight years*. ▶ Unit 37
6. *I've gone / I went* to look at some used cars two weeks ago. ▶ Unit 38
7. We've been *looked / looking* for a new car since January. ▶ Unit 39
8. Have *you searching / you been searching* for a sports car? ▶ Unit 39
9. Jack can't decide which new car to buy. He's *been looking / looked* at more than twenty different ones this month. ▶ Unit 40
10. I'm very tired. I've *been driving / driven* all morning. ▶ Unit 40

3 Check your answers below. Then go to the unit for more information and practice.

1 bought 2 on the Internet yet 3 just 4 I've ever owned 5 2003
6 I went 7 looking 8 you been searching 9 looked 10 been driving

⏻ Go online for a full diagnostic test

36 Present perfect for past experiences and present results

1 Form

We form the present perfect with *have* + past participle. The regular past participle ends in *-ed* (e.g. *finished*):

POSITIVE	I **have** (**'ve**) *finished*. She **has** (**'s**) *gone*. They **have** (**'ve**) *broken* it.
NEGATIVE	I **have not** (**haven't**) *finished*. He **has not** (**hasn't**) *gone*. We **have not** (**haven't**) *broken* it.
QUESTIONS	**Have** you *finished*? (*Yes, I have.*) **Has** he *gone*? (*No, he hasn't.*) Where **have** you *been*?

Have you driven an automatic car before?
No, I haven't.
OK, I'll explain how it works.

NATURAL ENGLISH In speech and informal writing, we usually use short forms of *has/have* in positive and negative statements:
I've finished. She hasn't gone.

🔊 Pronunciation ➤ 1.17

Many common past participles are irregular.

Irregular verbs ➤ page 348

	INFINITIVE	PAST PARTICIPLE
regular	play use visit want	played used visited wanted
irregular	be break come drive eat go have	been broken come driven eaten gone had

⚠ There is a difference in meaning between *been* and *gone*:
My parents **have gone** *to New York on holiday.* (= They are there now.)
My parents **have been** *to New York.* (= They have visited it in the past, and have returned home.)

2 Past experiences

We use the present perfect to talk about actions and experiences that have happened in our lives up to now:
Have you **driven** *an automatic car before?* *I've* **travelled** *a lot.*
My father **has worked** *for several different companies.*

We can use expressions like *often, once, twice* or *several times* to say 'how often':
I've eaten in that restaurant **several times**.   *My parents have visited Canada* **twice**.

3 *ever, never, before*

We often use *ever* to ask questions about past experiences. It means 'in your life':
Have you **ever** *driven a truck?*   *Has Kemal* **ever** *been to an opera?*

We use *never* in negative sentences. It means 'not in your life':
I've **never** *swum with dolphins.*   *Caroline's* **never** *eaten Chinese food.*

⚠ We put *ever* and *never* before the past participle:
✗ ~~Have you been ever to California?~~
✓ *'Have you* **ever been** *to California?' 'No. I've* **never been** *there.'*

We often use *before* to say whether it's the first time we've done something:
*We've been here **before**. We came for my birthday.*
(= We are here now and we've been here in the past as well.)
*I haven't stayed in a five-star hotel **before**.* (= I am going to stay in one soon – for the first time.)
We usually put *before* at the end of the statement or question: *Have you been here **before**?*

4 Past actions with present results

We can use the present perfect to talk about a past action that has a result in the present:
*My car**'s broken down**.* (= It broke down earlier, and it isn't working now.)
*They**'ve gone out**.* (= They went out earlier, and they aren't here now.)

Compare this with the past simple, where the action and the result are both in the past:
*My car **broke down** last year and I **couldn't drive** it for three weeks.*

My car**'s broken down**. Can you send a mechanic?

5 *just, already, recently*

We use *just* to talk about actions that happened a very short time ago:
*The plane has **just** landed. The passengers are getting off now.*
*The shop has **just** closed – you can't go in now.*

Already means 'before the expected time'. We use it in positive sentences:
*You've missed the match. It's **already** finished.*

 We usually put *just* and *already* before the past participle:
✗ *My car has broken down just.* ✓ *My car has **just broken** down.*
*Graham's train has **already arrived**.*
*You don't need to lock the car. I've **already done** it.*

We use *recently* to talk about actions that happened in the last few days or months:
*Have you seen them **recently**?*
*What's the place like now? I haven't been there **recently**.*

 We don't use *already* in negative sentences:
✗ *The parcel hasn't arrived already.* ✓ *The parcel hasn't arrived yet.*

6 *still, yet*

We use *yet* in questions to ask about something we expect to happen around now, but which hasn't happened at the time of speaking:
***Has** the six o'clock train **arrived yet**? It's five past six and I haven't seen it.*

We use *still* or *yet* in negative sentences when we expected something to happen before now:
*Our pizzas **haven't come yet**. We ordered them nearly half an hour ago!*
*I gave my teacher that essay last week but she **still hasn't marked it**.*

We usually put *yet* at the end of a question or negative statement; we put *still* before *hasn't/haven't*:
***Has** your car **been repaired yet**? We **still haven't had** our exam results.*

We can also use *still* in positive sentences to say that an earlier situation has not changed. We use the present simple or continuous, not the present perfect:
*Carlos is thirty, but he **still lives** with his parents. The bridge is closed; they**'re still repairing** it.*

 We don't use *yet* in positive sentences:
✗ *I've paid for the meal yet.* ✓ *I've already paid for the meal.*

American English *just/already/yet* ➤ page 353

36 PRESENT PERFECT: PAST EXPERIENCES AND PRESENT RESULTS

Practice

1 Write sentences and questions in the present perfect, using the words below. 🔊 3.07 Listen and check.

0	I / not finish / the report	*I haven't finished the report.*
00	you / see / my keys ?	*Have you seen my keys?*
1	we / play / five games this season	
2	you / eat / anything today ?	
3	our friends / not had / a pet before	
4	Sally / break / her mobile phone	
5	Clive / use / this computer ?	
6	I / never drive / an American car	
7	the children / see / all the Harry Potter films ?	
8	Mr Lopez / not come / to work today	

2 Match the sentences 1–7 with the explanations A–H.

0	My computer broke down.	A	So I have to water the garden.
1	My computer has broken down.	B	This is our first visit.
2	We've been here before.	C	He isn't here at the moment.
3	We haven't been here before.	D	I couldn't send any emails.
4	He's gone to the post office.	E	So I don't have to water the garden.
5	He's been to the post office.	F	This isn't our first visit.
6	It hasn't rained yet.	G	I can't send any emails.
7	It's just stopped raining.	H	He brought back some stamps.

3 **GRAMMAR IN USE** Complete the conversation with the words from the box. 🔊 3.08 Listen and check.

> already   been   before   ever   just   never   recently   still   ~~yet~~

MANDY How are the wedding plans going?
SARAH OK. But there are lots of things I haven't done (0) *yet*.
MANDY But you've (1) .... chosen your dress, haven't you?
SARAH No, I (2) .... haven't seen anything I like.
MANDY Have you (3) .... to Baxter's? They've got a good selection.
SARAH Really? Their clothes used to be very old-fashioned. But I haven't been there (4) ....
MANDY It's better now. Actually, there are lots of nice designs in the Nuptia catalogue. Perhaps you should get a dress from them.
SARAH I'm not sure. I've (5) .... bought a dress from a catalogue.
MANDY Well, at least have a look at it. They've (6) .... sent me the new edition. I can bring it around later.
SARAH All right.
MANDY What about the cake? Have you (7) .... tried that place on Randall Street? They do fantastic cakes.
SARAH I know. But they seemed a bit expensive to me. Of course, I don't really know how much a big wedding cake should cost. I've never bought one (8) ....!

4 Match the sentences with the pictures. Then write a suitable word in each gap.

 A  B  C  D  E

0 We're really nervous about the flight. We've *never* been on a plane before. *C*
1 I can't come out. I haven't finished my homework ....
2 I ordered this spare part three weeks ago and it .... hasn't arrived! ....
3 How is your brother? I haven't seen him ....
4 I don't want to rent that film. I've .... seen it. ....

5 **GRAMMAR IN USE** Find eight more mistakes in the conversation and correct them.

DAVE Have ~~brought you~~ *you brought* the new car?
ALICE Yes. I've park it outside. Come and have a look …
DAVE It's lovely. How fast does it go?
ALICE I don't know. I yet haven't driven it on the motorway.
DAVE I bet it's really fast. Pete's got one of these and he says he's did over 125 mph in it!
ALICE Oh, that's too fast for me. I've driven never over 80 or 90.
DAVE I haven't driven a car like this already. Could I have a go?
ALICE I'm afraid not. Just I've arranged the insurance and I'm the only person that's allowed to drive it.
DAVE That's a pity. How do you turn on the CD player?
ALICE Mmm, I'm not sure. I've looked at the manual yet.
DAVE Has it got air-conditioning?
ALICE Yes. I'm really looking forward to the hot weather so I can try it out. I've never had before a car with air-conditioning!

6 Write true sentences about yourself, using the words below.

0 have / shower / today   *I haven't had a shower today.*
1 have / cups of coffee / today   ....
2 visit / my grandparents / this month ....
3 see / the latest James Bond movie   ....
4 pass / the driving test   ....
5 go / to the doctor / recently   ....
6 have / a holiday / this year   ....
7 drive / an electric car   ....
8 send / text messages / this week   ....
9 phone / my best friend / today   ....
10 go / to the dentist / this year   ....

Go online for more practice

37 Present perfect for situations up to the present

I'm on my way to Toronto. **I've driven** 400 kilometres so far.

1 Unfinished time period + *(so far)*, *this morning*, *today*, etc.

We use the present perfect to talk about actions in a time period that is still continuing
- with time expressions (e.g. *today, this morning, this week, this year*):
  I've driven 500 kilometres **this week**. (The week has not finished.)
  Have you **spoken** to Ahmed **this morning**? (It is still morning.)
- with *so far* to mean 'up to now':
  We've had four holidays **so far this year**, and it's only September!

Compare:
PRESENT PERFECT **I've made** several phone calls this morning. (It is still morning.)
PAST SIMPLE I **made** several phone calls this morning. (It is now afternoon.)

2 Repeated actions

We use the present perfect to talk about repeated actions (that may happen again):
I've been there **many times**. (I might go there again one day.)
She's phoned five times already. (She may phone again.)
How many times have you **played** Grand Theft Auto? **How often has** she **been** here?

3 Situations up to the present + *for/since*, *how long*

We use *for* (and not *since*) with a period of time (e.g. *for an hour, for years*):
David has worked in Mexico **for many years**. I haven't seen Janice **for a long time**.

⚠ We don't use *for* before expressions beginning with *all* (e.g. *all day, all my life*):
✗ ~~I've worked there for all my life.~~ ✓ I've worked there **all my life**.

We use *since* with a particular time, day or date, or with a past event:
David has worked in Mexico **since January 2000**. I haven't seen Janice **since Tuesday**.
I haven't been to the beach **since we got here**.
- We can use *it's* (present simple) or *it's been* (present perfect) + time expression + *since*:
  It's two years since our wedding. **It's been two years since** our last meeting.
- The verb after *since* is usually in the past simple, not the present perfect:
  John has worked here since he **left** school. It's ages since I **saw** you.

We use *How long?* in questions, usually with state verbs: **How long** have you known Alan?

⚠ We use the present perfect (NOT the present simple or continuous) to talk about present situations that started in the past:
✗ ~~I am married for ten years.~~ ✓ **I've been married** for ten years.
✗ ~~We are living here since 2005.~~ ✓ **We've lived** here since 2005.

4 Superlatives, *the first time*

We often use the present perfect (+ *ever*) with superlative adjectives (▶ Unit 21.3):
That was the **worst** film I've **ever seen**! This is the **best** holiday we've **ever** had!

We also use the present perfect with *the first, the second*, etc:
This is **the third time** I've visited China, but it's **the first time** I've travelled in business class.

Practice

1 Match sentences 1 and 2 with A and B in each pair.

0 1 How far did you travel? → B A I'm asking about today.
   2 How far have you travelled? → A B I'm asking about yesterday.
1 1 The doctor called this morning. A It is still morning.
   2 We've been to the bank this morning. B It is now the afternoon.
2 1 How many criminals have you arrested, Sally? A Sally used to be a detective.
   2 How many criminals did you arrest, Sally? B Sally is a detective.
3 1 Mike did the reports. A He finished them and went home.
   2 Mike has done the reports. B He is doing the accounts now.
4 1 Sylvia has worn glasses for many years. A She wears contact lenses now.
   2 Samantha wore glasses for many years. B She's just bought a new pair.
5 1 We went there twice in the summer. A It is still the summer.
   2 We've been there several times this summer. B Now it is winter.

2 **GRAMMAR IN USE** Find six more mistakes in the conversation and correct them. 🔊 3.09 Listen and check.

LUCY So, how ~~much time~~ *long* have you known Caroline?
JANE I know her for about three months.
LUCY I see, for March then?
JANE Yes. March 12th. Caroline was my driving instructor for my first lesson!
LUCY How many lessons have you since then?
JANE I've had ten lessons far so. I think I'll pass the test this time.
LUCY What do you mean?
JANE Well, I've failed it twice before. But this is the first time I have proper lessons.
LUCY Good luck, then! Look, I'd better go – I haven't been shopping since several days and the fridge is empty!

3 Complete the second sentence so it means the same as the first, using the word in brackets. Use two to five words in your answer. 🔊 3.10 Listen and check.

0 It's Friday. We arrived here on Tuesday. (been)
   We *have been here for* four days.
1 I haven't seen her for six months. (since)
   It's .... I saw her.
2 I've lived in the same house since I was born. (life)
   I've lived in the same house ....
3 It's three o'clock. The shop closed at one. (two)
   The shop has been closed ....
4 It's years since I wore short trousers. (worn)
   .... short trousers for years.
5 The last time I smoked was in January. (since)
   I .... January.
6 Jane's been to the spa three times before. (time)
   This is the fourth .... to the spa.
7 I've never eaten such a bad meal. (ever)
   This is the worst meal ....
8 We got to the airport six hours ago. (it)
   .... since we got to the airport.

38 Present perfect or past simple?

1 Differences in use

PRESENT PERFECT	PAST SIMPLE
Single or repeated actions in the past, when we don't know the date of the action or it isn't important: I've **driven** an automatic car before. We've **been** to the theatre many times. Time expressions: *before, ever, already, just* and *yet*	Single or repeated actions that happened at a definite time in the past: I **drove** a racing car in the summer. We **went** to the theatre twice last month. Time expressions: *yesterday, last month, in 2007*, etc.
Situations that started in the past and are still continuing: Tom **has worked** at the garage for two years. (He's working there now.) with *for* + period of time, or *since* + date	Situations that started and finished in the past: Alex **worked** at the garage for two years. (He isn't working there now.) with *for* to say how long the situation lasted
One or more completed actions in a time period that is still continuing: He's **sold** fifteen cars this month. Time expressions: *this morning/evening, today, so far*, etc.	Completed actions in a time period that is finished: He **sold** twenty cars in August. I **sold** my Toyota two weeks ago. with *ago* to mean '(a period) before now'

 It is sometimes difficult to hear /v/ in *I've, we've, you've, they've* and /z/ in *he's* and *she's*.
It is easy to confuse the present perfect and past simple:
PAST SIMPLE I **finished** work. He **started** early. We **carried** the bags.
PRESENT PERFECT I've **finished** work. He's **started** early. We've **carried** the bags.
The other words around the verb can usually help you to understand which form you hear:
I finished work **an hour ago**. I've **just** finished work.

 Pronunciation ➤ 1.18

2 Giving news

We often use the present perfect to introduce new information:
I've **decided** to get a new car. I'm going to look at some tomorrow.
'Julian **has passed** his driving test.' 'Oh, that's good news!'

News reports often start a new item with the present perfect:
The Terracotta Army exhibition **has opened** in London.
There **has been** an earthquake in southern China.

After we have introduced new information with the present perfect, we usually give more details with the past simple:
Julian **has passed** his driving test. He **took** it on Wednesday.
The Terracotta Army exhibition **has opened** in Paris. It **was opened** by the Minister of Culture.

112

7

Practice

1 Choose the correct words in *italics*.
0 She's been to the doctor twice (*this month*) / *last month*.
1 I've driven this car *many times* / *in 2007*.
2 Jane *passed* / *has passed* her driving test last week.
3 Steve loves his job. He *did* / *'s done* it since he was twenty-two.
4 Caroline's bought a lot of clothes *this year* / *two years ago*.
5 Rick *has finished* / *finished* the course six months ago.
6 'George has arrived.' 'Really? When *has he got* / *did he get* here?'

2 **GRAMMAR IN USE** Complete the text with suitable forms of the words in brackets. Use the present perfect or past simple. In one place, both are possible.
🔊 **3.11** Listen and check.

Electric cars – Latest update

A small American car manufacturer (0) *has just announced* (just announce) that its experimental electric car, the Lexington X1, will go into production this year. Markton Automobiles, of Detroit, Michigan, (1) .... (make) the announcement at last month's Auto Show in Geneva.

Although there are now many electric cars on the market, so far manufacturers (2) .... (not be able) to produce one that can really compete with existing petrol cars. There are two major problems – speed and distance. Up until now, electric cars (3) .... (be) either too slow or unable to travel far enough without recharging their batteries. Markton Automobiles claim that they (4) .... (overcome) these difficulties with a new type of solar panel which continually recharges the batteries. The company (5) .... (not give) the press exact details yet, but they claim they (6) .... (already test) the car successfully under all kinds of weather conditions. A Japanese company (7) .... (first design) the engine in 2007. But over the last few years Markton (8) .... (adapt) the design and increased its power. The company (9) .... (invite) ten journalists to test-drive the new car last week. Their reports (10) .... (be) mainly positive, although we will have to wait for the full test results before we know if this really is the electric car that everyone is waiting for.

---

3 **GRAMMAR IN USE** Complete the conversation with words and phrases from the box. There are three extra words or phrases. 🔊 **3.12** Listen and check.

---

hasn't told   told   has told   have you done   've used   was   's been
happened   had just   has decided   ~~'ve just fallen~~   has given

---

ALEC   Hi, Judi, I'm home!
JUDI   Shh. Don't disturb the children. They (0) *'ve just fallen* asleep.
ALEC   OK. I'll be quiet. So, how are things? What (1) .... today?
JUDI   Not much. It (2) .... a quiet day really. What about you?
ALEC   Quite an exciting day. The boss (3) .... me a new job!
JUDI   Wow. That's fantastic. What (4) ....?
ALEC   Sylvia (5) .... to move Eddie to the Toronto office. So I've got his job!
       She (6) .... me about it at lunchtime. It (7) .... a real surprise!
JUDI   Well, I hope it's more money because we (8) .... all our savings!

⏻ Go online for more practice   113

39 Present perfect continuous

1 Form

We form the **present perfect continuous** with *have* + *been* + the *-ing* form of the verb:

POSITIVE	I **have** ('**ve**) **been waiting**. He **has** ('**s**) **been washing** the car. They **have** ('**ve**) **been cooking**.
NEGATIVE	I **have not** (**haven't**) **been waiting**. He **has not** (**hasn't**) **been washing** the car. We **have not** (**haven't**) **been cooking**.
QUESTIONS	**Have** you **been waiting**? (Yes, I **have**.) **Has** he **been washing** the car? (No, he **hasn't**.) What **have** you **been doing**?

🔊 Pronunciation ➤ 1.19

2 Actions/situations up to the present

We use the present perfect continuous to talk about actions or situations that started in the past and are still continuing now:
We've been waiting to hear from them. Clare's been living with her cousins.

We often use *for* or *since* to answer the question *How long?*:
We've been waiting for about an hour. I've been working since three o'clock.

We can also use the present perfect continuous if the action or situation finishes at the time of speaking:
I've been waiting in this queue for an hour! (… but now I've reached the ticket office.)
Clive's been driving all morning. (… but now he's arrived.)

⚠ We use the present perfect, NOT the present perfect continuous, when we say how many times we have done something, or how much we have done:
✗ *I've been washing the car twice this week.*   ✓ *I've washed the car twice this week.*
✗ *We've been having three lessons so far.*   ✓ *We've had three lessons so far.*

⚠ We don't usually use the present perfect continuous with *always*, *already* and *yet*:
✗ *I haven't been washing the car yet.*   ✓ *I haven't washed the car yet.*

3 Recent continuous actions with present results

We often use the present perfect continuous to talk about an activity in the recent past:
'*I haven't seen you in the office recently.*' '*I know. I've been working at home.*'

We often use this form to explain a present situation or result; it gives the cause:
'*Your clothes are all wet!*' '*I know. I've been washing the car.*'
'*Have you lost weight?*' '*Yes, I've been going to the gym a lot.*'

Sometimes the action is not complete:
I've been reading 'War and Peace' but I'm only half way through it.

⚠ We use the present perfect simple or continuous, NOT the present simple or continuous, for a situation that is still continuing:
✗ *I live here for five months.*   ✓ *I've lived here for five months.*
✗ *I am living here for five months.*   ✓ *I've been living here for five months.*

Practice

1 Write sentences, using the words below and the present perfect continuous form of the verbs. Then write true answers for questions 5 and 6. 🔊 3.13 Listen and check.

0   We / wait / for ages — *We've been waiting for ages.*
00 How long / you / wait ? — *How long have you been waiting?*
1   David / watch TV / all afternoon
2   What / he / do ?
3   Elizabeth / not work / this week
4   My grandparents / not feel well / recently
5   How long / you / study English ?
6   How long / you use / this book ?

2 Match the situations A–I with the explanations 1–8. Then complete the explanations with suitable verbs from the box. Use the present perfect continuous.

eat   lift   listen   not brush   ~~not live~~   not sleep   run   study   use

A   John's put on a lot of weight.
B   Aleesha's sweating and her legs ache.
C   Mike's ears hurt.
D   Clare's feeling tired.
E   ~~Rashid still doesn't speak much English.~~
F   Alec's got big muscles.
G   Marianne's looking very tanned.
H   Debbie expects to get an A in the test.
I   Marcus is at the dentist. He needs three fillings.

0   He *hasn't been living* in the UK for long.   E
1   She .... a sun bed.
2   He .... to loud music.
3   He .... too many desserts.
4   She .... very hard.
5   He .... his teeth properly.
6   She .... a marathon.
7   He .... weights at the gym.
8   She .... very well recently.

3 **GRAMMAR IN USE** Choose the correct words in *italics*.
🔊 3.14 Listen and check.

"You won't believe this but (0)(*I've*)/ *I'm* been learning to drive! I suppose it's a bit late to learn to drive at my age, but my husband used to do all the driving. So when he died I really needed to learn. In fact I've really been (1) *enjoyed / enjoying* it. I've (2) *had / been having* lessons for six months now. I suppose I've (3) *been having / had* about thirty lessons so far. I've (4) *gone / been going* to the local driving school. The instructors are very friendly and it's quite close to my house. But it's rather expensive. I've already (5) *spent/ been spending* over £500! After the first ten lessons I (6) *took / have been taking* my first test. It was a disaster! Of course, I didn't pass. Since then I've been (7) *tried / trying* to improve, but it isn't easy at my age. I find it's very difficult to change gears smoothly because of my bad leg – for the last ten years I (8) *am / 've been* suffering from arthritis, which makes my leg stiff. I've (9) *taken / been taking* some special vitamins which seem to help – I take two each day. My instructor says I should use an automatic car, but I think I prefer manual ones. Although in fact I've never (10) *driven / been driving* an automatic car, so perhaps I should give it a try …"

40 Present perfect simple or continuous?

1 Differences in use

PRESENT PERFECT SIMPLE	PRESENT PERFECT CONTINUOUS
An action that is completed: *I've driven an automatic car before.*	An activity that is still continuing, or has just ended: *I've been driving since nine o'clock.*
emphasis on the result of a past action: *The mechanic has repaired the car.* (It's ready for the customer now.)	emphasis on the cause of a present result: Why is Caroline dirty? *She's been repairing the car.*
To answer the questions 'how much?' or 'how many?' *We've played six games.* *Karl has driven 200 miles.*	To answer the question 'how long?' *We've been playing for three hours.* *Karl's been driving since nine o'clock.*
Time expressions: *always, recently, before, ever, already, just, still, yet, for* and *since* *I've always lived in that flat.* *I've lived there since I was born.*	Time expressions: *for, since* (NOT *always, yet*) ✗ *I've always been living in that flat.* ✓ *I've been living there for years.*

2 State verbs

With state verbs (e.g. *understand, know, be, own*) we use the present perfect simple, not the present perfect continuous:

  ✗ *I've been knowing Ben since I was six.*
✓ *I've known Ben since I was six.*

We can use *always* and *never* with these verbs:
*I've **always** liked ice cream. Switzerland has **never** had a king.*
*Have you **always** owned a car?*

State verbs ➤ Unit 29.3

Some verbs (e.g. *live, work, teach, study*) describe an action which continues over a period of time, not a single event. We can use these verbs with *for* or *since* in the present perfect simple or continuous. There's very little difference in meaning:
*'How long **have you lived/have you been living** here?' '**We've lived/We've been living** in this house since we got married.'*
*Alice **has studied/has been studying** maths for three years.*

Practice

1 Choose the correct words in *italics*. In two places both answers are possible.
🔊 3.15 Listen and check.

0 Jake doesn't have any family. He's always (*lived*) / *been living* on his own.
1 He never answers the phone. I've *called / been calling* six times!
2 Sorry I'm so late. I've *waited / been waiting* for a call from the New York office.
3 Debbie knows Seattle really well. She's *lived / been living* there for two years.
4 I'm afraid the house is a mess. We've *decorated / been decorating* it.
5 Look at the new garden lights. Sam's just *turned / been turning* them on.
6 Carol's an expert on economics. She's *studied / been studying* it for years.
7 Harry's an old friend of mine. I've *known / been knowing* him since we were kids.
8 Marking essays is hard work. I've *marked / been marking* twenty this evening.
9 I'm curious about the food here. I haven't *tried / been trying* Mexican food before.
10 I hate cabbage. I've never *liked / been liking* it.

2 Match sentences 1 and 2 with A and B in each pair.

0 1 Rick has had a nice time. — A He's been playing in the garden.
  2 Carlo needs a shower. — B He's played in the garden all day.
1 1 I've just read that detective story.   A So I know who the murderer is.
  2 I've been reading that detective story. B I don't know who the murderer is yet.
2 1 We can start making dinner now.   A I've been cleaning the kitchen.
  2 Sorry my clothes are dirty.   B I've cleaned the kitchen.
3 1 Jane's fixed the computer.   A You can use it now.
  2 Jane's been fixing the computer.   B It's taken her most of the day.
4 1 Your towels are ready.   A I've been washing them.
  2 Your towels are still damp.   B I've washed them.
5 1 The suitcases are empty.   A I've been unpacking.
  2 The suitcases are half empty.   B I've unpacked.

3 **GRAMMAR IN USE** Complete the conversation with suitable forms of the words in brackets.
🔊 3.16 Listen and check.

ROY You look tired. (0) *Have you been working* (you work) all day?
BEN Not exactly, I (1) .... (do) some research on the Internet.
    I (2) .... (try) to get some information about one of our old friends from college.
ROY Who?
BEN Dave Colston. Do you remember him?
ROY Yes. I (3) .... (not see) him for years! But what do you want to find out?
BEN Well. I (4) .... (just get) an email from Philip Markham. He wants to get in touch with Dave but he doesn't know where he is now. He thinks Dave (5) .... (live) in the Far East for the last few years.
ROY Yes. I remember he was always interested in oriental philosophy.
BEN Exactly. I (6) .... (look at) six or seven different websites already, but I (7) .... (not find) much information.
ROY (8) .... (you try) that website that reunites old college friends?
BEN Yes. I (9) .... (already look at) that one, but he's not on it. I posted a message for some of his other friends on some other websites and I (10) .... (wait) for a reply. But so far I've heard nothing …

Go online for more practice and a progress test

Review MODULE 7

1 UNITS 36 AND 37 Put the word in brackets into the correct position in each sentence.

0 I've ˄ been to a Mozart opera. (never) [never inserted]
1 We haven't heard from our grandson. (still)
2 Have you done the shopping? (yet)
3 No thanks, I've eaten. (already)
4 Have you tried Indian food? (before)
5 It's been two years I gave up eating sugar. (since)
6 Has she been horse-riding? (ever)
7 Have you seen your old geography teacher? (recently)
8 That's the doorbell – I think Carrie's arrived. (just)
9 I haven't been on a good holiday a long time. (for)
10 This is the best essay I've read. (so far)

2 UNITS 36, 37 AND 38 Find ten more mistakes in the email and correct them.

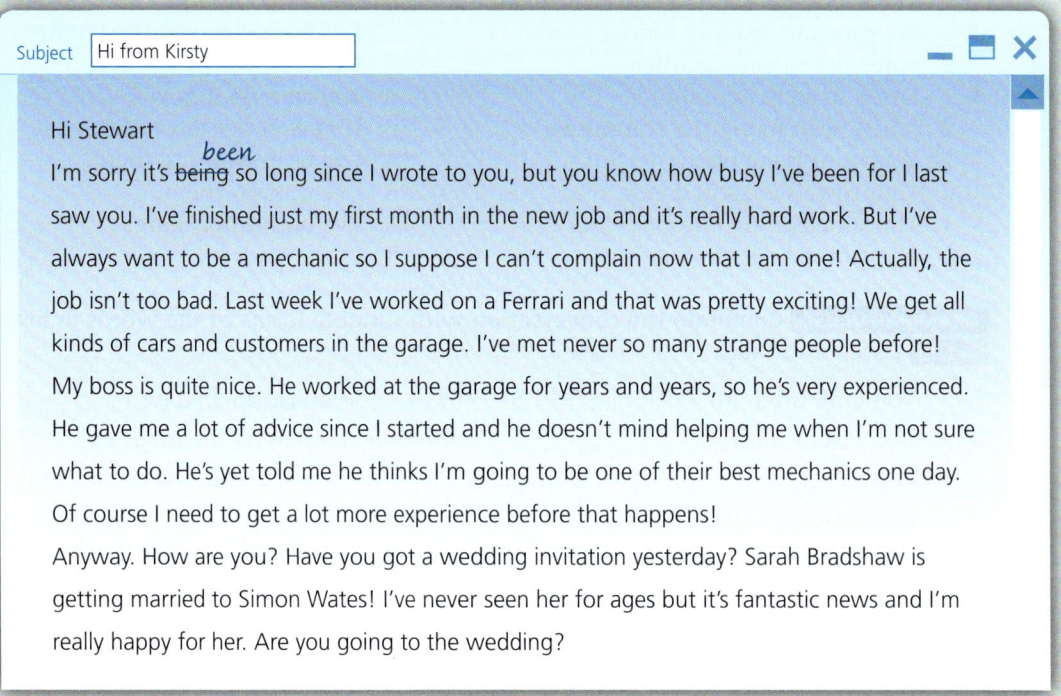

Subject: Hi from Kirsty

Hi Stewart

I'm sorry it's ~~being~~ **been** so long since I wrote to you, but you know how busy I've been for I last saw you. I've finished just my first month in the new job and it's really hard work. But I've always want to be a mechanic so I suppose I can't complain now that I am one! Actually, the job isn't too bad. Last week I've worked on a Ferrari and that was pretty exciting! We get all kinds of cars and customers in the garage. I've met never so many strange people before! My boss is quite nice. He worked at the garage for years and years, so he's very experienced. He gave me a lot of advice since I started and he doesn't mind helping me when I'm not sure what to do. He's yet told me he thinks I'm going to be one of their best mechanics one day. Of course I need to get a lot more experience before that happens!

Anyway. How are you? Have you got a wedding invitation yesterday? Sarah Bradshaw is getting married to Simon Wates! I've never seen her for ages but it's fantastic news and I'm really happy for her. Are you going to the wedding?

3 UNITS 39 AND 40 Complete the sentences using a present perfect simple or continuous form of the verbs in the box.

~~look at~~   not water   play   read   wash   work

0 'Why are there pictures all over the floor?' ' I **'ve been looking** at my old photos.'
1 'Your houseplants look very dry.' 'I know. I .... them recently.'
2 I .... this game for over two hours and I still haven't reached level 2!
3 I .... this shirt three times and I still can't get that stain out.
4 'What about this book?' 'No. I .... already .... that one.
5 'Your shoes are dirty.' 'Yes. I .... in the garden'.

4 **ALL UNITS** Complete the three conversations using suitable forms of the words in brackets.

SALESMAN Good morning. Can I help you?
CUSTOMER Yes. (0) *I've just seen* (I / just see) one of your cars on the Internet and I'd like to arrange a test drive.
SALESMAN Of course. (1) .... (you / take) a test drive with us before?
CUSTOMER No, (2) .... (I / not have).

CARRIE Hello. Carrie Simpson.
FRED Carrie. It's Fred here from the garage. (3) .... (I / work) on your car all morning and I can't find anything wrong with it.
CARRIE Oh. (4) .... (you / look) under the car?
FRED Yes. (5) .... (I / already do) that and it seems to be fine.
CARRIE Well, I heard a strange noise when (6) .... (I / drive) it yesterday!

MISHA I know I look dirty. (7) .... (I / clean) the attic all day.
JACQUI Oh really? (8) .... (I / not be) up there for ages.
MISHA Yes, there's dust and rubbish everywhere. (9) .... (I / already bring) most of the stuff downstairs.
JACQUI What about those old suitcases?
MISHA (10) .... (I / not look at) them yet. I'll do that tomorrow.

5 **ALL UNITS** Read the information and think of the best word for each gap. Write one word only.

Formula 1: Key facts

- Formula One (or F1) is the highest level of international car racing. For many years there (0) *has* been a world championship each year, involving a series of races around the world. Last year there (1) .... nineteen races. Each race is known as a Grand Prix.
- Formula One as we know it today has (2) .... in existence (3) .... 1946, although it goes back to the great races of the 1920s and 30s. (4) .... the last fifty years the sport (5) .... been under the control of the FIA.
  - In its early years the Formula One competition (6) .... mainly in Europe, but races now take place on almost every continent.
    - Formula One (7) .... often been described as the world's most expensive sport. Each car costs hundreds of millions of dollars to build, and costs (8) .... been increasing even more in recent years because of the use of advanced electronics.
      - Grand Prix racing can be a very dangerous sport. There have (9) .... several fatal accidents. One of the worst accidents (10) .... the death of Ayrton Senna at the San Marino Grand Prix in 1994.
        - The UK (11) .... produced the most world champions, but it is the German, Michael Schumacher, who has (12) .... the title most often (seven times).

Test MODULE 7

Present perfect

Choose the correct answer, A, B or C.

1. Have you .... the Egyptian pyramids?
   A saw   B seen   C seeing   ▶ Unit 36

2. Gerald .... to Italy. He gets back next week.
   A has been   B have been   C has gone   ▶ Unit 36

3. Has your sister .... an Italian car?
   A ever driven   B driven ever   C driven never   ▶ Unit 36

4. Have you ....?
   A been here before   B before been here   C being before here   ▶ Unit 36

5. I'm going to be late for the meeting. My car ....
   A broke down just   B has just broken down   C is just broken down   ▶ Unit 36

6. I don't know if I've passed the exam. I haven't had my result ....
   A already   B yet   C still   ▶ Unit 36

7. That house .... for more than two years. I wish somebody would buy it!
   A is for sale   B was for sale   C has been for sale   ▶ Unit 37

8. My cousin Claire .... a doctor for five years now.
   A is   B has been   C was   ▶ Unit 37

9. I think that was the best film ....
   A I've ever seen   B I ever see   C I've seen ever   ▶ Unit 37

10. Sandy's been to the opera ....
    A last year   B many times   C yesterday   ▶ Unit 38

11. Marcia had a great career as a dancer. She .... at the ballet company for twenty years.
    A has been working   B worked   C has worked   ▶ Unit 38

12. I .... the engineering course two weeks ago.
    A have started   B have been started   C started   ▶ Unit 38

13. Teresa is exhausted. She .... since eight this morning.
    A 's been worked   B 's been working   C 've been working   ▶ Unit 39

14. I haven't seen you for ages. What ....?
    A have you been doing   B have you been done   C have been you doing   ▶ Unit 39

15. 'Why are you so hot?' 'I .... at the gym.'
    A ran   B 've run   C 've been running   ▶ Unit 39

16. David loves San Francisco. He .... there for the last six months.
    A lives   B is living   C 's been living   ▶ Unit 39

17. You can collect your glasses now. The optician .... them.
    A has been repairing   B is repairing   C has repaired   ▶ Unit 40

18. Why didn't you answer the phone earlier? I .... you five times today.
    A 've been phoning   B 've phoned   C am phoning   ▶ Unit 40

19. We're old friends. I .... her since I was a small child.
    A 've known   B 've been knowing   C knew   ▶ Unit 40

20. .... in a big city?
    A Have you always been living   B Have you always lived   C Do you live always   ▶ Unit 40

Go online for a full exit test

Future forms

MODULE 8

Before you start

1 Read the conversation. Look at the highlighted grammar examples.

SALLY	Do you have any cheap flights to Malaga for Saturday, 14th June?
AGENT	**I'll look** on the computer ... Yes, there's one that **leaves at 7.30** in the morning.
PIETRO	That's no good. **I'm taking** the car to the garage first thing in the morning. Do you have anything later in the day?
AGENT	Let me see. ... OK, there's a flight at midday.
PIETRO	No, I **won't have got back** by then. Is there anything later?
AGENT	Most of the evening flights are full, I'm afraid. What about leaving on Friday evening?
SALLY	I'm afraid that's no good for me. **I'll be working** on Friday afternoon, so I won't get home until six. And Pietro has to take the car in on Saturday morning.
AGENT	Wait, there's one flight at seven on Saturday evening, …
SALLY	That sounds OK.
AGENT	What about a hotel? We have some very good offers at the moment. I can get you five nights at a four-star hotel for 250 euros.
PIETRO	Well, **we were going to stay** at the Hotel Luna, but your hotel sounds like better value. Is it near the beach?
AGENT	Yes, it is. **Shall** I book it for you?
PIETRO	Yes, please. Oh, do you have any day trips? We'd like to do some exploring while we're there.
AGENT	Sure. You can talk to our representative **when you arrive**. She**'ll have** all the details.

2 Now read the sentences and choose the correct words in *italics*. The highlighted grammar examples will help you.

1 I can't see you tomorrow – *I will spend / I'm spending* the day with my grandparents. ➤ Unit 41
2 'Does the show start at seven?' 'I'm not sure. *I check / I'll check* in my diary.' ➤ Unit 41
3 Why don't you talk to the manager? *He's going to / He'll* know what to do. ➤ Unit 41
4 Let's try that new Thai restaurant. *Will / Shall* I make a reservation for tonight? ➤ Unit 41
5 Don't phone us between seven and nine. We'll *watch / be watching* the football. ➤ Unit 42
6 They want the painting tomorrow, but *I won't have finished / I'm not finishing* it by then. ➤ Unit 43
7 The tour bus *is going to leave / leaves* at eleven, so be here by ten forty-five! ➤ Unit 44
8 Will the taxi be waiting when we *get / 'll get* there? ➤ Unit 44
9 We *were / are* going to visit our grandmother yesterday, but she was too sick to see us. ➤ Unit 45

3 Check your answers below. Then go to the unit for more information and practice.

1 I'm spending 2 I'll check 3 He'll 4 Shall 5 be watching
6 I won't have finished 7 leaves 8 get 9 were

⏻ Go online for a full diagnostic test

121

41 *going to*, present continuous and *will*

1 *be going to*

We use *am/is/are* + *going* + *to* + the infinitive form of the verb:

POSITIVE	I am ('m) going to be late. He is ('s) going to come later. They are ('re) going to sell it.
NEGATIVE	I am not ('m not) going to be late. It is not (isn't) going to arrive. We are not (aren't) going to see them.
QUESTIONS	Are you going to be late? (No, I'm not.) Is she going to take the bus? (Yes, she is.) What are you going to do?

NATURAL ENGLISH In informal conversation and in songs we often pronounce *going to* as 'gonna' /gənə/.

🔊 Pronunciation ➤ 1.20

Present continuous form ➤ Unit 28.1

2 Future plans and arrangements

We use *going to* or the present continuous to talk about future plans and arrangements:

going to	PRESENT CONTINUOUS
We intend to do something but we haven't made all the arrangements yet: *We're going to meet Joe's mother next week, but we haven't arranged a time yet. I'm going to be a doctor one day.*	We have already made arrangements to do something: *David sent me a text message. He's meeting us in front of the cinema at six o'clock. We're sitting in the front row. (We've already bought the tickets.)*
We plan to do something in the immediate future: *I'm going to make a sandwich – would you like one? I'm tired. I'm not going to stay any longer.*	To explain why we can't do something in the future: *'Can you come to lunch on Saturday?' 'No, I'm afraid I can't. I'm working on Saturday.'*

We usually use time expressions when we talk about plans with *going to* or the present continuous:
*I'm going to see Manchester United **on Saturday**.*
*What are you doing **this evening**?*

⚠ We don't use *will* to talk about personal arrangements:
✗ *We will sit in the front row.* ✓ *We're sitting/going to sit in the front row.*

FORMALITY CHECK In formal English we usually use *will*, not *going to*, for arrangements:
*The government **will meet** to discuss the situation tomorrow.*

3 will

We use *will (not)* + the infinitive form of a main verb:

POSITIVE	I **will ('ll) be** late. He **will ('ll) come** later. They **will ('ll) buy** it.
NEGATIVE	I **will not (won't) be** late. It **will not (won't) work**. We **will not (won't) take** it.
QUESTIONS	**Will** you **meet** him? (No, I **won't**.) **Will** she **see** us? (Yes, she **will**.) What **will** you **do**?

FORMALITY CHECK It is possible to use *shall* instead of *will*, but normally only after *I* and *we*. *Shall* is more formal than *will*. The contracted form is *'ll*, the same as we use for *will*. The negative form is *shall not* or *shan't*.

🔊 Pronunciation ➤ 1.21

4 Predictions

We use *going to* or *will* to talk about things we expect to happen:

going to	will
For predictions based on something we can see now, or that everybody knows: We're **going to get** soaked! (because it is raining now) I'**m going to be** late for work. (because my car has broken down)	For predictions based on our own personal opinion or knowledge: The rain**'ll stop** in a minute. (I know it never rains for long here.) In the future, people **will live** on other planets. (This is my opinion.)

NATURAL ENGLISH We often use *do you think* to ask what people expect to happen:
'**Do** you **think** he'll marry her? I **think** he will.' Who **do** you **think**'s going to win the election?
To make a negative prediction with *think* we usually make *think* negative:
I **don't think** he'll marry her.

5 *probably, certainly/definitely*

We often use *will* to talk about events that are certain to happen:
There **will be** a full moon tomorrow. New Year's Day **will fall** on a Tuesday next year.

We can make our predictions more or less certain by using the adverbs *probably, certainly* and *definitely*. Note the word order of the adverbs with a negative verb:
I'**ll definitely/certainly pass** the test. (I'm sure this will happen.)
We **definitely won't** go to Portugal. (I'm sure this will not happen.)
We're **probably going to move** to Spain next year. (I think this will happen, but I'm not sure.)

6 Immediate decisions

We use *will* when we decide to do something at the same time as speaking – something that we didn't plan:
'The manager isn't here right now. Can I take a message?' 'No thanks. I'**ll call back** later.'
'Do you want something to drink?' 'No, I'm tired. I think I'**ll go** to bed now.'

7 Offers, promises and warnings

We can use *will* to make offers, promises and warnings:
Don't worry about a taxi. We'**ll take** you to the hospital. (offer)
I'**ll work** harder next year, I promise. I **will** never do that again. (promise)
I **will not** allow bad behaviour in my house. (warning)
Don't lift that – you'**ll hurt** yourself! (warning)

We can also use *shall* (but not *will*) for suggestions:
It's hot in here. **Shall** I open a window? ✗ ~~Will I open a window?~~
Shall we get the earlier train?

More on *will* ➤ Unit 53.1/3

41 GOING TO, PRESENT CONTINUOUS AND WILL

Practice

1 Write the words and phrases in the correct order.

0 test Clare the isn't take to going — *Clare isn't going to take the test.*
1 won't this weekend rain probably it
2 a test tomorrow going have we to are ?
3 me meeting at the station she is ?
4 aren't to come to my party they going
5 phone I for a taxi shall ?
6 in a hotel I'm this time staying not
7 be they're late do you think to going ?
8 never I'll again there go

2 Match sentences 1 and 2 with A and B in each pair.

0 1 It's going to be cold tonight.   A It's always cold at night at this time of year.
   2 It'll be cold tonight.   B I can feel a cold breeze coming from the north.
1 1 He'll probably win.   A The race is almost over and he's at the front.
   2 He's going to win.   B He's won lots of races before.
2 1 I'm going to do a course at college.   A I've been looking at their websites.
   2 I'm doing a course at college.   B I enrolled yesterday.
3 1 We'll borrow Sally's tent.   A I'll phone and ask her if it's OK.
   2 We're borrowing Sally's tent.   B She's agreed to lend it to us.
4 1 I'm taking the children to the park.   A So I'm afraid I can't stay for lunch.
   2 I'm going to take the children to the park.   B Would you like to join me?
5 1 I'm leaving at ten.   A I'd like to have an early night.
   2 I'm going to leave at ten.   B I've arranged a taxi for that time.
6 1 He's going to be late.   A I know him. He's always late.
   2 He'll be late.   B There's a traffic jam on the motorway.

3 Complete the sentences with a form of *will* or *going to*.

0 'I don't think we *'re going to* get a seat.'

1 'Don't sit so close to the TV – you .... get a headache.'

2 'That ball .... land in the water!'

3 'Look at the cat. She can't get down.'
'Oh dear. I .... get a ladder.'

4 'I've used this machine before. Don't worry, the photos .... come out in a minute.'

5 'I .... call for an ambulance.'

4 **GRAMMAR IN USE** Read the notes and choose the correct words in *italics* in the conversation. 3.17 Listen and check.

VANESSA I hear you've booked your flights to Bangkok. When (0) *are you leaving* / *will you leave*?
PETER On Monday. We're (1) *getting* / *going to get* the overnight flight.
VANESSA (2) *Are you staying* / *Will you stay* long?
PETER A couple of weeks. We (3) *will fly* / *'re flying* back on the 26th.
VANESSA What about accommodation?
PETER We've booked a hotel for the first two nights. (4) *We're staying* / *We'll stay* at the Asia Hotel on Sukhumvit Road.
VANESSA That sounds nice. But I've heard Thailand can be terribly hot in February.
PETER No, I've been before, so I know it (5) *won't* / *isn't going to* be too hot then.
VANESSA What are your plans while you're in the city?
PETER Do you remember John? (6) *We're having* / *We'll have* lunch with him on the 14th.
VANESSA Give him my best wishes when you see him. What about after that?
PETER I'm not sure. (7) *We will* / *We're going to* look around and see what's available. We'd like to go to the beach.
VANESSA How are you going to get there?
PETER We'll (8) *probably* / *certainly* get the bus. I'm not sure really.
VANESSA (9) *Shall* / *Will* I look on the Internet? There might be a timetable or something.
PETER That's a good idea.
VANESSA OK. (10) *I'm getting* / *I'll get* my computer.

Feb 12th London – Bangkok. Flight 319
Feb 13th / 14th booked 2 nights, Asia Hotel
Feb 14th 12.30 – meet John for lunch
Feb 15th go to beach???
Feb 26th booked flight Bangkok – London. Leave Bangkok 11.30 p.m.

5 **GRAMMAR IN USE** Complete the conversations. Write one word (or a short form) in each gap. 3.18 Listen and check.

0 A How *are* you getting to the station tomorrow?
  B I don't know. I'll *probably* order a taxi. Actually, I *'ll* phone them now and see if I can book one.

1 A This bag's too heavy. I'm .... to hurt my back!
  B .... I help you carry it?
  A Thanks.

2 A Do you .... Davina will be here on time?
  B Yes, I'm sure she .... She's never late.

3 A Have the tickets arrived?
  B Yes. We .... sitting in row E. That's quite near the front.
  A Excellent. I .... call Pedro and tell him.

4 A I .... going to do the shopping later. Is there anything you want?
  B Yes. Quite a few things. .... I make a list?

5 A Have you asked Brian to the concert? I've got an extra ticket for him.
  B Yes, but I .... think he'll come. He hates classical music.
  A How annoying. Well, I .... waste money on an extra ticket again!

42 Future continuous

Come to the hotel lobby at nine o'clock tomorrow. Your guide **will be waiting** in reception.

1 Form

We form the future continuous with *will* + *be* + the *-ing* form of the verb:

POSITIVE	I will ('ll) be working. He will ('ll) be waiting. They will ('ll) be watching TV.
NEGATIVE	I **will not (won't) be coming** to the party. It **will not (won't) be working**. We **will not (won't) be leaving** then.
QUESTIONS	**Will** you **be waiting** for me? (No, I **won't**.) **Will** she **be arriving** tomorrow? (Yes, she **will**.) What **will** you **be doing**?

Spelling rules for *-ing* forms ➤ page 350

2 Actions happening at a future time

We use the future continuous to talk about an action that will be in progress at or around a time in the future:
*Come to the main door when you arrive at the theatre – we**'ll be waiting** for you inside.*

```
                    you arrive at the theatre
                              ▼
NOW ─────────────────────────────────────────────────▶
                     we'll be waiting inside
```

*Don't phone me at the office tomorrow. I**'ll be working** at home.*

⚠ We don't use *going to* with this meaning:
✗ *By this time next month I'm going to live in my new flat!*
✓ *By this time next month I**'ll be living** in my new flat!*

3 Future actions with possible results

We can use the future continuous to talk about a future action
- which may have a result:
  *I**'ll be meeting** my friends after work so I may be home late.*
- or which may make another action possible or necessary:
  *I**'ll be seeing** the doctor tomorrow. Do you want me to ask her about your prescription?*
  *We**'ll be turning off** the water supply for two hours at six o'clock. Please do not turn on your taps during this time.*

4 Asking about plans

We use the future continuous to ask polite questions about personal plans and arrangements. It is less direct than the present continuous or *going to*:
*Excuse me. **Will** we **be stopping** for a break during the journey?*
Compare:
*Are you **coming** to the party?* (present continuous: a direct question, to a friend)
Will you **be coming** to the party? (future continuous: a less direct question, to your boss)

FORMALITY CHECK We can also use the future continuous to say that we can't do something in a formal situation. Compare:
*Mr Jenkins is busy so I'm afraid he **won't be meeting** us.* (future continuous: formal situation)
*Sally's working so she **isn't coming** to the party tonight.* (present continuous: informal)

Practice

1 **GRAMMAR IN USE** Complete the captain's announcement with the future continuous form of the verbs in brackets. 🔊 3.19 Listen and check.

"Good afternoon, ladies and gentlemen. This is your captain speaking. Welcome on board today's flight to Las Palmas. Our flight time today will be around five hours and we (0) *will be flying* (fly) at an altitude of 35,000 feet. Weather conditions are good and we (1) .... (arrive) at Las Palmas at six o'clock local time.

During today's flight we (2) .... (show) a selection of films. You can find details in the in-flight magazine in the pocket of the seat in front of you. Our cabin crew (3) .... (pass) through the aircraft with refreshments shortly after take-off. I apologise for the fact that we (4) .... (not / serve) a hot meal on today's flight. This is due to a strike at the catering company. However, we (5) .... (offer) you sandwiches and the usual choice of drinks.

In a few moments the cabin crew (6) .... (demonstrate) the safety equipment. Please give them your full attention, then sit back, relax and enjoy the flight. Thank you."

2 Choose the best ending for each sentence, A or B. 🔊 3.20 Listen and check.

0 I'm afraid the head of finance won't be able to meet you tomorrow as
   A he'll attend a conference.   Ⓑ he'll be attending a conference.
1 By this time next week
   A we're going to lie on the beach.   B we'll be lying on the beach.
2 The au pair will be taking the children to school
   A if you're too busy.   B tomorrow morning.
3 Don't disturb me tomorrow evening because
   A I'll watch the match on TV.   B I'll be watching the match on TV.
4 I'll be giving you a lift home
   A so you don't need to bring your car.   B if you like.
5 You can deliver the dishwasher anytime tomorrow because
   A I'll be working from home.   B I'll work from home.

3 Rewrite these statements and questions so they are more polite.

0 Are you going to give us extra points for correct spelling?
   Will you be giving us extra points for correct spelling?

1 Do we get a pay rise next year?
   ....

2 I'm afraid we aren't sending you the documents until next week.
   ....

3 Are you going to stay the night?
   ....

4 Will you recommend me for a promotion when you see the boss?
   ....

5 Unfortunately, we aren't opening the day-care centre next summer.
   ....

6 Are you going to bring some food for the picnic?
   ....

Go online for more practice

43 Future perfect: simple and continuous

Shall I book the restaurant for seven this evening? We**'ll have got back** to the hotel and had a shower by then.

That's a good idea. We**'ll have been skiing** all day so we'll be ready for a meal!

1 Future perfect simple

We form the future perfect simple with *will* + *have* + past participle:

POSITIVE	I will ('ll) have worked. He will ('ll) have worked. They will ('ll) have arrived.
NEGATIVE	I will not (won't) have worked. It will not (won't) have finished. We will not (won't) have stopped.
QUESTIONS	Will you have worked? (No, I won't.) Will she have finished? (Yes, she will.) What will you have done?

2 Future perfect continuous

We form the future perfect continuous with *will* + *have* + *been* + the *-ing* form of the verb:

POSITIVE	I'll have been working. He'll have been waiting. They'll have been watching TV.
NEGATIVE	I will not (won't) have been waiting. It will not (won't) have been working. We will not (won't) have been skiing.
QUESTIONS	Will you have been swimming? (No, I won't.) Will she have been waiting? (Yes, she will.) What will you have been doing?

3 Completed actions

We use the future perfect simple for actions which we expect to be completed by a particular time in the future:
We'll have got back and had a shower by seven.
(= We will get back before seven o'clock.)
We usually use time expressions with the future perfect:
He'll have arrived by this evening.
Do you think your guests will have left before we get there?

4 Actions in progress

We use the future perfect continuous to talk about an action which is happening up to a particular time in the future. The action may stop at that time or it may continue after it.
By next Friday I'll have been waiting for my exam results for over two months!
We can use this form, usually with *so*, to explain the reason for a future situation:
We'll have been skiing all day so we'll be ready for a meal!
They'll have been working since eight o'clock so they'll be tired.
Compare the future perfect simple and continuous:
By ten o'clock I'll have finished my homework. (emphasis on a completed action)
By nine o'clock I'll have been working on my essay for four hours. (emphasis on 'how long')

8

Practice

1 Read the conversations and choose the correct word in *italics*.

1. A Shall we go out this evening?
   B OK, but only after seven. I (0) (*won't have*)/ *won't* finished my homework until then.
   A That's OK. I'm working on my project this evening but I'll (1) *done / have done* most of it by seven-thirty, so I can phone you then.
2. A Carol's lost a lot of weight!
   B Yes, she's been on a very good diet. By next week she'll have been (2) *go / going* to a weight loss class for over six weeks! If she carries on like this she'll (3) *have / has* lost over five kilos by the end of the month.
3. A Will you (4) *have / been* finished plastering this room by the weekend?
   B Yes, I hope so.
   A Great. So will we be able to paint the room on Monday?
   B No. Wait until Wednesday. The new plaster (5) *didn't dry / won't have dried* until then.
4. A Excuse me, nurse. I've been waiting here for ages.
   B I'm sorry. The doctor's very busy. She'll probably be able to see you after four.
   A And by then I'll (6) *be / have been* waiting here for more than six hours!

2 Complete the sentences with the verb in brackets. Use the future perfect or, where possible, the future perfect continuous form. 🔊 3.21 Listen and check.

0. By the end of next month I *'ll have been living* here in Spain for six years. (live)
1. I'll ask Jane to call you back at twelve. Her meeting .... by then. (end)
2. When he retires next year, Adam .... here for more than twenty years. (work)
3. I'll have more free time after September because the children .... to school by then. (go back)
4. My best friend is doing a 'round-the-world' trip. By this time next week she .... for more than six months. (travel)
5. Don't worry. By the time you get here, my mother-in-law ....! (leave)
6. .... the project in time for the meeting? (the team, complete)
7. It's a really long flight. We .... in the same seats for over fourteen hours so we'll be exhausted when we get there. (sit)
8. You can't stay here next week. We .... the decorating. (not finish)

3 GRAMMAR IN USE Find five more mistakes in the letter and correct them. 🔊 3.22 Listen and check.

> Dear Mr Sanderson,
> I am writing about the repairs which your company has been ~~made~~ *making* to the roof of our apartment building. The work started in March and it still isn't finished. By the end of this week the men will have working on the roof for over two months. This means we will suffered more than eight weeks of continuous noise and disruption, and we will be living for all that time with permanent cold draughts and dirt.
> As you know, my wife is pregnant and the baby is due next month. It looks as though the work will haven't been completed by the time the baby is born. This is unacceptable.
> I would like you to reassure us that work on the part of the roof that covers our flat will have finishing by the beginning of June at the latest. I think this is the least we can expect.
> Yours sincerely,
> Jeremy Brogan

44 Present simple with future meaning

Look, our gate **opens** at 6.30 so we've still got time for a coffee.

1 Fixed future events

We often use the present simple with a time or date to talk about future events on a timetable or fixed programme:
*The Dallas flight **arrives** at 9.45. Our next meeting **is** at 11.00 on Thursday.*
***Does** the tour bus **stop** in Ronda? **Do** we **get back** to the hotel by 6.00?*

We can use *will* in the same way: *'When **do/will** your classes **finish**?' 'The last one **will be/is** on December 5th.'*

We also use the present simple or *will* to talk about definite arrangements and things we can't change: *'What sort of party **is** it/**will** it **be**?' 'It's/It'll be a fancy dress party.'*
*New Year's Day **falls/will fall** on a Thursday next year.*

 When we are talking about personal arrangements we use the present continuous or *going to*, not the present simple:
✗ *We meet our friends at the cinema this evening.*
✓ *We're meeting our friends at the cinema this evening*

2 after, when, as soon as, etc.

We use the present simple to talk about future events after *when, as soon as, before, after, once* and *until*:
*I won't be able to use my phone **until** the plane **lands**. But **as soon as** I **get** there, I'll phone you.*
*I'll send you a text message **once** the parcel **arrives**.*

We can also use the present perfect after these expressions when we are talking about a completed action:
*I'll tell you what it's like **after** I've **seen** it.*
*We'll come down to reception **as soon as** we've **unpacked** our suitcases.*
*Don't leave **until** you've **spoken** to the manager.*

 We don't use *will* (or the present continuous for future meaning) after these expressions:
✗ *I'll see you when I'll arrive.*
✓ *I'll see you **when** I **arrive**.*
✗ *As soon as I will get there I'll phone you.*
✓ ***As soon as** I **get** there, I'll phone you.*
✗ *I'll phone you after I'm arriving.*
✓ *I'll phone you **after** I **arrive**.*

More on these linking words ➤ Unit 82.1

Form and present tense uses of the present simple ➤ Unit 27

8

Practice

1 Match the two parts of the sentences.

0 I've checked the timetable; our next exam — C
1 The government has announced that the election
2 The train to Edinburgh
3 My friend from university
4 We'll go the chemist's after
5 When we get to the hospital

A we'll see the doctor.
B is leaving tomorrow.
C is on Tuesday.
D we've seen the doctor.
E leaves at 4.45.
F will take place in May.

2 **GRAMMAR IN USE** Read the email. Then choose the correct words in *italics* in the conversation. 3.23 Listen and check.

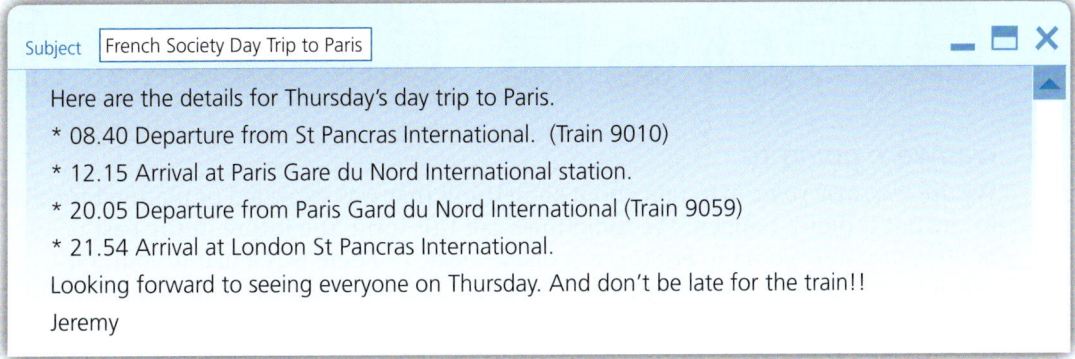

Subject: French Society Day Trip to Paris

Here are the details for Thursday's day trip to Paris.
* 08.40 Departure from St Pancras International. (Train 9010)
* 12.15 Arrival at Paris Gare du Nord International station.
* 20.05 Departure from Paris Gard du Nord International (Train 9059)
* 21.54 Arrival at London St Pancras International.
Looking forward to seeing everyone on Thursday. And don't be late for the train!!
Jeremy

CARRIE I'm so excited about Thursday's trip. I've just had Jeremy's email with the details.
EDDY Oh, I haven't, but I'm so pleased we (0) *sit /* ***'re sitting*** together on the train. Shall we meet up and have a coffee before the train (1) *leaves / is leaving*?
CARRIE No, we can get coffee on the train. But why don't you come to my house? We can get a taxi to the station together. The train (2) *'ll leave / leaves* at 8.40 so perhaps you should come here at about 8.00.
EDDY OK. What time (3) *does it arrive / is it arriving* in Paris?
CARRIE At quarter past twelve.
EDDY Perfect. Just in time for lunch! Do you know where we (4) *eat / 're eating*?
CARRIE Not exactly, but I know Jeremy's organised everything. We (5) *have / 're having* lunch at a place he knows near the Louvre. Apparently it's very nice but not too expensive.
EDDY That sounds great. I'd like to go to the museum after we (6) *have / 'll have* lunch.
CARRIE Good idea. But don't forget Jeremy (7) *'ll take / 's taking* us to the Eiffel Tower at 5.00.
EDDY I'm sure there'll be time. When do we have to be back at the station?
CARRIE The train back to London (8) *will leave / leaves* at five past eight.
EDDY How long (9) *is / will be* the trip back?
CARRIE The train (10) *gets / 's getting* back to London just before 10.00, so less than two hours.

3 Complete the sentences with the present simple, present continuous or *will* form of the verbs in brackets. 3.24 Listen and check.

0 I *'ll check* (check) with you before I buy the tickets.
1 We .... (meet) Sophie at 7.00. Would you like to join us?
2 I'll phone you as soon as I .... (hear) any news.
3 Because of unexpected demand, there .... (be) an extra show on Friday.
4 Once we .... (know) the survey results we'll be able to plan our campaign.
5 Next year, Thanksgiving Day .... (be) on Thursday, 26th November.
6 I can't come tomorrow. I .... (spend) the day with my cousins.
7 After I .... (pass) my driving test I'm going to buy a car.
8 I've checked the itinerary. The bus .... (get back) at 4.45.

45 Other ways to talk about the future

Well, we **were going to have** a skiing holiday this winter, but Judy broke her leg, so we're staying at home instead.

1 was/were going to

We use *was/were going to* to talk about something that was expected or planned for the future but it didn't happen. We sometimes call this form 'the future in the past':
In 2005 they **were going to build** a supermarket here. (= There was a plan to build it.)
When I was younger I **was going to be** a ballet dancer. (= I expected to do this in the future.)
I **wasn't going to work** today, but the boss called me in. (= I didn't expect to work today.)
We often use this form
- to talk about something we expected to happen but in fact didn't happen:
  I **was going to study** medicine but my grades weren't good enough for medical school.
- to make excuses about something we failed to do:
  I **was going to finish** my homework but I didn't have time.
  We **were going to buy** some more milk but we left our money at home. Sorry.

Past continuous for plans that did not happen ➤ Unit 31.4

2 Expressions with a future meaning

We use *am/is/are to* + infinitive in formal situations to talk about future events:
The president **is to talk** to the nation tomorrow.
The bridge **is to be opened** by the mayor on July 20th.

We often use this form in news reports and in instructions or orders:
The police **are to start** house-to-house enquiries this week.
The driver of the stolen car **is to appear** in court tomorrow.
These pills **are to be taken** three times a day.
You **are to report** for duty at 9.00 a.m.

We use *am/is/are about to* + infinitive to talk about an action that will happen in the immediate future:
Hurry up! The train's **about to leave**.
I can't talk now – my phone battery **is about to run out**.

Some verbs and other expressions also have a future meaning:

be due to	The new computer **is due to arrive** tomorrow.
be sure/certain to	The test isn't difficult. I'm **sure to pass** it.
be likely to	I don't think we're **likely to get** a refund as we don't have a receipt.
expect	The company **expects to announce** its annual results next month.
hope	I **hope to see** you on Friday.
want	They **want to visit** us next summer.

132

8

Practice

1 Match the sentences 1–5 with A or B.

0 She's certain to be promoted.
A I'm talking about the present. (B) I'm talking about the future.
1 We were going to go to their party.
A We went to their party.   B We didn't go to their party.
2 I can't talk now, I'm about to go out.
A I'm going out in a few minutes.   B I'm going out later this evening.
3 I wasn't going to wear that red dress.
A I didn't wear the red dress.   B My friend persuaded me to wear the red dress.
4 Four heads of state are to attend the opening ceremony.
A I read this in a newspaper.   B A friend said this.
5 The government was going to reduce taxes last year.
A They reduced taxes last year.   B They didn't reduce taxes last year.

2 **GRAMMAR IN USE** Complete the the recorded phone messages with the words and phrases from the box. 3.25 Listen and check.

> about to   due to   ~~hope~~   hope to   likely to be   sure to   want   was going to   were going to

A Hi Carla, it's Jane here. I (0) *hope* you get this message! Sorry I didn't call you earlier. I (1) .... phone, but it's been a really busy day. Anyway, I just wanted to tell you that I might be a bit late for the aerobics class this evening. I'm (2) .... finish a really important report for my boss for tomorrow and I need to spend a couple more hours on it to get it ready. But I'm (3) .... finish it by 7.00 so I'll see you around 7.30.

B Hello. Mr Carlton? This is Anthea from the electrical shop. You (4) .... collect your repaired toaster this morning but you didn't come in to the shop. Do you (5) .... us to send it to you or do you still want to collect it yourself? The thing is, we're (6) .... close for our annual holidays so if you don't collect it before the weekend it'll be too late.

C This is Karen from customer services with a message for Stephen Brook. I'm afraid we've had some problems with our suppliers and there's (7) .... a few weeks' delay in the delivery of your spare parts. I'm sorry about that. I (8) .... get a definite date from them in the next few days. I'll phone again when I've got a firm date for you.

3 Complete the second sentence so it means the same as the first, using the word in brackets. Use two to five words in your answer. 3.26 Listen and check.

0 They will definitely ask us about our holiday plans.   (sure)
They *are sure to ask us* about our holiday plans.
1 I planned to phone you but I didn't have time.   (was)
I .... but I didn't have time.
2 The new hospital will open next September.   (due)
The new hospital .... next September.
3 I think we're probably going to be there around 6.00.   (likely)
We .... there around 6.00.
4 The Prime Minister will make an announcement this evening.   (is)
The Prime Minister .... an announcement this evening.

Review MODULE 8

1 UNITS 41 AND 42 Complete the conversation with suitable forms of the verbs in brackets.

CELIA Hi, Celia. Nice to see you. (0) *Shall I get* (I get) you a coffee?
JAKE No, thanks, I've just had one.
CELIA I can't believe this weather. It's awful!
JAKE I know. And by the look of those clouds it (1) .... (get) worse.
CELIA Oh well, this time next week I (2) .... (sit) on a beach in the sun!
JAKE So you've booked your holiday then?
CELIA Yes. We (3) .... (leave) on Sunday.
JAKE Lucky you! I (4) .... (not think) we're going to go away this year. Sylvia's boss has given her a big project. She (5) .... (work) on it all summer.
CELIA That's a pity.
JAKE Yes. But her boss has promised that he (6) .... (give) her three weeks off in the autumn … Anyway, we should all get together before you leave. How about Friday?
CELIA I'm not sure. I (7) .... (look) in my diary… Well, I (8) .... (not do) anything on Friday but Mario (9) .... (go) to football training. So it (10) .... (just be) me. Is that OK?
JAKE Fine. We (11) .... (see) you on Friday. (12) .... (we meet) at seven?
CELIA Great. See you then.

2 UNITS 41, 42 AND 43 Read the email and choose the correct words in *italics*.

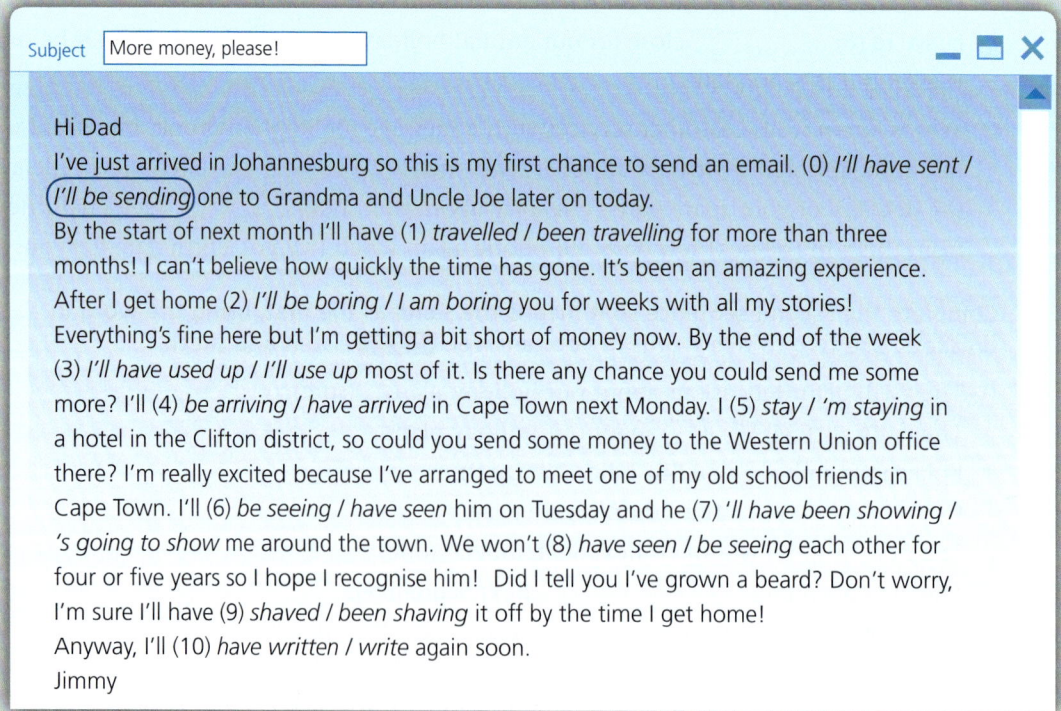

Subject: More money, please!

Hi Dad
I've just arrived in Johannesburg so this is my first chance to send an email. (0) *I'll have sent /* (I'll be sending) one to Grandma and Uncle Joe later on today.
By the start of next month I'll have (1) *travelled / been travelling* for more than three months! I can't believe how quickly the time has gone. It's been an amazing experience. After I get home (2) *I'll be boring / I am boring* you for weeks with all my stories! Everything's fine here but I'm getting a bit short of money now. By the end of the week (3) *I'll have used up / I'll use up* most of it. Is there any chance you could send me some more? I'll (4) *be arriving / have arrived* in Cape Town next Monday. I (5) *stay / 'm staying* in a hotel in the Clifton district, so could you send some money to the Western Union office there? I'm really excited because I've arranged to meet one of my old school friends in Cape Town. I'll (6) *be seeing / have seen* him on Tuesday and he (7) *'ll have been showing / 's going to show* me around the town. We won't (8) *have seen / be seeing* each other for four or five years so I hope I recognise him! Did I tell you I've grown a beard? Don't worry, I'm sure I'll have (9) *shaved / been shaving* it off by the time I get home!
Anyway, I'll (10) *have written / write* again soon.
Jimmy

134

3

UNITS 44 AND 45 Complete the sentences with words and phrases from A–K. There are two extra words or phrases.

0 Katie is an excellent driver. She ....C.... pass the test.
1 My sister .... become a scientist but she became a teacher instead.
2 New recruits .... report to the staff sergeant at 07.30 precisely.
3 The next train .... at ten forty-five.
4 'Today's main news: the government .... lower the tax on fuel.'
5 The final classes of the term .... at six o'clock on Thursday.
6 As oil runs out, electric vehicles .... become more and more popular.
7 We .... try bungee jumping but our friends persuaded us to do it!
8 The bridge .... open early in the New Year.

A are	B are to	C is sure to	D were going to
E is due to	F weren't going to	G leaves	H is about to
I was going to	J is to	K are likely to	

4

ALL UNITS Match the two parts of the sentences in each group.

1
0 I can't see you on Saturday,   A I'll have finished work by then.
1 I'll come and see you after   B I finish work.
2 We can meet at five because   C I'll be working.

2
1 We're not sure of our exact plans but   A we're going to go somewhere hot.
2 There's no shade here, so   B we're going to Mexico.
3 I've just got the tickets;   C we're going to get hot.

3
1 By the time he gets here, Harry will be tired;   A he's going to work all day.
2 I'm afraid Bill won't have time to see you;   B he'll be working all day.
3 Dave's determined to finish that essay;   C he'll have been working all day.

4
1 The sales director's instructions are as follows –   A we're meeting her at the café …
2 Everything's arranged,   B we are to meet her at the café.
3 We can go to the concert together after   C we meet her at the café.

5
1 We were going to take the plane but we   A 'll miss our connection.
2 We can't go on the later plane because we   B 're going to miss our connection.
3 Look at the time! We   C missed our connection.

5

ALL UNITS Complete the second sentence so it means the same as the first, using the word in brackets. Use two to five words in your answer.

0 The President will speak to the nation tonight. (is)
The President *is to speak to* .... the nation tonight.

1 I'm certain house prices will go down this year. (sure)
House prices .... this year.

2 James will leave before we get there. (left)
James .... by the time we get there.

3 We'll arrive at the resort and then we'll decide where to stay. (after)
We'll decide where to stay .... at the resort.

4 Next Saturday is Harry and Julia's twentieth wedding anniversary. (been)
By next Saturday Harry and Julia .... married for twenty years.

5 David planned to become an airline pilot but he failed the fitness test. (going)
David .... an airline pilot but he failed the fitness test.

6 I need to use my laptop tomorrow so I can't lend it to you. (be)
I can't let you borrow my laptop tomorrow because I .... myself.

Test MODULE 8

Future forms

Choose the correct answer, A, B or C.

1. I can't see you tomorrow afternoon. I .... a check-up at the dentist's.
   A 'll have   B 'm having   C have   ▶ Unit 41

2. The train's very late. I .... my appointment.
   A 'm going to miss   B am missing   C miss   ▶ Unit 41

3. Don't worry, the copier always makes that noise. It .... in a minute.
   A 's going to stop   B stops   C 'll stop   ▶ Unit 41

4. I .... that job – the pay isn't good enough.
   A don't think I'll take   B don't think I'm taking   C think I'm not taking   ▶ Unit 41

5. I fancy a snack. I think .... myself a sandwich.
   A I'm making   B I'll make   C I make   ▶ Unit 41

6. It's rather cold in here. .... turn on the heating?
   A Will I   B Am I going to   C Shall I   ▶ Unit 41

7. Come to the back door at 7.35 exactly. .... for you.
   A I'm waiting   B I wait   C I'll be waiting   ▶ Unit 42

8. I'm afraid we can't tell you anything yet. The board of directors .... an official announcement tomorrow.
   A is make   B will be making   C makes   ▶ Unit 42

9. Excuse me, Prime Minister. .... a statement about the crisis this evening?
   A Are you making   B Do you make   C Will you be making   ▶ Unit 42

10. By the end of August .... on the new bridge for over eighteen months.
    A they'll have been worked   B they'll been working
    C they'll have been working   ▶ Unit 43

11. You can come round at six. .... by then.
    A I will have been finishing work   B I'll have finished work
    C I'm finishing work   ▶ Unit 43

12. You won't have to wait for long. They .... it within the next few minutes.
    A 'll have repaired   B have repaired   C repair   ▶ Unit 43

13. According to the website there are three flights tomorrow. The earliest .... at 7.30 a.m.
    A is going to leave   B leaves   C will have left   ▶ Unit 44

14. Jack sent me an email. I'm afraid he .... on Saturday.
    A isn't coming   B won't come   C doesn't come   ▶ Unit 44

15. I .... you as soon as I hear any news.
    A phone   B 'll phone   C 'll have phoned   ▶ Unit 44

16. Don't open your presents until we .... there.
    A 'll get   B 're getting   C get   ▶ Unit 44

17. They .... going to build flats here but the builder went out of business.
    A have been   B will be   C were   ▶ Unit 45

18. As a condition of this contract you .... report a lost or stolen card within twenty-four hours.
    A are to   B will to   C be to   ▶ Unit 45

19. Hurry up! They .... the doors.
    A 're about close   B 're about to close   C about of closing   ▶ Unit 45

20. I .... the accounts to be ready by Friday at the latest.
    A have expected   B 'm going to expect   C expect   ▶ Unit 45

Modal verbs

MODULE 9

Before you start

1 Read the conversation. Look at the <mark>highlighted</mark> grammar examples.

MURAT   I <mark>can't find</mark> the episode of ER that we recorded yesterday.
KAREN   It <mark>must be</mark> there. I saw Max start the machine.
MURAT   No, it isn't. He <mark>must have done</mark> something wrong. How annoying!
KAREN   Don't worry. We <mark>can download</mark> it from the Internet. <mark>I'll do</mark> it for you if you like.
MURAT   That's nice of you. I was looking forward to watching it tonight.
KAREN   Well, I <mark>won't be able to do</mark> it until tomorrow – I've got <mark>to work</mark> on that geography project for college.
MURAT   But you <mark>don't have to hand</mark> it in until Friday.
KAREN   I know. But I'd <mark>better get on</mark> with it. You know how slow I am!
MURAT   Why don't I help you finish it?
KAREN   No, we'<mark>re not allowed</mark> to get help from anyone else. It has to be all our own work. But thanks for offering.

2 Now read the sentences and choose the correct words in *italics*. The <mark>highlighted</mark> grammar examples will help you.

1. Look at my new mobile phone. It *must / can* play movies! ➤ Unit 46
2. What's your new phone number? I *can't / mustn't* remember it. ➤ Unit 46
3. Can you change my appointment? I'm busy so I *won't be able to / don't have to* come at eleven o'clock tomorrow. ➤ Unit 46
4. Janine *can / must* be in the office now. I saw her go in ten minutes ago. ➤ Unit 47
5. My wallet's gone! Someone *can / must* have stolen it! ➤ Unit 48
6. *You've got / You're allowed* to show your driving licence when you rent a car. ➤ Unit 49
7. Take your time. We *can't / don't have to* be there until six. ➤ Unit 50
8. We're late. *We'd better / We might* hurry up. ➤ Unit 51
9. You *couldn't / aren't allowed* to drive without a licence in the UK. ➤ Unit 52
10. Are you hungry? *I make / I'll make* something for you. ➤ Unit 53

3 Check your answers below. Then go to the unit for more information and practice.

1 can 2 can't 3 won't be able to 4 must 5 must 6 You've got 7 don't have to 8 We'd better 9 aren't allowed to 10 I'll make

⏻ Go online for a full diagnostic test

46 Ability and possibility
can, could, be able to

CATHY	That's a smart new phone. Does it work in the USA?
TIM	Yes, you **can use** it anywhere in the world.
CATHY	So I suppose you've got a new phone number …
TIM	No. I **was able to transfer** my old number to the new phone.

1 *can* and other modal verbs

We use a modal verb with another verb to show that an action is possible, necessary or certain. We also use modal verbs to ask permission or to give advice.

POSITIVE	I **can** swim. You **must** leave. She **should** go.
NEGATIVE	I **cannot** (**can't**) dance. He **must not** (**mustn't**) stop. We **could not** (**couldn't**) leave.
QUESTIONS	**Can** you **speak** French? (No, I **can't**) **Should** they **leave**? (Yes, they **should**.) What **can** you **do**? Where **should** we **go**?

Modal verbs (*can, could, may, might, should, must, would, will* and *shall*) are different from other verbs.
- We use them + infinitive without *to*:
  ✗ *You can to use it anywhere.* ✓ You **can use** it anywhere.
- They have the same form for all subjects:
  ✗ *My brother cans swim.* ✓ My brother **can swim**.
- We form negatives with *not* or *n't* (not *doesn't* or *don't*):
  ✗ *I don't can speak Japanese.* ✓ I **can't speak** Japanese.
- We put the modal verb in front of the subject for questions. We don't use *do/does/did*:
  ✗ *Does she can play tennis?* ✓ **Can** she **play** tennis?
- They don't have infinitive or -*ing* forms. If we need to use an infinitive or -*ing* form, we use a form with a similar meaning, e.g. for *can* we use *be able to*:
  ✗ *I want to can play the guitar.* ✓ I want **to be able to play** the guitar.
  ✗ *I love can stay up late.* ✓ I love **being able to stay** up late.
- They don't have participle (-*ed*, -*ing*) forms, so we can't make continuous or perfect tenses with them. Instead we change the main verb:
  They can't **be waiting** *for us. They can't* **have used** *it yet.*

'Modal perfects', e.g. *He must have done it.* ➤ Units 51.3 and 84.1

- We can make modals passive. We use a modal verb + a form of *be* + past participle
  (➤ Unit 84.1): *Members can use this car park.* → *This car park* **can be used** *by members.*

2 *can* for present ability and possibility

We use *can* or *be able to* to say that it is possible to do something, or that somebody/something has an ability to do something:
You **can use** *this phone anywhere in the world.* **Can** *you* **speak** *Japanese?*
We usually pronounce *can* as /kən/ in statements and *Wh-* questions:
Karl can speak Japanese. When can we play tennis?
We sometimes use the strong form /kæn/ in *yes/no* questions and always in short answers:
Can Karl play tennis? Yes, he can.
The negative *can't* is /kɑːnt/ in most varieties of British English: *I can't read music.*

🔊 Pronunciation ➤ 1.22

- We use *be able to* when something is surprising or requires some effort:
  *It's amazing – some animals **are able to sleep** standing up!*
  *Because of her illness, Alice **isn't able to see** visitors.*
- We use *can/can't* with verbs of the senses (e.g. *see, hear, smell*) and some verbs of thinking (e.g. *believe, forget, remember*) to describe an action happening now:
  *I **can smell** something bad. **Can** you **remember** her name?*
  *I **can't believe** this computer's so slow!*

If we are NOT sure if something is possible, we use *may, might*, etc. (▶ Units 47 and 48):
*This phone **might work** in the USA, but I'm not sure.*

3 Future ability and possibility

To talk about what we can do in the future we use these modals:

be able to for situations that are certain	*After you receive your password, you'**ll be able to visit** our new website.* *I **won't be able to eat** for three hours after the operation.*
can for future personal arrangements	*The dentist **can see** you on Friday.* ***Can** you **meet** me at the airport on Tuesday?*
could for situations that are possible but unlikely	*We **could give up** our jobs and **live** on a desert island.* *I'm so angry I **could scream**. (NOT can)*
could or **would be able to** for conditional situations	*If you had a credit card, you **could buy** it on the Internet.* *If you learnt to sing, you'**d be able to join** the music group.*

Second conditional ▶ Unit 55

4 Past ability and possibility

To talk about past ability and possibility, we use *could/couldn't* or *was/were able to*:
*Before I got this job I **couldn't afford** a car.*
*When I was young I **was able to run** for miles without getting tired.*
***Could** the first cameras **take** colour photos?*

⚠ But if we are making a positive statement about a single event in the past, or asking a question about it, we use *was/were able to*, NOT *could*:
✗ I could transfer my old number.   ✓ *I **was able to transfer** my old number.*

For negative statements we can use *couldn't* or *wasn't/weren't able to*:
*We **weren't able to get** any cheap flights. We **couldn't get** any cheap flights.*

If something was particularly difficult, we can use *managed to*:
*I washed it twice but I'm afraid I **didn't manage to get rid of** that stain on your shirt.*

We often use *managed to* with expressions like *in the end, eventually* and *finally*:
*It took a while, but **in the end** we **managed to find** some cheap flights on the Internet.*

5 General truths

We use *can* for something that is generally possible:
*It **can be** very cold in New York in January. (= It is sometimes very cold.)*
*Life **can be** very hard for people on low incomes.*
*Bad weather **can cause** flight delays at any time.*

We use *could* to talk about general truths in the past:
*In the days of sailing ships it **could take** many months to travel across the Atlantic.*

46 CAN, COULD, BE ABLE TO

Practice

1 Complete the sentences with *can, can't, could, couldn't* or *will/won't be able to*. Then match them with the pictures below.

0 Jeff's great in the kitchen – he _can_ cook amazing meals!   E
1 Jeff .... cook at all when he was younger, not even simple things.   ......
2 Rob used to be a strong runner. He .... run a marathon in three hours.   ......
3 Rob .... run a marathon now. He gets very tired.   ......
4 Sandra .... repair her car – she doesn't know anything about cars.   ......
5 Sandra .... repair her car when she finishes her mechanics course.   ......

A NOW…
B NOW…
C TEN YEARS AGO…
D NEXT YEAR…
E NOW…
F TWENTY YEARS AGO…

2 Write statements and questions, using the words below and the modal verbs in brackets. 🔊 3.27 Listen and check.

0 I hate / not wear / jeans in smart restaurants   (be able to)
   I hate not being able to wear jeans in smart restaurants.

1 Their children / not read or write / yet   (can)
   ....

2 you / hear / that strange noise / ?   (can)
   ....

3 your old mobile phone / play videos / ?   (could)
   ....

4 you / arrange an appointment / with the dentist / yesterday / ?   (be able to)
   ....

5 we / not answer / your call / at the moment   (be able to)
   ....

6 we / get a flight / next Tuesday / ?   (be able to)
   ....

7 I'd love / play a musical instrument / really well   (be able to)
   ....

8 We really enjoy / swim / in our own pool / any time we like   (be able to)
   ....

9 It / be / very hot / in Madrid / in August   (can)
   ....

10 After the operation / I / not walk properly / for two weeks   (could)
    ....

3 **GRAMMAR IN USE** Read the article and choose the correct words in *italics*. In two places, both answers are possible. 🔊 3.28 Listen and check.

How technology has changed our lives …

Last week my wife suggested we should have a weekend break: Barcelona, or perhaps Prague. After a few minutes on my computer I (0) *was able to* / *could* book flights and a hotel, then print out airline tickets and a hotel voucher – all done in less than half an hour. Nothing surprising about that, you might say. But then I suddenly remembered how things were different when I was a child. If my parents wanted to go away they (1) *can't / couldn't* just use the Internet – because there was no Internet. Well, of course it existed, but ordinary people (2) *couldn't / weren't able to* use it, it was only used by a few universities and some government agencies. No, they had to phone a travel agent or drive into town and go to a travel agency.

It's the same thing with phones. I remember once, when I was a teenager, going out with some friends and missing the last bus home. Of course, none of us had a mobile phone. So we spent hours searching for a phone box so we (3) *could / can* call for a taxi. Eventually we (4) *could / managed to* find one, but by then it was 2 a.m. and we were freezing cold. In those days mobile phones were an expensive luxury. Even if you had one, you (5) *could only / were only able to* use it in big cities because there

was no signal in the countryside. And they were huge – not much smaller than a house brick. Now I have a phone that's no bigger than a box of matches. And I (6) *can / manage to* phone anyone, anywhere in the world, any time I feel like it. It can even (7) *using / be used* to look at the Internet. (8) *Do you can / Can you* imagine how exciting it was the first time an engineer managed (9) *to make / making* a phone small enough to put in your pocket? It must have been amazing. But I'm sure that in the future they (10) *can / will be able to* make them small enough to wear as a wristwatch!

4 Find eight more mistakes and correct them. Tick (✓) the correct sentences.

  0 You can hire bikes at the station. ✓
 00 Andrew <ins>was able to</ins> ~~could~~ get tickets for the film yesterday.
  1 Do you can drink the water from the taps in this country?
  2 We couldn't find an English-language newspaper at the shop.
  3 Erica could been really badly behaved when she was a child.
  4 Did you manage to calling your mother yesterday evening?
  5 To get the job you have to can speak fluent Spanish.
  6 We weren't able to buy water in bottles in those days.
  7 See you that man standing over there?
  8 I'm so angry I can kill him!
  9 London can be a very violent place in the nineteenth century.
 10 I could record the film for you last night. It's on this DVD.

47 Making a guess (1)
may, might, could, must, can't, should

1 Making a guess about a present situation

When we are completely certain about something, we don't use modal verbs:
The camera isn't working because the battery hasn't been charged.

But sometimes we make a guess. If we're certain our guess is correct, we use *must* or *can't*:
*'It **must be** the battery.' 'It **can't be** that. I recharged it yesterday.'*
*Lucy's just bought a new car – she **must be earning** plenty of money.*
*'Is that Marina at the door?' 'It **can't be** her, she's on holiday.'*

⚠ With this meaning, the opposite of *must* is *can't*, NOT *mustn't*:
I filled the petrol tank yesterday. ✗ *It mustn't be empty.* ✓ *It **can't be** empty.*

🔊 **Pronunciation ➤ 1.23**

If we are less certain that our guess is correct we use *may (not)*, *might (not)* or *could*:
*It **might be** the memory card. Perhaps it's full ...*
*There **could be** life on other planets.*
*The manager **may be** in a meeting. I'll just check for you.*
*Steve **might not be living** at home any more – I heard he was looking for a flat to rent.*

⚠ We use *may not* or *might not* (not *could not*) if we are not sure about our guess:
✗ *This small shop could not have batteries.*
✓ *This small shop **might not have** batteries.* (= Perhaps they don't have any batteries.)
We don't often ask people to guess with *must*, *may* or *might*. We prefer to use *Could* or *Do you think?*:
***Could** it **be** the battery?* ***Do you think** Jerry's at home today?*

2 Making a guess about the future

If we make a guess about the future, we use *may (not)*, *might (not)* or *could*, but NOT *couldn't*:
*If we wait for a few days, the prices **might be** cheaper.*
*I **could get** a part-time job next summer.* *The tickets **may not arrive** in time.*

⚠ ✗ *The engineer could not be able to fix it.* ✓ *The engineer **might not** be able to fix it.*

3 Expectations

When we expect something to be true, or have a strong feeling our guess is correct, we use *should* or *shouldn't*:
*You can phone Henry at work. He **should be** in the office by now.*
*Don't take any food. There **should be** plenty to eat once you get there.*
*Allow half an hour to get through security at the airport – it **shouldn't take** longer than that.*

Practice

1 Do the sentences in each pair have the same (S) or different (D) meaning? Write S or D.

0 A Could she be an engineer?
  B Do you think she's an engineer? *S*
1 A Perhaps we will buy some new computers for the office.
  B We may buy some new computers for the office. ....
2 A We are visiting our grandparents next weekend.
  B We might visit our grandparents next weekend. ....
3 A She can't be his daughter.
  B I'm sure she isn't his daughter. ....
4 A They might not get married in the spring.
  B They won't get married in the spring. ....
5 A He must be very angry.
  B Perhaps he's angry. ....
6 A She should be there on time.
  B I think she'll be there on time. ....

2 **GRAMMAR IN USE** Read the conversation and choose the correct words in *italics*. In two places, both answers are possible. 🔊 3.29 Listen and check.

LUCAS This is a nice painting. Wow. Five thousand pounds! It (0) *must* / *can* be by someone famous.
JODIE Let me see … er, it's by Darren Hudson. I've never heard of him.
LUCAS He (1) *could* / *might* be one of those new Canadian artists.
JODIE No, he (2) *mustn't* / *can't* be. All the artists in this exhibition are British.
LUCAS Oh. Look at this one. What do you think it is?
JODIE I don't know. It (3) *could* / *can* be a person. Yes. I think it's a woman.
LUCAS I'm not so sure. It (4) *could* / *might* not be a person. I think it looks more like a tree.
JODIE No, it (5) *mustn't* / *can't* be that. Look, you can see the eyes, just there.
LUCAS Oh, yes, I hadn't noticed them.
JODIE There's another one like it over there. (6) *May it be* / *Do you think it's* by the same artist?
LUCAS It (7) *might* / *may* be. Let's have a look … no, it's got a different name on it.
JODIE Well, I don't like any of these paintings, anyway. Why don't we go to the Bloomsbury Gallery? There (8) *can* / *should* be lots of nice pictures there.
LUCAS Yes, but it's already five o'clock. It (9) *might* / *could* not be open by the time we get there.
JODIE I think it's open until 6.30. I think we (10) *must* / *could* get there in time.

3 Look at the photos and complete the sentences below with your own ideas.

A 0 It could be *part of a jet engine* .
  1 It can't be ....
  2 It might not be ....
  3 It must be ....
B 1 It can't be ....
  2 It might be ....
  3 It could be ....
  4 It must be ....

143

48 Making a guess (2)
must, might, could, should + have

1 Past forms

The perfect form of modal verbs is modal verb + *have* + past participle:

POSITIVE	I **might have** (**might've***) **seen** him. You **should have** (**should've**) **been** there. She **must have** (**must've**) **done** it.
NEGATIVE	I **cannot** (**can't**) **have lost** it. He **might not** (**mightn't**) **have stopped**. We **could not** (**couldn't**) **have known**.*
QUESTIONS	**Could** you **have known**? (No, I **couldn't** (**have**).) **Should** they **have left**? (Yes, they **should** (**have**).) What **could** she **have done**? Where **should** we **have gone**?

* In spoken English we sometimes use short forms, e.g. *should've*, *shouldn't've*, *mightn't've*, etc.

🔊 **Pronunciation** ➤ 1.24

There is also a continuous form, modal verb + *have* + *been* + *-ing*:
He **must have been driving** too fast.   They **couldn't have been watching** us.

2 Making a guess about a past situation

If we're certain that our guess is correct we use *must*, *can't* or *couldn't* + *have* + past participle:
Everything's pink! You **must have put** something red in the machine.
I **can't have**. I always wash whites separately.
Lester **couldn't have been driving** the car – he doesn't even own a car!

If we are less certain, we use *may (not)*, *might (not)* or *could* + *have* + past participle:
'Where are the keys?' 'I don't know; I **may have left** them in the car.'
'Why isn't Ali here yet?' 'I don't know. **Could** he **have forgotten** the date?'
'Why haven't they phoned me back?' 'They **might not have been getting** their messages.'

 We use *mightn't have* + past participle, NOT *couldn't have* + past participle, if we are not certain:
I'm not sure; ✓ I **mightn't have passed** the exam. (= It's possible that I haven't passed it.)
✗ I couldn't have passed the exam.

3 Expectations about the past

We can talk about things we expected to happen in the past with *should* + *have* + past participle:
Check the post. That letter **should have arrived** by now.
You'd better phone the hospital. They **should have had** the test results this morning.
We can also use this form for an action that was planned but didn't happen:
We **should have had** our exam results last week, but they haven't arrived yet.
I **should have gone** swimming last Friday but the pool was closed for repairs.
Note that *was/were meant to* or *was/were supposed to* have a similar meaning:
The plane **was meant to leave** at six but there was a mechanical problem.
I **was supposed to send** her my email address but I forgot.

should have for criticism and regrets about the past   ➤ Unit 51.3   *was going to*   ➤ Unit 45.1

Practice

1 Use the words below to write sentences and questions that make guesses about the past. 3.30 Listen and check.

0 could / she / come / on the earlier bus? — *Could she have come on the earlier bus?*
1 Jackie / might / miss / the train
2 they / should / get home / by now
3 might / the children / stay / late at school?
4 I / must / leave the keys / in my coat pocket
5 Carol / might not / receive / your email

2 Choose the best meaning, A or B.

0 Sally might have taken the children to the park.
   A I'm sure this happened.   (B) I'm not sure this happened.
1 It must have been a wonderful party!
   A I went to the party.   B I didn't go to the party.
2 Ellen can't have been there.
   A I'm sure about this.   B I'm not sure about this.
3 Check your computer. They should have sent the email yesterday.
   A I think they sent an email.   B I don't think they sent an email.
4 That's a pity. They might not have known about it.
   A They didn't know about it.   B I don't know whether they knew about it or not.

3 **GRAMMAR IN USE** Choose the correct answer, A, B or C below. 3.31 Listen and check.

GABY Did you read about the 'man with no name' in the paper?
NICK No, what was the story?
GABY The police found this very confused man walking on the beach.
      He (0) .... remember his name or where he was from.
NICK He (1) .... a car accident or something.
GABY No, he (2) .... He doesn't have any injuries.
NICK Well, he (3) .... suffering from some sort of memory loss …
GABY Maybe. But he seemed to be quite healthy.
NICK What about his personal possessions? He (4) .... a wallet or something.
GABY No, he wasn't carrying anything.
NICK They (5) .... stolen by someone.
GABY I suppose so. But the police don't seem to think that was the case.
NICK How strange. (6) .... an illegal immigrant?
GABY No. He (7) .... He spoke to the police in fluent English, with a local accent.
NICK Don't the police have any idea who he is? I mean, they (8) .... looked at their missing persons records.
GABY Yes, but they didn't find a match. It's a real mystery …

0 A couldn't have   (B) couldn't   C must
1 A must have had   B must have   C might have been having
2 A could have   B might have   C couldn't have
3 A must have   B might have been   C can't have been
4 A must have had   B shouldn't have   C couldn't have had
5 A could being   B must to be   C might have been
6 A Could he have been B Might be he   C Could he being
7 A shouldn't have been B should be   C can't have been
8 A mightn't have been B must have   C shouldn't have

Go online for more practice

145

49 Rules *must, mustn't, have (got) to*

Do I have to buy a battery for it?

No, it's got a battery already. But you**'ll have to charge** the battery at home before you can use it.

1 Form

PRESENT	*must*[1]	I **must go** now. You **must not (mustn't) smoke** here. **Must** we **leave** now?
	have to	You **have to leave** now. They **don't have to work** today. **Do** I **have to pay**?
	have got to[2]	I **have ('ve) got to pay** my phone bill. He **hasn't got to work** today. **Has** she **got to work** today?
PAST	*had to*	We **had to buy** a new TV. We **didn't have to pay**. **Did** you **have to get** a visa?
FUTURE	*will have to*	You'**ll have to leave** soon. We **won't have to pay**. **Will** she **have to get** a visa?

[1] *Must* is a modal verb. *Have to* and *have got to* are not modal verbs.
[2] *Have got to* is not the same as *have got* (▶ Unit 26.2).

NATURAL ENGLISH We can ask questions with *must*, but it is more common to use *have to*:
Must we **answer** all the questions? → **Do** we **have to answer** all the questions?

2 Positive rules and necessary actions

We use *have to* to say that something is necessary, or is a rule:
The taxi's here. We **have to leave** *now.* (necessary)
All car passengers **have to wear** *a seat belt.* (a rule)
Do I **have to buy** *batteries?* (Is it necessary?)

NATURAL ENGLISH In informal British English we often use *have got to*. It means the same as *have to*.

We also use *must* but it is less common than *have (got) to*. We usually use *must* for
- a rule given by the speaker to another person, or to himself/herself:
  You **must wear** *your coat; it's cold outside.* (parent to young child)
  I **must lose** *some weight.* (I think I should do this.)
- instructions (often in writing and with a passive verb):
  Answers **must be written** *in ink.* (exam instructions)

We don't use *must* or *have got to* for past or future situations, we use forms of *have to*:
PAST *We* **had to have** *visas to visit China last year.*
FUTURE *You*'**ll have to charge** *the battery before you can use it.*

3 Negative rules

We use *can't* or *not allowed to* to say that there is a rule NOT to do something:
You **can't smoke** *here. We're* **not allowed to use** *calculators in the exam.*

We can also use *must not*, but usually only for explaining rules and in instructions:
Remember, children, you **mustn't ride** *your bikes on the grass.*
These lights **must not be used** *outdoors.*

To talk about negative rules in the past or future we use *be allowed to* (▶ Unit 52.3):
I **wasn't allowed to do** *that when I was a child. We* **won't be allowed to** *check in until later.*

⚠ If there is NO rule to say something is necessary, we use *don't have to*, NOT *mustn't*.
Compare: *You* **don't have to eat** *in here, you can eat outside if you prefer.* (You have a choice.)
You **mustn't eat** *in here.* (You don't have a choice. You have to eat somewhere else.)

More on *don't have to, need to, didn't need to/needn't* ▶ Unit 50

9

Practice

1 Write the words in the correct order to make sentences or questions. 🔊 **3.32** Listen and check.

0 has the see dentist Clare tomorrow to
   Clare has to see the dentist tomorrow.

1 got he has wear a uniform to ?
   ....

2 application form we to had get an
   ....

3 to will mobile phone a Serena have get new
   ....

4 did to wait you a long time have ?
   ....

5 leave guests before must midday their hotel rooms
   ....

2 **GRAMMAR IN USE** Choose the correct words in *italics*. In two places, both answers are correct. 🔊 **3.33** Listen and check.

FAQs

Setting up a broadband connection and wireless network in your home.

▶ **My wireless network is very slow and sometimes it doesn't work. What can I do to improve it?**

The most important thing is the position of your router (the machine that sends out the wireless signals). You (0) *are allowed to /* (have to) put it in the centre of the house. And it (1) *mustn't be / doesn't have to be* next to a TV or computer as they may interrupt the signals.

▶ **I've only got one phone line. (2)** *Do I have to / Must I* **have a second line for a broadband connection?**

No, you (3) *don't have to / mustn't* have a separate phone line, you can use one line.

▶ **I don't have a phone line in my house but my neighbour's phone line runs across the front of my house. (4)** *Am I allowed to / Have I got to* **use his line for my Internet connection?**

No. You (5) *don't have to / aren't allowed to* use somebody else's phone line; it's illegal! In any case, it wouldn't work. You will (6) *must / have to* get your own phone line, I'm afraid.

▶ **Is it true that (7)** *you have to / it must be to* **set up a special password?**

No, you (8) *haven't got to / don't have to* set up a password for your router, but it is a good idea to do so, as it will prevent other people using your connection.

3 Find five more mistakes and correct them. Tick (✓) the correct sentence.

0   Sylvia has to wear a uniform because she is a nurse. ✓
00 Henry has ~~get~~ *got* to wear glasses for reading.
1   Caroline must to do more exercise.
2   Do you got to take your holiday before the end of August?
3   You must lock the doors at night.
4   The car is very dirty; you've got wash it.
5   Have you allowed to park there?
6   Darren must wear glasses when he was young.

⏻ Go online for more practice and a progress test

50 Necessary and unnecessary actions
need, needn't, don't have to/need to

Sorry. I can't come out tonight. I **need to** finish this report for the meeting tomorrow.

You **needn't have** done that report, Celia – the meeting's cancelled.

1 *need* as a modal, *need to*

Need can be a modal verb (➤ Unit 46), but the only modal forms that we use are *needn't* and *needn't* + *have* + past participle:
You **needn't leave** yet, it's early.   You **needn't have done** that report.

We generally prefer to use *need to*, which is a regular verb, with the usual verb changes:
You **need to leave** now.   Do I **need to buy** batteries?
She **does not (doesn't) need to do** it.   We **didn't need to charge** the battery.

need + *-ing*/infinitive   ➤ Units 67.4 and 85.4

2 Necessary actions

We can use *need to*
- to say that something is physically necessary: *I'm tired. I **need to get** some sleep.*
- when we believe that something is necessary or important: *He really **needs to lose** weight.*
- to mean *have to* (➤ Unit 49): *You **need to score** 60% to pass the exam.*

PAST *Jane's condition was quite serious. She **needed to stay** in the hospital overnight.*
FUTURE *You'**ll need to get** some photos for this passport application.*

3 Unnecessary actions, present and future

We use *needn't/don't need to*, *don't have to* or *haven't got to* to say that something isn't necessary or isn't a rule:
You **needn't take** any food – lunch is provided. (It isn't necessary.)
You **don't need to buy** a battery – it already has one.
Men **don't have to do** military service in Britain. (It isn't a rule.)
There's no rush. We **haven't got to leave** yet.

We use *won't need to* or *won't have to* for unnecessary future actions:
You **won't need to bring** any extra money on Friday, everything is included in the price.
I won't **have to wait** for long; the bus comes every ten minutes.

4 Unnecessary actions in the past

We use *didn't need to* or *didn't have to* to say that something wasn't necessary in the past. We don't know if the action happened or not:
*The pain went away so I **didn't need to see** a doctor.   We **didn't have to pay** – it was free.*

We use *needn't* + *have* + past participle to say that an action happened in the past although it wasn't necessary:
You **needn't have brought** a camera. You can use mine.
You **needn't have gone** to a photographer's. There's a photo machine at the station.

Compare:
Carol **needn't have taken** a towel. The gym provides them free of charge.
(Carol took a towel but it wasn't necessary.)
Carol **didn't need to take** a towel. The gym provides them free of charge.
(We don't know whether Carol took a towel or not.)

9

Practice

1 Match the two parts of the sentences.

0 Tomorrow's meal is included in the price so
1 My rent is really high so
2 It's going to be an expensive evening so
3 The prices at the holiday resort were much cheaper than I expected so
4 My parents paid for everything yesterday so
5 We went on a really long holiday last year so

A I need to earn lots of money.
B I needed to take plenty of money.
C I needn't have taken so much money.
D I didn't need to take any money at all.
E I won't need to take any money.
F I'll need to take lots of money.

2 Match sentences A–H with 1–7. Then write a suitable form of *need* in the gaps.
🔊 3.34 Listen and check.

A There was no rain last summer and the grass didn't grow.
B John cut his hand badly while he was cooking yesterday.
C My parents changed their plans and didn't come to stay with us last month.
D My brother doesn't have any money.
E Helen is going on holiday next week.
F Maria's just painted her house.
G Adam's got fantastic eyesight.
H There are some tomatoes in the fridge.

0 E   She *'ll need to* .... buy a new suitcase before she leaves.
1 .... He .... get a job.
2 .... He .... wear glasses.
3 .... We .... tidied up the guest bedroom.
4 .... She .... paint it again for several years.
5 .... We .... cut it at all.
6 .... We .... call an ambulance.
7 .... You .... bought any.

3 **GRAMMAR IN USE** Complete the conversations with the words from the box.
🔊 3.35 Listen and check.

> didn't need to   do I need to   don't have   'll need to
> ~~need to~~   needn't have   needs to   won't need to

1 CUSTOMER   I'd like to join the sports club.

   RECEPTIONIST   Right. You (0) *need to* .... fill in this form. Then, after we've processed the form, you (1) .... make an appointment for a health check. Each new member (2) .... have a health check before using the equipment.

   CUSTOMER   Oh. I (3) .... do that at my previous club.

   RECEPTIONIST   Well, we have a very strict policy here. But don't worry, it's only an interview. You (4) .... to see a doctor or anything like that.

2 CUSTOMER   Here's my camera. I'd like to get some prints made.

   ASSISTANT   Oh, you (5) .... brought in the camera. All we need is the memory card.

   CUSTOMER   And I want to take some more photos. (6) .... buy more film?

   ASSISTANT   No, you (7) .... do that, it's a digital camera. You just delete the pictures and use the space on the memory card for your new photos.

Go online for more practice

51 Advice and criticism
should, ought to, must, had better

1 Forms

Must and *should* are modal verbs (▶ Unit 46.1): *You **should see** a doctor.*
We can also use the perfect form *should (not) + have +* past participle (▶ Unit 48.1):
*We **should have (should've) bought** it. **Should** we **have left**?*
*We **should not (shouldn't) have gone**.*

Ought to and *had better* have this word order:
*I **ought to** go. I **ought not to** go.* **Ought** I **to** go?*
*I **had better** go. I **had better not** go. **Had** I **better** go?**

* We don't usually use these forms in spoken English.

NATURAL ENGLISH We usually use short forms of *had better* and *should have* in spoken English: *You'**d better look** at the instruction book. We **shouldn't've spent** all our money!*

2 Advice and warnings

We use *should/shouldn't* and *ought to/ought not to* if we think something is a good or bad idea in general, and to give advice in a particular situation:
*People **shouldn't smoke** indoors. You look terrible – you **ought to see** a doctor.*
We usually use *should* to ask for advice:
***Should** I **ask** my boss for a pay rise?*

We can use *must* or *mustn't* to give strong advice and warnings. It is stronger than *should* or *ought to*:
*You **must try** this cake – it's delicious! I really **must lose** some weight!*
*We **mustn't forget** to take our passports. You **mustn't swim** there, it's dangerous.*

We use *had better (not)* to give advice and warnings in a particular situation. It usually means 'if you don't do/do this, something bad will happen':
*You'**d better check** the train times first. (If you don't do this, your journey might be difficult.)*
*That looks hot. You'**d better not touch** it. (If you touch it, you might get burnt.)*

⚠️ We don't use *had better (not)* to give general advice:
✗ *People had better not smoke indoors.* ✓ *People **shouldn't smoke** indoors.*

NATURAL ENGLISH In conversation, we often use *I (don't) think* and *do you think* with *should/ought to*: *It's expensive. **I don't think** we **should buy** it. (= We shouldn't buy it.)*
***Do you think** I **ought to wear** a suit to the interview?*

3 Criticism and regrets about the past

We can use *should/shouldn't + have +* past participle to criticise someone's past actions:
*You **should have done** more revision. You **shouldn't have bought** such a cheap machine!*
We also use *should/shouldn't have +* past participle to express regret for a past action:
*I **should have phoned** you but I was busy. I **shouldn't have shouted** at you. I'm sorry.*

⚠️ We don't use *must have* or *had better* to express regret or criticism:
✗ *You must have phoned me.* ✗ *You'd better phoned me.* ✓ *You **should have phoned** me.*

 Pronunciation ▶ 1.25

Practice

1 Choose the best meaning, A or B.

0 The bus is late. You'd better take a taxi.
  A Taxis are better than buses. (B) I think you should take a taxi.
1 We'd better not swim here.
  A It's dangerous.   B It's better than the other swimming pool.
2 You should have phoned your mother.
  A You phoned her this morning.   B You didn't phone her this morning.
3 The government should reduce taxes.
  A I think taxes aren't high enough.   B I think taxes are too high.
4 You ought to put on some suncream.
  A We went to the beach yesterday.   B We're going to the beach.
5 I really must look for a better job.
  A I think this is important for my future.   B My boss told me to do this.

2 **GRAMMAR IN USE** Read the problem page and choose the correct words in *italics*. 🔊 3.36 **Listen and check.**

> **Lulu's Problem Page**
>
> **Carla** I'm only 19 but I'm always tired and I haven't got any energy. I used to go to a gym but I'm a student so I spend most of my time sitting at my computer, and my diet is very bad. I know I (0) *can't / (shouldn't)* eat fast food but I hate cooking! What do you (1) *advice / think* I should do?
>
> **Lulu says** Well, you are right, you (2) *shouldn't / had better* eat fast food; it's very unhealthy! If you want to have more energy you (3) *should have / ought to* eat lots of fruit and vegetables. You (4) *mustn't / shouldn't* have stopped going to the gym! If you are more active, you'll feel better.
>
> **Andy** I work in a factory and in the evenings I stay at home and watch TV. Sometimes I go to the cinema. Last year I joined an evening class on photography but I only went for a few weeks. Perhaps I (5) *should have / had better* kept going to it, but it wasn't very interesting. What can I do to make my life less boring?
>
> **Lulu says** I (6) *think you shouldn't / don't think you should* stay at home all the time – you'll never make new friends if you do that! And you (7) *ought not to / don't ought to* go to an evening class if you aren't interested in it. Instead, you (8) *should / ought to have* join a club with people who are interested in the same things as you. I know you like the cinema. Why don't you join a film club?

3 Complete the second sentence so it means the same as the first, using the word in brackets. Use two to five words in your answer. 🔊 3.37 **Listen and check.**

0 It's a pity you didn't tell me about the party.   (told)
  You *should have told me* about the party.
1 Don't touch the top of the oven, it's still very hot.   (better)
  You .... the top of the oven, it's too hot.
2 I wish I hadn't ordered the soup; it tasted awful.   (have)
  I .... the soup, it was terrible!
3 You should ask Jack, he always gives good advice.   (to)
  You .... Jack, he always gives good advice.
4 I really think you should listen to this CD, it's fantastic!   (must)
  You .... this CD, it's fantastic!
5 Please tell me what to do with this old computer.   (think)
  What do you .... with this old computer?

52 Permission
can, may, might, could, be allowed to

Can I use my laptop?

I'm sorry. Passengers **aren't allowed** to **use** electronic devices during take-off.

1 Asking for and giving/refusing permission

	ASKING FOR PERMISSION	GIVING PERMISSION	REFUSING PERMISSION
informal	*Can I use* my laptop?	Yes, you **can**. Yes, of course (you **can**). Yes, sure.	No, you **can't**. No, I'm sorry.
formal/ polite	*Could I ask* a question? *May I make* a suggestion? *Might I interrupt* for a moment?	Yes, you **can/may**. Yes, of course/ certainly.	No, you **can't/may not**. No, I'm sorry/I'm afraid not.

FORMALITY CHECK To ask for permission
- we use *can* in most situations, but if we need to be polite, or if we think permission will be refused, we use *may, could* or *might*. *Might* is the most formal.
 May I leave early today? (to your boss) **Could** we stay an extra night? (to a hotel clerk)
 Might I ask a question? (in a formal business meeting)
- we can also use *Do you mind if ...* (formal), *Is it all right if ...* and *Is it OK to ...* :
 Do you mind if I open the window? **Is it all right if** I use your bathroom? **Is it OK to** bring a friend?

When we refuse permission we often give a reason:
'Can we park here?' 'No, I'm sorry. It's only for hotel guests.'

⚠ We don't use *could* or *might* when we give or refuse permission:
Could I use your bathroom? ✗ *Yes, you could.* ✗ *No, you couldn't.* ✗ *Yes, you might.*
Might I ask a question?   ✓ Yes, you **can**. ✓ No, you **can't**.

🔊 Pronunciation ➤ 1.26

2 Permission in rules and laws

We use *can/can't* or *be (not) allowed to* when we talk about permission in rules and laws:
In the USA you **can turn** right at a red traffic light.
You **can't ride** a motorbike without a helmet in the UK.
Are we **allowed to take** photos in the museum?
Passengers **aren't allowed to use** electronic devices during take-off.

We can also use *may/may not* to describe rules in written instructions:
Passengers **may use** electronic devices once the seat belt signs have been switched off.

3 Permission in the past and future

To talk about permission in the past, we use *could/couldn't* or *was/were allowed to*:
In the 1960s you **could drive** without a seat belt. You **couldn't wear** jeans at my old school.
I **was allowed to stay up** quite late when I was young.
In the nineteenth century women **weren't allowed to vote** in elections.

⚠ But to talk about permission for a single action in the past, we use *allowed to*, not *could*:
✗ *We could go home early last Friday.* ✓ We **were allowed to go** home early last Friday.

We can use *will/won't be allowed to* to talk about permission at a time in the future:
After you complete the training, you**'ll be allowed to use** the equipment on your own.
The play starts at eight o'clock. You **won't be allowed to enter** the theatre after that.

Practice

1 Match the sentences with the photos. Then write *can*, *can't*, *are allowed to* or *aren't allowed to* in each gap.

0 You *can't* use your mobile phone here but you *are allowed to* eat ice cream. *C*
1 You .... eat here but you .... bring your own food. ......
2 You .... drive a car here but you .... ride a bike. ......
3 You .... wear socks here but you .... wear shoes. ......
4 You .... look at things here but you .... touch them. ......

2 **GRAMMAR IN USE** Read each conversation and decide whether the situation is formal or informal. Then choose the best words in *italics*. 🔊 3.38 Listen and check.

1 A Good morning. This is Brinley Insurance. (*Could*)/ *Can* I speak to Mrs Canford?
   B This is Mrs Canford.
   A Hello, Mrs Canford. *May I / Am I allowed to* ask you some questions about your house insurance?
   A I'm sorry. I'm rather busy at the moment.
   B Well, *can / might* I you call back later?

2 A Now that everyone has given their opinion I think it's time to take a vote.
   B Mr Chairman. *Might / Can* I ask a question about these sales figures before we vote?
   A No, I'm afraid you *might not / can't*. We've already spent too long on this item.

3 A What's going to happen after the new anti-smoking law starts next month?
   B Well, people *can't / won't be allowed to* smoke in restaurants.
   A *Will they be allowed to / Can they* smoke in offices?
   B No, I don't think so.

4 A This old photo of you at school is so funny. Did you always wear old jeans to school?
   B No, we usually wore school uniform but we *could / were allowed to* wear jeans on that day because it was the last day of term.
   A Really? At my old school you *could / might* wear anything you liked!

3 Find six more mistakes and correct them. Tick (✓) the correct sentences.

0 People are allowed ~~carrying~~ *to carry* guns in many parts of the USA.
1 In my country you can't to smoke in the street.
2 In the UK, children aren't allowed have credit cards.
3 'Could I use your bathroom, please?' 'I'm afraid you couldn't. It's reserved for hotel guests.'
4 I'm not allowed to make personal calls from my office phone.
5 In my country people might vote once they reach the age of eighteen.
6 After next April we can't be allowed to bring mobile phones to school.
7 This device may not be used underwater.
8 I could use the boss's parking space last Friday because she was away.

53 Requests and suggestions; offers, promises and warnings *can, could, would, will, shall*

1 Requests

We use *can* to make requests in most situations:
Can you help me with these bags? Yes, of course (I can).
Can we have two coffees, please? Certainly/Sure.

We usually add *please* to requests to make them polite:
Can we have two coffees, **please**?

We put *please* in front of the verb to make a request stronger:
Can we **please** have a menu? Would you **please** be quiet?

We often use *will you* with people we know well:
Will you give me a hand with this?

FORMALITY CHECK We use *could* or *would* for more polite or formal requests:
Excuse me. **Could you** help me with this? (in a shop)
Would you sign this form? (talking to a customer in a bank)

 But we don't use *could* or *would* to reply to requests:
'Would you help me?' ✗ 'Yes, I would.' ✓ 'Yes, of course.'

Excuse me. **Could you** help me with this?

I'**ll** be with you in a minute. I'm helping this customer right now.

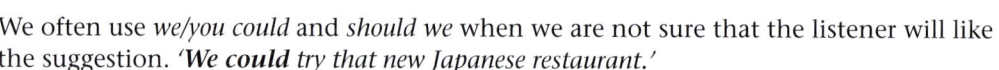

2 Suggestions

SUGGESTIONS AS STATEMENTS	We/You could	watch	a DVD.
	Let's		
SUGGESTIONS AS QUESTIONS	Why don't we	watch	a DVD?
	Shall/Should we		
	How/What about	watching	

We often use *we/you could* and *should we* when we are not sure that the listener will like the suggestion. '**We could** try that new Japanese restaurant.'

We can agree or disagree with the suggestion. If we disagree, we usually give a reason:
'**Shall we** get a pizza?' 'Yes, let's do that. / That's a good idea. / Great.'
'**How about** meeting up for coffee on Sunday?' 'Oh, I can't, I'm really busy. I'm sorry.'

3 *will* for offers, promises, warnings

to agree	'Will you sign this for me?' 'Yes, I **will**.' (✗ Yes, I'll.) 'Will you have some more cake?' 'No, thanks, I **won't**. I'm on a diet.'
to offer or promise to do something	We'**ll** drive you to the station if you like. We **won't** forget how kind you've been to us.
to say if someone else agrees or is able to do something (or not)	Take it to Marco – he'**ll** fix it for you. Ask my teacher about it – she'**ll** help you. Don't ask Carol. She **won't** know the answer.
promises/warnings	I'**ll** be with you in a minute. Don't touch the cooker – you'**ll** get burnt.

We can also make offers with *shall I/we* or *I/we could*. We use these forms when we are not sure that the listener will want to accept:
'**Shall we** help you with that?' 'No, thanks. I can manage on my own.'
'**I could** get Lucy's present for you.' 'That's kind of you, but I'd rather do it myself.'

 We don't use the present simple to make offers:
'My hair's wet.' ✗ 'I get you a towel.' ✓ 'I'**ll** get you a towel.' ✓ '**Shall I** get you a towel?'

🔊 Pronunciation ▶ 1.27

9

Practice

1 Write the requests, suggestions and offers in the correct order to complete the conversations. 🔊 3.39 Listen and check.

0 A I'm really late. I'm going to miss my train.
   B station you take I'll the to   *I'll take you to the station.*
1 A TV can please you the turn off ?   ....
   B Yes, sure.
2 A I really don't understand how to work out these maths problems.
   B give extra I lesson an you could   ....
3 A I don't really want to go out this evening.
   B getting pizza how a about ?   ....
4 A I don't think we're ready to order yet.
   B five in I back shall come minutes ?   ....
5 A it bag put would in a please you ?   ....
   B Yes, of course, Madam.

2 **GRAMMAR IN USE** Complete the conversation with the words from the box. 🔊 3.40 Listen and check.

> can   could you help   course   how about   I'll   ~~let's~~   shall   shall I   would you

LAURA Mmm. There are so many laptops to choose from.
NEIL (0) *Let's* ask somebody to help us.
LAURA OK. (1) .... we get one of the shop assistants? There's one over there. (2) .... go and ask him. ... Excuse me. (3) .... us?
ASSISTANT Of (4) .... I see you're looking for a laptop. (5) .... you tell me what you'll be using it for?
LAURA Yes. We want to replace our computer. It's old and it won't last much longer.
ASSISTANT Right. (6) .... looking at some of these ones?
NEIL Mmm. We also want to take it with us when we travel and those ones look pretty heavy. (7) .... get one down so we can try carrying it?
LAURA Oh, this one's quite heavy.
ASSISTANT (8) .... show you some of the lighter models?

3 Complete the conversations with one word only (or a short form) in the gaps. Use a different word each time.

1 A Mum. (0) *Can* you help me wrap this present?
   B OK, but there's no wrapping paper. I (1) .... get some next time I go to the shops.
   A Actually, I think there's some in the kitchen drawer. (2) .... don't we use that?
   B Oh, is there? (3) .... I go and get it?
2 A Right, Mr Parsons. (4) .... you put your cash card in the reader, please? Thanks. Now, (5) .... you type in your PIN number? Thank you.
   B Will you be able to give me the cash in twenty-pound notes?
   A Yes, of (6) ....

Go online for more practice and a progress test

155

Review MODULE 9

1 UNITS 46 AND 47 Choose the correct words in *italics*.

0 Although it took us a long time, we managed to (open)/ *opening* the old safe.
1 When I was younger, I *can / could* run very fast.
2 After he finishes the mechanics course, Dave *can / will be able to* service his own car.
3 Mr Webber *managed to / could* fit the carpet yesterday, with my brother's help.
4 Come this way. The nurse *might / can* see you now.
5 That restaurant was quite expensive. We *may not / could not* go there again.
6 'Why is Janine so late?' 'She *could not / might not* have the correct address.'
7 That *mustn't / can't* be David at the door. I know he's away on holiday.
8 My heating broke down yesterday but I *was able to / could* borrow a heater from next door.
9 Why don't you go up to Mr Gray's office? He *can / should* be back from lunch by now.
10 Look at old Mrs O'Leary. She *must / can* be at least ninety years old!

2 UNITS 46, 47 AND 48 Complete the sentences with the verbs from the box.

could   can   can't   could have   can't have   ~~must~~   must have
might not   should have   to be able   was able to

0 Elizabeth *must* be in; I can see the light in her window.
1 Perhaps you should take some cash with you. The restaurant .... accept credit cards.
2 Good news. The engineer .... fix your computer yesterday, so you can use it again.
3 You were very lucky. You .... been badly hurt.
4 We .... go to the museum today; it's closed.
5 There .... been a terrible storm. When Jeff got home he was soaking wet!
6 Those old photographs .... be in the cupboard. I haven't looked in there for ages.
7 Uncle Mike .... gone away. His car is still parked outside our house.
8 Turn on your TV. They .... announced the winner by now.
9 I'm having Spanish lessons. I want .... to speak the language when I go to Madrid.
10 Take some warm clothes. It .... be very cold there at this time of year.

3 UNITS 47 AND 48 Match the questions 1–5 with the replies A–F.

0 Is Mr Knight getting a pay rise?
1 Is it possible to see Mr Knight later today?
2 Is Mr Knight working at home today?
3 Was Mr Knight working at home yesterday?
4 Why wasn't Mr Knight at the meeting yesterday?
5 Is Mr Knight in his office?

A He can't have been. He was in the office.
B He could be. It depends on his sales results.
C Yes, he should be back by four-thirty.
D Yes, he should be there by now.
E He can't be. I've just seen him in the office.
F I don't know. He should have been there.

4 UNITS 49 AND 50 Read the article and choose the correct answer, A, B or C below. In two places more than one answer is possible.

How-to Guides
12 *Using Dry Ski Slopes*

Dry ski slopes are a cheap and effective way of learning to ski before you take the plunge and book that expensive holiday in the mountains. But, as with all sports, there are several *dos* and *don'ts* that you should know before you start.

- Skiers (0) .... be reasonably fit. Skiing can be physically demanding. If you are in any doubt about your fitness you (1) .... get a check-up from your doctor before using the slope.
- You (2) .... be an experienced skier – all levels of ability are welcome on the dry ski slope.
- You (3) .... wear skis at all times on the slope – it isn't safe to walk on it in ordinary shoes. (You (4) .... bring your own skis, they are available to hire.)
- You (5) .... wear special clothes when you are on the dry ski slope, but we recommend that you wear strong gloves as the surface of the slope can easily burn your hands if you fall. Because of safety regulations, children under the age of sixteen (6) .... wear protective helmets.
- Most dry ski slopes have a café or restaurant so you (7) .... to bring your own food or drinks. But remember that food and drinks (8) .... be taken onto the ski slope at any time, because of the risk of accidents.

0 A need	B mustn't	(C) have to
1 A will need to	B mustn't	C won't need to
2 A needn't	B must not	C don't have to
3 A need	B don't need to	C must
4 A have got to	B don't have to	C have to
5 A needn't	B mustn't	C don't have to
6 A didn't have to	B must	C need
7 A must not	B needn't	C don't need
8 A needn't	B must not	C don't need to

5 UNITS 46, 49 AND 50 Read the conversation and choose the correct words in *italics*.

MIKE I went skiing at the new dry ski slope last Wednesday. It was great fun.

DELLA Really? I didn't know you could ski!

MIKE Well, I (0) *can't* / *mightn't* really. But you (1) *mustn't* / *don't need to* be an experienced skier. Anyone (2) *can* / *may* do it. I mean, I've never skied before so I (3) *must* / *had to* have lessons. But they have really good instructors who teach you the basics. After about half-an-hour I (4) *can* / *managed to* start skiing reasonably well.

DELLA Did you (5) *have to* / *had to* wear special clothes?

MIKE Not really. I (6) *had to* / *must* wear skis, of course. But I (7) *was able to* / *could* hire them at the slope.

DELLA Did you have lunch there?

MIKE Well, I took some sandwiches. In fact, there's a really nice restaurant there, so I (8) *needn't* / *mustn't* have done that.

6 UNITS 49 AND 50 Match the sentences with the pictures, then complete the sentences with a suitable form of *must*, *have to* or *need*. If two answers are possible, write both.

0 We really *need to/must* get a new television.   *C*
1 He .... buy some warmer clothes before next week.   ....
2 You .... bought all that food. There's plenty in the fridge!   ....
3 You .... feed the animals. It's dangerous!   ....
4 We .... wear smart clothes. It was a very formal party.   ....
5 Mum, you .... pay, it's free.   ....
6 Mobile phones .... be switched off during the performance.   ....
7 Great. After next week I .... park in the street any more!   ....

7 UNITS 51, 52 AND 53 Complete this conversation at a conference hotel with phrases from the box. There are three extra phrases.

> aren't allowed to   could have   could you   how about   I'll   ~~may I~~   ought not to
> ought to   shall I   shouldn't have   why don't you   you'd better

CLERK Good afternoon, sir. (0) *May I* help you?

GUEST Hello. I'd like to check in, please. I'm here for the conference on technology in schools.

CLERK Certainly, sir. (1) .... complete this form, please?

GUEST Of course. Is my room ready?

CLERK No, I'm afraid not. It should be ready at half past two.

GUEST Oh, right. Well, I've got quite a lot of bags.

CLERK That's no problem. (2) .... leave them in the luggage room?
(3) .... ask the porter to take them there for you?

GUEST Yes, thanks. Er, I've parked my car on the street outside the back entrance of the hotel. Is that OK?

CLERK I'm sorry, sir. You (4) .... park there, it's against the fire regulations. You (5) .... block the access to the hotel. There's a car park for guests at the side of the hotel.

GUEST Oh. Do you think I (6) .... move it along a bit?

CLERK Well, that's a no-parking area so perhaps (7) .... put it straight in the car park.

GUEST OK. (8) .... go and do that now.

8 ALL UNITS Look at the signs and notices. Then complete the sentences below, using the words in brackets.

0 You *must keep your bags with you* at all times. (keep / bags / with you)
1 You .... in this park. (play football)
2 We .... – they are included. (buy / batteries)
3 I think we .... (cook / this / in the microwave)
4 How .... tomorrow evening? It might be fun. (try / keep fit class)
5 She ....; we were in the same year at school and I'm thirty-five! (be / thirty)
6 We'd .... from the garden – there's going to be frost tonight. (bring / those plants in)
7 Only adults .... (buy / this product)
8 What a pity I didn't go! I ....! (meet / someone famous)
9 That looks interesting. .... and have a look? (we / go / inside)
10 Why don't you go? This .... you've been waiting for. (be / the chance)

Test MODULE 9

Modal verbs

Choose the best answer, A, B or C.

1. I'd like to .... sing well.
   A can   B have ability to   C be able to ▶ Unit 46

2. We ran out of milk last night but I .... buy some at the corner shop.
   A could   B was able to   C can't ▶ Unit 46

3. The buses .... get very crowded before they built the new Underground.
   A could   B can   C were able to ▶ Unit 46

4. It took us a long time, but eventually we managed .... a refund.
   A to get   B get   C getting ▶ Unit 46

5. This .... be your book. It's got your name on it.
   A can   B must   C perhaps ▶ Unit 47

6. It's quite a popular course. There .... be any places left on it.
   A might not   B must not   C could not ▶ Unit 47

7. The heating's been on all day so there .... plenty of hot water for your bath.
   A could be   B should be   C can't be ▶ Unit 47

8. Everything's soaking wet. It .... have rained very heavily last night.
   A should   B could   C must ▶ Unit 48

9. I .... to football practice yesterday but I had a bit of a stomachache.
   A can't go   B should have gone   C couldn't have gone ▶ Unit 48

10. It's eight o'clock. We .... leave now.
    A 've got to   B are have to   C 've got ▶ Unit 49

11. When we arrived at the gate, we .... show our passports.
    A must   B had got to   C had to ▶ Unit 49

12. You .... take any of the confidential files home. It's against company rules.
    A don't have to   B haven't got to   C mustn't ▶ Unit 49

13. I'm really putting on weight. I .... some exercise.
    A need doing   B have need do   C need to do ▶ Unit 50

14. I .... my car so I left it at home and came on the bus.
    A needn't have brought   B didn't need to bring   C haven't needed to bring ▶ Unit 50

15. That cut looks bad. We .... phone for an ambulance.
    A 'd better   B must better   C should have ▶ Unit 51

16. I'm really sorry. I .... said all those terrible things about you.
    A shouldn't   B shouldn't have   C mustn't have ▶ Unit 51

17. 'Excuse me. May I take a photograph?' 'No, I'm afraid you ....'
    A mightn't   B couldn't   C can't ▶ Unit 52

18. Our teacher was sick, so we .... leave school early yesterday.
    A were allowed to   B could   C might ▶ Unit 52

19. One more thing, madam. .... you confirm your date of birth?
    A Would   B May I   C Shall ▶ Unit 53

20. 'I'm starving!' 'OK. I .... you something from the fridge.'
    A 'm getting   B 'll get   C get ▶ Unit 53

Go online for a full exit test

Conditionals

MODULE 10

Before you start

1 Read Danny's blog and his phone conversation with his father. Look at the highlighted grammar examples.

ARRESTED!
DANNY GOODMAN
21 May

Sorry it's been a long time folks, but I'm just back from my trip to the States to go to my cousin's 21st birthday party, and guess what … I was arrested! You see, I'd taken some medicine for my fear of flying – going to the States was the longest journey I'd done. The box said to take two, but it was a long flight and I thought 'I'll take four in case two don't last long enough.' Four was obviously too many: they made me aggressive and I behaved rather badly on the plane back. It's so annoying – if I wasn't so afraid of flying, I wouldn't have taken anything! Anyway, the police officer said, 'The airlines always call us if someone causes a problem on a plane. It's very serious.' I apologised, but they took me to the police station. I called my Dad …

DANNY The police have arrested me, Dad. I took some medicine for my fear of flying on the way home from Las Vegas, and apparently I became aggressive and upset the passengers next to me. I can't remember. Anyway, can you come? I'm sure the police would believe you if you talked to them. You know I wouldn't ask you to do this unless I had to, but I'm really worried.

DAD Of course. I'll come straight away. Are they treating you well?

DANNY Yes, but they want me to sign a written statement.

DAD I'd rather you didn't do that, Danny. I'll call my lawyer – wait until he gets there.

DANNY Oh, OK. It's stupid – if I hadn't taken that medicine, I'd be home now.

DAD Yes, well, if you hadn't accepted that invitation to your cousin's party, this wouldn't have happened …

2 Now read the sentences and choose the correct words in *italics*. The highlighted grammar examples will help you.

1 Notice: we always inform the police if you *will steal / steal* from us! ▶ Unit 54
2 It's freezing outside. Take your coat *if / in case* you have to wait for the bus. ▶ Unit 54
3 I would invite her to the party if I *know / knew* her phone number. ▶ Unit 55
4 We wouldn't ask you to help us *unless / in case* it was necessary. ▶ Unit 55
5 If you had arrived on time, we *won't / wouldn't* have missed the train. ▶ Unit 56
6 If we hadn't met in the hospital, we would both still *be / have been* single! ▶ Unit 57
7 I wouldn't have agreed to marry you if I *didn't / don't* love you! ▶ Unit 57
8 Do you have to stay in Canada? We'd rather you *come / came* home. ▶ Unit 58

3 Check your answers below. Then go to the unit for more information and practice.

1 steal 2 in case 3 knew 4 unless 5 wouldn't 6 be 7 didn't 8 came

⏻ Go online for a full diagnostic test

54 Present and future conditions

1 Present conditions (zero conditional)

A conditional sentence has two clauses.

the condition (*if*) clause	the result clause
If people steal from this shop,	the store detectives always catch them .

The *if* clause can come before or after the result clause.
We use the zero conditional to describe real situations that can happen at any time, or one event that always follows another. We can use *when* instead of *if*:
If/When we talk to the baby, she smiles.

We often use this conditional form, with the imperative in the result clause, for rules and to give instructions:
If the lift **breaks down**, **press** the alarm button.
If you **arrive** after the start of the performance, please **wait** outside until the first interval.

With this meaning, we use *if*, not *when*, in the *if* clause.
✗ *When a red light comes on, call the technician.*   ✓ **If** a red light comes on, **call** the technician.

2 Future conditions (first conditional)

We use the first conditional to talk about the results of a POSSIBLE future condition, one we think is likely to happen:
If they **catch** you, they**'ll call** the police.   If I **don't see** you at the gym, I**'ll give** you a call.

Note the comma after the conditional clause when it comes before the result clause. If the conditional clause comes after the result clause, a comma is not necessary:
They won't catch me if I run fast enough.

⚠ In the first conditional the *if* clause describes the future but uses the present tense, not *will* or *won't*:
✗ *If Jan will get the job, he'll move to New York.*   ✓ If Jan **gets** the job, he'll move to New York.

We can use the present continuous in the *if* clause, and *can* or *might* in the result clause:
If it**'s raining** tomorrow, we **might not** go to the festival.

We can make offers and warnings that depend on a future condition:
If you wait there for a minute, I**'ll get** you a few brochures.
If you children don't stop fighting, I**'ll come** and **stop** you myself!

3 Alternatives to *if*

unless	I won't wash your car **unless** you pay me. (if you don't pay me)
in case	Take an umbrella **in case** it rains. (It might/might not rain but you will be prepared.)
even if	I won't wash your car **even if** you pay me! (if you pay me or not)
provided/ as long as	You can borrow the car **provided** I have it back by six o'clock. (I must have the car back by six o'clock.)

10

Practice

1 Match the two parts of the sentences. 🔊 3.41 Listen and check.

0 When you book a superior room,   A we can provide a choice of meat-free dishes.
1 If you take items from the minibar,   B room service can provide snacks.
2 If the fire alarm sounds,   C we provide fresh fruit and flowers every day.
3 If you eat in the hotel every evening,   D we'll give you a discount on your meals.
4 If you require a vegetarian meal,   E we will add them to your bill on departure.
5 If you require a meal after 10.00 p.m.,   F leave the building immediately.
6 When you check out,   G don't forget to hand your key to reception.

2 **GRAMMAR IN USE** Write the verbs from the box in the correct form to make first conditional sentences. Use *will* or *might (not)* in the result clause. 🔊 3.42 Listen and check.

> be able to / not have   confuse / allow   not cover / see
> ~~get / steal~~   not have / not be   tell / not return

Credit card fraud – the facts

If a credit card thief _gets_ the chance, he _will steal_ your card or your money. How can you prevent this? There are several ways:

1 Always cover your PIN number when you use it. If you .... it, someone .... it.
2 Don't talk to people at the cash machine – a thief .... you by talking to you if you .... him to.
3 You need good security on your computer – thieves .... get into your accounts if you .... proper security.
4 When you buy something on the Internet, make sure the website has a 'locked' symbol. If it .... one, it .... secure enough.
5 Don't forget, if you .... your PIN number to another person and your money is stolen, your credit card company .... your money.

3 Find seven more mistakes and correct them. Tick (✓) the correct sentences.

0 If I get the job at Siemens, ~~I move~~ *I'll move* to Swansea.
1 Take your warm coat tonight if case it gets cold.
2 Mike really dislikes Luke and Pete. He won't come to your party unless they come.
3 When you go out, don't forget to lock the back door.
4 I'll meet you at 6.00, but when my bus is late, don't wait for me.
5 If the corner shop won't be open, I can go to the supermarket.
6 If I don't eat much during the day, I always get a headache.
7 Even my boss begs me to stay, I won't listen to him.
8 The taxi won't wait at the airport if your plane will be delayed.
9 I'll make some sandwiches provided you get hungry on the journey.
10 The match might be cancelled if the weather's really bad.

Go online for more practice

55 Unlikely/unreal conditions

If we **moved** out of the city, we**'d be** safer.

If this country **had** stricter laws against crime, we **wouldn't have to move!**

1 Second conditional

CONDITION *if* + past simple	RESULT *would (not)* + infinitive
If we **moved** out of the city,	we **would** (**we'd**) **be** safer.
If he **wasn't** so miserable,	he **might*** **have** more friends.
If you **lived** in the country,	you**'d be able to go**/you **could go** horse-riding.

* We use *might* in the result clause to make the result less certain.

2 Unlikely future conditions

We use the second conditional for future actions or situations that are possible, but UNLIKELY. Compare:
- FIRST CONDITIONAL *My boss is pleased with my work. If I get a pay rise this year, I'll buy a new car.* (I think I might get a pay rise.)
- SECOND CONDITIONAL *I know I've made a lot of mistakes at work, but if I got a pay rise this year, I'd buy a new car.* (I don't think I'll get a pay rise.)

3 Unreal present conditions

We can use the second conditional for present situations that are imaginary, not real:
*If they had stricter laws against crime, we **wouldn't have to move!*** (They don't have these laws.)
*We **wouldn't go** abroad if we **had** hot summers here.* (We don't have hot summers.)

4 Advice

We often use the expression *If I were you, I'd ...* to give personal advice:
***If I were you, I'd get** a taxi home from the party.* (= I think you should get a taxi.)

NATURAL ENGLISH Many people use *was* in this expression. Some people think this is incorrect:
[*I'd get more exercise **if I was you**.*] ✓ *I'd get more exercise **if I were you**.*

5 Alternatives to *if*

We can also introduce unlikely/unreal condition clauses with
- *unless* for unlikely conditions: ✓ *I wouldn't ask for your help **unless** I needed it.*
  but not unreal conditions:
  I would be more active ✗ *unless I had arthritis.* ✓ *if I didn't have arthritis.*
- *imagine/suppose* to ask about imaginary situations:
  ***Imagine** you had a million dollars, what would you spend it on?* (You don't have a million dollars.)
  ***Suppose** they lived in the country, would they feel safer?* (They don't live in the country.)

FORMALITY CHECK In informal British English, we can also use *say*:
***Say** you could live anywhere in the world, where would you live?*

PRACTICE

1 Choose the correct meaning, A or B.

0 If Charles got a pay rise, he'd buy a better car.
 A I think Charles will get a pay rise. (B) I think Charles is unlikely to get a pay rise.
1 If house prices rise, we'll sell our flat and buy a cottage in the country.
 A The speaker thinks house prices will probably rise.
 B The speaker thinks house prices probably won't rise.
2 If I were you, I'd take the train to Cornwall; it's more relaxing than driving.
 A I'm giving advice.   B You've taken the train before.
3 If I had a mobile phone, I'd call the police.
 A I might call the police.   B I can't call the police.
4 Suppose you had a yacht, where would you sail to?
 A You have a yacht.   B You don't have a yacht.
5 Pablo would be very disappointed if he didn't pass the exam.
 A Pablo expects to pass the exam.   B Pablo doesn't expect to pass the exam.

2 Write one word only (or a short form) in each gap to make second conditional sentences. 3.43 Listen and check.

0 If I *moved* to another country, I think I *would* go to Mexico.
1 If there .... more rain here, the countryside .... be much greener.
2 I .... talk to him right now if I .... you – he's in a terrible mood.
3 .... there were no borders between countries, wouldn't it .... wonderful?
4 The director wouldn't make any redundancies .... it .... really necessary.
5 If Jonas .... you to marry him, what .... you say?
6 I've got an awful voice, but if I .... sing, I .... join a choir.

3 **GRAMMAR IN USE** Read the letter and then complete the responses below, using the underlined parts of the letter to help you. 3.44 Listen and check.

This week's problem

We're really worried about our son at present. He's fifteen and he's just started going round with a gang of older boys who are involved in petty crime. (0) <u>We don't take him to school in the morning</u>, and we know that he doesn't actually go to school a lot of the time – he meets these boys. They go to the cinema and funfairs, and our son uses (1) <u>the money we give him</u> for lunch to go with them. (2) <u>We haven't talked to our son</u> about this yet, because we're sure (3) <u>he'd just lie to us</u> – he accuses us of treating him like a child and watching him all the time. (4) <u>We really don't know whether to talk to the police</u> about him – it seems so drastic. There's a parents' evening at school next week, so (5) <u>perhaps we should speak to his teachers</u> first. We don't know (6) <u>if there's any way they can help us</u>.

0 If *you took him to school* in the morning, you could make sure he goes inside.
1 He wouldn't be able to spend money on funfairs if you ....
2 I would talk to your son if I ....
3 He probably .... lie to you if you treated him like an adult.
4 If I were you I .... unless you know he has committed a crime. Your son is very young and you don't want the police involved at this stage.
5 It would be a good idea if you .... They might be worried, too.
6 The teachers know your son. If you speak to them, they ....

56 Past conditions

My client is innocent. If he **had stolen** the company plans, he **wouldn't have kept** them in his office. Someone else put them there.

1 Third conditional

CONDITION *if* + past perfect	RESULT *would (not)* + *have* + past participle
If we'd arrived on time,	we'd have flown to Majorca.
If we'd arrived on time,	we wouldn't have missed the flight.
If he hadn't stolen the money,	he wouldn't have lost his job.

We usually use short forms (*we'd*, *wouldn't*, etc.) in this conditional.

We can also use *could have/might have* + past participle in the result clause:
*If we hadn't lost the semi-final, we **might have won** the tournament.* (less certain than *would*)
*You **could have gone** to university if you'd studied harder.* (= you would have been able to)

NATURAL ENGLISH In American English it is possible to use *would have* + past participle in the *if* clause, but most British English speakers think that is incorrect:
[*I **would have spoken** to you if I **would have seen** you.*]
✓ *I would have spoken to you if I **had seen** you.*

Differences between British and American English ➤ page 352

2 Unreal past conditions

We use the third conditional to imagine situations or actions in the past that we know are the opposite of the facts:
*If he **had stolen** the company plans, he **wouldn't have kept** them in his office.*
(We know that he didn't steal the company plans, but we imagine a past where he did this.)

If the past condition happened, we use a negative verb. If it didn't happen, we use a positive verb:

	CONDITION	RESULT
condition happened (I got the job.)	If I hadn't got the job,	I might have stayed in London. I wouldn't have moved to Edinburgh.
condition didn't happen (I didn't get the job.)	If I had got the job,	I would have moved to Edinburgh. I couldn't have stayed in London.

Sometimes we use conditional forms of verbs on their own:
*We were really enjoying the party and **would have stayed** longer.* (… if we hadn't had to leave)
*I **would have liked** to meet your friends from Argentina.* (… if I had had the opportunity)

3 Regrets

We can use the third conditional to talk about regrets from our past, often with *could have*:
*I **could have got** a better job if I'd stayed at university.*
*We **might not have had** the accident if the weather had been better.*

I wish, if only ➤ Unit 58.2

Practice

1 Match the results 1–5 with the conditions A–F. Then complete 1–5 with *would have*, *wouldn't have* or *could have*.

0 I *would have* bought a faster car — D if I'd had enough money.
1 I .... called you yesterday   A if I'd studied harder.
2 I .... got a better degree   B if I'd practised the violin every day.
3 I .... left my parents' home   C if I'd remembered your phone number.
4 I .... played in an orchestra   E if I'd known how much renting costs.
5 I .... taken the job   F if I'd realised the company was in trouble.

2 **GRAMMAR IN USE** Complete the email, using the correct form of the verbs in brackets. 🔊 3.45 Listen and check.

Subject: Help!

Hi Mum and Dad
I'm afraid I have to ask you for some money – and I'm very ashamed to tell you about this. You see, I lost my job a few weeks ago. I deserved it because I upset a customer – if I hadn't been rude to the customer, my boss (0) *wouldn't have fired* (fire) me. And I was in debt because of the car – obviously, I wouldn't have got into debt if I (1) .... (not buy) the car, but I needed it for work. Then, one day recently I was in a local shop and I took some money from the till. If it hadn't been open, I (2) .... (not take) the money, but it was so easy. I left the shop before they noticed, but then, a couple of days later I went back into the shop and the shopkeeper saw me. That was really stupid – if I (3) .... (not go back), he wouldn't have recognised me. I denied taking the money, so he called the police, and they arrested me. If I'd admitted it to the shopkeeper and paid him back, he (4) .... (not call) the police. So … can I borrow £500 to pay the fine? I know I've been stupid – if I (5) .... (ask) for your help weeks ago, this wouldn't have happened.
Love Harry

3 Write what these people said. They are talking about their regrets with *would*, *might* or *could*. For 5 and 6, write sentences that are true for you. 🔊 3.46 Listen and check.

0 Pietro didn't get a place at college because he didn't apply in time.
   If I'd applied in time, I might have got a place at college.
1 Last year Olivia spent all her money on clothes and couldn't afford a holiday.
   ....
2 Samuel didn't notice the speed camera and he got a fine for driving too fast.
   ....
3 Patrice broke his leg on a skiing trip and he wasn't able to become a footballer.
   ....
4 Kimiko ate some fish which was bad, so she was very ill.
   ....
5 If I hadn't ....
6 If I had ....

57 Mixed conditionals

Honestly, I didn't do it. If that thief **hadn't tricked** me, I **wouldn't be** here in prison now.

I know. If I **didn't believe** you, I **would have left** you by now.

1 Mixed past to present conditional

We use this conditional to talk about present results of an imagined past condition/action:

If that thief **hadn't tricked** me, I **wouldn't be** in prison now.
(The thief did trick me.)   (I am in prison now.)

If I **had learnt** to play the violin, I **could be** in an orchestra now.
(I didn't learn to play the violin.)   (I'm not in an orchestra now.)

CONDITION *if* + past perfect	RESULT *would (not)* + infinitive
If that thief **hadn't tricked** me,	I **wouldn't be** in prison now.
If we **had missed** the train,	we **wouldn't be** here to enjoy your wedding.
If you **hadn't woken** me up,	I **might** still **be** in bed!

We can also use *could/might* + infinitive in the result clause:
If you hadn't had the operation, you **could be** really ill now.
We **might be** in a better financial position if you'd taken that job!

2 Mixed present to past conditional

We use this conditional to talk about imagined past results of a present condition/situation:

If I **didn't believe** you, I **would have left** you.
(I do believe you.)   (I didn't leave you.)

If you **were** a better student, you **could have gone** to university.
(You aren't a good student.)   (You didn't go to university.)

CONDITION *if* + past simple	RESULT *could/would (not)* + *have* + past participle
If I **didn't believe** you,	I **would have left** you.
If John **wasn't** a hard worker,	he **wouldn't have got** a promotion.
If I **had** a better memory,	I **could have won** the Mastermind competition.

We can also use *could have/might have* + past participle in the result clause:
If we **hadn't lost** the first match, we **might** still **have been** in the competition. (less certain than *would*)
You **could have gone** to university if you **were** a better student.
(= You would have been able to. / You aren't a good student.)

Practice

1 Read each sentence. Decide if each explanation, A and B, is true (T) or false (F).

0   Gary could have been a famous footballer if he was more prepared to train hard.
    A   Gary isn't a famous footballer.   T......   B   Gary doesn't like training hard.   T......
1   If Manfred's parents had moved to the UK, he might speak English now.
    A   Manfred's parents moved to the UK.   ....   B   Manfred doesn't speak English.   ....
2   If Noel and Jim had talked to each other more, they could still be friends today.
    A   They didn't talk to each other enough.   ....   B   They are still friends.   ....
3   If Juliet didn't believe her son's story, she might have called the police.
    A   Juliet doesn't believe her son's story.   ....   B   Juliet called the police.   ....
4   Joan might look really old now if she hadn't had cosmetic surgery.
    A   Joan has had cosmetic surgery.   ....   B   Joan doesn't look very old.   ....
5   Helen would have found a husband years ago if she wanted to get married.
    A   Helen wants to get married.   ....   B   Helen has found a husband.   ....

2 **GRAMMAR IN USE** Read the conversations and choose the correct words in *italics*.
🔊 **3.47** Listen and check.

0   A   I hear you lost that new laptop computer you'd bought.
    B   Yes, it was stolen. I feel really stupid now – I'd still have the computer and all my work on it if I *(hadn't left)* / *didn't leave* the bathroom window open.
1   A   Mum, can I play with my Xbox?
    B   Yes, go on. What *would you do* / *would you have done* in the evenings if they hadn't invented the Xbox?
2   A   Why are you here? I thought Jenny said that you'd cancelled the meeting?
    B   Well, no. If I *cancelled* / *had cancelled* the meeting, I wouldn't be here now, would I?
3   A   We've just bought a flatscreen TV.
    B   But you've already got one.
    A   No, if we already had one, we *wouldn't buy* / *wouldn't have bought* one, would we?
4   A   Gary said that his brother was very lazy.
    B   Neil, lazy? No, if that was true, I *didn't marry* / *wouldn't have married* him all those years ago!
5   A   Do you have any regrets about getting married when you were very young?
    B   Of course not! If we *didn't get married* / *hadn't got married* when we were young, we *couldn't enjoy* / *wouldn't have enjoyed* all our grandchildren and great-grandchildren now.

3 Write conditional sentences, using the words in brackets. Use *could* or *might* if possible.
🔊 **3.48** Listen and check.

0   There might have been more wars in recent years if (the United Nations / exist).
    There might have been more wars in recent years if the United Nations didn't exist.
1   If von Ohain and Whittle hadn't invented the jet engine we (have / mass air travel / today).
    ....
2   We wouldn't all use Windows today if (Bill Gates / start / Microsoft).
    ....
3   If there were still a lot of racial problems in the US, (they / elect / Barack Obama).
    ....
4   Fewer African people would have died if (we / have / a cure for malaria).
    ....
5   If Tim Berners-Lee hadn't created the World Wide Web, (the world / be / very different).
    ....

⏻ Go online for more practice

58 I wish, if only, it's time …

1 wish and if only + past simple/would

We use *wish* + past simple to talk about present situations, when we are unhappy with the situation:
*I **wish** we **were** still on holiday.* (We aren't on holiday now.)
*We **wish** we **didn't live** so far away.* (We live too far away to see our friends.)
*I **wish** we **had** a new car.* (Our car keeps breaking down.)

If only means the same but it can have a little more emphasis:
***If only** I **didn't get** angry so easily!* (= I get angry easily, but I don't like it.)

⚠ We don't use *wish* or *if only* with a present tense:
✗ *I wish I have a better job.* ✓ *I **wish** I **had** a better job.*

⚠ To express a wish about the future, we use *hope* + present tense verb, not *wish*:
✗ *I wish you have a good holiday.* ✓ *I **hope** you **have** a good holiday.*

We can use *wish/if only* + *would (not)* to talk about a habit in someone else that we would like to change:
***If only** Jenny **would talk** about her problems.* *I **wish** you **wouldn't bite** your nails!*

2 wish and if only + past perfect

We use *wish/if only* + past perfect to talk about a past situation or action that we regret:
*I've failed my exams. I **wish** I'**d studied** harder.*
***If only** I **hadn't left** all my jewellery here. I left it in the drawer and it's been stolen.*
*I'm really tired. I **wish** I'**d gone** to bed earlier.*

⚠ We don't use *wish/if only* with the past simple if we want to talk about the past:
✗ *If only I didn't shout at my boss last week.* ✓ ***If only** I **hadn't shouted** at my boss last week.*

3 it's time and would rather

We use the past tense after *it's time* and *would rather* when we are talking about the present.
- *it's (about) time* means we think that someone should do something:
  *Come on – **it's time** we **went** home. **It's about time** you **got on** the plane.*
- *it's high time* + a past simple verb is stronger and suggests that the action is urgent:
  ***It's high time** you **started** looking for a flat of your own! You can't stay here for ever.*
- We can also use the infinitive with *to* (with or without *for* + object pronoun):
  *Come on – **it's time** (for us) **to go** home. **It's about time** (for you) **to get on** the plane.*

We use *would rather* to say what we prefer:
*I'**d rather** we **stayed** at home.* (= I'd prefer to stay …)
*We'**d rather** we **didn't go** by plane.* (= We'd prefer not to go …)
***Would** you **rather** I **paid** you now or later?* (= Would you prefer me to pay you now or later?)

170

Practice

1 **GRAMMAR IN USE** Read the letter from a man in prison to his wife. Choose the correct underlined words. 🔊 3.49 Listen and check.

> My dearest Monique
> I can't begin to tell you how much I miss you. If only I (0) *didn't listen* / *(hadn't listened)* to Tommy Evans all those months ago when he said he wanted a driver to take him to the airport. Obviously, I wish the police (1) *didn't catch* / *hadn't caught* us at the warehouse, but I wish even more that I (2) *didn't believe* / *hadn't believed* his story.
> Well, I'm here now, and I suppose I'm lucky that it's only for two years. I just wish that I (3) *am* / *was* closer to home. If only you (4) *could visit* / *could have visited* me more often, then I'm sure life would be easier.
> Things aren't too bad here, really. I can work during the day and the evenings are OK, but the nights are awful – I really wish the other prisoners (5) *would make* / *wouldn't make* so much noise at night, and I wish I (6) *can* / *could* get some more sleep.
> Well, I'd better go. It's time (7) *I join* / *to join* the others for 'evening activities'. I do enjoy getting letters from you and I wish you (8) *would write* / *write* to me more often. I (9) *wish* / *hope* that I'll see you soon, but I'd rather (10) *you don't bring* / *you didn't bring* the children – I don't want them to see me here.

2 Complete the sentences with *would* / *wouldn't* and a verb from the box. 🔊 3.50 Listen and check.

| close   (not) leave   (not) make   (not) play   turn off   ~~wash up~~ |

0 I wish you *would wash up* after you've eaten.
1 I wish you .... your clothes in the living room.
2 I wish you .... phone calls late at night.
3 I wish you .... the fridge door.
4 I wish you .... music really loudly.
5 I wish you .... the TV and talk to me!

3 Find and correct the mistakes in each sentence.
0 I wish I ~~didn't turn down~~ *hadn't turned down* that job offer last week.
1 We'd rather you don't bring your children with you.
2 If only we have enough money for a new kitchen.
3 We wish you get good news from your son next week.
4 Would you rather went to the mountains this year?
5 I wish you won't criticise me in front of your friends.
6 Isn't it time the gas bill to come?

4 Complete the sentences so they are true for you.
0 I wish my parents *wouldn't treat me like a child*.
1 I wish my best friend ....
2 If only I hadn't bought ....!
3 I'd rather people didn't ....
4 I wish I could ....

Review MODULE 10

1 UNITS 54 AND 55 Choose the correct words in *italics*.

0 The director wouldn't call a special meeting *if /(unless)* it were really necessary.
1 People are always friendlier when the sun *is / was* shining.
2 It may be a good idea to take extra money *even if / in case* the museum isn't free.
3 If I were prime minister, I *will / would* increase taxes immediately.
4 Arsenal are doing well – they *will / would* win the group stage if they *don't / didn't* lose their next match.
5 *Suppose / When* Abba played together again, *do / would* you go to see them?
6 We will get to the airport in time *if / unless* there isn't much traffic on the motorway.
7 Provided this illness *has / doesn't have* time to develop, it is very easy to treat.
8 I know it's unlikely, but *will / would* you accept the job if they *offer / offered* it to you?

2 UNITS 56 AND 57 Rewrite the sentences, using past or mixed conditionals.

0 Tina owned a clothes shop but her business was in trouble, so she went to the bank. A man ran out of the bank and knocked her over, so she injured her shoulder.
   If Tina *hadn't gone to the bank*, she wouldn't *have been injured*.
1 The bank manager called a doctor. The doctor decided she should go to hospital.
   If the bank manager ...., Tina wouldn't ....
2 While Tina was waiting at the hospital, she met an old schoolfriend.
   If Tina ...., she ....
3 They had to wait for a long time so Tina told her friend about her business.
   If ....
4 Tina's friend had just received a lot of money and she invested in Tina's business.
   If Tina's friend ....
5 So, because Tina hurt her shoulder, she met her old friend, and Tina's business is now profitable. Tina's business might not ....

3 UNITS 57 AND 58 Look at the list and complete the past regrets and present wishes of a lonely person who lives in an old person's home.

Regrets
0 I never married and now I'm really lonely.
1 I didn't have any children and now I'm in an old people's home.
2 I didn't study when I was younger.
3 I lived a selfish life.

Wishes
00 I'd like to have more money.
4 I'd prefer to live in my own home.
5 I'd like the people here to be friendlier to me.
6 I don't like being old!

0 If I *had married, I wouldn't be so lonely now*.
1 If I ....
2 I wish I ....
3 If only I ....
00 I wish I *had more money* ....
4 I'd rather ....
5 I wish the people ....
6 If only I ....!

4 ALL UNITS Complete the article with one word (or a short form) in each gap.

End of the road for canoe couple

'Canoe couple' John and Anne Darwin are now both in prison, as the court decided they were both guilty of trying to cheat money out of an insurance company. John Darwin went canoeing in March 2002 and 'disappeared' – the canoe was found some weeks later, but there was no sign of John. In fact, he had already left the country. Some months later, Anne was able to claim £250,000 from their insurance. The couple had been in financial difficulties, and (0) _might_ not have committed the crime if things had (1) .... been so bad, a spokesman said.

Anne Darwin moved to Panama in 2007, to be with her 'dead' husband, but in December 2007 John Darwin came back to Britain and gave himself up – if he hadn't done this, they (2) .... still be free and living in Panama. Until this time, both their sons believed their father was dead. The couple now (3) .... they hadn't lied to their sons, and John Darwin (4) .... that one day they will forgive him. His wife Anne now says that she (5) .... he really (6) .... drowned that day.

John Darwin admitted his guilt and received a prison sentence of six years and three months, and his wife, who refused to admit guilt, received six years and six months – she would certainly (7) .... got a shorter sentence if she had admitted her part in the story. The court might have (8) .... more sympathetic (9) .... the couple hadn't lied to their sons. If the couple behave themselves in prison, they (10) .... be released in about four years. Whether they will be able to rebuild their lives is another story.

5 ALL UNITS Complete the second sentence so it means the same as the first, using the word in brackets. Use two to five words in your answer.

0 I can't come to the meeting because I'm ill. (would)
   If I _wasn't ill, I would_ come to the meeting.

1 You can go out tonight, but you must come back by 10.30. (as)
   You can go out tonight .... back by 10.30.

2 You should go to the doctor about your bad back. (were)
   If ...., I'd go to the doctor about your bad back.

3 I thought they'd have arrived by now. (time)
   It's about ....

4 I don't like the fact that you smoke in the house. (wish)
   I .... in the house.

5 That job involves moving to Berlin, but I don't think I'll get it. (move)
   I .... to Berlin if I got that job.

6 You didn't get the job because you're so lazy! (have)
   If you weren't so lazy, you .... the job.

7 Which sport would you play if you were really athletic? (suppose)
   .... really athletic, which sport would you play?

8 I have short legs and I hate it! (only)
   If .... short legs!

173

Test MODULE 10

Conditionals

Choose the correct answer, A, B or C.

1 I don't know what's wrong with this computer. If I press F1, it always .... down.
A close   B closes   C will close ➤ Unit 54

2 .... Mr Grainger arrives while I'm at lunch, please ask him to wait in my office.
A When   B Unless   C If ➤ Unit 54

3 If it's raining when you arrive, ... to the station and pick you up.
A I come   B I'll come   C you come ➤ Unit 54

4 I won't accept the job .... they offer me more money than I'm earning now.
A unless   B if   C when ➤ Unit 54

5 The manager won't give Kevin his job back, ... he gets on his knees and begs!
A as long as   B in case   C even if ➤ Unit 54

6 He would certainly buy a better car if he .... enough money.
A had   B would have   C didn't have ➤ Unit 55

7 Imagine you .... have a superpower, which one would you choose?
A could   B would   C can ➤ Unit 55

8 If I .... Geraldine, I'd definitely tell her son to leave home.
A am   B would be   C were ➤ Unit 55

9 Where would you go if you .... a holiday next year?
A had   B have   C will have ➤ Unit 55

10 The government .... lost the election if they hadn't put taxes up.
A won't have   B hadn't   C wouldn't have ➤ Unit 56

11 If you .... this question correctly, you would have passed the exam.
A answered   B had answered   C answer ➤ Unit 56

12 I'm not sure, but Heide .... here for the summer if we'd invited her.
A will have come   B would have come   C might have come ➤ Unit 56

13 If you .... at your boss that day, you'd probably still have the job now!
A hadn't shouted   B didn't shout   C don't shout ➤ Unit 57

14 Anne would have made more friends in the village if she .... so shy.
A isn't   B wasn't   C wouldn't be ➤ Unit 57

15 We .... in Greece now if the travel company hadn't gone out of business.
A would be   B were   C will be ➤ Unit 57

16 I'd really like to talk to Jim again. If only I .... his phone number!
A know   B knew   C didn't know ➤ Unit 58

17 I'm worried about Robert – I wish he .... us where he goes in the evenings.
A tell   B will tell   C would tell ➤ Unit 58

18 I'm sorry we offended you. We wish we .... such awful things.
A hadn't said   B didn't say   C had said ➤ Unit 58

19 Come on. It's time .... the plane now.
A get on   B we get on   C to get on ➤ Unit 58

20 We don't like those friends you hang around with. We'd rather .... with them again.
A you didn't go out   B you don't go out   C you not go out ➤ Unit 58

Go online for a full exit test

Word order and sentence patterns

MODULE 11

Before you start

1 Read the conversation. Look at the highlighted grammar examples.

TESS Hi, Phil. What's that you're reading?

PHIL Hi. It's *Time Magazine* – it's a really interesting article about the Burj Khalifa – a building in Dubai. I'll show you a photo of it. Amazing, isn't it?

TESS Wow! How tall is it?

PHIL It's over 800 metres tall, and it's now the tallest building in the world. There are more than 160 floors in it. It makes me dizzy just to look at it!

ANDY I've heard of it. Who designed it?

PHIL I think it was designed by an American architect.

TESS What's it for? Offices, maybe?

PHIL Well, it's got offices, apartments, a hotel, a restaurant … everything.

TESS It's so tall – I can't imagine the feeling at the top. Have you ever been to the top of a really tall building, Andy?

ANDY Yes, I have. I've been to the top of the Sears Tower in Chicago, but that's only 450 metres tall.

TESS What's it like?

ANDY Well, it's difficult to describe. You can feel it moving in the wind.

TESS It sounds exciting!

2 Now read the sentences and choose the correct words in *italics*. The highlighted grammar examples will help you.

1. Marianne and Jim showed *to us / us* their holiday photos. ► Unit 59
2. Don't talk to your father like that! It makes him *angry / to feel angry*. ► Unit 59
3. 'Is the class full?' 'Well, there *is/are* already twenty students on the register.' ► Unit 60
4. It was difficult *find / to find* anything in the sales. The shops were crowded. ► Unit 60
5. It's really sunny. *Have you put / You have put* the washing out? ► Unit 61
6. 'Has Jeremy started playing in the band yet?' 'Yes, *he's / he has*.' ► Unit 61
7. I've got a spare cup of coffee. Who *is it for / for is it*? ► Unit 62
8. Who *phoned / did phone* you at six this morning? ► Unit 62
9. The mountain we climbed was *1,000 metres high / high 1,000 metres*. ► Unit 63
10. I hear you've just been on a Caribbean cruise. What *did it like / was it like*? ► Unit 63

3 Check your answers below. Then go to the unit for more information and practice.

1 us 2 angry 3 are 4 to find 5 Have you put 6 he has 7 is it for 8 phoned 9 1,000 metres high 10 was it like

Go online for a full diagnostic test

59 Word order in statements

This is the Guggenheim Museum, Bilbao. It is an art gallery in the north of Spain. It contains an important collection of European and American paintings. Designed by architect Frank Gehry, the museum has made people interested in the industrial city of Bilbao, and a lot of tourists visit it now.

1 Subject + verb + object/complement

Word order is important in English because it helps us understand the meaning of a sentence. The basic order in statements is *subject + verb + object*. The subject and object are usually pronouns or noun phrases, and the object is a different thing/person from the subject:

SUBJECT	VERB	OBJECT
The gallery	contains	an important collection of paintings.

 We almost always need a subject before the verb: ✗ *Is building a new kitchen on his house.* ✗ *Is building a new kitchen in his house Ollie.* ✓ **Ollie** *is building a new kitchen in his house.*

- **Transitive verbs** (e.g. *contain, build, visit, take, like, leave, describe, say*) almost always need an object; but with some transitive verbs, we can leave out the object if the meaning is clear:
  'Where are the girls?' '*They've just left.*' (just left, e.g. the house/the room)
  Don't talk to Errol now – he's writing. (writing, e.g. a letter/an essay)
- **Intransitive verbs** (e.g. *come, go, arrive, fall, wait, land, happen, laugh, rain, swim*) do not usually have an object:
  Something **has happened.** *They* **weren't laughing.**
- Some verbs have a **complement**, not an object. The complement tells us something about the subject. Verbs like *be, become, seem, appear, remain, look, smell, taste* can have adjective complements:
  Fiona **remained unhappy** *about her exam results for weeks.*
  That cake **smells strange** *– have you burnt it?*
  After *be* and *become* the complement can also be a noun or noun phrase:
  The Tate Modern **is an art gallery**. *Joseph* **became a shop assistant** *when he left school.*

Word order in questions ➤ Units 61.1 and 62

2 Subject + verb + object + complement

Some verbs (e.g. *make, call, consider*) can be followed by an object AND a complement. The object is usually a person and the complement is usually an adjective:

SUBJECT	VERB	OBJECT	COMPLEMENT
The museum	has made	people	interested (in Bilbao).
The teacher	called	me	stupid.
We all	considered	her behaviour	really rude.

3 Subject + verb + (object / complement) + adverbial

An **adverbial** can be a one-word adverb or a phrase that often starts with a preposition. Adverbials answer questions such as *How? When?* and *Where?* They usually come after the verb (or after the object or complement if there is one):
The guests arrived **yesterday**. *The Guggenheim Museum is an art gallery* **in the north of Spain**.

4 Subject + verb + *that* clause

A lot of verbs expressing thoughts and speech (e.g. *think, believe, say, complain, know, promise*) are followed by *that* + a clause:

SUBJECT	VERB	*that* CLAUSE
He	believes	that children should be more polite.
I	complained	that my soup was cold.
The staff in the company	didn't know	that their jobs were in danger.

Verbs followed by *wh-* word + clause ➤ Unit 77.1
Verbs followed by another verb ➤ Module 12

5 Subject + verb + object + object

Some verbs can have an indirect object (usually a person) as well as a direct object (usually a thing):

SUBJECT	VERB	INDIRECT OBJECT (person)	DIRECT OBJECT (thing)
Jonathan	bought	his wife/her	a gold ring.
Panasonic	didn't offer	Chris/him	the job.
The local baker	made	Andy and me/us	a wedding cake.

 We use the word order above with a few common verbs (e.g. *ask, bring, buy, find, give, lend, make, offer, pay, promise, read, send, show, teach, tell, throw* and *write*). But with most verbs it is incorrect:
✗ ~~Judith described her visitors the house.~~   ✓ Judith described the house to her visitors.

If we put the indirect object second, we need to use a preposition, usually *to* or *for*:

SUBJECT	VERB	DIRECT OBJECT	PREPOSITION + INDIRECT OBJECT
Jonathan	bought	a gold ring	**for** his wife. / **for** her.
Panasonic	didn't offer	the job	**to** Chris. / **to** him.
The local baker	made	a wedding cake	**for** Andy and me. / **for** us.

When we give something to someone, we use *to*; when we do something for someone, we use *for*:
I'm just sending an email **to** my brother. I won't be long.
Can you find an interesting recipe **for** me?
This pattern is less common than *I'm sending my brother an email./Can you find me ...*, etc.

 We don't use a preposition before the indirect object when it comes first:
✗ ~~Jonathan bought for his wife a gold ring.~~   ✓ Jonathan bought **his wife** a gold ring.
✗ ~~Jonathan bought for her a gold ring.~~   ✓ Jonathan bought **her** a gold ring.

6 Adverbials and word order

Adverbials usually come at the end of the sentence:
The National Gallery is **in the centre of London**. There was no snow **last winter**.

We usually put adverbials in this order if there is more than one in a statement:

	MANNER (*how*)	PLACE (*where*)	TIME (*when*)
Let's have breakfast		in the Italian coffee bar	before the class tomorrow.
The next train will arrive		at platform 2	in five minutes.
Roger Federer didn't play	very well	at the French Open	last year.

If we want to emphasise an adverbial of time or place, we can put it at the beginning of the sentence:
Last year, Roger Federer didn't play very well. (But this year, unlike last year, he played well.)

More on adverbs and word order ➤ Unit 24

59 WORD ORDER IN STATEMENTS

Practice

1 Complete the sentences with the phrases from the box. Two sentences only need a full stop (.) – they are complete.

0 We went to the cinema last night and saw _a fantastic film._
1 We were so thirsty that we drank ....
2 Is everything OK? You don't seem ....
3 After Julie finished her course, she became ....
4 Quick! The train is leaving ....
5 It was a great holiday, but we spent ....
6 Tell me when the new guests arrive ....
7 The course was interesting, but I didn't read ....
8 What have you been doing? You look ....

> all the books
> a fantastic film
> a litre of water
> a nurse
> really tired
> too much money
> very happy

2 Show the best place in each sentence for the words in brackets.
🔊 **3.51** Listen and check.

0 Temperatures reached 38 degrees / last year. — (on the south coast)
1 The coach will meet us outside the school gates. — (at 8.30 in the morning)
2 Everyone in the train compartment was reading. — (a book or magazine)
3 Our friends didn't wait after the concert. — (for us)
4 Fabio called his friend. — (stupid)
5 The new doctor arrived yesterday. — (at the hospital)
6 The local council promised lower business taxes. — (the shopkeepers)
7 Ugh, your trainers smell. — (awful)
8 The children were playing in the back garden earlier. — (quite happily)

3 **GRAMMAR IN USE** Read the conversation and choose the correct words in *italics*.
🔊 **3.52** Listen and check.

RICK How's the band going?
CARL It isn't. I've left.
RICK Oh, I thought (0) *(that you were)* / *you were that* really enjoying it!
CARL I had (1) *at first a great time* / *a great time at first*. Everyone in the band (2) *appeared really friendly* / *really friendly appeared* and ambitious too, which I really liked.
RICK I know you were hoping it would work out. What happened?
CARL Well, we played (3) *last Friday at Conway's* / *at Conway's last Friday*, and …
RICK Conway's – that's great, it's really well-known.
CARL I know, and it was good – we played (4) *really well for over an hour* / *for over an hour really well*, and the audience (5) *really happy seemed* / *seemed really happy*.
RICK Go on.
CARL Then, at the end of the evening, Mr Conway himself offered (6) *to us* / *us* a regular Friday night job there.
RICK Fantastic!
CARL But the others turned it down – they didn't want to commit themselves to every Friday evening. They made (7) *me really angry* / *really angry me*! So next time we practised, I gave (8) *them a choice* / *a choice them* – either take the job at Conway's or I'd leave.
RICK And they told you that you could leave.
CARL Exactly. So I left. Stupid, isn't it?

4 Write the words in the usual order to make statements.

0 last term   head teacher of the local secondary school   became   Jeremy
Jeremy became head teacher of the local secondary school last term.

1 has had   the exhibition   a lot of interest
....

2 that   promised   he would call me   Errol
....

3 these days   Irina   quite sad   seems
....

4 their birthday presents   gave   the twins   Jan
....

5 at   was laughing   the clown   everyone
....

6 your father   has made   really angry   your terrible behaviour
....

7 to the insurance company   my lawyer   all the documents   sent
....

8 at the debate   Marco   his arguments   on Thursday   quite well   presented
....

5 GRAMMAR IN USE Read the text about Frank Gehry and find six more places where you can improve the word order.

Frank Gehry

Frank Gehry is one of the most famous architects in the world. He was born ~~in 1929 in Toronto~~ *in Toronto in 1929* but moved in 1947 to Los Angeles. He an architect became after studying architecture in California and design at Harvard, and his career has lasted over forty years. His designs have always been really large and very expensive to build. Some were so costly, such as the Walt Disney Concert Hall in Los Angeles, that many people considered 'unbuildable' them. His career really took off when the Guggenheim Museum was built in Bilbao in 1997, changing an old unused waterfront into an area that both modern and romantic looked. Gehry completed the Walt Disney Concert Hall in 2003 and it is now the home of the Los Angeles Philharmonic Orchestra. These two buildings, and others, have earned some important architectural awards him. One of Gehry's most recent projects is the Serpentine Gallery in London – this was in England his first project.

60 *there* and *it*

There's an interesting skyscraper in London. **It's** called the Swiss Re building. If you're in the City of London, **it's easy to see** this building as it is much higher than most of the others around it.

1 *there* + *be*

We use *there is/there are* to say that something happens or something exists, often when we talk about it for the first time:
There's *an interesting skyscraper in London.*
There are *several good restaurants near where we live.*

We can use *there* + a form of *be* in most tenses and forms:
There used to be *a post office here.* **There aren't going to be** *any more classes this week.*
There might be *an extra class for beginners next week.* **Is there** *a good film on TV tonight?*

⚠ We use *there* + *is*, not *there* + *are*, with a list that starts with a singular noun:
✗ ~~There are a pen, a ruler and some pencils on each desk.~~
✓ **There's** *a pen, a ruler and some pencils on each desk.*

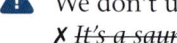 **Pronunciation** ➤ 1.28

2 *there* and *it*

There introduces new information; but we use *it* to say more about the information:
There's *a new cinema in town.* **It's** *got six screens.*

⚠ We don't use *it* to say something exists:
✗ ~~It's a sauna and a small gym at the hotel.~~   ✓ **There's** *a sauna and a small gym at the hotel.*

3 *it* as a subject

We use *it* as a subject in expressions for
- time: *What time is* **it**? **It's** *ten o'clock.*
  (+ *take*): *How long* **did it take** *to get here?* **It** only **took** *a few minutes.*
- days and dates: *What day is* **it**? **It's** *14th October.* **It's** *my birthday.*
- distances: **It's** *only 25 kilometres to Bordeaux.* **It** *isn't a very long way.*
- weather + verb: **It's** *snowing.* **It's** *really hot here.* **It** *rained all week.*
  BUT + noun: ✗ ~~It was a lot of rain on holiday.~~
  ✓ **There was** *a lot of* **rain** *on holiday.*
- identifying people: *Hi,* **it's** *Ginny here.* **It's** *Malcolm at the door.*
- descriptions: **It's** *boring here.* **It** *was a difficult time in my life.*

⚠ Although *it* has no real meaning in these sentences, we can't leave it out:
✗ ~~Is my birthday.~~   ✗ ~~Is raining.~~

4 *it* + *be* + adjective/noun + infinitive with *to*

We can use this pattern to describe how we feel about a situation:

It + be	ADJECTIVE	NOUN	INFINITIVE with *to*
It's It wasn't It will/would be It might be	nice possible difficult interesting		to see you. to get tickets for Saturday. to find a new secretary. to invite Joachim to give a talk.
It's It wasn't It has been		a pity a mistake a pleasure	to leave before the film ends. to change my course. to meet your family.

11

Practice

1 Complete the sentences with *There is*, *There are*, *It's*, or *It was*.

0 We'll have to open a new class. _There are_ too many students in this one.
1 .... an oven, a microwave and a fridge-freezer in the new apartment.
2 I hated being a teenager. .... the most embarrassing time of my life!
3 .... a mistake to think your boss won't notice if you don't go.
4 .... someone at the door for you. .... a young woman.
5 .... snowing again today. .... always snow here in January.
6 .... so many people here. .... wonderful to be so popular!

2 **GRAMMAR IN USE** Choose the correct words in *italics*.
🔊 3.53 Listen and check.

CRAIG Hi. Have you just come back from Croatia?
SONIA Yes, a place called Korcula. (0) *Is* / *It's* quite near Dubrovnik. (1) *It* / *There* was lovely there.
CRAIG How long (2) *did take* / *did it take* to fly there?
SONIA Not long – less than three hours.
CRAIG (3) *Was it* / *Was* useful for your architecture course?
SONIA Oh, yes. (4) *It's* / *There's* a fantastic old part of Korcula town that we visited. And (5) *there's* / *it's* on an island, with no cars.
CRAIG Oh?
SONIA Yes. (6) *There* / *It's* very hilly and (7) *are* / *there are* steps in most of the streets. The walls around the Old Town have got several towers – they're fascinating.
CRAIG A walled city – lovely. Did you visit any of the towers?
SONIA Yes, some of them. (8) *It was* / *There were* twelve originally, but there aren't so many now. There (9) *is* / *are* also some fantastic old buildings, like the Armeri Palace.
CRAIG (10) *Were there* / *Were* any beaches on the island?
SONIA Oh yes, it would be a pity (11) *going* / *to go* to the Mediterranean and not visit any beaches! We stayed at a beach resort. It had everything – there (12) *was* / *were* a beach, a hotel and some very good restaurants.
CRAIG Did you have good weather?
SONIA Mostly. (13) *There* / *It* was rain the day we arrived, but then (14) *was* / *it was* warm and sunny for the rest of the week.

3 Complete the second sentence so it means the same as the first, using the word in brackets. Use two to five words in your answer. 🔊 3.54 Listen and check.

0 Can I possibly start the course two weeks late? (possible)
Will _it be possible_ for me to start the course two weeks late?
1 We found a box of matches, some petrol and old clothes in the garage. (there)
.... a box of matches, some petrol and old clothes in the garage.
2 Was there a lot of rain while you were in Sri Lanka? (it)
.... much while you were in Sri Lanka?
3 We didn't have any difficulty in completing the deal in the end. (difficult)
In the end, it .... the deal.
4 Did you see anyone interesting at Veronica's party? (was)
.... anyone interesting at Veronica's party?
5 Finding the right person for this job won't be easy. (to)
It .... find the right person for this job.

⏻ Go online for more practice

61 Yes/No questions

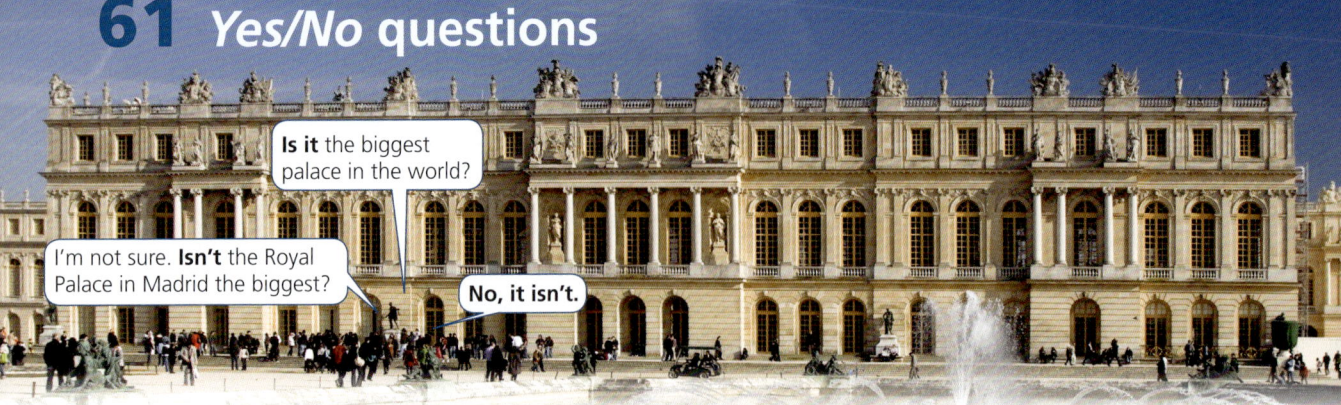

Is it the biggest palace in the world?

*I'm not sure. **Isn't** the Royal Palace in Madrid the biggest?*

No, it isn't.

1 Yes/No questions

Yes/No questions ask if something is true or not: *Is it the biggest palace in the world?*
- If a statement contains *be*, an auxiliary verb or a modal verb, this moves in front of the subject in questions:
  The water **is** from a bottle. → **Is** the water from a bottle?
  The builders **were** working here all day. → **Were** the builders working here all day?
- In present simple and past simple statements, there isn't an auxiliary verb, so we use *do/does/did*:
  My mother **worked** when I was at school. → **Did** your mother **work** when you were at school?

VERB TYPE		SUBJECT	VERB	COMPLEMENT/OBJECT
main verb *be*:	Is Was	the water the meal		from a bottle? enjoyable?
auxiliary verbs, e.g.	Is Have Did	the examiner you your mother	coming bought work	to the school? some fruit? when you were at school?
modal verbs, e.g.	Will Should	you the letters	clean be sent	your room this weekend? out today?

We usually say *yes/no* questions with a rising tone (↗): *Was the meal enjoyable?*

 Pronunciation ▶ 1.29

2 Short answers

We can answer *yes/no* questions with a short answer. The short answer uses *be*, an auxiliary verb or a modal verb:
'Is that an interesting book?' 'Yes, it **is**.'
'Have you bought some fruit?' No, I **haven't**. I forgot.
'Should I enter the competition?' 'Yes, you **should**.'
'Does Ella speak any foreign languages?' 'No, she **doesn't**.'

 We don't use short forms in positive short answers:
'Is it raining?' ✗ *Yes, it's.* ✓ 'Yes, **it is**.'

We usually use only the first auxiliary or modal verb in short answers, not the main verb:
'Have you bought some fruit?' ✗ *Yes, I have bought.* ✓ 'Yes, I **have**.'
'Should the letters be sent out today?' ✗ *Yes, they should be sent.* ✓ 'Yes, they **should**.'

3 Negative questions

We can make negative *yes/no* questions to check information or ask for agreement:
Isn't the Royal Palace in Madrid the biggest? '**Wasn't** the traffic awful?' 'Yes, it was.'
We can also use a negative question when we are surprised:
Didn't you know that? I thought everyone knew.

Note the answers to a negative question:
Didn't you know? Yes. (= I knew.) No. (= I didn't know.)

11

Practice

1 Match the questions 1–4 with the short answers A–J. There are two short answers for each question.

0 Does the park stay open in the winter? *B, G*
1 Did the flight arrive on time? ....
2 Hasn't the DVD recorded that show? ....
3 Will her book be published this year? ....
4 Should the form be sent back to this address? ....

A Yes, it has.
B ~~No, it doesn't.~~
C No, it hasn't.
D No, it won't.
E Yes, it should.
F Yes, it did.
G ~~Yes, it does.~~
H Yes, it will.
I No, it shouldn't.
J No, it didn't.

2 Read the information about Edinburgh Castle and write *yes/no* questions about it, using the words in brackets. Then write short answers. 3.55 Listen and check.

Edinburgh Castle – quick facts

- on an extinct volcano above the city of Edinburgh
- built by King David I in 1130
- James I of England was born in the castle
- more than 1.25 million visitors a year
- fantastic views over Edinburgh
- the ticket price includes a guided tour

0 (be / in / city)   *Is the castle in the city of Edinburgh? Yes, it is.*
1 (built / long time ago) ....
2 (James I / born) ....
3 (get / lot of visitors) ....
4 (can / see the city) ....
5 (the ticket price / include) ....

3 **GRAMMAR IN USE** Find six more mistakes in the conversation and correct them. 3.56 Listen and check.

JACK ~~Are going you~~ *Are you going* to join any clubs or societies at university this year, Vijay?

VIJAY Yes, I'm. I'm interested in joining the photography society. Why, you aren't going to join any?

JACK I'm not sure. Isn't the final year more difficult than the others?

VIJAY No, it is. At least, people say it is. They are having a 'club fair' to introduce all the clubs and societies this year?

JACK No, they not. All the information is online, and we can ask questions by email.

VIJAY That's a shame.

JACK Why? You not think it's a good idea? We can find out about the societies when we want.

VIJAY I suppose so, but I prefer to discuss things face to face.

Go online for more practice

62 Wh- questions

Q **When** was the Taj Mahal built?
A In the seventeenth century.
Q **Who** built it?
A Shah Jehan.
Q **Why** did he build it?
A To remember his wife after she died.

1 Wh- questions and question words

Wh- questions ask for information. They always start with a wh- word:

Wh- WORD	EXAMPLE
who, what	**Who** can you talk to about your course? **What** do you want to ask?
when, how	**When** did your visitors arrive? **How** did they get here?
where, why	**Where** have you been? **Why** did you leave so suddenly?
whose, which	**Whose** book are you using? **Which** chapter are you on?

⚠ We need to use *be*, an auxiliary verb or a modal verb in most wh- questions:
✗ ~~Where you living?~~ ✓ Where **are** you living? ✗ ~~How you get here?~~ ✓ How **did** you get here?
- With *what*, *whose* and *which* we can have a noun before the verb:
  What time is it? **Whose class** are you in? **Which subjects** are you taking this year?
- We can also make negative questions:
  What didn't you understand? **Why didn't** you say something?

⚠ We usually say wh- questions with a falling intonation (): Where have you been?

🔊 **Pronunciation** ➤ 1.30

2 Subject and object questions

In most wh- questions the wh- word is the OBJECT of the verb; we use the question word order:

object	auxiliary	subject	verb	(answer)
What	did	Shah Jehan	build ?	(the Taj Mahal)

Who, *what*, *which* and *whose* can be the SUBJECT of the verb; we use statement word order:

subject	verb	object	(answer)
Who	built	the Taj Mahal ?	(Shah Jehan)
What	ate	the strawberries ?	(the birds)
Whose car	hit	the gate ?	(Jack's)

Compare these subject and object questions:

Who invited Mary?   Jim invited Mary.   Who did Jim invite?   Jim invited Mary.

⚠ *Who* and *what* in subject questions take a singular verb:
✗ ~~Who live in this house?~~ ✓ Who **lives** in this house?
✗ ~~What happen after the interview?~~ ✓ What **happens** after the interview?

3 Wh- questions + prepositions

If we use a verb + preposition in a wh- question, we usually put the preposition at the end of the question:
Which hotel did they **stay at**? Who were you **living with** then?

With *when* and *where*, we don't usually use a preposition:
✗ ~~Where did they stay at?~~ ✓ Where did they stay?

11

Practice

1 Complete each question with one word only. 3.57 Listen and check.

0 _What_ is the name of the building in the photo?
1 .... was the castle built? Was it a long time ago?
2 .... idea was it to visit the castle?
3 .... built the castle – was it someone famous?
4 .... did they get all the bricks from?
5 .... long did it take to build it?
6 Who did the king build it ....? Was it one of his wives?
7 What .... do the castle gardens close?
8 Which .... do the guides speak?

2 Complete the questions about the article. You need to use both subject and object questions.

A disk containing details of government policies was stolen today in a dramatic car chase. The government car left the Home Office at 6.00 p.m., and a van immediately started to follow it. A high-speed chase ended when the government car crashed into a lamp-post. Two masked men jumped out of the van and grabbed the briefcase containing the disk before speeding off.

0 What _was stolen_ today? A disk containing details of government policies.
1 What time .... the Home Office? It left at 6.00 p.m.
2 What .... to follow it? A van.
3 When ....? It finished when the car crashed into a lamp-post.
4 Who .... out of the van? Two masked men.
5 What ....? They grabbed the briefcase containing the disk.

3 GRAMMAR IN USE Read the answers and write a suitable wh- question for each one. 3.58 Listen and check.

0 _What is the building in the photo?_
The building in the photo is the Statue of Liberty.
1 ....?
It is on Liberty Island, in New York Harbour.
2 ....?
Frédéric-Auguste Bartholdi, a French architect. He was commissioned by the French government to design it.
3 ....?
Because the French wanted to present a gift to the Americans, on the 100th anniversary of American independence.
4 ....?
It was finally opened ten years late – on 28 October 1886.

5 ....?
There are various things you can visit, apart from the Statue, such as a museum.
6 ....?
It is famous because it's one of the best-known images of the United States.

Go online for more practice

63 how, which/what, who and whose

*So you flew from Hong Kong International, **what's** it **like**?*

Fantastic – really modern. It's basically an artificial island in the sea.

*Wow! **How** did they build it?*

1 how

We usually use *how* to ask about the WAY something is done: **How** did they build it?

We use *how* + adjective/adverb when we expect the answer to be a number or a measurement of something:
'**How old** is the Taj Mahal?' 'It's 400 years old.' '**How long** is the film?' 'It's 90 minutes long.'
'**How often** are the classes?' 'Once a week.' '**How many** people work here?' 'About 200.'
'**How much** do the lessons cost?' 'They're £30 an hour.'

⚠ When the question contains the adjectives *tall, high, long, wide, deep*, we put the adjective in the answer. Notice the word order: **How tall** is Thomas now?
✗ ~~Thomas is tall 1.8 metres~~. ✓ Thomas is **1.8 metres tall**.

⚠ Notice the answer to a question asking about a person's age: ✗ ~~My daughter is seven years~~.
✓ My daughter is **seven**. / My daughter is **seven years old**.

We use *how* to ask about health, opinions and progress, often in set phrases:
'**How** are you?' 'Fine, thanks.'   '**How's** the hotel?' 'It's OK.'
'**How's** the new job going?' 'Well, thank you.'

2 which and what

Which and *what* both have similar meanings but *which* asks about one or more of a small number of things:

	small number	large number	+ noun	with people	with things
which	✓	✗	✓	✓	✓
what	✗	✓	✓	✗	✓

What's for dinner? **What** are they playing? **What sort** of shoes should I wear? **What time** is it?
Which airport did you fly from, Heathrow or Gatwick? **Which teacher** have you got for history?

- We do not need a noun if it is clear what we are asking about:
  'Our college offers language courses.' 'Really? **Which** do you teach?' (= which course)
- We use *what* + *do* to ask about a person's work:
  What do you **do**? **What did** your grandfather **do**?

⚠ We can use *what* + *be* + *like* (but not *how*) to ask for a description:
✗ ~~How is it like?~~ ✓ **What's** it **like**?
What was the exam **like**? ✗ ~~It was like easy!~~ ✓ It was easy!

Notice the difference between:
'**What's** she **like**?' 'She's young and attractive, and she's very clever.'
'**What does** she **like**?' 'She likes climbing – she goes every weekend.'

3 who and whose

We use *who* to ask about people, but we use *whose* (with or without a noun) to ask about relationships and possessions:
Who did you meet at the conference? **Who's** your favourite film star?
Whose daughter is she? **Whose newspaper** is this? **Whose** is that?

More on *whose* ➤ Unit 72.1

Practice

1 Complete the questions with *how* and an adjective or adverb if necessary. The answers will help you. 3.59 Listen and check.

0 '*How old* is your grandfather now?' 'He's nearly ninety.'
1 '.................. is the hotel from the beach?' 'It's about 500 metres.'
2 '.................. was your weekend at the health spa resort?' 'It was great, thanks.'
3 '.................. are the Belgian chocolates?' 'They're €25 a kilo.'
4 '.................. is your son now?' 'He's much better now, thank you.'
5 '.................. do you go to the theatre?' 'Only about twice a year.'
6 '.................. is your journey to work?' 'It takes about half an hour.'
7 '.................. is the swimming pool?' 'It's 1.8 metres at the deep end.'
8 '.................. bedrooms does the apartment have?' 'Three, but one is very small.'

2 Choose the correct words in *italics*.

0 It's an interesting house. (*Who*) / *Whose* does it belong to?
1 *Who's* / *Whose* the architect?
2 *What* / *Which* part of the house overlooks the pool?
3 What *does* / *is* it like inside?
4 *What* / *Which* does the owner do? Is he famous?
5 Oh, he manages a famous football team – *which* / *what* team does he manage?

3 GRAMMAR IN USE Complete the conversation with the words and phrases from the box. There are two extra words or phrases. 3.60 Listen and check.

| how long   how old   twenty-four   twenty-four old   what does |
| what   what's   which university   ~~who~~   who's   whose |

TOM (0) *Who* have you chosen as the new trainee?
ANNE It's a young woman – Sunita Patel.
KATE Oh, (1) .... she like?
ANNE Very intelligent with great ideas. I think she'll be good for us.
TOM (2) .... is she?
ANNE She's pretty young really – only (3) ....
TOM (4) .... did she study at?
ANNE Manchester.

TOM So (5) .... was she there?
ANNE I think it was six years – including her postgraduate studies.
KATE (6) .... did she do at postgraduate level?
ANNE Mainly industrial design.
KATE Good. (7) .... team will she be in?
ANNE Well, (8) .... got space for a new person at the moment? Tom, how about you?

4 Write questions, using the words below. Then write true answers.

0 how old / you?   *How old are you? I'm nineteen.*
1 what / phone number?   ....
2 how long / study English?   ....
3 how far / nearest cinema?   ....
4 what / like doing on holiday?   ....
5 whose songs (or music) / prefer?   ....

Review MODULE 11

1 UNITS 59 AND 60 Complete the conversation with words and phrases from the box. There are five extra words or phrases.

> at the school on Saturday evening   didn't take   gave me   gave to me
> ~~It was~~   It was   me so angry   on Saturday evening at the school   see
> There was   there were   took   to see   to you   were there   you

NICK Hi, Jan. How was your weekend?

JAN (0) *It was* great! I went to the school reunion.

NICK What school reunion?

JAN *Our* school reunion! Didn't you know about it? (1) **There was** an advert in the school magazine.

NICK Oh, I don't read that! How was it, anyway?

JAN Really good. It was lovely (2) **to see** everyone again.

NICK Did many people from our class go?

JAN Yes, (3) **there were** about twelve of our old classmates there.

NICK Where was it – and when?

JAN It was (4) **at the school on Saturday evening**.

NICK Did you go by train?

JAN No. (5) **It was** raining really heavily, so Stuart (6) **gave me** a lift. It (7) **didn't take** very long to get there – only about twenty minutes.

NICK And (8) **were there** any surprises?

JAN Well, yes. Just after we started eating, two people in really expensive clothes and jewellery came in. I didn't recognise them at first.

NICK And?

JAN But then I realised it was Leroy Watson and Shelley Miles – they're married now and they run their own business, obviously a very successful business!

NICK Leroy used to make (9) **me so angry** – he always thought he was better than the rest of us. Did you take any photos?

JAN Yes, I'll show them (10) **to you** at lunchtime.

2 UNITS 59 AND 60 Find six more mistakes and correct them. Tick (✓) the correct sentence.

0 When the speaker made a joke, the audience didn't laugh ^at^ it.
1 The protesters behaved at the demonstration really badly.
2 My grandfather showed to me his photos of the war.
3 Ella was with the architect's plans delighted.
4 Let's meet at the ticket office at nine in the morning.
5 There's someone on the phone for you. There's your mother, I think.
6 The children called Tibs their new cat.
7 There are a few useful things at the beach resort. It's a mini-market, a cash machine and several restaurants.

3 UNITS 61, 62 AND 63 Read the text and complete the questions for the answers below.

Chinese cave dwellers

For the next part of Dave Egerton's series on unusual communities, he visited China.

We arrived in Yan'an at 7.00 in the evening and night was already falling, but we were surprised that the area was quite light – the caves had electricity and bright lights! Mrs Yuang came to meet us and gave us tea and cakes in her living room. Mrs Yuang and her family live in one of the more modern caves, which has a living room, a kitchen and three bedrooms. The Yuang family lives in Shaanxi Province, China, where there are several million people living in caves, and most of them really like their cave homes. Most of the people there are farmers, and need to be near their work, so the caves are perfect. They are ecologically friendly because they're built directly in the ground, but they are also very comfortable because they protect the residents from both heat and cold. And we found out the next day that there are cave schools and shops there, too …

0 *What time did they arrive* in Yan'an?   They arrived at 7.00 in the evening.
1 .... surprised?   Because the area was quite light.
2 .... quite light?   Because they had electricity in the caves.
3 What ....?   She gave them tea and cakes.
4 .... her cave have?   It has three bedrooms.
5 .... the caves?   They are in Shaanxi Province.
6 .... in the caves?   Several million.
7 .... do there?   Most of them are farmers.
8 .... like?   They're very comfortable.
9 .... from?   From both heat and cold.
10 .... the next day?   That there are schools and shops there, too.

4 ALL UNITS Choose the correct answer, A or B.

0 Are the conference organisers going to discuss the arrangements with us?
   (A) Yes, they are.   B Yes, they're.
1 Who told you about our financial problems?
   A I told Christopher.   B Christopher told me.
2 What did you get for your birthday?
   A Well, Louis gave a new coat me.   B Well, Louis gave me a new coat.
3 Should we change some money here before we go to the States?
   A Yes, we should.   B Yes, we should change.
4 There was a phone call for you this morning.
   A Who was there?   B Who was it?
5 What's Michael's wife like?
   A She's very friendly.   B She enjoys opera a lot.
6 Have you set up a meeting with the people from Gallagher Brothers?
   A Yes, it's at their office on Monday morning.
   B Yes, it's on Monday morning at their office.

Test MODULE 11

Word order and sentence patterns

Choose the correct answer, A, B or C.

1. .... our friends at the pizzeria last night.
   A Met   B We met   C Met we   ▶ Unit 59

2. Have you had a hard week? You .... this evening.
   A seem tired   B tired seem   C seem to tired   ▶ Unit 59

3. The recent conflict has .... of the problems in the country.
   A made aware people   B made people aware   C people aware made   ▶ Unit 59

4. The manager promised .... a pay raise if we worked extra hours for a while.
   A at us all   B to us all   C us all   ▶ Unit 59

5. Can you throw ....? I'll get the things from the boot.
   A me the car keys   B the car keys me   C to me the car keys   ▶ Unit 59

6. Luciano was studying ....
   A really hard at the library yesterday   B at the library really hard yesterday
   C yesterday at the library really hard   ▶ Unit 59

7. The circus was pretty good. .... a clown, an acrobat and some jugglers.
   A There were   B There was   C It was   ▶ Unit 60

8. The ground here is very dry. .... hasn't rained much at all recently.
   A There   B It's   C It   ▶ Unit 60

9. I've heard a lot about you. It's a real pleasure .... you at last.
   A meet   B to meeting   C to meet   ▶ Unit 60

10. 'Has the film started yet?' 'Yes, ...
    A it did   B it's   C it has   ▶ Unit 61

11. 'Do you think we should take umbrellas with us tomorrow?' 'Yes, ...'
    A we should   B we take   C we should take   ▶ Unit 61

12. 'I wasn't able to give your note to the lecturer.' 'Why? .... to the lecture?'
    A Didn't you go   B Did you   C Did you go not   ▶ Unit 61

13. We haven't seen your son for ages. .... is he living now?
    A What   B Where   C Where place   ▶ Unit 62

14. I know Henry's got two brothers. .... married the soap opera star?
    A Which did   B What brother   C Which brother   ▶ Unit 62

15. 'I'm afraid I told someone about your wedding.' 'Oh dear. Who ....?'
    A you told   B did you tell   C told you   ▶ Unit 62

16. When you visited Stockholm, where did you ....?
    A stay   B stay at   C stay to   ▶ Unit 62

17. 'We're flying to London next weekend.' 'OK. Which airport will you ....?'
    A arrive   B arriving   C arrive at   ▶ Unit 62

18. 'How far is your new apartment from the sports centre?' 'Oh, only about ....'
    A 500 metres far   B 500 metres   C 500 metres sports centre   ▶ Unit 63

19. 'What was Dave's cousin from South Africa like?' '..........'.
    A She liked peanuts.   B She was like OK.   C She was OK.   ▶ Unit 63

20. I've never seen that car in the car park before. .... is it?
    A Who   B Whose   C Who's   ▶ Unit 63

Go online for a full exit test

Verbs with -ing forms and infinitives

MODULE 12

Before you start

1 Read the advertisement. Look at the highlighted grammar examples.

Paul Garrison

Do you enjoy cooking?
Do you want to learn something new?
Then come along and join one of Paul's cookery classes.

Learning a new skill can be very rewarding, and learning to cook new dishes can also be delicious! This autumn, Paul is offering classes in Thai cookery. Come and experience his unique method:

- Paul prepares all the ingredients first, including his special spice mix
- Then you watch Paul make a dish from beginning to end
- He teaches you to mix your own spices and curry powder for the dish
- Finally, you try copying Paul's recipe.

Paul lets you progress at your own pace, and if you'd prefer to watch and not to cook, that's also fine.

You also eat all the wonderful dishes you have prepared!

Autumn term 18 September–10 December, Thursday 6.30–9.30 p.m. Only £180.00, all ingredients included.

Cookery Classes

2 Now read the sentences and choose the correct words in *italics*. The highlighted grammar examples will help you.

1. Have you enjoyed *take / taking* part in this cookery class? ▶ Unit 64
2. *Speak / Speaking* a foreign language helps us understand other nationalities. ▶ Unit 64
3. The children really didn't want *to go / go* to the swimming club. ▶ Unit 65
4. I'd prefer not *to have / having* any oil on my salad. ▶ Unit 65
5. Will you teach *the children to / to the children* play chess? ▶ Unit 66
6. They wouldn't let me *join / to join* the club because I'm not yet sixteen. ▶ Unit 66
7. 'This phone doesn't work.' 'Try *to turn / turning* it on!' ▶ Unit 67
8. It all happened so fast – I saw the car *burst / bursting* into flames. ▶ Unit 67

3 Check your answers below. Then go to the unit for more information and practice.

1 taking 2 Speaking 3 to go 4 to have 5 the children to 6 join 7 turning 8 burst

⏻ Go online for a full diagnostic test

64 Verb + -ing form

1 Verb (+ adverb/preposition) + -ing form

When we use two verbs together, the second verb is often in the *-ing* form. After verbs with adverbs/prepositions (e.g. *give up, think of*), the second verb is always in the *-ing* form.

More on verb + preposition ➤ Units 89, 90 and 91

	COMMON VERBS	EXAMPLES
likes and dislikes	dislike can't stand enjoy hate* like* love* (not) mind prefer*	I **enjoy not doing** anything sometimes. Simon **doesn't mind working** late today.
ideas and opinions	admit consider imagine look forward to recommend suggest think of	Do you **admit stealing** that watch? I'd **recommend staying** near the beach. He **suggested paying** by credit card.
actions that start, stop or continue	begin* continue* delay give up start* stop* finish keep (on) practise put off spend (time)	Has he **given up smoking**? I **spent** two hours **preparing** this meal. Lena **practises singing** every day.
others	avoid can't help deny involve mention miss risk	You **can't risk losing** your job over a silly argument.

* These verbs can also be followed by an infinitive, sometimes with a difference in meaning (➤ Unit 67).

⚠ In the verb *look forward to, to* is a preposition, so we use an *-ing* form:
✗ *I'm looking forward to see you again.* ✓ *I'm looking forward to seeing you again.*

The *-ing* form sometimes needs to be
- negative: *I hate **not getting** to a station or airport on time.*
- perfect (for an earlier action): *Joe admitted **having sent** the wrong email.* (= that he had sent)
- passive: *Don't ring after 10.30 – I hate **being woken up** by the phone!*

2 The -ing form as subject, and as object

The *-ing* form can be
- the subject of a sentence: ***Swimming** is a good all-round exercise.*
  ***Living in the city** is more exciting than living in the country.*
- the object: *My job involves **listening to music**.* (object of *involves*)
  *I hate **being woken up** by the phone!* (object of *hate*)

3 go + -ing form; do the/some + -ing form

We sometimes use *go + -ing* form to talk about doing sports and other activities:
*The boys often **go fishing** at the weekend. I **go shopping** – it's the best way to relax!*

⚠ We usually use *go + -ing* form where there is a verb for the activity: *I sail → I go sailing.*
Where the activity is a game, or does not have a verb form, we use *play* or *do*:
✓ *I play football.* ✓ *I do karate.*

We use *do + the/some* with *-ing* forms to talk about work in the home:
*Have you done **the ironing**? We'd better do **some cleaning** this weekend.*

Spelling rules for *-ing* forms ➤ page 350   *do the shopping* or *go shopping*? ➤ Unit 92.1

Practice

1 Match the pictures with the sentences. Then complete each sentence with a suitable verb in the *-ing* form.

A B C D E

0 *Talking* on a mobile phone in a restaurant really annoys me – it's so rude. D
1 .... is very good exercise for strengthening your arms and legs. ......
2 We often go .... at the weekend – being in the countryside is lovely. ......
3 There's nothing more relaxing than .... by the sea, watching the waves. ......
4 I don't mind .... as long as it's in front of the TV! ......

2 Complete the sentences using the *-ing* form of the verbs in brackets. You will need to use the perfect or passive form for some of them. 🔊 3.61 Listen and check.

0 Did your secretary mention *having sent* (have sent) the package to me?
1 We're really looking forward to .... (have) two weeks off work in the summer.
2 I don't mind .... (not watch) *Sportsnight* if you want to see that film on Film 4.
3 .... (spend) too much time on their own often makes people depressed.
4 I can't imagine .... (be offered) a job like that.
5 The students admitted .... (have copied) their essays from the Internet.
6 I hate .... (work) here. I can't stand .... (be told) what to do all the time.

3 **GRAMMAR IN USE** Complete the conversation using the *-ing* form of the verbs in the box. 🔊 3.62 Listen and check.

call camp do go make not be play tell ~~try~~

JULES   I've got some information about that new club. Listen, it says: 'For young people who love (0) *trying* new things, and who enjoy (1) .... new friends! We offer lots of activities, so if you like (2) .... team sports and (3) .... martial arts like judo and karate, this is the club for you. In the summer, we also expect to go (4) .... and canoeing'.

NICK   Oh, OK. Sounds good. I like all of those things.

JULES   Me, too. I've really missed (5) .... to the sports centre since it closed down.

NICK   Yeah. Well, at least we've still got the bowling alley – can you imagine (6) .... able to go there with everyone on a Friday evening?

JULES   No, I can't! It would be awful. This new place opens next week. What do you think about (7) .... the others and (8) .... them about it?

NICK   Yes, let's do that.

Go online for more practice

65 Verb + infinitive

Oh, why did we **decide to go** camping?

Come on. I'll **help pack** your rucksack. It'll be OK.

1 Verb + infinitive without *to*

We use the infinitive without *to* after modal verbs (e.g. *can*, *will*):
We **can use** the swimming pool after 8.00 a.m.
We'**ll send** you an entry form in the post.

After the verb *help* we can use the infinitive with or without *to*. There is no change in meaning:
I'll **help pack** your rucksack.
We **helped to tidy up** after the party.

make and *let* + infinitive without *to* ▶ Unit 66.3

2 Verb + infinitive with *to*

	VERBS	EXAMPLES
mental states or activity	agree choose decide forget* learn remember* want wish	Did you **agree to help** them? Why did we **decide to go** camping?! I'm **learning to read** classical Arabic.
future arrangements	aim arrange expect hope offer plan prepare promise refuse threaten	The hotel **aims to provide** excellent service. The college **promised not to give up** my place. Our neighbours **are threatening to call** the police!
appearance	appear, pretend, seem, tend	Mr Knowles **doesn't seem to be** very confident. People round here **tend not to go** to bed early.
other	attempt (can/can't) afford ask deserve fail offer try*	We **can't afford to eat** out tonight. The letter **failed to arrive** on time.

* These verbs can also be followed by an *-ing* form, sometimes with a difference in meaning (▶ Unit 67).

Verb (+ object) + infinitive with *to* ▶ Unit 66

The infinitive sometimes needs to be
- negative: *She* **appears not to worry** *about her weight.* (NOT ~~to not worry~~)
- continuous: *I* **expect to be earning** *a lot of money when I'm forty!* (a continuous action)
- perfect: *We* **plan to have finished** *all of the decorating by July.* (an action that will be completed in the future)
- passive: *Jack drives over the speed limit all the time – he* **deserves to be caught**.

3 *would like*, etc.

We use the infinitive with *to* after *would* ('d) + *like/love/hate/prefer*:
I'**d really like to learn** a new skill – perhaps we could go sailing?
Jackie **would prefer not to go out** this evening as she's really tired.
We can use the *-ing* form after *like*, *love*, *hate* and *prefer* without *would* ('d) (▶ Unit 67.1). Compare:
I'**d love to go** mountain climbing. (in the future)
I **love going** mountain climbing. (= I enjoy the activity.)
I'**d prefer to stay in** tonight. (on this occasion)
I **prefer eating** at home to **eating** in restaurants. (in general)

4 *would rather* + infinitive without *to*

After *would rather* we can use the infinitive without *to*. We only use this if the subject of *would rather* and the second verb is the same:

same subject

We'd rather we went by plane. = **We'd rather go** by plane.

would rather + past simple ▶ Unit 58.3

Practice

1 Choose the correct words in *italics*. In one place, both answers are possible.
🔊 **4.01** Listen and check.

0 Do you think that the government might (*call*) / *to call* a general election soon?
1 Leila would love *to learn* / *learning* to play the saxophone.
2 The builders expect *have* / *to have* finished the roof by the end of next week.
3 If we wanted *sell* / *to sell* our house right now, we would *have* / *to have* to lower the price.
4 Children these days refuse *to told* / *to be told* how to do things.
5 My Canadian friend has offered to help *teach* / *to teach* our children English.
6 We'd prefer *to spend* / *spending* our holiday somewhere quiet and peaceful.
7 The writers threatened *not to* / *to not* complete the script for the next episode of the drama.
8 We'd rather *to spend* / *spend* holidays with friends than visit new places.

2 **GRAMMAR IN USE** Read the text and find eight more places where the word *to* is missing.
🔊 **4.02** Listen and check.

Avison Extreme Sports Holidays
Have you ever wanted ⌃to try a really different, adventurous holiday?
Would you love go parasailing or rock climbing, potholing or bungee jumping?
Why not try an Avison sports holiday?

This is how it works: you tell us what you can and can't do, and what you'd like be able to do. We assess your abilities and offer teach you at least two different extreme sports in one week. If you choose accept our offer, we decide on a date and then arrange collect you from the nearest station or airport.

Our promise to you: we promise provide you with all the equipment necessary and expert training in the chosen sports. We help you progress quickly because of the intensity of the training. You can expect be taught in a safe environment, with the minimum of risk.

Your promise to us: you promise not overestimate your abilities – we can only work with what is already there!

Interested? Then call us on the number below or visit our website.

3 Write the words in the correct order to make questions. Start with the underlined word or phrase.

0 would   like   can't afford   to do   <u>what</u>   but   you   to do   ?
  What would you like to do but can't afford to do?

1 do   you   in ten years' time   to be doing   want   <u>what kind of work</u>   ?
  ....

2 forgotten   recently   have   to do   <u>what</u>   you   ?
  ....

3 studying English   <u>when</u>   to have finished   hope   you   do   ?
  ....

4 aim   you   by the time you're sixty   <u>what</u>   do   to have done   ?
  ....

4 Now write true answers to the questions in Exercise 3.

0 *I'd like to travel round the world, but I can't afford to do it.*
1 ....
2 ....
3 ....
4 ....

66 Verb (+ object) + infinitive; *make* and *let*

Mrs Grant is **teaching Justin to play** the piano. She **makes him practise** every day.

1 Verb (+ object) + infinitive with *to*

With some verbs it is possible to put an object between the first verb and the infinitive:

ask beg dare expect help intend mean need require want wish would like/love/hate/prefer

verb + infinitive + *to*	verb + object + infinitive with *to*
Sami **wants to find** a better job.	Sami **wants his son/him to find** a better job.
I **didn't intend to spend** so much money.	I **didn't intend Lara/her to spend** so much money.

 We don't use a *that* clause after these verbs:
✗ <s>We begged Antonia that she didn't go out alone.</s>   ✓ We **begged Antonia not to go out** alone.

 We can use the infinitive with or without *to* after *help*:
I'll **help you carry** those bags. / I'll **help you to carry** those bags. (➤ Unit 65.1)

2 Verb + object + infinitive with *to*

With other verbs we ALWAYS put an object between the first verb and the infinitive:

advise allow cause encourage forbid force invite permit persuade recommend remind teach tell order warn

Mrs Grant is **teaching Justin to play** the piano.
We always **encourage the students to plan** their revision.
Can you **remind me to set** the alarm for 6.30 when we go to bed?

 To make the infinitive verb negative we put *not* BEFORE *to*:
✗ <s>The police persuaded the gunman to not shoot.</s>   ✓ The police **persuaded the gunman not to shoot**.

Some verbs (*advise, allow, forbid, permit, recommend*) can also be followed by an *-ing* form as an object (➤ Unit 64.2):
The management does not **allow staff to smoke**.
BUT The management does not **allow smoking**.
We **recommend students to use** a good dictionary.
BUT We **recommend using** a good dictionary.

3 *make* and *let*

The verbs *make* and *let* always have an object, and are followed by the infinitive without *to*:
Mrs Grant **makes Justin practise** every day. (= forces him to)
Our manager **lets us work** from home once or twice a week. (= allows us to)
The soldiers **made the prisoners walk** 50 kilometres.
But in the passive, we use *to* before the infinitive. For *let*, we use *allowed to* (➤ Unit 52.2/3):
The prisoners **were made to walk** 50 kilometres before **they were allowed to sleep**.
✗ <s>... they weren't let to sleep.</s>   ✓ They **weren't allowed to sleep**.

12

Practice

1 Write sentences about the pictures, using the words below.

0 she / encourage / jump *She encouraged the horse to jump the fence.*
1 she / teach / play ....
2 they / let / sleep ....
3 he / help / carry ....
4 he / warn / not skate ....

2 **GRAMMAR IN USE** Complete the conversation with the phrases from the box. 🔊 4.03 Listen and check.

> me follow   members to sell   ~~talking~~   to sell   to show
> to use   us to paint   you break   you to stay

STEVEN Davina, you know you recommended (0) *talking* to gallery owners about showing our paintings? Well, I've been invited (1) .... some of my paintings in an exhibition.

DAVINA That's wonderful news! Well done.

STEVEN Thank you. And I expect (2) .... quite a few of them.

DAVINA Ah, are these paintings that you've done in the art club, while we've been teaching you?

STEVEN Yes. Why?

DAVINA You know the club forbids (3) .... paintings done in club time?

STEVEN No, why on earth is that?

DAVINA Because our money comes from charities, we can't make a profit.

STEVEN So you teach (4) ...., but then we aren't allowed (5) .... our new skill?

DAVINA Well, not in order to make a profit. I'm sorry.

STEVEN Well, I suppose you can't make (6) .... the rules if I'm not a member, so I resign!

DAVINA That's a shame, you really are one of our best artists. I'd like (7) .... in the club, Steven, but if we let (8) .... the rules, everyone will want to do the same ...

3 Find and correct the mistake in each sentence. 🔊 4.04 Listen and check.

0 We want ~~that you~~ *you to* come home by eleven o'clock this evening.
1 My boss asked me work late last weekend.
2 We were made do an hour of extra homework after school.
3 The police officer was ordered to not arrest the man.
4 We would like that you do the washing-up sometimes!
5 After we'd filled out the forms and paid, we were let drive the hire car away.
6 Gina's friends persuaded her giving up smoking.
7 The police recommended to keep the doors and windows closed.
8 I had to remind the students not be late for the test the next day.

67 Verb + infinitive or -ing form

1 Infinitive or -ing form with similar meanings

After the verbs *begin, continue, hate, intend, like, love, prefer* and *start*, we can use an infinitive or an -*ing* form with little difference in meaning:
*Oh no! It's just **started to rain**. /*
*Oh no! It's just **started raining**.*

Notice this small difference in British English with *like*:
*We **like inviting** friends to dinner at the weekend.* (= We enjoy this.)
*I **like to save** a little bit of money every month.* (= It's a good habit and I choose to do it.)

Have you **stopped practising** now?

No, we've just **stopped to take a break** for five minutes. We've got another ten songs to practise!

2 Infinitive or -ing form with different meanings

VERB	+ -ing FORM	+ to + INFINITIVE
forget/ remember	for an event or situation in the past: *I'll never **forget riding** my first bike. Do you **remember learning** to swim?*	for something you should do/should have done: *Don't **forget to lock** the back door! Did you **remember to bring** the CDs?*
go on	continue an activity: *They stopped, but we **went on walking**.*	change from one action to another: *After a slow start, she **went on to win** the race.*
regret	feel sorry about something you did/ didn't do: *I **regret not studying** harder at school.*	say sorry, particularly in formal letters: *We **regret to inform** you that you have not been called for interview …*
stop	finish an action: *Have you **stopped practising** now?*	finish an action in order to do something else: *No, we've just **stopped to take** a break.*
try	do something as an experiment: *Try **turning** it off and on again.*	attempt to do something difficult: *I'm not an electrician, but I'll **try to mend** it.*

3 *feel, hear, see*, etc. + infinitive or -*ing* form

After sense verbs (e.g. *feel, hear, see*) we can use
- object + infinitive without *to*
- object + -*ing* form.

The meaning is slightly different:
*We were watching the runway and **saw your plane arrive**.* (= We saw the plane as it came down and landed.)
*We **saw your plane arriving** as we parked the car.* (= We saw the plane in the sky, but we didn't see it land.)

4 *need, help* and *can't help* + -*ing* form

The verbs *need* and *help* have different meanings, depending on their form:
*I **need to drink** some water.* (+ infinitive with *to* = physical necessity)
*This room **needs cleaning**.* (+ -*ing* form = someone should clean it)
*I **help (to) run** the local charity shop.* (+ infinitive with *to* = assist, aid)
*I **couldn't help laughing**.* (+ -*ing* form = couldn't avoid doing it)

More on *need* + -*ing* form ➤ Unit 85.4   *need to* ➤ Unit 50

Practice

1 Choose the correct meaning, A or B.

0 The TV presenter finished talking and went on to introduce her guests.
   A She continued doing one action.   (B) She started doing a second action.
1 The cleaner needs paying.
   A We should pay the cleaner.   B The cleaner should pay us.
2 I like to go to the dentist every six months.
   A I enjoy doing this.   B I choose to do this, to have my teeth checked regularly.
3 I've tried so hard to understand this science course, but I just can't.
   A I've made a lot of effort.   B I've done a lot of experiments.
4 I won't forget to pay the bills while you're away.
   A I remember this from my past.   B This is something I should do.
5 I saw you rehearsing for the play – you were really good.
   A I saw the whole of the rehearsal.   B I saw part of the rehearsal.

2 **GRAMMAR IN USE** Read the email and choose the correct words in *italics*. In two places, both answers are possible. 🔊 **4.05** Listen and check.

Subject: New hobby!

Hi Caroline

You know when we last spoke you said I should stop (0) *to feel* / *feeling* sorry for myself here and find something to do? Well, I have! I needed (1) *to get* / *getting* out to meet people, so I decided I'd try (2) *to join* / *joining* a group of some kind. I started (3) *to look* / *looking* for a 'Naturewatch' group in this area, and I found one.

It's really good – the people are nice and there are walks and other activities every weekend and some evenings. I love (4) *walk* / *walking* anyway, and I quite like (5) *to go* / *going* out in all weathers, or sometimes at night to see a badger or foxes (6) *to look* / *looking* for food. Last weekend, we actually saw an eagle (7) *fly* / *flying* over us – it was chasing something and it disappeared from sight in seconds. You can't help (8) *to get* / *getting* excited when you see something like that.

So you can stop (9) *to worry* / *worrying* about me – I really don't regret (10) *moving* / *to move* here, after all!

Susie 😊

---

3 Complete each sentence with the correct (infinitive or *-ing*) form of the verb in brackets. 🔊 **4.06** Listen and check.

1 A I love (0) *cooking* (cook) for friends. You must try my onion soup.
   B Well, I can smell something (1) .... (burn). Did you turn the cooker off?
   A Oh! I think I remember (2) .... (do) it, but I'd better go and check.
2 A I've had the letter. This is what they said: 'We regret (3) .... (inform) you that your application will not be taken any further.'
   B So what does that mean?
   A Well, they're trying (4) .... (tell) me nicely that I haven't got the job.
   B Oh, no. What will you do now?
   A I'll go on (5) .... (look), of course. I still need (6) .... (find) a job!

Review MODULE 12

1 **UNITS 64 AND 65** Complete the sentences with suitable verbs in the infinitive or -ing form.

0 Olivia is helping *to teach* children at her local school.
1 Larry is preparing .... his driving test tomorrow. We all hope he'll pass.
2 Pete is learning .... French – so he can talk to his new customers in Paris.
3 Fiona and Chris enjoy .... tennis at the club.
4 Steve goes .... at the new pool every Saturday afternoon.
5 Dave pretends .... classical music, but he hates it really.
6 Doreen's house is always perfect. She does some .... before work every day.

2 **UNITS 64, 65 AND 66** Write one word only in each gap.

JUDITH Hello, you're home early. How did the meeting go?
ALEX Awful! It all started to go wrong when the car broke down. I didn't want (0) *to* get my suit dirty so I gave up (1) .... to fix it after a few minutes..
JUDITH So then what did you do?
ALEX You know I hate (2) .... getting to a meeting on time ... so I took a taxi.
JUDITH Alex! That must have been really expensive!
ALEX I didn't intend (3) .... go all the way by taxi – just to the station as I knew there was a train at about nine o'clock. But there was an accident on the way, and I missed the train anyway.
JUDITH So you went all the way by taxi?
ALEX Yes, the driver didn't want (4) .... take me because he had another appointment, but I persuaded (5) .... to. Of course he made (6) .... pay the whole fare, and extra because he'd missed his appointment.
JUDITH Oh, Alex.
ALEX Then at the office they said I couldn't give my presentation because I was late – I didn't (7) .... them see I was annoyed, but I was! They were angry, too – they had hoped to (8) .... the meeting on time so that they could finish by lunchtime, and they had waited for me for over an hour. It was a completely wasted day.
JUDITH And a really expensive one!

3 **UNITS 64, 65 AND 67** Complete each sentence so it means the same as the sentence above it. Use an -ing form or an infinitive.

0 Christa likes swimming and ice-skating. She prefers the second activity.
   Christa prefers *ice-skating to swimming*.
1 The driver was tired and felt like having a break. So he stopped driving.
   The driver stopped driving .... a break.
2 Lucia was feeling very unhappy. She pretended she wasn't unhappy.
   Lucia pretended .... unhappy.

200

3 Karel is called 'Daddy' by his stepdaughter. He likes it.
   Karel likes .... 'Daddy' by his stepdaughter.
4 We went to Disneyland when I was young. I'll never forget it.
   I'll never forget .... to Disneyland when I was young.
5 Brad had taken the money from the shop. He admitted it.
   Brad admitted .... the money from the shop.
6 We will have finished building the house by March. Well, that's the plan!
   We plan .... building the house by March.
7 I heard what they were saying. I couldn't help it.
   I couldn't help .... what they were saying.
8 Jan's brother suggested that she went on holiday with him. She didn't agree.
   Jan didn't agree .... with her brother.

4 ALL UNITS Read the text and choose the best answer, A, B, C or D below.

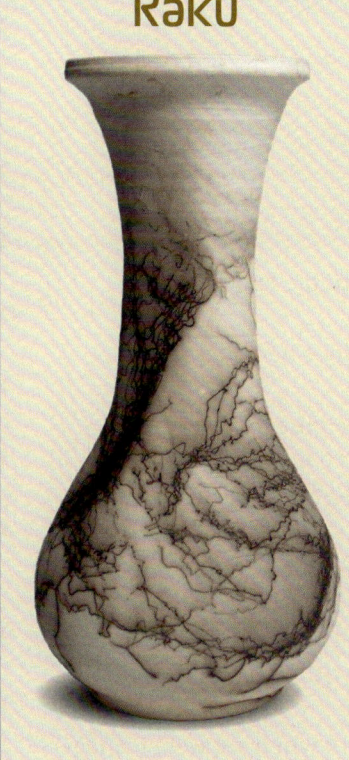

Raku

Course dates: 19 September – 15 December
Course fee: £150.00

Raku is a Japanese method of making pots which dates back to the sixteenth century, and which people have continued (0) .... to the present day. The pots may appear (1) .... cracked or broken, but Raku potters expect (2) .... slight imperfections – these result from the Raku process: Raku pots need (3) .... ('cooked') at very high temperatures – about 1000°C, which creates slight cracks. These are then repaired by painting the pots. Of course, with such high temperatures, we must (4) .... extreme care in making the pots.

Raku is suitable for anyone who enjoys (5) .... with their hands – we do not expect (6) .... any pottery before, as we teach (7) .... and create your pots. You can look forward (8) .... many creative hours on this course, and you will have a number of beautiful pots to take home at the end.

Due to increased demand, we advise (9) .... for a place soon.

Please note: this college does not allow (10) .... in any of the classrooms or studios.

	A	B	C	D
0	use	to using	using	to be used
1	be	being	was	to be
2	their pots to have	to have their pots	their pots have	having their pots
3	be fired	being fired	to be fired	are fired
4	taking	to take	take	taken
5	work	to work	to working	working
6	you to do	you to have done	you to be done	you to doing
7	you to design	to design you	to designing you	you to designing
8	to spend	spend	to spending	spending
9	to apply	apply	to apply you	you to apply
10	smoke	to smoke	smoking	to smoking

Test MODULE 12

Verbs with -ing forms and infinitives

Choose the correct answer, A, B or C.

1. We had to put off .... on the cruise until next year.
   A to go   B going   C go   ➤ Unit 64

2. Do you mind .... here? It's a non-smoking office.
   A not smoking   B not smoke   C not to smoke   ➤ Unit 64

3. Can you imagine .... your university degree before you're fifteen?
   A having finished   B have finished   C to have finished   ➤ Unit 64

4. .... is a cheap and easy way to relax – and catch your own food!
   A Go fishing   B Fish   C Going fishing   ➤ Unit 64

5. You should .... confirmation of your booking within three working days.
   A receive   B to receive   C receiving   ➤ Unit 65

6. The children decided .... their holidays with us last year.
   A not take   B not taking   C not to take   ➤ Unit 65

7. We don't expect .... for very long before we hear about the job.
   A to wait   B to waiting   C wait   ➤ Unit 65

8. Stop worrying about the promotion. You really deserve .... it.
   A get   B getting   C to get   ➤ Unit 65

9. Wouldn't you just hate .... in a factory?
   A work   B to work   C to working   ➤ Unit 65

10. We will do all we can to help you .... an unforgettable experience.
    A have   B having   C to having   ➤ Unit 66

11. Angelina begged her friends .... to the party without her.
    A not going   B not go   C not to go   ➤ Unit 66

12. You don't have to remind .... all the time – I am eighteen now!
    A to take me my key   B me my key to take   C me to take my key   ➤ Unit 66

13. We advise .... through the starter book before the course begins.
    A students to work   B to work students   C students working   ➤ Unit 66

14. We do not recommend .... only the minimum amount off your credit card each month.
    A to pay   B pay   C paying   ➤ Unit 66

15. Slaves were made .... for hours without rest and without food or drink.
    A to work   B work   C working   ➤ Unit 66

16. Do you remember .... to that concert in Hyde Park when we were teenagers?
    A to go   B we go   C going   ➤ Unit 67

17. Many people regret .... the opportunity to go to university.
    A not have   B not having   C not to have   ➤ Unit 67

18. We saw the plane .... out of the sky – it was really terrifying.
    A drop   B dropping   C to drop   ➤ Unit 67

19. I couldn't watch the animals .... each other in that documentary. I turned off halfway through.
    A attack   B to attack   C attacking   ➤ Unit 67

20. If you can't help .... unhelpful comments, then please don't say anything.
    A making   B make   C to make   ➤ Unit 67

Go online for a full exit test

Reported speech

MODULE 13

Before you start

1 Read the newspaper article. Look at the <mark>highlighted</mark> grammar examples.

Minister wins case against newspaper

Sports Minister Andrew Morgan won his court case today against *The Globe*. The newspaper claimed in March this year <mark>that Mr Morgan had used</mark> taxpayers' money to buy his new luxury apartment in London. Mr Morgan refused to <mark>admit doing</mark> anything illegal and said he would speak to his lawyers <mark>the following day</mark>. Although some of his political colleagues had <mark>advised him not to take</mark> *The Globe* to court, Mr Morgan decided against taking their advice. His lawyers supported his decision and today Judge Simmonds <mark>ordered the newspaper to pay</mark> the Minister £250,000. After the case <mark>we asked Mr Morgan how he felt</mark> about the result, and <mark>he told us</mark> he was delighted. When asked <mark>what his plans were</mark> now, Mr Morgan said he would be at work the following day as usual.

2 Now read the sentences and choose the correct words in *italics*. The <mark>highlighted</mark> grammar examples will help you.

1. My lecturer claimed that I *have / had* copied part of the last essay from someone. ▶ Unit 68
2. Sean told me last Monday that he would call me *the following day / tomorrow*, but he didn't call me till the weekend. ▶ Unit 68
3. Michelle asked me what *I thought / did I think* about her news. ▶ Unit 69
4. The staff want to know what *is your decision / your decision is*. ▶ Unit 69
5. The judge ordered *the girl to do / the girl should do* community service. ▶ Unit 70
6. My teacher advised me *don't apply / not to apply* for a university course yet. ▶ Unit 70
7. Bernie seems very unhappy but he won't tell *me / to me* what's wrong. ▶ Unit 71
8. We told the children's parents what they had said, but the children refused to admit *to say / saying* anything wrong. ▶ Unit 71

3 Check your answers below. Then go to the unit for more information and practice.

1 had   2 the following day   3 I thought   4 your decision is   5 the girl to do   6 not to apply   7 me   8 saying

⏻ Go online for a full diagnostic test

68 Reported statements

> Our members voted earlier today. The result will be available later this afternoon. I can't say any more than that.

The union leader said that **their** members **had voted** earlier and that the result **would be** available later in the afternoon, but he added that **he couldn't** say any more.

1 Reporting speech

When we repeat another person's words, we can use **direct speech** or **reported speech**.
- For direct speech, we use the exact words and we put quotation marks ("") or inverted commas ('') around them:
  'I'm really hungry because I haven't eaten since breakfast,' said Annabel.
- When we report speech with a **reporting verb** (e.g. *say*) in the present, we use the same tenses, but we have to change the pronouns and verb forms when necessary:
  Annabel **says** (that) **she's** really hungry because **she hasn't eaten** since breakfast.
- When we report another person's words some time after he/she said them, we usually use a past tense verb to introduce them, and we change the tense of the verbs as well:
  Annabel **said** (that) **she was** really hungry because **she hadn't eaten** since breakfast.
- We can use *that* after *said* but we often leave it out:
  Jake said he would meet us here.

2 Tense changes in reported speech

ORIGINAL WORDS	REPORTED STATEMENT
Present simple: 'We **work** for the town council.'	Past simple: → They said they **worked** for the town council.
Present continuous: 'I**'m doing** the washing.'	Past continuous: → She said she **was doing** the washing.
Past simple: 'We **decided** to leave earlier today.'	Past perfect: → He said they **had decided** to leave earlier that day.
Past continuous: 'I **wasn't telling** the truth.'	Past perfect continuous: → She admitted she **hadn't been telling** the truth.
Present perfect simple: 'My guests **haven't arrived** yet.'	Past perfect simple: → She said her guests **hadn't arrived** yet.
Present perfect continuous: 'We**'ve been waiting** for ages!'	Past perfect continuous: → They complained (that) they **had been waiting** for ages.
be going to: 'They**'re going to** stay at home tonight.'	was/were going to: → They said they **were going to** stay at home that night.
Most modal verbs (e.g. *can, will, must*): 'I **can't** say any more.' 'The result **will** be available later.' 'You **must** stop writing!'	could, would, had to; → He added that he **couldn't** say any more. → He said that the result **would** be available later. → She said we **had to/must** stop writing.

Some verb forms don't change.
- Past perfect: '*I* **hadn't met** your sister before.' → He said (that) he **hadn't met** my sister before.
- Modal verbs *could, would, should* and *mustn't*:
  'We **could** go to France for the day.' → Len suggested (that) we **could** go to France for the day.
  'You **mustn't** talk during the exam.' → He insisted (that) we **mustn't** talk during the exam.

204

3 Other changes in reported speech

We usually change pronouns and time and place words in reported speech:

PRONOUNS AND POSSESSIVES	
direct	reported
I	he/she
me	him/her
my	his/her
mine	his/hers
you	I/we
your	my/our
yours	mine/ours
we	they
us	them
our	their
ours	theirs

WORDS FOR TIME AND PLACE	
direct	reported
today	that day
tonight	that night
tomorrow	the next day / the following day
next (week, month, etc.)	the next/the following (week, month, etc.)
ago	before
yesterday	the day before/ the previous day
last (week, month, etc.)	the last/the previous (week, month, etc.)
now	then
here	there
this (place)	that (place)

Paul said, '*I* arrived **here** an hour **ago**.' → Paul said **he** had arrived **there** an hour **before**.
Angelique and Etienne said, '**We**'re starting **our** course at the college **next month**.'
→ They said **they** were starting **their** course at the college **the following month**.

FORMALITY CHECK We do not usually repeat *yes* and *no* in reported speech, except in informal speech for emphasis:
'Yes, we decided earlier today.' → He said that they had decided earlier that day.
→ (informal) Anyway, he said that yes, they had decided earlier that day.

4 Reasons for not changing the tense

There are times when we can choose not to change the tense of verbs in reported speech.
- When the situation or feelings/opinions in the original speech are still true:

  *My three sisters **have** bright red hair.* → He told me his three sisters **have** bright red hair.

  *I really **like** your friend.* → She said she really **likes** you.

  Compare:

  *We're **leaving** tomorrow at 6.30.*

  → They said they'**re leaving** tomorrow at 6.30. (reported on the same day as the original)
  → They said they **were leaving** the next day at 6.30. (reported some days after the original)

- When the verb follows the linking words *after* or *because*:

  I locked the door after I finished cleaning.

  → She told him she'**d locked** the door after she **finished** cleaning.
  OR She told him she'**d locked** the door after she'**d finished** cleaning.

  *I'm annoyed because I **was talking** and you **interrupted** me.*

  → She said she was annoyed because she **was talking** and I **interrupted** her.
  OR She said she was annoyed because she **had been talking** and I **had interrupted** her.

68 REPORTED STATEMENTS

Practice

1 **GRAMMAR IN USE** Read the newspaper report and choose the correct words in *italics*.

In court this week
Maggie Givans reports from Brentford Magistrates' Court

On Tuesday, local shopkeeper Barry Southgate appeared in court for dangerous driving. Police Constable Harriet Diamond said that on the night of 14 February she (0) *has seen / had seen* a dark blue Volkswagen Golf travelling at high speed through a residential area. She stopped the motorist, Mr Southgate, and asked him to tell her his driving speed. He replied that he (1) *has / had* no idea. When PC Diamond asked to see his driving licence, he replied that he (2) *would / will* bring it to the police station (3) *tomorrow / the following day*, closed his door and drove off, again at high speed.

In response to Magistrate Richard Pound's questions Mr Southgate said (4) *I / he* knew he had been over the speed limit, but he didn't know exactly what speed he (5) *was / had been* travelling at. He also said said that he (6) *has / had* forgotten to take his licence to the police station (7) *the next / next* day. The magistrate wanted to know how he could forget something important like that, and Mr Southgate explained that his wife (8) *has had / had had* their first baby that day, so he (9) *can't / hadn't been able* to take his licence to the police station. He added that he had been rushing to the hospital (10) *the evening before / yesterday evening*, and that was why he had been driving so fast. Magistrate Pound said that Mr Southgate still (11) *must / had to* pay the fine for speeding but that he (12) *wishes / wished* him and his new family all the best.

2 Complete the reported statements. Make all the changes you can.
🔊 4.07 Listen and check.

0 POLITICIAN (to reporters): I'm ready to answer your questions.
The politician told the reporters *that he was ready* to answer their questions.

1 REPORTER: People were offended by remarks in your speech.
A reporter said people .... remarks in the politician's speech.

2 POLITICIAN: I didn't make any offensive remarks in my speech yesterday.
The politician stated .... any offensive remarks in his speech ....

3 POLITICIAN: I was just describing my plans for next year.
He said that .... his plans for the next year.

4 REPORTER: You must know that people have asked for your resignation.
The reporter said that the politician .... for his resignation.

5 POLITICIAN: I can't understand it myself. I simply described the situation in the country.
The politician said .... himself.
He .... the situation in the country.

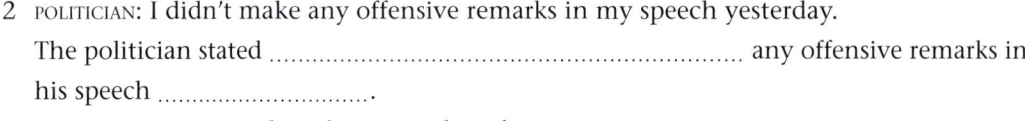

6 POLITICIAN: I have been working very hard and I see no reason to resign.
He added that .... and he saw no reason to resign.

7 POLITICIAN: I will make a full statement about my plans tomorrow afternoon.
He ended by saying that ....
....

3 Match the speech bubbles 1–8 with the reported statements A–L. Two more of the speech bubbles can match two statements.

Speech bubbles (girl):
0 I'm revising for an exam at the moment.
1 Adrian's revising for an exam at the moment.
2 I'm going to take the exam tomorrow.
3 I was revising for the exam yesterday evening.
4 I've already taken an exam this week.

Speech bubbles (boy):
5 I'm revising for an exam at the moment.
6 I'm going to take the exam this week.
7 I took an exam last week.
8 I'm revising for the exam this evening.

A She said she'd already taken an exam that week.
B He said he had taken an exam the week before.
C She said he's revising for an exam at the moment.
D He said he was revising for the exam that evening.
E She said she's already taken an exam this week.
~~F She said she was revising for an exam then.~~
G He said he was going to take the exam that week.
H She said she was going to take the exam the next day.
I He said he's revising for an exam this evening.
~~J She said she's revising for an exam at the moment.~~
K He said he was revising for an exam then.
L She said she was revising for the exam yesterday evening.

0 _F, J_   1 .... 2 .... 3 .... 4 .... 5 .... 6 .... 7 .... 8 ....

4 Rewrite the quotes in reported speech. Do not change the tense if it is possible not to.
🔊 4.08 Listen and check.

0 'You mustn't discuss the case outside the court room.'
The judge said that we _mustn't discuss the case outside the court room_.

1 'The museum was opened to the public in 1965.'
The guidebook says ....

2 'I'll take a taxi home after the film tomorrow evening.'
John told us last Friday ....

3 'Humans first walked on the moon in 1969.'
The lecturer said ....

4 'Samir's ill and can't come to school today.'
Mrs Richards, Samir's mother said ....

5 'Jason had been working for me for two years at that point.'
The manager told the police officer ....

6 'We're meeting our cousins from Vancouver at the weekend.'
Lou and Jane told us last week ....

5 Complete the sentences so they are true for you.

0 When my teacher gave back my last piece of homework, he/she said _that it was one of my best pieces of work_.
1 When my teacher gave back my last piece of homework, he/she said ....
2 A friend complimented me recently. He/She said ....
3 The last time I was upset, it was because someone said ....
4 The last time I went to the dentist, he/she said ....
5 The last person who spoke to me was .... He/She said ....

69 Reported questions

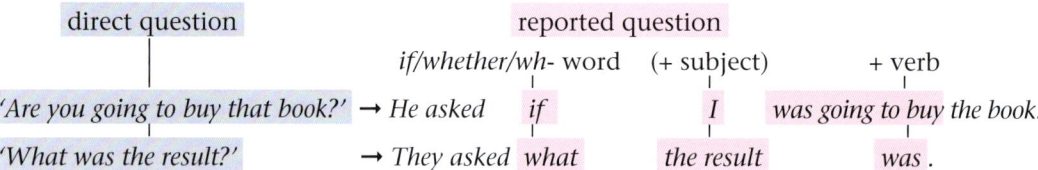

Miss Doyle was faced with a crowd of reporters yesterday. They asked her **why she wanted to move** to Paris and **whether she was leaving** the show. They also wanted to know **who her new agent was** – but she remained silent, and was quickly driven away from the studio.

1 Word order in reported questions

When we report a question, we change the word order of the question – it becomes the same word order as a statement:

direct question		reported question		
		if/whether/wh- word	(+ subject)	+ verb
'Are you going to buy that book?'	→ He asked	if	I	was going to buy the book.
'What was the result?'	→ They asked	what	the result	was.

 We do not use auxiliary *do, does* or *did* in reported questions:
✗ He asked what time did the flight leave Paris.   ✓ He asked what time the flight left Paris.

We make the same changes in tense, pronouns and time and place words as for reported statements:

The reporters asked, 'Did **you** *tell* **us** *the truth* **yesterday***, Minister?*
→ *The reporters asked the Minister if* **he** *had told* **them** *the truth* **the day before***.*

 We don't use question marks in reported questions:
✗ They asked if I was satisfied with the room?
✓ They asked if I was satisfied with the room.

2 Reported *yes/no* questions

We introduce reported *yes/no* questions with *ask/want to know* + *if* or *whether*:
'Has your union agreed the new pay deal?'
→ Reporters asked the leader **if** his union had agreed the new pay deal.
'Did the Minister answer your questions?'
→ She asked me **whether** the Minister had answered my questions.
'Have you always lived in this city? Why do you like it?'
→ They **wanted to know** if I had always lived in the city, and why I liked it.
With *if* and *whether*, we can add *or not* at the end of the question:
She asked **if/whether** the Minister had answered my questions **or not**.

3 Reported *wh-* questions

We introduce reported *wh-* questions with *ask/want to know* + *wh-* word:
- 'When will the article appear in the newspaper?'
  → They asked us **when** the article would appear in the newspaper.
  'Where's the cash desk?'
  → She **wanted to know** where the cash desk was.

 We don't use an object after *want to know*:
✗ They wanted to know me why I liked it.

General information on questions ➤ Units 61 and 62

Practice

1 Write the words in the correct order to make reported questions. Start with the underlined word or phrase. 🔊 4.09 Listen and check.

0 would be   asked   <u>my mother</u>   I   home   when
   My mother asked when I would be home.

1 <u>my friend</u>   couldn't come   why   to his party   asked   I
   ....

2 had   to know   <u>the officer</u>   if   wanted   the keys   I
   ....

3 how long   <u>she</u>   it   asked   had taken   to get there
   ....

4 he could have   his boss   a pay rise   asked   <u>John</u>   whether
   ....

5 <u>Maria</u>   to know   if   liked   her hairstyle   we   wanted
   ....

6 <u>the salesman</u>   whether we   the car   or not   asked   wanted to buy
   ....

2 **GRAMMAR IN USE** Read the reporter's questions and complete the text with reported questions. 🔊 4.10 Listen and check.

0 Are you going to leave the show?
1 Who caused the break-up?
2 Why can't you sort out your problems?
3 Are you unhappy because Annette gets more money than you?
4 Do you think Annette's a better singer than you?
5 What will you do next?
6 Have you thought about giving up singing?

❝That reporter was horrible. He wouldn't go away. He asked so many questions. He asked me whether (0) *I was going to leave the show or not*. He wanted to know who (1) .... and also why (2) .... Obviously, I didn't say anything. Then he asked me (3) .... because Annette got more money than me, and he was so rude – he asked (4) .... Imagine that! He wanted to know (5) .... and then he asked (6) ....! At that point I told him I wasn't going to answer any more questions and shut the door in his face. ❞

3 Think of four questions that people have recently asked you, and report them.

0 *My wife asked me what I wanted to have for dinner last night.*
1 ....
2 ....
3 ....
4 ....

⏻ Go online for more practice

70 Reported orders, requests and advice

So what did the doctor tell you?

Well, she **told me to stop** working so hard and she **advised me to go** to a gym. But she **warned me not to do** too much exercise at once …

1 Reporting orders

We can report orders, requests and advice with a reporting verb + infinitive with *to*. These reporting verbs all need an object.

We usually report instructions and orders with *tell*:
The doctor said, 'Stop working so hard.' → The doctor **told me to stop** working so hard.
We use *order* when the meaning is stronger:
The police officer shouted: 'Get out of the car!' → The police officer **ordered us to get out** of the car.

2 Reporting requests

We usually report requests with *ask*:
My mother said, 'Will you please tidy your room?' → My mother **asked me to tidy** my room.
We can use *beg* for a strong request:
'Please – oh, please – give us the sweets.' → The children **begged us to give** them the sweets.

With these verbs, we make the same changes to pronouns and time and place words as for reported statements. We also change the tense if necessary:
On Monday my mother said, 'Tidy **your** room when **you get** back from school **this** afternoon.'
→ My mother asked **me** to tidy **my** room when **I got** back from school **that** afternoon.

 We don't use *say* + *to* to report requests or orders: ✗ *My mother said me to tidy my room.*
To request information, we use *ask* (+ object) + *if/whether/wh-* word:
He **asked (me) if I had** everything I needed.

3 Reporting advice

We report advice with *advise*, *tell* or *warn*:
The doctor said, 'I think you should go to a gym.'
→ The doctor **advised me to go** to a gym.
The teacher said, 'You should all take the exam.'
→ The teacher **told all the students to take** the exam.
Dad said, 'Be careful – there's ice on the roads.'
→ Dad **warned me to be** careful because there was ice on the roads.

 We do not use this pattern with *suggest*. We use *suggest* + *should* or *suggest* + *-ing* form:
✗ *The doctor suggested me to get some exercise.*
✓ The doctor **suggested (that) I should get** some exercise.
✓ My friends **suggested going** to the gym.

4 Reporting negative orders, requests and advice

We report negative instructions, orders, requests and advice with verb + *not* + infinitive with *to*:
'Please don't bring food into the shop.' → The assistant **asked us not to bring** food into the shop.
'I wouldn't buy a new car if I were you.' → My father advised **me not to buy** a new car.

We can also use *warn* in a situation where there is some danger:
'Don't swim beyond the rocks.' → He **warned us not to swim** beyond the rocks.
'Don't do too much exercise at once.' → The doctor **warned me not to do** too much exercise at once.

Practice

1 **GRAMMAR IN USE** Read the email and choose the correct words in *italics*.
🔊 **4.11** Listen and check.

> **Subject** I hate exams!
>
> Hi Vicki
> I've just come back from my Spanish oral exam. It was awful! I was really nervous. Our teacher had advised us (0) *try to stay calm* / (*to try to stay calm*) but of course, that was really difficult. A group of us were waiting outside the exam room, when a woman came past and told (1) *us to* / *to us to* stop chatting – she warned (2) *that we don't* / *us not to* make too much noise or we'd be in trouble. Then she asked one of our group (3) *to go* / *go* in, and we realised that she was the examiner! She was so unfriendly. One of the teachers came past – she could see we were all nervous, but she told (4) *us not to* / *us to not* worry. After a few minutes, the door opened again and a man invited me to go inside. He was quite friendly, but of course the unfriendly woman was also in there – she ordered (5) *that I* / *me to* sit down, so I took the nearest chair. At first I couldn't understand their Spanish. After a couple of minutes I felt better and when they asked me (6) *that* / *to* talk about my last holiday in Spain, I was OK. But then the woman told me (7) *stop* / *to stop*, and started correcting my Spanish, so I felt awful again! The man advised (8) *me to* / *me* slow down – he said it wasn't a speed competition – and from then it seemed OK. I'll just have to wait for the results now …

2 Decide whether each sign is giving an order or advice, or making a request. Then use the words in the chart to describe each one.

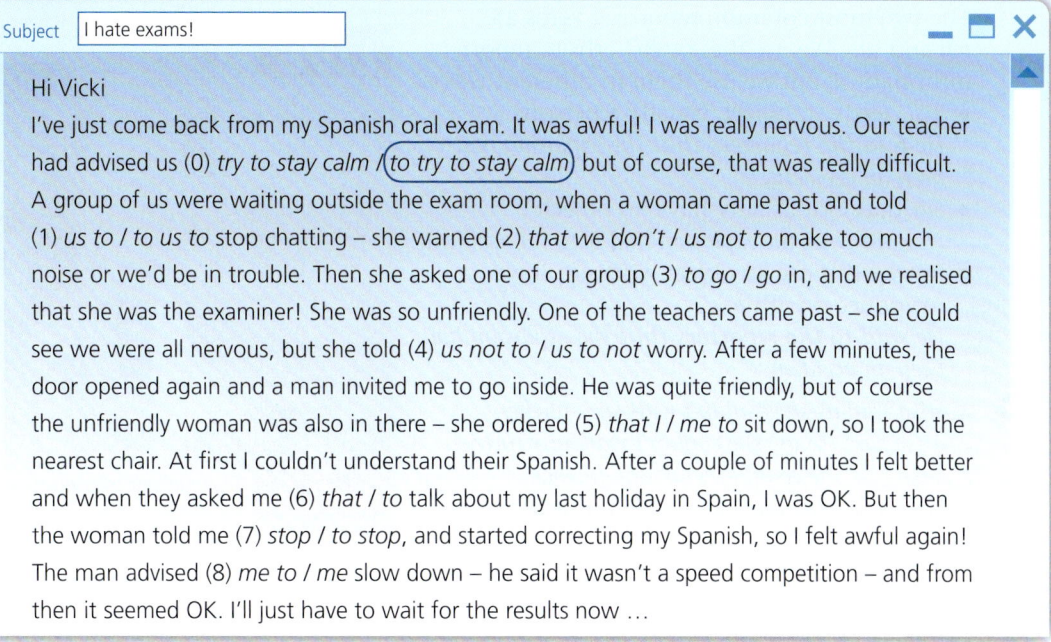

0 *This sign tells us not to smoke.*
1 *This sign asks* ....
2 ....
3 ....
4 ....

tells us warns us asks us advises us	to not to	feed the fish. smoke. wear a hard hat. queue from this side. touch the paint.

3 Complete the reported orders, requests, advice and warnings. Use *tell*, *ask*, *advise* or *warn*.
🔊 **4.12** Listen and check.

0 'Don't talk in the library.'
   The librarian *told us not to talk in the library* .

1 'I'd take some food for the journey, if I were you.'
   My mother ....

2 'Please have your tickets ready.'
   The clerk ....

3 'Don't go in the sea – it's dangerous.'
   The lifeguard ....

4 'It's best if you take the first train that arrives.'
   The guard ....

5 'Pick your rubbish up!'
   The police officer ....

71 Reporting verb patterns

1 *tell* and *say*

The two most common reporting verbs are *tell* and *say*. We use these two verbs to report information, but we use them in different ways.

- *Tell* needs an object, usually a person:
  He **told the reporters that** the explosion had been an accident.
- *Say* does not usually have an object:
  He **said that** the explosion had been an accident.
- But we can use an object with *say*, if we introduce it with *to*:
  He **said to the reporters that** the explosion had been an accident.

✗ Ailsa said us she couldn't walk any further.
✓ Ailsa said (to us) she couldn't walk any further.
✗ Ailsa told she couldn't walk any further.
✗ Ailsa told to us that she couldn't walk any further.
✓ Ailsa told **us** (that) she couldn't walk any further.

The minister refused to **admit sending** soldiers here. He **told reporters that** the desert exercises had stopped.

2 Reporting verb patterns

There are different ways of reporting speech, with different verbs:

PATTERN		VERBS
1 verb + *that* clause	no object	add admit announce claim complain insist reply respond say state suggest
	+ object	tell someone warn someone
2 verb + infinitive with *to*	no object	agree claim offer refuse
	+ object	advise someone ask someone beg someone encourage someone invite someone order someone persuade someone remind someone tell someone warn someone
3 verb + *-ing* form	no preposition	admit advise consider regret suggest
	+ preposition	admit to apologise for complain about insist on thank someone for

PATTERN 1 *'I'm getting married in July.'*
→ Simon **announced that he was getting married** in July.
PATTERN 2 *'You must remember to book the hotel later.'*
→ He **reminded me to book** the hotel later.
PATTERN 3 *'I'm sorry I lost your umbrella.'*
→ She **apologised for losing** my umbrella.

Some reporting verbs (shown in blue above) can have two or more patterns:
The boys **admitted that they had broken** the office window. / The boys **admitted breaking** the office window. / The boys **admitted to breaking** the office window.

When a reporting verb is followed by a preposition (e.g. *thank someone for*), we always use the *-ing* form of the verb that follows:
She thanked me for **helping** her.
You can check which preposition is used in a good dictionary.

Practice

1 Choose the correct words in *italics*. In four sentences, both answers are possible.

0 I agreed *to* / *him to* sign the bank forms for my son.
1 We told *you* / *to you* that we couldn't see you that evening.
2 The thief finally admitted *to stealing* / *that he had stolen* the painting from the gallery.
3 Your representative said *my husband* / *to my husband* that no payment would be taken.
4 The dentist suggested *that I should visit* / *visiting* him more regularly.
5 The programme makers apologised *upsetting* / *for upsetting* a lot of people.
6 Mario insisted *on buying* / *that he should buy* dinner for me as a 'thank you'.
7 She complained to my manager *that I was lazy* / *about my being lazy*.
8 The school encouraged *its students* / *to its students* to go to university.

2 **GRAMMAR IN USE** Complete the conversation with the verbs from the box.
🔊 4.13 Listen and check.

agreed announced apologised encouraged ~~insisted~~ regretted said told thanked

RASHID Sorry I'm late. Have you seen the news yet?
BEN No. My dad called – he (0) *insisted* on telling me all about his holiday. Why?
RASHID Well, you know there's been a bit of trouble with the TV company I work for?
BEN The complaints about that really violent series, yeah.
RASHID The managing director called the whole company to a meeting after work and (1) .... that he was going to resign this evening! He (2) .... that he took full responsibility for the problems, because he'd (3) .... to show the series although he knew how violent it was, so it was his fault.
BEN That's amazing, isn't it?
RASHID Yes, well, he's a very honourable man. He (4) .... for causing any difficulties for his staff, you know, with reporters, and (5) .... us all that he was very proud of the way we had behaved over the last two weeks.
BEN Did anyone ask how he felt about leaving?
RASHID Yes, he said he (6) .... having to make this decision, but it was the only one he could make. Anyway, he (7) .... us for supporting him, and (8) .... us to stay on and make the company a success.

3 Report the spoken words, using the verbs in brackets. You can report some of the sentences in more than one way. 🔊 4.14 Listen and check.

0 'OK, Dad. I did take £5 from your wallet, but it was to buy Mum a birthday card.' (admit)
The boy *admitted taking £5 from his father's wallet*.
1 'Would you like me to open the windows?' (offer)
The woman ....
2 'In answer to your question, the club accepts members of all ages.' (reply)
The assistant ....
3 'I really am the best electrician in the area.' (claim)
He ....
4 'Please try one of my cakes – they're delicious. You will? Good.' (persuade)
My friend ....
5 'We didn't tell the reporter about the company's financial problems.' (admit)
The managers ....

Review MODULE 13

1 **UNITS 68, 69 AND 70** Read the conversation between a student and her tutor, then complete the email below it with one word (or short form) in each gap.

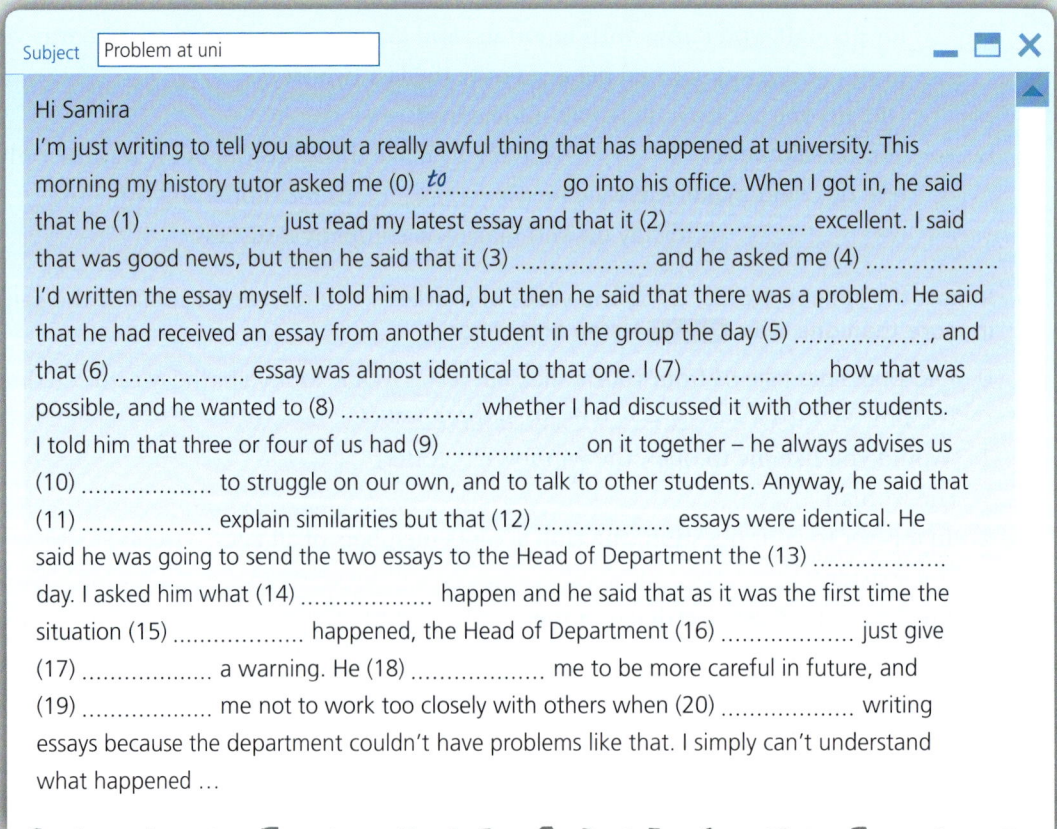

TUTOR   Jess, could you come into my office, please?
JESS   Of course.
TUTOR   Thanks. Jess, I've just read your essay, and it's excellent.
JESS   Thanks. That's really good news!
TUTOR   Well, actually, it isn't. Tell me, Jess, did you write that essay yourself?
JESS   Of course I did.
TUTOR   Well, there's a problem. I received an essay from another student in the group yesterday, and your essay is almost identical to that one.
JESS   I don't understand. How is that possible?
TUTOR   Well, did you discuss it with other students?
JESS   Yes, three or four of us worked on it together. You always say to us: 'Don't struggle on your own; talk to other students.'
TUTOR   True, that could explain similarities, but your two essays are identical. I'm going to send the two essays to the Head of Department tomorrow.
JESS   What will happen?
TUTOR   This is the first time this situation has happened, so the Head of Department might just give you a warning. But you really must be more careful in future, Ellen. You shouldn't work too closely with others when you're writing essays. The department really can't have problems like this.

Subject: Problem at uni

Hi Samira

I'm just writing to tell you about a really awful thing that has happened at university. This morning my history tutor asked me (0) *to* go into his office. When I got in, he said that he (1) .... just read my latest essay and that it (2) .... excellent. I said that was good news, but then he said that it (3) .... and he asked me (4) .... I'd written the essay myself. I told him I had, but then he said that there was a problem. He said that he had received an essay from another student in the group the day (5) ...., and that (6) .... essay was almost identical to that one. I (7) .... how that was possible, and he wanted to (8) .... whether I had discussed it with other students. I told him that three or four of us had (9) .... on it together – he always advises us (10) .... to struggle on our own, and to talk to other students. Anyway, he said that (11) .... explain similarities but that (12) .... essays were identical. He said he was going to send the two essays to the Head of Department the (13) .... day. I asked him what (14) .... happen and he said that as it was the first time the situation (15) .... happened, the Head of Department (16) .... just give (17) .... a warning. He (18) .... me to be more careful in future, and (19) .... me not to work too closely with others when (20) .... writing essays because the department couldn't have problems like that. I simply can't understand what happened …

2 UNITS 70 AND 71 Complete the second sentence so it means the same as the first, using the word in brackets. Use two to five words in your answer.

0 Gwyneth said: 'Would you like to join our team in the quiz competition?' (invited)
Gwyneth *invited us to join* their team in the quiz competition.

1 'Don't run in the school corridors,' the head teacher told us. (ordered)
The head teacher .... in the school corridors.

2 'I'm really sorry that I didn't remember your birthday,' Jennie told her sister. (remembering)
Jennie .... her sister's birthday.

3 'My advice is that you shouldn't give up your job yet,' Dad told me. (to)
Dad .... give up my job yet.

4 Our manager said to us, 'I'm going to pay for everyone's lunch and that's final.' (insisted)
Our manager .... for everyone's lunch.

5 'John, please don't ride that motorbike again,' said his father. (begged)
John's father .... ride that motorbike again.

3 ALL UNITS Choose the correct words in *italics*. In five places, both answers are possible.

MUM Alan, how many times has your father told you (0) *to not spend* / (*not to spend*) ages on the land line? That's what your mobile is for.

ALAN Sorry, Mum, but that was a reporter from the local newspaper. She phoned me.

MUM Oh, what did she want?

ALAN She wanted to know how I (1) *was feeling* / *am feeling* after winning the regional final of the Junior Musician of the Year competition.

MUM Oh, I see.

ALAN Yeah, she said she (2) *has been* / *had been* at the competition and she thought that (3) *I'd performed* / *I performed* really well. She asked when (4) *was I going* / *I was going* to the national final, so I told (5) *her* / *to her* that I might not go because I (6) *can't* / *couldn't* afford to go to London.

MUM What did she say?

ALAN She said that the local newspaper (7) *will* / *would* sponsor me if money was a problem. She invited me (8) *going* / *to go* to the office tomorrow and have my photo taken for the paper. I said (9) *I'm not* / *I wasn't* sure, you know, I said (10) *her* / *to her* that I (11) *had only done it* / *only did it* for a laugh. But then she told me what a good opportunity (12) *was it* / *it was* and she tried to persuade me (13) *to go* / *going* to the final.

MUM What did you say?

ALAN I told her I'd see her (14) *the next day* / *tomorrow* at her office, of course!

4 ALL UNITS Find four more mistakes and correct them. Tick (✓) the correct sentences.

0 The police officer asked me where ~~did you work~~. *you worked*
1 The doctor told that I should have an X-ray as soon as possible.
2 He phoned me last week and asked what I had been doing this morning.
3 He admitted to leaving a cigarette burning in an ashtray, which caused the fire.
4 That woman wanted to know where were the nearest toilets.
5 Our history teacher said that the Hundred Years' War lasted more than 100 years.
6 We can't go into the theatre yet – they told us to not.

Test MODULE 13

Reported speech

Choose the correct answer, A, B or C.

1. Maria said last Saturday that she .... her mother in hospital the day before.
   A had visited   B visited   C was visiting   ▶ Unit 68

2. Mike said yesterday that he .... us as soon as he had any news.
   A calls   B will call   C would call   ▶ Unit 68

3. The doctor told me that I .... drink less coffee.
   A shall   B should   C to   ▶ Unit 68

4. Jenna said the other day that she .... to your party this evening.
   A comes   B had come   C is coming   ▶ Unit 68

5. 'Are you and I both in the team for Saturday?' 'Yes, Lewis said he'd selected both of ....'
   A us   B you   C we   ▶ Unit 68

6. When I called the cinema the other day, they said all the tickets had sold out ....
   A the day before   B the next day   C yesterday   ▶ Unit 68

7. The receptionist asked us if .... upgrade to a better room.
   A we like to   B would we like to   C we would like to   ▶ Unit 69

8. My mum wanted to know which restaurant .... go to for Sunday lunch.
   A we want to   B we want   C do we want to   ▶ Unit 69

9. I asked that man where ...., but he doesn't know the city.
   A is the nearest metro   B was the nearest metro   C the nearest metro was   ▶ Unit 69

10. Your sister wants to know where .... her football boots.
    A you put   B did you put   C do you put   ▶ Unit 69

11. Salima asked us why .... to the club recently
    A we didn't go   B we hadn't been   C we weren't   ▶ Unit 69

12. The general ordered his soldiers ....
    A not to shoot   B not shoot   C to not shoot   ▶ Unit 70

13. 'Will you stay for supper?' → She asked .... for supper.
    A if I stayed   B me stay   C me to stay   ▶ Unit 70

14. There are signs warning .... the city centre this weekend.
    A drivers avoid   B drivers to avoid   C avoid drivers   ▶ Unit 70

15. The shop assistant advised .... the following day.
    A me to come back   B me come back   C me coming back   ▶ Unit 70

16. The presenter told .... the show was over.
    A to her guests that   B her guests that   C that   ▶ Unit 71

17. The woman at the front .... we could use the back entrance.
    A said us   B said to   C said   ▶ Unit 71

18. The gym instructor suggested that .... do forty minutes a day at first.
    A me to   B I should   C me doing   ▶ Unit 71

19. The managing director thanked all his staff .... him during the crisis.
    A for supporting   B for support   C to support   ▶ Unit 71

20. I was very tired when I got home, so Pete offered .... dinner.
    A me to cook   B to cook   C cooking   ▶ Unit 71

Go online for a full exit test

Relative, participle and other clauses

MODULE 14

Before you start

1 Read about Ian Fleming. Look at the highlighted grammar examples.

IAN FLEMING

Ian Fleming was the writer who invented James Bond. *Casino Royale*, published in 1953, was the first novel in which this character appeared. Fleming went on to write eleven more James Bond novels before his death in 1964.

As a young man, Fleming's ambition was to join the British Foreign Office. But he failed to get a job there, which was a great disappointment for him. Although he had never intended to be a writer, he got a job as a journalist for Reuters News Agency. Then, at the start of World War Two, Fleming became a secret information officer in the Royal Navy.

Leaving the navy in 1945, Fleming took the decision to write. But it was his work for the navy, which included several secret expeditions, that had given him the ideas for his James Bond novels.

The first James Bond novel to be made into a film was *Dr No*, in 1962. The film, starring Sean Connery, was a huge success.

Nobody really knows what makes the James Bond stories so successful. But now, half a century after Fleming's death, they are as popular as ever.

2 Now read the sentences and choose the correct words in *italics*. The highlighted grammar examples will help you.

1. Marie Curie was the scientist *which / who* discovered X-rays. ➤ Unit 72
2. That's the London house *in which / which in* Ian Fleming was born. ➤ Unit 72
3. We got the flights, *that / which* were very cheap, on the Internet. ➤ Unit 73
4. My best friend didn't come to the party, *who / which* was very annoying! ➤ Unit 73
5. 'Goldfinger', *made / which made* in 1964, was the third James Bond film with Sean Connery. ➤ Unit 74
6. Most of the James Bond films *featuring / featured* Sean Connery are now available on DVD. ➤ Unit 74
7. *To arrive / Arriving* at the railway station late at night, Clara couldn't find a taxi to take her home. ➤ Unit 75
8. The last James Bond novel *to be written / writing* by Ian Fleming was 'The Man With The Golden Gun'. ➤ Unit 76
9. My brother's main aim in life is *for to be / to be* rich. ➤ Unit 76
10. I don't understand *what / that* our teacher is saying. ➤ Unit 77

3 Check your answers below. Then go to the unit for more information and practice.

1 who 2 in which 3 which 4 which 5 made 6 featuring 7 Arriving 8 to be written 9 to be 10 what

⏻ Go online for a full diagnostic test

217

72 Relative clauses (1)

Arthur Conan Doyle is the writer **who invented Sherlock Holmes**. *The Hound of the Baskervilles* is a novel **he wrote in 1901**. It is set in the wild Dartmoor countryside.

1 Relative clauses

Relative clauses give us information about the subject or object of a main clause.

Defining relative clauses describe exactly which (or what kind of) person or thing we mean:

which writer?

Arthur Conan Doyle is *the writer* **who invented Sherlock Holmes**.

what kind of phone?

Do you have *a phone* **which takes photos**?

We introduce a relative clause with a **relative pronoun**:

RELATIVE PRONOUN	FOR	EXAMPLES
who	people	Mrs Lee was the woman **who** taught me to play the piano.
which	animals or things (but not people)	Their cat has killed the rat **which** was living under our house. I've got a water heater **which** uses solar power.
that	people, animals and things	He's the man **that** I spoke to. Sue's got a cat **that** loves coffee! It's a phone **that** takes photos.
whose	possession and relationships *his, her, its* or *their*	I know the woman **whose** husband used to be your boss. Hanna owns a horse **whose** coat is completely white. I'm working for a company **whose** head office is in Zurich.

FORMALITY CHECK *Whose* is quite formal. It is less formal to use *with*. We can also use *which has* for animals or things:
Hanna owns a horse **with** a completely white coat.
Steve's the boy **with** the red hair.
I work for a company **which has** its head office in Zurich.

⚠ We don't use *what* (▶ Unit 77.1) in the same way as *that*:
✗ ~~Frank's the man what owns our local gym.~~ ✓ Frank's the man **that** owns our local gym.

⚠ The relative pronoun REPLACES *he/him, she/her, they/them*, etc:
✗ ~~Karl is the teacher who he helped us.~~ ✓ Karl is the teacher who helped us.
✗ ~~I don't talk to people that I don't like them.~~ ✓ I don't talk to people that I don't like.

Non-defining relative clauses ▶ Unit 73

2 Leaving out the relative pronoun

The pronoun (e.g. *who, which, that*) in a relative clause can be the subject or object of the clause:

SUBJECT	Arthur Conan Doyle was the writer **who invented** Sherlock Holmes. (**Conan Doyle** invented Sherlock Holmes.)
OBJECT	'The Hound of the Baskervilles' is a novel **which he wrote** in 1901. (He wrote **the novel**.)

We can leave out the relative pronoun when it is an OBJECT, especially in speech and informal writing:
'The Hound of the Baskervilles' is a novel he wrote in 1901.

FORMALITY CHECK We usually include the object relative pronoun in formal writing:
*To activate your card you must use the new PIN number **which** we sent by recorded delivery.*

 We cannot leave out the relative pronoun when it is a SUBJECT:
✗ *Arthur Conan Doyle was the writer invented Sherlock Holmes.*
✓ *Arthur Conan Doyle was the writer **who** invented Sherlock Holmes.*

3 Clauses with *when*, *where*, *why*

We can also use *when*, *where* and *why* to introduce relative clauses.

- *When* introduces a relative clause about times, days, years, etc:
  *There was a storm on the day **when** my sister got married.*

- *Where* introduces a relative clause about places:
  *Do you know any shops **where** you can get designer jeans?*
  We can also use *which/that* (+ *in*) to talk about places:
  *That's the hotel **where** we stayed. That's the hotel **which/that** we stayed **in**.*

- *Why* introduces a relative clause about reason:
  *That's the reason **why** I'm late.*

We can leave out the noun before *when, where* and *why*:
*That was **when** I lived in London.* (the time when)
*This is **where** my best friend went to school.* (the building/place where)
*And that's **why** we're late.* (the reason why)

We can leave out *when* after *day, year, time,* etc. and *why* after *reason*:
*There was a storm on **the day my sister got married**. That's **the reason I'm late**.*

4 Prepositions in relative clauses

We sometimes form relative clauses using verbs with prepositions, such as *apply for*.
FORMALITY CHECK The position of the preposition is different in formal and informal English:

	INFORMAL		FORMAL
I applied for that job. →	That's the job **which** I applied **for**.		Below are the details of the job **for which** you applied.
I work with Steve. →	Steve's the man **who** I work **with**.		It's important to get on with the people **with whom*** you work.

* If we put a preposition before *who*, it changes to *whom*.

 We don't use prepositions in clauses beginning with *when* or *where*:
I used to live in this house. ✗ *This is the house where I used to live in.*
✓ *This is the house where I used to live.*

 We cannot put a preposition in front of *that*:
I've been looking for this book. ✗ *This is the book for that I've been looking.*
✓ *This is the book **that** I've been looking **for**.*

72 RELATIVE CLAUSES (1)

Practice

1 Choose the correct words in *italics*. In two places both answers are possible. 🔊 4.15 Listen and check.

0 Agatha Christie is the writer *who* / *which* invented Miss Marple.
1 Is this one of the DVDs *that* / *what* you've already seen?
2 Mike's the man *who* / *whose* wife writes detective novels.
3 What's the name of the hotel *which* / *that* you visited last summer?
4 Carol's the teacher *whose* / *who* will be taking over our class next term.
5 I prefer books *that* / *which* have a happy ending.
6 I could never live in a house *that* / *who* doesn't have a nice garden.
7 A whale is an animal *who* / *that* breathes air but lives underwater.
8 I'm afraid it's by an author *who* / *whose* name I can't remember.

2 **GRAMMAR IN USE** Find five more relative pronouns in the text that can be left out. 🔊 4.16 Listen and check.

> **The detective novel**
>
> For over a hundred years detective stories have been one of the most popular forms of writing. The books *that* they appear in are often called 'whodunits'. In many cases the detectives in these novels are professional police officers. A typical example is Inspector Morse, the famous Oxford detective who was created by the writer Colin Dexter.
>
> But many of these characters are private detectives who help the clients who they work for. Perhaps the best-known is Philip Marlowe – a private detective invented by the author Raymond Chandler in a novel which he wrote in 1939.
>
> Of course, not all detectives in fiction are professionals, many are amateurs. One of the most famous of these is Miss Marple, a character that Agatha Christie invented in 1927.
>
> In more recent years, scientists and psychologists have taken over the role of detectives in popular fiction. This is due to the increasingly important role which science plays in modern police work. One of the best-known of these 'detectives' is Dr Kay Scarpetta – the invention of American crime writer Patricia Cornwell. Cornwell introduced Scarpetta to the world in *Postmortem*, a book which she published in 1990.

3 Complete the sentences with *which*, *where*, *when* or *why*. Leave out the pronoun where possible.

0 This tastes awful. I don't know *why* I ordered it!
1 It was raining by the time .... we got there.
2 Is this the place .... we're supposed to meet them?
3 She works in a building .... used to be a hospital.
4 Is that the reason .... she never answers your emails?
5 This is the house .... my grandmother was born.
6 1969 was the year .... human beings first landed on the moon.
7 What a terrible thing to say! I don't know .... she's always so rude to me.
8 It was a film .... seemed to last forever.
9 Do you remember the day .... we met?
10 There were a couple of questions .... were too difficult for me to answer.

14

4 Complete the second sentence so it means the same as the first.
Sentences 4–6 are more formal English.

0 We used to go to that school.
   That's the school *we used to go to*.
1 I told you about that woman.
   She's the woman ....
2 You were interested in a musical. Is it *Mamma Mia*?
   Is *Mamma Mia* the musical .... ?
3 We walked under that old railway bridge.
   That's the old railway bridge ....
4 The insurance company has already paid for those repairs.
   Those are the repairs .... has already paid.
5 The committee has no control over this matter.
   This is a matter .... has no control.
6 The bank has lent money to those customers.
   Those are the customers .... has lent money.

5 **GRAMMAR IN USE** Look at the text about a TV show below and complete it with this information.

(0) The Internet and mobile phones didn't exist in the nineteenth century.
(1) Sherlock Holmes lives in the flat at 221B Baker Street.
(2) Conan Doyle invented the basic plots.
(3) Sherlock Holmes uses his powers of observation to solve crimes.
(4) Benedict Cumberbatch has starred in many recent films and TV shows.
(5) Dr Watson's career in the army has ended.
(6) Martin Freeman became famous for his part in *The Office*.

A 21st Century Sherlock Holmes

Sherlock is a new BBC television series based on the novels of Arthur Conan Doyle, but set in present-day London. Of course, the original stories were written in the late nineteenth century, a time (0) *when the Internet and mobile phones didn't exist*. In this new version all kinds of modern technology are used.

Although the stories have been updated to the twenty-first century, lovers of the original novels will be pleased to know that many of the familiar characters and places have been kept for the new series. For instance, the flat (1) .... is still 221B Baker Street.

The writers of the series have used the basic plots (2) ...., but they have been made more exciting and modern. The main characters are:

Sherlock Holmes: Holmes is a brilliant detective (3) .... The part of Holmes is played by Benedict Cumberbatch, a young actor (4) ....

Dr Watson: Watson, a doctor (5) ...., is Sherlock Holmes' best friend. The part of Watson is played by Martin Freeman. He's an actor (6) .... in the hit comedy series *The Office*.

Go online for more practice

73 Relative clauses (2)

Alexander Solzhenitsyn, **who was awarded the Nobel Prize in 1970**, wrote several novels about the Soviet labour camps in Siberia.

1 Non-defining relative clauses

Non-defining relative clauses do not describe exactly who or what we mean. Instead they give us extra information about the subject or object of a main clause:
*Alexander Solzhenitsyn, **who was awarded the Nobel Prize in 1970**, wrote several novels.*
If we remove the clause, the sentence still makes sense:
Alexander Solzhenitsyn wrote several novels.

Compare this with defining relative clauses:
*Angela Green is the woman **who lives next door**.*
Angela Green is the woman. [which woman?]

⚠ We don't use *that* or *what* in non-defining relative clauses:
✗ ~~The painting, that is now restored, can be seen in the National Gallery.~~
✓ The painting, which is now restored, can be seen in the National Gallery.

Because non-defining relative clauses do not identify the subject in the main clause, there is a difference in meaning:

DEFINING *The passengers **who were injured in the crash** were taken to hospital.*
(Only the injured passengers were taken to hospital. We know that some were not injured.)
NON-DEFINING *The passengers, **who were injured in the crash**, were taken to hospital.*
(All the passengers were taken to hospital. We know that they were all injured.)

2 Punctuation and use of prepositions

Unlike defining relative clauses, non-defining relative clauses are separated from the rest of the sentence by commas. We usually put the clause immediately after the subject it refers to:

⚠ ✗ ~~The author of the novel lives in Edinburgh, which you can buy for €20.~~
✓ The author of the novel, **which you can buy for €20**, lives in Edinburgh.

We use prepositions in non-defining relative clauses in the same way as in defining relative clauses (➤ Unit 72.4):
*Sue recently won a prize, **which she never stops talking about**.*
*That house, **which we used to live in**, has been sold.*

🔊 Pronunciation ➤ 1.31

3 Comment clauses with *which*

We can use a non-defining relative clause, usually at the end of the sentence, to say something about the whole of the main clause:
*The army team was unable to make the bomb safe, **which meant everyone had to leave the area**.*
*Solzhenitsyn wrote his books while he was still a prisoner, **which was very brave**.*

⚠ We use *which*, NOT *who*, *whose*, *that* or *it*, to introduce a comment clause.
We put a comma before *which*:
✗ ~~Solzhenitsyn wrote his books while he was still a prisoner, who was very brave.~~
✓ Solzhenitsyn wrote his books while he was still a prisoner, **which** was very brave.

14

Practice

1 Choose the correct meaning, A or B.

0 Emma's sister, who isn't married, lives in New York.
  A Emma has several sisters. (B) Emma only has one sister.
1 This building is part of the Riverside development, which has just won a design award.
  A The building has won an award. B The Riverside development has won an award.
2 We stayed at the first hotel we saw which had a swimming pool.
  A We only looked at one hotel. B We looked at other hotels without pools.
3 I chose the grey suit, which cost $100.
  A The colour was more important.   B The price was more important.
4 Two students who took the exam passed with distinction.
  A More than two students took the exam. B Only two students took the exam.

2 Rewrite the sentences, using non-defining relative clauses.

0 I went to university in Cambridge. Cambridge is a beautiful city.
  I went to university in Cambridge, which is a beautiful city.
1 *Humaniqueness* is the first book that Glauco Ortolano has written in English. Ortolano is Brazilian.
  ....
2 Harlitt's chocolate factory has closed down. It used to employ over a thousand people.
  ....
3 You can't smoke in restaurants any more. I'm pleased about that.
  ....
4 They've closed down our local library. This is really annoying.
  ....
5 The course starts on Monday 12th January. The course lasts ten weeks.
  ....
6 The new company president will be Sandra Jackson. Sandra Jackson's period as creative director was very successful.
  ....

3 **GRAMMAR IN USE** There are four more missing commas and three more incorrect pronouns in the text. Write the correct words and the missing commas. 🔊 4.17 Listen and check.

> The nineteenth century, ~~that~~ *which* was the golden age of Russian literature**,** produced the world-famous novelists Leo Tolstoy and Fyodor Dostoevsky, the poet Alexander Pushkin and the playwright Anton Chekhov. Tolstoy's novel *War and Peace* what was written in 1869 is often considered to be the greatest novel of the nineteenth century.
>
> Russian literature continued to flourish in the twentieth century. Internationally, the two Russian novelists who were most successful were Boris Pasternak and Vladimir Nabokov.
>
> Nabokov, that spent much of his life in the United States also wrote novels in English.
>
> Pasternak was the author of *Dr Zhivago* that was made into a hugely successful film in 1965. He was awarded the Nobel Prize in 1958 but refused to accept it.

74 Clauses after the noun

Robinson Crusoe is a novel **based** on the true story of a Scottish pirate, Alexander Selkirk.

1 Reduced relative clauses

We often make relative clauses shorter, like this:
'Robinson Crusoe' is **a novel** *which is based* on the true story of Alexander Selkirk.
→ 'Robinson Crusoe' is **a novel** *based* on the true story of Alexander Selkirk.
It's about **a man** *who lives* on a deserted island.
→ It's about **a man** *living* on a deserted island.

- If the verb in the original relative clause is active, we use the *-ing* form:
  It's a shop that **sells** designer jeans. → It's a shop **selling** designer jeans.
- If the verb is passive we use the *-ed* form:
  It's a novel which **is based** on a true story. → It's a novel **based** on a true story.
- We can only make clauses shorter when the noun we are describing is the same as the subject of the relative clause, NOT if it is different:
  noun we are describing ≠ subject of relative clause
  This is a photo of **the hotel** that **we** stay in every year.
  ✗ *This is a photo of the hotel staying in every year.*

More on other participle clauses ➤ Unit 75

⚠ We only use the *-ing* form if the action is happening now or is continuing. We cannot use it for single actions in the past:
That was the customer **who phoned yesterday**. (single completed action)
✗ *That was the customer phoning yesterday.*

⚠ We don't use *-ing* forms with state verbs (➤ Unit 29.3/4):
✗ *He's the man owning the factory.*   ✓ He's the man **who owns** the factory.

2 Infinitive clauses

We often replace a relative clause with an *infinitive clause* after a superlative, after *the first, the second,* etc., or after *one, next, last, few* and *only* (➤ Unit 76.2):
Yuri Gagarin was the first man **that went into space**.
→ Yuri Gagarin was the first man **to go into space**.
She was the only one **who helped me**. → She was the only one **to help me**.

3 Using prepositions instead of relative clauses

We often shorten sentences with the help of prepositions:
- relative pronoun + *have* → *with*:
  This queue is for passengers **who have EU passports**.
  → This queue is for passengers **with EU passports**.
  Is there a restaurant **that has a vegetarian menu** near here?
  → Is there a restaurant **with a vegetarian menu** near here?
- relative pronoun + *be* + preposition → *in/at/on*, etc.:
  I like the painting **which is on** the bedroom wall. → I like the painting **on** the bedroom wall.
  What are those plants **that are in** your garden? → What are those plants **in** your garden?

224

14

Practice

1 **GRAMMAR IN USE** Choose the correct words in *italics*. In two places, both answers are possible. 🔊 4.18 Listen and check.

ANNA   What's the name of the book (0) *reading* / *that you're reading* at the moment?

KARL   *Imperium* by Robert Harris. It's a book (1) *recommending* / *recommended* by my history teacher.

ANNA   That's about the people (2) *who were killed* / *killed* by the volcanic eruption in Pompeii, isn't it?

KARL   No, it's a historical novel (3) *basing* / *based* on the true story of Cicero.

ANNA   Who was he? Wasn't he the first person (4) *became* / *to become* an emperor?

KARL   No. He was one of the politicians (5) *living* / *lived* in Rome at the end of the Republic.

ANNA   Was it an expensive book?

KARL   No. I got it from the market. There's a stall there (6) *that has* / *with* lots of bargain books.

2 Complete the second sentence so it means the same as the first, using a reduced relative clause, an infinitive clause or a preposition + noun. 🔊 4.19 Listen and check.

0   It's a poem that somebody wrote in the sixteenth century.
    It's a poem *written in the sixteenth century*.

00 Was she the only person that visited you?
    Was she the only person *to visit you*?

000 Is there a bank near here that has a cash machine?
    Is there a bank near here *with a cash machine*?

1   Daniel was the first person that spoke to me.
    Daniel was the first person _____.

2   There was an old letter that was found under the floor.
    There was an old letter _____.

3   What is the name of the building that's next to the library?
    What's the name of the building _____?

4   My grandfather gave me that watch.
    That is the watch _____ by my grandfather.

5   This is the third DVD player that has broken down!
    This is the third DVD player _____!

6   I need a computer that has a bigger hard drive.
    I need a computer _____.

3 Replace the <u>underlined</u> phrases with reduced relative clauses, infinitives or prepositions. Then match the descriptions with the writers and characters from fiction.

0   A scientist /<s>who has</s> *with* two different personalities.   Madame Bovary
1   A man <u>who was left</u> on a deserted island.   Boris Pasternak
2   The only Russian writer <u>that refused</u> the Nobel Prize.   Dr Jekyll/Mr Hyde
3   A police detective <u>who lives</u> in Oxford.   William Shakespeare
4   A writer <u>who was born</u> in Stratford-upon-Avon in 1564.   Robinson Crusoe
5   A secret agent <u>who has</u> the code name 007.   Inspector Morse
6   A woman <u>who is married</u> to a country doctor in nineteenth-century France.   James Bond

⏻ Go online for more practice and a progress test

75 Participle clauses

> **Written** in 1961, *Catch-22* is a novel about a young American soldier, John Yossarian. In the middle of World War Two he is sent to fight in Italy, **leaving** his friends and family behind.

1 Participle clauses

Participle clauses give more information about a noun. We use the *-ed* or *-ing* form of the verb. Participle clauses don't have a subject because their subject is the noun/pronoun in the main clause:

participle clause   subject

Written in 1961, *'Catch-22'* is a novel about a young American soldier, John Yossarian.

                     subject   participle clause

In the middle of World War Two, he is sent to fight in Italy, **leaving his friends and family behind.**

FORMALITY CHECK In written English we often put participle clauses in front of the main clause. We use a comma to separate the two clauses.

Participle clauses are common in written English because they let us give a lot of information in a single sentence.

More on sentence-building ➤ Module 19

2 Participle clauses of reason, result, time, etc.

	FULL CLAUSE	PARTICIPLE CLAUSE
reason	**Because he's a student** he can get a discount on rail travel.	**Being a student,** he can get a discount on rail travel.
result	A snowstorm covered the motorway. **The result was that dozens of drivers were trapped in their cars.**	A snowstorm covered the motorway, **trapping dozens of drivers in their cars.**
condition	**If you give it enough water and sunlight,** the plant will grow to three metres.	**Given enough water and sunlight,** the plant will grow to three metres.
time/ sequence	**As I walked into the room** I noticed the flowers by the window.	**Walking into the room,** I noticed the flowers by the window.

There is also a perfect form, *having* + past participle (➤ Unit 64.1), which we can use to talk about an action that happened earlier:
Having paid the entrance fee, we walked into the museum.
(= After we had paid the entrance fee, we walked into the museum.)

3 Forms for active and passive meanings

In participle clauses the *-ing* form has an active meaning:
The bank manager **opened** the safe and noticed something strange inside. (active verb)
→ **Opening** the safe, the bank manager noticed something strange inside.

The *-ed* form has a passive meaning:
The flood victim stood on the roof. He **was trapped** by the rising water. (passive verb)
→ The flood victim stood on the roof, **trapped** by the rising water.

Practice

1 **Choose the correct meaning, A or B.**

0 Jake fell over, breaking his glasses.
  A Jake fell over because his glasses were broken.
  B Jake's glasses broke because he fell over.
1 Having read the book, I don't need to see the film.
  A I have to read the book but I don't need to see the film.
  B It isn't necessary to see the film because I've already read the book.
2 Stored in a fridge, the dish will stay fresh for four days.
  A If you store it in a fridge, the dish will stay fresh for four days.
  B I stored the dish in a fridge for four days.
3 Being a doctor, people often ask me for advice.
  A Doctors often ask me for advice.
  B People ask me for advice because I'm a doctor.
4 Having passed the driving test, I was able to buy a car.
  A I was able to buy a car because I'd passed the driving test.
  B I bought a car before I passed the driving test.

2 **GRAMMAR IN USE** Complete the article with words from the box. There are three extra words. 4.20 Listen and check.

> annoyed arrested arresting being ~~born~~ having become
> joining leaving left needing used using

The true story of Alexander Selkirk

(0) _Born_ in Scotland in 1676, Selkirk was the son of a shoemaker, and very different from the character he inspired in the novel *Robinson Crusoe*. As a teenager he was very badly behaved. (1) .... for causing trouble in 1695, he was ordered to appear in court, but he ran away to sea, (2) .... the crew of the pirate ship, *Cinque Ports*. He was a skilled sailor and was quickly promoted.
(3) .... sailing master in 1703, Selkirk soon started arguing with Thomas Stradling, the ship's captain. In October 1704, (4) .... to collect fresh food and water for his ship, Captain Stradling decided to stop at one of the deserted islands of Juan Fernandez. (5) .... an old ship, the *Cinque Ports* also needed repairs. Selkirk wanted the crew to repair the ship, but the captain refused, and, (6) .... by Selkirk's continued demands, sailed away without him.
(7) .... alone on the island for more than four years, Selkirk had to find ways to stay alive. Fortunately, he was able to make his own clothes and tools, (8) .... the skills he had learnt from his father.

3 **Complete the sentences with participle clauses, using the information in brackets.** 4.21 Listen and check.

0 _Having three children_, we don't get much free time. (because we have three children)
1 ...., we left the restaurant. (after we'd paid for the meal)
2 ...., *Invictus* is based on a true story. (it was filmed in 2009)
3 Karen ran out of the building, ... (she called for help)
4 ...., I noticed two people arguing. (as I looked out of the window)
5 ...., this rose can grow to a height of two metres.
   (if you plant it in a sunny spot)

76 Infinitive clauses

And Then There Were None was the first book by Agatha Christie **to sell** more than 100 million copies. It is one of the few books **not to feature** her famous characters Hercule Poirot or Miss Marple.

1 Infinitive clauses (infinitive + *to*)

We often use infinitive clauses after the verb *be*:
As a child, my ambition was **to study medicine**. *My ambition is* **to become a vet**.
There are active and passive forms of the infinitive:

	ACTIVE INFINITIVE	PASSIVE INFINITIVE
simple*	The most important thing is **to tell** the truth.	I hate **to be told** lies.

* There is a perfect form *to have told* and a continuous form *to be telling* (▶ Unit 65.2).

To make the negative form we put *not* in front of the infinitive:
It is one of the few books **not to feature** *her famous characters Hercule Poirot or Miss Marple.*
President Solano was the only head of state **not to be invited** *to the conference.*

⚠ We don't usually include a subject in an infinitive clause:
✗ *It is important you to tell the truth.*   ✓ *It is important* **to tell the truth**.
But if the subject of the infinitive clause is different from the subject of the sentence, we can use *for* + subject + infinitive with *to*:
I think it's important **for politicians to tell** *the truth. My aim is* **for my children to be** *happy.*

NATURAL ENGLISH There are some well-known expressions with infinitive clauses that we use to make a comment about something we are saying:
I really don't like him, **to be honest**. **To tell the truth**, *the show was disappointing.*

Infinitives which follow certain verbs, e.g. *I refuse to leave* ▶ Unit 65

2 Infinitives after superlatives, adjectives, etc.

We often use infinitive clauses to replace relative clauses after a superlative, after *the first, the second*, etc. or after *one, next, last, few* and *only*:
It was the first book by Agatha Christie which sold more than 100 million copies.
→ *It was* **the first** *book by Agatha Christie* **to sell** *more than 100 million copies.*
We also use infinitives after adjectives which describe people's feelings and opinions:
We're **delighted to be** *here. I'm* **happy for them to join** *the class.*

3 Infinitive of purpose

We can use an infinitive clause to describe the purpose or reason for an action:
Carlos went to college **to study law**. *I took a pill* **to get rid of my headache**.

⚠ We don't use *for* + infinitive of purpose:
✗ *He went to the corner for to get a taxi.*   ✓ *He went to the corner* **to get** *a taxi.*

FORMALITY CHECK In more formal English we can also use *in order to* or *so as to*:
We moved to Brighton **in order to be** *nearer our grandchildren.*
Please move to the front **so as to allow** *more room for the late arrivals.*

We can put the infinitive clause before the main clause for instructions:
To make a call, *press the green button.* **To inflate the life jacket**, *pull on the red cord.*

Practice

1 Write the words in the correct order to make sentences. Start with the underlined word(s).

0 an email   to   <u>Daniella</u>   the Internet café   went   send   to
Daniella went to the Internet café to send an email.

1 the first man   on the moon   walk   to   <u>Neil Armstrong</u>   was

2 to university   to   chemistry   <u>my brother</u>   went   study

3 not   a mess   to   <u>I</u>   make   promise

4 the third person   to   <u>Harry</u>   is   this morning   phone me

2 Choose the correct words in *italics*. In two places, both answers are possible.
🔊 **4.22** Listen and check.

1 A We're going to Skytrip Tours (0) *for booking* / *to book* our next holiday.
   B Really? Why are you going there?
   A It's the only travel company (1) *to charge not* / *not to charge* for children under sixteen.
2 A I've put lemon juice round my plants (2) *for* / *to* stop the cats digging them up.
   B Does it work?
   A I'm not really sure, (3) *telling* / *to tell* the truth.
3 A Are you applying for university?
   B Yes. I'm trying to get a place (4) *to study* / *that studies* economics.
   A Good for you. It's so important (5) *that people* / *for people to* get a good education.
4 A I'm looking for something (6) *to give* / *for giving* to my cousin for his birthday. I've heard there's a good video game called 'Space Warriors' – do you have that?
   B I'm not sure. You're the first person (7) *that's asked* / *to ask* me for that one. I'll just check on the computer. No, we're out of stock at the moment. I could order it for you.
   A Oh, how long would that take?
   B I don't really know, (8) *that I'm* / *to be* honest.

3 **GRAMMAR IN USE** Find six more mistakes in the conversation and correct them.
🔊 **4.23** Listen and check.

ANGELA I'm going to the library ~~for~~ *to* get some books on Marco Polo. Do you want to come?
BELLA   Sure. Who's Marco Polo?
ANGELA He was one of the first Europeans visiting the Far East. He wrote a book about his adventures in 1298.
BELLA   I think I've heard about that. It was the first book for to describe China and Kublai Khan, wasn't it?
ANGELA Yes. I'm writing an essay on him for my course. It's really important because I need to get a good grade for the essay in order for pass the course. I don't want to be the only person in my year to pass not!
BELLA   Well, it sounds like a fascinating subject, anyway. It's my ambition visit China onc day.
ANGELA I'd love to do that, too. Listen. Do you want to go for a coffee later?
BELLA   I'm not sure. I'm supposed to be meeting Helena.
ANGELA That's OK. I'd be happy her to join us.

⏻ Go online for more practice

77 Other noun structures

The Grapes of Wrath, by John Steinbeck, is a fascinating book. It describes **what life was like** for poor American farmers in the 1930s.

1 Wh- clauses

Wh- clauses can express the same as a noun or noun phrase, but we tend to use them more in informal English.

NOUN PHRASE	Wh- CLAUSE
I don't agree with **their decision**.	→ I don't agree with **what they decided**.
Have you been to **our house**?	→ Have you been to **where we live**?
They told us about **the designer**.	→ They told us about **who designed it**.
I don't understand **this method**.	→ I don't understand **how you do it**.

- *Wh-* clauses are not the same as relative clauses:
  *I don't agree with **their decision**.* (noun phrase)
  → *I don't agree with **what they decided**.* (wh- clause)
  → *I don't agree with the decision **that they made**.* (relative clause)
- The *wh-* clause acts like a noun, so it can be the subject or object of a verb:
  ***What he did** made us very angry.* (= His actions made us angry.)
  *It describes **what life was like** for poor farmers in the 1930s.*
  (= It describes poor farmers' living conditions.)

What usually means 'the thing(s) that':
What we do is more important than **what we know**.
(= The things we do are more important than the things we know.)
*I don't know much about art, but I know **what I like**.* (= I know the things that I like.)

⚠ We don't include the noun in a clause beginning with *what*:
✗ ~~I don't agree with the decision what they decided.~~   ✓ *I don't agree with **what they decided**.*

Relative clauses with *when*, *where* and *why* ➤ Unit 72.3

2 Comparison clauses with nouns

We usually make comparisons using adjectives and adverbs (➤ Units 21, 22).
But we can also compare nouns:
*She's **richer** than me.* → *She's got **more** money than me.*
*Their house **is bigger** than ours.* → *Their house **has more** space than ours.*
*Nowadays it **doesn't take as long** to get there.* → *Nowadays it **takes less** time to get there.*

We can also make superlative forms using *the most/the least* + noun:
*Of all our staff, Jackie had **the fewest** complaints.*
*Sally has **the least** money, so we should let her have the cheapest ticket.*

More on *more/less* and *the most/the least* ➤ Unit 12.3   *less* ➤ Units 21 and 25

Practice

1 **Rewrite the underlined phrases, using *who, what, where, why* or *how* and a phrase from the box.** 🔊 **4.24** **Listen and check.**

> she decided   he did   he knows   you live   wrote it   he's doing it
> she does   they're going   they did it

0 I'm not very pleased with <u>his actions</u>.   *what he did*
1 Do you know <u>their destination</u>?   ....
2 Can you explain <u>their method</u>?   ....
3 Is that <u>his reason</u>?   ....
4 I don't know <u>the author of that book</u>.   ....
5 Excuse me. Is this <u>your address</u>?   ....
6 <u>Her job</u> isn't very exciting.   ....
7 <u>Her decision</u> seems rather selfish to me.   ....
8 <u>His knowledge</u> is important.   ....

2 **Choose the correct words in *italics*.**

0 I'm amazed by *which / (what)* he knows.
1 *What / That* we need is a really good dictionary.
2 The person with *the most / more* correct answers wins the competition.
3 I don't care *where / which* we go for our holiday, so long as it's near a beach.
4 Sarah *more earns money / earns more money* than me.
5 *The thing what / What* that man did is outrageous.
6 Can you explain *that / how* he solved the puzzle?
7 Which house has *most the / the most* bedrooms?
8 *What / Why* she left him is something we'll never know.

3 **GRAMMAR IN USE** **Complete the text with one word only in each gap.** 🔊 **4.25** **Listen and check.**

The Embarrassment of Riches by Simon Schama

This is a book about Holland in the seventeenth century, the golden age of Dutch history. Simon Schama, a professor of history at Columbia University, uses this book to tell us about (0) ___*what*___ he thinks is a key moment in European history – the birth of the first modern society. The book explains (1) .... Holland built the world's first maritime empire and created a tolerant society which has lasted until the present day. He describes the people that created this society: (2) .... they were and (3) .... they achieved it.

He is particularly strong on cultural history. He has clearly done (4) .... research than most historians because his knowledge of Dutch art is enormous. In fact, (5) .... we know about most Dutch artists is fairly limited, but Schama uses the evidence very well. He tells us (6) .... the artists came from and (7) .... they managed to create such amazing works of art. But he doesn't ignore the ordinary people of that time; he describes (8) .... life was like for people at all levels of society.

This is a big book and has (9) .... facts and figures than most history books. But, because Schama is such a master storyteller, it never seems dull or academic. If you want a history book that is thoroughly researched, but has all the excitement of a novel, then *'The Embarrassment of Riches'* is probably exactly (10) .... you are looking for.

Go online for more practice and a progress test

Review MODULE 14

1 UNITS 72 AND 73 Complete the sentences with one word only in each gap.

0 The traffic was bad. That's *why* we're so late.
1 That's the hospital .... I was born.
2 What was the name of the man .... killed President Kennedy?
3 This photo was taken in the year .... my parents got married.
4 Is she the girl .... brother used to teach you football?
5 We didn't get a room with a sea view, ... was disappointing.
6 I don't know .... I failed the test. Perhaps I didn't do enough revision.
7 Fleming had never been back to the city in .... he grew up.
8 The hero of the film wasn't good-looking, ... is unusual in a Hollywood film.
9 My uncle, ... used to be an actor, loves telling funny stories.
10 The 'Dark Lady' is the mysterious woman for .... Shakespeare wrote some of his best poems.

2 UNITS 72 AND 73 Match the sentences 1–5 with the meanings A–F.

0 The candidate who I spoke to was only twenty-one.
1 The candidate, who I spoke to, was only twenty-one.
2 The candidates who were under twenty-one didn't have enough experience.
3 The candidates, who were under twenty-one, didn't have enough experience.
4 The candidates, who had been to university, wanted higher salaries.
5 The candidates who had been to university wanted higher salaries.

A Some of the candidates had enough experience.
B Some of the candidates wanted higher salaries.
C All of the candidates wanted higher salaries.
D There were several candidates for the job, but the one I spoke to was twenty-one.
E None of the candidates had enough experience.
F There was only one candidate for the job.

3 UNITS 72 AND 73 Complete the descriptions, using the information. Each description must contain all the information in one sentence only, with a relative clause.

← she was the first woman to be prime minister of Pakistan
← she died in 2007

← it was taken by Marianne's father
← it shows her playing on the beach with her brother

0 This politician *, who was the first woman to be prime minister of Pakistan, died in 2007.*

1 This photo ....

232

← it was painted hundreds of years ago
← it shows a man riding a horse

← it belonged to Queen Marie Antoinette
← it is now worth a million dollars

2 This picture ....
....
....

3 This antique chair ....
....
....

← Winston Churchill lived in it
← it belongs to the National Trust

← her father was in the group Aerosmith
← she's been in lots of Hollywood films

4 This house ....
....
....

5 This actress ....
....
....

← they filmed 'Lord of the Rings' here
← it's in New Zealand

← it's the only one to stay open at night
← it sells all kinds of food and drink

6 This valley ....
....
....

7 This shop ....
....
....

4 UNITS 72, 73, 74 AND 75 Find seven more mistakes and correct them. Tick (✓) the correct sentences.

0 He wrote a book, ~~what~~ *which* I haven't read, when he was a young man.
1 The computer which I bought it last week has broken down.
2 Having eaten a large main course, I had no desire for a dessert.
3 The Wright brothers were the first people flying an aeroplane.
4 I prefer meals making with fresh ingredients.
5 Dorothy is often late, that the boss finds really annoying.
6 Can I see the sales assistant that I spoke to him yesterday?
7 Those parking spaces are for people with young children.
8 *Labyrinth* is the best book I've read recently.
9 Walked into the room, I noticed something strange in the corner.
10 Apparently Susan was the last person speak to her before she left.

233

5 UNITS 75, 76 AND 77   Complete the second sentence, so it means the same as the first, using the word in brackets. Use two to five words in your answer.

0   This was the first novel that was published on the Internet. (be)
    This was the first novel *to be published* on the Internet.

1   I'll never forget the advice which my grandfather gave me. (given)
    I'll never forget .... by my grandfather.

2   Because she is so pale, Caroline gets sunburnt very easily. (being)
    ...., Caroline gets sunburnt very easily.

3   I needed some toothpaste so I went to the corner shop. (get)
    I went to the corner shop ....

4   This is the only place that doesn't charge for parking. (to)
    This is the only place ....

5   Can you tell me the way I should set up this DVD recorder? (how)
    Can you tell me .... this DVD recorder?

6   The car can be quite noisy if you drive it at high speed. (driven)
    ...., the car can be quite noisy.

7   Can you describe the things that were stolen in the robbery? (what)
    Can you describe .... in the robbery?

6 ALL UNITS   Complete the article, using the words in brackets. If necessary, add pronouns and make changes to the words in brackets.

Who was the real Sherlock Holmes?

Sherlock Holmes is probably the most famous detective in literature. Of course, he wasn't a real person. His character is based on a real man (0) *whose career had* (career / have) a huge influence on Arthur Conan Doyle, (1) .... (be) the author of the Sherlock Holmes books. The man's name was Joseph Bell and he was a leading surgeon (2) .... (teach / medicine) at Edinburgh University. Conan Doyle first met Joseph Bell when he went to one of Bell's lectures in 1877. (3) .... (notice) Conan Doyle's ability and intelligence, the great doctor decided to make him his assistant. This gave Conan Doyle the chance to observe Bell and to see (4) .... (he / treat) his patients.
Bell believed that the most important thing was (5) .... (find out) as much as possible about a patient. He did this by very close observation of (6) .... (they / move), acted and talked, and by looking closely at their bodies, hands and clothing. For example, by looking at someone's hands he could often work out (7) .... (job / they / do). By listening carefully to their accent it was possible to find out (8) .... (they / come from).
This technique of deducing information from very detailed observation was the inspiration for Sherlock Holmes. Holmes notices things (9) .... (the ordinary person / be) usually unaware of, and this is often the key to solving crimes. (10) .... (live /in an age) before DNA and scientific evidence, Holmes must use his own intelligence and powers of observation.

7 ALL UNITS Read the text and choose the correct answer, A, B or C below.

J K Rowling

J K Rowling, (0) .... first name is actually Joanne, is one of the world's most successful writers. She is the author of the Harry Potter books, (1) .... have sold over 400 million copies worldwide. (2) .... figures published in the Sunday Times Rich List, Rowling is one of the few writers (3) .... a fortune of more than a billion dollars.

Rowling was born in England on 31 July 1965 and went to school in the west of the country. She studied French and Classics at Exeter University, (4) .... in Paris for a year as part of her course. After her degree she worked as a bilingual secretary in London. Then, from 1991 to 1994 she lived in Porto, Portugal, (5) .... she taught English as a foreign language. While she was in Portugal she met and married Portuguese journalist Jorge Arantes. In 1993 they had a daughter (6) .... they named after Jessica Mitford, the author (7) .... The couple divorced later that year. In December 1994, Rowling moved to Edinburgh, (8) .... unable to find work, and lived on state benefits. (9) .... without a job, Rowling had plenty of time to devote to writing, and it was in Edinburgh that she started to write the Harry Potter books.

Rowling's first book was *Harry Potter and the Philosopher's Stone*, (10) .... in 1997. It soon became popular and Rowling went on to write six more Harry Potter books. The last book, *Harry Potter and the Deathly Hallows*, sold eleven million copies on its first day of publication, (11) .... is a world record. Now she is writing a new book, but (12) .... it is about, nobody knows.

0	A who her	(B) whose	C that's
1	A which	B that	C that they
2	A Basing on	B Which basing on	C Based on
3	A to have earned	B who she has	C whose having
4	A lived	B who lived	C living
5	A in which	B that	C where
6	A whose	B who	C which
7	A most admire Rowling	B Rowling most admires	C Rowling most admires her
8	A where she was	B who was	C that she was
9	A To be	B Being	C Been
10	A published	B to publish	C publishing
11	A that	B which it	C which
12	A which	B what	C that

Test MODULE 14

Relative, participle and other clauses

Choose the correct answer, A, B or C.

1 She's the film star .... husband is a famous writer.
   A who's   B whose   C which   ▶ Unit 72

2 Who is the plumber .... your leaking tap?
   A fixed   B what fixed   C that fixed   ▶ Unit 72

3 We always go to the shop .... has the lowest prices.
   A that it   B where   C that   ▶ Unit 72

4 Clive is the man .... my cousin Lucy.
   A married   B which married   C who married   ▶ Unit 72

5 That's the hotel where we used to ....
   A stay in   B stay   C stay in it   ▶ Unit 72

6 The airline displayed their new uniform .... at the press conference.
   A which is bright red   B ,which is bright red,   C that is bright red,   ▶ Unit 73

7 His first novel, ... was made into a film, was written in 1936.
   A which   B that   C which it   ▶ Unit 73

8 I haven't had a single job offer, ... is very disappointing.
   A that   B which   C for which   ▶ Unit 73

9 I've been visiting all the places .... in the guidebook.
   A that mentioned   B mentioned   C which they are mentioned   ▶ Unit 74

10 There are no theatres in the town ....
   A living in   B that living in   C that he lives in   ▶ Unit 74

11 David was the first person .... to me when I arrived.
   A to talk   B which talking   C that he talked   ▶ Unit 74

12 .... in 1980, this photo shows the Prime Minister at university.
   A Taken   B Which it was taken   C To be taken   ▶ Unit 75

13 There was a strange man .... in the doorway.
   A to stand   B standing   C who standing   ▶ Unit 75

14 What's the name of the actor .... James Bond in this film?
   A playing   B played   C who playing   ▶ Unit 75

15 It's important .... anyone your PIN number.
   A to tell not   B not to tell   C that to not tell   ▶ Unit 76

16 Patrick was the only student .... 100% in the test.
   A to get   B that getting   C who to get   ▶ Unit 76

17 Marion moved house .... nearer to her elderly parents.
   A for to be   B that to be   C to be   ▶ Unit 76

18 .... they said to me was really surprising.
   A Which   B What   C That   ▶ Unit 77

19 Why don't you show me .... you bought today?
   A the things what   B which   C what   ▶ Unit 77

20 These days I read .... than I used to.
   A the more books   B more books   C the most books   ▶ Unit 77

Go online for a full exit test

Linking words

MODULE 15

Before you start

1 Read the extract from a geography textbook. Look at the highlighted grammar examples.

The Indian monsoon

The Indian monsoon is rain caused by hot air blowing over India from the Arabian Sea. Monsoon rains are very heavy in India **because of** the Himalayan mountains in the north of the country. The mountains are **too high for the clouds to pass over**, so all the rain falls on the south side – over central and northern India. **In addition to the rain**, there are high winds and frequent storms.

The monsoon begins some time **during June** and lasts for several months. Up to 10,000 millimetres of rain can fall during this period. **Even though** Indians are used to the monsoon, there are many towns that still can't deal with all the water. In fact, there is **so much rain that** most cities get flooded. **After falling** continuously for two or three months, the rain eventually stops in September. **Although** people in most countries complain about rain, Indians are pleased to get the monsoon. **Not only does it cool** the air, but it provides the water that is necessary for growing crops. **Since** 80 percent of the year's rain falls during the monsoon, farmers have learned to grow suitable crops – mostly rice and cotton.

2 Now read the sentences and choose the correct words in *italics*. The highlighted grammar examples will help you.

1. We didn't go to the beach *because of / because* the bad weather. ➤ Unit 78
2. *For / Since* we have a large garden, we should have the party at our house. ➤ Unit 78
3. There was so much sun *that we got / to get* sunburnt. ➤ Unit 79
4. The suitcase was too heavy *me / for me* to carry. ➤ Unit 79
5. Not only *he arrived / did he arrive* late, but he didn't bring a present. ➤ Unit 80
6. In addition to *we paid the hotel bill / the hotel bill*, we had to pay for parking. ➤ Unit 80
7. *Despite / Although* it is hot in August, we enjoy going to the beach then. ➤ Unit 81
8. The manager refused to give us a refund *despite / even though* we had a receipt. ➤ Unit 81
9. We usually take our holidays *during / while* the summer. ➤ Unit 82
10. After *living / to live* in Thailand for a year, we got a taste for spicy food. ➤ Unit 82

3 Check your answers below. Then go to the unit for more information and practice.

1 because of 2 Since 3 that we got 4 for me 5 did he arrive 6 the hotel bill 7 Although 8 even though 9 during 10 living

⏻ Go online for a full diagnostic test

78 Reason and purpose

> **Because there is plenty of sunshine and rain**, farmers in some parts of Asia can grow two rice crops a year. They flood the rice fields with water **in order to protect the young plants**.

1 Joining clauses

We always use linking words (e.g. *because*, *since*) to join a subordinate clause to the main clause in a sentence. The subordinate clause gives us more information about the main clause:

main clause	linking word	subordinate clause
Farmers can grow two crops a year	**because**	*there is plenty of sunshine and rain.*

We can put the subordinate clause (+ comma) at the beginning of the sentence for emphasis:
Because there is plenty of sunshine and rain, *farmers can grow two crops a year.*
or we can use it to talk about something we've already mentioned (▶ Unit 103):
They always ask to see a membership card. **Since we don't have one**, *we can't get into the club.*

2 Introducing a reason

We use *because* to introduce the reason for something:
I don't use trains **because they are too expensive**. *The show was cancelled* **because it rained**.

If we use a noun for the reason, we use *because of*:
I don't use trains **because of the cost**. *The show was cancelled* **because of the rain**.

We use *as* or *since* to introduce a reason we already know:
As we're late, *we'd better get a taxi.* (We know we are late.)
We can't get into this club **since we don't have a membership card**. (We know we don't have it.)

Other meanings of *as* ▶ Units 22.2/3 and 82.1 and *since* ▶ Unit 37.3

3 Introducing a purpose

We use *in order to*, *so as to*, *in order that* and *so that* to say why we do something.

MAIN CLAUSE	LINKING WORDS	+ SUB CLAUSE	+ INFINITIVE
They flood the rice fields with water	to / in order to / so as to		protect the young plants.
They've changed the law	in order that / so that	the police can listen to calls.	

- We often use modal verbs (e.g. *can*, *could*, *will*, *would*) after *so that* and *in order that*:
  I'm buying a magazine **so that I'll have something to read on the flight**.
- We can use all these expressions to introduce a negative result:
  I caught the earlier train **so as not to be late** *for my interview.*
  We took plenty of dollars **so that we wouldn't run out of cash** *while we were in the US.*

Infinitive of purpose (e.g. *I went to the shop to get some milk.*) ▶ Unit 76.3

15

Practice

1 **GRAMMAR IN USE** Choose the correct words in *italics*. In one place, both answers are possible. 🔊 4.26 Listen and check.

AMANDA Hello, Elizabeth. What are you doing here?
ELIZABETH I've come (0) *to* / *for* buy one of those patio heaters.
AMANDA Really?
ELIZABETH Yes, we thought we'd buy one (1) *because of* / *as* it's getting cooler now. We need one (2) *in order* / *so that* we'll be able to carry on sitting outside in the evenings … and – well, it's (3) *because* / *because of* the grandchildren, too. They love playing in the garden when they come to us after school. I want to be able to sit outside (4) *in order* / *so that* to watch them. What about you?
AMANDA Oh, I'm looking for a hosepipe. (5) *As* / *Since* the garden's so large, it's really rather hard work with just a watering can – and I'm not getting any younger! But the ones here are all too short. I need an extra long one (6) *so as to* / *in order that* reach the plants at the back of the garden.
ELIZABETH What about an automatic watering system? (7) *Because of* / *Because* this summer has been so dry, we've put one in our garden. It's very good. It comes with an automatic timer (8) *so that* / *since* you don't have to worry about turning it on or off.
AMANDA What a good idea! I'll see if they've got one here.

2 Match the two parts of the sentences.

0 We water the plants because — A we water the plants.
1 We water the plants because of   B make them grow.
2 Because it doesn't rain very often, → C it doesn't rain very often.
3 We water the plants so as   D that they will grow.
4 In order to make the plants grow, E the lack of rain.
5 We water the plants so   F we water them.
6 We water the plants to   G to make them grow.

3 Find six more mistakes and correct them. Tick (✓) the correct sentences. 🔊 4.27 Listen and check.

0 Carrie wore a big hat so ~~for~~ *as* not to get her hair wet in the rain.
1 We arrived at the theatre early that we could get good tickets.
2 I'm going swimming every day for to lose weight.
3 Since you don't have any money, I'll have to pay for your meal.
4 I got up early so not to be late for the job interview.
5 The fish are packed in ice so as to stay fresh for the journey.
6 I couldn't play football for six months because my broken leg.
7 Louis studied English in order understand American films.
8 We didn't have a holiday last summer because of we didn't have enough money.

4 Complete the sentences so they are true for you.

0 I'm studying English so that *I can read English books at university*.
1 I'm studying English so that ....
2 I enjoy .... because ....
3 I'd like to .... in order to ....
4 I can't stand .... because of ....

Go online for more practice   239

79 Causes and results

Hurricane Katrina passed just east of New Orleans with winds of over 200 km per hour. **As a result**, local canals were damaged in fifty places. The damage was **so bad that** more than 80 percent of the city was flooded.

1 therefore, as a result

In formal English we can use *Therefore* or *As a result* (+ comma) to introduce a result in a new sentence:

cause/reason		result
There was a major hurricane.	**As a result**,	local canals were damaged in fifty places.
Trains have become very expensive.	**Therefore**,	more people are travelling by bus.

2 so, such a (lot of)

We often use *so* to introduce a result:
There was a lot of rain **so the city was flooded**. *I slept late* **so I was late for work**.

We can also use *so* and *such* + a *that* clause to give more information about the cause and link it to the result. In spoken English we often leave out *that*.
- *so* + adjective/adverb: *The damage was* **so bad (that)** *the city was flooded.*
- *such* + *a/an* (+ adjective) + noun: *It was* **such a strong hurricane (that)** *the city was flooded.*
- *so much/little* + uncountable noun: *He ate* **so much food (that)** *he felt sick.*
- *so many/few* + plural noun: *There were* **so many people (that)** *we couldn't get in.*
- *such a lot of* + noun: *There was* **such a lot of noise (that)** *I just couldn't sleep.*

3 too, enough

We use *too* and *enough* + infinitive with *to* to say why a result is/isn't possible:

POSSIBLE	EXAMPLES
not too + adjective adjective + *enough* adverb + *enough* *enough* + noun	I'm **not too old to dance**! My new laptop is **light enough to carry** anywhere. I worked just **hard enough to pass** the course. There's **enough food to feed** everybody at the party.

NOT POSSIBLE	EXAMPLES
too + adjective *too* + adverb *too much/many* + noun	The lake is **too cold to swim** in. Caroline types **too slowly to be** a secretary. This is **too much work to do** in one day.
not + adjective + *enough* *not* + adverb + *enough* *not enough* + noun	The lake **isn't warm enough to swim** in. Kevin **doesn't exercise often enough to get** fit. There **isn't enough money to pay** for it.

To introduce a different subject before the infinitive we can use *for* + subject + infinitive:
There isn't enough work **for us to do** *today.* *It's too far* **for him to come**.

⚠ Adjectives and adverbs always go BEFORE *enough*:
✗ *I'm not enough strong to carry that bag.* ✓ *I'm not* **strong enough** *to carry that bag.*

240

15

Practice

1 Complete the sentences with the words and phrases from the box.

> a lot of   as a result   for   many   ~~much~~   so   such

0 There was so *much* flooding that we couldn't get back to our homes.
1 There was such .... snow we couldn't see out of the windows.
2 The waiter behaved .... rudely that I walked out of the restaurant.
3 It didn't rain for four months. ...., the lakes dried up completely.
4 It was .... a lovely picture I really had to buy it.
5 The shop had so .... brands of shampoo I just didn't know which one to get.
6 That car's much too expensive .... us to buy.

2 Complete the second sentence so it means the same as the first, using the word in brackets. Use four or five words in your answer. 🔊 4.28 Listen and check.

0 We can't go outside today because it's really cold.   (for)
   It's *too cold for us* to go outside today.
1 The chair is too uncomfortable to sit in.   (comfortable)
   The chair .... sit in.
2 It's possible to read the book in fifty minutes because it's short.   (that)
   The book .... you can read it in fifty minutes.
3 Because I'm only sixteen, I can't vote.   (young)
   I'm .... because I'm only sixteen.
4 We can't swim across the river because the water is moving very fast.   (too)
   The water .... for us to swim across the river.
5 There was such a strong wind that I could hardly stand up.   (windy)
   It .... could hardly stand up.

3 **GRAMMAR IN USE** Complete the text with one word only in each gap. 🔊 4.29 Listen and check.

Tsunami

One of the greatest natural disasters of recent years was the tsunami that occurred on 26 December 2004. It was (0) ...*so*... destructive
(1) .... more than 225,000 people were killed.
The tsunami (or tidal wave) was caused by (2) .... a powerful earthquake that it was felt as far away as Alaska. The result was a 30 metre-high wave which hit all the countries bordering the Indian Ocean. There was almost no warning of the tsunami. (3) ...., very few people were prepared for it. Many houses were destroyed because they weren't strong (4) .... to resist the huge wave. People who were (5) .... young or weak to hold on to solid objects were swept out to sea. Many of the beaches hit by the tsunami were popular with tourists. (6) .... a result, more than 9,000 of the casualties were European visitors. Most of the countries around the Indian Ocean didn't have (7) .... resources to cope with the disaster (8) .... it was necessary for international agencies to help in the rescue operation.
Fortunately, there was (9) .... much publicity that more than $7 billion were raised worldwide – enough (10) .... many people to rebuild their homes.

🔌 Go online for more practice

241

80 Adding information and giving alternatives

> December is a hard month for the people of Finland. **Not on**[ly] is it very cold, **but** the sun only shines for two hours a day.

1 and, both, not only

To add extra information we use *and*:
*Dave turned the key **and** opened the door.*

To connect two similar actions, things or people we can use *both … and*:
*Clint Eastwood **both** acted in the film **and** directed it.*
*We stock **both** gas **and** electric cookers.* ***Both** Melanie **and** her sister are doctors.*

To emphasise two pieces of information we can use *not only … (but/but also)*:
*It's **not only** expensive, it's badly made.*
***Not only** is it very cold, **but** the sun only shines for two hours a day.*
***Not only** does the machine wash your clothes, **but** it **also** dries them.*

⚠ If there is a subject and verb after *not only* we put *be* or an auxiliary/modal verb (e.g. *do, does, did, can*) BEFORE the subject (▶ Unit 102.2):
It is very cold. → ✗ *Not only it is very cold* ✓ *Not only **is it** very cold …*
He gave me flowers. → ✗ *Not only he gave me* ✓ *Not only **did he give** me flowers, …*

2 as well as, in addition to

We also use the expressions *as well as* and (in formal English) *in addition (to)*:
*She has a car **as well as** a bicycle.* ***As well as** a bicycle, she has a car.*
*You must supply proof of your current address **in addition to** proof of identity.*
We offer a range of phone services. ***In addition**, we can supply Internet access.*

⚠ If we use a verb after *as well as* and *in addition to*, we use the *-ing* form:
✗ *Harry sings as well as plays the violin.* ✓ *Harry sings **as well as playing** the violin.*

3 or, either … or, neither … nor

We use *or* to introduce a choice between two or more things:
*Which do you prefer – tea **or** coffee? I'd like a holiday in Spain, Portugal **or** Morocco.*

When there are only two choices we can use *either … or*:
*You can **either** come with me **or** stay here. We can go **either** by bus **or** by train.*

For two negatives, we can use *neither … nor*:
*She has no talent – she can **neither** sing **nor** dance!* (= She can't sing and she can't dance.)
***Neither** the chairman **nor** his assistant usually attends the conference.*

If there is a subject and verb after *neither* or *nor* we put *be* or an auxiliary/modal verb (e.g. *do, did, have, should*) BEFORE the subject (▶ Unit 107.1):
*Sandy hasn't got any children and **neither/nor have I**.*
*They don't watch TV and **nor/neither do we**.*

⚠ We don't repeat the verb after *neither/nor*: ✗ *They don't watch TV and nor do we watch.*

Practice

1 **GRAMMAR IN USE** Complete the information with one or two words in each gap.

[0] **Apollo Theatre**
Neither cameras ..*nor*.... recording devices are allowed inside the auditorium.

[1] Special tour packages available for 10 days only! You can book .... on our website or by phone.

[2] .... T-shirts and posters are available for sale in the theatre foyer.

[3] **New account holders:** you will need to provide proof of identity as .... proof of your current address.

[4] Not only .... **SuperLux** clean your clothes, it also leaves them smelling as fresh as summer flowers.

[5] **City Car Parks**
Please pay at the machine before returning to your car.
.... to the machine in the car park, there is a machine inside the station.

2 Complete the sentences below, using the information from the questionnaire. 🔊 **4.30** Listen and check.

What do you do in the evenings?	Steve	Debra	Claudio	Anna
watch TV	✗	✓	✗	✓
listen to music	✗	✓	✓	✗
play computer games	✓	✗	✓	✗
use the Internet	✓	✓	✗	✗
read magazines	✗	✗	✓	✓

0 Steve doesn't watch TV and neither *does Claudio*.
1 Neither .... nor .... plays computer games.
2 Both .... use the Internet.
3 In the evenings Anna either ....
4 .... Claudio and .... read magazines.
5 Steve doesn't listen to music and .... Anna.
6 .... Steve play computer games, he also .... the Internet.
7 .... Debra and Claudio listen to music.
8 Steve .... read magazines and .... Debra.

3 Complete the sentences so they are true for you.

0 At the weekends I *go shopping* as well as *visiting my grandparents*.
1 I don't .... and neither does ....
2 I can both .... and ....
3 I don't have .... or ....
4 Not only ...., I also .... !

⏻ Go online for more practice

81 Showing differences

Although it often rains in the summer, Britain has many popular holiday resorts. People usually enjoy themselves **despite** the bad weather.

1 Simple differences *but, while, whereas*

We use *but* to show a simple difference between two pieces of information:
*The weather was cold **but** it didn't rain.   The latest Batman movie is exciting **but** very violent.*
*My mobile phone has a camera **but** it doesn't play music.*

We can use *whereas* or *while* in more formal English:
*Flight BA101 leaves from Heathrow, **whereas/while** flight BA206 leaves from Gatwick.*

Clauses with *while* and *whereas* can come at the start or end of the sentence. We don't start a sentence with *but* unless *but* refers to information in the previous sentence:
✓ **While** the food there is very good, it isn't expensive.
✗ But the food there is very good, it isn't expensive.
✓ The food in that new restaurant is very good. **But** it isn't as expensive as you might expect.

2 Surprising differences *although, even though, despite, in spite of*

We use *although*, *though* and *even though* to introduce a surprising difference:
***Although** it often rains in the summer, Britain has many popular holiday resorts.*
*We enjoyed our holiday **even though** it rained.*
*They're great jeans, **though** they're expensive.*

We don't use a noun phrase after these expressions:
✗ We liked our walk even though bad weather.   ✓ *We liked our walk **even though** it rained.*

We use *despite* and *in spite of* before a noun phrase or an *-ing* verb:
*People usually enjoy themselves **despite the bad weather**.*
***Despite its huge success**, the website is quite difficult to use.*
*I passed the exam **in spite of not answering** all the questions.*

⚠ If we want to include a subject and verb after *despite* or *in spite of* we add *the fact that*:
✗ In spite it rained, we liked our walk.   ✓ *In spite of **the fact that it rained**, we liked our walk.*

NATURAL ENGLISH In spoken and informal English we often use *though* at the end of a sentence to express a difference:
*We had a great holiday. It rained most of the time **though**!*

3 Formal differences *however, nevertheless*

In more formal English we can use *however* or *nevertheless* to emphasise a difference. We usually put the two pieces of information in separate sentences and use *however* or *nevertheless* (+ comma) to introduce the second sentence:
*Credit cards are very useful for travellers. **However**, the interest rates can be very high.*
*Egypt has very little rainfall. **Nevertheless**, farmers grow many crops using water from the River Nile.*

Using linking words in writing ➤ Unit 101

Practice

1 Choose the correct words in *italics*. 🔊 4.31 Listen and check.

0 Marion enjoys her life *however* / *even though* she doesn't earn a lot of money.
1 We had a nice swim *although* / *despite* the water in the pool was rather cold.
2 Dave got the job in spite of *he wore* / *wearing* jeans to the interview.
3 Your phone bill has not been paid for two months. *Nevertheless,* / *Even though*, we are prepared to give you one more month in which to pay before disconnecting your line.
4 My best friend's a brilliant footballer *despite* / *but* he's useless at swimming!
5 *But* / *While* the Vestra may not be the cheapest model, it's the most reliable.
6 We enjoyed the show despite *we missed* / *missing* the first twenty minutes.
7 In spite of *it* / *the fact that it* was brand new, the car broke down after only one week.
8 Our classes are designed for intermediate skiers. *However,* / *Although,* we can provide one-to-one lessons for complete beginners.

2 **GRAMMAR IN USE** Complete the facts with the words and phrases from the box. 🔊 4.32 Listen and check.

~~although~~   but it   despite   even though   however
in spite of the fact   nevertheless   whereas   while it

Strange facts!

- (0) *Although* the USA only has 5% of the world's population, it uses 26% of the world's energy.
- The valleys near Ross Island in the Antarctic are covered in snow and ice, (1) .... it hasn't rained there for two million years.
- Severe storms in the Atlantic are called hurricanes, (2) .... severe storms in the Pacific are called typhoons.
- The Amazon occupies only 1.5% of the world's surface. (3) ...., it produces 20% of the earth's oxygen.
- The famous leaning tower of Pisa has never fallen over, (4) .... that it leans at an angle of almost four degrees.
- (5) .... being 27 times smaller than the USA, Norway has a longer coastline.
- (6) .... is inside just one country, Istanbul is in fact situated on two continents.
- New York is an American city. (7) ...., it contains more Irish inhabitants than Dublin – Ireland's capital city.
- The Atlantic Ocean is much smaller than the Pacific (8) .... has saltier water.

3 Find six more mistakes in the conversation and correct them.

JAN   How was the folk music festival?
RUBY Not bad. It rained most of the time ~~although~~! *though*
JAN   That's no fun when you're in a tent.
RUBY I know! In spite of my tent's quite a good one, it still let the rain in.
JAN   Were the bands good?
RUBY Well, but some of the first few acts weren't great, most of them were. Actually, even however we were quite near the front, it wasn't always easy to hear the music.
JAN   Was there a problem with the sound system?
RUBY I think so, yes. Oh, one thing that was great was the food. It was delicious, despite to be mainly vegetarian!
JAN   So you've developed a taste for vegetarian food, have you?
RUBY Not really. Although enjoying it at the festival, I don't think I could eat it all the time.

Go online for more practice   245

82 Ordering events

We saw the hurricane warning **when** we turned on the TV. **As soon as** we knew the storm was coming, we closed the shutters on the windows. **Then** we went to the basement and stayed there **until** it had passed over us.

1 Common linking words for time

	LINKING WORDS	EXAMPLES
a series of events	before after	We closed the shutters **before** we went to the basement. We went to the basement **after** we closed the shutters.
one event immediately after another	as soon as when	**As soon as** we knew the storm was coming, we closed the shutters. We saw the warning **when** we turned on the TV.
event(s) in a period of time	when while during (+ noun) until	Mandy saw her cousin **when** she was in New York. I sent a lot of emails **while** I was on holiday. I sent a lot of emails **during** my holiday. (✗ ~~during I was on holiday~~.) We stayed in the basement **until** the storm had passed.
at the same time	while	Luisa fed the baby **while** Daniel made the supper.

We can use *after/before* + *-ing* verb to show the order of events:
We went to the basement **after closing** the shutters.
After closing the shutters, we went to the basement.
We closed the shutters **before going** to the basement.

When, before, after and *while/during* can mean 'whenever', or 'every time that':
I always get headaches **when** the weather's hot. (every time that the weather is hot)
Jackie used to feel nervous **during** exams. (every time she took an exam)

⚠ After linking words which refer to the future we use the present tense, not *will* or *going to*:
✗ ~~I'll phone you as soon as I will arrive~~.   ✓ I'll phone you **as soon as** I **arrive**.

2 Describing a series of events

When we describe a series of events in the past, we can use the linking words *first, then, after that, afterwards, later, in the end* and *eventually* (meaning 'after a long time'):
First, we closed the window shutters. **Then** we went to the basement and waited there.
Eventually, we were able to go back upstairs. **Later**, we went outside to look at the damage.

⚠ We put these linking words at the beginning or end of the sentence, not in the middle:
✗ ~~Steve paid the bill after that we left the restaurant~~.
✓ Steve paid the bill. **After that**, we left the restaurant.
✓ Steve paid the bill. We left the restaurant **after that**.

We can use *first, next, then, after that* and *finally* in a series of instructions:
Put the DVD into the machine. **Then** press 'select channel'. **After that**, you can choose …
First, put the potatoes in a pan of boiling water. **Then** slice the tomatoes. **Next**, take an onion …

NATURAL ENGLISH We don't usually use more than two or three of these linking expressions in a paragraph.

More on linking words in written English ➤ Unit 101

15

Practice

1 **GRAMMAR IN USE** Read the information and choose the correct words in *italics*. 4.33 Listen and check.

Vesuvius: a volcano erupts

Mount Vesuvius today, overlooking the ruins of Pompeii.

On a hot summer morning in the year AD 79 the citizens of the Roman town of Pompeii were woken by a sudden earthquake. (0) *As soon as* / *Before* people felt the earth shake, they ran out of their houses to see what was happening. Vesuvius, the mountain which lay behind the town, seemed to be on fire.
(1) *During* / *While* the people watched, a huge column of black smoke rose from the top of the mountain.
(2) *After* / *Then* the smoke had covered the sky, huge chunks of grey ash and rock started to rain down on the city. The terrified citizens began to run into their houses or along the streets of the city. (3) *After that* / *While* they were running, a huge cloud of grey poisonous smoke filled the air around the town, killing everybody within a few seconds.
(4) *When* / *Later*, long streams of red-hot rock began to run down the sides of Vesuvius, burning the trees and vegetation. (5) *Eventually,* / *Next*, after eighteen hours, the smoke cleared. Nothing was left. All the citizens of Pompeii were dead and the town had disappeared, buried under three metres of grey ash. It was not seen again (6) *while* / *until* it was rediscovered in the eighteenth century.

2 **GRAMMAR IN USE** Complete the conversations with a linking word from A, and a phrase from B. 4.34 Listen and check.

A ~~after~~ after that as soon as before then until while

B they asked ~~I finish~~ I'm waiting they called I began they had you leave

MUM Right, Lorna. I'm going to work. Don't be late for your interview.
LORNA I won't. I'll leave (0) *after I finish* my breakfast.
MUM Have you read all the information they sent you?
LORNA Yes, Mum, I have. But I'll read it again (1) .... for the train.
MUM OK. And don't forget to call me (2) .... the interview.
LORNA I won't, Mum. I promise.

LATER THAT DAY …

LORNA Mum, it's me. I was the last one. I had to wait (3) .... interviewed all the others. But it wasn't a problem. I managed to read everything carefully again (4) .... me.
MUM How did it go? Were you nervous?
LORNA Yes, I was a bit nervous at first. But they were very friendly and started with some easy questions. (5) .... to relax. (6) .... me about my previous experience, so that wasn't too bad. Oh, the train's coming. I'd better go now.

Review MODULE 15

1 UNITS 78 AND 79 Match each sentence beginning 1–8 with one of the endings A–E. Some of the endings can be used more than once.

0 In Britain it is so cold in the winter that
1 Farmers can't grow oranges in Britain because of
2 Farmers can't grow oranges in Britain because
3 In Britain it is too cold
4 In Britain it isn't warm enough
5 It's cold in Britain in the winter. As a result,
6 In Britain people build special glasshouses in order
7 In Britain people build special glasshouses so that
8 Britain has such a cold winter that

A oranges and lemons can be grown there.
B oranges and lemons can't be grown there.
C to grow oranges and lemons.
D the cold weather.
E it is cold in the winter.

2 UNITS 80 AND 81 Complete the sentences with a suitable word or phrase. Match them with the pictures.

A   B   C   D   E   F   G

0 This shows that you're married _and_ it's usually made of gold. _F_
1 .... it has wings, it can't fly. ....
2 It can send emails .... it can't make a cup of coffee. ....
3 People often use this to pay for things in shops. ...., it can be used to get money from cash machines. ....
4 You could .... buy this from a shop or make it yourself. ....
5 Not only .... this allow you to breathe underwater, but it also helps you to see the fish. ....
6 This will keep you dry in the rain. ...., it doesn't work very well if it's windy. ....

3 UNITS 80, 81 AND 82 Join the sentences, using the linking words in brackets. Make any other necessary changes.

0 Would you like a view of the sea? Would you like a garden room? (or)
   Would you like a view of the sea or a garden room?

1 We can go to the museum. We can have a walk by the river. (either ... or)

2 I finished my essay. Then I sent those emails. (before)

3 Andrea lives in this part of the city. She works in this part of the city. (both ... and)

4 The company's head office is in New York. Its biggest factory is in Texas. (while)

5 I was wearing a smart suit. I wasn't allowed into the hotel. (even though)

6 I heard the news on the radio. I immediately phoned my best friend. (as soon as)

7   The President didn't resign. The Vice President didn't resign.   (neither … nor)
   ....

8   The children all caught colds. They all went swimming in the lake the day before.   (after)
   ....

9   Karl is very experienced. He can't find a good job.   (despite)
   ....

10   I felt rather sick. It happened while I was flying to Moscow.   (during)
   ....

4   ALL UNITS   Read the email and choose the correct words in *italics*.

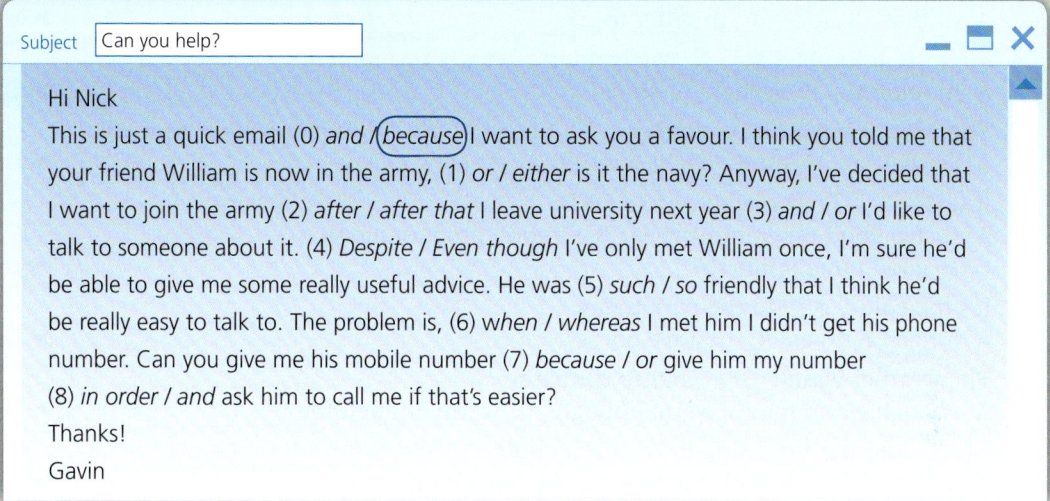

Subject: Can you help?

Hi Nick

This is just a quick email (0) *and / (because)* I want to ask you a favour. I think you told me that your friend William is now in the army, (1) *or / either* is it the navy? Anyway, I've decided that I want to join the army (2) *after / after that* I leave university next year (3) *and / or* I'd like to talk to someone about it. (4) *Despite / Even though* I've only met William once, I'm sure he'd be able to give me some really useful advice. He was (5) *such / so* friendly that I think he'd be really easy to talk to. The problem is, (6) *when / whereas* I met him I didn't get his phone number. Can you give me his mobile number (7) *because / or* give him my number (8) *in order / and* ask him to call me if that's easier?
Thanks!
Gavin

5   ALL UNITS   Complete the text with one word only in each gap.

THE GREAT STORM

(0) *Although* Britain is a place that rarely has extreme weather, there have been a few exceptions over the years. They include the great storm of October 1987. Dozens of people were (1) .... killed or injured and billions of pounds of damage was caused to buildings (2) .... property.
The bad weather began over the Bay of Biscay. (3) .... increasing in strength for a few days, this became a huge storm which started to move north. (4) ...., on the evening of 15 October it hit the English Channel. Neither the BBC (5) .... the Meteorological Office had predicted the storm earlier. (6) ...., when it arrived, nobody was prepared. Suddenly, in the middle of the night, hurricane winds (7) .... torrential rain swept over southern England.

London was badly affected (8) .... of the large number of tree-lined streets. The winds were (9) .... strong that thousands of trees were knocked over, falling on top of cars or buildings that were close to them.
(10) .... the storm there were power cuts as the high winds and falling trees destroyed electricity cables. As a (11) ...., many places were in complete darkness, which made things difficult for (12) .... the fire and ambulance services.
Surprisingly, even (13) .... there were hurricane force winds throughout the night, several people were completely unaware of what was happening. Not (14) .... did they sleep through the storm, they didn't even hear the falling trees crashing onto their cars on the street. Of course, as (15) .... as they woke up, they received a nasty shock!

Test MODULE 15

Linking words

Choose the correct answer, A, B or C.

1 .... we know the owner of the shop, we always get a good price.
   A Because of   B Because that   C Because   ➤ Unit 78

2 .... the house is old, it can get very cold in winter.
   A As   B Because that   C So that   ➤ Unit 78

3 We got up early .... be on time for the flight.
   A so that   B so as   C in order to   ➤ Unit 78

4 We took an umbrella .... we wouldn't get wet if it rained.
   A in order to   B so that   C since   ➤ Unit 78

5 There was a bus strike yesterday. .... most of my colleagues walked to work.
   A So that   B As result,   C As a result,   ➤ Unit 79

6 It was .... I recorded it onto a DVD.
   A such a good programme that   B so good programme that
   C so good programme to   ➤ Unit 79

7 It's too cold .... to the park today.
   A for go   B to go   C that we go   ➤ Unit 79

8 The weather wasn't .... her to sunbathe.
   A enough warm for   B warm enough   C warm enough for   ➤ Unit 79

9 .... and her sister sing in the local choir.
   A Melanie also   B Both Melanie   C Melanie both   ➤ Unit 80

10 Not only .... a new sports car, but he also bought a speedboat.
   A did he buy   B he bought   C he did buy   ➤ Unit 80

11 Alan goes jogging every morning as well as .... to the gym regularly.
   A he goes   B going   C goes he   ➤ Unit 80

12 I don't wear glasses and neither ....
   A do my brothers   B my brothers do   C wear my brothers   ➤ Unit 80

13 .... the hotel was comfortable, it was rather a long way from the beach.
   A But   B In spite of   C While   ➤ Unit 81

14 We got home in time even though ....
   A a traffic jam   B there was a traffic jam   C being a traffic jam   ➤ Unit 81

15 The singer performed well despite .... a sore throat.
   A that she had   B having   C to have   ➤ Unit 81

16 The garden is rather small. ...., they manage to grow quite a lot of vegetables.
   A Nevertheless   B Despite   C Whereas   ➤ Unit 81

17 I saw my old school teacher .... I was in Rome.
   A during   B until   C when   ➤ Unit 82

18 .... I got into bed, I turned off the light and fell asleep.
   A As soon as   B While   C During   ➤ Unit 82

19 After .... the back door, I went upstairs to my bedroom.
   A that I locked   B to lock   C locking   ➤ Unit 82

20 In the morning we went down to the beach. .... at the beach café.
   A We had later an ice cream   B Later, we had an ice cream
   C Later that we had an ice cream   ➤ Unit 82

Passive forms

MODULE 16

Before you start

1 Read about Yves Saint Laurent. Look at the highlighted grammar examples.

Great fashion designers of the 20th century

Yves Saint Laurent **is considered to be** one of the most influential fashion designers of the twentieth century. His designs **have been copied** many times and his ideas form the basis of many of today's most famous fashion labels. Saint Laurent was born in Algeria but at the age of seventeen he moved to Paris to work for the famous clothes designer, Christian Dior. At first Dior **had him copy** patterns and help with details, but it was clear that this young man had a great talent for design. So, when Christian Dior died in 1957, **the job of chief designer was given to Saint Laurent** by the directors of the Dior fashion house.

Saint Laurent created his first fashion collection for Dior in 1958. His designs for Dior were a huge success and within a few years he was making plans to start his own business. The new company **was set up by Saint Laurent** in 1962 and quickly became the most successful French fashion house of the 1960s and 70s.

But it wasn't enough for Saint Laurent to design clothes for the rich and famous. He wanted to create designs that anybody could afford. So in 1966 he formed a new company called *Rive Gauche* and **had his clothes mass-produced** in different sizes, so that anybody could wear them.

Saint Laurent always wanted to be different from other designers. For example, **it is said that** he was one of the first French designers to use black models in his shows. And he was certainly the first designer to put women in trouser suits and dinner jackets – clothes that **had previously only been worn by men**.

Yves Saint Laurent 1936–2008

2 Now read the sentences and choose the correct words in *italics*. The highlighted grammar examples will help you.

1. Your car isn't here. It has *taken / been taken* to the garage. ➤ Unit 83
2. Do you think that jacket was designed *by / of* a man? ➤ Unit 83
3. That ring was *given to / given* my mother by my father. ➤ Unit 84
4. My application for a loan was turned *by the bank down / down by the bank*. ➤ Unit 84
5. I have *cut my hair / my hair cut* once a month. ➤ Unit 85
6. My boss had me *take / to take* the report to the printers. ➤ Unit 85
7. Paris is thought *being / to be* the most beautiful city in Europe. ➤ Unit 86
8. It is *saying / said* that the city is more beautiful than Venice. ➤ Unit 86

3 Check your answers below. Then go to the unit for more information and practice.

1 been taken 2 by 3 given to 4 down by the bank 5 my hair cut 6 take 7 to be 8 said

Go online for a full diagnostic test

83 The passive

What about this wedding dress? It **was designed** by Sara O'Neill.

Yes, it's lovely.

1 Forming the passive

We use a form of *be* + past participle (➤ page 348–350) of the verb. The object of the active verb becomes the subject of the passive verb:

active verb + object   subject + passive verb

They **buy** their clothes in the sales.   Their clothes **are bought** in the sales.

We don't usually repeat the same subject and form of *be* in a sentence:
The cars **are taken** to the port, [the cars are] **loaded** onto ships and [they are] **sent** to their destinations.

	ACTIVE	PASSIVE
simple tenses	They **import** all the clothes from China. **Did** Fabio **design** her dress?	All the clothes **are imported** from China. **Was** her dress **designed** by Fabio?
continuous tenses	Somebody's **washing** her jeans. They **weren't selling** those designs last year.	Her jeans **are being washed**. Those designs **weren't being sold** last year.
perfect tenses	I **haven't ironed** your shirt yet. People **had seen** that design before.	Your shirt **hasn't been ironed** yet. That design **had been seen** before.
will and infinitives	They **will post** the results tomorrow. We need **to repair** your shoes. I'm not going **to finish** the report today.	The results **will be posted** tomorrow. Your shoes **need to be repaired**. The report **isn't going to be finished** today.
-ing forms	I hate people **shouting** at me.	I hate **being shouted** at.

More on passive infinitives and *-ing* forms ➤ Units 64.1, 65.2, 75.3 and 76.1

NATURAL ENGLISH In spoken and informal written English, we sometimes use a form of *get* instead of *be* to form the passive. We can only do this to describe actions, not states:
What happened? Did he **get beaten** up? We **got stuck** in the lift for an hour!

Other uses of *get*, e.g. *get married* ➤ Unit 92.3

If we want to say who or what does an action when using a passive verb, we use *by* + noun. We usually put this at the end of the clause or sentence:
Katie Holmes' wedding dress was designed **by Giorgio Armani**.
Did you buy that sweater from a shop or was it knitted **by your mother**?

⚠ Verbs with no object (intransitive verbs, e.g. *arrive, come, grow up, happen, wait*) cannot be made passive:
✗ ~~I was grown up in Edinburgh.~~ ✓ I **grew up** in Edinburgh.
✗ ~~An email has been arrived.~~ ✓ An email **has arrived**.
Born is always passive:
I **was born** in 1990. Where **were** your parents **born**?

252

2 Reasons for using the passive

We often use the passive when we want to talk about an action rather than the person or thing that does the action. We do this when
- it doesn't matter who does the action:
  *The votes **will be counted** at the end of the meeting.*
  *Have the parcels **been delivered**?*
- we know or can guess who does the action:
  *Here's your skirt. It**'s been dry-cleaned**.* (obviously by the dry cleaner's)
  *I brought my car to your garage yesterday. **Has** it **been repaired** yet?* (by the garage)
- we don't know, or we don't want to say who does the action:
  *My bicycle **has been stolen**!* (I don't know who stole it.)
  *I see the washing-up **hasn't been done** again!* (I don't want to say who hasn't done it.)
- we want to talk about general feelings or beliefs (➤ Unit 86):
  *The building **is believed** to date from the thirteenth century.* (Most people believe this.)
- we want to be polite or we are in a formal situation:
  *Have the reports **been typed** yet?* (more polite than *Have you typed the reports yet?*)
  *Your application **will be assessed** by the manager.* (more formal than *The manager will assess your application.*)

3 Using passives in writing

Passives are more common in writing than in speech.
- We usually prefer to start a sentence with known information (something that has already been mentioned) and then put new information at the end. The passive helps us to do this:

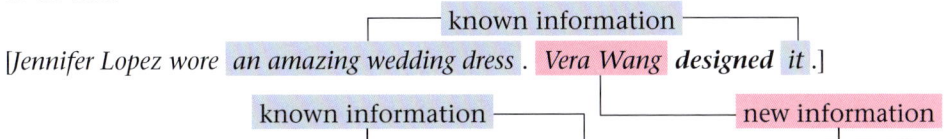

✓ Jennifer Lopez wore an amazing wedding dress. It **was designed** by Vera Wang.

- We generally don't like to put a long subject before the verb, so we often use the passive to move the subject towards the end of the sentence, after the verb:
  [*The low prices on a selection of summer suits in the shop window **attracted** us.*]
  ✓ *We **were attracted** by the low prices on a selection of summer suits in the shop window.*

More on the use of passives in writing ➤ Units 103 and 105.2

4 Common uses of the passive

We often use the passive in these situations:

news reports	Three men **have been arrested** by the police. The missing child **has not been seen** for three days. The results **were announced** early this morning.
academic and scientific writing	Three possibilities **have been suggested** and these **will be examined** in Chapter 3. The crystals **were heated** to a temperature of 150°.
instructions and rules	This plant **needs to be watered** daily. The doors **are locked** at 10.30 p.m.
describing methods, ways of working	Staff expenses **are recorded** on form SE11 and **supported** by receipts. The employees **are paid** monthly by cheque.

83 THE PASSIVE

Practice

1 Complete the second sentence so it means the same as the first, using passive forms. 4.35 Listen and check.

0 They were painting that wall yesterday. — That wall *was being painted yesterday*.
1 We've turned off the lights. — The lights ....
2 We will send you an email tomorrow — You ....
3 They aren't making that model any more. — That model ....
4 Do I have to fill in this form? — Does this form ....?
5 They haven't repaired your computer yet. — Your computer ....
6 They're going to close the road for 24 hours. — The road ....

2 Complete the descriptions of the pictures, using passive forms of the verbs in the box.

| build   count   ~~decorate~~   finish   repair   wash |

0 This house *is being decorated*. 3 The roof needs ....
1 The votes .... 4 The bridge .... next year.
2 This castle .... in 1250. 5 The dishes .... yet.

3 Use the information in the email to complete the sentences below.

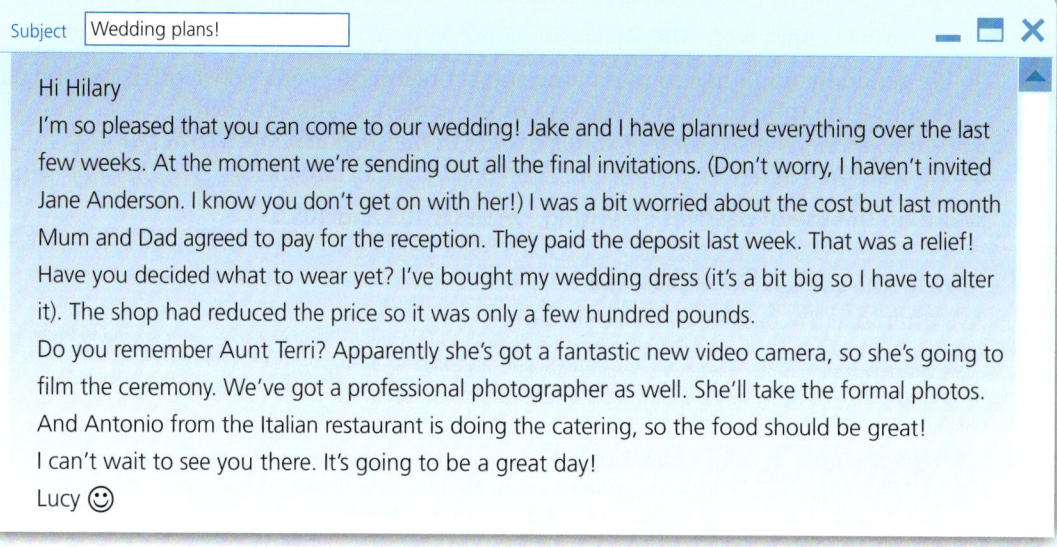

Subject: Wedding plans!

Hi Hilary
I'm so pleased that you can come to our wedding! Jake and I have planned everything over the last few weeks. At the moment we're sending out all the final invitations. (Don't worry, I haven't invited Jane Anderson. I know you don't get on with her!) I was a bit worried about the cost but last month Mum and Dad agreed to pay for the reception. They paid the deposit last week. That was a relief! Have you decided what to wear yet? I've bought my wedding dress (it's a bit big so I have to alter it). The shop had reduced the price so it was only a few hundred pounds.
Do you remember Aunt Terri? Apparently she's got a fantastic new video camera, so she's going to film the ceremony. We've got a professional photographer as well. She'll take the formal photos. And Antonio from the Italian restaurant is doing the catering, so the food should be great!
I can't wait to see you there. It's going to be a great day!
Lucy ☺

0 Everything *has been planned* by Jake and Lucy.
1 The final invitations .... at the moment.
2 Jane Anderson .... to the wedding.
3 The deposit for the reception .... last week.
4 Lucy has bought her wedding dress but it has ....
5 The price of the dress .... by the shop.
6 The ceremony .... by Lucy's aunt.
7 The formal photos .... by a professional photographer.
8 The catering .... by Antonio.

16

4 **GRAMMAR IN USE** Choose the best word in *italics*. Sometimes both are grammatically correct, but one answer is more suitable. 🔊 4.36 Listen and check.

HOW IS PAPER MADE?

Everyone enjoys reading fashion magazines and newspapers. But have you ever thought about how the paper (0) *we print them / (they are printed)* on is made?
Most paper is (1) *made / making* from wood. First, (2) *they cut the wood / the wood is cut* into small pieces. These (3) *mix / are mixed* with water and heated to produce a kind of thick paste. Then chemicals (4) *we add them / are added* to clean the paste and make it white. Next the paste is spread on a screen and (5) *dried / is dried*. The water drains away or evaporates and (6) *are left / leaves* a thick layer of paper. (7) *We then pass this / This is then passed* between two large rollers (circular machines) to make it thinner and flatter.
(8) *The paper can then be cut / They can then cut the paper* into the correct sizes.

5 Three more of these paragraphs would be improved if the second sentence used a passive form. Decide which paragraphs they are and rewrite the second sentence.

0 Philip Green bought the famous British clothes store, Moss Bros, in 2008. Because they ran out of money, the original owners sold it.
It was sold by the original owners because they ran out of money.

1 Live Aid was the most successful fund-raising event of the 1980s. A group of well-known British and American musicians organised it in July 1985.
....

2 The Laurentian Library in Florence is one of the greatest buildings of the Italian Renaissance. Michelangelo designed it in the 1520s.
....

3 Jeans first became popular when they were worn by film stars and singers in the 1950s. Elvis Presley and James Dean were the two stars who had the most influence on young people's fashion at that time.
....

4 In recent years several high street stores have started selling copies of designer jeans. People who can't afford to buy real designer clothes often buy them.
....

6 Rewrite these sentences so they are true for you. Change the underlined part.

0 My watch was made in <u>Australia</u>.   *My watch was made in Switzerland.*
1 My school was built <u>in the 1960s</u>.
2 My old photos are stored <u>in the garage</u>.
3 My favourite shirt is made of <u>nylon</u>.
4 My hair is usually cut by <u>my mother</u>.
5 I don't like food that <u>has been fried</u>.

⏻ Go online for more practice

84 Passives with modal and other verbs

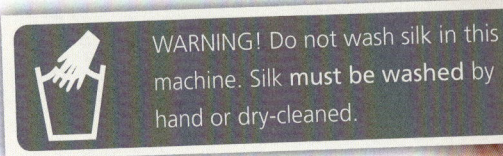

WARNING! Do not wash silk in this machine. Silk **must be washed** by hand or dry-cleaned.

1 Modal verbs

We make the passive form of modal verbs with the modal verb (+ *not*) + *be* + past participle. There is a perfect form – modal verb (+ *not*) + *have been* + past participle.

	ACTIVE	PASSIVE
Present	You **must wash** silk by hand. You **should not iron** this jumper.	Silk **must be washed** by hand. This jumper **should not be ironed**.
Perfect	They **might have turned** the electricity off. She **couldn't have washed** it yet.	The electricity **might have been turned** off. It **couldn't have been washed** yet.

We often use modal present passives for written instructions and rules:
Silk **must be washed** by hand or dry-cleaned. These lights **cannot be used** outside.

We often use modal perfect passives to make guesses about the past or to talk about past expectations (➤ Unit 48.2/3):
I don't know why the cake's burnt. It **may have been left** in the oven for too long.
This computer still isn't working; it **should have been repaired** ages ago!

2 Verbs with two objects

With these verbs, e.g. *give, offer, buy* (➤ Unit 59.5), there are two ways of forming the passive.

- The 'person' object becomes the subject of the passive verb:

subject		object	
Amanda	was given	*first prize*	(by the judges).
Sylvia	is going to be offered	*a new job*	(by her boss).
The children	were bought	*a new kitten*	(by their aunt).

- The 'thing' object becomes the subject of the passive verb, and we put *to* or *for* in front of the 'person' object:

First prize	was given **to**	*Amanda*	(by the judges).
A new job	is going to be offered **to**	*Sylvia*	(by her boss).
A new kitten	was bought **for**	*the children*	(by their aunt).

3 Verb + adverb/preposition

We can usually make passive forms of phrasal verbs (➤ Unit 91) if they have an object:
They **pulled down** the old school in 2005. → The old school **was pulled down** in 2005.
Sally **has given away** Kemal's CDs. → Kemal's CDs **have been given away** (by Sally).

⚠ We don't separate the verb and adverb:
✗ *Kemal's old clothes have been given by Sally away.*

There are a few prepositional verbs (➤ Unit 90) that are common in the passive:
The old Hoover factory **has been used as** a supermarket for several years.
New York **is known as** 'The Big Apple'.
Coco Chanel **was regarded as** the best designer of the 1920s.

16

Practice

1 Write the words in the correct order. 🔊 4.37 Listen and check.

0 the questions all be answered must
   All the questions must be answered.

1 down by the committee our proposal been has turned
   ....

2 left was by my grandfather to me that house
   ....

3 a pay rise hasn't Geraldine given been
   ....

4 be in the USA can this mobile phone used ?
   ....

5 taken couldn't that photo been at our wedding have
   ....

2 Rewrite these historical facts, using passive forms. Begin with the underlined word.

0 The French government gave <u>the Statue of Liberty</u> to the United States in 1886.
   The Statue of Liberty was given to the United States by the French government in 1886.

1 The Spanish brought <u>potatoes</u> to Europe in the sixteenth century.
   ....

2 Neil Armstrong took <u>an American flag</u> to the moon in 1969.
   ....

3 Thomas Wolsey gave <u>Hampton Court Palace</u> to King Henry VIII in 1525.
   ....

4 The South African government sent <u>Nelson Mandela</u> to prison in 1962.
   ....

5 France sold <u>Louisiana</u> to the United States in 1803.
   ....

3 **GRAMMAR IN USE** Find six more mistakes in the conversation and correct them. 🔊 4.38 Listen and check.

EXPERT Well, this is an interesting fashion print. Did you buy it?

OWNER No, it was given to me 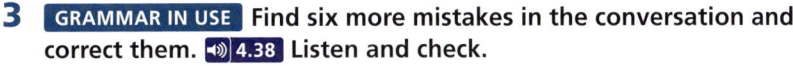 ~~of~~ *by* my grandmother just before she died.

EXPERT So she was the person who bought it?

OWNER Not exactly. She found it. It had left on the side of the road by somebody.

EXPERT How amazing. Tell me, is this the original frame?

OWNER No, I think it may been changed when my grandparents moved house. They had a really good carpenter and he made new frames for all their pictures. It might have been put into a new frame from him.

EXPERT That's a pity. These prints are always worth more if they've been keep in their original frames. It shouldn't have been taken of the original frame out, really. But if it was for sale put up I expect it might fetch several hundred pounds …

Go online for more practice   257

85 have something done

1 have/get something done

We use *have something done* (*have* + object + past participle) when somebody does something for us (something we want or ask them to do):
Gerald **has all his suits made** for him. (His tailor makes them.)
We're going to have our kitchen painted. (Decorators are going to do it.)

We can use this pattern with all tenses of *have* and make questions and negatives:
Will they **have their house painted** next year?
What **has** she **had done** in the garden?
Have you **had your hair cut**?
We **haven't had our car repaired** yet.
We **didn't have our house painted** last year.

Gerald **has all his suits made** for him by a tailor in London. Today Gerald**'s getting him to make** a winter suit.

FORMALITY CHECK In informal English we can use *get something done* with the same meanings:
Your hair's lovely. Where **do you get it cut**? Can I **get my car washed** here?

We also use *have/get something done* when somebody does something to us that we didn't want or ask for, often something bad.
Sergei **got his passport stolen** yesterday. (= A thief stole it.)

⚠ We always use *have* (not *get*) *something done* in the present perfect tense:
✗ We've got our water supply disconnected.
✓ We've had our water supply disconnected. (= The water company did it.)

2 have somebody do something, get somebody to do something

In formal English we use *have* + object + infinitive to talk about making someone do something:
The customs officer **had me open** my suitcase. (= He made me open my case.)
I'm sorry about the mess in your room, sir. I'**ll have someone clean** it immediately.

In informal English we use *get* + object + *to* + infinitive with the same meaning:
Gerald**'s getting him to make** a suit. I **got the children to clear out** their rooms yesterday.

If we tell a person to make something happen, we use the imperative:
Teresa, **have the new patients fill in** forms, please.
When you go to the shop, **get them to give** your money back.

The forms with *get* are more common in British English and the forms with *have* are more common in American English.

3 need + -ing

We can use an *-ing* form or infinitive after *need* in order to give a passive meaning:
These dirty clothes **need to be washed**. (= It is necessary for somebody to wash them.)
→ These clothes **need washing**.
My hair is very long. It **needs to be cut**. → My hair **needs cutting**.

More on *need* for necessity ➤ Unit 50

Practice

1 Complete the sentences, using a form of *have*, *get* or *need* and suitable forms of the verbs in the box.

| break | ~~paint~~ | show | test | wash |

0 Isabel *is having* her nails *painted*.
1 Karl .... his eyes ....
2 That van ....
3 The police officer .... me .... him my driving licence.
4 Barry .... his nose .... in a boxing match last year.

2 **GRAMMAR IN USE** Read about the club and choose the correct words in *italics*.
🔊 4.39 Listen and check.

THE SPOIL YOURSELF CLUB

- **What is the Spoil Yourself Club?**
  The Spoil Yourself Club is there for your every need. Once you pay the $10,000 membership fee you can call us at any time and get us (0) *arrange* / (*to arrange*) almost anything you want.

- **What can you get for me?**
  We can get almost anything for you. For example, if you need a new designer dress for a special party we can have a top designer (1) *produce* / *produced* something for you within a few days. If you need a table at a five-star restaurant we can (2) *have had* / *have* the best table (3) *reserved* / *to reserve* for you at just an hour's notice. If you've had (4) *cancelled a flight* / *a flight cancelled*, we can get one of our pilots (5) *to fly* / *fly* you anywhere you desire in our private jet.

- **What about other services?**
  If you've had a hard day at the office and just want a relaxing massage, we have a team of excellent therapists ready to help. You can have your hair and make-up (6) *to be done* / *done* by our expert beauticians. But we haven't forgotten about those everyday problems. So, if your central heating system breaks down we will get a plumber (7) *coming* / *to come* to your house in half an hour. If your car needs (8) *servicing* / *to service*, we can have a mechanic collect your car and return it to you later the same day.

3 Complete the sentences, using suitable forms of the words in brackets.
🔊 4.40 Listen and check.

0 Your room is filthy! *Get it cleaned up* at once! (get / it / clean up)
1 I'm going grey, so I .... every six weeks. (have / my hair / colour)
2 Sindy .... while she was at the gym. (get / phone / steal)
3 Something is wrong with your TV. I think .... (it / need / check)
4 .... while you were out? (get / those documents / copy)
5 I .... your bags up to your room now, sir. (have / the porter / take)
6 Excuse me. Can I .... here? (get / my passport photos / take)

Go online for more practice

86 Passive reporting verbs

It **is said that** Ralph Lauren is the richest fashion designer in the world. His company **is thought to be** worth almost three billion dollars.

1 Using passive reporting verbs

We can use passive reporting verbs
- to talk about general feelings or beliefs:
  His company **is thought to be** worth almost three billion dollars. (= Many people think this.)
- when we don't know (or we don't want to say) who made the statement originally:
  It **was suggested that** the factory should be closed.
  I'm afraid your fees **were considered to be** too expensive.

2 Patterns with passive reporting verbs

We usually use the reporting verbs *believe, consider, expect, know, report, understand, say, state* and *think*. There are two patterns.
- It + passive verb + *that* clause:
  It is said that Ralph Lauren is the world's richest fashion designer.
  Yesterday **it was reported that** three prisoners had escaped from the island.
- Subject + passive reporting verb + *to* + infinitive:
  The American team **is expected to win**. (= Most people expect them to win.)
  His company **is thought to be** worth almost three billion dollars.

To talk about the past, we use the perfect infinitive (➤ Unit 65.2); there is an active and a passive form:
People say the Romans **built** the town. → The Romans are said **to have built** the town.
People believe the town **was built** by the Romans. → The town is believed **to have been built** by the Romans.

FORMALITY CHECK These patterns are used mainly in news reports and in academic and scientific English:
These poems **are considered to be** Shakespeare's finest works.
The new software **is expected to require** more memory.

3 *supposed to, meant to*

Supposed to and *meant to* have several meanings
- We often use them for something that was arranged or expected but didn't happen:
  He **was supposed to phone** me yesterday. (= I expected him to phone but he didn't.)
  Where are the keys? They **were supposed to have been left** on my desk.
  Where's John? He **was meant to be** here half an hour ago!
- We also use *supposed to/meant to* for things we should or shouldn't do. We often use it when people 'break the rules' or do things we think are wrong:
  You can't go in there. You**'re meant to wait** outside.
  Shh! We **aren't supposed to talk** in the library.
- But *supposed to/meant to* can also describe a general belief:
  Try their lamb curry. It**'s supposed to be** really good.
  You should take the train; it**'s meant to be** less stressful than flying.

More on reporting verbs and patterns ➤ Module 13

Practice

1 Choose the correct meaning, A or B.

0 Phillipe Starck is considered to be the world's greatest designer of household objects.
A Phillipe Starck thinks this. (B) Many people think this.
1 Tom Cruise is said to be the richest film star in the world.
A People think this, but it may not be true. B This is a fact.
2 We're supposed to take a present with us.
A Our hosts expect us to take a present. B We forgot to take a present.
3 It is believed that the government will cancel the high speed railway line.
A The government believes this will happen. B Some people believe this will happen.
4 How annoying. We were meant to have seats in the front row!
A They've given us seats in the front row. B They haven't given us seats in the front row.
5 It has been suggested that Martin stole £100,000 from his employer's bank account.
A Some people say Martin did this. B Martin says he did this.

2 Complete the second sentence so it means the same as the first, using the word in brackets. Use four or five words in your answer. 🔊 4.41 Listen and check.

0 I expected Harriet to send me a parcel, but she didn't. (supposed)
Harriet ...*was supposed to send*... me a parcel.
1 Many fashion writers think that New York is the top fashion city in the world these days. (said)
New York .... the top fashion city in the world these days.
2 My landlord doesn't like me smoking in the house. (meant)
I'm .... in the house.
3 The TV news says that the football club has a new owner. (reported)
The football club .... a new owner.
4 They wanted me to go to their party but I was too busy. (supposed)
I .... their party but I was too busy.
5 I've been told that Armani designs all her clothes. (believed)
All her clothes .... by Armani.

3 **GRAMMAR IN USE** Rewrite the underlined phrases in the talk, using the words in brackets. 🔊 4.42 Listen and check.

'Welcome to Candleburgh Hall, the historic home of the Westmoor family. (0) <u>The house is said to have been designed by Robert Smythson</u>, although we don't have any proof of that. But we certainly know it was built around 1570. (1) <u>We were going to visit the stables today</u>, but I'm afraid they are currently closed for repairs. (2) <u>We think they'll be finished in April</u>, so you'll be able to see them then. Today we're starting in the main drawing room. In fact, (3) <u>many people think it is the most beautiful room in the house</u>. But it holds a dark secret. (4) <u>Some people believe that Sir Henry Westmoor died here</u>. In fact, (5) <u>they say he was killed by his own brother</u>. Now, if you'll all follow me, we'll move to the Queen's Bedroom … this room got its name because (6) <u>we think that Queen Elizabeth I slept here</u> in the 1580s …'

0 The house *is supposed to have been designed by Robert Smythson*. (supposed)
1 We .... (meant)
2 The work .... (expected)
3 It .... (considered)
4 Sir Henry Westmoor .... (believe)
5 It .... (said)
6 Queen Elizabeth I .... (thought)

Review MODULE 16

1 UNITS 83 AND 84 There is a mistake in each of these signs and labels. Find the mistakes and correct them.

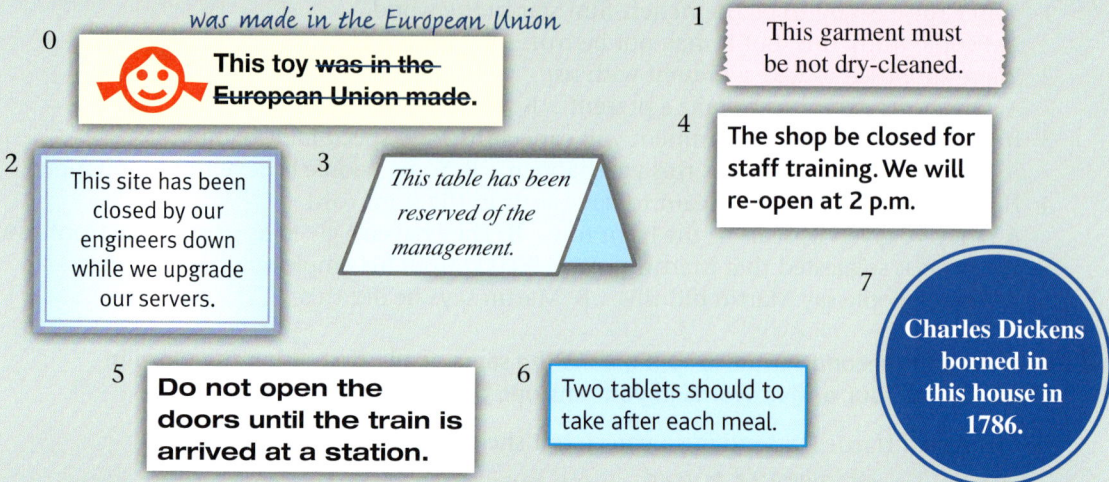

0 *was made in the European Union*
This toy ~~was in the European Union made~~.

1 This garment must be not dry-cleaned.

2 This site has been closed by our engineers down while we upgrade our servers.

3 This table has been reserved of the management.

4 The shop be closed for staff training. We will re-open at 2 p.m.

5 Do not open the doors until the train is arrived at a station.

6 Two tablets should to take after each meal.

7 Charles Dickens borned in this house in 1786.

2 UNITS 85 AND 86 Complete the article, using suitable forms of the words in brackets.

Fake fashions
(0) *It is said that* .... (it / say / that) most designer goods sold in street markets these days are fakes. It isn't surprising; most designers only sell their goods through upmarket shops. There is even more of a problem on the Internet. In June 2008 a French court found eBay guilty of allowing fake goods to be sold on their website. The court (1) .... (have / eBay / pay) €40 million to the luxury brands Louis Vuitton and Christian Dior in compensation.
Of course, the people who buy these items often don't know that they are fakes. A man who paid £500 for a 'Rolex watch' only discovered it was a fake when he (2) .... (have / it / repair) by a local jeweller. People often find that clothes are fakes when they (3) .... (need / wash). They wash them and discover that they shrink or the colour changes – something that would never happen with a real designer product.
(4) .... (It / often / argue) that designer brands are much too expensive. People don't like paying such high prices and don't seem to care that designers are losing money. But the truth is that buying fake goods does have serious consequences because the people who deal in these fakes are often serious criminals. They (5) .... (have / the goods / make) in small factories in the Far East or South America and then import them to Europe and the USA. Some of the people making the goods (6) .... (think / be) children who work in terrible conditions for almost no money. They are the ones who pay the real price for our fake designer clothes.

3 UNITS 83 AND 86 Choose the best sentence to continue each paragraph, A or B.
0 Marek brought a beautiful carved wooden table back from India.
   A An old Indian carpenter in Delhi made it.
   B It was made by an old Indian carpenter in Delhi.
1 Davina was really thrilled when she got her first car.
   A It was given to her by her parents just before she went to university.
   B Just before she went to university her parents gave it to her.

262

2 Susie and Jim were shocked when they visited their old school.
   A Somebody had demolished it and built a block of flats in its place.
   B It had been demolished and a block of flats built in its place.
3 *Guernica* is one of Pablo Picasso's most famous paintings.
   A He painted it while he was living in France.
   B While he was living in France it was painted.
4 The Member of Parliament for Warton North was arrested by the police this morning.
   A He is reported to have sold government secrets to the *Enquirer* newspaper.
   B Some people say he has sold government secrets to the *Enquirer* newspaper.

4 ALL UNITS Read the note and the letter. Choose the best answer, A, B or C below.

Redding Lexton Student Loans Ltd.
Redding House
Loughborough
LX8 9OM

Dad,
Section 9 of this form (0) ………..
by you as my next of kin. Could
you do it for me? It was (1) ………..
last month but I've only just
received it. See you later,
Bill X

Dear Mr Kingston,
Thank you for choosing Redding Lexton Student Loans. (2) …………… over one million adult students with loans in the UK, so we know that there is a wide choice of student loans on the market. We believe that our *Student Loan Plus* is the best choice available.
We apologise for the fact that you did not receive the application form last month. There was a postal strike in Loughborough and we believe (3) …………… in the post.
The application form (4) …………… with this letter. The form (5) …………… in black ink and signed at the bottom. Please (6) …………… by your next of kin.. The form then needs (7) …………… to our Loughborough office. The bottom section (8) …………… and kept as a receipt.
The completed contract (9) …………… our customer service department in due course.
The first instalment of the loan (10) …………… direct to your bank account as soon as your application has been approved.
Yours sincerely,

JDunn

Jacob Dunn
Sales Executive

0 A has filling in   (B) has to be filled in   C has to been filling in
1 A supposed to have been sent B supposing to be sent   C supposed to been sent
2 A We think there are   B There are thought being   C There are thought to be
3 A it may to be lost   B we may lose it   C it may have been lost
4 A is enclosed   B enclosing   C be enclosed
5 A you should complete   B should be completed   C should you complete
6 A section 9 have completed B have completed section 9   C have section 9 completed
7 A being posted   B to be posted   C that it is posting
8 A can be torn off   B can torn off be   C can be off torn
9 A is sending to you from   B to you will send by   C will be sent to you by
10 A can making   B can to make   C can be made

Test MODULE 16

Passive forms

Choose the correct answer, A, B or C.

1. Sorry. Your clothes .... yet.
   A didn't been ironed   B haven't done iron   C haven't been ironed ▶ Unit 83

2. Film stars love ....
   A been photographing   B being photographed   C being photograph ▶ Unit 83

3. .... in the 1960s?
   A Did the house build   B Was the house built   C Was built the house ▶ Unit 83

4. What happened? .... hurt?
   A Did he get   B Did he been   C Got he ▶ Unit 83

5. The novel was ....
   A by Charles Dickens written   B written of Charles Dickens
   C written by Charles Dickens ▶ Unit 83

6. The experiment .... under strict medical supervision.
   A we carried out   B was carried out   C was carrying out ▶ Unit 83

7. Thanks for the medicine. .... before or after meals?
   A Should it be taken   B It should take   C Should be taken it ▶ Unit 84

8. This heater .... in a bathroom.
   A can't to use it   B not can be used   C cannot be used ▶ Unit 84

9. David ....
   A a car was given by his uncle   B to his uncle was given a car
   C was given a car by his uncle ▶ Unit 84

10. I'm not surprised your camera isn't working. It .... out in the rain!
    A shouldn't have left   B shouldn't have been left   C shouldn't to be left ▶ Unit 84

11. Rome is often ....
    A as the Eternal City known   B known as the Eternal City
    C as known the Eternal City ▶ Unit 84

12. Mrs Osbourne .... once a month.
    A her hair coloured   B has coloured her hair   C has her hair coloured ▶ Unit 85

13. I .... serviced next week.
    A am being the car   B am having the car   C have done the car ▶ Unit 85

14. Don't worry, sir. I .... you the contract this afternoon.
    A will have my assistant fax   B will have faxed my assistant
    C have my assistant done fax ▶ Unit 85

15. Those curtains are very dirty. They really need ....
    A to wash   B washing   C have washed ▶ Unit 85

16. The painting .... worth at least fifty million dollars.
    A is thought to be   B it is thought to be   C is thought being ▶ Unit 86

17. The ancient Romans .... central heating.
    A are believed to invent   B are believed have invented
    C are believed to have invented ▶ Unit 86

18. We were expected .... the match against the army team.
    A to lose   B losing   C to be lost ▶ Unit 86

19. You can't park there. You .... at the side of the building.
    A supposing to park   B are supposed parking   C are supposed to park ▶ Unit 86

20. Where's the report? It was supposed .... by this morning.
    A to being finishing   B to have been finished   C to have done finished ▶ Unit 86

Go online for a full exit test

Word combinations

MODULE 17

Before you start

1 Read the information about curling. Look at the ==highlighted== grammar examples.

UNUSUAL SPORTS NO 27

Curling

Famously described once as '==doing the housework== on ice' because of its similarity to sweeping the floor, curling is an old Scottish sport. The game consists of two teams playing against each other, moving ten stones down an ice path, trying to get them as close to the home circle as possible. The teams ==take turns== to 'throw' the stone down the ice, with players 'sweeping' the ice in front of the stone to make it smoother. The team with most stones closest to their home wins the match.

Most people have ==heard of== curling, but not many people have a detailed ==knowledge of== the sport. In the Winter Olympics of 2002, the Great Britain women's team (consisting of Scots) enjoyed ==great success== and ==brought the gold medal home== to Scotland. Many people were ==amazed at== just how exciting this sport could be, and were ==looking forward to== the next Winter Olympics.
It is also quite a gentle sport, and players are unlikely to be ==hurt== while playing it. People often ==take it up== when they are children and continue playing it into their 70s or 80s! If you ==feel like trying== curling yourself, but you don't like ==getting cold==, you could try playing a game of curling on your computer!

2 Now read the sentences and choose the correct words in *italics*. The ==highlighted== grammar examples will help you.

1 We usually *have / take* turns to put the children to bed. ▶ Unit 87
2 The American runners always have *great / big* success at the Games. ▶ Unit 87
3 We were really amazed *at / with* the prices in Greece this year. ▶ Unit 88
4 Evans said that he had no knowledge *about / of* the robbery at all. ▶ Unit 88
5 Have you heard *from / of* that Icelandic band called Sigur Rós? ▶ Unit 89
6 I really don't feel *like working / working like* this afternoon as it's so sunny. ▶ Unit 90
7 I've read quite a lot about curling and I think I'd like to take *up it / it up*. ▶ Unit 91
8 'Are you coming to our party?' 'Yes, I'm looking forward *to it / it to*.' ▶ Unit 91
9 I'm nearly ready. I just want to *do / make* the washing-up. ▶ Unit 92
10 I never use saunas because I really don't like *going / getting* hot. ▶ Unit 92
11 The team will be *bringing / taking* their medals to show us tomorrow. ▶ Unit 93
12 Be careful when you get into the pool – don't slip and *damage / hurt* yourself. ▶ Unit 94

3 Check your answers below. Then go to the unit for more information and practice.

1 take 2 great 3 at 4 of 5 of 6 like working 7 it up 8 to it 9 do 10 getting 11 bringing 12 hurt

87 Common collocations

Aren't you going to **take part in** the swimming competition?

No, I'm not a very **strong swimmer**.

1 Verb + noun

Collocations are words that often go together. Verb + noun collocations sometimes change the meaning of the verb, e.g. *run + a business*.

VERB + NOUN		EXAMPLES
take	a photo an exam turns action a chance	When do you **take** your final medical **exams**? In this game, you **take turns** to throw the dice and answer questions. The police need to **take action** against these thieves.
miss	the bus a penalty the point a person	I was late for work because I **missed the bus** again. You've **missed the point** of my argument – you don't understand.
run	a race a shop a business	Radcliffe **ran** a good **race** and won by over thirty seconds. My brothers and I have been **running the** family **business** for years.
tell	a story the truth a joke	Go to bed! Your father won't **tell** you **a story** if you misbehave. There's no point in discussing this if you don't **tell the truth**.
start	work the car an argument	Why couldn't you **start the car** this morning? I knew that he wanted to **start an argument**, so I refused to speak.
make	a mistake the bed a promise	I think you've **made a mistake** in these accounts. Don't **make promises** if you can't do what you say!

2 Verb + noun + preposition

VERB + NOUN + PREPOSITION		EXAMPLES
take	part in pity on care of	Aren't you going to **take part in** the swimming competition? I don't **take care of** the children much because I work full-time.
make	friends with the most of	I haven't **made friends with** many people here. The weather's awful here but we're trying to **make the most of** it.
run	the risk of	You **run the risk of** hurting yourself if you don't rest after your injury.
have	confidence in	The company has problems, but I **have confidence in** my managers.

3 Adjective + noun

ADJECTIVE + NOUN		EXAMPLES
strong	swimmer smell wind coffee	I'm not a very **strong swimmer**. Last night's **strong wind** has blown down a lot of trees.
heavy	rain traffic smoker industry meal	There was very **heavy traffic** on the motorway last night. The **heavy industry** outside the town creates employment.
great	difficulty time interest success	I had a **great time** at your party – thanks for inviting me. The athletics team had **great success** at the Olympics.
good/bad	habit luck news	Biting your nails is a really **bad habit** – I wish you'd stop.
light	meal rain coat	The weather wasn't too bad – just a little **light rain** most days.

⚠ You often can't translate directly from other languages. Always check in a good dictionary:
✗ *We had a little thin rain yesterday.*   ✓ We had a little **light rain** yesterday.

17

Practice

1 Put a line through the incorrect collocation in each group.

0 take ... care of / an exam / ~~the risk of~~ / turns
1 make ... friends with / a mistake / a photo / a promise
2 (a) heavy ... industry / luck / smoker / traffic
3 (a) great ... difficulty / interest / smoker / time
4 tell ... a joke / a promise / a story / the truth
5 (a) strong ... coffee / rain / swimmer / wind

2 Now complete the correct collocations for the words/phrases you have put a line through in Exercise 1. Add a verb or adjective.

0 *run the risk of*   2 ....   4 ....
1 ....   3 ....   5 ....

3 Read the sentences and complete the collocations. Use a verb in the correct form, or an adjective. 🔊 4.43 Listen and check.

0 Will you *make* the beds before you go out this morning?
1 The secret of .... a good joke is not to laugh when you get near the end.
2 It isn't very cold in Milan in March, so a .... coat or jacket should be enough.
3 That new perfume has such a .... smell that I find it annoying.
4 We urge you to .... confidence in your government in these difficult times.
5 This workshop will teach you all you need to know to .... your own business.
6 Please listen – you're .... the point. I'm not trying to criticise you at all.
7 We advise early booking as there is always .... interest in this excursion.
8 We've only got a day's holiday left, so we'd better .... the most of it.

4 **GRAMMAR IN USE** Complete the email with collocations. Take a word from Box A and one from Box B. 🔊 4.44 Listen and check.

A ~~bad~~ great great heavy started strong strong take took

B argument coffee difficulty ~~luck~~ part pity rain success swimmers

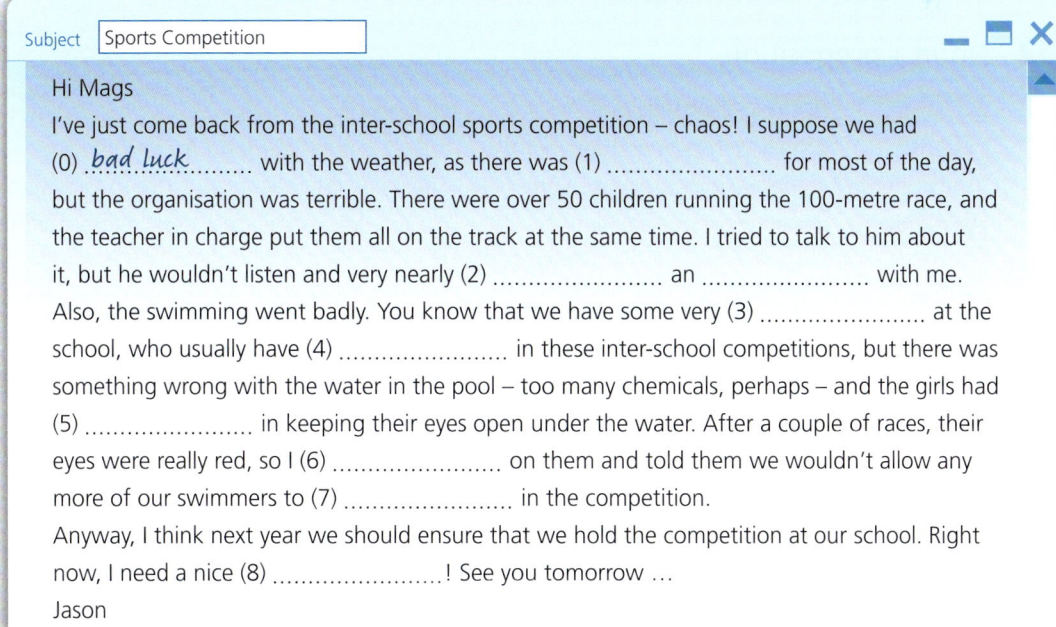

Subject: Sports Competition

Hi Mags
I've just come back from the inter-school sports competition – chaos! I suppose we had (0) *bad luck* with the weather, as there was (1) .... for most of the day, but the organisation was terrible. There were over 50 children running the 100-metre race, and the teacher in charge put them all on the track at the same time. I tried to talk to him about it, but he wouldn't listen and very nearly (2) .... an .... with me. Also, the swimming went badly. You know that we have some very (3) .... at the school, who usually have (4) .... in these inter-school competitions, but there was something wrong with the water in the pool – too many chemicals, perhaps – and the girls had (5) .... in keeping their eyes open under the water. After a couple of races, their eyes were really red, so I (6) .... on them and told them we wouldn't allow any more of our swimmers to (7) .... in the competition.
Anyway, I think next year we should ensure that we hold the competition at our school. Right now, I need a nice (8) ....! See you tomorrow …
Jason

Go online for more practice   267

88 Adjective or noun + preposition

The UK's main **hope of** success in the Olympic sailing event lies with Lucy McGregor, Annie Lush and Ally Martin (*pictured*).

1 Adjective + preposition

	ADJECTIVE + PREPOSITION	EXAMPLES
feelings	afraid/scared/terrified + *of* proud/ashamed/jealous + *of* annoyed/worried/upset + *about*	Sally is **terrified of** spiders. I'm really **ashamed of** your behaviour. I'm not really **upset about** my team's results.
	delighted/bored/pleased + *with/at/by* surprised/amazed/shocked + *at/by*	I was **bored by** the lesson. We weren't **pleased with** the builders' progress. Aren't you **shocked at** the violence in the film? I was really **surprised by** Samantha's news.
behaviour	nice/kind/unfriendly/mean + *to*	She's very **kind to** animals.
ability	good/bad/excellent + *at* capable/incapable + *of*	Nathan is **excellent at** painting. Julia is **incapable of** making a decision.
similarity	similar/identical + *to* different + *from/to*	That car is very **similar to** your last one. Spoken Portuguese is **different from** Spanish.
likes	keen + *on*, fond + *of* interested/involved + *in*	Lisa is **keen on** tracing her family tree. You aren't very **involved in** that book, are you?
other	full/short/tired + *of* ready/fit/famous/late/sorry + *for*	Gary can't come – he's **short of** money. He has only recently become **fit for** the competition.

More on preposition + *-ing* form ➤ Unit 14.1

⚠ Some adjectives (e.g. *good*, *bad*) can have more than one preposition, with different meanings, for example
- ability: *She's quite **good at** working out maths problems.*
- an advantage: *Doing regular exercise is **good for** you.*
- behaviour: *Salima is very **good to** her mother – she does all her shopping.*

2 Noun + preposition

	NOUN + PREPOSITION	EXAMPLES
needs	demand/request/need/wish + *for*	There's a great **demand for** cheap houses.
movement	rise/fall/increase/decrease + *in*	The bank has announced a **rise in** interest rates.
response	reaction/response/solution/ attitude + *to*	Do you get a severe **reaction to** insect bites? We need to find a **solution to** the problem.
contact	relationship/contact + *with*	She has a good **relationship with** the students.*
other	cause/cost/example + *of* opinion/knowledge/hope + *of* advantage/disadvantage + *of*	The **cause of** the flooding was heavy rain. Britain's main **hope of** success ... lies with ... He's got the **advantage of** speaking Chinese.
	matter/trouble/problem + *with* belief/trust/confidence + *in*	What's the **matter with** you today? People don't have **confidence in** the government any more.

* We use *relationship* + *between* before two people/groups/things:
*The **relationship between** Alex and his brother has always been difficult.*
*I don't understand the **relationship between** global warming and wetter summers.*

For preposition + noun, e.g. *at home, on time, for sale* ➤ Unit 18

17

Practice

1 Match the two parts of the sentences. 🔊 4.45 Listen and check.

0	The government is very worried	A	to his father, Kirk.
1	Princess Diana didn't have a good relationship	B	about the state of the economy.
2	There has been a huge rise	C	for relaxation.
3	Pete Sampras was extremely good	D	in house prices this year.
4	Michael Schumacher is famous	E	with finding enough water.
5	Some countries have awful problems	F	with the press.
6	Michael Douglas looks very similar	G	for motor racing.
7	Some breathing exercises are very good	H	of playing the saxophone.
8	Former US president Bill Clinton is fond	I	at playing tennis.

2 **GRAMMAR IN USE** Write the correct prepositions. 🔊 4.46 Listen and check.

COACH   Everyone's fit (0) *for* Saturday's match except for Wayne.

MANAGER   Wayne? Why? What's the matter (1) .... him?

COACH   His left ankle is painful. We don't know the cause (2) .... it yet – he's having a scan this afternoon – but we may not have him for Saturday.

MANAGER   OK, so we need a new captain for Saturday. How about Ewan?

COACH   I'm not sure. The relationship (3) .... him and some of the others isn't great. He's not good (4) .... talking to the referee. I think Thierry might be better.

MANAGER   You're right about Ewan, but I'm still annoyed (5) .... Thierry's comments to the press recently, and his attitude (6) .... the team in general. You know, he's been late (7) .... training every day this week.

COACH   OK. Perhaps we could try Roberto. It might be good (8) .... him to have some responsibility. He's become a lot calmer since he's been involved (9) .... that charity he supports.

MANAGER   You're right. It's time to show more confidence (10) .... him. I'll tell him later.

3 Answer the questions about yourself. Use full sentences.

0 What kind of relationship do you have with your colleagues / classmates?
  I have a good relationship with my colleagues.

1 What kind of relationship do you have with your colleagues / classmates?
  ....

2 What were you last really surprised by?
  ....

3 What's the main advantage of studying English for you?
  ....

4 Are you involved in any organisations? What?
  ....

5 Do you get an allergic reaction to anything? What?
  ....

6 What are you most scared of?
  ....

⏻ Go online for more practice

89 Verb + preposition (1)

Peter Edwards **succeeded in** winning first prize in this year's 'Young Baseball Star' competition. His father and grandfather were there to **congratulate him on** his success.

1 Verb (+ preposition) + object

With many verbs in English we can put a noun/pronoun object straight after the verb:
British people **discuss** *the weather every time they meet!*
But other verbs need a preposition before the object:
British people **talk about** *the weather every time they meet!*

⚠ There are many verbs that don't need a preposition in English, (e.g. *answer, demand, discuss, enter, expect, leave, phone, request*):
✗ *Everyone clapped when he entered to the room.*   ✓ *Everyone clapped when he entered the room.*

2 Verb + preposition combinations

Some verbs can be followed by different prepositions, (e.g. *talk to/talk about*). It is a good idea to check these in a dictionary.

+ about	complain hear know read speak talk think write
+ at	arrive laugh look shout stay
+ for	apologise apply ask care look pay search wait work
+ in + into	arrive believe stay succeed bump crash drive run
+ of	approve consist hear think
+ on	concentrate decide depend rely insist
+ to	belong explain happen listen speak talk write
+ with	agree deal stay

The Prime Minister **apologised for** *Britain's involvement in the slave trade.*
The music next door is so loud that I can't **concentrate on** *my work.*
Ahmed's job is to **deal with** *difficult customers.*

It is possible to have more than one preposition + noun combination after a verb:
I **spoke to** *the manager last week* **about** *the problem with the car.*

3 Verb + object + preposition + object

Some verbs can have two objects after them, one with a preposition and one without:
- *congratulate* + person + *on*: *Peter's father* **congratulated him on** *his success*.
- *accuse/remind* + person + *of*: *She* **reminded the player of** *his appointment with the coach.*
- *ask/blame/criticise/punish* + person + *for*: *Don't* **blame me for** *your mistakes!*
- *compare/provide/share* + person/thing + *with*: *The assistants will* **provide you with** *paper.*
- *borrow/translate/prevent* + person/thing + *from*: *Do you* **translate texts from** *English?*

Notice the difference between *to* and *at* after *throw, kick, shout* and *point*:
He threw the ball **to** *the girl.* (for her to catch it)
He threw the ball **at** *the girl.* (to hit her)

Verbs with two objects ➤ Unit 59.5

Practice

1 Match the two parts of the sentences. 🔊 4.47 Listen and check.

0	Does this mobile phone belong	A	on where to go for your holiday?
1	You don't have to pay	B	of a kitchen, living room and two bedrooms.
2	My mother's always complaining	C	for children to visit the museum.
3	The police car crashed	D	in good luck and bad luck.
4	Did you and your friends decide	E	into a tree at the side of the road.
5	What time does the train arrive	F	with each other on the runway.
6	I find it difficult to believe	G	to anyone in this class?
7	The two planes didn't collide	H	at London Paddington station?
8	The apartment consists	I	about the clothes I wear.

0 → G

2 **GRAMMAR IN USE** Complete the newspaper article with one word in each gap if necessary. There are two places where you do not need a word. 🔊 4.48 Listen and check.

18 August 2008

CHINESE ATHLETE WITHDRAWS FROM RACE

In the biggest shock of the Beijing Olympics so far, Chinese athlete Liu Xiang withdrew from the 110-metre hurdles this morning. Many people in the packed stadium had been waiting (0) ...*for*... Liu – wanting to see this great Chinese hero – and they walked out once it was clear he could not run. Everyone has been talking (1) .... Liu since he won his first title in the 2004 Olympics and then broke the world record in 2006, and they were all expecting (2) .... an easy victory for the young athlete. Although China has the most medals, a win by Liu was hugely important to them because Chinese athletes rarely succeed (3) .... track events. As soon as Liu walked off the track, questions were being asked and the press demanded (4) .... answers. What had happened (5) .... their great athlete? How could he disappoint the 1.3 billion people who were relying (6) .... him? It appeared that Liu had a damaged ankle, and despite the fact that three doctors were dealing (7) .... his injury, it prevented (8) .... from even starting the race.

3 Find and correct the mistakes. The preposition may be unnecessary, incorrect, or missing.

0 We decided ⌃on a vote to choose the class representative.
1 Has your friend apologised of his behaviour at the party yet?
2 I think I might apply a job at the local sports centre.
3 Do you think that Carol is keen on entering into competitions?
4 We don't really agree our neighbour's political views.
5 The kittens are so cute – you can't help laughing to them.
6 The police are searching the missing child all over the town.
7 If you're unhappy, why don't you phone to the shop and tell them?
8 Don't throw stones to other children – you might hurt them.

⏻ Go online for more practice

90 Verb + preposition (2)

The driver braked too hard and **ran into** the barriers.

Imagine **running into** you here, after all this time!

1 Prepositional verbs

Prepositional verbs are a very common type of verb + preposition combination. Generally, with these verbs, the preposition loses its usual meaning. Compare:
We **arrived at** the station an hour early. (verb + preposition; *at* = preposition of place)
We **arrived at** the solution very quickly. (prepositional verb; *at* has lost its meaning of 'place')

2 Prepositional verbs with a small change of meaning

With some verbs, the preposition often makes only a small change in the meaning of the verb. We can work out the meaning of many common prepositional verbs:

> ask for   believe in   care for   go for   happen to   listen to   look at   look like
> say to   speak to   stare at   talk to   think about   think of   wait for

'Have you **thought of** a name for the baby yet?' (*think of* = produce an idea)
'No, we've been **thinking about** it but haven't decided on one.' (*think about* = consider)

3 Prepositional verbs with complete change of meaning

Sometimes the preposition changes the meaning completely. Compare:
The driver braked too hard and **ran into** the barriers. (*into* = movement)
We **ran into** some friends of ours the other day. (= met by chance)
We managed to **get through** the crowd and get close to the stage. (*through* = movement)
I don't know how the people there **will get through** the winter. (= survive)

VERB	MEANING	EXAMPLE
arrive at	reach	Have you **arrived at** a decision about the new teacher yet?
come across	find, meet	I **came across** her diary when I was cleaning her room.
feel like	want	'Do you want to go swimming tonight?' 'No, I don't **feel like** it.'
get over get through	recover survive	Has your daughter **got over** the flu yet? I don't know how I **got through** that interview – it was really tough!
look after look into look like	take care of investigate be similar to	Can you **look after** the children tomorrow evening? The police are **looking into** the woman's disappearance. The baby really **looks like** his father, doesn't he?
run into	meet (by chance)	Amazingly, we **ran into** some old friends when we were visiting Rome!
see to	organise	Will you **see to** the flowers at Gail and Carl's wedding?
stand for stand for	mean accept	What do the letters BBC **stand for**? We won't **stand for** this kind of behaviour on the streets of our city!
take after	be similar to	Everyone says that Cheryl **takes after** her grandmother.

Practice

1 Match the verbs in these sentences with their meanings, A or B.

- 0 1 The soldiers got over the fence. → A climbed
-     2 Has Simon got over his illness? → B recovered from
- 1 1 The police will look into it.   A focus your eyes in this direction
-     2 Look into the camera viewfinder.   B investigate
- 2 1 The bus arrived at the Lovell Road bus station. A reached an answer
-     2 Have you arrived at a conclusion yet?   B got to
- 3 1 What does OPEC stand for?   A mean
-     2 Please stand for the National Anthem. B get onto your feet
- 4 1 Will they get through the journey?   A pass from one side to the other
-     2 Can you get through this gap in the fence? B survive
- 5 1 We ran into her at the supermarket. A met
-     2 The car ran into a woman at the crossing. B hit

2 Write the words in the correct order. 🔊 5.01 Listen and check.

0 family you like do anyone your look in ?
Do you look like anyone in your family?

1 me strange a this morning really to thing happened
....

2 on the bus at please people don't the stare
....

3 my daughter I'm staying for at home care to
....

4 Heather's think you new what of apartment did ?
....

5 take all of him grandchildren Bert's after
....

6 going to dreadful for I'm not behaviour your stand
....

3 **GRAMMAR IN USE** Complete the letter with the correct form of the verbs in the box. 🔊 5.02 Listen and check.

> ask   come   feel   look   see   talk   think   think   ~~wait~~

Dear Lesley
How are you? I'm just writing you a quick note while I'm (0) *waiting* for my plane back to Toulouse. I know I haven't been in touch with you recently, but I've been (1) .... about you a lot since we moved to France, and we should get together soon. So, do you (2) .... like coming to the men's final of the French Open tennis with me? I know you're a tennis fan, and you could make a weekend of it. I was walking in the park here recently when I (3) .... across an old friend who likes tennis, and as we were (4) .... to each other, she mentioned that she had two tickets that she couldn't use. She offered them to me and didn't (5) .... for any money for them, which was so nice of her. Anyway, if you're interested, all you need to do is book your flight – I'll (6) .... to all the other arrangements, like a hotel in Paris for us. I'm sure that François will (7) .... after the children that weekend. What do you (8) .... of the idea?
Let me know!
Nikki

Go online for more practice and a progress test

91 Phrasal verbs

The Canadians are **falling behind** now but the Danish boat is just **keeping up with** the Slovakians. Can they **turn** the race **round** and win the gold medal?

1 Two-part phrasal verbs

A **phrasal verb** is a verb + adverb/preposition (e.g. *fill in, take off*):
Could you **fill in** this form and return it to us by post?
Don't **take** your coat **off** – we're going shopping now.

Phrasal verbs are similar to prepositional verbs, but the word order is sometimes different.
- In prepositional verbs, the preposition comes immediately after the verb and before the object: *She's **looking after** the children. She's **looking after** them.*
- In phrasal verbs, the adverb/preposition can come AFTER the noun object, and it ALWAYS comes after a pronoun object:
*Did you **look up** that word? Did you **look** that word **up**? Did you **look** it **up**?*

	VERB	+ NOUN OBJECT	+ PRONOUN OBJECT
prepositional verb	work for (be employed by)	I **work for** Gerald Bryant & Sons. ✗ I work Gerald Bryant & Sons for.	I **work for** them. ✗ I work them for.
	take to (like)	I **took to** my teacher immediately. ✗ I took my teacher to immediately.	I **took to** her. ✗ I took her to.
phrasal verb	work out (solve)	I've **worked out** the solution. I've **worked** the solution **out**.	✗ I've worked out it. I've **worked** it **out**.
	take off (remove)	He **took off** his boots. He **took** his boots **off**.	✗ He took off them. He **took** them **off**.

You can work out from a good dictionary whether a verb is prepositional or phrasal. Look at the position of the object (*sth*) in these dictionary entries:

> **take to** sth to start to like someone or something.
>   *Sandra took to it straight away.* (*prepositional*)
> **take** sth **off** to remove a piece of clothing.
>   *He sat on the bed to take his boots off.* (*phrasal*)

A lot of two-part phrasal verbs are intransitive – they don't have an object:
Come in, we're almost ready.   The plane **took off** nearly three hours late. (= left)
We often use them in exclamations:
Look out! There's a car coming!   **Hurry up!** The taxi's here.   **Go on**, I'm listening.

⚠ We don't use an object with intransitive phrasal verbs: ✗ The plane took off the runway.

2 Three-part phrasal verbs

There are also some phrasal verbs which have an adverb and a preposition (e.g. *look forward to, keep up with, cut down on*). We don't separate the parts of these verbs:

⚠ ✓ I'm **looking forward to** my holiday.
  ✗ I'm looking forward my holiday to. ✗ I'm looking my holiday forward to.

274

3 Change in meaning

A phrasal verb usually has a different meaning from the verb on its own:
*While he was exercising, the gymnast **fell** and broke his leg.* (= dropped to the ground)
*The Canadians are **falling behind** now.* (= going more slowly than the others)

A lot of phrasal verbs combine with different adverbs/prepositions and have different meanings:

PHRASAL VERB		MEANING	EXAMPLE
give	in	deliver	You were supposed to **give** this essay **in** yesterday.
	up	stop	Why don't you **give up** eating chocolate?
make	out	understand	I couldn't **make out** what I had done to annoy her.
	up	invent	When you're the boss you can **make up** your own rules.
	up for	make better	You'd better **make up for** forgetting my birthday!
turn	down	reject	They offered her the job but she **turned** it **down**.
	round	change	Can they **turn** the race **round** and win the gold medal?
	up	arrive	Steve **turned up** late as usual.

Some phrasal verbs can have more than one meaning:
*You were supposed to **give** this essay **in** yesterday.* (+ object = deliver)
*I know I can't beat you at chess. I **give in**!* (no object = surrender)

If an object is very long, we put it after the adverb/preposition:
✓ *I couldn't make out **what I had done to annoy her**.*
✗ ~~I couldn't make what I had done to annoy her out.~~

4 Phrasal verbs in informal English

Many phrasal verbs have the same meaning as another, more formal verb (e.g. *find out* (information) = discover, *take off* (your coat) = remove).

FORMALITY CHECK Phrasal verbs are more common in informal English.

INFORMAL	FORMAL
I **took** the damaged CD **back** to the shop.	Please **return** damaged goods within ten days.
We can't **put up with** his behaviour.	Staff will not **tolerate** rude behaviour.
Carrie **turned down** Sean's proposal.	Tutors may **reject** unsuitable topics for essays.
They **left** me **out** of the hockey team this year!	Unfortunately, our agents **omitted** this information.
I think I'm going to **cut down** my hours at work.	The management intends to **reduce** working hours.
Can you **throw** these old things **away**?	We ask visitors to **dispose of** their rubbish.

5 Adverb/preposition meaning

The adverb/preposition sometimes helps us to work out the meaning of a phrasal verb:
*stand **up** / get **up** / lift **up** / pick **up*** (movement in an upwards direction). But many of them have other meanings:

	MEANING	EXAMPLES
up	complete an amount/ a distance	Come on, **finish** your dinner **up**; there's isn't much left. If we run fast enough, we'll be able to **catch** them **up**.
	maintain sth	The Danish boat is just **keeping up with** the Slovakians.
down	reduce, movement downward	The business was losing money so we decided to **run** it **down**. He **fell down** and hit his head. **Note** your answers **down** on a piece of paper.
out	remove	Can you **take** the rubbish **out** when you leave later?
	do completely	I think I've managed to **work out** the answer to this problem.
off	stop connection	**Turn** the TV **off**! I can't hear myself think.
	depart	We're **setting off** really early tomorrow morning.

91 PHRASAL VERBS

Practice

1 Complete the sentences with a suitable adverb/preposition. 5.03 Listen and check.

0 Are you going *out* with your friends this evening?
1 This report isn't very clear. I can't make .... what he's saying.
2 This new diet involves giving .... fat and sugar.
3 The talks failed when the union turned .... the company's last offer.
4 This new type of engine cuts .... on carbon dioxide.
5 When you fly, wear several layers so that you can take them .... as you get hotter.
6 I'd better finish my assignment this evening so that I can give it .... tomorrow.
7 Our friends were astonished when we turned .... at their door.
8 Hannah was always very good at making .... stories.

2 **GRAMMAR IN USE** Complete the race report with the correct form of the phrasal verbs in the box. 5.04 Listen and check.

> catch up   give up   keep up with   ~~leave out~~   look out
> make out   make up for   set off   turn round

"Welcome to the 155th Oxford and Cambridge Boat Race. The crews are on the river beneath me – I'm standing on Putney Bridge. Oxford are the favourites this year, but they've had to (0) *leave* their strongest rower *out* of the boat as he has been unwell recently. Right, they're ready to (1) ....
And they're off! Cambridge immediately take the lead and Oxford are falling behind ... it seems that they're struggling to (2) .... Cambridge today ... It's a bit foggy on this bend; I can't (3) .... them .... very clearly, but I think that Oxford are getting faster.
Yes! They had a very slow start but they're (4) .... it now. (5) .... Cambridge! They're (6) .... you .... !
Now Cambridge are starting to speed up again, but Oxford are right behind them. Don't (7) ...., Oxford, you're nearly there! You're coming to the last bend. ...
There's the finish line and it's neck and neck, but Oxford are pulling ahead. Yes, that's it! After a terrible start, Oxford have (8) .... the race .... and won! Well done, Oxford!"

3 Write the words in the correct order. Where there are two lines, there are two possible word orders.

0 fill   form   could   in   application   you   the   ?
   Could you fill in the application form?   *Could you fill the application form in?*
1 already   in   it   have   filled   I
2 meaning   dictionary   look   the   a   up   in
   ....
3 up   looked   in   I   dictionary   it   the
4 you   forward   holiday   are   to   your   looking   ?   ....
5 been   it   weeks   forward   for   I've   looking   to   ....
6 address   you   down   can   the   write   me   for   ?
   ....

4 Underline the phrasal verb in each sentence. Then choose the correct meaning from the words in *italics*.

0 Please <u>leave out</u> that part of the email.   complete / move ↓ /(remove)
1 What time are we setting off in the morning?   move ↑ / depart / complete
2 They're going to pull down the old cinema.   complete / move ↓ / remove
3 Eat up – we've got to leave in five minutes.   move ↑ / depart / complete
4 Please lift me up, so I can see what's happening!   move ↑ / depart / complete
5 The dentist is going to take my tooth out.   complete / move ↓ / remove
6 My feet hurt! I really must sit down.   complete / move ↓ / remove

5 Rewrite the formal extracts in informal English by completing the sentences below. Use suitable phrasal verbs.

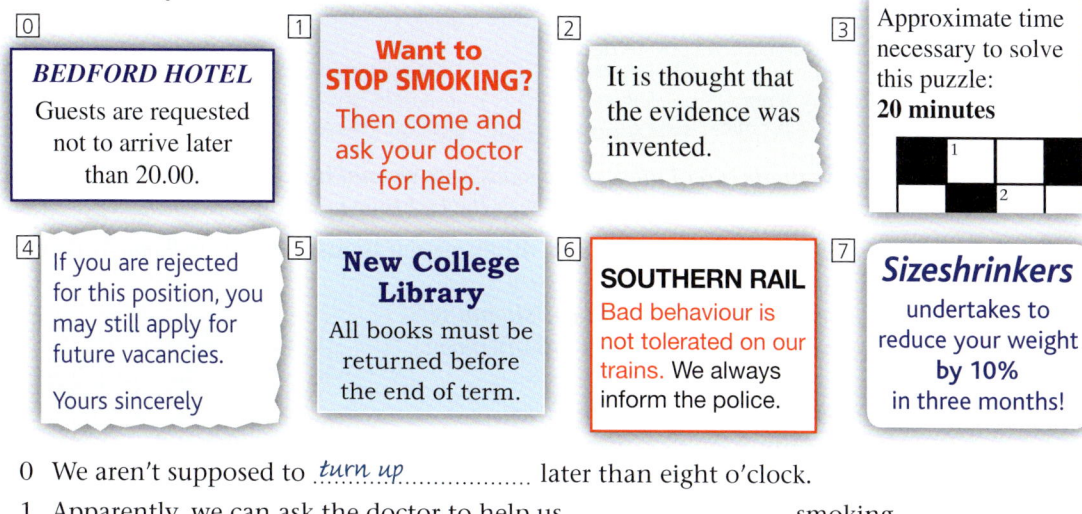

0 We aren't supposed to *turn up* .... later than eight o'clock.
1 Apparently, we can ask the doctor to help us .... smoking.
2 They think that the evidence was ....
3 It should take about twenty minutes to .... the answer to the puzzle.
4 It says I can apply in future even if they .... me .... this time.
5 We have to .... all our books .... before the end of term.
6 I don't blame them if they don't .... bad behaviour, do you?
7 They say they can .... our weight .... by about 10 percent.

6 Find six more mistakes and correct them. Tick (✓) the correct sentences.

0 We're looking forward ~~your party to~~. *to your party*
1 I've decided to cut on sweets and chocolates down.
2 What time did the plane take off in the end?
3 What does that sign say? I can't quite make out it.
4 Come on! Run faster! You have to keep up them with.
5 You know, I can never work the answers to these awful number puzzles in this magazine out.
6 The children next door are so noisy. I don't think I can put up with it for much longer.
7 Your boots are filthy! Please take off them before you come in the house.
8 I know I've had a lot of time off work, but I'm going to make it up for.

92 Confusing verbs (1)

1 make and do

We often use the verb *make* to talk about creating something or causing something to happen.
*What do they **make** in that factory?*
*Have you **made a decision** about the job yet?*

We often use *do* to talk about carrying out or completing any activity:
*Are you **doing** anything exciting at the weekend?   All the students **did** the essay this time.*

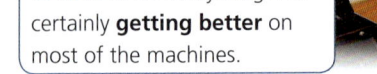

I **do** a lot of **exercise** as I want to **get fit**. I come to the gym regularly, and it **takes** a lot of **time** to do everything. I'm certainly **getting better** on most of the machines.

make +	do +
an appointment the bed a copy a decision friends a meal (lunch, dinner, etc.) a mess a mistake money a noise a phone call a plan progress a promise a suggestion	a course an exam/test (an) exercise/homework the housework (the ironing, shopping, etc.) research someone a favour well/badly your hair/make-up

*The workmen have **made a real mess** of the roads.   Are we **making** enough **money** at the moment?*
*I **do** a lot of **exercise** as I want to get fit.   That's the last time I **do you a favour**!*

⚠ We **do the** shopping (usually for food and other regular items) but we **go** shopping (usually a specific shopping trip):
*Will you get some biscuits when you **do the shopping**?*
*I'm **going shopping** for some new shoes this afternoon.*

2 have and take

We can use *have* and *take* with some actions, but only *take* with others:

have/take +	take +
a bath/a shower a break an exam/test a holiday a look a rest a seat time off	action a bus/train care (of) a decision medicine a message part in a photo

Note the difference between *have time* and *take time*:
***Do** you **have time** to help me with the gardening today?   We **don't have time** to wait.*
*'How much **time does it take** to cross the Channel?'   'It only **takes** twenty minutes by Eurostar.'*

have + noun for action ➤ 26.2   it + takes for time ➤ 60.3

3 get

The verb *get* has several different meanings:

receive	We **get** a lot of junk mail. I **got** a call from my friend in Argentina yesterday.
find, buy	We need to **get** help quickly. I **got** this jacket from the local market.
arrive at / reach	We didn't **get** home until midnight. I've almost **got** to the end of the book.
fetch	Can you **get** my glasses from the bedroom? Hold on, I'll **get** a pen.
become	Eat your dinner before it **gets** cold. Young people are **getting** more aggressive.

FORMALTIY CHECK *Get* is more informal than other words that have the same meaning:
*I **received** your communication.* (formal) → *I **got** your letter.* (informal)

We use *get* + an adjective to talk about changes:

get changed/dressed   get engaged/married   get fit   get ready   get well/better/worse

*Hurry up and **get dressed** or we'll miss the train!*
*I'm certainly **getting better** on the rowing machine.*

17

Practice

1 Write a sentence about each picture, using the word in brackets and a suitable verb.

(phone call) (exam) (make-up) (medicine) (shower) (mess)

0 *He's making a phone call.*
1 ....
2 ....
3 ....
4 ....
5 ....

2 The underlined phrases below are too formal. Rewrite the sentences, using a form of *get* and the word(s) from the box. 🔊 5.05 Listen and check.

> the answer   better   ~~an email~~   help   older   ready

0 We <u>received an electronic communication</u> from our daughter in Bali this morning.
   We got an email from our daughter in Bali this morning.
1 Come on, kids! Haven't you <u>prepared yourselves</u> for the party yet?
   ....
2 I think I've broken my leg. Can you <u>obtain assistance</u>, please?
   ....
3 He's quick! He <u>arrived at the solution</u> much faster than the rest of us.
   ....
4 It's more difficult to climb stairs as <u>your age increases</u>.
   ....
5 Has your husband<u>'s health improved</u> after his fall?
   ....

3 **GRAMMAR IN USE** Complete the conversations with suitable verbs in the correct forms. 🔊 5.06 Listen and check.

1 JOHN   Have you (0) *made* a decision about the new team coach yet?
  ANDREW   No, but I've (1) .... an appointment to interview someone tomorrow.
  JOHN   Oh, really. Who?
  ANDREW   Martin Adams. He's (2) .... all the coaching courses and he's (3) .... a lot of progress with his present club. I think he'd be a good choice.

2 ALEX   Dad, will you (4) .... me a favour? Will you be my tennis partner? Joe's ill.
  DAD   I'm busy, Alex. I don't (5) .... time. Sorry.
  ALEX   How much time does it (6) .... to play a game of tennis? You're always saying you want to (7) .... fitter.
  DAD   Oh, all right, then. I'll go and (8) .... changed.

3 PILAR   Are you (9) .... anything tomorrow, Carmen?
  CARMEN   Yes, I'm training. I'm going to (10) .... part in the marathon next month, so I'm (11) .... a lot of exercise at the moment.
  PILAR   You must be (12) .... a lot faster, then.

93 Confusing verbs (2)

I'm **going** for a ride round the lake today.

OK, Tina. **Take** your mobile, and **remember** to be careful. And don't **leave** the gate **open**!

1 come or go, bring or take?

Come/bring and *go/take* have opposite meanings.

come/bring = movement towards the speaker:	go/take = movement away from the speaker:
Can I **come** and ride your horse this evening? They're **bringing** their children with them so we'll meet them for the first time.	I'm **going** for a ride. I'll see you later. His wife went to Australia, **taking** the children with her.

We can also use *come/bring* to mean 'with the speaker':
We're going to the cinema this evening – would you like to **come** with us?
You'd better **bring** a coat on our walk tomorrow – it's likely to rain.

2 live and stay

- We use *live* to talk about permanent situations or long periods of time:
  Lions **live** in social groups called 'prides'. Rosie **lived** with her grandparents when she was a child.
- We use *stay* for temporary periods of time:
  Have you ever **stayed** in the Waldorf Hotel in New York?

3 remind and remember

- *Remember* means 'to bring something into your mind': *I must **remember** to post Jen's birthday card. Some older people find it easier to **remember** things that happened long ago.*
- *Remind* means 'to make someone else remember': *Will you **remind me** to get some milk later?*
- *Remind of* + noun means 'to make you think of another thing/person':
  *Daniel Radcliffe really **reminds me of** my brother.*

4 keep

The verb *keep* has different meanings:

not lose something	Don't throw that book away. I want to **keep** it.
remain, stay (usually with an adjective or phrase)	I'm exhausted. I can't **keep awake**. **Keep off the grass!**
continue (+ -ing form) also with *on*	I **keep telling** you but you refuse to listen! She pretended not to hear and **kept on walking**.

5 leave

The verb *leave* can be used with different meanings, and in different ways:

go away from somewhere	The plane **leaves** at 12.30.
stop something (usually a long-term activity)	Students can **leave** school at sixteen. Are you going to get a job as soon as you **leave** university?
not change/move something (usually + adjective)	Don't **leave** the gate **open**. We don't want to change from electricity to gas so **leave** us **alone**!

The phrase *be left* means 'remaining': *There **isn't** much money **left**. Are there any biscuits **left**?*

Practice

1 Choose the correct words in *italics*.

0 Should we *bring /(take)* some presents when we go to visit your family in Canada?
1 Have you *lived / stayed* in this house all your life?
2 Your brother *remembers / reminds* me of Brad Pitt.
3 We need some building work done. Could you *go / come* here and look at it for us?
4 I'm so tired. It's difficult to *keep / leave* awake.
5 You'd better apply for that course soon. There isn't much time *left / kept*.
6 When you go to the shops, *remember / remind* to get a birthday card for Harry.
7 Don't *leave / keep* the lights on when you go out – it's a waste of electricity.
8 Where did your cousins from Kenya *live / stay* when they were here last summer?

2 **GRAMMAR IN USE** Complete the article with the correct forms of the verbs in the box.
🔊 **5.07** Listen and check.

| bring | ~~come~~ | keep | keep | live | leave | remember | remind | stay |

Tennis USA: *Martina Navratilova*

Born in Prague, in 1956, Martina Navratilova turned professional in 1975. In the same year she (0) *came* to the United States to play in the US Open, and decided to (1) .... Czechoslovakia for good and stay in the United States. Because of the political situation, she wasn't able to (2) .... her parents with her, although she managed to (3) .... in touch with them. She took US citizenship, which meant, unfortunately, that she couldn't (4) .... her Czech citizenship. Since then she has (5) .... in the United States. She played for this country for twenty years, when she won all of the most important tennis tournaments. Most tennis fans (6) .... the intense but entertaining rivalry she had first with Chris Evert and later with Steffi Graf. In 2008, she moved into reality TV when she (7) .... in the Australian jungle for a few weeks during a series of *I'm A Celebrity, Get Me Out Of Here*. She did very well, perhaps because the tests in the jungle (8) .... her of her competitive years playing tennis.

3 Complete the second sentence so it means the same as the first, using a verb from this unit. Use one to three words in your answers. 🔊 **5.08** Listen and check.

0 Flight AF384 to Paris will be delayed until 22.30.
   Flight AF384 to Paris ......*will leave*...... at half past ten.
1 Dogs are not allowed into this shop.
   You can't .... into this shop.
2 Close the windows when you go out tonight.
   Don't .... open when you go out tonight.
3 All the rooms in the Tregarth Hotel are half price in December.
   You can .... the Tregarth Hotel very cheaply in December.
4 Don't forget to switch your headlights on in the tunnel.
   You should .... to switch your headlights on in the tunnel.
5 Do not leave baggage unattended in the station.
   You should .... with you in the station.
6 In this game, you can't stop talking for one minute.
   In this game, you have to .... talking for one minute.

94 Confusing adjectives

Unfortunately, Gareth Farnham is badly **injured** and won't be able to play for some weeks. He has a **damaged** ankle.

1 injured, hurt, wounded and damaged

It is easy to confuse adjectives that have similar meanings. We use *injured*, *hurt* and *wounded* to talk about people or animals.
- *Injured* and *hurt* are similar – we can be injured or hurt in accidents and natural disasters:
  Gareth Farnham is badly injured. Sometimes horses get hurt when they are racing.
- We use *wounded* when we are hurt by a weapon, such as a gun or a knife:
  They set up a hospital for wounded soldiers.
- We use *damaged* to talk about things and parts of the body:
  The cause of the flood was a damaged pipeline. He has a damaged knee.

⚠ We don't usually put *hurt* before a noun: ✗ ~~There's a hurt horse in this race.~~

More on adjectives ending in *-ed* ▶ Unit 19.3

2 sensible and sensitive (to)

Sensible means 'showing good judgement': *It's sensible to keep a note of your passport number.*
Sensitive means 'easily upset or offended': *Victoria's very sensitive about her red hair.*
- Note that *sensitive to* = affected by something, often physically: *My skin is very sensitive to the sun – I go red very easily.*

⚠ I can't eat spicy food.   ✗ ~~I've got a sensible stomach.~~   ✓ I've got a **sensitive** stomach.

3 likeable and sympathetic

We use *likeable* about people to mean 'pleasant and friendly': *Jason's a really likeable guy.*
We use *sympathetic* about people who are able to feel sorry about another person's problems: *My boss was very sympathetic when I told him about my bad back.*

⚠ I've become really friendly with my new neighbour.   ✗ ~~She's very sympathetic.~~
✓ She's very **likeable**.

4 amusing and enjoyable

We use *amusing* when we find something funny (it makes us laugh):
That new comedy series is very amusing, isn't it?
Your father's got a great sense of humour – he's very amusing to listen to.

We use *enjoyable* when something is a pleasant activity:
Thanks for inviting us to your party. It was very enjoyable.
That was an enjoyable evening – Geoff and Sue are always good company.

⚠ We can use *amusing*, but not *enjoyable*, to describe a person: ✗ ~~Your father's very enjoyable.~~

5 expensive and valuable

Expensive means 'costing a lot of money': *Kyle bought me some expensive perfume.*
We don't often go to that restaurant. It's very expensive.

Valuable means 'worth a lot of money': *My grandmother left me a valuable antique ring.*
I found this old painting at a charity shop. It wasn't expensive but I think it could be really valuable.

17

Practice

1 Choose the correct words in *italics*. 🔊 5.09 Listen and check.

0 Don't buy your food at the new shop in the main road – it's really *valuable* / (*expensive*).
1 Damon can't play in the badminton competition because he's *injured* / *damaged*.
2 It isn't very *sensible* / *sensitive* to go walking in high-heeled shoes.
3 I can't talk to my best friend about my problems. She isn't very *likeable* / *sympathetic*.
4 I like Harry because he makes me laugh – he's very *amusing* / *enjoyable*.
5 You can borrow my pearl necklace tonight but don't lose it – it's very *expensive* / *valuable*.
6 I've got *a hurt* / *an injured* shoulder from last night's judo class.
7 Those onions are making me sneeze – my nose is very *sensible* / *sensitive*.
8 The builder says our roof is badly *wounded* / *damaged*, and we need a new one.

2 Complete the sentences, with the adjectives from the box. There are two extra adjectives.

> damaged   enjoyable   injured   hurt   likeable
> sensible   sensitive   ~~sympathetic~~   valuable

0 A couple of my friends are very *sympathetic* listeners.
1 Visiting an art gallery is a(n) .... way of spending an afternoon.
2 My eyes are very .... to the sun so I have to wear sunglasses.
3 My daughter would like a job caring for .... animals.
4 Please return immediately any goods that have been .... in the post.
5 My most .... possession is a gold watch.
6 I think you'll get on with Judy's brother; he's very pleasant and ....

3 **GRAMMAR IN USE** Complete the telephone conversation with suitable adjectives from this unit. 🔊 5.10 Listen and check.

A Good morning. Frobisher Martial Arts Institute.
B Oh, hello. I'm calling to ask about your self-defence classes. Are they (0) *expensive* ?
A Well, our group classes are £10 an hour. Tell me, why do you want to learn self-defence?
B Well, there've been a lot of muggings round here recently and I walk home every night.
A Mmm. Do you carry anything (1) .... with you?
B No, well, only my laptop; it was quite (2) .... when I bought it, but it's old now. To be honest, I'm more worried about getting (3) ....
A That's understandable. It's certainly (4) .... to get some kind of training in case you're ever in a dangerous situation. Would you like to enrol for a class with Peter? He's very experienced. All his students say he's very (5) .... – very pleasant, and that his classes are (6) .... – everyone has a good time in them.
B OK, when can I start?

4 Write sentences about yourself, using the words in brackets.

0 (sensible) *I think I'm a very sensible person.*
1 (most valuable) ....
2 (been injured) ....
3 (sensitive) ....
4 (enjoyable) ....

Review MODULE 17

1 UNITS 87, 88 AND 89 Read the article and choose the correct words in *italics*.

Man v. Horse Marathon

If a man (0) *did / ran* a race against a horse, who would win? I expect your response (1) *to / for* that question would be 'the horse', like mine was, but think again! It is possible for the man to win, and this has been proved by the annual man versus horse marathon in Llantwryd Wells in Wales. I first heard (2) *about / in* this race a few years ago and it fascinated me. The competitors start in the town square and go along farm tracks, paths and roads, and across open land, arriving (3) *to / at* the finish line back in the town after 22 miles (about 35 kilometres). This race has generated (4) *great / big* interest among runners in the UK and Europe, especially those who are interested (5) *in / at* taking part (6) *of / in* strange challenges. From the first race in 1980, the times of the human runners were slower than the horses' times, though perhaps more similar (7) *to / from* them than you would expect. But when a man first won the race in 2004 I was quite surprised, to (8) *say / tell* the truth. Huw Lobb, a marathon runner, passed the finish line in two hours and five minutes, two minutes faster than the first horse!

2 UNITS 89, 90 AND 91 Write the words in the correct order. Be careful! Some sentences contain prepositional verbs and some contain phrasal verbs.

0 a long time over it to took the flu get   *It took a long time to get over the flu.*
1 told give the doctor me it up to   ....
2 the garden I across it came in   ....
3 I'll about him write the problem to   ....
4 turned I last week them down   ....
5 can me you on always rely   ....
6 for we stand this behaviour any more won't   ....

3 UNITS 90 AND 91 Match the underlined words in the sentences with a verb from Box A and a preposition/adverb from Box B.

A   cut ~~get~~ get give keep set stand take turn

B   after down down on for in off over ~~up~~ up

0 Go to bed. We need to <u>rise</u> early in the morning.   *get up*
1 What do the letters UNESCO <u>represent</u>?   ....
2 It's difficult to <u>maintain</u> the payments at present.   ....
3 Has the rebel army agreed to <u>surrender</u> yet?   ....
4 I think we should <u>reduce</u> our spending.   ....
5 How long does it take to <u>recover from</u> this illness?   ....
6 Who do you <u>resemble</u> most in your family?   ....
7 Please <u>reduce the volume of</u> the television.   ....
8 The runners <u>departed</u> from the town at 8.00 a.m.   ....

4 UNITS 92, 93 AND 94 Find eight more mistakes in the conversation and correct them.

SAM I've just ~~gone~~ *done* the shopping and I think they've done a mistake in the bill. It seems very valuable.

MUM Let me have a look. Which supermarket did you come to?

SAM The usual one. But I paid with a £50.00 note and I've only got £3.00 kept.

MUM Well, be sensitive, there must be a mistake. The shopping's usually only just over £20.00. Did you stay the receipt?

SAM Yes, it's here.

MUM Take it to me then. Look – this says £27.00. They should have given you £23.00 change, not £3.00. Didn't you remind to check the change in the shop?

SAM No, I was in a hurry.

5 UNITS 87, 92, 93 AND 94 Use the sentence clues to complete the word puzzle.

Clues

0 Next year I'm doing a ... in advanced mathematics.
1 Sit still. I want to take a ... of you all.
2 Ballack missed a ... and Germany lost the match.
3 Sorry we're late – we were stuck in heavy ... on the motorway.
4 The government will run the ... of losing the election if they raise taxes.
5 Sally and Michael have just got ... ; they're going to get married next year.
6 I've just met Anya's brother. He's a very ... person, very pleasant, isn't he?
7 Can you ... me when your birthday is? I've forgotten the date.
8 The council must take ... soon about the rubbish, or it will spread diseases.
9 I must go to bed. I'm finding it really difficult to ... awake.
10 I'm terrified of doing the parachute jump really, but I have ... in my instructor.

6 ALL UNITS Match A or B to the meaning given below.

0   A Alan is very sensible.   B Alan is very sensitive.
    Alan is a logical, rational person. *A*

1   A We've cut down our smoking.   B We've cut down the tree in the garden.
    We've reduced something we do. ....

2   A He kicked the ball to me.   B He kicked the ball at me.
    He intended to hit me with the ball. ....

3   A Prakesh lives in Delhi.   B Prakesh is staying in Delhi.
    Delhi is his permanent home. ....

4   A That watch was very expensive.   B That watch is valuable to me.
    The watch means a lot to me, but might not have cost very much. ....

5   A You should have a light meal.   B You should have a heavy meal.
    You should only eat a little. ....

6   A I remind him of his sister.   B I remember his sister.
    I think about his sister sometimes. ....

7   A I ran into a tree on the road.   B I ran into some friends.
    I had an accident. ....

8   A Bring some money with you.   B Take some money with you.
    I'm going to be with you. ....

7 ALL UNITS Complete the second sentence so it means the same as the first, using the word in brackets. Use two to five words in your answer.

0   Would you mind completing this form, please, sir? (in)
    Would you mind *filling in* this form, please, sir?

1   We haven't decided which colour we want to paint the kitchen. (decision)
    We haven't .... about which colour we want to paint the kitchen.

2   How many people are participating in the competition? (part)
    How many people are .... the competition?

3   Many people continue to work into their sixties now. (keep)
    Many people .... into their sixties now.

4   His health was poor because of a childhood disease. (cause)
    The .... his poor health was a childhood disease.

5   Rebecca can swim very well. (swimmer)
    Rebecca is a ....

6   We need to reduce our weekly expenses. (cut)
    We need to .... our weekly expenses.

7   Have you considered a change in your career? (thought)
    Have you .... your career?.

8   Stop being silly and put your clothes on! (get)
    Stop being silly and ....!

9   'Have you finished that puzzle?' 'Yes, I've just solved it.' (out)
    'Have you finished that puzzle?' 'Yes, I've ....

10 The children are really excited about the trip to the circus. (forward)
    The children .... the trip to the circus.

8 ALL UNITS Read the advert for a form of exercise and choose the best answer, A, B or C below. Sometimes more than one answer is correct.

The Ashoka Health and Well-Being Centre

- Have you always wanted to (0) .... more exercise?
- Do you want to (1) .... fit, but you don't want to (2) .... yourself?
- As you (3) .... older, do you find yourself becoming more and more anxious about your health and fitness?

Then maybe pilates is for you.

Pilates is an (4) .... form of exercise that strengthens the deep inner muscles in the abdomen and back. Many people believe it is partly responsible for the decrease (5) .... back problems for many people in recent years.

It consists (6) .... controlled, slow movements combined with careful breathing. It borrows some of its movements (7) .... other forms of exercise, and you may find that it's not very different (8) .... general fitness classes you have done. Started during World War One by Joseph Pilates to help (9) .... soldiers regain full fitness, it has become increasingly popular since the 1990s.

It can work for anyone, however fit or unfit. It will get rid of your (10) .... habits, and will help you to take better care (11) .... your body.

Why don't you enrol for a class now? You'll be amazed (12) .... the results!

```
 0  Ⓐ do          B make        Ⓒ take
 1  A leave       B go          C keep
 2  A hurt        B wound       C injure
 3  A get         B stay        C keep
 4  A amusing     B enjoyable   C expensive
 5  A at          B in          C of
 6  A from        B with        C of
 7  A to          B from        C with
 8  A to          B from        C of
 9  A damaged     B injured     C hurt
10  A weak        B strong      C bad
11  A to          B of          C with
12  A by          B about       C at
```

287

Test MODULE 17

Word combinations

Choose the correct answer, A, B or C.

1. We were late at the bus station so we .... the bus.
   A passed   B lost   C missed   ➤ Unit 87

2. It's difficult to make friends .... people in a large city.
   A with   B of   C to   ➤ Unit 87

3. There's a lot of .... industry on the outskirts of the town.
   A big   B strong   C heavy   ➤ Unit 87

4. You know, you can be really mean .... the children sometimes.
   A with   B to   C at   ➤ Unit 88

5. Dr Mackenzie has a really good relationship .... his patients.
   A to   B with   C between   ➤ Unit 88

6. They said at the interview that they would phone .... within a week.
   A me   B to me   C at me   ➤ Unit 89

7. The government did not provide .... food or clothing.
   A with the refugees   B the refugees with   C the refugees for   ➤ Unit 89

8. Have you got the car keys? Can you throw them ....?
   A to me   B me   C at me   ➤ Unit 89

9. That was dreadful! I thought I'd never ....!
   A get the evening through   B the evening get through
   C get through the evening   ➤ Unit 90

10. Gerry's at home with the children while his wife's in hospital. He cares .... very well.
    A them   B for them   C them for   ➤ Unit 90

11. We watched as the plane took ....
    A off   B off the runway   C the runway off   ➤ Unit 91

12. The cat's been in all day. Can you .... now?
    A let out him   B let him out   C let take out   ➤ Unit 91

13. I know I've had to take a lot of time off work recently but I will ....
    A make it up for   B make up it for   C make up for it   ➤ Unit 91

14. I'm really looking forward .... at the weekend.
    A to the party   B the party to   C the party   ➤ Unit 91

15. The Minister .... a promise at the last election, so the government has to keep it.
    A did   B made   C got   ➤ Unit 92

16. Mr Davis, I .... a message for you earlier from Mr Lewis.
    A took   B made   C did   ➤ Unit 92

17. Your father's in the garden, can you .... this sandwich to him?
    A fetch   B bring   C take   ➤ Unit 93

18. 'The window's open.' 'I know. .... it open – it's too hot in here.'
    A Stay   B Leave   C Keep   ➤ Unit 93

19. I'd like to return this book because some of the pages are ....
    A hurt   B wounded   C damaged   ➤ Unit 94

20. You'll like Jane's cousin – he's very witty and ....
    A enjoyable   B valuable   C amusing   ➤ Unit 94

Go online for a full exit test

Word formation

MODULE 18

Before you start

1 Read the advertisement. Look at the highlighted grammar examples.

Prior Lodge College

Prior Lodge is a private college dedicated to the needs of adult students. Our courses are part-time and run in the evenings and at weekends.

Courses
We run courses in languages, science and arts. We have an excell**ent** record of preparing students for public examin**ations**.

Facilities
In the last two years we have completely modern**ised** our facilities and now have a media centre with fifty workstations and Internet access.

Teaching and study programmes
Our teachers are friendly, experienced and dedicated. Each student receives an individual study programme and your **coursework** is continuously graded so we can help you achieve your highest potential.

Dates and fees
Our next **twelve-week course** begins in September. Applic**ants** will be interviewed in July. See our website for details of fees and payment.

If you **dis**liked school and you prefer to learn in an **in**formal atmosphere then Prior Lodge College is the place for you!
www.priorlodgecollegeinfo.org

2 Now complete the sentences with a suitable word or words, using the ideas in brackets ( ). The highlighted grammar examples will help you.

1 My boss is incredibly busy. She needs a full-time ....
   (a noun from *assist*) ▶ Unit 95
2 Do you have any .... on part-time courses?
   (a noun from *inform*) ▶ Unit 95
3 I don't like this model. Have you got something .... ?
   (an adjective from *differ*) ▶ Unit 96
4 We can't accept this form; it's .... (not *complete*) ▶ Unit 96
5 You're wrong. I completely .... with you. (not *agree*) ▶ Unit 97
6 The whole process is now .... ; so we no longer give paper tickets to passengers. (verb from *computer*) ▶ Unit 97
7 Tonight's .... is exercise 2 on page 98. (*work* you do at *home*) ▶ Unit 98
8 I'm exhausted! I've just done a .... test. (lasting *two hours*) ▶ Unit 98

3 Check your answers below. Then go to the unit for more information and practice.

1 assistant 2 information 3 different 4 incomplete 5 disagree 6 computerised 7 homework 8 two-hour

Go online for a full diagnostic test

95 Forming nouns

1 Using suffixes

Suffixes are short additions to the end of words, to make new words:
bank → banker, govern → government
Sometimes the spelling of the original word changes when a suffix is added:
cycle + ist → cyclist, argue → argument

Karl is a **trainee** doctor. He hopes to be a **consultant** one day.

2 Jobs, beliefs and languages

	VERB OR NOUN	+ SUFFIX	= PERSON/JOB
verbs	build drive teach wait	-er	builder driver teacher waiter
	employ interview pay train	-ee	employee interviewee payee trainee
	act educate instruct visit	-or	actor educator instructor visitor
	apply assist consult study	-ant/ent	applicant assistant consultant student
nouns	art cycle guitar journal	-ist	artist cyclist guitarist journalist

⚠ Not all nouns that end in *-er* or *-or* describe people or jobs:
a *cooker* (= a machine that cooks things) a *calculator* (= a machine that can add, etc.)
Nouns that end in *-er* often have an active meaning and nouns that end in *-ee* have a passive meaning. For example, a *payee* is the person who is paid, not the person who pays.

We often add *-ism* to nouns and adjectives to describe a belief or a set of ideas:
social → socialism, nation → nationalism, impression → impressionism

COUNTRY	+ SUFFIX	= NATIONALITY (adjective)/LANGUAGE
China Malta Portugal Vietnam	-ese	Chinese Maltese Portuguese Vietnamese
Italy Hungary Russia Slovakia	-(ia)n	Italian* Hungarian* Russian* Slovakian
Finland Poland Spain Turkey	-ish	Finnish Polish Spanish Turkish

* These can also be used as nouns describing nationality: *Italian* → *an Italian*

⚠ The names of some languages do not follow these patterns: *The Netherlands* → *Dutch*, *Greece* → *Greek*, *France* → *French*

3 Nouns from verbs and adjectives

VERB	+ SUFFIX	= NOUN
argue govern move treat	-ment	argument government movement treatment
communicate educate produce	-(t)ion	communication education production
examine explain inform invite	-ation	examination explanation information invitation
decide discuss	-(s)ion	decision discussion

ADJECTIVE	+ SUFFIX	= NOUN
blind dark happy ill	-ness	blindness darkness happiness illness
able active equal national	-ity	ability activity equality nationality
distant ignorant important	-ance	distance ignorance importance
different independent silent	-ence	difference independence silence

 Pronunciation ▶ 1.32

18

Practice

1 Complete each sentence with nouns formed from words in Box A and suffixes in Box B.
🔊 5.11 Listen and check.

A   assist   ~~China~~   ill   independent   inform   Italy   journal   national   train   treat   wait

B   -ant   -ation   -ee   -ence   -er   ~~-ese~~   -ian   -ist   -ity   -ment   -ness

0 My best friend is studying *Chinese* at university.
1 Debbie's working as a ………………… for the local newspaper.
2 Mexico gained its ………………… from Spain in 1821.
3 Chickenpox is an ………………… which often affects young children.
4 Mrs Greenberg isn't here today. Would you like to speak to her …………………?
5 Don't let Carla cut your hair – she's only a ………………… so she's not very experienced.
6 Excuse me. Do you have any ………………… on computer courses?
7 I don't know if you need a visa. It depends on your ………………… .
8 My sister married an …………………; they live in Milan now.
9 Shall I ask the ………………… for the bill now?
10 She's had a lot of therapy at the hospital, but the ………………… wasn't very successful.

2 Read the clues and complete the crossword.

CLUES ACROSS
7 The opposite of *similarity*.
8 When you decide something.
11 A test where you are examined on something.
14 Someone who applies for something, e.g. a job.
15 The language spoken in Poland.
16 It governs a country.
17 A person who you pay money to.

CLUES DOWN
1 Someone who studies at college.
2 A person who rides a bicycle.
3 A noun from *silent*.
4 A style of painting used by artists like Cezanne and Monet.
5 The language spoken in Russia.
6 Most people who live in Athens speak this language.
8 The language spoken in the Netherlands.
9 The opposite of *knowledge*.
10 When several people talk about something together.
12 The language spoken in Portugal.
13 A noun from *blind*.

96 Forming adjectives

> The government has set up these courses to solve the growing problem of **ill**iterate adults. The courses are **in**expensive and suit**able** for all adults who struggled with reading and writing at school.

1 Adjectives from nouns and verbs

We can add suffixes to some nouns and verbs to make adjectives:

NOUN OR VERB	+ SUFFIX	= ADJECTIVE
centre music nation	-al	central musical national
beauty care help pain use	-ful	beautiful careful helpful painful useful
care help pain use	-less	careless helpless painless useless
comfort drink fashion suit	-able	comfortable drinkable fashionable suitable
dirt health rain sun thirst wind	-y	dirty healthy rainy sunny thirsty windy
continue danger fame	-ous	continuous dangerous famous
depend differ excel insist	-ent	dependent different excellent insistent
act attract expense relate	-ive	active attractive expensive relative

Note the suffix *-less* means 'without/not', *-ful* can mean 'displaying/containing' and *-able* after a verb often has the meaning of 'it is possible to'.

NATURAL ENGLISH In informal spoken English we can add the suffix *-ish* to some short adjectives to make the meaning weaker or less exact:
He's got **darkish** hair. (dark but not very dark)
I'm not sure how old she is – she's **youngish**. (fairly young but not very young)

Adjectives, e.g. *interesting/interested* ➤ Unit 19.3

2 Changing the meaning of adjectives

We can use **prefixes** (short additions to the beginning of words) to change the meaning of some adjectives. These prefixes usually mean 'not', e.g. *displeased* = not pleased.

PREFIX	+ ADJECTIVE	= ADJECTIVE WITH NEGATIVE MEANING
dis-	honest loyal pleased	dishonest disloyal displeased
un-	happy tidy usual	unhappy untidy unusual
in-	complete correct formal	incomplete incorrect informal
im-	patient polite possible	impatient impolite impossible
ir-	replaceable responsible	irreplaceable irresponsible
il-	legal literate logical	illegal illiterate illogical

- We can add a prefix to an adjective that already contains a suffix:
  unmistake**able**, **un**help**ful**, **ir**replace**able**, **in**expens**ive**, **in**depend**ent**
- If the adjective begins with the sound /p/ we often use *im-*, not *in-*, to make the negative form:
  polite → ✓ **im**polite ✗ ~~inpolite~~ perfect → ✓ **im**perfect ✗ ~~inperfect~~
- We use *ir-* before the sound /r/ and *il-* before the sound /l/:
  responsible → ✓ **ir**responsible ✗ ~~inresponsible~~ logical → ✓ **il**logical ✗ ~~inlogical~~

⚠ With nouns and verbs, the prefixes *in-/im-* do not always mean *not*, they can mean 'into' or 'inside':
to **im**port (= bring things into a country) **in**come (= money you receive)
to **in**put (= put information into a computer)

Practice

1 **GRAMMAR IN USE** Complete the letter with suitable adjectives, made from the words in brackets. 🔊 5.12 Listen and check.

Summerdean School Wellsby Northants NP23 5GS

Dear Mrs Smithers,

 I am writing to you about your son, Matthew. In the last few weeks we have become more and more (0) _displeased_ (not pleased) with his attitude. On several occasions he has been (1) .... (not polite) to me or other members of staff at the school. This (2) .... (not usual) bad behaviour has come as a shock to us as Matthew had previously been an (3) .... (excel) student.

 In recent weeks I have also noticed that his clothes are (4) .... (not tidy) and he seems (5) .... (not happy). He used to be very neat and (6) .... (care) when doing his assignments, but now he seems to have developed an (7) .... (not responsible) and (8) .... (not care) attitude to his work.

 I think it would be (9) .... (help) if we could discuss the situation. If you phone me, we can arrange a (10) .... (suit) time to meet.

Yours sincerely,
Hilary Carlton
Form Tutor

---

2 Find six more mistakes and correct them. Tick (✓) the correct sentences.

0 I'm sorry but this answer is completely ~~uncorrect~~. *incorrect*
1 Maria's a model so she always wears fashionful clothes.
2 What an unusual jacket! I've never seen anything like it before.
3 When babies are born they are totally helpful.
4 Her children are so unpolite. They never never say 'please' or 'thank you'.
5 Is there anything to drink? I'm terribly thirstful.
6 I'm very patient. I hate waiting for things!
7 Although she's got blond hair, her skin is quite darkish.
8 There's nothing to worry about; the operation is completely painful.

3 Complete the second sentence so it means the same as the first. Use one word only and choose a word from the box to help you. 🔊 5.13 Listen and check.

| continue   drink   expense   legal   literate   possible   ~~replace~~ |

0 Nothing could take the place of our cat.   Our cat is _irreplaceable_.
1 I'm afraid her son can't read or write.   Her son is ....
2 Dan's car cost a lot of money.   Dan's car was ....
3 The rain didn't stop for two weeks.   The rain was .... for two weeks.
4 You can't live without water.   It's .... to live without water.
5 Don't do that, it's against the law.   Don't do that, it's ....
6 The water is salty, but you can drink it.   The water is ...., although it's salty.

⏻ Go online for more practice

97 Forming verbs

This is the British Library. The collection **outgrew** its old home in the British Museum and has now been **rehoused** in a modern building. The catalogue **has been computerised** and can be searched on the Internet.

1 Verbs from nouns and adjectives

We can make some nouns and adjectives into verbs by adding suffixes:

STEM NOUN/ADJECTIVE	+ SUFFIX	= VERB
commercial computer critic modern special summary	-ise/ize*	commercialise computerise criticise modernise specialise summarise
awake flat length short	-(e)n	awaken flatten lengthen shorten
active different valid	-(i)ate	activate differentiate validate
example false note sign solid	-(i)fy	exemplify falsify notify signify solidify

* The spelling -ize is more common in American English.

The meaning of the verb is related to the original adjective or noun:
*This dress is too long. Can you **shorten** it?* (= make it shorter)
*We had to **summarise** the chapter.* (= make a summary)
*The application forms **have been computerised**.* (= changed to an electronic system)

2 Changing the meaning of verbs

We can use prefixes to change the meaning of some verbs:

PREFIX	MEANING	VERB	EXAMPLES
re-	do again	reappear rebuild rehouse reorganise repay reproduce rethink reunite	The painting **has been rehoused** in the new gallery. (= put into a new home) I had to **reorganise** the files in alphabetical order. (= organise them again)
dis-	not/stop	disagree dislike disconnect	I **dislike** pasta. (= I don't like it.) Our electricity **has been disconnected** (= stopped)
over-	too much	overeat overcharge overheat	They always **overcharge** in that shop. (= charge too much money) The engine **overheated** and blew up.
un-	opposite or reverse action	undress unfold unpack	I opened the envelope and **unfolded** the letter. Have you **unpacked** your suitcase yet?
mis-	badly/ wrongly	misbehave misinform misjudge	The children always **misbehave** when they are tired. (= behave badly) I'm afraid you've been **misinformed**. (= given wrong information)
out-	more/ better/ further	outdo outgrow outperform	The collection **outgrew** its old home. (= grew bigger than the space it was in) Their team easily **outperformed** us. (= performed better than us)

The most common prefixes are shown in the chart. Other, less common prefixes include:
under- (= not enough) *The workers in that factory **are underpaid**.*
inter- (= between) *Members of the two tribes rarely **intermarry**.*

18

Practice

1 Complete the sentences with a suitable form of a verb, using the words in brackets. Form the correct verb by using a prefix from Box A or a suffix from Box B. 🔊 5.14 Listen and check.

A | dis- mis- over- ~~re-~~ un- | B | -ate -en -ify -ise |

0 After the hurricane the victims were *rehoused* in temporary homes. (house)
1 I .... people who shout at waiters. I think it's very impolite. (like)
2 They've really .... this place, it used to be free! (commercial)
3 These trousers are a little too short. Can you .... them for me? (length)
4 If you freeze water, it will .... and turn into ice. (solid)
5 Welcome home. Put those heavy suitcases down – you can .... them later. (pack)
6 I have to phone the bank in order to .... my new credit card. (active)
7 Children who .... will be punished. (behave)
8 I'm sure they've .... me. My electricity bill is usually much lower. (charge)

2 Complete the sentences, using the prefix or suffix in brackets. Use the pictures to help you.

0 Ed's trying to *flatten* his stomach. (-en)
1 After an hour in a traffic jam the engine started .... (over-)
2 Our local delicatessen .... in cheese from all over the world. (-ise)
3 Roger .... the TV aerial before he took the TV to be repaired. (dis-)
4 Jack's growing so fast now. He's .... everything I bought for him last winter. (out-)
5 Miranda is .... her kitchen cupboards so that she can find things more easily. (re-)

3 **GRAMMAR IN USE** Find six more mistakes in the text and correct them. 🔊 5.15 Listen and check.

Bartholomew News
BARTHOLOMEW ROAD SCHOOL PARENTS' NEWSLETTER

- Next term we will be ~~disorganising~~ *reorganising* our modern languages department and introducing two new languages. Mrs Birkin will be taking Spanish and Mr Dawson will teach Mandarin. Mr Dawson has recently joined us from Frobisher High School where he specialated in Asian languages. If you wish your child to enrol in either of these classes, please notificate the deputy head.

- As some of you may know, we have overgrown our existing computer room. We will be dehousing the computers in a new computer centre and work will begin on this in January. While we are doing this we will be modernifying our own computer systems and making changes to the school's website.

- One last piece of good news. In this month's exam results we have reperformed all other schools in the area, achieving 65 grade A results! Congratulations to all Year 8 students.

98 Compound nouns and adjectives

Lois is a **self-employed** accountant.

It's **well-paid** work and I have a small office in my **living room**.

1 Compound nouns

A **compound noun** is a noun made from two words. The first word is usually singular and gives more information about the second word:
a dishwasher = a machine for washing dishes   *a firefighter* = a person who fights fires
✓ There are a lot of **taxi drivers** in London.   ✗ ~~There are a lot of **taxis drivers** in London.~~

- Some compound nouns are written as one word (e.g. *classroom, dishwasher*) and some are two separate words (e.g. *bank account, car park*). It is best to check the correct form in a dictionary.
- We can make compound nouns by adding a noun, verb, preposition, adverb or adjective to a noun or verb. Here are some common examples:

noun + noun	alarm clock bank account classmate computer science credit card eyelashes film star history teacher homework record shop science fiction shop assistant sunglasses traffic jam website
noun + verb(-er)	DVD player dishwasher firefighter hairdresser screwdriver taxi driver
noun + verb(-ing)	hairdressing horse-riding scuba diving window shopping
verb(-ing) + noun	living room shopping centre swimming pool washing machine
adjective + noun	blackbird grandfather high school supermarket whiteboard
preposition/adverb + verb/noun	bypass downstairs outfit overdraft overtime underground upbringing
verb + preposition/adverb	checkout sleepover turnover dropout walkabout kickoff

The stress is usually on the first syllable of the compound noun: **tra**ffic jam, **horse**-riding, **un**derground. Compare:
She's an **English** teacher. (a teacher of English)
He's an English **teach**er. (a teacher who is English)

 Pronunciation ➤ 1.33

2 Compound adjectives

Compound adjectives can be made from nouns, adjectives, verbs and adverbs.
They usually have a hyphen (-) between the words when they come before a noun:

number/measurement + noun	two-hour five-day ten-kilometre tenth-century two-seater 250-gramme 600-dollar half-price part-/full-time ten-year-old
adjective + noun	high-quality high-level high-speed low-price low-calorie
noun + adjective	user-friendly child-friendly colour blind duty-free worldwide
adjective/adverb + -ed/-ing participle	right-handed short-tempered well-known well-paid good-looking loose-fitting fast-moving best-selling hard-working
verb + preposition/adverb	drive-in burnt-out built-up worn-out broken-down
self + verb/adjective/noun	self-employed self-confident self-service self-assembly

 The noun in a compound adjective is usually singular:
✗ ~~He's a ten-years-old boy.~~   ✓ He's a ten-**year**-old boy.
✗ ~~It was a three-hours film.~~   ✓ It was a three-**hour** film.

18

Practice

1 Complete the sentences. Use words from Box A and Box B to make suitable compound nouns or adjectives. 🔊 5.16 Listen and check.

A	bank credit duty- ~~eighteenth~~ scuba short two- well- worn	B	account card ~~century~~ diving free out paid seater tempered

0 Samantha inherited a valuable *eighteenth-century* clock from her aunt.
1 I can't give you all a lift. I've only got a .... car.
2 I enjoy ...., but only if the water is warm!
3 We should replace that old sofa. It's completely ....
4 Be careful what you say to him. He can be very ....
5 Can I pay my phone bill by ....?
6 The full amount will be paid into your .... in the next five working days.
7 Let's buy some perfume from the .... shop before we get on the plane.
8 If you like expensive things, you need a .... job.

2 Use compound words to complete the sentences. Part of the word has been given in brackets.

0 Celia's bought a house in a very crowded and *built-up* part of town. (up)
1 Let's go to the sales. Everything's .... today! (half)
2 At the end of the course there will be a .... exam. (three)
3 I'm training to be a .... I know it's a dangerous job. (fire)
4 When you are expecting a baby you have to wear .... clothes. (fitting)
5 Sorry I'm late. There was an awful .... on the motorway. (traffic)

3 **GRAMMAR IN USE** Complete the compound nouns and adjectives in *italics*. The first letter of each missing part is given. 🔊 5.17 Listen and check.

Famous people who didn't go to college No. 14: Mark Zuckerberg

Mark Zuckerberg is the world's youngest billionaire. He is the co-founder of the famous *Facebook* Internet site. He started studying psychology and (0) *c omputer science* at Harvard University but didn't finish his course.
Zuckerberg was born in 1984 and grew up in Dobbs Ferry, New York. Even as a child he loved computers and he designed several programs at (1) *high s....................* . His favourite subjects at school were Latin and Ancient Greek. As a child he wasn't particularly (2) *good-l....................* or (3) *s....................-confident*, and he was slightly (4) *colour b....................* . But he was very intelligent and (5) *hard-w....................* and in 2002 he won a place at Harvard University in Boston.
In 2004, while he was at Harvard, he realised there was a need for a (6) *webs....................* where students could contact each other, show their photographs and leave messages. He invented *Facebook* with his (7) *classm....................* Dustin Moscovitz, Eduardo Saverin and Chris Hughes. At first the website was only designed for university students, but it soon spread. Now *Facebook* is a (8) *w....................wide* phenomenon; it has more than 600 million members around the world and is worth billions of dollars.

⏻ Go online for more practice and a progress test

Review MODULE 18

1 UNITS 95 AND 96 Make adjectives and nouns from the pairs of words in the box. Use them to write descriptions for the pictures.

> danger / active   ~~not happy / study~~   attract / Italy   expense / decide
> fame / art   success / apply   pain / treat   not complete / inform

0
an unhappy student

1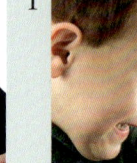
....

2 ....

3
....

4
....

5
....

6 **SPORTS DAY**
PLACE: Turnley Park
DATE: July
START: 2.00 pm
....

7
....

2 UNITS 95, 96 AND 97 Write the missing words in the chart.

NOUNS	VERBS	ADJECTIVES
thirst		(0) *thirsty*
	(1)	modern
	(2)	false
(3)	instruct	
nation		(4)
(5)	insist	insistent
(6)	communicate	
	(7)	short
(8)		ignorant

3 UNIT 97 Complete the sentences, using the verbs in brackets and a suitable prefix.

0 I don't know if he'll ever *repay* (pay) the money he owes me.
1 The children have .... (grow) their summer clothes – everything's too small.
2 I won't buy anything from a company that .... (pay) its workers like that.
3 Although he was the youngest, Lucas always .... (do) his brothers in maths.
4 It took years for people to .... (build) their lives after the earthquake.
5 I thought the tickets were free, but it seems I was .... (inform).
6 Andy's a really nice, kind person. How can you .... (like) him?

298

4 UNITS 95, 98 Complete the second sentence so it means the same as the first, using the word in brackets. Use three or four words in your answer.

0 Maurice has gone on a run that lasts for ten kilometres. (kilometre)
   Maurice has gone on _a ten-kilometre run_.

1 You'll probably be able to find that CD in a shop that sells records. (record)
   You can probably find that CD in ....

2 When you write the cheque, don't forget the name of the person you are paying the money to. (of)
   Remember to write the name .... on the cheque.

3 I need an Internet connection that works very fast. (high)
   I need .... Internet connection.

4 I think looking at things in shop windows is just as much fun as buying them. (shopping)
   I think .... as much fun as buying things.

5 That factory began producing electric cars in 2004. (of)
   The .... at that factory began in 2004.

6 Because she works for herself, Linda doesn't need to go into the office every day. (employed)
   Linda doesn't need to go into the office every day because ....

7 This tool is only suitable for people who use their left hand to do things. (can)
   Only .... use this tool.

8 That machine was invented by somebody who comes from Hungary. (invented)
   A .... machine.

5 ALL UNITS Complete the blog using the words in brackets. You will need to add a suffix or prefix, or make a compound word.

Melinda's Blog for today

Education isn't just for children!

In recent years the government has been (0) _criticised_ (critic) for its treatment of adult (1) .... (educate). It has poured money into the system, but the money has all gone into schools rather than colleges. The adult education system has been (2) .... (organise) several times, but the result has been fewer colleges and less choice.

Many older people had a bad experience at school and want to have a second chance. In the old days each town had its own adult education college which provided (3) .... (quality which is high) teaching and (4) .... (price which is not high) courses. It was (5) .... (expense) for the government to provide this, but it made a big (6) .... (differ) to people who had no qualifications. Because the courses were aimed at adults, even people who had (7) .... (not like) learning at school were able to enjoy the lessons. Many even took and passed (8) .... (examine) which they had previously failed. Most of the courses were (9) .... (didn't take all your time) or took place in the evenings. I think it is a (10) .... (nation) disgrace that we have allowed this crucial part of our education system to become so neglected.

Test MODULE 18

Word formation

Choose the correct answer, A, B or C.

1. Everyone is always searching for ………… .
   A happyness   B happy   C happiness → Unit 95

2. Our company has over five thousand ………… .
   A employees   B employments   C employers → Unit 95

3. The Prime Minister was on TV last night – the ………… asked her some difficult questions!
   A interviewee   B interviewing   C interviewer → Unit 95

4. Although Jana is Norwegian, she speaks fluent ………… .
   A Finish   B Finnish   C Finlandian → Unit 95

5. What's the ………… between iron and steel?
   A differing   B difference   C different → Unit 95

6. What's the ………… between Paris and Berlin?
   A distant   B distence   C distance → Unit 96

7. Have you seen Sarah's little girl? She's very ………… .
   A attractive   B attraction   C attracting → Unit 96

8. I don't remember the make of the car but it was a ………… colour.
   A darkly   B darkish   C darkful → Unit 96

9. In this country it's ………… to drive without a proper licence.
   A unlegal   B dislegal   C illegal → Unit 96

10. Don't give the keys to Dennis, he's too ………… .
    A irresponsible   B inresponsible   C unresponsible → Unit 96

11. Selma's a surgeon. She ………… in heart operations.
    A specialates   B specialises   C specialifies

12. To ………… the alarm, press the red button.
    A activate   B activify   C activise → Unit 97

13. Since Lucy ………… the files, I haven't been able to find anything!
    A outorganised   B reorganised   C overorganised → Unit 97

14. You're wrong. I completely ………… with you.
    A disagree   B unagree   C misagree → Unit 97

15. The baby's getting so big – she's ………… most of her clothes.
    A overgrown   B outgrown   C disgrown → Unit 97

16. How much money have you got in your …………?
    A bank's account   B account of bank   C bank account → Unit 98

17. I've just bought a pair of expensive designer ………… .
    A glasses for sun   B sunglasses   C sun's glasses → Unit 98

18. It's based on a book by a ………… author.
    A good-known   B known-well   C well-known → Unit 98

19. Actors have to be very ………… .
    A self-confident   B confident of self   C self-confidence → Unit 98

20. It was a ………… flight so I'm feeling quite tired now.
    A seven-hours   B seven-hour   C seven-hourly → Unit 98

Formal and written English

MODULE 19

Before you start

1 Read the newspaper article. Look at the highlighted grammar examples.

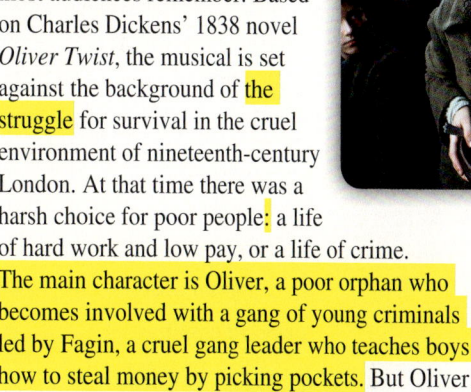

Music News

A revival of the musical *Oliver!* is due to open on Broadway next month. **This** is a new production of a show which was originally staged in London in 1960. Despite its age, the show is not out of date or irrelevant to today's problems. **On the contrary**, it tackles an issue which is still of great concern today – the problem of deprived young men who become tempted by a life of crime.

Most people **are familiar with** the 1968 film version of the musical. **Not only did it win** six Oscars, it was also one of the most successful British films of the 1960s. The music and lyrics were written by Lionel Bart. The original stage production was directed by Peter Coe **and the film by Carol Reed**. There are many wonderful songs in the film but **it is** the remarkable characters that most audiences remember. Based on Charles Dickens' 1838 novel *Oliver Twist*, the musical is set against the background of **the struggle** for survival in the cruel environment of nineteenth-century London. At that time there was a harsh choice for poor people**:** a life of hard work and low pay, or a life of crime. **The main character is Oliver, a poor orphan who becomes involved with a gang of young criminals led by Fagin, a cruel gang leader who teaches boys how to steal money by picking pockets.** But Oliver is an honest boy and does not want to be a criminal. **Consequently**, the story contains all the ingredients for a classic battle between good and evil.

2 Now read the sentences and choose the correct, or most suitable, option in *italics*. The highlighted grammar examples will help you.

1. There were two teams on the field *: / ;* the whites and the reds. ▶ Unit 99
2. Next season we will be offering our 'Highlights of Andalusia' tour. *This / Our 'Highlights of Andalusia' tour* has always been one of our most popular tours. ▶ Unit 100
3. Amy's dad taught her the piano and *her mum / her mum taught her* the guitar. ▶ Unit 100
4. It is not true that Paul McCartney only writes popular songs. *Therefore / On the contrary*, he has composed a complete classical symphony. ▶ Unit 101
5. Your outstanding debt has not been *paid consequently / paid. Consequently*, your electricity will be disconnected. ▶ Unit 101
6. Luciano Pavarotti released many records. But *his recording / it is his recording* of 'Nessun Dorma' that everyone knows. ▶ Unit 102
7. Not only *we were / were we* late, we also forgot to take our passports. ▶ Unit 102
8. 'The Marriage of Figaro' is Mozart's most famous opera. *A clever servant who tricks his employer, Count Almaviva, is the main character. / The main character is a clever servant who tricks his employer, Count Almaviva.* ▶ Unit 103
9. In the first act of 'Hamlet' the young prince learns of his father's murder. This *learning about his father's murder / event* leads to terrible consequences. ▶ Unit 104
10. Please ensure you *are familiar with / 've looked at* our terms and conditions before signing this insurance document. ▶ Unit 105

3 Check your answers below. Then go to the unit for more information and practice.

1 : 2 This 3 her mum 4 On the contrary 5 paid. Consequently, 6 it is his recording 7 were we 8 The main character is a clever servant ... Almaviva. 9 event 10 are familiar with

⏻ Go online for a full diagnostic test

99 Punctuation

1 Punctuation symbols

We use **punctuation** to divide written language into units (e.g. clauses and sentences):

SYMBOL	NAME	USE
A, B, etc.	capital letter	shows the start of a sentence
.	full stop or period (Am E)	shows the end of a sentence
,	comma	separates parts of the same sentence
?	question mark	used after a direct question (➤ Unit 61)
!	exclamation mark	usually informal, used after an order, an exclamation or something surprising (➤ Unit 108)
:	colon	introduces a list or further information
;	semi-colon	divides two main clauses
–	dash	usually informal, can be used in the same way as colons, semi-colons and brackets
-	hyphen	joins the parts of compound words, can be used between dates, etc.
'	apostrophe	used in short forms and possessive forms (➤ Unit 6)
" "	quotation marks	enclose words of direct speech (➤ Unit 68.1)
' '	inverted commas	enclose speech, names such as book titles, or something we want to point out
( )	brackets or parentheses	enclose additional information, references or dates

- In website and email addresses we pronounce . as 'dot' and @ as 'at',
  e.g. chairman@pearson.com is said as 'chairman at pearson dot com'
- In numbers (but not prices) we read . as 'point':
  16.15 = 'sixteen point one five' $16.15 = 'sixteen dollars (and) fifteen cents'

2 Dividing a sentence

Commas separate items in a list. We don't usually put commas in front of *and* and *or* at the end of a list:
*David Bowie is **a singer, a songwriter, an actor and** an Internet entrepreneur.*

We use a comma if we put a subordinate clause before a main clause:
***Although he was German,** Handel spent most of his life in England.*

We also use a comma to divide non-defining relative clauses (➤ Unit 73.2) and some linking words and phrases (➤ Unit 101) from the rest of the sentence:
*Mozart**, who was born in Salzburg,** spoke German. **However,** most of his operas are in Italian.*

If a sentence has two main clauses, we can separate them with a semi-colon:
*We didn't spend much money. I bought an opera CD**; my brother** bought some folk music.*

🔊 Pronunciation ➤ 1.34

3 Introducing information

We use a colon to introduce a list:
There are four musicians in the group: a guitarist, a violinist, a pianist and a drummer.

We use brackets to enclose short pieces of extra information such as dates and explanations:
*W. A. Mozart **(1756–1791)** was the greatest composer of the classical period.*
*The BBC **(British Broadcasting Corporation)** has just launched a new digital channel.*

We use quotation marks or inverted commas to enclose direct speech. We separate the reporting verb from the direct speech with a comma. Note the position of the punctuation:
He said, "That musical was fantastic."   "Really? I didn't like it very much," she replied.

Practice

1 Look at the punctuation and tick (✓) the correct sentence in each pair, A or B.

0 A You will need a notebook, a pencil, a calculator and a ruler. ✓
   B You will need a notebook, a pencil a calculator: and a ruler. ✗
1 A We have two fruit trees in our garden: an apple and a pear.
   B We have two fruit trees in our garden; an apple and a pear.
2 A Oh, no! The house is on fire!
   B Oh, no. The house is on fire.
3 A <Come with me> said the teacher.
   B "Come with me," said the teacher.
4 A My uncle is the CEO (Chief Executive Officer) of a big corporation.
   B My uncle is the CEO 'Chief Executive Officer' of a big corporation.
5 A Despite being Spanish, Placido Domingo usually sings in Italian.
   B Despite being Spanish – Placido Domingo usually sings in Italian.
6 A (To be or not to be) is one of Shakespeare's most famous quotes.
   B 'To be or not to be' is one of Shakespeare's most famous quotes.

2 **GRAMMAR IN USE** Use the punctuation marks A–G from the box to punctuate the text.

A '   B)   C ?   D ,   E :   F .   G ;

Guitar Players

Who was the greatest guitarist of all time (0) ?........ For many people the answer is Jimi Hendrix (1942–1970 (1) .... Hendrix was born in Seattle and grew up in a poor neighbourhood (2) .... his parents divorced when he was only ten. Although he never had guitar lessons (3) .... he learned to play by watching other musicians and listening to records (4) .... He joined the US army in 1961 but only stayed for one year. After leaving the army, he became a professional musician.

Hendrix had some success in New York in the early 1960s but it was in 1966 that he hit the big time. Spotted in the UK by a top music producer, he was given a recording contract and made his first album, (5) .... Are You Experienced'. He was to make two more albums (6) .... 'Axis: Bold As Love' and 'Electric Ladyland'. Success in America came after his appearances at the Monterey and Woodstock festivals in 1967 and 1969. Unfortunately, he did not live long enough to enjoy the fame which he eventually achieved.

3 Write a suitable punctuation mark in the boxes, where necessary.

0 Be careful [!] You're going to fall [!]
1 Is this the bus to the airport [ ]
2 We've got two televisions [ ] one in the living room [ ] and one in the kitchen.
3 Although it was expensive [ ] my Danish stereo was worth every penny [ ]
4 What a disgusting thing to say [ ]
5 I packed a toothbrush [ ] some clean clothes [ ] my shaver [ ] and a warm scarf [ ]
6 Alison went upstairs [ ] the children stayed in the garden [ ]
7 [ ] I don [ ] t know the answer [ ][ ] she replied [ ]
8 How do you spell [ ] charisma [ ][ ]
9 George Washington [ ] 1732 [ ] 1799 [ ] was the USA [ ] s first president [ ]
10 Do you have a pen [ ] or a pencil [ ] in your bag [ ]

⏻ Go online for more practice   303

100 Ways to avoid repeating words

Before the invention of powerful computers, **musicians had to play** their own instruments. Now **they don't need to**.

1 Replacing nouns and verbs

Replacing one word or phrase with another is very common in written and spoken English:
It didn't take long for Rossini to compose 'The Barber of Seville'. He composed 'The Barber of Seville' in thirteen days.
→ *It didn't take long for Rossini to compose 'The Barber of Seville'. He **did it** in thirteen days.*

Replacing a noun/noun phrase:

pronoun	*My husband loves **jazz** but I hate **it**. (it = jazz)*
	*__Janis Joplin__ died in 1970. **She** was only twenty-seven. (She = Janis Joplin)*
one(s)/some (▶ Units 8/10)	*David bought a large **ice cream** and I got a small **one**. (one = ice cream)*
	*There are ten **tracks** on the album. **Some** are very short. (some = tracks)*
this/that/those (▶ Unit 5)	*The best **songs** are **those** she recorded early in her career. (those = the songs)*
a word with the same meaning	*Mozart wrote several **operas**. Some of the early **works** are rarely performed these days. (works = operas)*

Replacing a verb/verb phrase:

present simple verb → do	*He **likes** the same music as I **do**. (do = like)*
past simple verb → did	*They **didn't go** but I **did**. (did = went)*
do/did it for a single action	*It didn't take long for Rossini to compose 'The Barber of Seville'. He **did it** in thirteen days. (did it = composed 'The Barber of Seville')*
(not) do/did that	*They asked me to go on holiday with them but I didn't want to **do that**. (do that = go on holiday with them)*
an object pronoun after comparisons (▶ Unit 21.2)	*Blur had several hits. But Oasis were much more popular than **them**. (them = Blur.)*

2 Leaving out a word or phrase

- We can usually leave out the same subject and/or (auxiliary) verb in clauses after *and*:
  Andrew Lloyd Webber wrote 'Cats' and *(he wrote)* 'Phantom of the Opera'.
  I bought the first album and Caroline *(bought)* the second one.
  We were watching TV and *(we were)* eating popcorn.
  We often take the children to the cinema and *(we often take them to)* the theatre.
- We don't have to repeat the same verb phrase after an auxiliary or modal verb:
  *Our neighbours **might** get satellite TV. We **might** (get satellite TV), too.*
  *I play the violin but my brother **doesn't** (play the violin).*
- We don't have to repeat the infinitive after *to*:
  *Before the invention of powerful computers, musicians had **to play their own instruments**. Now they don't need **to** (play their own instruments).*
  *I wanted **to get tickets** for the concert but I wasn't able **to** (get tickets for the concert).*
- After reporting verbs which take the infinitive with *to* (e.g. *ask, forget, promise, refuse*) we can also leave out *to*:
  *They asked him to produce another album but he **refused** (to produce another album).*
  *I meant to record that programme but I **forgot** (to record that programme).*

304

19

Practice

1 **GRAMMAR IN USE** Read the text and underline the parts that the *italic* words refer to.

> **Why is a CD 74 minutes long?**
> In the early days of CDs, the president of Sony, Norio Ohga, insisted on increasing the size of a CD *(0)* to 12 cm so it could contain 74 minutes of music. Nobody knows why he did (0) *this*. One theory is that (1) *he* wanted the disc to be big enough for Beethoven's Ninth Symphony – it is said that (2) *this* was his wife's favourite piece of music. (3) *Another* is that Herbert von Karajan, the famous conductor, was involved. (4) *He* was a well-known supporter of the (5) *larger size* CD, and his best Beethoven recordings are (6) *the ones* you can still buy on CD today.

2 Read the sentences and put a line through all the words that can be left out.

0 I used to wear braces on my teeth but now I don't need to ~~wear them~~.
1 Caroline has been to the surgery and she has spoken to the doctor.
2 I was going to phone my mother but I forgot to do it.
3 The children were laughing and they were smiling as they ran out of the door.
4 I can't speak Spanish but my best friend can speak Spanish.
5 Dario wanted to come to your party but he wasn't able to come to your party.
6 You could put it in a plastic bag and you could throw it in the bin.
7 Hank chose the blue jacket and Laurence chose the grey one.
8 I have to visit my grandmother because I promised to visit her.

3 **GRAMMAR IN USE** Improve this text in two ways. Cross out three more words/phrases that aren't necessary, and replace seven more repeated words/phrases with substitute words. 🔊 **5.18** Listen and check.

> ### Susan Boyle, Glasgow 14 June
>
> This venue was the ideal place to see for myself if all the media hype about this new Scottish singer was true. It didn't take me long to find out it was ~~true~~!
> From the opening number 'I Dreamed A Dream' it was clear that the fans were determined to have a good time and that is exactly what (the fans) *they* did! Susan Boyle may be new to performing but Susan Boyle certainly knows how to please a crowd. The audience were standing up and they were clapping at the end of 'I Dreamed A Dream' – the song that first made Susan famous around the world. In fact 'I Dreamed A Dream' reached number 1 in the US. Not many new singers reach number 1 in the US with their first record, especially singers who are not American.
> The concert ended with the song 'Memory' from the musical *Cats*. 'Memory' is a beautiful song which really shows Susan's powerful voice and shows her emotional power.
> Many critics have compared Susan Boyle to Barbra Streisand and they have compared her to Celine Dion, but Susan Boyle is unique. You are going to be hearing a lot more about Susan Boyle very soon!

Go online for more practice

101 Using linking words in writing

Musical talent shows are very popular on TV. **As a result**, previously unknown singers such as Will Young (*pictured*) have become pop stars.

1 Linking sentences

In writing, we often use linking words and phrases to connect two pieces of information.

LINKING WORDS	USE	EXAMPLES
Furthermore, *In addition,*	giving extra information (➤ Unit 80)	This month we are offering you five CDs for the price of three. **In addition,** we will send you 'The 20 Greatest Folk Songs' free of charge.
However, *Nevertheless,* (= despite this)	introducing a difference (➤ Unit 81)	Singers don't earn as much money from selling albums as they used to. **However,** they can now make money from selling their music on the Internet.
On the contrary,	correcting or adding to a statement (usually negative)	Musicians thought computers would never become widespread in the music industry. **On the contrary,** they have become an essential tool for many singers.
Consequently, *For this reason,* *As a result,* *Therefore,*	introducing a result (➤ Unit 79)	Musical talent shows are very popular on TV. **As a result,** previously unknown singers have become famous.
After that, *Then* *Finally,* *In the end,*	ordering events (➤ Unit 82)	In the last act of 'The Sound of Music' the von Trapp family travel to sing in a concert. **Finally,** as they realise the danger they are in, they escape to freedom across the mountains.

We often use these common linking words at the beginning of a sentence. We put a comma between the linking word or phrase and the rest of the sentence:
As a result, previously unknown singers have become famous.

 We don't usually use a comma after *then*:
*We queued up and bought tickets at the box office. **Then** we made our way to our seats.*

2 Linking clauses

We use some linking words (e.g. *after, because, although*) to link a main clause with a subordinate clause (➤ Unit 78.1). If we put the subordinate clause at the beginning of the sentence we use a comma to separate it from the rest of the sentence:
*People prefer to download music from the Internet **because it's convenient.***
OR ***Because it's convenient**, people prefer to download music from the Internet.*

We use the linking words *and*, *but* or *or* to link main clauses and we can often put either of the clauses (but not the linking word) first:
✓ *The song is long **but** it is well-performed.*   ✓ *The song is well-performed **but** it is long.*
✗ *But the song is long it is well-performed.*

We can also use the 'two-part' linking phrases *both ... and, either ... or, neither ... nor* and *not only ... but (also)*:
*Diana Ross **both** acted in the film 'Lady Sings the Blues' **and** performed the title song.*
*The new musical has **neither** good songs **nor** an exciting plot.*

More on linking clauses ➤ Module 15

19

Practice

1 Choose the correct words in *italics*.

0 I waited in the queue for hours and hours. *After / (In the end,)* I decided to give up and go home.
1 My wool suit was rather expensive *but / however* it is very comfortable.
2 We have checked your credit rating and found it to be insufficient. *As a result, / Although* we are not able to give you a credit card at this time.
3 You can park your car in the long-term car park *in addition / and* take the shuttle bus to the airport.
4 You have only scored 42 percent in the test. *Nevertheless, / But* we are prepared to give you a second chance to take the test on Friday.
5 I take the Underground to work *consequently / because* it is quick and convenient.
6 We do not want to lose your business. *On the contrary, / Then*, we value you as a customer, and would like to offer you a discount on your next purchase.
7 The customer service manager is on holiday this week. *Therefore, / Furthermore*, we will be passing on your complaint to her assistant.
8 I enjoyed the concert *furthermore / although* I had never heard their music before.

2 **GRAMMAR IN USE** Read the letter and think of the best word for each gap. Write one word only. You can use the same word more than once. 🔊 **5.19** Listen and check.

Quest TV Productions

Dear Stephen

Thank you for sending us your audition video. We are pleased to tell you that your application has been successful. As a (0) ..... *result* ....., we would like to invite you to the regional auditions for this year's *Young Musician of the Year*.

The auditions will be held at the National Theatre Centre in Station Road, Manchester, on Saturday 21st October. Please come to entrance A at 10.30 a.m. You will be interviewed by our staff (1) .... given a name badge. (2) .... you will be taken to a waiting room where you will be told the time of your audition. We have a lot of contestants to audition, so we cannot guarantee what time you will be free to leave. (3) ...., we will try to be as accurate as possible.

We have very strict age restrictions for the competition. For this (4) ...., we ask you to bring proof of your age (birth certificate (5) .... passport) with you to the audition. (6) .... addition, please do not wear any clothes with visible brand labels as these are not allowed under broadcasting regulations.

Space in the centre is very limited. (7) ...., we cannot allow contestants to bring a large number of guests to the audition. (8) ...., you may bring <u>one</u> friend or a member of your family with you.

(9) .... there will be strict security in the centre, we cannot be responsible for lost or stolen valuables. Please keep your belongings with you (10) .... do not leave any valuables unattended.

Good luck with the audition.

Yours sincerely,

Damon Fulbright

Production Assistant

⏻ Go online for more practice

102 Using word order for emphasis

There were hundreds of successful singer-songwriters in the 1960s. But **it is Bob Dylan** that everybody remembers.

1 Using *it* for emphasis

We sometimes want to emphasise part of a sentence that introduces new or different information:
Many people think of Phil Collins as the singer of Genesis. But in fact it was **Peter Gabriel** *who sang on their early albums.* (emphasis on Peter Gabriel)

We use sentences beginning with *it* to emphasise the subject or object of a sentence. Compare these examples:
Pink Floyd recorded 'Dark Side of the Moon'.
→ *It was* **Pink Floyd** *that recorded 'Dark Side of the Moon'.* (emphasising the subject)
→ *It was* **'Dark Side of the Moon'** *that Pink Floyd recorded.* (emphasising the object)

2 Changing the usual word order

We sometimes change the usual order of subject + verb. This gives emphasis to the clause or phrase. We do this after negative adverbs such as *not only*, *neither/nor* and *never*.

not only (▶ Unit 80.1)	*The concert started late and the sound quality was terrible.* → **Not only did the concert start late**, *the sound quality was terrible.*
neither/nor (▶ Unit 80.3)	*Their previous album didn't contain any good songs and their current album doesn't contain any either.* → *Their previous album didn't contain any good songs and* **neither does their current album**.
never	*She has never had to sing such a difficult role.* → **Never has she had to sing** *such a difficult role.*

 Not only, *neither/nor* and *never* have a negative meaning, so we use them with positive verbs:
✓ *Radiohead didn't release an album this year and nor* **did** *Franz Ferdinand.*
✓ ~~*Radiohead didn't release an album this year and nor didn't Franz Ferdinand.*~~

For the verb *be* we just put the verb in front of the subject:
***It is** very expensive ...* → *Not only* **is it** *very expensive, ...*   ✗ ~~*Not only it is expensive*~~ *...*
***The song was** terrible ...* → *Not only* **was the song** *terrible, ...*

For present and past simple verbs we use *do* or *did* followed by the subject (and verb):
***She listens** to my music ...* → *Not only* **does she listen** *to my music, ...*   ✗ ~~*Not only she listens*~~ *...*
***He bought** me a CD ...* → *Not only* **did he buy** *me a CD, ...*

For perfect and continuous verbs we use the auxiliary verb:
***They have won** the competition ...* → *Not only* **have they won** *the competition, ...*
***She is singing** in the opera ...* → *Not only* **is she singing** *in the opera, ...*
✗ ~~*Not only she is singing in the opera*~~ *...*

We also change the usual word order in questions (▶ Units 61 and 62) and in short answers after *so*, *neither* and *nor*. (▶ Unit 107.1)

Practice

1 Rewrite the sentences, using *it* to emphasise the underlined word or phrase.

0 Leonardo da Vinci painted the *Mona Lisa*, not Michelangelo.
It was Leonardo da Vinci who painted the Mona Lisa, not Michelangelo.

1 Shirley Bassey sang many of the James Bond theme songs.
....

2 Michael took those photos.
....

3 Sally is married to Fred's best friend, not his cousin.
....

4 Mozart's most famous opera is *The Marriage of Figaro*.
....

2 Complete the second sentence so it means the same as the first.

0 My parents don't smoke.   My father doesn't smoke and neither *does my mother*.
1 The house is old and it is small.   Not only .... old, it is also small.
2 I have never been treated so badly!   Never .... so badly!
3 My sister and I didn't buy any CDs.   I didn't buy any CDs and neither ....
4 The children made a mess and they shouted at the babysitter.
   Not only ...., they also shouted at the babysitter.
5 I'm not talking to her and my friends aren't talking to her either.
   I'm not talking to her and neither ....

3 **GRAMMAR IN USE** Complete the text with phrases from the box. There are four extra phrases. 🔊 5.20 Listen and check.

> it was   it wasn't   ~~did they~~   neither didn't   what are
> that are   it is   they could   could they   neither did

Take That

Take That were the most successful young British musicians of the 1990s. Not only (0) *did they* sell a huge number of records, they were also nominated for the Mercury Music Prize. Between 1991 and 1996 they sold more than 30 million albums.
Take That was a 'boy band', that is a group of young men who have been put together by a manager. The members of a typical boy band are usually performers, not musicians.
(1) .... their good looks and appearance (2) .... important, not their ability to play musical instruments. Take That were different. In fact, it was quite a shock to discover that not only (3) .... sing, they could also write songs.
But (4) .... just their music that the band was famous for. The personality clashes in the band were frequently in the newspapers. Robbie Williams made international headlines by leaving the group in July 1995. The band continued until Gary Barlow left to become a solo artist in 1996. He didn't have much success, and (5) .... the other members of the group. Robbie Williams, on the other hand, went on to become a big star. Four members of the band regrouped in 2006 and achieved new success. Then, when Williams rejoined them in 2010 and their sixth studio album, *Progress* was released, it became the fastest-selling album of the century.

103 Organising information in writing

> The electric folk movement began in England in the late 1960s. **It** was led by a small group of musicians who wanted to revolutionise folk music.

1 The order of information

Compare these examples:

A

The electric folk movement began in England in the late 1960s. *It* was led by *a small group of musicians who wanted to revolutionise folk music.*

(known information: *The electric folk movement ... It*; new information: *a small group of musicians who wanted to revolutionise folk music*)

Here we start the second sentence with *it* (for something we have already mentioned – electric folk).

B The electric folk movement began in England in the late 1960s. A small group of musicians who wanted to revolutionise folk music started it.

Here we start the second sentence with new information and end with *it* (electric folk).

In writing we usually begin a sentence with information we already know about and end with something new, as in the first example. It makes the writing easier to understand, especially in long sentences with subordinate clauses.

2 Short phrases and long phrases

We usually prefer to put short phrases before the verb and long phrases at the end of the sentence:

short phrase	verb	long phrase
Most rock bands	*include*	*a vocalist, a guitarist, a bass guitarist and a drummer.*

Long phrases at the start of a sentence can seem clumsy and less clear:
A vocalist, a guitarist, a bass guitarist and a drummer are included in most bands.

3 Using different grammar forms

In order to follow the two points above, we sometimes have to choose different grammar forms. These are the common forms we use to put known information at the beginning of the sentence:

GRAMMAR FORM	EXAMPLES
known information as the **subject** of the sentence	'OK Computer' was Radiohead's most successful record. **The album** caused a sensation when they recorded it.
a **passive form** to bring an object to the beginning of the sentence (▶ Unit 83)	Radiohead released OK Computer in 1997. When **the album was released**, it caused a sensation.
it as a subject (▶ Unit 60.3)	When **it was released**, it caused a sensation.
a **noun phrase** that refers to the known information (▶ Unit 104)	**The release of the album** came at an important time for the group. **Releasing the album** proved to be a turning point for the group.

310

Practice

1 In the following short paragraphs, underline the words or phrases that refer to known information. Start with the second sentence in each paragraph.

0 Placido Domingo's new album, *Italia Ti Amo*, contains sixteen Italian songs. Some of <u>them</u> are well-known Italian favourites and <u>others</u> are traditional songs from Naples. <u>This beautiful city</u> in Italy has produced some of the world's greatest songs.

1 *Chinese Democracy* is the latest album by music legends Guns N'Roses. The album follows fourteen years in which the band has not made any recordings. It has been a difficult period, the low point of which was the arrest of singer Axl Rose in 2006.

2 Folk music is often neglected by critics. Less commercially profitable than other forms of modern music, the music is considered to be of interest only to a minority. However, those who like it are often fanatical about it.

2 Choose the best second sentence, A or B. Which order of information is the clearest?

0 We moved to northern Alaska four years ago.
   (A) Life there was much more difficult than it had been back home.
   B Life back home wasn't as difficult as it was there.

1 Nobody likes our awful new boss.
   A Something which can be very annoying is his unfriendly attitude.
   B His unfriendly attitude can be very annoying.

2 One of the greatest pictures in the Prado museum is 'The Third of May 1808'.
   A Painted by Francisco Goya in 1814, it shows the true horrors of war.
   B Francisco Goya painted it in 1814 and it shows the true horrors of war.

3 Beyoncé Knowles was a member of Destiny's Child until 2005.
   A To pursue a solo career was her reason for leaving the group.
   B She left the group in order to pursue a solo career.

3 **GRAMMAR IN USE** Rewrite the underlined sentences so that the known information is at the beginning of the sentence. Use the words in brackets. 5.21 Listen and check.

The Salzburg Festival

The Salzburg Festival is the world's greatest summer festival of classical music. <u>Every summer for five weeks beginning in late July is when it takes place.</u> (0) (*It ... .*)

It takes place every summer for five weeks beginning in late July.

The Festival is held in Salzburg, Austria. <u>Wolfgang Amadeus Mozart was born in the town</u>.
(1) (The town ... birthplace of ...)

....

The picturesque town features several beautiful concert venues. <u>Opened in 1926, the most important venue is the Festival Hall.</u> (2) (The most ..., which)

....

The festival was started by a group of professional musicians in 1877. <u>The famous Austrian composer Richard Strauss was one of the founders.</u> (3) (One of ...)

....

Since its earliest days the festival has concentrated on the works of Mozart. <u>It put on all twenty-two Mozart operas in 2006 to celebrate the 250th anniversary of his birth.</u> (4) (To celebrate ...)

....

104 Using nouns instead of verbs

African musician Thomas Mapfumo **decided** to move to the USA in 2004. **The decision** disappointed his fans at home in Zimbabwe but they still love his music.

1 Using noun phrases

We can sometimes replace a verb with a noun which has the same meaning. We can then get the same information into a shorter sentence:
He **decided** to move and this **disappointed** his fans. (two clauses, two verbs)
The **decision** to move **disappointed** his fans. (one clause, one verb)

A noun or noun phrase often summarises known information from an earlier sentence. This is useful when we are developing an argument or explanation in writing:
Hundreds of fans started to push towards the stage. **The situation** became dangerous.
(the situation = hundreds of fans pushing)

Other examples include *event, situation, things, activity*:
Apple opened their online music store in 2003. **This event** changed the way music was sold.
After their number one hit, the group received an invitation to tour the USA. **Things** were getting better and better.

2 Making nouns from verbs

It is often possible to make verbs into nouns by adding a suffix, e.g. *arrive* → *arrival*, *decide* → *decision*, *educate* → *education*, *teach* → *teacher* (▶ Unit 95).

FORMALITY CHECK In informal English we sometimes use verbs as nouns after *do, have, get, give,* etc.
Can you **call** her tomorrow? → Can you give her **a call** tomorrow?
We **walked** around the park. → We had **a walk** around the park.

We can sometimes make nouns from phrasal and prepositional verbs:
The taxi **broke down** just outside the airport. → The **breakdown** happened just outside the airport.
When did he **take over** the company? → When was the **takeover**?

-ing forms of verbs as subjects and objects ▶ Unit 64.2

3 Making nouns from verb phrases

To make a noun phrase from a verb phrase we often use two nouns linked by a preposition:

VERB PHRASE	NOUN PHRASE
They released the video in 2009 and this helped to increase their album sales.	*The release of the video* in 2009 helped to increase their album sales.
The rules were changed last week, which annoyed the public.	*The change to the rules* last week annoyed the public.
The government became unpopular after *they increased taxes*.	The government became unpopular after *the increase in taxes*.

Practice

1 Match the noun phrases 1–8 with the verb phrases A–I.

0 their departure _C_
1 the purchase ......
2 their wedding ......
3 his visit ......
4 her decision ......
5 the argument ......
6 his performance ......
7 their breakup ......
8 his regret ......

A they got married
B they broke up
C ~~they left~~
D he sang and told jokes
E she decided to do it
F they argued about it
G somebody bought it
H he wished he hadn't done it
I he went to see them

2 Rewrite these sentences, replacing the underlined verb phrase with a noun phrase. Make any other necessary changes.

0 <u>The company was sold, which</u> resulted in the loss of 200 jobs.
   The sale of the company resulted in the loss of 200 jobs.

1 Everything changed after <u>the war ended</u>.
   ....

2 <u>We arrived late, which</u> meant that we missed the start of the show.
   ....

3 Silvia worked as my assistant before <u>she was promoted</u>.
   ....

4 Our company has been much more successful since <u>it was taken over</u>.
   ....

5 <u>Taxes have been reduced, which</u> has pleased people on low incomes.
   ....

3 **GRAMMAR IN USE** Improve this article by replacing the underlined words with noun phrases A–G below. 🔊 **5.22** Listen and check.

Concert tragedy: December 3, 1979 – Cincinnatti, Ohio

It was the worst (0) <u>bad thing that happened</u> ...F..... at a music concert. Eleven fans were killed and many others injured shortly before a concert by British musicians The Who. At that time most concert tickets for large concerts didn't provide numbered seats. (1) <u>Not having a numbered seat</u> .... meant that people always rushed forward in an attempt to find an empty seat near the stage, and (2) <u>the fact they rushed forward</u> .... was a recipe for (3) <u>something awful to happen.</u> .... The concert was due to start at 8 p.m. By three o'clock in the afternoon, there were already 8,000 people waiting outside the concert hall. By seven o'clock, the crowd had increased and people were getting very impatient. (4) <u>The large number of impatient waiting people</u> .... was becoming dangerous. Somebody smashed through one of the glass doors and there was a stampede, with everybody frantically trying to find the best seats. At the same time, the organisers opened one of the main doors and another crowd of several thousand fans surged past the barriers. (5) <u>With so many more people rushing in,</u> .... the police officers on duty were unable to do anything. Sadly, eleven fans in the crowd died of (6) <u>not being able to breathe</u> ....

A this stampede   B This additional wave of eager fans meant that
C The situation   D disaster   E Suffocation   F ~~tragedy~~   G This uncertainty

105 Formal language

ROYAL OPERA

Ms Starkova is unwell and will be unable to perform the role of Elvira this evening.

1 Informal and formal language

We show formality through our choice of grammar and vocabulary. Compare:

INFORMAL   Ludmila 's sick – she won't be going on stage tonight .
FORMAL   Ms Starkova is unwell and will be unable to perform this evening .

We use language that is suitable for the situation we are in:
- informal → talking or writing to friends and members of your own family
- formal → talking and writing to strangers or people in authority, business letters and reports, talking to an audience, academic writing

2 Formal grammar

IN WRITTEN ENGLISH	
impersonal pronouns (➤ Unit 9.4)	*One should not judge people by their appearance.*
passives (➤ Unit 83)	*Your application will be assessed by the manager.*
infinitive clause subjects (➤ Unit 76)	*To create a fairer society is the party's main aim.*
non-defining relative clauses (➤ Unit 73)	*The singer, who performed the same role in Milan, will be appearing in tonight's performance.*
IN SPOKEN ENGLISH	
indirect questions instead of direct questions (➤ Unit 106.3/4)	*Can you tell me when the performance ends?* *I'm afraid I don't know who wrote that opera.*
* past tenses for a present situation; using *would* and *could*: (➤ Unit 53.1)	*Did you want to ask me something?* *We weren't sure about which model to choose.* *It would be helpful if you could send me a copy.*
* continuous forms of verbs to talk about arrangements, etc. (➤ Units 28, 31, 41, 42)	*Excuse me. Will we be stopping during the journey?* *Will you be coming to the party?* *I'm afraid I can't come on Friday, I'm working.*

* We often use these forms in spoken English to be more polite, or if we are not sure about something.

⚠ In formal English we don't usually use passives with *get* (➤ Unit 83.1), longer contractions (e.g. *shouldn't've*) or sentences ending with prepositions (➤ Unit 72.4).

3 Formal vocabulary

We can use most words in any situation. However, there are some words which are usually only used in formal language. Here are some examples:

nouns	*performance* (show), *remuneration* (salary), *spouse* (husband/wife)
verbs	*anticipate* (expect), *be possible to* (can), *commence* (start), *inform* (tell), *terminate* (finish)
adjectives	*delightful* (lovely), *extensive* (large) *personable* (friendly), *unwell* (sick),

INFORMAL *Carrie **turned down** Sean's invitation.*
FORMAL *Universities have to **reject** many excellent candidates.*

19

Practice

1 Match 1 and 2 with A and B in each pair and decide if each statement is formal (F) or informal (I).

```
0  1  The accused was taken to court and     A  they've sent her to jail.   I
   2  She's been to court and                B  given a prison sentence.   F
1  1  Do you think your workmates are        A  coming with us?   ........
   2  Do you know if your colleagues will be B  going to come with us?   ........
2  1  The performance will be                A  starting in a few minutes' time.   ........
   2  The show is                            B  commencing in ten minutes.   ........
3  1  Can you                                A  lend us some money?   ........
   2  Would you be able to                   B  offer us a loan?   ........
4  1  We do not tolerate                     A  impolite behaviour in this institution.   ........
   2  We won't put up with                   B  bad behaviour in our house.   ........
```

2 These sentences are all too formal for the situation. Make them informal by changing the underlined parts. Use the words in brackets. 🔊 **5.23** Listen and check.

0 Sorry, Sue. I'm afraid <u>I am unable to assist you</u> with your project. I'm much too busy. (help)
Sorry, Sue. I can't help you with your project.

1 <u>The keys have been left under the doormat by my grandmother.</u> ('s left)
....

2 Dad, <u>would it be possible for you to let me</u> use the car tonight? (can)
....

3 <u>To win the competition is my greatest desire.</u> (really like)
....

4 OK, Jim. <u>Your request will be considered</u> and I'll let you know later. (think about)
....

5 Come in. <u>Remove</u> your coat and relax here by the fire. (take)
....

3 **GRAMMAR IN USE** This formal letter contains unsuitable informal language. Correct it with the words and phrases from the box. 🔊 **5.24** Listen and check.

> ~~Dear~~   Thank you   submitting   regret to inform you   are unable to offer   at this time
> it would be advisable   perform cover versions of other artists' songs   every success
> returning   Yours sincerely

ABC RECORDS • 345 CRAWSHAW ST • LONDON W1

Dear
~~Hi~~ Mr Sheldrake,

Thanks for sending in the CD of your group's music. My colleagues and I have listened to it carefully and I'm afraid that we can't give you a recording contract right now. We feel that it's a good idea to write your own material rather than copy other groups' stuff.

We wish you loads of luck with your future. We are sending back your CD with this letter.

Best wishes,

Allie Henshaw, ABC Records

Review MODULE 19

1 UNITS 99 AND 100 Put a punctuation mark in each box and write one word only in each gap.

LOST IN A RECORD STORE

Have you ever gone into a record store without really knowing what you wanted (0) [?] You know you want to buy a CD, but you don't quite know which (00) *one*. I have, many times. Each time I end up regretting (1) .... There's just so much to choose from but where does one start (2) [ ] All those thick boxes in the classical section with their fat booklets and their gorgeous covers (3) [ ] hours of listening pleasure there. (4) .... look so promising – but then you notice the prices. Way too expensive for me!
So you turn to the bargain shelves instead – what a disappointment (5) [ ] Most of (6) .... look as though (7) .... contain music to play in lifts and supermarkets. Then you see the wall of CDs described as 'the top 30 albums'. Well (8) [ ] some of (9) .... look interesting. Then you notice that most of (10) .... are Greatest Hits compilations by bands whose albums you've already got, or more boring cover versions of old songs from the winners of the latest TV talent show contest.
Of course (11) [ ] eventually you find an album you're curious about. So you go over to the 'listening' stations and attempt to listen to (12) .... Have you ever managed to get one of those machines to work properly (13) [ ] I never have.
One thing is sure (14) [ ] I'll use the Internet next time!

2 UNITS 100 AND 102 Complete the second sentence so it means the same as the first, using the word in brackets. Use two to five words in your answer.

0 There are two slow songs on the album and the slow songs are my favourites. (those)
 There are two slow songs on the album and *those are my favourites*.

1 They walked out of the restaurant and refused to pay the bill. (only)
 .... walk out of the restaurant, they also refused to pay the bill.

2 I've cleaned the floors; I washed them this morning. (did)
 I've cleaned the floors; I .... this morning.

3 David slept in the big bedroom and Mike slept in the small bedroom. (one)
 David slept in the big bedroom and Mike slept ....

4 Celine Dion sang the theme song for the movie *Titanic*. (it)
 .... who sang the theme song for the movie *Titanic*.

5 Recent albums are usually more expensive than older albums. (ones)
 Recent albums are usually more expensive ....

6 They asked me to move to the Edinburgh office but I wasn't prepared to go there. (that)
 They asked me to move to the Edinburgh office but I didn't want to ....

7 Robbie Williams recorded *Millennium*, not *Rock DJ*, in 1998. (it)
 .... Robbie Williams recorded in 1998, not *Rock DJ*.

8 Susie wasn't hungry but I wanted to eat something. (did)
 Susie didn't want to eat anything ....

19

3 UNITS 101 AND 102 Choose the correct words in *italics*.

0 I'm afraid you're wrong. *That /(It)* was John Travolta that starred in the film 'Saturday Night Fever'.
1 Julie Andrews both acted in the film 'The Sound of Music' *or / and* sang many of the songs.
2 Not only *she was / was she* late for my party, she didn't even bring a present.
3 In any orchestra, *it is the conductor / the conductor is it* that is the most important person.
4 You have not paid this year's membership fee. *After that, / Consequently,* we are terminating your club membership.
5 *Nevertheless / Although* I go to the gym regularly, I never seem to lose any weight.
6 I didn't get a pay rise this year and neither *got / did* any of my colleagues.
7 It was Oasis *they / that* recorded 'Wonderwall', not Blur.
8 Cats don't have good eyesight *nevertheless / but* their hearing is excellent.
9 Never *have I / I have* seen such a terrible performance!
10 If you take up this offer you will receive two DVDs a month free of charge *and / in addition* a discount voucher for the first month.

4 UNITS 100 AND 105 Improve this text by replacing the highlighted words and rewriting the underlined words in more formal language.

What are MP3s?

In the last few years there has been a revolution in the way people listen to music. (0) ~~The revolution~~ *This* is largely thanks to a breakthrough in the way (00) ~~we can record and compress sounds~~ *sounds can be recorded and compressed* into a very small file. (1) <u>We call this technology</u> MPEG – 1 Audio Layer 3, or MP3. MP3 is a development of the technology that brought us CDs in the 1980s. That technology was digital recording. (2) Digital recording changes sound into a digital file that (3) <u>a computer can read</u>. When music is recorded, it usually contains many sounds that the human ear cannot actually hear. MP3 technology (4) takes away (5) the sounds humans cannot hear and compresses the music to a tenth of (6) the music's previous size. This means that a single CD can contain hundreds of songs instead of just ten or twelve.

The reduction in the size of music files has also meant that (7) <u>you can</u> transfer music over the Internet. People can now download music from a website and record (8) the music onto a CD or an MP3 player. Apple developed their own version of MP3s and used the technology in their famous iPods. (9) iPods were a huge success and (10) <u>Apple has sold more than 500 million of them</u> around the world.

---

5 UNITS 103 AND 104 Choose the best second sentence, A or B, to continue each paragraph.

0 The children wouldn't stop shouting and running around the classroom.
 A The children running around was beginning to annoy the teacher.
 (B) Their behaviour was beginning to annoy the teacher.
1 London's parks are full of rhododendron bushes.
 A These beautiful plants were imported from Asia in the eighteenth century.
 B In the eighteenth century somebody imported these beautiful plants.

2 The airline has decided to put up the cost of its flights.
  A The increase will not be popular with their customers.
  B The airline putting up costs will not be popular with customers.
3 The managing director, John Travers, resigned last week.
  A John leaving has upset many members of staff.
  B His departure has upset many members of staff.
4 Pedro showed his boarding pass to the attendant and walked up the steps to the aircraft door.
  A There was a strange smell which he noticed when he walked onto the plane.
  B Walking onto the plane, he suddenly noticed a strange smell.
5 Hanford has a brand-new hospital.
  A Last month the Minister of Health opened it.
  B It was opened by the Minister of Health last month.
6 Last year the Grayson family decided to sell their house and move to a small apartment.
  A Within a few months they had begun to regret their decision.
  B Within a few months they had begun to regret that they'd decided to do it.

6 ALL UNITS Read the short text and match the descriptions A–I with the highlighted words.

THE GREATEST DIVA

Many people consider Maria Callas to be the greatest diva (0) (female opera singer) of all time. Not only (1) was she a great singer, she also had the rare ability to act convincingly on stage. (2) This, combined with her strong and (3) delightful personality, made her one of the few opera singers to become a truly international star.

(4) Although she died more than thirty years ago (5), her albums are still some of the best-selling of all classical records.

Callas achieved tremendous success as a singer, but (6) it was her celebrity lifestyle that most interested the public. (7) Her battle to lose weight led to headlines around the world. But Callas disliked being in the newspapers. (8) Consequently, she slowly began to retire from public life. She spent the last ten years of her life living alone in Paris and died in 1977.

A punctuation marks which enclose an explanation *0*
B a word which replaces a noun phrase ....
C a punctuation mark that separates two parts of the same sentence ....
D a sentence with *it* used to emphasise an object ....
E a noun phrase ....
F a word linking two clauses ....
G a word linking two sentences ....
H changing word order after a negative adverb ....
I a formal adjective ....

7 ALL UNITS Write the words in the correct order.

0 she's intelligent, not only she beautiful is
   Not only is she intelligent, she's beautiful.

1 can't my brother I can swim but
   ....

2 to lend her he refused but she asked her father some money
   ....

3 changed the electric guitar for ever the invention of music
   ....

4 Amy Winehouse it who recorded *Back to Black* was
   ....

5 the teachers the children went on strike were sent home because
   ....

6 does like I spicy food don't and neither my wife
   ....

7 his favourite composer my best friend is classical music; Bach loves
   ....

8 ALL UNITS Choose the best word or phrase, A, B or C below. Be careful! Some answers may be grammatically correct but are less suitable.

GOOD NEWS FOR ABBA FANS

Fans of Abba's music have been delighted by the news that *Mamma* (0) .... featuring the group's songs, has now broken all box office records for a musical. Since (1) .... in 2008, the movie has earned more than 600 million dollars.

Mamma Mia stars Oscar-winner Meryl Streep. Most filmgoers think of (2) .... as a serious actress who doesn't work in musicals. (3) .... she loves comedy roles and is a fine singer. (4) .... since she first heard their music as a teenager.

Abba was one of the biggest groups of the 1970s. (5) .... began when they won the Eurovision Song Contest in 1974. (6) .... ensured that their winning song, *Waterloo*, would become a huge hit in every European country and the USA. (7) ...., they went on to release a string of hit singles and albums, selling more than 400 million copies worldwide.

Abba were famous for their flamboyant costumes and videos, but (8) .... that people remember. Abba had four (9) .... Agnetha Faltskog, Anni-Frid Lyngstad, Benny Andersson and Bjorn Ulvaeus. Not only (10) .... in the group, they also composed all the songs.

0   A *Mia* the film   B *Mia*; the film   Ⓒ *Mia*, the film
1   A its release   B the releasing of the film   C it did release
2   A Meryl Streep   B the Oscar-winner   C her
3   A Furthermore,   B On the contrary,   C Consequently,
4   A Abba was loved by her   B She has loved Abba   C Abba it was loved by her
5   A Their career   B The career of Abba   C Abba's working
6   A Winning the contest   B Abba winning   C The victory
7   A However   B After   C After that
8   A the songs are   B are the songs   C it is the songs
9   A members;   B members: C members
10 A did Benny and Bjorn play   B played Benny and Bjorn   C did play Benny and Bjorn

Test MODULE 19

Formal and written English

Choose the correct answer, A, B or C.

1. I'm afraid I don't like popular .... music.
   A music: or classical   B music; or classical   C music or classical   ▶ Unit 99

2. I bought .... bought an MP3 player
   A a camera. my friend   B a camera; my friend   C a camera: my friend   ▶ Unit 99

3. Elizabeth I .... was one of England's greatest rulers.
   A (1533–1603)   B 1533–1603   C 1533–1603:   ▶ Unit 99

4. She gave me a present and I opened .... immediately.
   A present   B it   C that   ▶ Unit 100

5. My husband likes the same bands as I ....
   A do like   B do   C like them   ▶ Unit 100

6. She asked me to go to the cinema but I didn't want ....
   A to   B to go to it   C go there   ▶ Unit 100

7. The flights were expensive. .... decided not to go.
   A As a result, we   B As a result we   C Because we   ▶ Unit 101

8. The solicitor claimed Mr Grant had been unaware of the decision. .... is proof that he had received the relevant letter several weeks earlier.
   A Nevertheless there   B Therefore, there   C On the contrary, there   ▶ Unit 101

9. .... the singer was disappointing.
   A But the band was good   B The band was good but
   C But, the band was good,   ▶ Unit 101

10. .... produced all the Beatles' albums.
    A It George Martin was   B George Martin was   C It was George Martin that   ▶ Unit 102

11. Not only ...., she also composes most of the songs.
    A she sings   B sings her   C does she sing   ▶ Unit 102

12. I didn't get a pay rise this year and neither .... my colleagues.
    A did   B didn't   C didn't get   ▶ Unit 102

13. *Bohemian Rhapsody* is one of the biggest-selling singles of all time. ....
    A In 1975 Queen recorded it.   B It was recorded by Queen in 1975.
    C Queen was the band that recorded it in 1975.   ▶ Unit 103

14. My sister went on holiday to Casablanca in January, but ....
    A the weather disappointed her.   B she was disappointed by the weather.
    C there was weather which disappointed her.   ▶ Unit 103

15. The fans began to scream and shout. .... was becoming difficult.
    A Fans screaming and shouting   B The situation   C That   ▶ Unit 104

16. Alex bought an old farmhouse in Romania. .... was quite complicated.
    A Buying of that house   B He bought the house   C The purchase   ▶ Unit 104

17. Ladies and gentlemen. .... will be delayed due to airport congestion.
    A Our arrival   B Our plane arriving   C Arriving of our plane   ▶ Unit 104

18. Prime Minister. .... us more about your tax proposals?
    A Why not tell   B How about telling   C Could you tell   ▶ Unit 105

19. Hi, Mum. How was the job interview? Is the .... good?
    A pay   B remuneration   C financial compensation   ▶ Unit 105

20. Continued poor performance will result in the .... of your employment.
    A termination   B stopping   C finish   ▶ Unit 105

Spoken English

MODULE 20

Before you start

1 Read the conversation. Look at the <mark>highlighted</mark> grammar examples.

Family health check
Our representative will visit you in your own home …

MR SMART	… Do come in. We're in the living room.
REPRESENTATIVE	Thank you … <mark>Right,</mark> let me start by asking how much exercise you all do.
MR SMART	Well, we do quite a lot, <mark>don't we?</mark> We all go cycling and walking together. I swim twice a week and <mark>so does my wife.</mark> And the kids do sports at school, too.
ANNIE	Well, I <mark>did do</mark> sport until last year, Dad, but I don't have to now I'm in the final year.
MR SMART	I didn't know that. <mark>How ridiculous!</mark>
REPRESENTATIVE	Can you tell me something about your diet?
MR SMART	Well, <mark>we never eat junk food, do we?</mark>
MRS SMART	We try to eat rice and pasta and <mark>stuff</mark> like that sometimes. We eat healthily, don't we?
MR SMART	<mark>I think so.</mark> We don't eat fruit and vegetables every day. <mark>Personally,</mark> I don't think it's necessary.
REPRESENTATIVE	Mmm. Next question … I'd like to know <mark>if you take</mark> any vitamins.
MR SMART	Why would we do that? We're healthy enough without them.

2 Now read the sentences and choose the correct or most suitable words in *italics*. The <mark>highlighted</mark> grammar examples will help you

1. You eat a lot of healthy food, *don't you? / don't you eat?* ▶ Unit 106
2. We never go to the gym at the weekend, *don't we? / do we?* ▶ Unit 106
3. The doctor would like to know *do you / if you* want a morning appointment. ▶ Unit 106
4. I went to the local school and *so my friends did / so did my friends.* ▶ Unit 107
5. 'Is the fish and chip shop open on Sunday evenings?' '*I think yes. / I think so.*' ▶ Unit 107
6. 'Our school doesn't teach any foreign languages in the first year.'
   '*What / How* stupid! It's best to learn when you're young.' ▶ Unit 108
7. *Personal / Personally*, I'd rather not take any medicine at all. ▶ Unit 108
8. 'Why didn't you tell me you were coming?' '*I told you! / I did tell you!* You just didn't listen.' ▶ Unit 109
9. We use a lot of spices in our cooking – we like Indian and Mexican food and *stuff / what* like that. ▶ Unit 110
10. Have you all finished writing? *Right, / Yes,* I'll collect your exam papers now. ▶ Unit 110

3 Check your answers below. Then go to the unit for more information and practice.

1 don't you? 2 do we? 3 if you 4 so did my friends 5 I think so. 6 How 7 Personally 8 I did tell you! 9 stuff 10 Right.

⏻ Go online for a full diagnostic test

106 Spoken question forms

1 Question tags

We add a **question tag** (e.g. *are you?/aren't you?*) to change a statement into a *yes/no* question (➤ Unit 61). We use *be*, an auxiliary verb or a modal verb.

TAG TYPE	+ VERB FORM	→ STATEMENT	+ QUESTION TAG
with *be*	be	I'm in the advanced class,	aren't I?
		You aren't still getting those headaches,	are you?
	there is	There weren't many people there,	were there?
with auxiliary verbs	present simple	Alice comes from France,	doesn't she?
	past simple	The doctor didn't say much,	did he?
	present continuous	They're developing a new drug,	aren't they?
	be going to	She isn't going to marry him,	is she?
	present perfect	The girls haven't been ill again,	have they?
with modal verbs	will	You'll call us when you get there,	won't you?
	can	Brad can speak fluent Spanish,	can't he?

- With a negative statement we use a POSITIVE tag:
  *The doctor didn't say much, **did** he?*
  *You've **never** met my son, **have** you?* *Nobody wants this last biscuit, **do** they?*
- With a positive statement we use a NEGATIVE tag:
  *Brad can speak Spanish, **can't** he?*

⚠ The tag always refers back to the subject: ✗ *He's English, no?* ✗ *He's English, isn't it?*
✓ *He's English, **isn't he**?*

We can make informal suggestions and requests with question tags:
***Let's sort out** this ordering problem, **shall** we?* ***Open** the door for me, **would** you?*

Question tags have two different meanings, depending on the intonation we use.
- With a rising tone (↗) they can ask for information:
  The last performance of the film is after 9.00, isn't it? (I'm really not sure of the answer.)
- With a falling tone (↘) they can ask for agreement:
  You're coming with us to see the film tonight, aren't you? (I think you are but I want you to agree.)

We answer question tags with *yes/no*, a short answer and other information if necessary:
'*You aren't still getting those headaches, are you?*' '*Yes, I am. The doctor says they're caused by stress.*'
'*Charles hasn't been to football practice recently, has he?*' '*No, he hasn't. Actually, he's been ill.*'

 Pronunciation ➤ 1.35

2 Reply questions

Reply questions are like question tags in form, but we use them to show we are listening and to continue the conversation:
'The doctor says the headaches are caused by stress.' **'Does she?** *I wonder if you're spending too much time on the computer.'*
'My computer's been causing problems all week.' **'Has it?** *What's wrong?'*

Reply questions are positive if the statement is positive, and negative if the statement is negative: *'My doctor* **doesn't** *like giving antibiotics.'* **'Doesn't he?'**
We usually use a rising tone (↗), and we stress the auxiliary verb: <u>Does</u> she? <u>Has</u> it?

🔊 **Pronunciation ➤ 1.36**

3 Indirect questions

The form of **indirect questions** is similar to the form of reported questions (➤ **Unit 69.1**):
Could you tell me where Studio 5 is?
We can use indirect questions to be polite or if we think the person we are asking may not know the answer to the question. We introduce the question with a polite phrase, for example:
Excuse me, **can/could you tell me** *if this is the correct platform for Edinburgh?*
Do you know *what time the film finishes?*
I'd like to know *what you think about my idea.*

The word order after the polite phrase is the same as in reported questions:

direct question	indirect question
	if/whether/wh- word (+ subject) + verb:
'Is this the road for Cardiff?'	*'Can you tell me if this is the road for Cardiff, please?'*
'Who is the manager here?'	*'Do you know who the manager is here?'*

 We ALWAYS use statement word order in indirect questions, and we do NOT use *do/does* or *did*:
✓ *Can you tell me* **what the correct time is?**   ✗ ~~Can you tell me what is the correct time?~~
✓ *I'd like to know* **where you heard that.**   ✗ ~~I'd like to know where did you hear that.~~

We can also use the infinitive in indirect questions:
'How do you turn this machine on?' → *'Do you know* **how to turn** *this machine on?'*
'Where do we buy tickets for the play?' → *'Can you tell us* **where to buy** *tickets for the play?'*
'What should I buy?' → *'I'd like to know* **what to buy.'**
In spoken English, we often say *Could you ...?* and *Do you ...?* very fast and the words run together: *could you* /kədjuː/ *do you* /djuː/.

🔊 **Pronunciation ➤ 1.37**

4 Indirect question forms in statements

If we don't know the answer to a question, we can use a polite phrase such as *I'm not sure* or *I don't know* + an indirect question form:
'What time does the film start?' *'I'm afraid* **I'm not sure** *what time it starts. I'll just check.'*
'Is it raining in London?' → *'***I can't tell you** *if it's raining here – I'm in the studio!'*
'How do I get to Studio 5?' *'I'm sorry.* **I don't know** *how to get there.'*

We can also make a statement with an indirect question if we are 'thinking aloud' or asking ourselves something:
'Where did I put my glasses?' → *'***I wonder** *where I put my glasses.'*
'Are you spending too much time on the computer?' → *'***I wonder** *if you are spending too much time on the computer.'*
'Did I turn the iron off?' → *'***I can't remember** *if I turned the iron off.'*
'What time are the builders coming?' → *'***I don't know** *what time the builders are coming.'*

106 SPOKEN QUESTION EXAMS

Practice

1 Match the sentences 1–8 with their question tags A–I. 🔊 5.25 Listen and check.

0 You won't be late home tonight, —   A shall we?
1 There's something good on at the theatre at the moment,   B have you?
2 You've never met my parents-in-law,   C does it?
3 You took part in the quiz competition at the school,   D isn't there?
4 Let's take the afternoon off and go shopping,   E can't you?
5 You can pick up the kids from school later on,   F didn't you?
6 I'm invited to Gianni's party as well as you,   G shouldn't we?
7 We really should spend more time with the family,   H will you?
8 Nothing ever seems good enough for her,   I aren't I?

2 Match the questions and answers, then practise saying them. 🔊 5.26 Listen and check.

0 Is it a powerful computer? I can use it to play games, can't I?   [↗] ...B....
1 Fabulous weather! It's been really sunny today, hasn't it?   [↘] ....
2 Five hundred euros for a vase? That's rather expensive, isn't it?   [↗] ....
3 How much further must we walk? It isn't too far to the station, is it?   [↗] ....
4 2 + 2 = 5. You've made a mistake, haven't you?   [↘] ....

    A Not really, not for an antique one.   C Um, yes, obviously I have.
    ~~B Yes, you can. You can play all the popular games on it.~~   D Yes, it's been a lovely day.
                                    E No, it's only another 500 metres.

3 **GRAMMAR IN USE** Read the dialogue and think of the best word for each gap. Write one word only. 🔊 5.27 Listen and check.

WOMAN   Excuse me. I wonder (0) _if_ you could help me. I'm new to this town. Could you tell me where (1) .... find a good supermarket?
MAN   Of course. There's one in the shopping centre on the main road out of town.
WOMAN   Oh, (2) .... there? Thank you. You don't (3) .... what time it closes, (4) .... you?
MAN   I'm sorry, I don't know (5) .... it opens or closes.
WOMAN   That's OK. There isn't a department store in the shopping centre, is (6) ....?
MAN   Yes, there is, but I can't (7) .... you what it's like, I'm afraid. I never go there.
WOMAN   Really? (8) .... you? Oh, just one more question. Do you (9) .... which bus I should take for the shopping centre?
MAN   I'm sorry, I'm really not sure (10) .... bus goes there. I hate shopping centres, you see.

4 Find and correct the mistake in each sentence. 🔊 5.28 Listen and check.

0 You won't go to that awful club, ~~won't~~ _will_ you?
1 'We aren't going out now, after all.' 'Are you?'
2 Let's have a pizza tonight, do we?
3 You phone your friends in Spain a lot, no?
4 Can you tell me where is the nearest bank?
5 Well, Jake's never had a better job, hasn't he?
6 I'd like to know where did she get that ring.
7 Drinking a lot of water is good for you, yes?
8 'The storms last year did a lot of damage.' 'Didn't they?'

5 **GRAMMAR IN USE** Complete each spoken question with a suitable verb.
🔊 **5.29** Listen and check.

MOIRA   I've been thinking about having a health check.
KIM   (0) *Have* you? Why? Is everything OK?
MOIRA   Oh, yes. But there's a company in town offering them, and you can't be too careful with your health, (1) .... you?
KIM   I suppose not. Do you (2) .... how much it costs?
MOIRA   A basic one costs £250.
KIM   (3) .... it? Really?
MOIRA   That's not too expensive, (4) .... it?
KIM   Well, if there's nothing wrong with you, it's a lot of money. Anyway, you can get a health check at the doctor's, (5) .... you?
MOIRA   (6) .... you? I'm not sure.
KIM   I think so. There's no harm in asking, (7) .... there?
MOIRA   No, you're right, and I suppose my doctor knows me best.
KIM   Exactly. I'd better go. It's getting late.
MOIRA   (8) .... it? Oh, yes, so it is. Listen, are you busy on Saturday morning?
KIM   No …
MOIRA   Let's meet for coffee, (9) .... we? We can have a long chat then.

6 Complete the polite questions that the researcher asks. Use the notes to help you.
🔊 **5.30** Listen and check.

0 Excuse me, can *you tell me what types of media you use, please*?
1 OK, and could you .... ?
2 Thank you. I'd also ....
3 That's great. Do you know .... ?
4 And can .... ?
5 Right, and could .... ?
6 Finally, I'd ....

Media survey
Ask people the following questions:
(0) what types of media do you use?
(1) how much TV do you watch every week?
(2) do you listen to the radio?
(3) how many newspapers do you read every week?
(4) do you read the same newspaper every day?
(5) do you prefer to get the news from the TV, radio or newspapers?
(6) why do you prefer that method of getting news?

107 Agreeing and disagreeing

1 Agreeing with *so/neither* and *too/either*

When we want to reply to a statement by saying that something is the same, or agreeing, we use the pattern *So/Neither* + *be*/auxiliary verb/modal verb + subject:

	STATEMENT	REPLY
positive	I feel awful now! My daughter's going to pass all her exams.	So do I!* So is my son.
negative	I'm not very good with new technology. I can't go to the company dinner.	Neither am I. Neither can I.

* stressed words in the replies are underlined.

We can also use *nor* instead of *neither*, especially with pronouns:
'We haven't been to the theatre for ages'. '**Nor** have we.'

⚠️ In these statements, we use an auxiliary verb and we put it before the subject:
'We got tickets for the Olympics!' ✓ 'So did we!' ✗ 'So did we get!' ✗ 'So got we!' ✗ 'So we did!'

🔊 Pronunciation ➤ 1.38

We can also use *too* after a positive verb and *either* after a negative verb:

	STATEMENT	REPLY
positive	I really must start going to the gym more frequently.	'Yes, I must, too.'
negative	My mobile phone doesn't store music.	'Mine doesn't either.'

2 Disagreeing

To say something is different, or to disagree, we use *be*/the auxiliary verb or the modal verb from the statement, and we change the verb from positive to negative/negative to positive:

	STATEMENT	REPLY
positive	The sea **is** much too cold for swimming today.	No, it isn't! It's lovely!
negative	We **don't** really **like** living in the country.	Oh, we do. We love it.

NATURAL ENGLISH We often use *Oh* or *Really?* before we disagree. It sounds a little more polite: 'I'm bored.' '**Oh**, I'm not.' / **Really?** I'm not.

3 *think so, hope so*

We can use *so* after *think, hope, expect, suppose* to avoid repeating a longer phrase:
'Will all your students pass the exam?' 'I think so.' (= I think they will all pass the exam.)

⚠️ We don't use *so* with a clause: ✗ 'I expect so (that) he will.'

If we want to give a negative reply, we usually make the auxiliary verb negative:
'Did the Vikings come to Britain before the Romans?' ✓ '**I don't think so**.' ✗ 'I think not.'
'Do you think Chelsea will win tonight?' ✓ '**I don't expect so**.' ✗ 'I expect not.'

But we use *not* after *hope*: 'Is it going to rain tomorrow?' 'I hope **not**.'

20

Practice

1 Match the statements 1–8 with the replies A–I. 🔊 **5.31** Listen and check.

0 We weren't expecting you to arrive so early. — B
1 We won't be able to afford a holiday this year.
2 My boss is always asking me to stay late.
3 I've never had to stay in hospital.
4 Our teacher doesn't give us a lot of homework.
5 I'd really like to go to the end-of-year party.
6 My boss didn't go to university.
7 We believe that everyone should enjoy work.
8 Our teacher taught in South America.

A Ours doesn't either.
B No, neither were we.
C I know. I would, too.
D Yes, so do we.
E No, we won't either.
F Nor have I.
G Really? So did ours.
H Is he? Mine is, too.
I No, neither did my boss.

2 GRAMMAR IN USE Complete the conversation with the words from the box. 🔊 **5.32** Listen and check.

> I am, too.   I expect so.   I'm not.   I think so.   I won't either.
> ~~Neither did I.~~   No, I don't!   So did I!   Well, I did!

MUM   What's the time?
DAD   It's half past two. Goodness! I didn't think it was so late!
MUM   (0) *Neither did I*. I was having so much fun that I didn't notice the time!
JOE   (1) .... I noticed the time all evening!
DAD   I thought it was a great evening! Do you think everyone enjoyed themselves?
MUM   Yes, (2) .... They stayed quite a long time after dinner, didn't they?
DAD   Mmm, in the end I wanted them to leave.
JOE   (3) .... The whole evening was boring.
DAD   You think everything's boring.
JOE   (4) .... But you only ever talk about other people in the family and friends.
MUM   Well, we like that. You didn't have to stay here. Anyway, I'm really tired now.
DAD   (5) .... Time for bed.
JOE   (6) .... I want to stay up and watch a DVD.
MUM   OK, but you'll be tired tomorrow, won't you?
JOE   (7) ...., but it doesn't matter – it's Sunday.
DAD   Well, I'm going to bed. I'm really tired so I won't clear up now, Ann.
MUM   No, (8) .... We can do it in the morning.

3 Complete the replies. Use one word only (or a short form). 🔊 **5.33** Listen and check.

0 'I don't go to the doctor very often.' 'Really? I *do*.'
1 'My kids are always falling over and hurting themselves.' '................ are mine!'
2 'We take a lot of vitamins and minerals.' 'Do you? We ....'
3 'Do you think exercise keeps you healthy?' 'I .... so, but I think good food is important, too.'
4 'I've spent a lot of time in hospital.' 'Have you really? I ....'
5 'Do you think you'll live to 120?' 'No, I .... think so.'
6 'We don't think it's a good idea to smoke.' 'No, ... do we.'
7 'Will you have to take antibiotics?' 'Well, I certainly hope ....! I hate them.'

Go online for more practice

108 Expressing our feelings and ideas

The Government has revealed that it will reduce the budget for the health service by £3.5 billion …

That's awful! So lots of people won't get the treatment they need …

Personally, I think it's our own fault. If we want a better health service, we have to pay for it.

1 Expressing our feelings

When we feel strongly about something, or when we are surprised or shocked. We can express it like this:
- What (a/an) + (adjective) + noun: 'Eddie went swimming in the sea on New Year's Day.'
  'What a stupid thing to do! It must have been freezing!'
  What a lovely day! What good friends you have! **What a pity! What a mess! What good advice!**
- That's/How + adjective: 'I won the tennis championship last week.' **'That's fantastic!'**
  'Stan has to take ten pills a day.' **'How dreadful!'** (How makes the adjective stronger.)

	GOOD	BAD	SURPRISING
That's/ How	wonderful! great! fantastic! fabulous! really cool!	awful! terrible! dreadful! disastrous! shocking!	crazy! amazing! incredible! unbelievable! ridiculous!

There are also some single words which we use to express feelings:
'Jamie's been offered the job of managing director of the company.'
→ **'Wow! That's amazing!' 'No! You're joking!' 'Really? That's great news.'**

⚠ We use *Wow!* only to reply to something positive:
'Our cat died last week.' ✗ *Wow! I'm really sorry.*' ✓ 'No! I'm really sorry.'

🔊 **Pronunciation ➤ 1.39**

2 Expressing our ideas

Some adverbs, like *personally, to be honest* and *obviously,* are used mostly in speech. They show that the sentence contains an opinion or comment. With *personally* and *to be honest*, we often use *I think/believe/feel*:

ADVERB	MEANING	EXAMPLE
personally	in my opinion	*Personally,* I think it's our own fault.
to be honest	this is what I really think	*To be honest,* I think you paid too much for that car.
obviously	It's clear that	*Obviously,* he had no idea what you were talking about.

🔊 **Pronunciation ➤ 1.40**

3 Other adverbs

Adverbs like *anyway* and *by the way* help to make a conversation more natural:

ADVERB	USE	EXAMPLE
so anyway	to change subject/ end conversation	… and I've been really busy. *So,* how are things with you? *Anyway,* I'd better go now.
by the way	to start a new topic	*By the way,* have you heard anything from Katy since her trip?

20

Practice

1 Read the reactions to the newspaper headlines and choose the correct words in *italics*. 🔊 5.34 Listen and check.

0 **FIVE MORE CASES OF CHOLERA FOUND**   That's *great /* (*terrible*). I thought it had disappeared.
1 **OFFICIAL! CHOCOLATE IS GOOD FOR YOU!**   Wow! *That / What* fantastic news! I love it!
2 **WOMAN HAS BABY AT 65**   *That's / How's* awful; it's much too old.
3 **HOSPITALS' BUDGETS CUT BY 20%**   *Wow! / Really?* How dreadful!
4 **LIFE EXPECTANCY NOW UP TO 95**   *What a / That's* good, but I hope we'll be healthy.
5 **SCIENTISTS DISCOVER NEW CANCER TREATMENT**   *What / How* wonderful! We need better drugs.

2 **GRAMMAR IN USE** Complete the conversation with A–I below. 🔊 5.35 Listen and check.

PAULA Hi, Jim. How are you feeling?

JIM Well, not bad. I went to the doctor yesterday – I got an appointment straightaway.

PAULA (0) *F*......... . What did the doctor say?

JIM I'm anaemic – that's why I've been feeling so tired.

PAULA Oh, that (1) ....! Discovering you're anaemic. (2) .... shock!

JIM (3) ...., it doesn't bother me. I was worried it might be something more serious.

PAULA Mmm, I suppose it's quite easy to treat.

JIM Well, I have to take some tablets for a while, and I need to eat more food with iron in it, so (4) ...., I need to improve my diet a bit.

PAULA Mmm. (5) ...., I think diet is so important.

JIM You're right, and I haven't paid enough attention to mine. (6) ...., enough about me. How are things with you?

PAULA Well, we're all fine, but my mother's getting worse. She's got dementia.

JIM Oh, how (7) ....! I'm so sorry.

PAULA Thanks. It isn't too bad at the moment but it will get worse. (8) ...., did you see that TV programme the other day about caring for the elderly?

A obviously	D Anyway	G 's terrible
B What a	E By the way	H Personally
C awful	F ~~Really? That's good!~~	I To be honest

3 Find six more mistakes and correct them. Tick (✓) the correct sentences. 🔊 5.36 Listen and check.

   What a shame
0 ~~What shame~~ you can't come to the company's dinner and dance.
1 Have you heard about the earthquake in China? How a terrible thing!
2 He weighs about 140 kilos, so, personally, he has to lose some weight.
3 'I've just won a holiday home.' 'That's fantastic news!'
4 'I've just lost my job.' 'Wow! That's terrible.'
5 'Sheila didn't get the job she applied for.' 'Really? What shame.'
6 'What do you think of Frank?' 'Well, anyway, I don't like him at all.'
7 'Someone tried to break into our house last night.' 'That dreadful!'
8 That's really interesting. Anyway, I'd better go now.

109 Emphasis

1 Emphasising verbs

We can emphasise most verbs simply by stressing *be*, an auxiliary or a modal:
'We can start the meeting when Kyra's here.' 'I <u>am</u> here, Tim! Over here. In the corner.'

⚠ We don't use short forms for positive verbs when we emphasise them:
✗ ~~I'm here!~~ ✓ I <u>am</u> here!

- To emphasise a positive verb in the present or past simple, we use *do*, *does* or *did*:
  Yes, that's sensible, but it **does** look *strange!* (= Although it is sensible, it looks strange.)
  You **do** say *some silly things!* (= You have a habit of saying silly things.)
  'Weren't you going to tell everyone about the meeting?' 'I **did** tell *everyone*.'
  I said I'd remember to book tickets and I **did** remember. (You think I didn't, but I did.)

- To emphasise a negative, we stress *not* (or another negative word) or a short form with *not*:
  I'm sorry but your behaviour in this class is <u>not</u> good enough! You've made <u>no</u> effort at all.
  'I thought Ahmed wasn't coming with you.' 'He <u>wasn't</u>, but he changed his mind.'

🔊 Pronunciation ➤ 1.41

2 Emphasising adjectives, adverbs and nouns

We often use words such as *really* and *so* to emphasise adjectives and adverbs:
More flowers for me? You're <u>so</u> good to me! You should read this book – it's <u>really</u> interesting.
The musicians performed <u>really</u> well last night. Eva Cassidy used to sing that song <u>so</u> beautifully.

We can use *such* (*a/an* + adjective) to emphasise nouns (➤ Unit 79.2):
That was <u>such</u> a good holiday! I feel terrible – I've got <u>such</u> a bad headache.
'Mum, I got the job.' 'That's <u>such</u> wonderful news! I'm really happy for you.'

3 Emphasising questions

We can use *on earth* or *ever* after a question word to emphasise a question, usually when we are surprised or annoyed about something:

What	What on <u>earth</u> was that politician talking about? What<u>ever</u> have you done to your hair? It looks awful!
Who	Who on <u>earth</u> would pay $1,000 for a coat like that? Who<u>ever</u> told you that I was leaving my job? That's rubbish!
Where	Where on <u>earth</u> have you put the keys? I can't find them anywhere! Wher<u>ever</u> did Jeremy sleep last night? Under a hedge?
How	How on <u>earth</u> do you expect me to remember all your phone numbers? How<u>ever</u> do they get those little sailing ships into glass bottles?
When	When<u>ever</u> does your mother get the time to work and bake these wonderful cakes?
Why	Why on <u>earth</u> are you wearing that mask? Why <u>ever</u> would anyone want to have a holiday in space?

We do not usually say [When on earth …?] We prefer to use *Whenever* …?

Practice

1 **GRAMMAR IN USE** Add one word for emphasis in each gap. 🔊 5.37 Listen and check.

ERROL How's your work experience going?
NIKKI Oh, it's (0) _really_ awful, actually.
ERROL Awful? Why?
NIKKI You know my tutor said I'd be going to a 'state-of-the-art' computer company? Well, it is most definitely (1) .... state of the art! It's (2) .... old-fashioned, and I'm not learning anything new.
ERROL Oh, that's (3) .... ridiculous! The whole point of work experience is to learn something about work, and use your skills.
NIKKI I know. What on (4) .... were they thinking of when they sent me there? Anyway, I've told the managing director that I'm leaving on Friday.
ERROL What? Why (5) .... did you do that? You know the teachers at the college get really annoyed if you don't make an effort.
NIKKI That's the point. I (6) .... make an effort. I tried really hard, but they weren't interested in listening to my ideas or anything. It was all (7) .... unfair!
ERROL So, what are you going to do?
NIKKI Well, I (8) .... want to continue with a work placement, so I'm going to talk to the college tomorrow about working somewhere else.

2 Emphasise the underlined parts of the sentences. Add a word or phrase, and make any other necessary changes. 🔊 5.38 Listen and check.

0 'Gavin didn't come to the meeting.' 'He <u>came</u> to the meeting.' _did come_
1 Your little daughter is <u>delightful</u>. ....
2 Don't lie to me. You're <u>a terrible liar</u>. ....
3 'That film doesn't look very good.' 'It <u>looks</u> good.' ....
4 <u>Where</u> did you ride that horse? It's filthy! ....
5 'You didn't hear the story.' 'I <u>heard</u> it.' ....
6 Of course Penny didn't pass the test. She drove <u>badly</u>. ....
7 The travel agent gave us <u>bad advice</u>. ....
8 'The school's closed today.' '<u>Who</u> told you that?' ....

3 **GRAMMAR IN USE** Find five more mistakes in emphasis and correct them. 🔊 5.39 Listen and check.

CATHY What ^on earth are you doing?
DAVINA I'm soaking my feet. Isn't it obvious?
CATHY Yes, but ever what for?
DAVINA I've been out running and my feet got such cold.
CATHY Running? You don't go running!
DAVINA I go running! I've been running quite a lot recently.
CATHY Whenever do you find the time to run?
DAVINA Early mornings, before work. Today I've had such long run in the park …
CATHY But why are you doing it? You're not interested in exercise.
DAVINA I'm interested in it! I want to get fit and run a marathon.

Go online for more practice

110 Other spoken features

SID: How are you feeling now?
DAISY: **Mustn't complain**, a bit better.
SID: What did the doctor say?
DAISY: Well, I can't come home yet. **I mean**, he wants to do some more tests …
SID: **Mmm.**
DAISY: **You know**, blood tests, to see if I've got enough iron and things in my blood.
SID: I see. Oh, yes. **Bunch of flowers** for you.
DAISY: Thanks.

1 Leaving out words

We sometimes leave out words when we are speaking: *Mustn't complain. Bunch of flowers for you.*
We only do this in very informal speech, and rarely in writing.
To be more exact, we say: *I mustn't complain. Here's a bunch of flowers for you.*

The words that we leave out are often the words that come at the beginning of a sentence (e.g. pronouns (*I, you*) and/or the auxiliary verb (*do, is*)) as these are usually clear from the situation:

A *How you doing?*	(How are you doing?)
B *Fine, thanks.*	(I'm fine, thanks.)
A *Coming to the party at the weekend?*	(Are you coming to the party …?)
B *Don't know yet.*	(I don't know yet.)

2 Common words and phrases

There are a few words and phrases that we use a lot in spoken English, but not in writing:

Well,	to pause before saying something to start talking about a subject that you have just mentioned	It was quite … er, **well**, it was embarrassing. Do you remember Chloe? **Well**, I've just heard that she's getting married.
Right,	to get everyone's attention	**Right**, have you all finished?
I mean,	to explain/to correct something	**I mean**, he wants to do some more tests. She plays the violin, **I mean**, the guitar …
You know,	to ensure the listener understands	We went to the shop, **you know**, the one on the corner.

3 Listening and responding

We often make noises or say things in a conversation to show we are listening:
'… he wants to do some more tests …' '**Mmm.**'
'They're back over here for the summer …' '**Really?**'
'And we want to see them but …' '**Yeah, I know. It's difficult when you're working, isn't it?**'

4 *things, stuff, kind of*

There are times when we don't know or can't think of the exact words for what we want to say. If we don't know the words for nouns, we can use words like *thing(s)* or *stuff*:
- *thing(s)* for countable nouns: *… to see if I've got enough iron and **things** …* (e.g. minerals)
- *stuff* for uncountable nouns: *Have we got enough food and **stuff** for the party?* (e.g. drink)

We often use the word *thing* if we want to explain something but don't know the word for it:
*It's a **thing** you use **to open bottles**. Have you got a **thing for opening bottles**?*

We can use *sort of* or *kind of* before a word if we don't want to be exact: *It's **a sort of** piano. He's **kind of** difficult – he wants everything to be exactly right. She just **sort of** walked out.*

 Pronunciation ➤ 1.42

Practice

1 Number the speeches in the correct order. 🔊 5.40 Listen and check.

☐ Wife: Yes, you know, like he suddenly fainted or something.
[1] Doctor: What happened?
☐ Doctor: Yes, I mean, things like a bad heart or …
☐ Doctor: That's good. Right, we'll take him to hospital now. Coming?
☐ Wife: Don't know, really. He just sort of fell over.
☐ Wife: … Oh, no, nothing like that. He's usually very healthy.
[10] Wife: Well, I'd better get the car and follow you. Won't be a minute.
☐ Doctor: Does he have any medical problems?
☐ Doctor: Fell over, just dropped to the ground?
[6] Wife: Medical problems?

2 **GRAMMAR IN USE** Complete the conversations with the words and phrases from the box. 🔊 5.41 Listen and check.

Coming   Don't   ~~Everything~~   I mean   Mmm   sort of   stuff   thing   Well   ~~Yeah~~   You know

1 A Hi, how are things?
　B Fine. (0) _Everything_ OK with you?
　A (00) _Yeah_ , things are going really well.

2 A (1) .... to the gym this evening?
　B I'm not sure really. I'm (2) .... tired today.
　A (3) ...., call me before 8.00 to let me know, OK?

3 A I had a package from Janie this morning.
　B (4) ....
　A She sent me this for my birthday.
　B What exactly is it?
　A (5) .... know, really. It looks like a (6) .... for putting on lipstick.
　B But you don't wear lipstick and (7) .... like that.
　A I know!

4 A Have you got everything for the party?
　B I don't know. What do we need?
　A (8) ...., all the paper plates and glasses, and so on.
　B We don't need plates, do we? (9) ...., we're only having crisps and nuts.

3 Rewrite the speeches with one word in each gap. Use all the spoken English features from this unit that you can. 🔊 5.42 Listen and check.

0 Jan, are you going to the shops later? _Going_ to the shops later, Jan?

1 'Are you ready to leave? We're late.' 'Yes, I'm coming now.'
　'.................. to leave? We're late.' '.................., ... now.'

2 Have you got the tent and sleeping bags, etc. for the trip?
　.................. the .... for the trip?

3 Do you remember Clark? He's left the company!
　.................. Clark? ...., he's left the company!

4 The new manager is a little odd. Let me explain, he looks really strange.
　The new manager is .... of odd. I ...., he looks really strange.

⏻ Go online for more practice and a progress test

333

Review MODULE 20

1 UNITS 106 AND 107 Read the conversation and choose the correct words in *italics*. Sometimes both are correct but one is more natural.

A Look at this quiz in my magazine: 'Do you have a healthy lifestyle?' Well, I think I do.
B (0) *So do I* / *So I do*, I think. But there's so much confusing information, (1) *no / isn't there*?
A Yes. I always eat five portions of fruit and vegetables, but they say here it should be nine.
B (2) *Do they / Are they*? That's a lot to eat in one day, (3) *isn't there / isn't it*?
A Mmm. And I try to buy organic food when I can.
B Oh, (4) *I don't / me either*. It's too expensive. Do you know if (5) *is it / it is* really better for you?
A Well, I think (6) *so / it is better for you*, but I buy a lot from the local farm.
B (7) *You do / Do you*? That sounds good. It must be fresh, (8) *doesn't it / mustn't it*?
A I certainly (9) *so hope / hope so*! Look at the time. I'd better go.
B Yes, (10) *me too / so me*. I've got a class now and I don't like rushing.
A No, neither (11) *I do / do I*. Do you know when (12) *finishes your class / your class finishes*?
B At 12.30. Shall we meet for lunch afterwards?

2 UNITS 108 AND 109 Choose the most suitable reply to each statement, A or B.

0 The only person who didn't contribute to the present was Jonas.
   A No, he contributed. He gave £5.00.   (B) No, he did contribute. He gave £5.00.
1 I fell over and broke my wrist yesterday.
   A No! What a pain!   B Wow! What a pain!
2 I've done the shopping and picked up the stuff from the dry cleaner's.
   A When did you do all that?   B Whenever did you do all that?
3 What do you think of my new hair colour?
   A Well, obviously, I think it's rather bright.   B Well, to be honest, I think it's rather bright.
4 Maggie won't come with us because she can't ski.
   A She can ski! She learnt last year.   B She skis! She learnt last year.
5 We had an email from Tony. He seems to be doing well.
   A Yes, he's enjoying himself. Anyway, must go. See you soon.
   B Yes, he's enjoying himself. Personally, must go. See you soon.
6 I'm going to volunteer to help elderly people.
   A When on earth will you find the time to do that?
   B Whenever will you find the time to do that?

3 UNITS 108 AND 110 Find a mistake in each speech bubble and correct it.

[0] ... and then he left. ~~Frankly~~ *By the way*, have you seen that new film with Scarlett Johannsen?

[1] That's odd. It's a sort car, isn't it?

[2] What nice to see you here! I didn't expect you to be here.

[3] Half past four. You know, that's the end of the exam. Please stop writing.

[4] You ran over a cat in the driving test? Wow! That's awful!

[5] Have you got one of those stuff you use to open jars?

4

ALL UNITS Read the voicemail message below and choose the best answer, A, B or C. Sometimes two answers are possible.

❝Hi Jackie! I'm really sorry I haven't been in touch, but I've been (0) .... busy. You know what it's like. Things have been (1) .... difficult recently – I told you that Grandad's living with us now, (2) ....? (3) ...., a couple of weeks ago, Mum asked me to take him to the doctor's for his flu injection. It was pouring with rain so Grandad didn't want to walk, and, frankly, (4) .... so we took the car. When we got to the doctor's, I parked in the only space I could find. Grandad was a bit concerned and asked if it was OK to park there, and I said I (5) .... – I should've listened to him! So, we were in the waiting room, and someone came in and started shouting about 'these thoughtless people' and he called out the number of my car. Well, you can imagine, I was really embarrassed! Apparently, the space was reserved for doctors, and this man was a doctor: he accused me of not looking where I was parking – but I (6) ...., honestly. Well, I went outside then and pointed out to him that the reserved sign was covered by bushes, and asked him to tell me how (7) .... seen it. He said I should've realised that an empty space was a doctor's space! (8) ...., I think these doctors can be so arrogant. I told him so and he told me to leave, and said that he didn't want to see me or my family at the surgery again. (9) .... mess! So, now we don't have a doctor, Grandad hasn't had his flu jab, and everyone in the family blames me. Well that's enough about me. How are things with you? Do you know (10) .... ? I've been meaning to contact him as well ...❞

0	(A) so	B such	(C) really
1	A sort of	B kind of	C how
2	A didn't you	B didn't I	C haven't I
3	A Anyway	B Right	C Well
4	A I did too	B I didn't either	C neither did I
5	A thought so	B so thought	C thought so it was
6	A looked	B didn't look	C did look
7	A could I have	B I could have	C I have could
8	A So	B To be honest,	C Obviously
9	A How	B That's	C What a
10	A where Patrick	B where is Patrick	C where Patrick is

5

ALL UNITS Read the four conversations about the photo. Write one or two words in each gap.

1. A I don't understand why they do it, (0) *do you* ?

   B No, I think it's (1) .... awful!

2. A I (2) .... if they're doing it for political reasons.

   B I expect (3) ...., but they're causing (4) .... awful problems for ordinary people. I don't think it's right.

   A No, (5) .... I.

3. A (6) .... dreadful mess! Do you (7) .... why people behave like that? They don't have any reason.

   B Well, actually, I think they (8) .... a reason. They're protesting about the environment.

4. A I find photos like this (9) .... disturbing, (10) ....?

   B Well, no, I don't. I agree with street protests.

Test MODULE 20

Spoken English

Choose the best answer, A, B or C.

1. The rubbish collectors aren't coming this Monday, ...?
   A come they B are they C aren't they → Unit 106

2. Let's just try one more shop, then go home, ...?
   A shall we B will we C do we → Unit 106

3. Pay for the coffees while I go to the toilet, ...?
   A do you B are you C would you → Unit 106

4. There's no reason to worry about this interview, ...?
   A isn't there B is there C is it → Unit 106

5. 'Ross wants to come with us tomorrow.' '..........? That's fine.'
   A Does he B Wants he C Doesn't he → Unit 106

6. I'm not sure whether .... dinner this evening.
   A want all the guests B do all the guests want C all the guests want → Unit 106

7. Don't ask Gerald to help you – he doesn't even know what time ....!
   A it is B is it C is → Unit 106

8. 'We don't think a holiday together is a good idea.' '.........., really.'
   A Nor we B Nor we do C Nor do we → Unit 107

9. 'Elena wants to have the meeting after work.' 'Jane ...., so let's do that.'
   A is too B does too C too does → Unit 107

10. 'Let's leave now. I'm exhausted.' '..........! Just one more dance, please.'
    A Oh, me not B Oh, me too C Oh, I'm not → Unit 107

11. 'Can I try the advanced class, then?' 'OK, I ....'
    A suppose so you can B suppose it is C suppose so → Unit 107

12. 'We can't go into the school during the holiday.' '..........! How are we supposed to get all our preparation done?'
    A What crazy B That's crazy C How's crazy → Unit 108

13. 'Shall we get a red tablecloth?' '.........., I prefer white.'
    A Personally B By the way C Obviously → Unit 108

14. So, that's today's session finished. ...., what time are you coming on Wednesday?
    A To be honest B Personally C By the way → Unit 108

15. 'You completely forgot to tell me about the meeting!' 'I .... you!'
    A did tell B told C didn't tell → Unit 109

16. 'The builder wants £100 an hour.' 'But that's .... ridiculous!'
    A not B so C such → Unit 109

17. 'Bob has cancelled the order for the music system.' 'Why .... has he done that?'
    A earth B for C ever → Unit 109

18. Have you seen the new celebrity magazine, ..., the one with Orlando Bloom on the cover?
    A well B so C you know → Unit 110

19. What's this ....? Is it a kind of sugar?
    A stuff B sort C thing → Unit 110

20. Is that all clear then? ...., let's move on to the next topic.
    A By the way B I mean C Right → Unit 110

Go online for a full exit test

Grammar check

This section will help you with your work on the practice exercises; it will help you with revision for exams, too.

APPENDIX 1	Quick checks	
QUICK CHECK 1	Pronouns	338
QUICK CHECK 2	Prepositions	338
QUICK CHECK 3	Verb tenses	340
QUICK CHECK 4	Modal verbs	342
QUICK CHECK 5	Conditionals	344
QUICK CHECK 6	Verbs + -ing form and infinitive	345
QUICK CHECK 7	Linking words	346
QUICK CHECK 8	Verbs + prepositions	347
QUICK CHECK 9	Phrasal verbs	347

APPENDIX 2	Irregular verbs	348

APPENDIX 3	Spelling rules	350

APPENDIX 4	British and American English	352

APPENDIX 1

QUICK CHECK 1 MODULE 2 **Pronouns**

	SUBJECT PRONOUNS	OBJECT PRONOUNS	POSSESSIVE ADJECTIVES	POSSESSIVE PRONOUNS	REFLEXIVE PRONOUNS
singular	*I*	*me*	*my*	*mine*	*myself*
	you	*you*	*your*	*yours*	*yourself*
	he	*him*	*his*	*his*	*himself*
	she	*her*	*her*	*hers*	*herself*
	it	*it*	*its*		*itself*
plural	*we*	*us*	*our*	*ours*	*ourselves*
	you	*you*	*your*	*yours*	*yourselves*
	they	*them*	*their*	*theirs*	*themselves*

QUICK CHECK 2 MODULE 3 **Prepositions**

PREPOSITION	POSSIBLE MEANINGS	EXAMPLE
about	1 near to 2 the subject of something	Meet me at about six tonight. This book's about the French Revolution.
above	in a higher position	He lives in the flat above the supermarket.
across	from one side to the other	They're building a new bridge across the river.
after	a time later than	Let's have dinner after the film this evening.
against	1 (place) next to, touching 2 opposition	Leave your bike against the wall – it'll be safe. I'm really against the new tax increases.
along	following the line of	You can walk along the disused railway tracks.
among	surrounded by three or more things/people	I've got a suit somewhere among all these clothes.
apart from	1 not including 2 separated from	I like all music apart from jazz. The club members sit apart from the other visitors.
around	about	The online test takes around an hour to complete.
as	in the role of	Janine works as a market researcher.
at	1 (place) exact position 2 direction 3 time	I'll wait for you at the bus stop. Did you just throw something at me? The coach will leave at 8.30 exactly.
away from	in a direction leaving somewhere	He turned and walked away from the hotel.
before	a time earlier than	I like to do some exercises before going to bed.
behind	in a position further back	Stop walking behind me – it annoys me!
below	in a lower position	The people in the flat below us have got a dog.
beside	close to, touching	Dave and Alice live in a cottage beside the river.
besides	as well as	There are important things in life besides money.
between	with someone/thing either side	He was holding the ball between his feet.
by	1 (place) close to, touching 2 (time) at/on or before 3 means	Dave and Alice live in a cottage by the river. Arrive by 7.30 so we can get good seats. I'll contact you by phone or email.
despite	showing difference	We arrived on time despite the delays.

APPENDIX 1 GRAMMAR CHECK

PREPOSITION	POSSIBLE MEANINGS	EXAMPLE
down	in a lower position	They live down the hill.
except (for)	not including	Everyone has arrived except for Jane.
facing	opposite, looking out on	I'd love a house facing the sea.
for	1 (time) + a period 2 purpose 3 supporting	They've lived in the house for fifty years. You use a thesaurus for finding similar words. Are you for the government's proposals or not?
from	1 direction 2 origin 3 material	He came from the river. Naoko comes from Japan. The soup is made from the finest vegetables.
from ... to	period of time	The exam will last from 10.00 to 1.00.
in	1 (place) inside borders 2 (time) + month, year, etc. 3 (time) within a period	Bob's in the garden. The course starts in August. I'll be finished in five minutes.
in front of	in a position further forward	Lucas sits in front of the other students.
in spite of	showing difference	We arrived on time in spite of the delays.
into	direction (to somewhere)	Put the card into the slot, then key in your number.
like	comparison	Salma looks like her mother.
near	close to	If you play outside, stay near the house.
next to	close to, touching	Dave and Alice live in a cottage next to the river.
of	material	My coat is made of leather.
off	direction (down from somewhere)	Take your feet off the coffee table, please.
on	1 (place) above, touching 2 (time) + date, day 3 (AmE) + *the weekend*	The newspaper's on the sofa. My interview is on Friday, 13th July. Mom and Dad are coming to stay on the weekend.
onto	direction (up from somewhere)	Climb onto this wall – the view is lovely.
on top of	above and directly touching	The large saucepan is on top of the cooker.
opposite	looking towards each other	There's a café opposite the school.
out of	direction (away from somewhere)	Can you get the meat out of the oven?
over	in a higher position	The plane flew over the Alps.
past	from one side to the other	There's a delicious smell when you walk past that cake shop.
round/ around	in a circular movement	Go round the roundabout and take the third exit.
since	+ a point in time	Julian has worked here since 2005.
through	1 from one side to the other 2 (AmE) until/to	Have you ever been through the Channel Tunnel? He has to work from 8.00 through 6.30.
throughout	the whole time the whole place	I'm afraid I slept throughout the whole film. The fire spread throughout the building.
to	direction	Throw the ball to me.
towards	in the direction of	He turned round and walked towards the door.
under	in a lower position	I think the newspaper is under those books.
until (till)	to a later time	Don't move until I get back!
up	in a higher position	The newsagent's is up the street from here.
with	1 together 2 instrument	I went on holiday with my two best friends. The man was killed with a shotgun.
within	in a period of time	Can you do the job within a week?
without	not including, not having	I prefer tea without sugar.

Note: *after, as, before* and *since* can also be conjunctions of time:
I like to do some exercises **before** I go to bed. We started talking **as** we were waiting for the bus.

GRAMMAR CHECK APPENDIX 1

QUICK CHECK 3 MODULES 5, 6, 7 AND 8 Verb tenses

TENSE	USE	EXAMPLE	UNIT
present simple	facts/permanent situations	Water boils at 100°C.	27.2
	thoughts/feelings/opinions	I think New York is exciting.	27.2
	likes and dislikes	I prefer the city to the countryside.	27.2
	regular activities, routines	We usually start at eight o'clock.	27.3
	describing/telling stories	The film takes place in the US.	27.4
	describing states (state verbs)	They seem very nice.	29.3
present continuous	actions happening now (as we speak)	Hurry up! The taxi's waiting.	28.2
	temporary situations	Trudi's studying animal behaviour now.	28.2
	criticising someone	You're always losing your keys.	28.2
	changes and trends	The economy is getting worse.	28.3
	describing pictures	A woman is walking into the room.	28.4
past simple	finished actions in the past	I passed my driving test last week.	30.2
	repeated actions in the past	She phoned her parents every day.	30.2
	a series of past actions	We arrived in Rome and took a taxi to the apartment.	30.2
	past situations	He lived from 1500 to 1539.	30.2
past continuous	actions at around a time in the past	I wasn't feeling well that day.	31.2
	temporary situations in the past	We were living in Beijing at the time of the 2008 Olympics.	31.2
	one action interrupted by another action	The bus was going too fast and it hit the car.	31.3
	plans that did not happen	I was hoping to study medicine.	31.4
	a scene in the past	When we arrived, the sun was shining.	31.5
past perfect simple	an earlier action in the past	Before I found a job, I had been to thirty interviews.	34.2
	giving reasons for past actions/feelings	Emily was unhappy because her husband hadn't bought her a present.	34.4
past perfect continuous	continuing past actions that were happening before another action/time	Julia had been working in sales for two years when Phil joined the team.	35.2
	emphasising time	It had been selling well for ten years.	35.3
	giving reasons for past actions/feelings	He was tired as he'd been driving all afternoon.	35.3

APPENDIX 1 GRAMMAR CHECK

TENSE	USE	EXAMPLE	UNIT
present perfect	actions/experiences in our lives until now	My father has worked for several different companies.	36.2
	a past action with present results for recent events	They've gone out. (So they're not here now.)	36.4
	actions in a time period that is still continuing	The plane has just landed. I've driven 500 kilometres this week.	36.5 37.1
	repeated actions in the past (which may be repeated in the future)	We've been there many times. (We may go there again.)	37.2
	with *for* or *since* for situations that started in the past and continue now	He's worked here for ten years. I haven't seen Janice since Tuesday.	37.3
	giving news	The Terracotta Army exhibition has opened in London.	38.2
present perfect continuous	continuing actions/situations until now emphasising time	Clare's been living with her cousins. We've been waiting for hours!	39.2
	to explain a present situation	I'm wet because I've been washing the car.	39.3
future with *going to*	future plans	I'm going to be a doctor one day.	41.2
	things we expect to happen (because of something in the present)	It's raining. We're going to get soaked!	41.4
future with *will*	things we think will happen	In the future, people will live on other planets.	41.4
	certain future	New Year's Day will fall on a Tuesday next year.	41.5
	immediate decisions	I'm tired. I think I'll go to bed now.	41.6
	offers, promises and warnings	I'll get you a drink. What would you like?	41.7
future with present continuous	future arrangements	I've got the tickets. We're sitting in the front row.	41.2
	to say why we can't do something	I can't come. I'm working on Saturday.	41.2
future continuous	continuing actions at/around a time in the future	Come to the main door – we'll be waiting for you.	42.2
	future actions with possible results	I'll be meeting my friends after work so I may be home late.	42.3
	to ask polite questions about plans	Will we be stopping for a break?	42.4
future perfect	actions completed by a time in the future	We'll have got back to the hotel by seven o'clock.	43.3
future perfect continuous	continuing action up to a time in the future	By next Friday, I'll have been waiting for over two months.	43.4
	to explain the reason for a future situation	We'll have been skiing all day, so we'll be starving!	43.4
future with present simple	fixed future events (on timetables and schedules)	The Dallas flight arrives at 9.45.	44.1
	after *when*, *as soon as*, etc.	As soon as I get there, I'll phone you.	44.2
was/were going to (future in the past)	something that was in the future from the point of view of a time in the past	In 2005, they were going to build a supermarket here.	45.1
	something we expected to happen but which didn't happen	I was going to study medicine but my grades weren't good enough.	45.1

QUICK CHECK 4 MODULE 9 Modal verbs

VERB	USE	EXAMPLE	UNIT
able to	future ability or possibility	After you receive the password, you'll be able to log on to our website.	46.3
	past ability or possibility	We weren't able to get any cheap flights to Malaga.	46.4
can/can't	present ability	Can you speak Japanese?	46.2
	present possibility	You can use this phone anywhere in the world.	46.2
	arrangement	The dentist can see you on Friday.	46.3
	general truths	Bad weather can cause delays at any time.	46.5
	asking permission	Can I use your phone?	52.1
	negative rules	You can't smoke here.	49.3
can	requests	Can you help me with these bags?	53.1
can't	certain	It can't be her, she's on holiday.	47.1
can't + have + past participle	certain about the past	It can't have been her – she was on holiday.	48.2
could/ couldn't	past ability and possibility	Could the first cameras take colour photos?	46.4
	permission (formal)	Could we stay an extra night in the hotel?	52.1
	past permission/prohibition	In the 1960s, you could smoke in cinemas. You couldn't wear jeans at my old school.	52.3
could	possible but unlikely to happen	We could give up our jobs and live on a desert island.	46.3
	making a guess about the future	I could get a part-time job next summer.	47.2
	suggestion	We could watch a DVD.	53.2
	offer	I could get Lucy's present for you.	53.3
	requests (formal)	Could you help me with this?	53.1
	making a guess	There could be life on other planets. Who knows?	47.1
could + have + past participle	making a guess about the past	David could have overslept.	48.2
couldn't + have + past participle	almost certain about the past	Lester couldn't have been driving the car – he doesn't even own a car!	48.2
had to/ didn't have to	past action necessary/not necessary	We had to have lots of vaccinations when we went to Borneo last year.	49.2
		We didn't have to pay for the tickets. They were free.	50.4
have to/ don't have to	present action necessary/ not necessary	All car passengers have to wear a seat belt.	49.2
		You don't have to get a licence to ride a bicycle.	50.3

APPENDIX 1 GRAMMAR CHECK

VERB	USE	EXAMPLE	UNIT
had better (not)	advice and warnings in a particular situation	That looks hot. You'd better not touch it.	51.2
may/ may not	permission (formal)	May I leave early today?	52.1
	uncertain (present) making a guess about the future	The manager may be in a meeting. I'll just check. The tickets may not arrive in time.	47.1 47.2
might/ might not	uncertain (present) making a guess about the future	This small shop might not have batteries. If we wait a few days, the prices might be cheaper.	47.1 47.2
must/ must not	positive rules negative rules	All answers must be written in ink. These lights must not be used outdoors.	49.2 49.2
must	recommending something	You must try this cake – it's delicious!	51.2
must	certain (present)	It's not working. It must be the battery.	47.1
must + have + past participle	certain (past)	Everything's pink! You must have put something red in the washing machine.	48.2
need to/ don't need to/needn't	present action necessary/ not necessary	He really needs to lose weight. You needn't take any food. Lunch is provided.	50.2 50.3
needed to/ didn't need to	past action necessary/not necessary	Carl needed to go to hospital when he broke his leg. The pain went away so I didn't need to see a doctor.	50.2 50.4
needn't + have + past participle	past action that was taken but wasn't necessary	You needn't have taken a towel. The gym provides them free of charge.	50.4
ought to/ ought not to	advice	You look terrible. You ought to see a doctor. You ought not to sit in the sun all day.	51.2
shall	suggestion offer	Shall we get a pizza this evening? Your hands are wet. Shall I get you a towel?	53.2 53.3
should/ should not	expectations advice	Phone Henry at work. He should be in the office by now. Should I ask my boss for a pay rise?	47.3 51.2
should + have + past participle	expectations, regrets and criticism about the past	That letter should have arrived by now. I should have phoned you. I'm sorry. You shouldn't have bought such a cheap machine!	48.3 51.3 51.3
will	offers, promises, warnings	We'll drive you to the station, if you like. Don't touch the cooker. You'll get burnt.	53.3 53.3
would	requests (formal)	Would you tell the manager that I called?	53.1

343

GRAMMAR CHECK **APPENDIX 1**

QUICK CHECK 5 MODULE 10 **Conditionals**

CONDITIONAL	USE	EXAMPLE	UNIT
present conditions (zero conditional)	things that can happen at any time giving instructions for a situation	*If we talk to the baby, she smiles.* *If the lift breaks down, press the alarm button.*	54.1 54.1
first conditional (future conditions)	possible future situations offers and warnings	*If I don't see you at the gym, I'll call you.* *If you don't stop fighting, I'll stop you myself!*	54.2 54.2
second conditional (unlikely/unreal conditions)	unlikely future conditions unreal present conditions giving advice	*If I got a pay rise this year, I'd buy a new car.* *We wouldn't go abroad for our holidays if we had hot summers here.* *I'd get more exercise if I were you.*	55.2 55.3 55.4
third conditional (past conditions)	imaginary past actions and situations regrets	*If I hadn't got the job, I might have stayed in London.* *I could have got a better job if I'd stayed at university.*	56.2 56.3
mixed conditionals	present result of an imaginary past action imaginary past result of a present action	*If you hadn't had the operation, you could be really ill now.* *If I didn't believe you, I would have left you.*	57.1 57.2

QUICK CHECK 6 MODULE 12 Verbs + *-ing* form and infinitive

PATTERN	SAMPLE VERBS	EXAMPLE	UNIT
verb (+ preposition) + *-ing* form	admit avoid can't help can't stand consider delay deny dislike enjoy finish give up involve keep (not) mind miss practise put off recommend	Simon can't stand talking about politics. The politician denied talking to the press. Don't put off saving money.	64.1
verb + infinitive without *to*	modal verbs help	We can use the swimming pool after 8.00 a.m. I'll help pack your rucksack.	65.1
verb + object + infinitive without *to*	make let	They made the prisoners walk thirty kilometres. Our manager lets us work from home.	66.3
verb + infinitive with *to*	agree appear arrange can/can't afford deserve expect fail learn offer prepare promise refuse seem tend threaten wish	The letter failed to arrive on time. People round here tend not to go to bed early.	65.2
verb (+ object) + infinitive with *to*	ask beg dare expect help mean want would like/love/hate/prefer	I didn't intend (her) to spend so much money. They expect (you) to finish the work today.	66.1
verb + object + infinitive with *to*	advise allow cause encourage forbid invite order tell warn	We always encourage the students to plan their revision.	66.2
verb + infinitive or *-ing* (similar meanings)	begin continue hate intend like love prefer propose start	It's just started raining/to rain.	67.1
verb + infinitive or *-ing* (different meanings)	forget remember go on regret stop try	Vanya regrets not studying harder. We regret to inform you that you have not been called for interview.	67.2
sense verb + infinitive or *-ing* form	feel hear notice see watch	We saw the plane land. We saw the cars passing.	67.3

GRAMMAR CHECK APPENDIX 1

QUICK CHECK 7 MODULE 15 Linking words

TYPE OF LINKING	LINKING WORDS	EXAMPLES	UNIT
adds something	and both ... and not only ... (but ...)/ but ...also) as well as/in addition (to)	Dave turned the key and opened the door. We stock both gas and electric cookers. Not only does the machine wash your clothes, but it also dries them. She has a car as well as a bicycle.	80.1 80.1 80.1 80.2
shows a difference between two things	but while/whereas although/though/even though However, Nevertheless	The weather was cold but it didn't rain. While the food there is very good, it isn't expensive. We enjoyed our holiday even though it rained. Credit cards are useful for travellers. However, the interest rates can be very high.	81.1 81.1 81.2 81.3
gives a choice	or either ... or neither ... nor	Which do you prefer – tea or coffee? You can either come with me or stay here. She can neither sing nor dance.	80.3 80.3 80.3
gives a reason	because because of as/since	I don't use trains because they are too expensive. The show was cancelled because of the rain. As/Since we're late, we'd better get a taxi.	78.2 78.2 78.2
gives a result	As a result, Therefore, so so ... (that) such ... (that) too/enough	There was a hurricane. As a result, 80 percent of the city was flooded. Trains have become expensive. Therefore, more people are travelling by bus. I overslept so I was late for work. He ate so much (that) he was sick. There was such a lot of noise (that) I couldn't sleep. The lake is too cold to swim in. The lake isn't warm enough to swim in.	79.1 79.1 79.2 79.2 79.2 79.3 79.3
gives a purpose	to in order to/so as to in order that/so that	They flood the fields to protect the plants. I caught the earlier train in order not to be late for my interview. I'm buying a magazine so that I'll have something to read on the flight.	78.3 78.3 78.3
links times/events	before/after as soon as/when while until	We closed the shutters before we went down to the basement. As soon as we knew the storm was coming, we closed the shutters. I sent a lot of emails while I was on holiday. We stayed in the basement until the storm had passed.	82.1 82.1 82.1 82.1
shows a series of events	first then after that later in the end eventually	First, we closed the window shutters. Then we went down to the basement and waited there. Eventually, the storm passed over us and we were able to go back into the house. Later, we went outside and opened the window shutters.	82.2
shows stages in a process	First Then Next After that Finally	First, put the potatoes in boiling water. Then slice the tomatoes. Next, take an onion ...	82.2

346

APPENDIX 1 GRAMMAR CHECK

QUICK CHECK 8 MODULE 17 Verbs + prepositions

COMMON VERBS + PREPOSITIONS — UNIT 89.2

verb + *about*	complain about hear about know about read about talk about think about	British people often complain about the weather.
verb + *at*	arrive at laugh at look at shout at stay at	We're staying at a small hotel.
verb + *for*	apologise for apply for ask for care for look for pay for search for wait for work for	The Prime Minister apologised for Britain's involvement in the slave trade.
verb + *in*	arrive in believe in stay in succeed in	Do you believe in luck?
verb + *into*	bump into crash into drive into run into	I crashed into a tree on my bike and hurt my shoulder.
verb + *of*	approve of consist of hear of think of	What do you think of her new flatmate?
verb + *on*	concentrate on decide on depend on insist on rely on	The music is so loud that I can't concentrate on my work.
verb + *to*	belong to explain to happen to listen to speak to talk to write to	That house belongs to my uncle.
verb + *with*	agree with collide with deal with stay with	Ahmed's job is to deal with awkward customers.

VERB + OBJECT + PREPOSITION + OBJECT — UNIT 89.3

verb + *of*	accuse remind	The police accused the boy of stealing.
verb + *for*	ask blame criticise punish	Don't blame me for your mistakes!
verb + *with*	compare provide share	We will provide you with paper.
verb + *from*	borrow discourage prevent translate	Do you translate texts from English?

PREPOSITIONAL VERBS — UNIT 90.3

get over get through	Has your daughter got over the flu yet? I don't know how I got through that interview – it was really tough!
look after look into look like	Can you look after the children tomorrow evening? The police are looking into the woman's disappearance. The baby really looks like his father, doesn't he?
stand for	1 (= mean) What does BBC stand for? 2 (= accept) We won't stand for this kind of behaviour on the streets of our city!

QUICK CHECK 9 MODULE 18 Phrasal verbs

COMMON PHRASAL VERBS — UNIT 91

intransitive phrasal verbs	come in go out hurry up look out sit down stand up take off watch out	Look out! There's a car coming. The plane took off three hours late. Come in. We've been expecting you.
transitive phrasal verbs	give back give in give up make out make up turn down turn up	Why don't you give up smoking? They just make the rules up as they go along! Sorry, but I have to turn your kind offer down.
three-part phrasal verbs	cut down on keep up with look forward to make up for put up with	I'm looking forward to my holiday. I'll make up for missing your birthday. We can't put up with this behaviour.

APPENDIX 2

Common irregular verbs (1) A–Z list

INFINITIVE	PAST TENSE	PAST PARTICIPLE
be	was/were	been
beat	beat	beaten
become	became	become
begin	began	begun
break	broke	broken
bring	brought	brought
build	built	built
burn	burnt/burned	burnt/burned
buy	bought	bought
catch	caught	caught
choose	chose	chosen
come	came	come
cost	cost	cost
cut	cut	cut
dig	dug	dug
dive	dived	dived (dove AmE)
do	did	done
draw	drew	drawn
dream	dreamt/dreamed	dreamt/dreamed
drink	drank	drunk
drive	drove	driven
eat	ate	eaten
fall	fell	fallen
feel	felt	felt
fight	fought	fought
find	found	found
fly	flew	flown
forget	forgot	forgotten
forgive	forgave	forgiven
freeze	froze	frozen
get	got	got (gotten AmE)
give	gave	given
go	went	gone
grow	grew	grown
have	had	had
hear	heard	heard
hide	hid	hidden
hit	hit	hit
hold	held	held
hurt	hurt	hurt

INFINITIVE	PAST TENSE	PAST PARTICIPLE
keep	kept	kept
know	knew	known
learn	learnt/learned	learnt/learned
leave	left	left
lend	lent	lent
let	let	let
lose	lost	lost
make	made	made
mean	meant	meant
meet	met	met
pay	paid	paid
put	put	put
read	read	read
ride	rode	ridden
ring	rang	rung
rise	rose	risen
run	ran	run
say	said	said
see	saw	seen
sell	sold	sold
send	sent	sent
shine	shone	shone
show	showed	shown
sing	sang	sung
sit	sat	sat
sleep	slept	slept
speak	spoke	spoken
spell	spelt/spelled	spelt/spelled
spend	spent	spent
stand	stood	stood
steal	stole	stolen
swim	swam	swum
take	took	taken
teach	taught	taught
tell	told	told
think	thought	thought
throw	threw	thrown
understand	understood	understood
wear	wore	worn
win	won	won
write	wrote	written

Common irregular verbs (2) list of forms

1 Past tense form = past participle

INFINITIVE	PAST TENSE	PAST PARTICIPLE
buy	bought	bought
say	said	said
send	sent	sent
sleep	slept	slept
tell	told	told
win	won	won

2 Infinitive + (e)n

INFINITIVE	PAST TENSE	PAST PARTICIPLE
beat	beat	beaten
draw	drew	drawn
eat	ate	eaten
know	knew	known
see	saw	seen
take	took	taken

3 Past tense form + (e)n

INFINITIVE	PAST TENSE	PAST PARTICIPLE
break	broke	broken
choose	chose	chosen
forget	forgot	forgotten
hide	hid	hidden
speak	spoke	spoken

4 No change

INFINITIVE	PAST TENSE	PAST PARTICIPLE
cost	cost	cost
hit	hit	hit
hurt	hurt	hurt
put	put	put
read	read	read

* For *read*, the spelling doesn't change, but the pronunciation does: /riːd/ /red/ /red/

5 Vowel change

INFINITIVE	PAST TENSE	PAST PARTICIPLE
begin	began	begun
drink	drank	drunk
ring	rang	rung
swim	swam	swum

6 Two participle forms

INFINITIVE	PAST TENSE	PAST PARTICIPLE
burn	burnt/burned	burnt/burned
dream	dreamt/dreamed	dreamt/dreamed
learn	learnt/learned	learnt/learned
spell	spelt/spelled	spelt/spelled

APPENDIX 3

Spelling rules

1 Spelling of nouns/verbs + s
(plural nouns and present simple verbs after *he/she/it*)

most nouns and verbs	add -s	cat → cats house → houses eat → eats sleep → sleeps
nouns and verbs ending in -ch, -s, -sh, -x, -o	add -es	beach → beaches bus → buses dish → dishes box → boxes potato → potatoes teach → teaches miss → misses wash → washes go → goes
nouns and verbs that end in consonant + -y	take away -y and add -ies	city → cities family → families carry → carries fly → flies
nouns and verbs that end in vowel + -y	add -s	holiday → holidays key → keys enjoy → enjoys play → plays
nouns that end in -f or -fe	take away -f(e) and add -ves	wife → wives loaf → loaves (BUT roof → roofs)

2 Spelling of -ing forms of verbs

most verbs	add -ing to the infinitive form	eat → eating go → going sleep → sleeping
verbs that end in -e	take away -e and add -ing	take → taking use → using
verbs that end in -ie	take away -ie and add -ying:	lie → lying die → dying
verbs of one syllable that end in a short vowel + consonant	double the consonant and add -ing	swim → swimming sit → sitting
verbs with more than one syllable that end in a <u>stressed</u> short vowel and consonant (not y, w or x) e.g. be<u>gin</u>*	double the consonant and add -ing	begin → beginning forget → forgetting

*We don't normally repeat the consonant if the final syllable is not stressed: <u>vis</u>it → visiting.
BUT BrE: travel → travelling   AmE: travel → traveling

3 Spelling of regular verbs
(past simple endings and past participles)

verbs ending in -e	add -d	die → died live → lived like → liked
verbs ending in a consonant + y	take away -y and add -ied	carry → carried study → studied
verbs ending in a vowel + y	add -ed	enjoy → enjoyed play → played
verbs of one syllable that end in a short vowel + consonant	double the consonant and add -ed	stop → stopped plan → planned rob → robbed
verbs with more than one syllable that end in a <u>stressed</u> short vowel and one consonant (NOT y, w or x) e.g. pre<u>fer</u>*	double the consonant and add -ed	prefer → preferred

*We don't normally repeat the consonant if the final syllable is not stressed: <u>vis</u>it → visited.
BUT BrE: travel → travelled   AmE: travel → traveled

4 Spelling of comparative adjectives

most short adjectives	add -er	tall → tall**er** rich → rich**er**
most short adjectives ending in e	add -r	nice → nic**er** late → lat**er**
short adjectives ending in one vowel + one consonant (except w)	double the consonant, add -er	big → bi**gger** hot → ho**tter** (slow → slow**er** low → low**er**)
short adjectives ending in consonant + y	change y to i, add -er	dry → dr**ier** funny → funn**ier**

5 Spelling of superlative adjectives

most short adjectives	add -est	tall → tall**est** rich → rich**est**
short adjectives ending in e	add -st	nice → nice**st** late → late**st**
short adjectives ending in one vowel + one consonant (except w)	double the consonant, add -est	big → bi**ggest** hot → ho**ttest** (slow → slow**est** low → low**est**)
short adjectives ending in consonant + y	change y to i, add -est	dry → dr**iest** lucky → luck**iest**

APPENDIX 4
British and American English

Group nouns + verb ➤ Unit 1

In informal British English, nouns we use to describe groups, e.g. *government, family, company, team*, can be followed by a singular or plural verb.
My family is/are quite wealthy.
In American English and more formal British English we usually use a singular verb:
The Federal government is announcing new taxes.

at/on the weekend ➤ Unit 16

BrE: **at** the weekend
*What are you doing **at** the weekend?*
AmE: **on** the weekend
*We're visiting our cousins in Ohio **on** the weekend.*

to/through ➤ Unit 16

BrE: **from** (day/date) **to** (day/date)
*The shop will be closed **from Wednesday to Friday**.*
AmE: (day/date) **through** (day/date)
*The shop will be closed **Wednesday through Friday**.*

different to/from/than ➤ Unit 22

BrE: different **from**/**to**:
*CDs are **different from** DVDs. CDs don't have films on them.*
AmE: different **than**:
*Text messages are **different than** emails.*

have/have got ➤ Unit 26

We can use *have got* in American English but *have* is more common.
BrE: **Has** your house **got** a garden?
AmE: **Does** your house **have** a garden?

have/take a shower ➤ Unit 26

BrE: **have** a shower/bath/holiday
*Jack can't come to the phone; he's **having** a shower.*
AmE: **take** a shower/bath/holiday
*Jack can't come to the phone; he's **taking** a shower.*

just/already/yet ➤ Unit 36

In British English we usually use the present perfect with *just*, *already* and *yet*. We don't use the past simple.

✓ *We've **just finished** eating.*	✗ *We just finished eating.*
✓ *Graham's train **has already arrived**.*	✗ *Graham's train already arrived.*
✓ ***Have** you **seen** that film **yet**?*	✗ *Did you see that film yet?*

In American English we can use the present perfect OR the past simple:

✓ *We've **just finished** eating.*	✓ *We **just finished** eating.*
✓ *Graham's train **has already arrived**.*	✓ *Graham's train **already arrived**.*
✓ ***Have** you **seen** that film **yet**?*	✓ ***Did** you **see** that film **yet**?*

would have ➤ Unit 56

In British English we form the third conditional with *If* + past perfect, *would have* + infinitive:
If I'd known, I would have phoned you.

In informal American English we can also use *would have* in the *If* clause:
If I would have known, I would have phoned you.

Index

A
a/an 6, 8, 10
a bit 58, 62, 64, 68
a few 30
a little 30, 58, 62, 64, 68
a lot 4, 62
a lot of 30, 240
a whole 32
ability
   adjective + preposition: *good at* 268
   future: *be able to* 138, 139
   future: *can* 139
   past: *could/couldn't* 139
   past: *managed to* 139
   past: *was/were able to* 139
   present: *be able to* 138, 139
   present: *can/can't* 138, 139
-able adjectives 292
about 348
   adjective + *about* 268
   be about to + verb 132
   How/What about? 154
   verb + *about* 270, 272, 347
above 41, 338
across 44, 64, 338
action verbs 82
active forms 226, 228
add in reported speech 212
addition in addition (to) 242, 306
adjectives 56–60
   + adverbs of degree 58
   + *enough* 240
   + noun 56, 266
   + preposition 268
   of age 58
   as + adjective + *as* 62
   changing into nouns 290
   changing into verbs 294
   of colour 58
   comparative adjectives 60, 62, 351
   compound adjectives 296
   confusing adjectives 282
   demonstrative adjectives 12
   -ed form 56
   emphasising 330
   formation 292, 296
   How? + adjective 186
   -ing form 56
   of material 58
   of nationality 8, 58, 290
   of opinion 58
   of origin 58
   possessive adjectives 20, 338
   prefixes 292
   of purpose 58
   the same (as) 62
   of shape 58
   of size 58
   suffixes 292
   superlative adjectives 60, 98, 110, 224, 353
   the + adjective + *one(s)* 22
   too + adjective 240
   of type 58
   used as nouns 8
   verbs + adjective 56
   word order 58, 240
admit 192, 212
advance: *in advance* 50
adverbials 176, 177
adverbs 64–8
   + *enough* 240
   already 107
   as + adverb + *as* 68
   certainly 123
   comparative adverbs 68
   definitely 123
   of degree 58, 62, 64
   of direction 64
   emphasising 330
   of frequency 64, 66, 96
   irregular adverbs 64
   just 107
   of manner 64, 66, 68
   of place 64, 66
   probably 123
   in speech 328
   superlative adverbs 68
   of time 64, 66, 90
   too + adverb 240
   verb + adverb 66
   very 58, 64
   word order 66, 240
   yet 107
advice
   had better 150
   If I were/was you 164
   must 150
   ought to 150
   reporting verbs 210
   should 150
advise 196, 210, 212
after 90, 130, 246, 338
After that, 246, 306
afterwards 246
against 40, 338
age 58, 186
ago 90
agree (to) 194, 212
agreeing and disagreeing 154, 326
agreement
   noun–verb 2

question tags 322
-al adjectives 292
all 26, 32
all of 26
allow 196
allowed to 146, 152
almost as ... as 62
along 44, 338
already 107
although 244
always 66, 80
am 76
am to + verb 132
American English 352–3
among 41, 62, 338
amusing or *enjoyable* 282
an see *a/an*
-an nouns 290
and 242, 306
animals, referring to 218
announce 212
another (one) 22
   one another 24
-ant nouns 290
any 26
   anybody 28
   anyone 28
   anything 28
   Anyway, 328
   anywhere 28
apart from 40, 48, 338
apologise for 212
apostrophe (') 302
appear 83, 194
are 76
   are to + verb 132
   are you? 322
   aren't I/they? 76, 322
around 348
arrangements 126, 194
arrive at 272
articles
   definite: *the* 6, 8, 10, 60, 68
   indefinite: *a/an* 6, 8, 10
   no article 6, 10
   pronunciation 6
as
   as + adjective + *as* 62
   as + adverb + *as* 68
   or *like* 48
   as long as 162
   for reason 238
   As a result, 240, 306
   in the role of 338
   so as to 238
   as soon as 130, 246
   as well as 242
   or *while* 94

ask
   ask for 272
   ask to 194, 196
   in reported speech 210, 212
at
   + noun phrases 50
   adjective + *at* 268
   movement 44, 338
   place 40, 338
   time 46, 64, 338
   verb + *at* 270, 347
at (@) 302
-ate verbs 294
-ation nouns 290
auxiliary verbs see *be*; *do*; *have*
away from 40, 338

B

bad 60, 266, 268
be 76, 83
   + infinitive clause 228
   be able to 138, 139
   be allowed to 146, 152
   be going to 122, 123, 132, 341
   be used to doing 96
   for future 132
   for passive 252
   past participle 106
   past simple 90
   present simple 76, 132
   question forms 76
   there + be 180
   Yes/No questions 182
because/because of 40, 238
been 106
before
   + *-ing* 246
   future events/time 130
   order of events 107, 246, 338
beg 196, 212
begin 192, 198
beginning: *at the beginning (of)* 50
behaviour 268
behind 338
beliefs 83, 290
believe 83, 272
belong 83
below 41, 338
beside 41, 338
besides 48, 338
best: *the best* 60, 68
better 60, 68
   had better (not) 150
between 41, 338
bit: *a bit* 58, 62, 64, 68
both 32, 242
   both ... and 242, 306
   both of 32

brackets ( ) 302
bring or *take* 280
British and American English 352–3
business: *on business* 50
but 244, 306
by
  + noun phrases 50
  adjective + *by* 268
  by far 62
  by means of 40, 48
  by myself/himself 24
  means 338
  passive + *by* 252
  place 40, 41, 338
  time 46, 338
  By the way, 328

C

can 138
  ability 138, 139
  after *so that* 238
  arrangements 139
  general truths 139
  get something done 258
  permission 152
  possibility 138, 139
  pronunciation 138
  reported statements 204
  requests 154
cannot/can't
  ability 138
  cannot/can't have 144
  can't he? 322
  can't help + -ing 192
  making a guess 142
  possibility 138, 139
  prohibition 146, 152
  pronunciation 138
  rules 146
capital letters 2, 302
care for 272
case: *in case* 162
cause
  have something done 258
  linking words 240
cause 196
certain to 132
certainly 123
certainty
  definitely 123
  going to 122, 123
  must be 142
  probably 123
chance: *by chance* 50
charge: *in charge (of)* 50
choice: *linking words* 242
claim 212

clauses
  comparison clauses 230
  infinitive clauses 224, 228
  linking words 238, 306
  main clauses 238
  participle clauses 226
  relative clauses 218–24
  subordinate clauses 238
  wh- clauses 230
collocations 266
colon (:) 302
come 106
  come across 272
  Come in, 274
  come or *go* 280
comma (,) 222, 302, 306
comparative adjectives 60, 62, 351
comparative adverbs 68
comparative structures 62
comparison clauses with nouns 230
complain (about) 212
complements 176
compound adjectives 296
compound nouns 18, 296
conditionals 162–70, 344
  advice 164
  first conditional 162
  future conditions 162
  mixed past to present 168
  mixed present to past 168
  participle clauses 226
  past conditions 166
  present/real conditions 162
  regrets 166
  second conditional 164
  third conditional 166
  unlikely future conditions 164
  unreal past conditions 166
  unreal present conditions 164
  zero conditional 162
conjunctions *see* linking words
Consequently, 306
consider 192, 212
consonants 6
contain 83
containers: uncountable nouns 3
continue 192, 198
contractions *see* short forms
contrary: *On the contrary,* 306
contrast: linking words 244
could/couldn't 138
  conditional situations 139, 166
  couldn't help + -ing 198
  future possibility 139
  indirect questions 323
  making a guess 142, 144
  offers 154
  passive form 256

past ability/possibility/truths 139
permission 152
reported statements 204
requests 154
suggestions 154
uncertainty 142
could/couldn't have 144, 166
countable nouns 3, 332
cut down (on) 274, 275

D

damaged 282
dare (object) *to* 196
dash (–) 302
dates: *It's …* 180
days: *It's …* 180
decisions: *I'll …* 123
definite article: *the* 6, 8, 10, 60, 68
definitely 123
demonstrative adjectives 12
demonstrative pronouns 12
describing events/process 246
despite 244, 238
did he? 322
didn't have to 146
different (from/to) 62, 268, 352
different (than) 352
direct objects 177
direct questions 182–6, 323
direct speech 204, 302
dis- adjectives 292
dis- verbs 294
disagreeing 326
distances: *It's …* 180
do
 do + the/some + -ing form 192
 do/don't 76
 do or *make* 278
 do they? 322
 in indirect questions 323
Do you mind if … ? 152
does/doesn't 76
 doesn't she? 322
don't have to 146, 148
don't need to 148, 198
dot (.) 302
down 275, 339
due to 40, 132
during 46, 246, 338

E

each 32
each other 24
early 64, 68
earth: *How/What on earth?* 330
-ed adjectives 56
-ed form of verb 90, 98, 106, 224, 226, 352

-ee nouns 290
either 32
 after negative verb 326
 either … or 32, 242, 306
else 28
email addresses 302
emphasis 308, 330
-en verbs 294
encourage 196, 212
end
 at the end of 50
 in the end 50, 139, 246, 306
enjoy + -ing form 192
enjoyable or *amusing* 282
enough 240
 not enough 30, 240
-ent adjectives 292
-ent nouns 290
-er comparative adjectives 60, 351
-er nouns 290
-ese nouns 290
-est superlative adjectives 60, 351
even if 162
even though 244
eventually 139, 246
ever
 for ever 50
 hardly ever 66
 Have you ever … ? 106
every 32
 everybody 26, 28
 everyone 26, 28
 everything 28
 everywhere 28
except (for) 48, 339
exclamation mark (!) 302
exclamations 328
expect so 326
expect to 132, 194, 196
expectations 142, 144, 256
expensive or *valuable* 282
extremely 58, 64

F

facing 339
fact: *the fact that* 244
fairly 58, 64
far 60
 + comparative adjectives 62, 68
 by far 62
 so far 110
far or near? (*this* or *that?*) 12
farther 60, 68
farthest: *the farthest* 60, 68
fast 64, 68
feel 83, 198
 feel like 272
feelings 83, 180, 268, 328

357

few 224, 228
  a few 30
  so few + plural noun 240
Finally, 139, 306
fire: *on fire* 50
First
  describing past events 246
  the first 110, 224, 228
first conditional 162
for
  + indirect object 177
  + noun phrases 50
  + past perfect continuous 100
  + past simple 90
  + present perfect continuous 114
  + present perfect simple 110
  + subject + infinitive with *to* 228, 240
  noun + *for* 268, 339
  or *to* 177
  preposition 40, 46, 48, 268
  For this reason, 306
  verb + *for* 270, 272, 347
forbid 196
force 196
forget 83, 194, 198
formal language 314
forward: *look forward to* 192, 274
frequency
  adverbs 64, 66, 96
  How often? 64, 66, 68
  present simple 78
frequently 66, 68
friendly 64
from
  + material 48, 339
  away from 40, 339
  different from 62
  (*from*) … *to* 90, 339, 352
  (*from*) … *until* 46
front: *in front of* 40, 41
-ful adjectives 292
full stop (.) 302
further 60, 68
Furthermore, 306
furthest: *the furthest* 60, 68
future forms 122–32, 341
  ability 138, 139
  arrangements 126, 194
  certainty 123
  conditions 162, 164
  decisions 123
  events 130
  expressions 132
  future continuous 126, 341
  future in the past 132, 341
  future perfect continuous 128, 341
  future perfect simple 128
  going to 122, 132, 341

  linking words 130
  necessity 146
  offers, promises, warnings 123
  plans 126
  possibility 126, 139
  predictions 123
  present continuous 122, 341
  present simple 130, 132, 341
  probability 123
  verbs in present tense 132
  will 123, 341
-fy verbs 294

G

get 278
  get over 272, 347
  get somebody to do something 258
  get something done 258
  get through 272, 347
  get used to doing 96
  for passive 252
give in 275
give up 192, 275
go 106
  go + *-ing* form 192
  go for 272
  go on 198, 274
  go or *come* 280
going to 122, 123, 132, 341
good 60, 266, 268
  for good 50
got: *have got* 76, 83, 146, 148
great + noun 266

H

had 106, 204
had better/had better not 150
had to/didn't have to 146, 210
happen to 272
hard 64, 68
hardly ever 66
hate 83, 192, 198
  I'd hate (object) *to* 194, 196
have 76
  + noun + preposition 266
  have got 76, 83
  have got to/haven't got to 146, 148
  have or *take* 278
  have somebody do something 258
  have something done 250, 258
  have they? 322
  have to/don't have to 146, 148
  will have to 146
having 83
  + past participle 192, 226
he 20
hear 83, 198
heavy + noun 266

help 194
   can't/couldn't help + *-ing* 192, 198
   help (object) *to* 194, 196, 198
her
   object pronoun 24
   possessive adjective 20
hers 20
herself 24
high 64, 68
him 24
himself 24
his 20
holiday: *on holiday* 50
honest: *to be honest,* 228, 328
hope
   hope so 326
   hope to 132, 194
   I hope not. 326
   was/were hoping 92
How? 64, 184, 186
   + adjective 186
   How about ... ? 154
   How long? 110
   How much? 64
   How often? 64, 66, 68
   How old? 186
   How on earth? 330
How + adjective! 328
However, 244, 306
However? 330
Hurry up! 274
hurt 282
hyphen (-) 302

I

I 20
I don't know 323
I mean, 332
I (don't) think so 326
I wonder 323
-ian nouns 290
-iate verbs 294
ideas 192, 328
if
   advice 164
   alternatives 162, 164
   even if 162
   if + past perfect, *would (not)* + *have* + past participle 166
   if + past perfect, *would (not)*+ infinitive 168
   if + past simple, *could/would (not)* + *have* + past participle 168
   if + past simple, *would (not)* + infinitive 164
   if + present tense, present tense 162
   if + present, *will/won't* + infinitive without *to* 162
   If I were/was you ... 164
   indirect questions 323

   reporting requests 210
if only 170
-ify verbs 294
il- adjectives 292
I'll 123
im- adjectives/verbs 292
I'm afraid ... 323
I'm not sure 323
imagine 164, 192
imperatives 162, 228, 246
in
   + noun phrases 50
   movement 268
   noun + *in* 268
   place 40, 339
   time 46, 339
   verb + *in* 270, 275, 347
in- adjectives/nouns/verbs 292
in addition (to) 242, 306
in case 162
in front of 40, 41, 349
in love (with) 50
in order that 238
in order to 238
in spite of 40, 244, 349
in the end 50, 139, 246, 306
in time 50
indefinite article: *a/an* 6, 8, 10
indefinite pronouns 28
indirect objects 177
indirect questions 323
indirect speech
   indirect questions 323
   reported statements 204–5
   reporting verbs for orders, requests, advice 210, 212
infinitive clauses 224, 228
infinitive with/without *to* 194, 196
informal language 275, 314
information
   adding information 242
   asking for information 184
   giving alternatives 242
   question tags 322
   reporting information 6, 204–5, 253
   showing differences 244
   Wh- questions 184, 186
   in writing 310
-ing form
   adjectives 56
   after/before + *-ing* 246
   need + *-ing* form 198, 258
   as object 192
   in participle clauses 226
   passive forms 252
   past continuous 92
   present continuous 80

    in reduced relative clauses 224
    spelling 350
    as subject 192
    verb + *-ing* form 192, 224, 345
    verb + preposition + *-ing* form 192
injured 282
insist: *insist on* 212
instructions
    imperatives 162, 228, 246
    infinitive clauses 228
    linking words 246
    modal passives 256
    must/must not 146
    reporting instructions 210
intend 196, 198
inter- verbs 294
interrupted actions 92, 94
into 44, 270, 339
    verb + *into* 296, 347
intonation
    compound nouns 296
    for emphasis 330
    question tags 322
    reply questions 323
    short answers 326
    Wh- questions 184
    Yes/No questions 182
    see also pronunciation
intransitive verbs 176
inverted commas (") 302
invite 196, 212
-ion nouns 290
ir- adjectives 292
irregular forms
    adverbs 64
    comparative adjectives 60
    comparative adverbs 68
    plural nouns 2
    superlative adjectives 60
    superlative adverbs 68
    verbs 90, 106, 348–9
is 76
    is he/she? 322
    Is it all right if … ? 152
    Is it OK to … ? 152
    is to + verb 132
    isn't he/she? 322
-ise verbs 294
-ish adjectives 290
-ist nouns 290
it
    for emphasis 308
    as object 24
    as subject 20, 180
    and *there* 180
it's (= *it is*) 20
    + adjective/noun + *to* 180
    it's and *there is* 180

    It's time + past tense 170
its (possessive adjective) 20
itself 24
-ive adjectives 292
-ize verbs 294

J
jobs 8, 290
just 107

K
keep 192, 280
    keep on + *-ing* 192
    keep up with 274
kind
    kind of 332
    kind to 268
know 83
    I don't know 323
    You know, 332

L
languages 10, 290
last 228
    at last 50
    last for 46
    last week 64
late 64, 68
later 246
latest: *at the latest* 50
least
    at least 50
    the least 60, 68, 230
leave 280
    leave out 275
left
    be left 280
    left out 275
    on the left 40
less 60, 68
-less adjectives 292
let 196
Let's + infinitive 154
light + noun 266
like 83, 192, 198
    feel like 272
    I'd like (object) *to …* 194, 196
    look like 272, 349
    or *as* 48
    What is it like? 186
likeable or *sympathetic* 282
likely to 132
linking words 238–46, 346
    adding information 242
    for causes 240
    for choice 242

for contrast 244
describing a process 246
for future 130
for instructions 246
joining clauses 238, 306
joining sentences 246, 306
for purpose 238
for reason 238
for results 240
for sequence 98, 246
showing differences 244
for time 246
in writing 306
listen to 272
listener responses 332
lists 302
little
  a little 30, 58, 62, 64, 68
  so little 240
live or *stay* 280
lonely 64
long 64, 68
  How long? 110
  as long as 162
look after 272, 347
look at 272
look for 270
look forward to 192, 274
look into 272, 347
look like 272, 347
Look out! 274
lot
  a lot 62, 64, 68
  a lot of 30, 240
lots of 30
love 83, 192, 198
  I'd love (object) *to* 194, 196
  in love (with) 50
lovely 64
low 64, 68
-ly adverbs 64

M

main clauses 238
make 90
  + noun (+ preposition) 266
  + object + infinitive without *to* 196
  make out/up/up for 275
  or *do* 278
making a guess
  about the future 142
  about the past 144, 256
  about the present 142
  expectations 142
managed to 139
many 30
  so many 240
  too many 30

may (not) 138
  making a guess 142
  permission 152
  possibility 142
  prohibition/rules 152
  uncertainty 142
me 24
mean 83, 196
  I mean, 332
means: *by means of* 40
meant to 144, 260
measurement 3, 10
media 8
-ment nouns 290
mental states/activity 194
might (not) 138
  making a guess 142
  possibility 142
might (not) have 144, 166
  passive form 256
might: permission 152
mind
  Do you mind if … ? 152
  (*not*) *mind + -ing* 192
mine 20
mis- verbs 294
miss
  + *-ing* form 192
  + noun 266
mistake: *by mistake* 50
Mmm. 332
modal verbs 138–54, 342–3
  + infinitive 194
  ability 138–9
  advice 150
  certainty and uncertainty 142
  criticism 150
  expectations 142, 144, 256
  instructions 146
  making a guess 142–4
  necessity 146, 148
  offers 154
  passive forms 256
  past tenses 144
  permission 152
  possibility 138–9
  present tenses 142, 144
  prohibition 142, 152
  promises 154
  regrets 150
  in reported speech 204
  requests 154
  rules 146, 152, 256
  suggestions 154
  warnings 150, 154
  Yes/No questions 182
more 60, 68

most 26
   the most + adjective 60
   the most + noun 230
   most of 26
   (the) most + adverb 68
movement: prepositions 40, 44
much 30
   + comparatives 62, 68
   + uncountable noun 30
   How much? 64
   so much 240
   too much 30
   (very) much 64
must 138
   advice 150
   have something done 250
   instructions 146
   making a guess 142
   must be 142
   necessity 146
   opinion 142
   passive form 256
   reported statements 204
   rules 146
   warning 150
must (not) have 144
must not/mustn't
   advice 150
   instructions 146
   prohibition 146
   reported statements 204
   rules 146
   warning 150
my 20
myself 24

N

-n verbs 294
names 10
nationalities 8, 58, 290
near 41, 64, 68, 339
near or far? (*this* or *that?*) 12
nearly: *not nearly as … as* 62
necessity
   future: *will have to* 146
   past: *didn't have to* 148
   past: *didn't need to* 148
   past: *had to* 146
   past: *needn't have* 148
   present: *have to/don't have to* 146, 148
   present: *haven't got to* 148
   present: *must* 146
   present: *need to/don't need to* 148
need 83
   + *-ing* form 198, 258
need to/don't need to 148, 196, 198
needn't/needn't have 148

negative forms
   cannot/can't 138, 144
   could not/couldn't 139, 144, 166
   future continuous 126
   future perfect continuous 128
   future perfect simple 128
   future with *going to* 122
   future with *will* 123
   have 76
   modal verbs 138, 144
   needn't/needn't have 148
   nothing 28
   past continuous 92
   past perfect continuous 100
   past perfect simple 98
   past simple 90
   present continuous 80
   present perfect continuous 114
   present perfect simple 106
   present simple 78
   present simple: *be* 76
   present simple: *have/have got* 76
   question tags 322
   questions 182
   reporting orders, requests, advice 210
   rules 146, 152
   used to 96
   wasn't/weren't able to 139
neither 32, 308
   neither … nor 32, 242, 306, 308
   Neither am I./Neither do I. 242, 323, 326
-ness nouns 290
never 64, 66, 100, 106, 308
Nevertheless, 244, 306
next 228
   next to 40, 41, 339
no 26
No! 328
no one 26, 28
nobody 26, 28
none 26
none of 26
nor: *neither … nor* 32, 242, 306, 308
normally 66
not
   I hope not. 326
   not as … as 62
   not enough 30, 240
   not only 242, 306, 308
nothing 28
noun clauses *see wh-* clauses
noun phrases
   avoiding repetition 304
   used instead of verbs 312
nouns 2–3
   adjective + noun 56, 266
   avoiding repetition 304
   changing nouns into adjectives 292

changing nouns into verbs 294
comparison clauses 230
compound nouns 18, 296
countable nouns 3, 332
emphasising 330
formation 290, 296, 312
-ing form as noun subject/object 192
noun + noun 296
noun + preposition 268
noun + *'s/'* 18
noun–verb agreement 2
of + noun 18
plural 2, 350
possessive forms 18
prefixes 292
singular 2
suffixes 290, 312
uncountable nouns 3, 332
used instead of verbs 312
now or then? (*this* or *that*?) 12
nowhere 28

O

object
  direct object 177
  indirect objects 177
  -ing form as object 192
  it as an object 24
  object pronouns 24, 338
  object questions 184
  relative pronoun as object 219
  verb + object + infinitive 196
  verb (+ object) + preposition + object 270, 346
  verb + two objects 177
  wh- clauses 230
obligation *see* rules
Obviously, 328
occasionally 66
of
  + noun + *'s* 20
  adjective + *of* 268
  both of 32
  material 339
  noun + *of* 268
  verb + *of* 48, 270, 347
off 44, 275, 339
offer to 194, 212
offers
  future condition 162
  I/we could 154
  Shall I/we? 154
  shall/will 123, 154
often
  How often? 64, 66
  more often 68
omitting words/phrases 304
on
  + noun phrases 50, 330
  place 40, 41, 339
  time 46, 339
  verb + *on* 270, 347
On the contrary, 306
on top of 40, 41, 339
once (= *when*) 128
one 228
  = people in general 24
  another one 22
  one another 24
  one of 62
  one/ones 22
  the other one(s) 22
only 228
  not only 242, 306, 308
onto 44, 339
opposite 41, 339
or 242, 306
-or nouns 290
order
  + object + *to* 196
  in order that/to 238
  out of order 50
  in reported speech 212
order of events 98, 246
orders in reported statements 210
other
  each other 24
  the other one(s) 22
ought to/ought not to 150
  reported statements 210
our 20
ours 20
ourselves 24
-ous adjectives 292
out 275
  Look out! 274
out- verbs 294
out of 40, 44, 50, 339
over 41, 44, 339
  get over 272
over- verbs 294
own 83
  a/an + noun + *of my own* 20

P

parentheses ( ) 302
participle clauses 226
passive forms 252–60
  be + past participle 252
  by + noun 252
  common uses 253
  get + past participle 252
  get something done 258
  have something done 258
  modal verbs 256
  -ing forms 252
  in participle clauses 226

past tenses 252
perfect tenses 252
phrasal verbs 256
present tenses 252
reasons for using 253
reporting verbs 260
verb + object(s) 252
verb + preposition 256
verbs + two objects 256
will and infinitives 252
in writing 253
past 44, 339
past conditions 166
past continuous 92, 340
modal verbs 144
passive 252
or past perfect continuous? 100
or past simple? 94
reported statements 204
past experiences 106
past participles 98, 106, 350
irregular forms 106, 348–9
regular forms 350
past perfect continuous 100, 340
past perfect 98, 340
+ superlative adjectives 98
passive 252
or past perfect continuous? 100
or past simple? 98
past simple 90, 340
+ adverbs of time 90
be 90
for + period of time 90
from ... to 90
irregular verbs 90, 348–9
modal verbs 144
passive 252
or past continuous? 94
or past perfect simple? 98
or present perfect simple? 112
regular verbs 90, 350
reported statements 204
then 246
time expressions 90
or *used to*? 96
past tenses 90–100, 340
irregular verbs 348–9
linking words 246
passive 252
past continuous 92, 100, 340
past simple 90, 94, 98, 112, 340, 350
used to 96
period (.) 302
permission
be allowed to 152
can/can't 152
could/couldn't 152
in the future 152

might 152
permit 196
Personally, 328
persuade 196, 212
phrasal verbs 274–5, 347
passive form 256
phrases: order in writing 310
place
adverbs 64, 66
prepositional phrases 50, 176, 177
prepositions 40–1
in reported statements 204
place names 10
plan
plan to 194
was/were planning 92
plans and arrangements 126, 194
please 154
plural nouns 2, 350
point (.) 302
politeness
indirect questions 323
please 154
possess 83
possessives
adjectives 20, 338
nouns 18
pronouns 20, 338
in reported statements 205
's/' 18
possibility
future: *can* 139
future conditional 139
future continuous 126
future: *could* 139
future: *will/won't be able to* 139
general truths 139
may 142
might 142
past: *could/couldn't* 139
past: *was/were able to* 139
present: *can/can't* 138
predictions 123
prefer 83, 192, 198
I'd prefer (object) *to* 194, 196
prefixes 292, 294
prepositional phrases 50, 176, 177
prepositional verbs 272, 347
passive forms 256
and phrasal verbs 274
prepositions 40–50, 338–9
adjective + preposition 268
as adverbs 40
in American English 352
of instrument 40
of means 40
of movement 40, 44
of place 40–1

of purpose 40
in relative clauses 219, 222
instead of relative clauses 224
of time 40, 46
verb + preposition 219, 270, 272, 347
with other meanings 48
present conditions 162
present continuous 80, 340
describing pictures 80
for future 122, 341
passive 252
or present simple? 82–3
time expressions 80
verbs not using 83
present perfect continuous 114, 341
or present perfect simple? 116
present perfect 106–12, 341
with *ever, never, before* 106–7
with *for, since* etc. 110
with *just, already, recently* 107
for new information 112
passive 252
for past experiences 106–7
or past simple? 112
or present perfect continuous? 116
with present results 107
for repeated actions 110
reported statements 204
for situations up to the present 110
with *still, yet* 107
with superlative adjectives 110
with time expressions 110
present simple 76–8, 340
be 76, 132
can/can't 138
describing films, plays and books 78
facts, permanent situations and opinions 78
for future 130, 132, 341
have/have got 76
negative 78
passive 252
positive 78
or present continuous? 82–3
questions 78
regular actions, habits and routines 78
spelling 350
present tenses 76–83, 340
passive 252
present continuous 80, 340
present simple 76–8, 340
pretty (= *rather*) 58
private: *in private* 50
probably 123
prohibition 146, 152
promises
promise to 194
will 123, 154

pronouns 20–4, 338
another (*one*) 22
demonstrative pronouns 12
indefinite pronouns 28
object pronouns 24, 338
one/ones 22
possessive pronouns 20, 338
reflexive pronouns 24, 338
relative pronouns 218, 219, 224
in reported statements 205
in short answers 182, 322
subject pronouns 20, 338
pronunciation
the 6
Could you … ? 323
Do you … ? 323
-ed form of verb 90
going to 122
of punctuation 302
weak/strong forms 138
see also intonation
provided 162
public: *in public* 50
punctuation 204, 222, 302
purpose
infinitive clauses 228
linking words 238
prepositions 40
on purpose 50
put 90
put off + *-ing* 192
put up with 275

Q

quantifiers
all 26, 32
any 26
both 32, 242, 306
each 32
either 32
every 32
a few 30
a little 30
a lot of 30
many 30
most 26
much 30
neither 32
no 26
none 26
none of 26
not enough 30, 240
some 26
question mark (?) 302
question: *out of the question* 50
question tags 322
questions
alternative questions (*or*) 242

with *be* 76
can 138
closed questions 182
could/couldn't 144
direct questions 182–6, 323
emphasising 330
future continuous 126
future perfect continuous 128
future perfect simple 128
future with *going to* 122
future with *will* 123
have 76
have something done 258
How? 64, 184, 186
indirect questions 323
for information 184
modal verbs 138, 144
negative questions 182
object questions 184
open questions 184, 186
past continuous 92
past perfect continuous 100
past perfect simple 98
past simple 90
present continuous 80
present perfect continuous 114
present perfect simple 106
present simple 76, 78
reply questions 323
reported questions 208
should 144
spoken forms 322–3
subject questions 184
used to 96
Wh- questions 184, 186
word order 182, 184, 323
Yes/No questions 182, 322
quite
  + adjective/adverb 58, 64
  not quite as … as 62
quotation marks (" ") 204, 302

R

rarely 66
  more rarely 68
rather
  + adjective/adverb 58, 64
  would rather + infinitive without *to* 194
  would rather + past tense 170
re- verbs 294
real conditions 162
really 58, 64, 330
Really? 328, 332
reason
  + past perfect continuous 100
  + past perfect simple 98
  infinitive clauses 228
  linking words 238

not … enough 240
participle clauses 226
with *so* 128
For this reason, 306
too 240
why 219
recently 107
recommend 192, 196
reflexive pronouns 24, 338
refuse to 194, 212
regret 198, 212
regrets
  could have 166
  might not have had 166
  should/shouldn't have 150
relative clauses 218–24
  defining relative clauses 218–19, 222
  non-defining relative clauses 222
  prepositions in 219, 222, 224
  punctuation 222
  reduced relative clauses 224
  with *when, where, why* 219
  with *which* 222
  with *who, which, that, whose* 218, 219
relative pronouns 218
  + *be* + preposition 224
  + *have* 224
  omitted 219
  as subject/object 219
remember 83, 194, 198, 280
remind 196, 212, 280
reply: in reported speech 212
reply questions 323
reported questions 208
reported speech 204–12
reported statements 204–5
reporting verbs 204
  for orders, requests, advice 210, 212
  passive form 260
  patterns 212, 260
  tell and *say* 210, 212
requests
  can/can't 154
  could/couldn't 154
  please 154
  in reported statements 210
  Will you … ? 154
  Would you … ? 154
require (object) *to* 196
respond: in reported speech 212
result
  linking words 240
  participle clauses 226
  As a result, 240, 306
Right, 332
  on the right 40
round 339

rules
    allowed to 152
    can/can't 152
    have got to 146
    have to 146
    may/may not 152
    must 146
    negative rules 146, 152
    with passive verbs 256
run + noun (+ preposition) 266
run into 272

S

's/' (possessive) 18
-s, -es verb endings 78, 350
sale: for sale 50
same: the same (as) 62
say 90
    in reported speech 212
    Say ... 164
    say to 272
second conditional 164
see 83, 90, 198
    see to 272
seem 83
    seem to 194
seldom 66
semi-colon (;) 302
sense verbs 83, 139
    + infinitive 198
    + object + -ing form 198
sensible 282
sensitive (to) 282
sentences 176–86
    imperatives 162
    it as subject 180
    linking words 246, 306
    main clause 238
    punctuation 222, 302
    statements 176–7
    subordinate clause 238
    there + be 180
    verbs with two objects 177
    word order 176–7
    see also clauses; passive forms; questions
shall 123, 138
    offers 123, 154
    shall we? 154, 322
    suggestions 123, 154
she 20
short answers 182, 322, 326, 332
short forms
    be 76
    have got/got to 76, 83
    question tags 322
    spoken English 314
    see also short answers

should/shouldn't 138
    advice 150
    expectations 142
    passive form 256
    reported statements 204
should/shouldn't have 144, 150
silly 64
similar (to) 62, 268
since
    + reason 238
    preposition 339
    present perfect continuous 114
    present perfect simple 110
singular nouns 2
-sion nouns 290
slightly 58, 62, 68
smell 83, 198
so 128
    for emphasis 330
    expect so 326
    hope so 326
    for reason 128
    for result 240
    So, 328
    So am I./So do I. 326
    so as to 238
    so far 110
    so many/few 240
    so much/little 240
    so (+ adjective) + that 238, 240
some 26
    some of 26
    somebody 28
    someone 28
    something 28
    sometimes 64, 66
    somewhere 28
soon 64, 68
    as soon as 130, 246
sort of 332
speak to 272
speculation see making a guess
spelling 350–1
spite: in spite of 40, 244
spoken English 322–32
    agreeing and disagreeing 326
    common words and phrases 332
    either 326
    emphasis 330
    exclamations 328
    expressing feelings/ideas/opinions 328
    grammar 314
    indirect questions 323
    listener responses 332
    neither 326
    omitting words 332
    polite phrases 154, 323
    question tags 322

reply questions 323
short forms 322, 326
so ... 326
thing(s), stuff, kind of 332
too 326
stand: can't stand + -*ing* 192
stand for 272, 372
stare at 272
start 192, 198, 266
state: in reported speech 212
state verbs 83, 116
statements
   reported statements 204–5
   word order 176–7, 246
stay or *live* 280
still 107
stop 192, 198
stress: compound nouns 296
   see also intonation
strong + noun 266
stuff 332
subject
   + verb (no object) 176
   + verb + (object/complement) + adverbial 176
   + verb + object/complement 176
   + verb + *that* clause 177
   + verb + two objects 177
   in infinitive clauses 228
   -*ing* form as subject 192
   it as subject 20, 180
   pronouns 20, 338
   questions 184
   relative pronouns 219
   wh- clauses 230
subordinate clauses 238
such
   such + *a/an* (+ adjective) + noun 240
   such (a/an + adjective) + noun 330
   such a (lot of) 240
   such a/an ... that 240
suffixes
   adjectives 292
   nouns 290, 312
   verbs 294
suggest
   + -*ing* form 192
   in reported speech 210, 212
suggestions
   Could I ... ? 154
   How/What about ... ? 154
   Let's + infinitive 154
   Shall ... ? 154
superlative adjectives 60
   + past perfect simple 98
   + present perfect simple 110
   first, second, etc. 110, 224
   spelling 351
superlative adverbs 68

superlative nouns 230
suppose
   Suppose ... 164
   suppose so 326
   supposed to 144, 260
sure
   I'm not sure 323
   sure to 132
sympathetic or *likeable* 282

T

tags (questions) 322
take 90
   + noun (+ preposition) 266
   How long did it take? 180
   take after 272
   take back 275
   take off 274
   take or *bring* 280
   take or *have* 278
   take to 274
talk to 272
taste 83, 198
teach 196
tell 90, 196, 210, 212, 266
   To tell the truth, 228
tenses 340–1
   changes in reported speech 204, 205
   future forms 122–32, 341
   past tenses 90–100, 340
   present perfect 106–12, 340
   present tenses 76–83, 340
than 60
thank someone for 212
that
   + clause 177
   After that, 246, 306
   demonstratives 12
   relative pronoun 218
   in reported statements 204
   so that 238, 240
   such a/an that 240
   That's + adjective! 328
the 6, 8, 10, 60, 68
the best 60, 68
the farthest/furthest 60, 68
the least/most 60, 68, 230
the same (... as) 62
the whole 32
the worst 60, 68
their 20
theirs 20
them 24
themselves 24
then 246, 306
then or *now?* (*this* or *that?*) 12
there + *be* 180
there and *it* 180

Therefore, 240, 306
these 12
they 20
   = people in general 24
thing(s) 332
think 83
   think about 272
   think of + *-ing* 192
   think so 326
third conditional 166
this 12
   this one 22
those 12
though 244
through
   in American English 352
   = *from ... to* 339
   direction 64
   get through 272
   movement 44
throughout 339
throw away 275
till 46
time
   adverbs 64, 66, 90
   of the day 10
   for + period of time 90, 100
   How long? 110
   in time 50
   It's ... 180
   It's time + past tense 170
   linking words 246
   on time 50
   phrases 177
   prepositions 40, 46
   in reported statements 204
   spend (time) + *-ing* form 192
time expressions 46
   + future 132
   + past simple 90
   + present continuous 80
   + present perfect simple 110
   + present simple 78
-tion nouns 290
to
   adjective + *to* 268
   direction 339
   (from) ... to 90, 352
   infinitive with/without *to* 194
   movement 44
   noun + *to* 268
   or *for* 177
   verb + *to* 270
To be honest, 328
today 64, 110
too 240
   after verb 326
too many 30

too much 30
top: *on top of* 40, 41
towards 40
transitive verbs 176
transport 10, 48
try 194, 198
turn down/round/up 275

U

un- adjectives 292
un- verbs 294
uncertainty 142
uncountable nouns 3, 332
under 41, 339
under- verbs 294
units: uncountable nouns 3
unless 162, 164
until 46, 130, 246, 339
up 275, 339
us 24
used to 96
usually 64, 66

V

valuable or *expensive* 282
verb phrases
   avoiding repetition 304
   to make noun phrases 312
verbs
   + adjective 56
   + adverb 66
   + complement 176
   + indefinite pronouns 28
   + infinitive or *-ing* form 198
   + infinitive with/without *to* 194, 345
   + *-ing* form 192, 224, 345
   + no object 176
   + noun (+ preposition) 266
   + object 176
   + object + complement 176
   + (object/complement) + adverbial 176
   + (object) + infinitive with *to* 196, 345
   + object + preposition + object 270, 347
   + preposition + *-ing* form 192, 345
   (+ preposition) + object 270
   + prepositions 219, 270, 272, 347
   + reflexive pronouns 24
   + *that* clause 177
   + two objects 177
   action verbs 82
   active verbs 226
   all + verb 26
   auxiliary verbs 182
   avoiding repetition 304
   changing verbs into adjectives 292
   changing verbs into nouns 290
   confusing verbs 278, 280
   -ed form 90, 106, 224, 226, 350

emphasising 330
-es form 350
formation 294
infinitive form 194, 196
-ing form 226, 350
intransitive verbs 176
irregular verbs 90, 106, 348–9
noun–verb agreement 2
passives 252–60
past continuous 92, 100, 340
past participles 98, 106, 348–9, 350
past simple 90, 94, 98, 112, 340
phrasal verbs 256, 274–5, 347
prefixes 292, 294
prepositional verbs 256, 272, 274, 347
present continuous 80, 340
present perfect continuous 114, 116, 341
present perfect 106–12, 116, 341
in reported statements 204, 210, 212, 260
spelling 348, 350
state verbs 83, 116
suffixes 294
transitive verbs 176
uncountable nouns 3
see also modal verbs 342–3
very 58, 64
vowels 6

W

wait for 272
want 83
 want (object) to 132, 194, 196
warn 196, 210, 212
warnings
 first conditional 162
 had better/had better not 150
 must/mustn't 150
 will 123, 154
was/were able to 139
was/were going to 132, 341
was/were meant to 144
was/were supposed to 144
way: By the way, 328
we 20
weather: It's … 180
website addresses 302
weekend: at/on the weekend 64
Well, 332
well (= better) 60, 64
well: as well as 242
were
 If I were … 164
 were there? 322
wh- clauses 230
Wh- questions 184, 186
 + do, does and did 184
 + have 184
 + have got 76

 + prepositions 184
 indirect questions 323
 intonation 184
 past simple 90
 present continuous 80
 present perfect continuous 114
 present perfect simple 106
 present simple 76, 78
 reported Wh- questions 208
wh- words 184, 218
what 230
What? 184, 186
 What about … ? 154
 What on earth? 330
What a/an + (adjective) + noun! 328
Whatever? 330
when
 + past continuous 94
 + past simple 90
 future events/time 130
 order of events 94, 100, 246
 period of time 246
 present conditions 162
 relative clauses 219
 and while 94
When? 64, 184
Whenever? 330
where 219
Where? 64, 184
 Where on earth? 330
whereas 244
Wherever? 330
whether 323
which 218, 222
Which? 184, 186
 Which one/ones? 22
 Which way? 64
while
 = at the same time 246
 for difference 244
 or as 94
 or during 246
 period of time 94, 246
who 184, 218
Who? 184
 or Whose? 186
 Who on earth? 330
Whoever? 330
whole: a/the whole 32
whose 218
Whose? 184
 or Who? 186
why 219
Why? 184
 Why ever? 330
 Why on earth? 330
will 123, 138, 341
 certainty 123

decisions, offers, promises, warnings 123, 154
predictions 123
reported statements 204
requests 154
will have something done 258
will/won't be able to 139
will/won't have to 146
wish 83, 170
  wish (object) *to* 194, 196
with 40, 46, 48, 218, 268, 270, 339, 347
within 46, 339
without 339
wonder: *I wonder* 323
won't you? 322
word combinations 266–82
  adjective + preposition 268
  common collocations 266
  confusing adjectives 282
  confusing verbs 278, 280
  noun + preposition 268
  phrasal verbs 274–5, 347
  verb + preposition 270
word formation 290–6
  adjectives 292, 296
  compound adjectives 296
  compound nouns 296
  nouns 290, 296, 312
  verbs 294
word order
  adjectives 58, 240
  adverbials 177
  adverbs 66, 240
  for emphasis 308
  infinitive clauses 228
  linking words 246
  passives 253
  questions 182, 184, 323
  relative clauses 222
  reported questions 208
  statements 176–7, 246
words, avoiding repetition 304
words, omitting 304
work
  at work 50
  work for 274
  work out 274
worse 60, 68
worst: *the worst* 60, 68
would 138
  + infinitive for past actions 96
  + *like/love/hate/prefer* (object) *to* 194, 196
  reported statements 210
  requests 154, 322
  would you? 154, 322
would be able to 139
would rather
  + infinitive without *to* 194
  + past tense 170

would/wouldn't
  reported statements 204
  second conditional 164
  third conditional 166
wounded 282
Wow! 328
written English 302–14
  avoiding repetitions 304
  formal language 314
  linking clauses 306
  linking sentences 306
  nouns instead of verbs 312
  organising information 310
  passives 253
  punctuation 302
  word order for emphasis 308

Y

-y adjectives 292
Yeah/Yes, 332
Yes/No questions 182, 322
  future with *going to* 122
  future with *will* 182
  have 182
  have something done 258
  indirect questions 323
  past continuous 92
  past simple 90
  present continuous 80
  present perfect continuous 114
  present perfect simple 106
  present simple 78
  present simple: *have got* 76
  reported *Yes/No* questions 208
  short answers 182
  used to 96
yet 107
you
  = people in general 24
  object pronoun 24
  subject pronoun 20
You know, 332
your 20
yours 20
yourself 24
yourselves 24

Z

zero conditional 162

Pearson Education Limited
Edinburgh Gate
Harlow
Essex CM20 2JE
England
and Associated Companies throughout the world.

www.pearsonelt.com

© Pearson Education Limited 2012

The right of Mark Foley and Diane Hall to be identified as authors of this Work has been asserted by them in accordance with the Copyright, Designs and Patents Act 1988.

All rights reserved; no part of this publication may be reproduced, stored in a retrieval system, or transmitted in any form or by any means, electronic, mechanical, photocopying, recording, or otherwise without the prior written permission of the Publishers.

First published 2012
This edition published 2014

ISBN: 9781447979487

Set in Frutiger and ITC Stone Serif

Printed in Slovakia by Neografia

Illustrated by Paul Boston, Joanna Kerr and Roger Penwill

Picture Credits

The publisher would like to thank the following for their kind permission to reproduce their photographs:

(Key: b-bottom; c-centre; l-left; r-right; t-top)

Alamy Images: Ace Stock Limited 62r, Art Directors & TRIP 115, Asia Images Group Pte Ltd 287, Andrew Bain 61, Howard Barlow 292, Ben Molyneux Sports 280, Adrian Brockwell 57, Ian Dagnall 176, Danita Delimont 70, Diana Bier British Library 294, Lisa F. Young 214, Glow Wellness 80, Jeff Greenberg 6, Peter Horree 59, Image Source 12l, 12r, 196, Image Source 12l, 12r, 196, Image Source 12l, 12r, 196, Boris Karpinski 153cr, Matthew Noble Studio 137, mediablitzimages (uk) Limited 33l, Jeff Morgan 8, North Wind Picture Archives 89r, Alberto Paredes 22, Patrick Bishop / PB Productions 157, Trevor Payne 142, PCL 28, David Pearson 2, Photofusion Picture Library 233br, Chris Rout 321, Royal Geographical Society 92, 96, Royal Geographical Society 92, 96, Alex Segre 29, 155, Alex Segre 29, 155, Uwe Skrzypczak 64, David Taylor 153cl, Urikiri-Shashin-Kan 272r; **The Art Archive:** Victoria and Albert Museum London / V&A Images 257; **Bridgeman Art Library Ltd:** British Library, London, UK / © British Library Board. All Rights Reserved 89l, Museo de America, Madrid, Spain / Index 100b; **Corbis:** Balan Madhavan / Robert Harding World Imagery 237, Bettmann 230r, Bettmann 230r, Daisy Gilardini / Science Faction 222 (Background), Araldo de Luca 233tr, Kevin Fleming 15, Hinrich Baesemann / dpa 242, HO / Reuters 173r, Image Source 65, 266, Jim Sugar / Science Faction 95, Liu Liqun 189, Walter Lockwood 152, Don Mason 18, moodboard 278, Nick Daly / cultura 244, North Carolina Museum of Art 231, Ocean 203, Tim Pannell 166, Peter Barritt / SuperStock 99, Radius Images 107, Terry Vine / Blend Images 252; **Mary Evans Picture Library:** The Women's Library 103; **Fotolia.com:** ambrits 146, Yuri Arcurs 144l, Martin Bech 5/1, Dual Aspect 218 (Background), Dzmitry Fedarovich 274l, Maximino Gomes 298/0, Louella Folsom 5/6, lunamarina 31, Ilja Masik 152 (Background), Kablonk Micro 164, Monkey Business 84, Sergey Peterman 112, Victoria Short 257 (Frame), WavebreakMediaMicro 48; **Getty Images:** 173l, 217, 218 (Arthur Conan Doyle), 233cr, 265, 276, 306, 318, AFP 98, 119, 222 (Alexander Solzhenitsyn), 335, AFP 98, 119, 222 (Alexander Solzhenitsyn), 335, altrendo images 322, Chris Baker 333, Ron Chapple 141, Comstock 106, Winston Davidian 282l, De Agostini 247, DEA / G. Cigolini / Veneranda Biblioteca Ambrosiana 100t, Jason Dewey 128, GK Hart / Vicky Hart 144r, Franck Guiziou 181, Andrew Holt 180, Inti St Clair 304, Jupiterimages 26, Serge Krouglikoff 258, LatinContent 282r, Scott Montgomery 110, New York Daily News 179l, Redferns 308, 310, 319, Anatoly Sapronenkov 233tl, Bob Thomas 121; **iStockphoto:** Kelly Cline 33r, Chris Cousins 37t, deepblue4you 5/7, Niko Guido 191, kali9 56r, locke_rd 56l, maodesign 161, Kristian Sekulic 163, travellinglight 32l, Baldur Tryggvason 153c; **Kobal Collection Ltd:** Channel 4 / Pathe 75b, Paramount / Filmways 226; **Masterfile UK Ltd:** Pete Webb 130; **Pearson Education Ltd:** 230l, Trevor Clifford 5/8; **Photolibrary.com:** 204, 328, Andrew Ward / Life File 11, Atlantide SN.C. 153r, Blend Images 75t, Christine Besson / Photononstop 43, Tom Evans 298/5, FSG 255, Glow Images, Inc 20, Hill Street Studios 270, Norman Hollands 17, Image100 39, Imagesource 212, Kordcom 13, Javier Larrea 81, Wayne Lynch 68, Nancy Ney 127, Paul Paul 138, Peter and Georgina Bowater 78, Pixtal Images 186l, Radius Images 44, 298/3, Stockbroker 332, Tom & Dee Ann McCarthy 256, Daniel Torrello 46, Whisson / Jordan 298/7, Peter Widmann 1, Jeremy Woodhouse 330, Yukiko Yamanote 238; **Photoshot Holdings Limited:** NHPA 66; **Press Association Images:** Barry Batchelor / PA Archive 284, Christof Stache / AP 97, Liam Creedon 87, DPA Deutsche Press-Agentur / DPA 272l, Kirsty Wigglesworth / PA Archive 79, Li Ga / Landov 271, Matt Crossick / EMPICS Entertainment 179r, Neal Simpson / EMPICS Sport 76; **Reuters:** Mike Cassese 312, David Gray 274r, Gary Hershorn 281, Issei Kato 298/4, Enrique Marcarian 143r, Ho New 186r, Pool New 235, Darren Whiteside 55; **Rex Features:** 58, 105, Ingrid Abery 268, Action Press 241, Antti Aimo-Koivisto 73, BDG 305, c.20thC.Fox / Everett 37b, c.Columbia / Everett 301, CSU Archv / Everett 228c, Denkou Images 232r, Don Hammond / Design Pics Inc. 289, Everett Collection 224, 228l, 303, Everett Collection 224, 228l, 303, FremantleMedia Ltd 168, Image Source 143l, ITV 228r, Sipa Press 232l, 240, 251, 297, 316, Sipa Press 232l, 240, 251, 297, 316, Sipa Press 232l, 240, 251, 297, 316, Sipa Press 232l, 240, 251, 297, 316, Startraks Photo 208, Charles Sykes 260, Ray Tang 27; **Science Photo Library Ltd:** Jonathan Burnett 93; **Shutterstock.com:** AMA 187, Anyka 71, Yuri Arcurs 192r, ATurner 207t, Big Pants Production 5/3, cameilia 62cr, Tony Campbell 62l, Christopher Meder Photography 233bl, Rafal Cichawa 184, Elnur 5/2, Jonathan Gaynes 201, godrick 183, Margo Harrison 239r, IvicaNS 210, Wojtek Jarco 239l, Amy Johansson 153l, Muellek Josef 32r, KENCKOphotography 175, Agita Leimane 47, MarkMirror 195, Monkey Business Images 296, Orange Line Media 192l, Andrey Shadrin 207b, Smit 298/1, sokolovsky 185, Michaela Stejskalova 5/5, Simone van den Berg 62cl, wavebreakmedia ltd 290, Kelly Young 77; **SuperStock:** Image Asset Management Ltd. 94; **Thinkstock:** 182, 233cl, John Foxx 5/4, PhotoObjects.net 5/0; **TopFoto:** © 2006 Alinari 298/2, The Granger Collection 90

All other images © Pearson Education

Every effort has been made to trace the copyright holders and we apologise in advance for any unintentional omissions. We would be pleased to insert the appropriate acknowledgement in any subsequent edition of this publication.